## PART THREE  *Writing Effectively*  317

# PART SEVEN   *Writing When English Is a Second Language*     799

CENTRAL TEXAS COLLEGE EDITION

# SIMON & SCHUSTER
# HANDBOOK FOR WRITERS

## LYNN QUITMAN TROYKA • DOUGLAS HESSE

Taken from:

*Simon & Schuster Handbook for Writers*, Eighth Edition
by Lynn Quitman Troyka and Douglas Hesse

# CENTRAL TEXAS COLLEGE

PEARSON
Custom
Publishing

PEARSON
Prentice
Hall

PEARSON CUSTOM PUBLISHING
75 Arlington Street, Suite 300, Boston, MA 02116
A Pearson Education Company

# The Pathway to Success in Your College Courses

Your journey through college can be winding, filled with detours and potholes, or it can be relatively straight and smooth. The information below will help you have a pleasant experience along the way.

## Time Management

*I am definitely going to take a course on time management . . . just as soon as I can work it into my schedule.*
— Louis E. Boone

The time you spend preparing to study relates directly to a successful outcome. But time, or lack thereof, is a common complaint. How often do you comment that you don't have enough time to accomplish everything you wish to do?

### How Do You Spend Your Time?

The first step in time management is to see how you currently spend your time. Have you ever taken the time to add up all of the hours you spend on your regular activities? Take a moment to write down everything you do during a seven-day period. These questions will help you consider all of the activities you do.

- You may spend 40 hours a week on your job, but what about commute time?
- You have to fuel your body. How many hours a week do you spend eating?
- Good grooming is essential. How many hours a week do you spend bathing and dressing?
- How much time do you give to your friends and family?

Remember, there are only 168 hours in a week. Is there any time left to sleep?

### How Can I Make More Time?

You can't add hours to the day or days to the week, but if you learn to plan your time wisely, you should be able to make better use of the time you have. As an added bonus, you should feel less stress. Scheduling your time is a step in the right direction.

### Develop schedules:

Long term
- Include fixed commitments only
- Include weekly obligations-job, classes, church, meetings, etc.
- Plan enough time for study-as a minimum, use two hours for every one hour in the classroom.
- Plan for weekly reviews-at least one hour each week for each class.

**Intermediate**

- One per week
- List major events and amount of work to be accomplished in each subject.
- Try to study at the same time every day.
- Make use of free hours between classes.
- Include non-study activities.

**Short term**

- Daily
- Use small note card you can carry with you.
- Write specifically what you need to accomplish that day.
- Mark out each item as it is completed.

## Study Environment

Where you study and how you study is as important as how often you study.

- Identify a quiet place with a desk or table, a chair, and good lighting.
- Your bed might be inviting, but remember your goal is to stay awake and concentrate.
- Although music or some type of background noise might be ok, avoid the TV.
- It's too easy to get engrossed in a show rather than your course work.
- Watching CSI can be interesting, but it probably won't help you with your Introduction to Criminal Justice final exam.
- Make sure you have everything you need: your textbooks, notes, paper and pencil, and a clock.
- Why a clock? To help you manage your time.
- And, don't forget to take regular breaks.

## Learning Styles

- If you are assembling a toy or using a new computer program, do you put instructions aside and refer to them only when you run into trouble?
- Do you have to see a name or address in writing in order to remember it?
- Do you enjoy audio books, or do you find your mind wandering as you listen?

Your answers to these questions relate to your preferred learning style, and like clothing, one learning style doesn't fit all. If you have access to the Internet, you can take a learning style inventory at *http://www.vark-learn.com/english/index.asp* and then view helpsheets at *http://www.vark-learn.com/english/page.asp?p=helpsheets* related to your preferred learning style.

### Visual Learners

- learn through seeing
- need to see the teacher's body language and facial expression to fully understand the content of a lesson.
- tend to prefer sitting at the front of the classroom to avoid visual obstructions (e.g. people's heads).
- may think in pictures and learn best from visual displays including: diagrams, illustrated text books, overhead transparencies, videos, flip charts and hand-outs.
- During a lecture or classroom discussion, visual learners often prefer to take detailed notes to absorb the information.

If you are a visual learner, here are some suggestions just for you:

- use visual materials such as pictures, charts, maps, graphs, etc.
- have a clear view of your teachers when they are speaking so you can see their body language and facial expression
- use color to highlight important points in text
- take notes or ask your teacher to provide handouts
- illustrate your ideas as a picture or brainstorming bubble before writing them down
- write a story and illustrate it
- use multi-media (e.g. computers, videos, and filmstrips)
- study in a quiet place away from verbal disturbances
- read illustrated books
- visualize information as a picture to aid memorization

## *Aural Learners*

- learn through listening
- learn best through verbal lectures, discussions, talking things through and listening to what others have to say.
- interpret the underlying meanings of speech through listening to tone of voice, pitch, speed and other nuances. Written information may have little meaning until it is heard.
- often benefit from reading text aloud and using a tape recorder.

If you are an aural learner, here are some suggestions just for you:

- participate in class discussions/debates
- make speeches and presentations
- use a tape recorder during lectures instead of taking notes
- read text out aloud
- create musical jingles to aid memorization
- create mnemonics to aid memorization
- discuss your ideas verbally
- dictate to someone while they write down your thoughts
- use verbal analogies, and story telling to demonstrate your point

## *Read/Write Learners*

- learn through reading and writing
- learn best by reading and re-reading the textbook and their notes, writing and rewriting their notes, and in general, organizing items into lists.

## *Kinesthetic Learners*

- learn through moving, doing, and touching
- learn best through a hands-on approach, actively exploring the physical world around them.
- may find it hard to sit still for long periods and may become distracted by their need for activity and exploration.

If you are a tactile/kinesthetic learner, here are some suggestions just for you:

- take frequent study breaks

- move around to learn new things (e.g. read while on an exercise bike, mold a piece of clay to learn a new concept)
- work at a standing position
- chew gum while studying
- use bright colors to highlight reading material
- dress up your work space with posters
- if you wish, listen to music while you study
- skim through reading material to get a rough idea what it is about before settling down to read it in detail.

### Multimodal Learners

- don't have a single preferred learning style.
- learn best through combinations.

If you have multiple preferences, you are in the majority as somewhere between fifty and seventy percent of any population seems to fit into that group.

## Reading Skills and Strategies

Good reading skills are essential to your success in your college-level classes. Here are a couple of reasons why:

- In high school, you may have been able to get good grades without reading much of the text. Now that you're in college, professors will expect you to read the textbook and they may test you on information not discussed in class but covered in the reading. In fact, many professors test on assigned readings as a check to make sure students are using their texts.
- The average freshman is assigned over 250 pages of reading each week, so clearly you're going to need to keep up with your reading assignments. If you do not read during week one, that means that you will need to read 500 pages the next week-just to stay caught up! If you choose not to read during the second week either . . . well, you can see how the work can just snowball.

### Improving Your Reading Skills and Applying Reading Strategies

A good reader:

- seizes the main ideas.
- thinks about what the author is saying
- is active, not passive.
- concentrates on what is being read.
- remembers as much as possible.
- applies what is being read to personal experience.

Go to *http://www.how-to-study.com/pqr.htm* for more on reading skills.

**SQ3R** is one recommended method for improving your reading comprehension. The letters in the name stand for these five steps:

Survey: Before you read, scan the titles, headings, pictures, and summaries. Consider using the heading and subheadings as an outline for notes as you read.

Question: Ask yourself questions based on Step 1 and look for answers as you complete Step 3. For example, if a subheading is entitled "Basic Concepts of Reading," change it to read, "What are the Basic Concepts of Reading?"

__R__ead:  Read and take notes.

__R__ecall:  Without referring to the book or your notes, think about what you have read. See if your questions were answered. Could you explain the content to someone else? Try putting major concepts in your own words.

__R__eview:  Look at your questions, answers, notes and book to see how well you did recall. Observe carefully the points stated incorrectly or omitted. Fix carefully in mind the logical sequence of the entire idea, concepts, or problem. Finish up with a mental picture of the WHOLE.

Another method is **PQR3**, which stands for

__P__review: Preview what you are going to read.

__Q__uestion: Question what you are going to learn after the preview.

__R__ead: Read the assignment.

__R__ecite: Stop every once in a while, look up from the book, and put in your own words what you have just read.

__R__eview: After you have finished, review the main points.

(Sounds similar to SQ3R, doesn't it?) Go to *http://www.how-to-study.com/pqr.htm* to learn more about this method.

There is even a related study method known as **M.U.R.D.E.R.**

__M__ood:  Set a positive mood for yourself to study in.

__U__nderstand:  Mark any information you don't understand in a particular unit and keep a focus on one unit or a manageable group of exercise.

__R__ecall:  After studying the unit, stop and put what you have learned into your own words.

__D__igest:  Go back to what you did not understand and reconsider the information. Contact external expert sources (e.g., other books or an instructor) if you still cannot understand it.

__E__xpand:  ask three kinds of questions concerning the studied material:

- If I could speak to the author, what questions would I ask or what criticism would I offer?
- How could I apply this material to what I am interested in?
- How could I make this information interesting and understandable to other students?

__R__eview:  Go over the material you've covered. Review what strategies helped you understand and/or retain information in the past and apply these to your current studies.

Check this system out at *http://www.studygs.net/murder.htm*.

## Notetaking

### *Why take notes?*

- It triggers basic lecturing processes and helps you to remember information.
- It helps you to concentrate in class.
- It helps you prepare for tests.
- Your notes are often a source of valuable clues for what information the instructor thinks most important (i.e., what will show up on the next test).
- Your notes often contain information that cannot be found elsewhere (i.e., in your text-book).

Evaluate your present notetaking system. Ask yourself:

- Did I use complete phrases or sentences that mean something to me later?
- Did I use any form at all?
- Are my notes clear or confusing?
- Did I capture main points and all subpoints?
- Did I streamline using abbreviations and shortcuts?

If you answered "no" to any of these questions, you may need to develop some new notetaking skills!

## Guidelines for Taking Notes

- Concentrate on the lecture or on the reading material.
- Take notes consistently.
- Take notes selectively.
  - Do NOT try to write down every word.
  - Remember that the average lecturer speaks approximately 125-140 words per minute, and the average note-taker writes at a rate of about 25 words per minute.
- Translate ideas into your own words.
- Organize notes into some sort of logical form.
- Be brief. Write down only the major points and important information.
- Write legibly. Notes are useless if you cannot read them later!
- Don't be concerned with spelling and grammar.

There are many reasons for taking lecture notes.

- Making yourself take notes forces you to listen carefully and test your understanding of the material.
- When you are reviewing, notes provide a gauge to what is important in the text.
- Personal notes are usually easier to remember than the text.
- The writing down of important points helps you to remember then even before you have studied the material formally.

Instructors usually give clues to what is important to take down. Some of the more common clues are:

- Material written on the blackboard.
- Repetition
- Emphasis
  - Emphasis can be judged by tone of voice and gesture.
  - Emphasis can be judged by the amount of time the instructor spends on points and the number of examples he or she uses.
- Word signals (e.g. "There are **two points of view** on . . . " "The **third** reason is . . . " " In **conclusion** . . . ")
- Summaries given at the end of class.
- Reviews given at the beginning of class.

Each student should develop his or her own method of taking notes, but most students find the following suggestions helpful:

- Make your notes brief.
  - Never use a sentence where you can use a phrase. Never use a phrase where you can use a word.

–Use abbreviations and symbols, but be consistent.
- Put most notes in your own words. However, the following should be noted exactly:
  –Formulas
  –Definitions
  – Specific facts
- Use outline form and/or a numbering system. Indention helps you distinguish major from minor points.
- Date your notes. Perhaps number the pages.
- If you miss a statement, write key words, skip a few spaces, and get the information later.
- Don't try to use every space on the page. Leave room for coordinating your notes with the text after the lecture. (You may want to list key terms in the margin or make a summary of the contents of the page.)

Here are some hints ("Do not's") regarding taking notes on classroom lectures that can save time for almost any student.

**Do not plan to rewrite or type your notes later.** To do so is to use a double amount of time; once to take the original notes a second to rewrite them. The advice is simple: DO IT RIGHT THE FIRST TIME!

**Do not take notes in shorthand.** Though shorthand is a valuable tool for a secretary, it is almost worthless for a student doing academic work. Here's why. Notes in shorthand cannot be studied in that form. They must first be transcribed. The act of transcribing notes takes an inordinate amount of time and energy but does not significantly contribute to their mastery. It is far better to have taken the notes originally in regular writing and then spend the time after that in direct study and **recitation** of the notes.

**Do not record the lesson on a cassette tape or any other tape.** The lecture on tape precludes flexibility. This statement can be better understood when seen in the light of a person who has taken his/her notes in regular writing. Immediately after taking the notes this person can study them in five minutes before the next class as s/he walks toward the next building, as s/he drinks his/her coffee, or whatever. Furthermore, this student, in looking over his/her notes, may decide that the notes contain only four worthwhile ideas which s/he can highlight, relegating the rest of the lecture to obscurity. Whereas the lecture on tape has to be listened to in its entirety including the worthwhile points as well as the "garbage," handwritten notes may be studied selectively. A student who takes the easy way out - recording the lecture on tape as he or she sits back doing nothing—will box him or herself into inflexibility.

Learning to make notes effectively will help you to improve your study and work habits and to remember important information. Often, students are deceived into thinking that because they **understand** everything that is said in class they will therefore remember it. This is dead wrong! Write it down.

As you make notes, you will develop skill in selecting important material and in discarding unimportant material. The secret to developing this skill is practice. Check your results constantly. Strive to improve. Notes enable you to retain important facts and data and to develop an accurate means of arranging necessary information.

## Hints on Note Making

- Don't write down everything that you read or hear.
  –Be alert and attentive to the main points.
  –Concentrate on the "meat" of the subject and forget the trimmings.
- Notes should consist of key words or very short sentences. If a speaker gets sidetracked it

is often possible to go back and add further information.
- Take accurate notes.
    - You should usually use your own words, but try not to change the meaning.
    - If you quote **directly** from an author, quote **correctly**.
- Think a minute about your material before you start making notes.
    - Don't take notes just to be taking notes!
    - Take notes that will be of real value to you when you look over them at a later date.
- Have a uniform system of punctuation and abbreviation that will make sense to you.
    - Use a skeleton outline and show importance by indenting.
    - Leave lots of white space for later additions.
- Omit descriptions and full explanations.
    - Keep your notes short and to the point.
    - Condense your material so you can grasp it rapidly.
- Don't worry about missing a point.
- Don't keep notes on oddly shaped pieces of paper.
    - Keep notes in order and in one place.
- Shortly after making your notes, go back and rework (not redo) your notes by adding extra points and spelling out unclear items.
    - Remember, we forget rapidly. Budget time for this vital step just as you do for the class itself.
- Review your notes regularly. This is the only way to achieve lasting memory.

These are only a few of the many methods for taking notes.

- the Cornell Method
- the Outline Method
- the Mapping Method (or Mindmapping)
- the Charting Method
- the Sentence Method

For details on these methods, go to *http://www.sas.calpoly.edu/asc/ssl/notetaking.systems.html.* Also check out this resource about note taking: *http://www.how-to-study.com/Taking%20Notes%20in%20Class.htm*

## Memory Techniques

We hope that the information on preparing to study has been helpful, but do you feel that your real problem is remembering?  Don't worry. There are ways to help you build your memory skills too.

### Acronym

- An *acronym* is defined as "a word formed from the initial letters of a name," such as PCS for permanent change of station or SOC for Servicemembers Opportunity Colleges, "or by combining initial letters or parts of a series of words," as radar for radio detecting and ranging.
- Can you think of other acronyms?

## *Mnemonic*

- A *mnemonic* is defined as "a device, such as a formula or rhyme, used as an aid in remembering."

**Examples**

As a child, you might have determined the number of days in a given month

- by reciting the rhyme "Thirty days hath September, April, June, and November . . . ." or
- by using your knuckles ("peaks" have 31 days and "valleys" have 30, except February, of course).

If you have studied music, you might have used these techniques for remembering the names of the notes:

- FACE represents the names of the notes in the spaces on the staff.
- The first letters of the words in sentence "Every good boy does fine" represent the names of the notes on the lines on the staff.

A mnemonic used to recall the steps for simplifying algebraic expressions is "Please excuse my dear Aunt Sally."

- Perform operations within the innermost parentheses and work outward.
- Evaluate all exponential expressions.
- Perform multiplications and divisions as they occur, working from left to right.
- Perform additions and subtractions as they occur, working from left to right.

Use the sentence "My Very Educated Mother Just Served Us Nine Pizzas" to recall the order of the planets from the sun

- Mercury
- Venus
- Earth
- Mars
- Jupiter
- Saturn
- Uranus
- Neptune
- Pluto

Big Brown Rabbits Often Yield Great Big Vocal Groans When Gingerly Slapped for the color codes for resistors

- Black
- Brown
- Red
- Orange
- Yellow
- Green
- Blue
- Violet
- Gray
- White
- Gold
- Silver

## Preparing For and Taking Tests

If you have practiced the strategies we have outlined in this orientation, you should be reviewing on a regular basis as you study rather than waiting to cram right before a test.

- Try to anticipate what is important and will be on the test, and use any review materials that are available, such as practice tests or review sheets.
- This doesn't mean that you don't need to study right before a test, but you shouldn't have to stay up all night to prepare for it, and you should feel more confident when you take the test.

### Do You Suffer From Test Anxiety?

- Do you do great on homework assignments, but you dread test days?
- Do you forget everything you know when you sit down to take a test?
- Does it seem like what you studied has nothing to do with the test you are taking?

Once you are sitting in the hot spot with your pencil in hand, use the DETER strategy for taking tests as described at *http://www.how-to-study.com/A%20Strategy%20for%20Taking%20Tests.htm.*

Directions: Read and understand the test directions.
Examine: Examine the entire test to see what is required.
Time: Determine how much time to allow for each item.
Easiest: Answer the easiest items first.
Review: Allow time to review the test to check your answers for accuracy and completeness.

Again, practice makes perfect. There are several web sites for taking practice tests. Here are a few:

- *http://www.actstudent.org/testprep/index.html*
- *http://4tests.com/*
- *http://www.collegeboard.com/*
- *http://www.ets.org/*

## Computer Basics

For many classes, you need to know the basics about using a computer and possibly even surfing the Internet in order to complete certain assignments. If you are taking a distance learning class, you MUST have some basic knowledge of computers and the Internet.

You must be able to

- prepare, save, and retrieve files
- send and receive emails with attachments
- deposit files in an electronic drop box
- locate and navigate web sites
- download software and plug ins
- participate in discussion boards.

A good resource for learning about these items is *http://www.learnthenet.com/english/index.html.*

- Once you have reached this site, note the "How To" list at the left side of the screen.
- If you are a novice, you might want to start with "How to Use this Site."
- Otherwise, start with "Master the Basics" and then work your way down the list.

You will find information ranging from making the connection to the Internet to building your own web site.

- Click on each underlined word or title to access the information.
- This information is also available as the "Animated Internet."

*Jan's Illustrated Computer Literacy 101* at *http://www.jegsworks.com/Lessons/index.html* includes lessons on the topics listed on the next screens, and the approach is very detailed yet easy to understand. Even if you have never touched a mouse before, you should be able to follow along.

Do you want to learn about specific items; i.e., WindowsXP or MSWord2003?

- These are Microsoft products.
- You can go to *http://www.microsoft.com/* and find training on just about every product produced by Microsoft—even older versions.

The information above is just a teaser. We have included only a few websites because websites come and go. To learn more, check out the Internet and use a search engine, such as GOOGLE (*www.google.com*), to find sites on the topics we have referenced.

# *Personal Message to Students*
## from Lynn Quitman Troyka and Doug Hesse

As writers, many of you have much in common with both of us. Sure, we've been at it longer, so we've had more practice, and most rules have become cemented in our heads. However, we share with you a common goal: to put ideas into words worthy of someone else's reading time.

We also share the constant desire to become better writers. Given our extensive teaching experience, this probably sounds odd. However, writing is a lifelong enterprise. Just as we did, you'll write not only in composition classes, but also in other courses throughout college. Writing will likely be an important part of your career, of your role as a public citizen, and even of your personal life. It has certainly been central to ours. Whenever we get stuck in an unfamiliar writing situation or while learning new writing technology, we rummage through strategies we've developed over time. We talk to friends and colleagues, in person, by phone, and by e-mail, and they consult us, too.

We offer this book to you, then, as our partners in the process of writing. We hope that its pages help you give voice to your thoughts—now and years from now. We trust you'll find our advice useful in the wide range of writing situations you're bound to encounter in college and in life. You're always welcome to write us at <troykalq@nyc.rr.com> or <ddhesse@ilstu.edu> to share your reactions to this book and your experiences as writers. We promise to answer.

Each of us would like to end this message with a personal story.

*From Doug:* I first glimpsed the power of writing in high school, when I wrote sappy—but apparently successful—love poems. Still, when I went to college, I was surprised to discover all I didn't know about writing. Fortunately, I had good teachers and developed lots of patience. I needed it. I continue to learn, especially from Lynn.

*From Lynn:* When I was an undergraduate, handbooks for writers weren't common. Questions about writing nagged at me. One day, browsing in the library, I found an incorrectly shelved, dust-covered book whose title included the words *handbook* and *writing*. I read it hungrily and kept checking it out from the library. Back then, I could never have imagined that someday I might write such a book myself. Now that we've completed the eighth edition of the *Simon & Schuster Handbook for Writers*, I'm amazed that I ever had the nerve to begin. This proves to me—and I hope to you—that anyone can write. Students don't always believe that. I hope you will.

With cordial regards,

*Lynn Quitman Troyka*        *Doug Hesse*

# How to Use the *Simon & Schuster Handbook for Writers*

The ***Simon & Schuster Handbook for Writers*** is designed to help you navigate the road to becoming a better writer. You will find many features to guide you along your journey. We are confident you will find this an invaluable reference in college and beyond.

▦ **The detailed Overview of Contents** on the inside front cover lists all parts and chapters in the book. Locate the specific topic you need to reference and then turn to the page indicated.

▦ **A list of supplementary material** available with this book, including information about the book's Web site, can be found in the **Preface**.

▦ **Highlight Boxes** (Summary 📷, Checklist ✓, and Pattern 📷) throughout give easy access to some of the most common and important issues that will come up as you write. You will also find a **List of Boxes by Content** at the end of the book.

▦ **Documentation Source Maps** are designed to clearly illustrate the process for citing different types of sources. Annotated replications of original sources are presented along with step-by-step guidelines. Color is used carefully to help students see where information is pulled from a source and then where it is placed in a citation. Visual tools are provided throughout the research and documentation sections to simplify the research writing process.

▦ **The Terms Glossary** toward the back of the book is an easy way to find the definitions for common writing-related terms. Words and phrases called out in SMALL CAPITAL LETTERS throughout the book can be found in the Terms Glossary.

▦ **Two Indexes** provide quick and convenient navigation by topic. The **ESL Index** 🌐

puts a list of topics for multilingual students in one convenient place. An easy-to-reference and comprehensive **Subject Index** covers virtually everything found in the book.

▦ **Quick Notes** pages, provided at the end of the book, are a convenient place to take notes and highlight the page numbers you refer to most often.

▦ **An access code** at the back of the book gives you access to **a valuable Web site**, which includes an electronic version of the book and many more online resources. Turn to the back endpaper for a detailed list of what is available to you on this Web site.

▦ **The one-of-a-kind Quick Card** at the end of the book puts some of the most useful information from the book in a more portable format. Take the card to class, to the writing lab, or on the road with you!

▦ **A list of Proofreading Marks and Response Symbols** is provided on the inside back cover. Consult this list if your instructor uses revision and proofreading symbols when commenting on your writing.

▦ **The Common Error Quick Find** feature on the back cover is like a compass directing you to the section of the book that will help you find your way through some of the most common errors made by all writers. Look for the error you are struggling with and then turn to the page referenced in the **Quick Find list**.

**The sample page to the right illustrates features that help you navigate the *Simon & Schuster Handbook for Writers*.** ➤

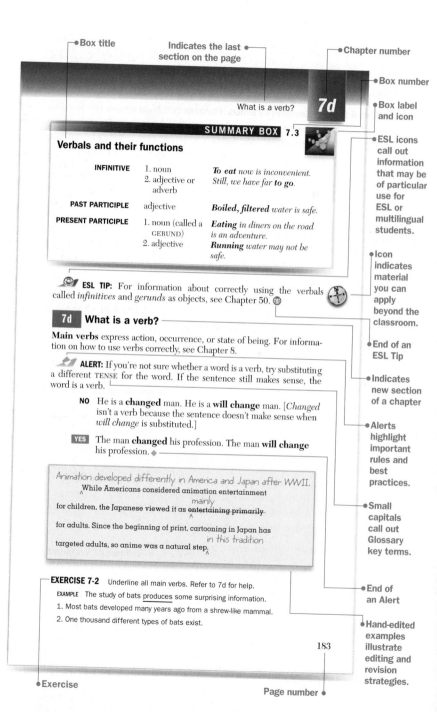

Box title — Indicates the last section on the page — Chapter number

Box number

What is a verb? **7d**

Box label and icon

**SUMMARY BOX 7.3**

ESL icons call out information that may be of particular use for ESL or multilingual students.

**Verbals and their functions**

| INFINITIVE | 1. noun | *To eat now is inconvenient.* |
| | 2. adjective or adverb | *Still, we have far to go.* |
| PAST PARTICIPLE | adjective | *Boiled, filtered water is safe.* |
| PRESENT PARTICIPLE | 1. noun (called a GERUND) | *Eating in diners on the road is an adventure.* |
| | 2. adjective | *Running water may not be safe.* |

Icon indicates material you can apply beyond the classroom.

**ESL TIP:** For information about correctly using the verbals called *infinitives* and *gerunds* as objects, see Chapter 50.

End of an ESL Tip

Indicates new section of a chapter

**7d  What is a verb?**

**Main verbs** express action, occurrence, or state of being. For information on how to use verbs correctly, see Chapter 8.

**ALERT:** If you're not sure whether a word is a verb, try substituting a different TENSE for the word. If the sentence still makes sense, the word is a verb.

Alerts highlight important rules and best practices.

**NO** He is a **changed** man. He is a **will change** man. [*Changed* isn't a verb because the sentence doesn't make sense when *will change* is substituted.]

**YES** The man **changed** his profession. The man **will change** his profession. ◆

Small capitals call out Glossary key terms.

End of an Alert

Animation developed differently in America and Japan after WWII. While Americans considered animation entertainment for children, the Japanese viewed it as entertaining primarily [mainly] for adults. Since the beginning of print, cartooning in Japan has targeted adults, so anime was a natural step [in this tradition].

Hand-edited examples illustrate editing and revision strategies.

**EXERCISE 7-2**  Underline all main verbs. Refer to 7d for help.

EXAMPLE  The study of bats <u>produces</u> some surprising information.

1. Most bats developed many years ago from a shrew-like mammal.

2. One thousand different types of bats exist.

Exercise

183

Page number

v

# *Preface*

This eighth edition of the *Simon & Schuster Handbook for Writers* gives you comprehensive access to the information you need about the writing process, from mastering grammar to using correct punctuation, from writing research papers to documenting sources, and from writing for the Web to writing using visuals. The **organizational structure** corresponds to the way that writers actually use the topics and strategies. The *Simon & Schuster Handbook* is carefully designed for usability in college and beyond, as illustrated in this Preface.

**Accessible and proven tone.** Lynn Troyka and Doug Hesse make topics accessible and welcome students into a conversation about becoming a better writer. Consider these quotes from just a few of the book's reviewers:

> "There is a real sense of commitment to the reader and helping the reader understand and negotiate his or her way through the myriad of information about academic writing, especially the research paper."
> —Joyce Boatright, North Harris College

> "I really like the author's voice as well as the multilayered approach to making the information accessible."
> —Gina Claywell, Murray State University

> "I like the 'I was once in your shoes' approach. It's often difficult for students—and instructors—to realize that no one is born knowing how to write and that writing is a process that can be learned."
> —Ruth Gerik, University of Texas, Arlington

> "I think the authors' approach represents a departure from traditional handbooks in that they come across as peers in the campaign to make students better writers. I think students will be more responsive to this type of approach than the traditional didactic voice that most handbooks employ."
> —Joel Henderson, Chattanooga State Technical Community College

> "The authors' approach is friendly, nonthreatening, and inviting. . . . The book itself is attractive and eye-catching but not glitzy or lacking in substance."
> —Dorothy Minor, Tulsa Community College

> "I especially like the approach the authors have taken. . . . Their information about their own writing experience is an attempt to connect with the readers, something I try to do in my own Composition and Rhetoric class."
> —Patricia Cearley, South Plains College

**Emphasis on critical thinking from page one.** A new Chapter 1, "Thinking Like a Writer," and a revised Chapter 4, "Thinking, Reading, and Writing Critically," more explicitly connect critical thinking with the kinds of strategies and habits that writers practice.

**Comprehensive coverage of argument.** An updated and more comprehensive Chapter 5, "Writing Arguments," reflects current theory, research, and practice.

**Easy access to common errors integrated throughout the text.** Common errors that most writers make are often called out as **Alerts** or in **Boxes** throughout the text. Students can use the **Quick Find** feature on the back cover to locate the sections of the book that address specific common errors.

**Coverage and support for writing with technology.**

- Updated Chapter 41, "Making Oral Presentations and Using Multimedia," explains how and why to use various strategies for effective oral presentations. This chapter also discusses how to use several types of multimedia and the pitfalls associated with them.

- Updated Chapter 42, "Document and Visual Design," helps students make effective and ethical uses of technology.

- Revised Chapter 43, "Writing for the Web," shows students how to produce effective online texts for various audiences and purposes.

**Support for multilingual writers integrated throughout.** Whether English is your native language or you are multilingual, you'll find answers in the *Simon & Schuster Handbook for Writers* to your questions about standard American English grammar, punctuation, and sentence correctness and style. **ESL Tips** are integrated throughout, and there's a built-in **mini ESL handbook** (Part 7) devoted to questions of special concern to multilingual students.

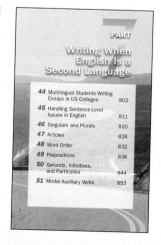

**Coverage of analyzing visuals and writing using visuals.** A new chapter on viewing images critically (Chapter 6) provides practical and theoretically sound strategies for students to analyze the images that are increasingly a part of the texts they encounter. New coverage of writing using images (integrated in Chapters 41, 42, and 43) prepares students to use visuals in their own documents.

**Research and documentation sections that provide applicable strategies and are designed for utility.** We know from talking to instructors and students that the research and documentation sections of a handbook are the most often referenced. Therefore, we have taken great care in designing these sections to be as useful as possible.

- Thoroughly revised research chapters emphasize the distinction between scholarly sources (such as those found in libraries and professionally edited databases) and less reliable sources, including strategies for recognizing and integrating credible sources.
- The use of computer research strategies is fully integrated throughout the book.
- Four new full-color documentation maps illustrate original sources and provide guidelines for evaluating and citing a variety of print and electronic sources.
- Chapter 33, "Using Sources and Avoiding Plagiarism," helps students appreciate the importance of citing sources and provides useful strategies for avoiding plagiarism.

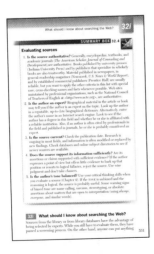

You can easily locate coverage of **MLA documentation, APA documentation, Chicago Manual (CM) documentation,** and the **Council of Science Editors (CSE) documentation** by referring to the Overview of Contents. New examples and updated models have been provided throughout.

**Student and professional writing samples.** The *Simon & Schuster Handbook for Writers* contains eight complete samples of student writing, five of which are new papers, on fresh topics of interest. This book also includes new examples of professional writing. Below is a list of just a few of the examples you will find throughout the book.

- Three drafts of a student essay to illustrate drafting and revising strategies (Chapter 2)
- A student's argument research paper (Chapter 5)
- Students' literature essays (Chapter 38)
- Various examples of business and public writing (Chapter 40)
- New examples of a student-made flyer (Chapter 42) and Web site (Chapter 43)
- New student MLA-style research paper (Chapter 34)
- New student APA-style research paper (Chapter 35)

Figure 42.2 A Flyer for The Nature Club

**Extensive coverage of Writing Across the Curriculum.** Part 6, "Writing Across the Curriculum—and Beyond," was thoroughly revised to connect writing in the composition classroom to writing in other disciplines and in the world beyond. Look for the **Writing for the World icon** throughout the text to identify integrated coverage.

- Chapter 37, "Comparing the Disciplines," more fully connects the writing students do in other classes, thereby providing a resource for students throughout their college years.
- Updated Chapter 38, "Writing About the Humanities and Literature," which includes sample student literature papers, explains the types of writing that students do in the humanities.
- Chapter 39, "Writing in the Social Sciences and Natural Sciences," reflects the current range of practices and theories for teaching and writing in these disciplines.
- Substantially revised Chapter 40, "Business and Public Writing," explains characteristics of business and professional writing and offers specific advice, along with examples, of several common types of workplace and public writing.
- Updated Chapter 41, "Making Oral Presentations and Using Multimedia," explains how and why to use various strategies for effective oral presentations. This chapter also discusses how to use several types of multimedia and the pitfalls associated with them.

- Revised Chapter 43, "Writing for the Web," shows students how to produce effective online texts for various audiences and purposes.

**A contemporary visual and functional design.** Greater use of full-color images and illustrations throughout not only enhances interest for students but also conforms to the increased use of visual rhetoric in composition.

- A new visual and functional design was carefully crafted to make navigation quick and easy (see the sample page at the beginning of the Preface for an illustrated walk-through of the design).
- The **Overview of Contents** on the inside front cover provides a comprehensive list of parts, chapters, and sections. To find a specific topic, use the **List of Boxes by Content**, the **ESL Index**, and the **Subject Index** at the end of the book.
- **Seven Parts** separate major topics into sections. Each part opener contains a list of contents for that specific part. Numbered chapters contain uncomplicated discussions in small "chunks" of information. Every chunk has a chapter number plus a letter in alphabetical order within the chapter.
- **Major headings are worded to resemble Frequently Asked Questions (FAQs)** you're likely to be asking when you consult the *Simon & Schuster Handbook for Writers.* Look for the FAQ repeated in a "running head" at the top of each right-hand page to help you navigate smoothly through the book. You can also use the colored rectangle at the top outside corner of each page to check which chapter you're using.
- Each of the **Boxes** offers a quick way to find important information. Look for **Summary Boxes** 📊, **Pattern Boxes** 📋, and **Checklist Boxes** ✅ throughout the text. And if you ever need to locate a box by topic, you can turn to the **List of Boxes by Content**. Also, you will find **Alerts** ➔ throughout the book to remind you about a rule or other relevant information. For example, in a sentence discussion, an Alert might remind you of a comma rule that applies.

**A valuable and integrated Web site to help students get better grades and instructors manage their courses.** Every page of the eighth edition of the *Simon & Schuster Handbook for Writers* is available online for you to search effortlessly by index, part number, and chapter number. (More information on the Web site is provided under the list of supplements.)

## Supplements

The following supplements accompany the eighth edition to aid in teaching and learning:

## FOR THE INSTRUCTOR

- **Annotated Instructor's Edition (AIE)**. Annotations in the margins of the AIE for the *Simon & Schuster Handbook for Writers*, Eighth Edition, offer instructors and teaching assistants teaching tips, annotated bibliographic citations from major journals in composition, thought-provoking quotations about writing, and answers to the in-text exercises.

- **Instructor's Manual**. *Strategies and Resources for Teaching Writing with the Simon & Schuster Handbook for Writers* offers practical, hands-on advice for new and experienced composition instructors for organizing their syllabi, planning, and teaching.

- **Prentice Hall Resources for Writing**. This series is a specially designed set of supplements for the instructor that support timely classroom and composition topics. These supplements are available upon adoption of the *Simon & Schuster Handbook for Writers*, Eighth Edition.

  - *Teaching Writing Across the Curriculum* by Art Young is written for college teachers in all disciplines and provides useful advice on teaching writing across the curriculum.

  - *Teaching Civic Literacy* by Cheryl Duffy offers advice on how to integrate civic literacy into the composition classroom.

  - *Teaching Visual Rhetoric* by Susan Loudermilk provides an illustrated look at visual rhetoric and offers guidance on how to incorporate this topic into the classroom.

  - *Teaching Writing for ESL Students* by Ruth Spack addresses various strategies that can be employed to teach writing to non-native speakers.

## FOR THE INSTRUCTOR AND STUDENT

- **NEW!** *Web Site with Tutoring, Personal Study Plan, and Interactive eBook* (**<www.prenhall.com/troyka>**). Every copy of the *Simon & Schuster Handbook for Writers*, Eighth Edition, is packaged with an access card that allows you to register for instant access to the book's Web site. This comprehensive, easy-to-use, valuable Web site offers the following resources and tools in one place:

  - **Interactive eBook**. The Web site includes a complete online version of the book unlike any other. Whenever you write or do research, the eBook is just a click away. The eBook can be searched by table of contents, index, and heading number. Students can also annotate and highlight their eBook, just as they would a print book. The eBook is linked to thousands of interactive exercises, videos, course management tools, research tools, and more.

  - **Diagnostics and Personal Study Plan**. The book's Web site includes before and after tests available for student self-assessment. These comprehensive tests are automatically graded, and the results are broken down by the student's particular strengths and weaknesses. In areas where the student might want more practice, the software will automatically generate a custom eBook, a personal set of quizzes, and topic-specific videos. The table of contents is customized and aligned to the quizzes and videos to help students master each topic. The result is an "intelligent" study plan specific to each student's needs.

- *English Tutor Center*. Actual composition instructors will review student papers for structure, style, organization, and grammar, providing feedback for the revision process. Tutors will also help students use the handbook and Web site resources when writing and researching.

- *Exchange*. This resource provides instructor commentary and peer review.

- *Research Navigator*™. This tool is the easiest way for students to start a research assignment or research paper. Students get extensive help on the research process and access to exclusive databases of credible and reliable source material, including the EBSCO Academic Journal and Abstract Database, *New York Times* Archive, "Best of the Web" Link Library, and the *Financial Times* Article Archive and Company Financials.

- *Interactive, Self-Graded Exercises*. This resource provides additional exercises tied to every topic of every chapter in the handbook.

- *Writing and Grammar Practice for ESL Students*. This additional set of exercises has over 700 interactive activities on topics that ESL students find most difficult.

- *Blue Pencil Exercises*. This popular editing software provides contextual grammar and punctuation editing exercises at the paragraph level.

- *Optional Plagiarism Detection Software*. MyDropBox allows instructors to submit papers for plagiarism detection or set up class accounts so that students can submit their papers themselves. MyDropBox provides its users with comprehensive plagiarism reports on all submitted documents, alerting the user to identified plagiarism. MyDropBox can be used not only to catch plagiarism, but to help students learn to avoid it altogether.

- *Understanding Plagiarism*. This section of the Web site helps students understand what plagiarism is and how to avoid committing plagiarism.

- **NEW!** *Writing Matters Videos*. This video series includes anecdotes from instructors and students with tips on teaching and writing from the handbook, as well as interviews with professionals who discuss the importance of writing in their jobs.

- *Research and Documentation Web Site*. This site provides a quick guide to writing a research paper and documenting sources.

- **Course Management**. All the resources available on the book's Web site are also available in CourseCompass™, BlackBoard™, and WebCT™. Contact your Prentice Hall sales representative for more information.

- **Student Workbook and Answer Key**. *The Simon & Schuster Workbook for Writers* contains hundreds of additional exercises and activities with answers to help improve writing skills.

- **NEW! *The Prentice Hall WAC PAC***. A compilation of resources, designed to facilitate teaching and learning Writing Across the Curriculum (WAC), includes *Papers Across the Curriculum* (edited by Judith Ferster), a series of sample student papers, and *A Prentice Hall Pocket Reader: Writing Across the Curriculum* (by Stephen Brown, University of Nevada Las Vegas). If you would like to put additional emphasis on WAC in your composition course(s), please contact your Prentice Hall sales representative for more information.

**Dictionary, Thesaurus, Writer's Guides, Workbooks, and Pocket Readers.** The following resources can be packaged with the *Simon & Schuster Handbook for Writers*, Eighth Edition. These valuable student resources provide additional depth on specialized topics that may only be touched upon in the text, and allow you to customize the handbook to your specific needs. Contact your local Prentice Hall representative for additional information.

- *The New American Webster Handy College Dictionary*
- *The New American Roget's College Thesaurus*
- *A Writer's Guide to Research and Documentation*
- *A Writer's Guide to Oral Presentations and Writing in the Disciplines*
- *A Writer's Guide to Document and Web Design*
- *A Writer's Guide to Writing About Literature*
- *The Prentice Hall Grammar Workbook*
- *The Prentice Hall ESL Workbook*
- *Applying English to Your Career (Workbook)*
- *A Prentice Hall Pocket Reader: Argument*
- *A Prentice Hall Pocket Reader: Literature*
- *A Prentice Hall Pocket Reader: Patterns*
- *A Prentice Hall Pocket Reader: Themes*
- *A Prentice Hall Pocket Reader: Purposes*
- *A Prentice Hall Pocket Reader: Writing Across the Curriculum*
- *Papers Across the Curriculum*

## *Acknowledgments*

With this eighth edition of the *Simon & Schuster Handbook for Writers*, we heartily thank all those students who, to our great luck, have landed in our writing courses. We admire how they and their counterparts in classrooms around the world strive to write skillfully, think critically, and communicate successfully, in college and beyond. We especially thank the individual students who have given us permission to make them "published authors" by including their exemplary writing in this handbook.

Hundreds of students have contacted us by e-mail or letter with their reactions to, and questions about, the *Simon & Schuster Handbook for Writers* or related matters. We deeply appreciate these messages. We take your comments seriously and use them to improve our teaching and this book. Any student now using the *Simon & Schuster Handbook for Writers* is welcome to get in touch with us at <troykalq@nyc.rr.com>, at <ddhesse@ilstu.edu>, or c/o Executive English Editor, Pearson Education, One Lake Street, Upper Saddle River, NJ 07458. We promise to answer.

Along with our colleagues at Prentice Hall, we'd like to call special attention to an expert team of advisors and contributors who helped us shape and polish this eighth edition to be a truly great resource for instructors and students alike. We could not have completed this challenging task without the meaningful contributions of this team:

Melinda Reichelt, University of Toledo, helped write new chapters and integrated content for multilingual writers.

Dorothy Minor, Tulsa Community College, and Leslie Leach, College of the Redwoods, skillfully revised and added to the exercises throughout the book and the answers in the AIE.

Georgia Newman, Polk Community College, a colleague and dear friend, meticulously updated the AIE to be relevant for today's instructors.

Plentiful appreciation goes to members of Prentice Hall's Advisory Board for this text, who continue to share perspectives on teaching writing.

For their helpful analytic reviews of the seventh edition of the *Simon & Schuster Handbook for Writers* and drafts of this eighth edition, we sincerely thank Linda de Roche, Wesley College; Andy Anderson, Johnson County Community College; Mailin Barlow, Valencia Community College; Pauline Uchmanowicz, State University of New York, New Paltz; Monroe Lerner, Milwaukee Area Technical College; Carolyn Kinslow, Cameron University; Colleen Lloyd, Cuyahoga Community College; Nate Gordon, Kishwaukee Community College; Muriel Fuqua, Daytona Beach Community College; and James McWard, Johnson County Community College.

We're also grateful to past contributors, advisors, and reviewers of this handbook and related projects: Esther DiMarzio, Kishwaukee

Community College; Carolyn Calhoun-Dillahunt, Yakima Valley Community College; Kip Strasma, Illinois Central College; Cy Strom, Colborne Communications Centre in Toronto, Ontario; Mary Angelo, University of South Florida; Martha Bachman, Camden County College; Sandra Barnhill, South Plains College; Nancy Blattner, Longwood University; Brian J. Benson, A & T State University; Ken Claney, Tulsa Community College; Gary Christenson, Elgin Community College; Nita Danko, Purdue University, Calumet; David Elias, Eastern Kentucky University; Diana Grahn, Longview Community College; Jean Harmon, Chemetka Community College; Lola Harmon, Greenville Technical College; Sarah Harrison, Tyler Junior College; Gary Hatch, Brigham Young University; Elaine Kromhout, Indian River Community College; Patrick McMahon, Tallahassee Community College; Dorothy Minor, Tulsa Community College; Catherine C. Olson, Tomball College; Lindee Owens, University of Central Florida; Michael Suwak, College of Southern Maryland; Carolyn West, Daytona Beach Community College; Kathleen Bell, University of Central Florida; Jon Bentley, Albuquerque Technical-Vocational Institute; Don Jay Coppersmith, Internet consultant; Jo Ellen Coppersmith, Utah Valley State College; Ann B. Dobie, University of Southwestern Louisiana; David Fear, Valencia Community College; Michael J. Freeman, Director of the Utah Valley State College Library; Kathryn Fitzgerald, University of Utah; Barbara Gaffney, University of New Orleans; D. J. Henry, Daytona Beach Community College; Scott Leonard, Youngstown State University; Dorothy V. Lindman, Brookhaven College; Alice Maclin, DeKalb College; Darlene Malaska, Youngstown Christian University; Marilyn Middendorf, Embry Riddle University; Patricia Morgan, Louisiana State University; Mary Ruetten, University of New Orleans; Matilda Delgado Saenz; Phillip Sipiora, University of South Florida; Maggy Smith, University of Texas at El Paso; Martha Smith, Brookhaven College; Paulette Smith, Reference Librarian, Valencia Community College; Donnie Yeilding, Central Texas College; Valerie Zimbaro, Valencia Community College; Westrich Baker, Southeast Missouri State University; Marilyn Barry, Alaska Pacific University; Norman Bosley, Ocean Community College; Phyllis Brown, Santa Clara University; Judith A. Burnham, Tulsa Community College; Robert S. Caim, West Virginia University at Parkersburg; Joe R. Christopher, Tarleton State University; Marilyn M. Cleland, Purdue University, Calumet; Thomas Copeland, Youngstown State University; Janet Cutshall, Sussex Community College; Dawn Elmore-McCrary, San Antonio College; Joanne Ferreira, State University of New York at New Paltz and Fordham University; Sheryl Forste-Grupp, Villanova University; Carol L. Gabel, William Paterson College; Joe Glaser, Western Kentucky University; Michael Goodman, Fairleigh Dickinson University; Mary Multer Greene, Tidewater Community College at Virginia Beach; Jimmy Guignard, University of Nevada at Reno; Julie Hagemann, Purdue University, Calumet; John L. Hare, Montgomery College; Kimberly Harrison,

Florida International University; Lory Hawkes, DeVry Institute of Technology, Irving; Janet H. Hobbs, Wake Technical Community College; Frank Hubbard, Marquette University; Rebecca Innocent, Southern Methodist University; Ursula Irwin, Mount Hood Community College; Denise Jackson, Southeast Missouri State University; Margo K. Jang, Northern Kentucky University; Peggy Jolly, University of Alabama at Birmingham; Myra Jones, Manatee Community College; Rodney Keller, Brigham Young University, Idaho; Judith C. Kohl, Dutchess Community College; James C. McDonald, University of Southwestern Louisiana; Martha Marinara, University of Central Florida; Michael J. Martin, Illinois State University; Michael Matto, Yeshiva University; Susan J. Miller, Santa Fe Community College; Pamela Mitzelfeld, Oakland University; Rosemary G. Moffett, Elizabethtown Community College; Rhonda Morris, Lake City Community College; Roarck Mulligan, Christopher Newport University; Alyssa O'Brien, Stanford University; Jon F. Patton, University of Toledo; Pamela T. Pittman, University of Central Oklahoma; Nancy B. Porter, West Virginia Wesleyan College; Stephen Prewitt, David Lipscomb University; Kirk Rasmussen, Utah Valley State College; Edward J. Reilly, St. Joseph's College; Mary Anne Reiss, Elizabethtown Community College; Peter Burton Ross, University of the District of Columbia; Eileen Schwartz, Purdue University, Calumet; Lisa Sebti, Central Texas College; Eileen B. Seifert, DePaul University; John S. Shea, Loyola University at Chicago; Tony Silva, Purdue University; Beverly J. Slaughter, Broward Community College; Martha A. Smith, Brookhaven College; Scott R. Stankey, Anoka Ramsey Community College; Bill M. Stiffler, Harford Community College; Michael Strysick, Wake Forest University; Jack Summers, Central Piedmont Community College; Susan Swartwout, Southeast Missouri State College; Vivian A. Thomlinson, Cameron University; Michael Thro, Tidewater Community College at Virginia Beach; William P. Weiershauser, Iowa Wesleyan College; Joe Wenig, Purdue University; Carolyn West, Daytona Beach Community College; Roseanna B. Whitlow, Southeast Missouri State University; and the late and wildly admired Sally Young, University of Tennessee at Chattanooga.

A project as complicated as the *Simon & Schuster Handbook for Writers* cannot be undertaken without the expertise and dedication of many professionals. We would like to thank the exceptional people at Prentice Hall who facilitated our work on the eighth edition. We're especially grateful for the expertise of Paul Crockett, Veronica Tomaiuolo, Tara Culliney, Melissa Casciano, Marta Tomins, Windley Morley, Shelly Kupperman, Judy Kiviat, Ann Marie McCarthy, Anne Nieglos, Leah Jewell, Brandy Dawson, Yolanda De Rooy, Rochelle Diogenes, and Alexis Walker. All have worked creatively, tirelessly, and with good cheer.

Doug values Lynn Troyka's vast knowledge, skill, dedication to teaching, and patience with a greenhorn. He appreciates the support of the

Honors Program staff at Illinois State University, the insights of his long-time colleagues Jan Neuleib, Ron Fortune, Ron Strickland, and Jim Kalmbach, and the energies of his Illinois State students. He further states, "Carol Rutz, Erika Lindeman and, foremost and always, Kathi Yancey, have been exemplary professional and personal friends. Dan Graybill, Michelle Staley, Susan Bellas, and Lawrence Bellas are constant sources of support and friendship. My children, Monica, Andrew, and Paige, amaze me with their creativity, as does the best writer I know: Becky Bradway, my wife."

Lynn is especially grateful to her coauthor Doug Hesse for his gentle friendship and invaluable participation in revising the *Simon & Schuster Handbook for Writers* for its eighth edition. Lynn also places on the record her gratitude to Ida Morea, her administrative assistant and special pal, Lynn's central support with her solid expertise and clever problem solving; Kristen Black, along with Dan, Lindsey, and Ryan, the beloved, ever-present joy of her life; Avery Ryan, Lynn's superb friend and "niece," along with Jimmy, Gavin, and Ian, for being irreplaceably woven into the texture of her life; and Edith Klausner, Lynn's sister and grand friend, a vital part of her life. Other exceptional folks include Susan Bartelstone; Florence Bolden; Rita and Hy Cohen; Esther DiMarzio; Alan, Lynne, Adam, and Josh Furman; Edie and Alan Lipp; JoAnn Lavery; Roberta Moore; Betty Renshaw; Magdelena Rogalskaja; Joseph W. Thweatt; Lisa and Nathaniel Wallace; Muriel Wolfe; and extraordinary Douglas Young III and his wife Anna. Principally, Lynn thanks her husband and sweetheart, David Troyka, for being her treasured companion and most discerning critic.

**Lynn Quitman Troyka**
**Doug Hesse**

# About the Authors

**LYNN QUITMAN TROYKA,** Adjunct Professor in the Graduate Program in Language and Literature at the City College (CCNY) of the City University of New York (CUNY), has also taught at Queensborough Community College. Former editor of the *Journal of Basic Writing,* she has had her writing and research published in major journals and various scholarly collections. She also conducts workshops in the teaching of writing. Dr. Troyka is coauthor of *Quick Access Reference for Writers,* Fifth Edition, Prentice Hall (2007); *QA Compact,* Prentice Hall (2007); the Canadian editions of her *Simon & Schuster Handbook for Writers* and *Quick Access Reference for Writers; Structured Reading,* Seventh Edition, Prentice Hall (2007); and *Steps in Composition,* Eighth Edition, Prentice Hall (2004).

Dr. Troyka is a past chair of the Conference on College Composition and Communication (CCCC); the Two-Year College Association (TYCA) of the National Council of Teachers (NCTE); the College Section of NCTE; and the Writing Division of the Modern Language Association (MLA). She received the 2001 CCCC Exemplar Award, the highest CCCC award for scholarship, teaching, and service; the Rhetorician of the Year Award; and the TYCA Pickett Award for Service.

"This information," says Dr. Troyka, "tells what I've done, not who I am. I am a teacher. Teaching is my life's work, and I love it."

**DOUG HESSE,** Professor of English and Director of Writing at the University of Denver as of Fall 2006, previously held several positions at Illinois State University, including Director of the Honors Program, Director of Writing Programs, and Director of the Center for the Advancement of Teaching. Dr. Hesse earned his PhD from the University of Iowa. He has also taught at the University of Findlay, Miami University (as Wiepking Distinguished Visiting Professor), and Michigan Tech.

Dr. Hesse is a past chair of the Conference on College Composition and Communication (CCCC), the nation's largest professional association of college writing instructors. A past president, as well, of the Council of Writing Program Administrators (WPA),

Dr. Hesse edited that organization's journal, *Writing Program Administration.* He is a member of the executive committees of the National Council of Teachers of English (NCTE) and the Modern Language Association (MLA) Division on Teaching as a Profession.

He is the author of forty-five articles and book chapters, in such journals as *College Composition and Communication, College English, JAC, Rhetoric Review,* and the *Journal of Teaching Writing* and in such books as *Essays on the Essay; Writing Theory and Critical Theory; The Writing Program Administrator's Sourcebook; Literary Nonfiction; The Private, the Public, and the Published;* and *Passions, Pedagogies, and 21st Century Technologies.* He is also coauthor with Lynn Quitman Troyka of *Quick Access Reference for Writers,* Fifth Edition, Prentice Hall (2007) and *QA Compact,* Prentice Hall (2007). Illinois State University recently named him Outstanding University Researcher.

"Of all these accomplishments," says Dr. Hesse, "the one that matters most to me is being named Distinguished Humanities Teacher at Illinois State. That one came from my students and suggests that, in however small a way, I've mattered in their education and lives."

# PART 1

# The Writing Process

# Chapter 1

## THINKING LIKE A WRITER

### 1a    What is the current scene for writers?

We live in an age when people do more writing than they have at any other time in history. Computers have not only made it easier to produce clean texts, but they've also allowed average writers to create documents that twenty years ago would have required professional designers. Just as important, the Internet and devices such as cell phones and personal data assistants have made it easier for people to share writing, both formally and informally.

As writers and writing teachers, we find it particularly interesting—and heartening—to witness the explosion of writing that people choose to do on their own, without any prompting. You might be among the millions of people who regularly write e-mails and text messages, keep journals, craft stories or poems, create Web sites on hobbies, or write **blogs** (Web logs)—all without anyone asking you to do so. The Internet is filled with ordinary people who write about their favorite television programs, analyze politics, or simply share their experiences and thoughts. Figure 1.1 shows part of a blog that a college student, Jillian, keeps to entertain herself and her friends—and sometimes to blow off steam.

Digital photography and scanning allow people to blend words with photographs and images to make scrapbooks, newsletters and posters, or memorable keepsakes. Of course, many people continue to enjoy the simple pleasure of writing by hand—as we do ourselves from time to time.

The writing that people choose to do on their own complements the kind of writing that they do for college and work. As a student, you can expect to write in a variety of courses across the curriculum, not just in English. Writing is also vital in your career. A 2004 survey of business leaders by the National Commission on Writing found that "people who cannot write and communicate clearly will not be hired and are unlikely to last long enough to be considered for promotion." Recent surveys of people in a variety of jobs and professional fields say that they spend an average of 30 percent of each day writing. Most commonly, they write letters, memos, product evaluations, and technical manuals, but they

Bloggers can freely write down thoughts in the same way they might write in a print journal.

Blogs often have profile sections in which bloggers can tell others about themselves.

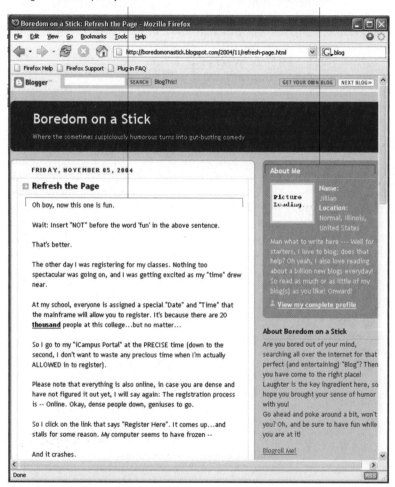

Figure 1.1 A student's blog

may also write business-trip reports, proposals, meeting minutes, feasibility reports, lab reports, Web pages, newsletters, or brochures.

Skilled writers move effectively from one kind of writing to another—writing for family, friends, and personal enjoyment; for college instructors; and for employers and colleagues. Skilled writers participate as informed citizens, using writing for everything from appealing parking tickets to influencing the outcomes of elections. A measure of your skill as a writer is the ability to move back and forth between the kinds of writing you choose to do and the kinds you're obliged to do. The opportunities to make a difference with your writing are limitless, even if that prospect at times might seem a bit intimidating.

If you're one of the many people who choose to write out of personal interest, we respect you and offer this book to help you stretch. If you're someone who doesn't very much like to write, we hope that you might explore the satisfaction of putting your thoughts into words—and we hope this book helps ease your way. We've composed these pages because we have repeatedly seen in our classes that everyone has the capacity to make the concentrated effort needed to become an effective writer. Certainly, if you spend some time and energy improving your writing skills, your efforts will bring you academic, professional, and personal rewards.

We'd like to make a recommendation to you before you dive into this book: Keep a portfolio of your writing during your college years. For some of you, a portfolio might be assigned as part of your college-course routine. If it's not, we urge you to keep a personal record of your work so that you can monitor your evolution as a writer and thinker. Little can be as compelling as looking back over the years to see where you've been and how far you've come as a writer. For an example of the opening screen of a required digital portfolio in a freshman English class, see section 1h.

## 1b   What are the major purposes for writing?

A writer's purpose for writing motivates what and how he or she writes. In college, the purposes for writing are far more than to fulfill an assignment. The purposes relate to the academic reason you're writing. Every writer needs to get under way by choosing one of the four major overall purposes for writing, listed in Box 1.1.

---

**SUMMARY BOX** 1.1

### Purposes for writing*

- To express yourself
- To inform a reader
- To persuade a reader
- To create a literary work

*Adapted from James L. Kinneavy, in *A Theory of Discourse* (1971; New York: Norton, 1980).

---

In this handbook, we concentrate on the two major purposes you need for most academic writing: to inform a reader (1b.2) and to persuade a reader (1b.3). The two remaining purposes listed in Box 1.1 are important for contributing to human thought and culture, but they relate less to what most college writing involves.

## 1b.1   What is expressive writing?

**Expressive writing** is writing to express your personal thoughts and feelings. Much expressive writing is for the writer's eyes only, such as that in diaries, personal journals, or exploratory drafts. When expressive writing is for public reading, it usually falls into the category of literary writing. The excerpt here comes from a memoir intended for public reading.

> For much of her life my mother longed, passionately longed, for a decent house. One with a yard that did not have to be cleared with an ax. One with a roof that kept out the rain. One with a floor that you could not fall through. She longed for a beautiful house of wood or stone. Or of red brick, like the houses her many sisters and their husbands had. When I was thirteen she found such a house. Green-shuttered, white-walled. Breezy. With a lawn and a hedge and giant pecan trees. A porch swing. There her gardens flourished in spite of the shade, as did her youngest daughter, for whom she sacrificed her life doing hard labor in someone else's house, in order to afford peace and prettiness for her child, to whose grateful embrace she returned each night.
>
> —Alice Walker, "My Mother's Blue Bowl"

## 1b.2   What is informative writing?

**Informative writing** seeks to give information to readers and usually to explain it. Another name for this type of writing is *expository writing* because it expounds on—sets forth in detail—observations, ideas, facts, scientific data, and statistics. You can find informative writing in textbooks, encyclopedias, technical and business reports, nonfiction books, newspapers, and many magazines.

The essential goal of informative academic writing is to educate your readers about something. Like all good educators, therefore, you want to present your information clearly, accurately, completely, and fairly. In section 3i of this handbook, we show you many strategies that writers use for informative writing. These strategies can help you deliver your message, but above all, your success depends on whether your readers can verify your information as accurate. Box 1.2 (p. 6) gives you a checklist to assess your informative writing. But first, here's a paragraph written to inform.

> "Diamonds in the rough" are usually round and greasy looking. But diamond miners are in no need of dark glasses to shield them from the

dazzling brilliance of the mines for quite another reason: even in a diamond pipe, there is only one part diamond per 14 million parts of worthless rock. Approximately 46,000 pounds of earth must be mined and sifted to produce the half-carat gem you might be wearing. No wonder diamonds are expensive!

—Richard B. Manchester, "Diamonds"

As informative writing, this paragraph works because it focuses clearly on its TOPIC* (diamonds in the rough), presents facts that can be verified (who, what, when, where), and is written in a reasonable tone.

---

CHECKLIST BOX **1.2**

## Informative writing

- Is its information clear?
- Does it present facts, ideas, and observations that can be verified?
- Does its information seem complete and accurate?
- Is the writer's tone reasonable and free of distortions? (1d)

---

### 1b.3  What is persuasive writing?

**Persuasive writing**, also called *argumentative writing*, seeks to persuade readers to support a particular opinion. When you write to persuade, you deal with debatable topics, those that people can consider from more than one point of view. Your goal is to change your readers' minds about the topic—or at least to bring your readers' opinions closer to your point of view. To succeed, you want to evoke a reaction in your audience so that they think beyond their present position (for example, reasoning why free speech needs to be preserved) or take action (for example, register to vote). Examples of persuasive writing include newspaper editorials, letters to the editor, opinion essays in newspapers and magazines, reviews, sermons, books that argue a point of view, and business proposals that advocate certain approaches over others.

In Chapter 3 of this handbook, we show you strategies of paragraph development that effective writers use in their persuasive writing. Also, Chapter 5 of this handbook offers you a whole chapter that discusses ways to write effective arguments.

In general terms, persuasive writing means you need to move beyond merely stating your opinion. You need to give the basis for that

---

*Words printed in SMALL CAPITAL LETTERS are discussed elsewhere in the text and are defined in the Terms Glossary at the back of this book.

opinion. You support your opinion by using specific, illustrative details to back up your **generalizations**, which are usually very broad statements. The first sentences of sections 1b.1, 1b.2, and 1b.3 in this chapter are examples of generalizations.

Box 1.3 gives you a checklist to assess your persuasive writing. But first, here's a paragraph written to persuade.

> It is a widely accepted fact that many of America's schools are doing a poor job of educating the nation's young people. Research studies indicate that about 30 percent of American high school students drop out before graduating. In some high school systems, fewer than half of the students who enter ever graduate. We should not be surprised, then, that one in four Americans is illiterate—unable to read and write at the most basic level. What can be done? American schools should take a lesson from Japan, where strict rules of behavior, very demanding school schedules, and high academic standards have produced nearly 100 percent literacy.
>
> —Nancy-Laurel Pettersen, "American Schools
> Should Take a Lesson from Japan"

As persuasive writing, this passage works because it provides undistorted information on literacy; it expresses a point of view that resides in sound reasoning (American schools should emulate Japanese schools); it offers evidence (a logical line of reasoning); and it tries to get the reader to agree with the point of view.

CHECKLIST BOX **1.3**

## Persuasive writing

- Does it present a point of view about which opinions vary?
- Does it support its point of view with specifics?
- Does it base its point of view on sound reasoning and logic?
- Are the parts of its argument clear?
- Does it intend to evoke a reaction from the reader?

**EXERCISE 1-1**    For each paragraph, decide if the dominant purpose is *informative, persuasive,* or *expressive.* Then, answer the questions in Box 1.2 or 1.3 in relation to the paragraph and explain your answers.

A.    Trees are living archives, carrying within their structure a record not only of their age but also of precipitation and temperature for each year in which a ring was formed. The record might also include the marks of forest fires, early frosts and, incorporated into the wood itself, chemical elements the tree removed from its environment. Thus, if we only knew how to unlock its secrets, a tree could tell us a great deal about what was happening in its neighborhood from the time of its beginning. Trees can tell us what was happening before written records became available. They also have a great deal to tell us about our future. The records of past climate that they contain can help us to understand the natural forces that produce our weather, and this, in turn, can help us plan.

—James S. Trefil, "Concentric Clues from Growth Rings Unlock the Past"

B.    We know very little about pain, and what we don't know makes it hurt all the more. Indeed, no form of illiteracy in the United States is so widespread or costly as ignorance about pain—what it is, what causes it, and how to deal with it without panic. Almost everyone can rattle off the names of at least a dozen drugs that can deaden pain from every conceivable cause—all the way from headaches to hemorrhoids. There is far less knowledge about the fact that about ninety percent of pain is self-limiting, that it is not always an indication of poor health, and that, most frequently, it is the result of tension, stress, idleness, boredom, frustration, suppressed rage, insufficient sleep, overeating, poorly balanced diet, smoking, excessive drinking, inadequate exercise, stale air, or any of the other abuses encountered by the human body in modern society.

—Norman Cousins, *Anatomy of an Illness*

C.    Although Littleman, my eleven-year-old poodle, has never been separated from his thirteen-year-old mother, Simone, they are remarkably different. Simone weighs in at about five kilograms with very delicate, sophisticated features and coarse, curly hair. Slightly shorter, Littleman tops the scale at no more than three kilograms and is quite handsome with his teddy-bear features and soft wavy hair. Simone was the first dog in the family and is a pedigreed poodle. In many ways she is the picture of a thoroughbred, with her snobby attitude and nonchalant manners. On the other hand, Littleman came into the family a year later with four other puppies of pure breeding, but they were never registered. Unlike his mother, Littleman is very friendly, almost to the point of being pesty at times.

—Linda Neal, student

**EXERCISE 1-2**    Consulting section 1b, write on each of these topics twice, once to inform and once to persuade your reader: diets, tastes in music, tourists, good manners, road rage. Be prepared to discuss how your two treatments of each topic differ.

## **1c** What does "audience" mean for writing?

Your **audience** consists of everyone who will read your writing. Thinking like a writer about audience means figuring out how to successfully reach your audience in various kinds of situations. For example, papers that you write for a history course differ in form and style from lab reports that you write in biology, and both differ from memos that you write on the job, letters that you write to a newspaper editor, or e-mails that you write to a friend. Effective writers know they need to adjust their writing for different tasks and audiences.

After college, your audiences are likely to be readers of your business, professional, and public writing (Chapters 40–43). In college, you'll surely address a mix of audience types that expect to read ACADEMIC WRITING. Here's a list of categories of those audiences, each of which is detailed in the section listed in parentheses.

- Your peers (1c.1)
- Your general audiences (1c.2)
- Your specialist audiences (who are much like your business audiences) (1c.3)
- Your instructor (who represents your general or specialized readers) (1c.4)

The more specifics you can assume about each of your audiences for your academic writing, the better your chances of communicating with them successfully.

**ESL TIPS:** (1) If you do not share a cultural background with your readers, it may be difficult for you to estimate how much your readers know about your topic. Discussing your topic with friends or classmates might help you decide what background information you need to include in your paper.

(2) As someone from a non-US culture, you might be surprised—even offended—by the directness with which people speak and write in the United States. If so, we hope you'll read our open letter—it introduces Part Seven of this handbook—to multilingual students about honoring their cultures. You may come from a written-language tradition that expects elaborate, formal, or ceremonial language; that reserves the central point of an academic essay for the middle; that requires tactful, indirect discussions (at least in comparison with the US style); and, in some cultures, that accommodates digressions that might, or might not, lead back to the main point. In contrast, US writers and readers expect language and style that are very direct, straightforward, and without embellishment (as compared with the styles of many other cultures). US college instructors expect essays in academic writing to contain a thesis

statement (usually at the end of the introductory paragraph). They further expect your writing to contain an organized presentation of information that moves tightly from one paragraph to the next, with generalizations that you always back up with strong supporting details, and with an ending paragraph that presents a logical conclusion to your discussion. Also, for writing in the United States, you need to use so-called edited American English. This means following the rules used by educated speakers. In reality, the United States has a rich mixture of grammar systems, but academic writing nevertheless requires edited American English. If you want to hear these forms spoken, listen to the anchors of television and radio news programs. You also need to choose words for your writing that are accurate in meaning and spelled correctly. ☻

To analyze your audience, you might ask yourself whatever questions in Box 1.4 you think will be useful in each situation.

---

**SUMMARY BOX** 1.4

## Ways to analyze your audience

**WHAT SETTING ARE THEY READING IN?**
- Academic setting? Specifically, what subject?
- Workplace setting? Specifically, what business area?

**WHO ARE THEY?**
- Age, gender
- Ethnic backgrounds, political philosophies, religious beliefs
- Roles (student, parent, voter, wage earner, property owner, veteran, and others)
- Interests, hobbies

**WHAT DO THEY KNOW?**
- Level of education
- Level of knowledge: Do they know less than you about the subject? as much as you about the subject? more than you about the subject?
- Beliefs: Is the audience likely to agree with your point of view? disagree with your point of view? have no opinion about the topic?
- Interests: Is the audience eager to read about the topic? open to the topic? resistant to or not interested in the topic?

## 1c.1 What is a peer audience?

Your peers are other writers like you. In some writing classes, instructors divide students into **peer-response groups**. Participating in a peer-response group makes you part of a respected tradition of colleagues helping colleagues. Professional writers often seek comments from other writers to improve their rough drafts. As a member of a peer-response group, you're not expected to be a writing expert. Rather, you're expected to offer responses as a practiced reader and as a fellow student writer who understands what writers go through.

The role of members of a peer-response group is to react and discuss, not to do the work for someone. Hearing or reading comments from your peers might be your first experience with seeing how others read your writing. This can be very informative, surprising, and helpful. Also, when peers share their writing with the group, each member gets the added advantage of learning about other students' writing for the same assignment.

Peer-response groups are set up in different ways. One arrangement calls for students to pass around and read one another's drafts silently, writing down reactions or questions in the margins or on a response form created by the instructor. In another arrangement, students read their drafts aloud, and then each peer responds either orally or in writing on a response form. Yet another arrangement asks for focused responses to only one or two features of each draft (perhaps each member's thesis statement, or topic sentences and supporting details, or use of transitional words, for example). Still another method is for the group to brainstorm a topic together before writing, to discuss various sides of a debatable topic, or to share reactions to an essay or piece of literature the class reads, and so on.

Whatever the arrangement of your group, you want to be clear about exactly what you are expected to do, both as a peer-responder and as a writer. If your instructor gives you guidelines for working in a peer-response group, follow them carefully. If you've never before participated in a peer-response group, or in the particular kind of group that your instructor forms, here are ways to get started: Consult the guidelines in Box 1.5 on the following page; watch what experienced peers do; and ask questions of your instructor (your interest shows a positive, cooperative attitude). Otherwise, just dive in knowing that you'll learn as you go.

Now to the sometimes sticky issue of how to take criticism of your writing: Here's our personal advice as writers for being able (or at least appearing able) to take constructive criticism gracefully. First, know that most students don't like to criticize their peers. They worry about being impolite or inaccurate, or losing someone's friendship. Try, therefore, to cultivate an attitude that encourages your peers to respond as freely and as helpfully as possible. Show, also, that you can listen without getting angry or feeling intruded on. Second, realize that most people tend to

## Guidelines for participating in peer-response groups

One major principle needs to guide your participation in a peer-response group: Always take an upbeat, constructive attitude, whether you're responding to someone else's writing or receiving responses from others.

### AS A RESPONDER

- Think of yourself as a coach, not a judge.
- Consider all writing by your peers as "works in progress."
- After hearing or reading a peer's writing, briefly summarize it to check that you and your peer are clear about what the peer said or meant to say.
- Start with what you think is well done. No one likes to hear only negative comments.
- Be honest in your suggestions for improvement.
- Base your responses on an understanding of the writing process, and remember that you're reading drafts, not finished products. All writing can be revised.
- Give concrete and specific responses. General comments such as "This is good" or "This is weak" aren't much help. Say specifically what is good or weak.
- Follow your instructor's system for putting your comments in writing so that your fellow writer can recall what you said. If one member of your group is supposed to take notes, speak clearly so that the person can be accurate. If you're the notetaker, be accurate and ask the speaker to repeat what he or she said if the comment went by too quickly.

### AS A WRITER

- Adopt an attitude that encourages your peers to respond freely. Listen and try to resist any urge to interrupt during a comment or to jump in to react.
- Remain open-minded. Your peers' comments can help you see your writing in a fresh way, which, in turn, can help you produce a better-revised draft.
- Ask for clarification if a comment isn't clear. If a comment is too general, ask for specifics.
- As much as you encourage your peers to be honest, remember that the writing is yours. You "own" it, and you decide which comments to use or not use.

be a little (or quite a bit) defensive about even the best-intentioned and most tactful criticism. Of course, if a comment is purposely mean or sarcastic, you and all others in your peer-response group have every right to say so and not tolerate such comments. Third, if you don't understand a comment fully, ask for clarification. Otherwise, you might misunderstand what's suggested and go off in the wrong direction.

Finally, no matter what anyone says about your writing, it remains yours alone. You retain "ownership" of your writing always, and you don't have to make every suggested change. Use only the comments that you think can move you closer to reaching your intended audience. Of course, if a comment from your instructor points out a definite problem, and you choose to ignore it, that could have an impact on your grade—though many instructors are open to an explanation of your rationale for deciding to ignore what they said.

**ALERT:** Some instructors and students use the terms *peer-response group* and *collaborative writing* to mean the same thing. In this handbook, we assign the terms to two different situations. We use *peer-response group* (1c.1) for students getting together in small groups to help one another write and revise. We use *collaborative writing* (2x) for students writing an essay, a research paper, or a report together in a group. ◆

**ESL TIP:** Students from cultures other than those in the United States or Canada might feel uncomfortable in the role of critic or questioner of other people's writing. Please know, however, that peer-response groups are fairly common in schools and at jobs because people usually think that "two heads are better than one." Sharing and questioning others' ideas—as well as how they are expressed in writing—is an honorable tradition in the United States and Canada. Peer-response groups help writers politely but firmly explore concepts and language, so please feel free to participate fully. In fact, some instructors grade you on your open participation in such activities. 🌐

## 1c.2  What is a general audience?

A **general audience** of readers is composed of educated, experienced readers. These are people who regularly read newspapers, magazines, and books. These readers, with general knowledge of many subjects, are likely to know something about your topic. However, if you get too technical, you're writing for readers who possess specialized knowledge on a particular subject (1c.3). Consequently, avoid specialized or technical terms, although you can use a few as long as you include everyday definitions.

In addition, general readers approach a piece of writing expecting to become interested in it. They hope to learn about a new topic, to add to their store of knowledge about a subject, and, often, to see a subject from a perspective other than their own. As a writer, you need to fulfill those expectations. Of course, there are also readers who are not particularly well-read or open to new ideas, but in most academic writing not intended for specialized audiences, you want to target a general audience, as defined above.

## 1c.3  What is a specialist audience?

A **specialist audience** is composed of readers who have expert knowledge of specific subjects or who are particularly committed to those subjects. Many people are experts in their occupational fields, and some become experts in areas that simply interest them, such as astronomy or raising orchids. People from a particular group background (for example, Democrats, Republicans, Catholics, or military veterans) are knowledgeable in those areas.

Specialist readers, however, share more than knowledge: They share assumptions and beliefs. For example, suppose you're writing for an audience of immigrants to the United States who feel strongly about keeping their cultural traditions alive. You can surely assume your readers know those traditions well, so you won't need to describe and explain the basics. Similarly, if you intend to argue that immigrants should abandon their cultural traditions in favor of US practices, you'll want to write respectfully about their beliefs. Additionally, whenever you introduce a concept that's probably new to a specialist audience, explain the concept thoroughly rather than assuming the audience will understand it right away.

## 1c.4  What is my instructor's role as audience?

As your audience, your instructor functions in three ways. First, your instructor assumes the role of your target audience, either as a general reader (1c.2) or a specialist reader (1c.3). Second, your instructor is a coach, someone committed to helping you improve your writing. Third, your instructor is the eventual evaluator of your final drafts.

Instructors know that few students are experienced writers or experts on the subjects they write about. Still, instructors expect your writing to reflect your having taken the time to learn something worthwhile about a topic and then to write about it clearly. Instructors are experienced readers who can recognize a minimal effort almost at once.

As important, instructors are people whose professional lives center on intellectual endeavors. You need, therefore, to write on topics that contain intrinsic intellectual interest (2d) and to discuss them according to the expectations for academic writing.

If you're a relatively inexperienced college writer, you don't want to assume that your instructor can mentally fill in what you leave out of your writing. Indeed, you might think that it's wrong, even insulting to your instructor, if you extend your discussion beyond simple statements. Instructors—indeed, all readers—can't be mind readers, so they expect students to write on a topic fully. If you think you might be saying too little, ask your peers to read your writing and tell you if you've developed your topic sufficiently.

## 1d    What is "tone" in writing?

**Tone** is more than what you say; tone is *how* you say it. As a writer, your tone reveals your attitude toward your AUDIENCE as well as toward the topic. Tone in writing operates like tone of voice, except in writing you can't rely on facial expressions and voice intonations to communicate your message.

Your DICTION (choice of words), LEVEL OF FORMALITY, and writing style create your tone. While you can use SLANG and other highly INFORMAL LANGUAGE in a note to your roommate or a close friend, such a relaxed tone isn't appropriate for ACADEMIC WRITING or BUSINESS WRITING. As a rule, when you write for an audience about whom you know little, use more formality in your tone. "More formality," by the way, doesn't mean dull and drab. Indeed, lively language in a serious discussion enhances your message.

Problems with tone result from combining words into certain phrases. It's the combination and location, not the words taken separately, that create a tone. For example, you want to avoid sarcastic language in an academic or business setting that calls for a reasonable tone. If you were to write "He was a regular Albert Einstein" to describe a person interviewed for a paper, those sarcastic words would say more about you than about the person interviewed. Such a tone implies that you have an overly critical or nasty streak. Conversely, you could introduce irony if you wrote "The chief assistant to Governor Marie Ghoti claimed that the governor could give me up-to-date information about my topic, but then the assistant turned out to know much more than the governor."

In business and professions, if you write a memo to your supervisor about a safety hazard in your workplace, you want to avoid writing a chatty message with a joke about an accident that could happen. Using such a tone directed at your supervisor would be considered flippant or irresponsible. Equally important, if you include minute details of background information that your supervisor already knows, your tone would probably seem condescending and your supervisor might become annoyed with you.

Academic writing usually calls for a medium-to-formal tone (21b), which is a reasonable, even-handed tone. It's somewhat formal and

15

serious but never pompous. Also, such a tone avoids language that attempts to manipulate your readers. Distorted facts or SLANTED LANGUAGE (21h)—for example, *the corrupt, deceitful politician* rather than *the politician under investigation for taking bribes*—jumps off the page, making your readers decide immediately that your message isn't objective or trustworthy.

Additionally, in all types of writing, GENDER-NEUTRAL LANGUAGE (21g) that represents both men and women fairly—for example, replace *policeman* with *police officer,* and replace *doctors' wives* with *doctors' spouses*—demonstrates an even-handed tone. Similarly, avoid SEXIST LANGUAGE, which involves words with sexist overtones (21g), or you'll alienate your readers because you appear to be insensitive to gender issues or crude in your understanding about the effects of language choices.

Another type of language that carries a message larger than the words themselves is pretentious language (21h). Its use implies either that you're showing off to impress people (which always backfires) or that you're obscuring a message. Choose straightforward rather than extravagant words (use *concert,* not *orchestral event*) if you want readers to take you seriously. Also, readers usually assume that you want to conceal something unpleasant if you use EUPHEMISMS (21l), such as *downsizing* or *rightsizing* instead of *cutting jobs.* Box 1.6 lists guidelines for handling tone in your writing.

---

**SUMMARY BOX  1.6**

### How to use tone in writing

- Reserve a highly informal tone for conversational writing.
- Use a formal or medium level of formality in your academic writing and when you write for supervisors, professionals, and other people you know from a distance.
- Avoid an overly formal, ceremonious tone.
- Avoid sarcasm and other forms of nastiness.
- Choose language appropriate for your topic and your readers.
- Choose words that work with your message, not against it.
- Whatever tone you choose to use, be consistent in each piece.

---

**EXERCISE 1-3**   Using the topics listed here, work individually or with your peer-response group to think through specific ways the tone of an essay would differ for the following three audiences: a college instructor, a close friend, and a supervisor at a job. Be ready to discuss in some detail how the three essays on each topic would differ for each audience. For help, consult sections 1c and 1d.

1. Suggestions for a fair way to evaluate each person's work
2. Benefits of having a more casual dress code
3. An explanation of why you were absent from class yesterday

## 1e   What does "sources for writing" mean?

**Sources for writing** consist of material that contains someone else's ideas, not yours. Sources, often called *outside sources,* include credible information on the Internet, library collections, and the spoken words of experts. Sources can add authority to what you write, especially if the topic is open to debate. But be careful: Different instructors have differing policies on students' using outside sources. Some instructors want students to draw on sources only when writing a research paper (Chapters 31–36). Other instructors encourage "source-based writing" for most assignments. Still other instructors never want students to use outside sources. Find out your instructor's stand on the use of sources so you can fulfill the requirements of your course successfully.

Some students wonder whether consulting sources for their writing might suggest that they can't come up with ideas of their own. Actually, the opposite is true. When students use sources well, they demonstrate their ability to locate relevant sources, assess whether the sources are credible and worth using, integrate the material with skill, and credit the sources accurately. To achieve this, follow the guidelines in Box 1.7 (p. 18).

Of course, no matter how many outside sources you refer to, you remain your own first source. Throughout your life, you've been building a fund of knowledge by reading, going to school, attending cultural and sports events, hearing speeches, watching television, and exploring the Internet. The basis for your writing is the information you have, as well as your ideas, reflections, reactions, and opinions. Sources offer support and additional information and points of view, but you're always the starting point for your writing.

When you use sources in your writing, never plagiarize. As a student, you want to become a full participant in the community of knowledge seekers and makers. The expected honorable standard for participants is always to credit thinkers who have come before you and on whose shoulders you stand as you learn and create. You therefore never want to behave unethically by stealing someone's thinking or language.

PLAGIARISM occurs when you take ideas or words from a source without revealing that you used a source. Always reveal your source and credit it by using DOCUMENTATION to tell your readers the exact place where your thinking is influenced by a source. Adhering to the requirements of the DOCUMENTATION STYLE you're using (Chapters 34–36), state the name of the source and where anyone who wishes to consult it can find it.

**SUMMARY BOX** 1.7

## Guidelines for using sources in writing

- Evaluate sources critically. Not all are accurate, true, or honest (4g, especially Box 4.6).
- Represent your sources accurately. Be sure to quote, paraphrase, and summarize well so that you avoid distorting the material (Chapter 33).
- Never plagiarize (Chapter 33).
- Know the difference between writing a SUMMARY and writing a SYNTHESIS (4e). A summary means all you do is report the source material. That is not enough. A synthesis means you make intelligent connections between a particular source or a variety of sources and your ideas. Synthesizing is what college writers are expected to do.
- Credit your sources with documentation that names them clearly and completely. Ask your instructor which documentation style to use. Five widely used styles are presented in Chapters 34–36.

If you forget to document your sources, you're plagiarizing (Chapter 33). Using quotation marks without naming your source is a form of plagiarizing. Leaving out quotation marks from a direct quotation that you take from a source, even if you name the source, is a form of plagiarizing. Plagiarism is a major academic offense. A student who plagiarizes can instantly fail a course or be expelled from college.

New computer technologies make plagiarism especially easy to detect today. If ethical reasons aren't enough to prevent you from plagiarizing, then the real chance of strong punishment definitely should be.

**ESL TIP:** In many cultures other than those in the United States and Canada, instructors expect students to respect and copy the thoughts and exact language of scholars, without naming the people who wrote the scholarship. This practice is not acceptable in the United States and most British-based educational systems. You always need to use documentation to credit your source. Otherwise, you're plagiarizing (that is, "stealing" the ideas of others), which is a major offense. ●

### 1f  What resources can help me with writing?

Your personal bookshelf needs to contain three essential volumes: a dictionary, a thesaurus, and a handbook for writers. A **dictionary** is indispensable. Most college bookstores offer a variety of hardback "college dictionaries." Before buying one, browse through a few to read some definitions you want to learn or to understand more clearly. Choose the book you like best. Also, a lightweight paperback abridged dictionary in your book bag can be very handy for checking unknown words on the spot. Unabridged dictionaries list all recognized words in standard use in English. Being comprehensive, they're usually heavy and oversized, so the reference section of every library usually stocks one for all students to consult (21e.1). Another valuable resource for writers is a **thesaurus**, which is a collection of SYNONYMS. The alphabetically arranged ones are the easiest to use. Check for this feature, as it isn't an automatic arrangement for a thesaurus. *Roget's 21st Century Thesaurus* is an excellent volume arranged alphabetically.

A **handbook for writers** is also vital for you to own. A handbook—such as the one you're holding as you read this—gives you detailed information about rules of grammar and punctuation and about other writing conventions. It also offers extensive advice about how to write successfully, whether for college, business, or the public. It shows you step by step how to write and document research papers. Some handbooks, including this one, contain guidance on how to write for a variety of courses other than English. You need all this information to write successfully in courses other than English and in your career after college.

Finally, **college libraries**, sometimes called *learning resource centers,* are essential for writers. Libraries are fully stocked with all manner of reference books, circulating books, resources for online access, and more. Some of the books listed above are available online through computers, although you'll probably need to connect to them by going through the library's Web site. Before you actually use the library, spend some time getting to know what's available. Then, you can dive right in when you need to get information. Chapter 32 provides extensive advice on using the library.

## 1g   How do computers shape the writing process?

Almost all writing projects, whether in college or in the workplace, require computers. Some instructors make allowances when getting to a computer is impossible, but the clear preference is for word-processed final drafts. If you own a computer or live with someone who does, you enjoy some obvious conveniences. If you don't, however, you can use computers on most campuses (often in libraries and student centers), in public libraries, and in Internet cafés.

Computers are important tools for creating documents, finding resources, managing work, and communicating with others.

### 1g.1  Creating documents

A computer's word processing software (for example, Microsoft Word or WordPerfect) offers invaluable help at various stages of the WRITING PROCESS. Word processing allows you easily to add, delete, revise, or move around material, even from one document to another. Some writers prefer to print their drafts to revise or edit them by hand and then enter the changes in the computer; other writers do almost all their revising and editing on the screen.

Word processing also allows you to make quick format changes. You can easily shift between single-spacing and double-spacing or put a WORKS CITED page into the correct DOCUMENTATION STYLE (Chapters 34–36). The toolbar at the top of the word processing window contains numerous formatting options, and exploring how they work can save you time in the long run.

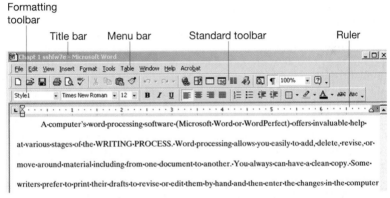

**Figure 1.2  Microsoft Word for Windows toolbar and document**

Be careful using the special aids for writers that are built into word processing software, as they have limitations.

- **Spell-check programs** show you words that don't match the dictionary in the software. These programs are a big help for spotting a misspelling or mistyping (called *typos*), but they won't call your attention to your having typed *form* when you intended to type *from*. Therefore, always remember to read your work carefully after you use a spell-check program.

- **Thesaurus programs** give you SYNONYMS for words. They can't, however, tell you which ones fit well into your particular sentences. Whenever a synonym is unfamiliar or hazy, look it up in your dictionary. You don't want to use words that strike you as attractive options but then turn out to distort your communication. For example, a synonym for *friend* is *acquaintance,* but these words have different senses.

- **Grammar- or style-check programs** check your writing against the software's strict interpretations of rules of grammar, word use, punctuation, and other conventions. Can you always rely on those standards?

No. These signals call attention to a possible error. The decision to change the usage, however, is yours. Consult this handbook when you're not sure what a program is suggesting or whether you're justified in deviating from the program's rules.

## 1g.2 Finding resources

In addition to helping you produce and revise writing, computers help you find SOURCES. Most library catalogs and databases are searchable with computers, both from within the library and remotely, through the Internet. Catalogs and databases are large collections of references that experts have gathered and organized. Often they lead to sources that are available online. Many companies also subscribe to database and information services. Chapter 32 explains how to use catalogs and databases.

Computers also help you find sources on the World Wide Web (the Web), a vast collection of materials that are accessible through the Internet. Chapter 32 explains how to use the Web—and how to avoid misusing it. Especially keep in mind that anyone can post anything online. Some of what you find is plain wrong.

## 1g.3 Managing your work

Computers allow you to save drafts of your papers or to organize your work into various folders. For example, you might create a folder for each document you write and also keep all notes, drafts, and ideas related to that project in the folder. Figure 1.3 (p. 22) shows how one student has started a folder for all the projects in her writing course. In the subfolder for project 2, she has ideas, notes, peer comments, and drafts. She created this folder in the "My Documents" directory in Microsoft Windows.

Computers and associated technologies also allow you to store vast quantities of your own writing and research, in forms even more portable than laptops. Storage devices such as thumb/jump/keychain drives, compact flash cards, PDAs (personal digital assistants), or even MP3 players allow you to store cheaply hundreds of megabytes of information, in something small enough to keep in your pocket. Not only can you potentially keep every word you ever write (as a lifelong portfolio), but you can store photos and other images that you might need for a certain writing project, and you can download vast quantities of source materials from databases.

## 1g.4 Communicating with others

E-mail, instant messaging, and similar technologies not only help you communicate with friends but also help you prepare formal writing projects. For example, discussing a topic online with others can generate

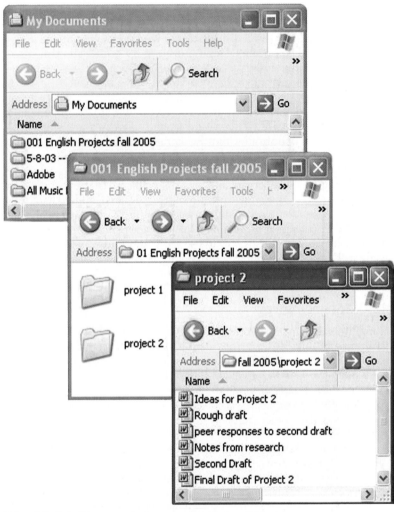

Figure 1.3 Using the computer to manage writing projects

ideas. Some college instructors organize such discussions in Web-based programs such as WebCT or Blackboard. People in all walks of life often exchange ideas on discussion boards, listservs, and BLOGS.

You want to realize, however, that a large number of college instructors never allow students to share and discuss their writing outside of class, whether by computer or other means, because they such activities as forms of PLAGIARISM. Protect yourself well, therefore, by clarifying each instructor's rules about such matters. Pleading ignorance of a law is rarely sufficient defense in life or in college.

Computers allow you to share drafts of your work without physically meeting with others. You can send a draft as an e-mail attachment or save it on a community server or Web site. That way, classmates or colleagues—or even instructors or supervisors—have access to it and can offer suggestions for revision. Certainly, if you're working on a collaborative project, the ability to share drafts and to discuss revisions online has many advantages.

## 1h    What forms of writing do computers enable?

For decades, formal writing has consisted of essays and reports containing only words. These forms will always remain essential, and you need to master them. However, computers enable different kinds of writing, both in college and beyond. You can copy and paste photographs or illustrations into documents. You can easily create tables and graphs, and you can use different fonts and graphical elements such as lines or textboxes. As a result, writers can more easily produce brochures, pamphlets, or other documents that, in the past, required a graphic artist (Chapter 42).

Other forms of writing are designed to appear on computers rather than on paper. Sometimes they contain audio or video files, or they connect to other documents and Web sites. The Web site of the National Park Service, shown in Figure 1.4 (p. 24), incorporates several images to create a pleasing effect, and it has links to many other pages. Some writing situations may call for you to make a Web page rather than write a traditional paper.

A Web log (or **blog**) is a Web site on which a writer posts a series of messages that anyone can read through the Internet. Some people create blogs to serve as a diary of their daily experiences; others offer sites geared toward comments about a particular hobby or interest. Blogs can be very personal, written to an audience of friends and family. Other blogs have taken on a national readership, as is the case with particular news, political, and author blogs. For an example of a blog, see Figure 1.1.

A **wiki** is a Web site that allows multiple readers to change its content. Several people can work on the same document from remote places around the globe. Figure 1.5 (p. 25) is an image from the Wikipedia, an online encyclopedia; anyone can post an article to this site, and anyone can revise an article already posted there. For this reason, use caution when considering any Wikipedia content, and ask your instructor whether he or she will permit you to use it for scholarly research.

Links to audio
or video files

Eye-catching
image

Links to
other pages

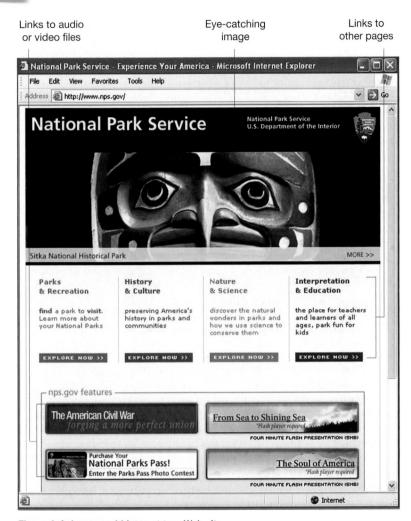

Figure 1.4  Images add interest to a Web site.

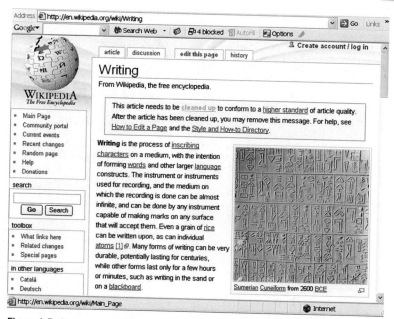

Figure 1.5 A screen capture from Wikipedia, an online encyclopedia

A **digital portfolio** is a collection of several texts in electronic format that you've chosen to represent the range of your skills and abilities. Unlike regular paper portfolios, digital versions contain links between—and within—individual texts; they can be modified and shared easily and cheaply; and they can be put online for wide reading. Figure 1.6 (p. 26) shows the opening screen of one student's digital portfolio for a first-semester writing course. Note that all the paper titles are links to the papers themselves.

**Presentations**, using software such as PowerPoint, allow you to create slides to project while you speak, providing visuals to accompany your oral remarks. PowerPoint slides can incorporate both words and images, as well as sounds. Chapter 41 provides more advice on creating presentations.

**Podcasts** are brief sound files that are shared over the Internet, somewhat like online radio broadcasts. Their name comes from Apple's

# New Vistas

## Final Portfolio

By Corey Sawyer

English 101

Dr. Hesse

May 2005

## Contents

Figure 1.6  Opening screen of a student's digital portfolio

Figure 1.7 A screen capture of Yahoo's podcast directory at podcasts.yahoo.com

familiar iPod player and the fact that you can download podcasts for listening anywhere. What do podcasts have to do with writing? A good number of podcasts are miniature essays or commentaries that their writers have carefully polished and then read, as a script. You might view podcasts as the oral form of blogs. Figure 1.7 shows one of many podcast directories available on the Internet. People who click on the button "listen" or "subscribe" get to the listed podcasts; the directory on the right shows other topic categories.

Always check with instructors before integrating audiovisual elements into your writing. And don't worry if your knowledge about producing any of these types of writing is limited. Instructors who require such projects can tell you how to proceed.

# Chapter 2

## PLANNING, SHAPING, DRAFTING, AND REVISING

### 2a  What is the writing process?

Many people think that professional writers can sit down at their computers, think of ideas, and magically produce a finished draft, word by perfect word. Experienced writers know better. They know that writing is a process, a series of activities that starts the moment they begin thinking about a subject and ends with proofreading the final draft. Experienced writers also know that good writing is rewriting, again and yet again. Their drafts are filled with additions, deletions, rewordings, and rearrangements.

For example, see in Figure 2.1 how Lynn revised the paragraph you just read. Lynn didn't make all the changes at the same time, even though it looks that way on the example. She went through the

---

~~Chapter One discusses what writing is. This chapter explains~~
~~how writing happens.~~ Many people think that professional writers
can sit down at their computers, think of ideas, and ^magically^ produce a
finished draft, word by perfect word. Experienced writers know
better. They know that writing is a process. ~~The writing process is~~
                                             ^they begin^
a series of activities that starts the moment ~~thinking~~ about a subject
          ^proofreading^
~~begins~~ and ends with the ^final draft. Experienced writers also know
that good writing is rewriting, again and yet again. Their drafts
are filled with additions, deletions, rewordings, and rearrangements.

---

Figure 2.1  Draft and revision of Lynn Troyka's first paragraph in Chapter 2

paragraph four times before she was satisfied with it. Notice that she deleted two sentences, combined two sentences, added a sentence at the end, and changed wording throughout.

Writing is an ongoing process of considering alternatives and making choices. The better you understand the writing process, the better you'll write; and the more you feel in control of your writing, the more you'll enjoy it.

In this chapter, we discuss each part of the writing process separately. In real life, the steps overlap. They loop back and forth, which is why writing is called a recursive process. Box 2.1 lists the steps.

---

**SUMMARY BOX** 2.1

## Steps in the writing process

- **Planning** means discovering and compiling ideas for your writing.
- **Shaping** means organizing your material.
- **Drafting** means writing your material into sentences and paragraphs.
- **Revising** means evaluating your draft and then rewriting it by adding, deleting, rewording, and rearranging.
- **Editing** means checking for correct grammar, spelling, punctuation, and mechanics.
- **Proofreading** means reading your final copy to eliminate typing or handwriting errors.

---

Do you like, as we do, to visualize a process? If so, see the drawing in Figure 2.2. The arrows show movement. You might move back before going ahead (perhaps as you revise, you realize you need to plan some more); or you might skip a step and come back to it later (perhaps in the middle of revising, you jump into editing for a few minutes because a punctuation or grammar rule affects how you express your point); and so on.

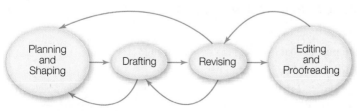

Figure 2.2 Visualizing the writing process

As you work with the writing process, allow yourself to move freely through each step to see what's involved. Notice what works best for you. As you develop a sense of your preferred writing methods, adapt the process to fit each writing situation. No single way exists for applying the writing process.

Our personal advice from one writer to another is this: Most writers struggle some of the time with ideas that are difficult to express, sentences that won't take shape, and words that aren't precise. Be patient with yourself. Don't get discouraged. Writing takes time. The more you write, the easier it will become—though writing never happens magically.

## 2b    What terms describe different kinds of writing?

Terms that describe different types of writing are often used interchangeably. Most instructors attach specific meanings to each one. Listen closely so you can sort out what terms your instructor uses. If your instructor's use of terms isn't clear, ask for clarification. For example, the words *essay, theme,* and *composition* usually—but not always—refer to written works of about 500 to 1,500 words. In this handbook, we use *essay.* Similarly, the word *paper* can mean anything from a few paragraphs to a complex research project. In this handbook, we use *paper* for longer writing projects, such as research papers. Also, we sometimes use the general term *piece of writing* to refer to all types of writing.

## 2c    What is a "writing situation"?

The writing situation of each assignment is the place to start with thinking about your writing. Its four elements are *topic, purpose, audience,* and *special requirements.* The questions in Box 2.2 cover each aspect.

---

**SUMMARY BOX** 2.2

### Analyzing each writing situation

- **Topic:** What topic will you be writing about?
- **Purpose:** What is your purpose for writing? (1b)
- **Audience:** Who is your audience? (1c)
- **Special requirements:** How much time do you have to complete the assignment? What is the length requirement?

A **topic** is the foundation of every writing situation. As you think through a topic, you want to remain within the constraints of academic writing. Whatever your topic, stick to it, and resist any temptation to bend it in another direction.

The PURPOSE of most college writing is to inform or persuade (1b.2 and 1b.3). Some assignments state the writing purpose, while some only imply it. For example, if you were asked to "Describe government restrictions on cigarette advertising," your purpose would be informative. In contrast, if you were asked to respond to the statement "Smoking should (or should not) be banned in all public places," your purpose would be persuasive.

But suppose your assignment doesn't indicate a writing purpose—for example, "Write an essay on smoking." Here, you're expected to choose a purpose and think about what you intend to write on the topic. As you plan how to develop the topic, you'll begin to see whether your purpose is informative or persuasive. It's normal to find yourself deciding to switch purposes midstream to better suit what you are saying.

Your reading AUDIENCE (1c) consists of everyone who will read what you write. According to your assignment and the procedures in your class, your audience includes your PEER-RESPONSE GROUP (1c.1), friends, readers who have specialized knowledge (1c.3) about your topic, and your instructor (1c.4). Think through the characteristics and expectations of your audience so that your writing will successfully deliver its intended meaning.

**Special requirements** are practical matters such as how much time you're given to complete the assignment and how long your writing should be. For example, for an assignment due in one week, your reading audience expects more than one day's work. However, if an assignment is due overnight, your reading audience realizes you had to write in relative haste, though readers never expect sloppy or careless work. Perhaps the highest expectations in a reading audience are applied to an assignment that calls for reading or other research, so be sure to build time for that early in your schedule.

Some instructors put each assignment in writing, either on the board or in a handout. But other instructors give assignments orally during class, expecting you to write them down. Try to record every word. Don't hesitate to ask questions if you don't catch all the words or if something isn't clear—and be sure to write down the answers because they often tend to slip from memory. Listen, too, to questions other students ask, and write down the answers. Such notes can serve as useful springboards when you start writing. In the rest of this chapter, we present the writing processes of two college students, Sara Cardini and Lacie Juris, as they plan and shape their material. You'll see Cardini's essay evolving through three separate, complete drafts. Later, in Chapter 5, you'll see how Juris's essay developed. To start, here are the written assignments each student received.

### Sara Cardini received this assignment:

Addressing an educated audience, write an essay of 900 to 1,300 words discussing something you learned outside of a classroom. Your writing purpose can be informative or persuasive. Expect to write three drafts. (1) Your first draft, typed double-spaced, is due two classes from today. (2) Your clean second draft, typed double-spaced, without notes or comments, is due two classes later. Clip to it your first draft showing all notes you made to yourself or from comments your peer-response group made; you can handwrite notes and comments. I'll read your second draft as an "essay in progress" and will make comments to help you toward a third (and final) draft. (3) The third draft, typed double-spaced, is due one week after I return your second draft with my comments.

### Lacie Juris was given this assignment:

Write an essay of 1,000 to 1,500 words that argues for a particular action on an issue that interests you. Your final draft is due in two weeks.

Cardini's first step was to analyze her writing situation (Box 2.2). She looked at the very general topic—explain to an educated audience something you learned outside of a classroom—and she saw that she needed to narrow it considerably. She tentatively decided her purpose would be informative, though she thought she might have to switch to a persuasive purpose as she went along. She knew that she would share her first draft with her peer-response group to help her toward her second draft. She also understood that her instructor would be her final audience. She was aware of the requirements for time and length.

Juris also read her assignment and analyzed her writing situation. Because the topic was very broad, she knew she would have to spend a good deal of time deciding what she wanted to write about. On the other hand, she understood that her assigned purpose was persuasive. The audience was not specified; she knew that her instructor would be the main audience, but she also decided to write in a way that would address a broader public audience. She kept in mind the requirements for time and length.

**EXERCISE 2-1**   For each assignment below, work individually or with a peer-response group to list the elements in the writing situation. Consult section 2c for help.

1. *Family and Consumer Science:* Write a 500- to 700-word essay that explains important safety procedures to day-care providers. This assignment is due in one week.

2. *Journalism:* Write a 300-word editorial for the student newspaper (to be published next week) supporting or attacking your college's plan to replace the food court with bookstore space for selling software and CDs. Draw on your personal experience or that of students you know.

3. *Art:* You have twenty minutes in class to discuss the differences between a photograph and a painting of the same scene, using a specific example from the textbook or class discussions.

4. *Politics:* Write a one-paragraph description of what is meant by "freedom of the press."

5. *Computer Science:* Write a 1,500-word paper that argues that computers will or will not simulate most aspects of human intelligence in the next ten years. Read and draw on sources to support your argument. Be sure to document your sources. This assignment is due in two weeks.

## 2d    How can I think through a writing topic?

Situations vary. Some assignments are very specific. For example, here's an assignment that leaves no room for choice: "Explain how oxygen is absorbed in the lungs." Students need to do precisely what's asked, taking care not to wander off the topic. Only rarely, however, are writing-class assignments as specific as that one. Often, you'll be expected to select your own topic (2d.1), broaden a narrow topic (2d.2), or narrow a broad topic (2d.3). Regardless of the situation, keep in mind that what separates most good writing from bad is the writer's ability to move back and forth between general statements and specific details.

### 2d.1  Selecting your own topic

If you have to choose a topic, don't rush. Take time to think through your ideas. Avoid getting so deeply involved in one topic that you cannot change to a more suitable topic in the time allotted.

Not all topics are suitable for ACADEMIC WRITING. Your topic needs to have inherent intellectual interest: ideas and issues meaty enough to demonstrate your thinking and writing abilities. Think through potential topics by breaking each into its logical subsections. Then, make sure you can supply sufficiently specific details to back up each general statement. Conversely, make sure you aren't bogged down in so many details you can't figure out what GENERALIZATIONS they support.

Work toward balance by finding a middle ground. Beware of topics so broad that they lead to well-meaning but vague generalizations (for example, "Education is necessary for success"). Also, beware of topics so narrow that they lead nowhere after a few sentences (for example, "Jessica Max attends Tower College").

## 2d.2 Broadening a narrow topic

You know a topic is too narrow when you realize there's little to say after a few sentences. When faced with a too-narrow topic, think about underlying concepts. For example, suppose you want to write about Oprah Winfrey. If you chose "Oprah Winfrey's television show debuted in 1986," you'd be working with a single fact rather than a topic. To expand beyond such a narrow thought, you could think about the general area that your fact fits into—say, the impact of television shows on American culture. Although that is too broad to be a useful topic, you're headed in the right direction. Next, you might think of a topic that relates to Oprah's influence, such as "What impact has Oprah Winfrey's television show had on American culture since she began broadcasting in 1986?" Depending on your WRITING SITUATION (2c), you might need to narrow your idea further by focusing on Oprah's impact in a single area, such as how her book club influenced publishing and reading habits, how her guests and topics brought certain issues to national visibility, or how the style of her show affected other talk shows.

## 2d.3 Narrowing a broad topic

Narrowing a broad topic calls for you to break the topic down into subtopics. Most broad subjects can be broken down in hundreds of ways, but you need not think of all of them. Settle on a topic that interests you, one narrowed enough—but not too much—from a broad topic. For example, if you're assigned "marriage" as the topic for a 1,000-word essay, you'd be too broad if you chose "What makes a successful marriage?" You'd be too narrow if you came up with "Alexandra and Gavin were married by a justice of the peace." You'd probably be on target with a subtopic such as "In successful marriages, husbands and wives learn to accept each other's faults." You could use 1,000 words to explain and give concrete examples of typical faults and discuss why accepting them is important. Here are two more examples.

| | |
|---|---|
| **SUBJECT** | *music* |
| **WRITING SITUATION** | freshman composition class |
| | informative purpose |
| | instructor as audience |
| | 500 words; one week |
| **POSSIBLE TOPICS** | "How music affects moods" |
| | "The main characteristics of country music" |
| | "The relationships between plots of Puccini's operas" |

| SUBJECT | *cities* |
|---|---|
| WRITING SITUATION | sociology course |
| | persuasive purpose |
| | peers and then instructor as audience |
| | 950 to 1,000 words; ten days |
| POSSIBLE TOPICS | "Comforts of city living" |
| | "Discomforts of city living" |
| | "Importance of city planning for open spaces" |

Sara Cardini, the student whose essay appears in this chapter, knew that her very general assigned topic—"Explain to an educated audience something you learned outside of a classroom"—was too broad. To narrow it, she used the following structured techniques for discovering and compiling ideas: browsing her journal (2f), FREEWRITING (2g), and MAPPING (2j). They helped her decide that she wanted to discuss how she learned about a culture other than her own. She realized that even her narrower topic "Japanese culture" would still be too broad. She considered "Japanese music" or "Japanese schools." In the end, she chose "Japanese videos" and, even more specifically, a kind of Japanese animation called "anime" (commonly pronounced AN-a-may). Extensive experience had taught her about the topic, and she could think of both generalizations and specific details to use in her essay. In addition, Cardini knew that if she needed to do research, she could find sources in books and magazines and on the Internet.

Lacie Juris also needed to narrow her topic to suit a 1,000- to 1,500-word essay. To explore several possible topics, she used BRAINSTORMING (2h). Once she had chosen a topic (whether wild animals should be kept as pets), she used the "journalist's questions" (2i) to compile more ideas and then a subject tree (2p) to check whether she was ready to begin drafting.

## 2e What can I do if no ideas occur to me?

If you've ever felt you'll never think of anything to write about, don't despair. Instead, use structured techniques, sometimes called *prewriting strategies* or *invention techniques*, for discovering and compiling ideas. Professional writers use them to uncover hidden resources in their minds. For a list of the techniques, see Box 2.3 on the following page. (The parentheses after each technique tell you where to find more explanation and an example.)

Try out each one. Experiment to find out which techniques suit your style of thinking. Even if one technique produces good ideas, try another to see what additional possibilities might turn up.

Save all of the ideas you generate as you explore possible topics. You never know when something you have initially rejected might

## Ways to discover and compile ideas for writing

- Keep an idea log and a journal (2f).
- Freewrite (2g).
- Brainstorm (2h).
- Ask the "journalist's questions" (2i).
- Map (2j).
- Talk it over (2k).
- Do an Internet search (2l).
- Incubate (2m).

become useful from another point of view. Computers make it easy to keep a folder labeled, for example, "explorations," in which you can store your ideas.

**ESL TIP:** The structured techniques discussed here aim to let your ideas flow out of you without your judging them right away. If it's difficult for you to implement these techniques using English, consider doing several in your primary language. Then, choose one that seems to have potential for your writing and do it over again in English. ☻

## 2f    How do I use an idea log and a journal?

As you develop the habits of mind and behavior of a writer, your ease with writing will grow. One such habit is keeping an idea log. Professional writers are always on the lookout for ideas to write about and details to develop their ideas. They listen, watch, talk with people, and generally keep an open mind. Because they know that good ideas can evaporate as quickly as they spring to mind, they're always ready to jot down their thoughts and observations. Some carry a pocket-size notepad, while others use a PDA (personal digital assistant, such as a Palm Pilot) or a laptop. If you use an idea log throughout your college years, you'll see your powers of observation increase dramatically.

Additionally, many professional writers keep a daily writing **journal**. Doing this will allow you to have a conversation in writing with yourself. Your audience is you, so the content and tone can be as personal and informal as you wish. Even fifteen minutes a day can be enough. If you don't have that chunk of time, write in your journal before you go to bed, between classes, on a bus. Some people find that the feel of pen on paper, perhaps in a bound blank journal, is important to this kind of writing. Others keep journals in computer files. Several people even put their journals online as BLOGS (short for "Web logs"). For examples of blogs (or to start one of your own), go to <http://www.blogger.com>.

Unlike a diary, a journal isn't a record of what you do each day. A journal is for your thoughts from your reading, your observations, even your dreams. You can respond to quotations, react to movies or plays, or reflect on your opinions, beliefs, and tastes. Keeping a journal can help you in three ways. First, writing every day gives you the habit of productivity; the more you write and the more you feel words pouring out of you onto paper, the more easily you'll write in all situations. Second, a journal instills the practice of close observation and discovery, two habits of mind that good writers cultivate. Third, a journal is an excellent source of ideas for assignments.

Figure 2.3 shows an excerpt of a journal entry Sara Cardini had made before she got the assignment to write about something she had learned outside the classroom (2c). Even though she hadn't thought of her entry as a potential subject for a later essay, when she read through her journal for ideas, she realized that one of her great interests had started beyond classroom walls.

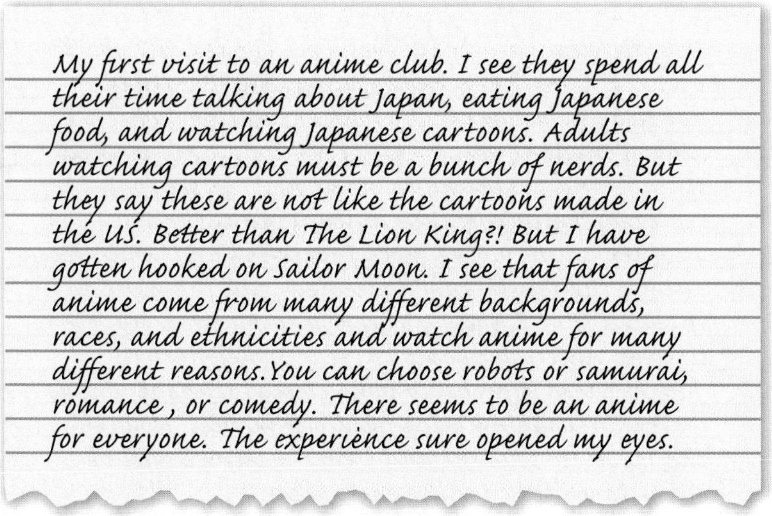

> My first visit to an anime club. I see they spend all their time talking about Japan, eating Japanese food, and watching Japanese cartoons. Adults watching cartoons must be a bunch of nerds. But they say these are not like the cartoons made in the US. Better than The Lion King?! But I have gotten hooked on Sailor Moon. I see that fans of anime come from many different backgrounds, races, and ethnicities and watch anime for many different reasons. You can choose robots or samurai, romance, or comedy. There seems to be an anime for everyone. The experience sure opened my eyes.

Figure 2.3  Excerpt from Sara Cardini's journal

## 2g What is freewriting?

**Freewriting** is writing nonstop. You write down whatever comes into your mind without stopping to wonder whether the ideas are good or the spelling is correct. When you freewrite, don't do anything to interrupt the flow. Don't censor any thoughts or flashes of insight. Don't go back and review. Don't delete.

Freewriting helps get you used to the "feel" of your fingers rapidly hitting computer keys or your pen moving across paper. Freewriting works best if you set a goal—perhaps writing for fifteen minutes or filling one or two pages. Keep going until you reach that goal, even if you have to write one word repeatedly until a new word comes to mind. Some days when you read over your freewriting, it might seem mindless, but other days your interesting ideas may startle you.

In **focused freewriting**, you write from a specific starting point—a sentence from your general freewriting, an idea, a quotation, or anything else you choose. Except for this initial focal point, focused freewriting is the same as regular freewriting. Write until you meet your time or page limit, and don't censor yourself. If you go off the topic, that's fine: See where your thoughts take you. Just keep moving forward.

Like a journal, freewriting is a good source of ideas and details. When Sara Cardini thought her growing interest in Japanese animation might qualify for her assignment (2c), she explored the topic through focused freewriting on watching anime (Figure 2.4).

> In watching anime, my eyes were opened to a world I would never have known otherwise. I learned not to be so judgmental about animation (which I always thought was for kids). While anime seemed strange and confusing to me at first, before long I realized the importance of studying art from another country. The more I watched and understood anime, the less strange it seemed, and the more I realized that I had just been judging from my limited American point of view. Somewhere in Japan, there is probably some college student who is learning about America from our movies. Now, if the Japanese student and I ever meet, we will be closer to understanding each other.

**Figure 2.4 Excerpt from Sara Cardini's freewriting**

## **2h**   **What is brainstorming?**

**Brainstorming** means listing everything you can think of about a topic. Let your mind roam freely, generating quantities of ideas. Write words, phrases, or sentence fragments—whatever comes to you. If you run out of ideas, ask yourself exploratory questions, such as *What is it? What is it the same as? How is it different? Why or how does it happen? How is it done? What causes it or results from it? What does it look, smell, sound, feel, or taste like?*

After you've compiled a list, go to step two: Look for patterns, ways to group the ideas into categories. You'll probably find several categories. Set aside any items that don't fit into a group. If a category interests you but has only a few items, brainstorm that category alone.

You can brainstorm in one concentrated session or over several days, depending on how much time you have for an assignment. Brainstorming in a PEER-RESPONSE GROUP can be especially fruitful: One person's ideas bounce off the next person's, and collectively more ideas come to mind.

When brainstorming or FREEWRITING on a computer, try "invisible writing." Temporarily turn off your computer monitor. A blank screen can help you focus on getting the words out without the temptation to stop and criticize, but the computer will still be recording your words. When you can write no more, turn on the monitor to see what you have.

Brainstorming was a technique Lacie Juris used to find her topic about keeping wild animals as pets (5b). Brainstorming helped her think through several topics and generate some ideas about the one that most appealed to her (Figure 2.5).

- women on TV commercials: realistic?
- health care for poor people—don't know much on that
- holidays are too commercial
- parking situation at this college—solutions?
- protecting wild animals
- wild animals as pets—that bothers me; why?
- is it healthy for the animals? for people? is it fair?
- ~~famous people and their pets nope~~
- laws about pets and pet owners

Figure 2.5  Lacie Juris's brainstorming

**EXERCISE 2-2**   Here's a list brainstormed for a writing assignment. The topic was "Ways to promote a new movie." Working individually or in a peer-response group, look over the list and group the ideas. You'll find that some ideas don't fit into a group. Then, add any other ideas you have to the list.

| | |
|---|---|
| coming attractions | suspense |
| TV ads | book the movie was based on |
| provocative | locations |
| movie reviews | Internet trailers |
| how movie was made | adventure |
| sneak previews | newspaper ads |
| word of mouth | stars |
| director | dialogue |
| topical subject | excitement |
| special effects | photography |

## 2i   What are the "journalist's questions"?

When journalists report a story, they gather and write about information by asking who did what, when it happened, where it happened, and why and how it happened. The same questions come in handy for writers exploring a topic. The **journalist's questions** are *Who? What? When? Where? Why?* and *How?*

Lacie Juris used the journalist's questions to expand her thinking on the problems of keeping wild animals as pets. Her answers, listed below, showed her that she had enough material for a good essay.

WHO?   **Who** benefits from keeping wild animals as pets?

WHAT?   **What** kinds of pets do people keep?

WHEN?   **When** did the practice of owning wild animals begin?

WHERE?   **Where** can I find evidence that wild animals make dangerous pets?

WHY?   **Why** do some people think they have a right to do this?

HOW?   **How** exactly would we stop this process?

## 2j   What is mapping?

**Mapping**, also called *clustering*, is a visual form of brainstorming. When some writers actually see ways that their ideas connect, they begin to think more creatively. Other writers like mapping to help them check the logical relationships between ideas.

To map, write your topic in the middle of a sheet of paper and draw a circle around it. Now, moving out from the center, use lines and circles to show ideas that are subtopics of the topic in the center circle. Continue to subdivide and add details. At any time, you can move to a blank space on your map and start a new subtopic. Try to keep going without censoring yourself.

Sara Cardini used mapping to prompt herself to discover ideas about Japanese animation. When she finished, she was satisfied that she'd have enough to say in her essay. Figure 2.6 shows part of Sara Cardini's clustering for the second paragraph of her essay about Japanese anime.

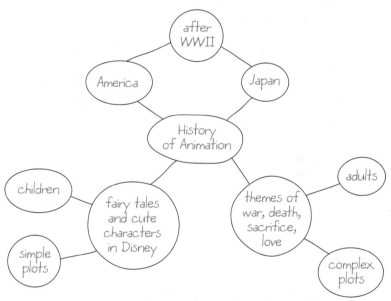

**Figure 2.6  Part of Sara Cardini's mapping for her essay on anime**

## 2k  How can "talking it over" help?

**Talking it over** is based on the notion that two heads are better than one. The expression "bouncing ideas off each other" captures this idea. When you discuss a topic with someone interested in listening and making suggestions, you often think of new ideas. You can collaborate with others while brainstorming, asking the journalist's questions, or mapping. Ways of approaching a point of discussion include debating, questioning, analyzing (4b), evaluating (4c), synthesizing (4e), and assessing reasoning (4i).

People you trust can serve as "sounding boards" and tell you if your ideas are complete and reasonable. If your instructor sets up PEER-RESPONSE GROUPS in your class, you might ask the other members to serve as sounding boards. Otherwise, talk with a good friend or another adult.

Chatting, in the traditional sense, means talking. In a more recent sense, however, chatting also refers to "talking" online through instant messaging, e-mail, and so on. Exchanging ideas online not only stimulates your thinking but also acts as a writing warm-up. Figure 2.7 is an excerpt from an online chatting session.

Figure 2.7  Instant messaging screen capture

## 2I   How can an Internet search help?

**Internet searches** help you find topics to write about; understand your subject's categories from the most general to the most specific; and locate specific information. Internet searches scan the WORLD WIDE WEB using **search engines**, which are software programs that rapidly search and find online information sources. Some instructors want students to think of ideas on their own, without searching the Web. If that's the case, don't.

Chapter 32 provides extensive guidelines for searching the Internet. Briefly, however, try <http://www.google.com>. When you get there, click the "Directory" button to see a screen that lists broad subject areas.

Next, click on "Society" to see a number of slightly more specific topics. Note that each of them would be much too broad to write about.

However, if you keep clicking on topic headings, you'll move to more and more specific subjects. Browsing through the layers of topics can help you think of several ideas for your writing. If you know a general topic area, you can type it in the search window of the program and then click on more specific subcategories.

**EXERCISE 2-3**  On a computer connected to the Internet, go to <http://www.google.com>. Click on "Directory" and then choose one of the headings. Continue to click on topics under that heading to create a "path" to a specific possible topic. Be ready to explain the sequence (or path) you used, what you found, and what you think the strengths and weaknesses of the topics you identified would be. Finally, go back to the opening "Directory" page and repeat the process with a different heading.

**EXERCISE 2-4**  Explore some of the following topics by typing them into the search window of a search engine. You can use Google, as for Exercise 2-3, or you can try a different search engine. Be ready to explain the sequence of topics you discover.

1. global warming
2. intelligence
3. plagiarism
4. New Age music
5. disability

## 2m   How can incubation help me?

**Incubation** refers to giving your ideas time to grow and develop. This technique works especially well when you need to step back and evaluate what you've discovered and compiled for your writing. For example, you might not see how your material can be pulled together at first, but if you let it incubate, you might discover connections you didn't see originally. Conversely, if some parts of your essay seem too thin in content, incubation gives you distance from your material so that you can decide what works. Ideally, incubate your ideas overnight or for a couple of days; but even a few hours can help.

If you don't have the luxury of a lengthy incubation period, some strategies may help you jump-start it. One method is to turn your attention to something entirely unrelated to your writing. Concentrate hard on that other matter so that you give your conscious mind over to it totally. After a while, relax and guide your mind back to your writing. Often, you'll see what you've discovered and compiled for writing in a different way. Another strategy for incubation is to allow your mind to wander without thinking about anything in particular. Relax and open your mind to random thoughts, but don't dwell on any one thought very long. After a while, guide your mind back to your writing. Often, you'll see solutions that hadn't occurred to you before.

**EXERCISE 2-5**  Try each structured technique for discovering and compiling ideas discussed in 2e through 2m. Use your own topics or select from the suggestions below.

1. A dream trip
2. An important personal decision
3. Professional sports
4. Advertisements on television
5. What you want in a life partner

## 2n  How can shaping help me?

**Shaping** writing means organizing your material. Like a story, an essay needs a beginning, a middle, and an end. The essay's introduction sets the stage; the essay's body paragraphs provide the substance of your message in a sequence that makes sense; the conclusion ends the essay logically. The major elements in an informative essay are listed in Box 2.4. (For the major elements in a persuasive essay using classical argument, see Box 5.1 in 5e.)

---

**SUMMARY BOX** 2.4

### Elements in an informative essay

1. **Introductory paragraph:** Leads into the topic of the essay and tries to capture the reader's interest (3b).

2. **Thesis statement:** States the central message of the writing. The thesis statement (2q) usually appears at the end of the introductory paragraph.

3. **Background information:** Provides a context for understanding the points that a writer wants to make. You can integrate background information into the introductory paragraph. More complex information may require a separate paragraph of information (as in the second paragraph in Sara Cardini's essay, in section 2y).

4. **Points of discussion:** Support the essay's thesis statement. They're the essential content of the body paragraphs in an essay (3c). Each point of discussion consists of a general statement backed up by specific details.

5. **Concluding paragraph:** Ends the essay smoothly, flowing logically from the rest of the essay (3k).

---

Each paragraph's length in an informative essay needs to be in proportion to its function. Introductory and concluding paragraphs are usually shorter than body paragraphs. Body paragraphs need to be somewhat approximate to each other in length. If one body paragraph becomes overly long in relation to the others, consider breaking it into two paragraphs. (We discuss paragraph writing extensively in Chapter 3.)

## 2o    How can looking for "levels of generality" help me?

**Generality** is a relative term. Concepts exist in the context of—in relationship with—other concepts. More general concepts belong together (can be grouped), while less general concepts belong grouped together. When you look for **levels of generality**, you're figuring out which ideas or concepts can be grouped. Levels of generality start with the most general and work down to the most specific. Conversely, **levels of specificity** start with the most specific and work up to the most general. Being aware of levels, particularly when writing body paragraphs, gives you a sensible sequence for presenting your material. Use whichever pattern works for you because each sequence is merely the reverse of the other. Here's an example.

**LEVELS OF GENERALITY (BIG TO SMALL)** ∨

| | |
|---|---|
| **MOST GENERAL: LEVEL 1** | a bank |
| **LESS GENERAL: LEVEL 2** | money in the bank |
| **LESS GENERAL: LEVEL 3** | bank account |
| **LESS GENERAL: LEVEL 4** | checking account |
| **LEAST GENERAL: LEVEL 5** | account #123456 at Bank EZCome, EZGo |

**LEVELS OF SPECIFICITY (SMALL TO BIG)** ∧

| | |
|---|---|
| **MOST SPECIFIC: LEVEL 5** | account #123456 at Bank EZCome, EZGo |
| **LESS SPECIFIC: LEVEL 4** | checking account |
| **LESS SPECIFIC: LEVEL 3** | bank account |
| **LESS SPECIFIC: LEVEL 2** | money in the bank |
| **LEAST SPECIFIC: LEVEL 1** | a bank |

## 2p    How can a subject tree help me?

A **subject tree** shows you visually whether you have sufficient content, at varying levels of generality or specificity, to start a first draft of your writing. A subject tree also visually demonstrates whether you have a good balance of general ideas and specific details. If what you have are mostly general ideas—or, the other way around, mostly specific details—go back to techniques for discovering and compiling ideas (2e through 2m) so that you can come up with the sorts of materials that are missing.

Lacie Juris created a subject tree, shown in Figure 2.8, using tools available in Microsoft Word, to help her shape the fifth paragraph in her essay (5n).

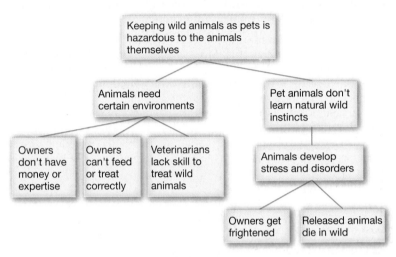

Figure 2.8  Lacie Juris's subject tree for her essay

## 2q  What is a thesis statement?

A **thesis statement** is the central message of an essay. It's the essay's main idea. As a writer, you want to write a thesis statement with great care so that it prepares your readers for what follows in the essay. This means your thesis statement has to reflect with some accuracy the content of your essay. Box 2.5 lists the basic requirements for a thesis statement.

### SUMMARY BOX  2.5

**Basic requirements for a thesis statement**

- It states the essay's subject—the topic that you discuss.
- It conveys the essay's purpose—either informative or persuasive.
- It indicates your focus—the assertion that presents your point of view.
- It uses specific language, not vague words.
- It may briefly state the major subdivisions of the essay's topic.

Some instructors add to these basic requirements for a thesis statement. You might, for example, be asked to put your thesis statement at the end of your introductory paragraph (as in the final draft of Sara Cardini's essay, in section 2y.3). Some instructors require that the thesis statement be contained in one sentence; other instructors permit two sentences if the topic is complex. All requirements, basic and additional, are designed to help you develop a thesis statement that will guide the writing of your essay and help you communicate clearly with your reader. By the way, never confuse the role of a thesis statement with the role of an essay's title (2u.3).

**ESL TIP:** A thesis statement, especially in the introductory paragraph, is commonly found in the ACADEMIC WRITING of North American and some other cultures. Readers and writers from some cultures prefer not to state their main idea so bluntly at the beginning of a piece of writing. Because US readers of academic writing generally expect such a statement, using one will probably help your readers better understand your writing.

Most writers find that their thesis statement changes somewhat with each successive draft of an essay. Still, when you revise its language, be sure to stick to the essential idea you want to communicate. A thesis statement is a guide; it helps you stay on the topic and develop your ideas in an essay. To start, make an **assertion**—a sentence stating your topic and the point you want to make about it. This assertion focuses your thinking as you develop a preliminary thesis statement. Next, move toward a final thesis statement that most accurately reflects the content of your essay.

Following is the evolution of Sara Cardini's thesis statement from a simple assertion to the final version in her essay on anime. The final version fulfills all the requirements described in Box 2.5.

**NO**   I think Japanese animation is interesting. [This assertion is a start, but simply proclaiming something "interesting" is dull.]

**NO**   Most people think cartoons are simple entertainments for kids, but there are exceptions to that rule. [This statement draws readers in by promising to show them how their expectations may be inadequate and that there really isn't a "rule" involved.]

**NO**   Anime films are sophisticated Japanese cartoons. [This statement is closer to a thesis statement because it's more specific. It promises to show that anime is sophisticated. However, the concept that anime contrasts with American cartoons is an important part of Sara's paper, and that concept is missing here.]

**NO**    The purpose of this paper is to explain Japanese anime and how anime films differ from American cartoons. [This version clearly states a main point of the paper, but it's inappropriate because it announces what the writer is going to do.]

**YES**    Anime has traditions and features that distinguish it from American cartoons and make it sophisticated enough to appeal to adults. [The final version serves as Cardini's thesis statement by effectively conveying the main ideas and point of her essay.]

## THESIS STATEMENTS FOR INFORMATIVE ESSAYS

For essays with an informative purpose (1b.2), here are more examples of thesis statements for 900- to 1,300-word essays. The NO versions are assertions or preliminary thesis statements. The YES versions are good because they fulfill the requirements in Box 2.5.

**TOPIC**   *suing for malpractice*

**NO**    There are many kinds of malpractice suits.

**YES**    Because many people have heard about medical malpractice suits, they are becoming aware of cases against lawyers, teachers, and even parents.

**TOPIC**   *women artists*

**NO**    Paintings by women are getting more attention.

**YES**    During the past ten years, the works of the artists Mary Cassatt and Rosa Bonheur have finally gained widespread critical acclaim.

## THESIS STATEMENTS FOR PERSUASIVE ESSAYS

For essays written with a persuasive purpose (1b.3), here are examples of thesis statements written for 900- to 1,300-word essays. Again, the NO versions are assertions or preliminary thesis statements. The YES versions fulfill the requirements in Box 2.5.

**TOPIC**   *discomforts of city living*

**NO**    The discomforts of living in a large modern city are many.

**YES**    Rising crime rates, increasingly overcrowded conditions, and rising taxes make living comfortably in a large modern city difficult.

**TOPIC**   *deceptive advertising*

**NO**    Deceptive advertising can cause many problems for consumers.

**YES**    Deceptive advertising costs consumers not only their money but also their health.

**EXERCISE 2-6**    Each set of sentences below offers several versions of a thesis statement. Within each set, the thesis statements progress from weak to strong. The fourth thesis statement in each set is the best. Referring to requirements listed in Box 2.5, work individually or with a peer-response group to explain why the first three choices in each set are weak and the last is best.

A. 1. Advertising is complex.
   2. Magazine advertisements appeal to readers.
   3. Magazine advertisements must be creative and appealing to all readers.
   4. To appeal to readers, magazine advertisements must skillfully use language, color, and design.
B. 1. Tennis is excellent exercise.
   2. Playing tennis is fun.
   3. Tennis requires various skills.
   4. Playing tennis for fun and exercise requires agility, stamina, and strategy.
C. 1. *Hamlet* is a play about revenge.
   2. Hamlet must avenge his father's murder.
   3. Some characters in the play *Hamlet* want revenge.
   4. In the play *Hamlet,* Hamlet, Fortinbras, and Laertes all seek revenge.
D. 1. We should pay attention to the environment.
   2. We should worry about air pollution.
   3. Automobile emissions cause air pollution.
   4. Congress should raise emissions standards for passenger cars and SUVs.
E. 1. Many people are not interested in politics.
   2. Adults have become increasingly dissatisfied with the political process.
   3. Fewer adults than ever vote in local elections.
   4. Fewer college students participated in state primaries and voted in state elections this year than in either of the last two elections.

**EXERCISE 2-7**    Here are writing assignments, narrowed topics, and tentative thesis statements. Alone or with a peer-response group, evaluate each thesis statement according to the basic requirements in Box 2.5.

1. *Marketing assignment:* 700- to 800-word persuasive report on the cafeteria. *Audience:* the instructor and the cafeteria's manager. *Topic:* cafeteria conditions. *Thesis:* The college cafeteria could attract more students if it improved the quality of its food, its appearance, and the friendliness of its staff.
2. *Theater assignment:* 300- to 500-word review of a performance. *Audience:* the instructor and other students in the class. *Topic:* a touring production of the musical *Rent. Thesis:* The recent performance of *Rent* was very interesting.

3. *Chemistry assignment:* 800- to 1,000-word informative report about the ozone layer. *Audience:* the instructor and visiting students and instructors attending a seminar at the state college. *Topic:* recent research on the ozone layer. *Thesis:* The United States should increase efforts to slow the destruction of the ozone layer.

4. *Journalism assignment:* 200- to 300-word article about campus crime. *Audience:* the instructor, the student body, and the college administration. *Topic:* recent robberies. *Thesis:* During the fall term, the number of campus robberies at the college equaled the number of robberies that took place in the prior five years combined.

5. *Nursing assignment:* 400- to 500-word persuasive report about technology changes in nursing. *Audience:* nursing students and professionals. *Topic:* using handheld computers to track patient information. *Thesis:* More hospitals require nurses to use handheld computers to enter patient data instead of using traditional charts.

## 2r    What is outlining?

An **outline** lays out the relationships among ideas in a piece of writing. Outlines can lead writers to see how well their writing is organized. Many instructors require outlines either before or with an essay.

Some writers like to outline; others don't. If you don't, but you're required to write one, tackle the job with an open mind. You may be pleasantly surprised at what the rigor of outline writing does to your perception of your essay.

An outline can be *informal* or *formal.* Try outlining at various steps of the WRITING PROCESS: before drafting, to arrange ideas; while you draft, to keep track of your material; while you revise, to check the logical flow of thought or to reveal what information is missing, repeated, or off the topic; or in whatever other ways you find helpful.

### INFORMAL OUTLINES

An **informal outline** is a working plan that lays out the major points of an essay. Because it's informal, it doesn't need to use the numbering and lettering conventions of a formal outline. Complete sentences aren't required; words and phrases are acceptable. Sara Cardini used an informal outline for planning her essay. Here is part of an informal outline for the third paragraph of her essay.

### SARA CARDINI'S INFORMAL OUTLINE

*Thesis statement:* Anime has traditions and features that distinguish it from American cartoons and make it sophisticated enough to appeal to adults.

    qualities of anime
        quick movements
        jazz and rock music

large eyes for characters
complicated drawings
Samurai X as an example

## FORMAL OUTLINES

A traditional **formal outline** follows long-established conventions for using numbers and letters to show relationships among ideas. MLA STYLE doesn't officially endorse using an outline or, indeed, any one outline style. However, many instructors do assign outlines, and they prefer the traditional format shown here. Increasingly, some instructors prefer a less traditional format for a formal outline, one which includes the content of the introductory paragraph and the concluding paragraphs. An example of such an outline appears in section 34e.2, written by a student whose instructor required that format for an MLA-style research paper. Either of these styles of formal outline—the traditional or the less traditional—can be a sentence outline, composed entirely of complete sentences, or a topic outline, composed only of words and phrases. So that you can compare the two styles of outlines, both examples below outline the third paragraph of Sara Cardini's essay on Japanese anime. Never mix the two styles in one outline.

Writers who use formal outlines say that a sentence outline brings them closer to drafting than a topic outline does. This makes sense because topic outlines carry less information. But you have to find out which type works better for you.

### TOPIC OUTLINE

*Thesis statement:* Anime has traditions and features that distinguish it from American cartoons and make it sophisticated enough to appeal to adults.

I. Anime qualities
 A. Quick images
 B. Jazz and rock soundtracks
 C. Character eyes and features
 D. Colorful, complicated art
  1. Samurai X as example
  2. Samurai X about nineteenth-century warrior
  3. Samurai X art like old Japanese prints

### SENTENCE OUTLINE

*Thesis statement:* Anime has traditions and features that distinguish it from American cartoons and make it sophisticated enough to appeal to adults.

I. Complex plots are but one of the distinctive features of anime.
 A. Anime images move quickly, with a style often more frantic than in American cartoons.
 B. Their soundtracks frequently use jazz and rock music rather than symphonic music.
 C. Most striking are the large eyes and sharp features of the characters.

    D.  The drawing is more colorful, more complicated, and often more abstract than that in most American cartoons.

        1.  A TV series called <u>Samurai X</u> is one of the most popular anime series with both American and Japanese audiences.

        2.  <u>Samurai X</u> is set in the nineteenth century and tells the story of one warrior's life.

        3.  <u>Samurai X</u> art is drawn beautifully to look both like older Japanese art prints and like more contemporary movies such as <u>Crouching Tiger, Hidden Dragon</u>.

**EXERCISE 2-8**   Here is a sentence outline. Individually or with your peer-response group, revise it into a topic outline. Then, be ready to explain why you prefer using a topic outline or a sentence outline as a guide to writing. For help, consult 2r.

*Thesis statement:* Because noise pollution causes many problems in our society, it must be reduced.

  I.  Noise pollution comes from many sources.

    A.  Noise pollution occurs in many large cities.

       1.  Traffic rumbles and screeches.

       2.  Construction work blasts.

       3.  Airplanes roar overhead.

    B.  Noise pollution occurs in the workplace.

       1.  Machines in factories boom.

       2.  Machines used for outdoor construction thunder.

    C.  Noise pollution occurs during leisure-time activities.

       1.  Headphones blare directly into eardrums.

       2.  Film soundtracks bombard the ears.

       3.  Music in discos assaults the ears.

 II.  Noise pollution causes many problems.

    A.  Excessive noise damages hearing.

    B.  Excessive noise alters moods.

    C.  Constant exposure to noise limits learning ability.

III.  Reduction in noise pollution is possible.

    A.  Pressure from community groups can support efforts to control excessive noise.

    B.  Traffic regulations can help alleviate congestion and noise.

    C.  Pressure from workers can force management to reduce noise.

    D.  People can wear earplugs to avoid excessive noise.

    E.  Reasonable sound levels for headphones, soundtracks, and discos can be required.

## 2s   What can help me write a first draft?

In the WRITING PROCESS, drafting and revising come after PLANNING and SHAPING. **Drafting** means you get ideas onto paper or into a computer file in sentences and paragraphs. In everyday conversation, people use the word *writing* to talk about drafting, but writing is too broad a term here. The word *drafting* more accurately describes what you do when you write your first attempt—your first *draft*—to generate words. **Revising** means you look over your first draft, analyze and evaluate it for yourself, and then rewrite it by composing a number of subsequent versions, or drafts, to get closer to what you want to say. Revising involves adding, cutting, moving material, and, after that, EDITING and PROOFREADING.

A **first draft** is the initial version of a piece of writing. Before you begin a first draft, seek out places and times of the day that encourage you to write. You might write best in a quiet corner of the library, or at 4:30 a.m. at the kitchen table before anyone else is awake, or outside alone with nature, or with a steady flow of people walking by. Most experienced writers find they concentrate best when they're alone and writing where they won't be interrupted. But individuals differ, and you may prefer background noise—a crowded cafeteria, with the low hum of conversation at the next table or in the next room, for example.

A caution: Don't mislead yourself. You can't produce a useful first draft while talking to friends and stopping only now and then to jot down a sentence. You won't draft smoothly while watching television or being constantly interrupted.

Finally, resist delaying tactics. While you certainly need a computer or a pad of paper and a pen or pencil, you don't need fifteen perfectly sharpened pencils neatly lined up on your desk.

Box 2.6 (p. 54) offers suggestions for ways to move from planning and shaping into drafting. Experiment to see what works best for you. And be ready to adjust what works according to each WRITING SITUATION.

Now, dive in. Using the planning and shaping you've done as a basis, start writing. The direction of drafting is forward: Keep pressing ahead. If you wonder about the spelling of a word or a point of grammar, don't stop. Use a symbol or other signal to alert you to revisit later. Use whatever you like: boldface, underlining, a question mark before and after, an asterisk, or all capital letters. If the exact word you want escapes you while you're drafting, substitute an easy synonym and mark it to go back to later. If you question your sentence style or the order in which you present supporting details, boldface or underline the passage or insert a symbol or the word *Style?* or *Order?* nearby so that you can return to it later. If you begin to run out of ideas, reread what you have written— not to start revising prematurely, but only to propel yourself to keep moving ahead with your first draft. Once you finish your draft, search for the boldfaces, underlines, symbols, or words that you've used to alert yourself to reconsider something. If it's a word, you can use the "Edit>Find" function on your word processing program toolbar.

When drafting on the computer, use your "Save" function often to protect your work, at least every five minutes. (This can be set up as an automatic function.) To prevent losing what you've written, back up your files diligently. Also, print your work regularly—very definitely at the end of each work session—so that you always have a hard copy in case your computer develops problems (a not unusual occurrence).

A first draft is a preliminary or *rough draft*. Its purpose is to get your ideas onto disk or into computer memory or on paper. Never are first drafts meant to be perfect.

---

**SUMMARY BOX** 2.6

## Ways to start drafting

- **Write a discovery draft.** Put aside all your notes from planning and shaping, and write a discovery draft. This means using FOCUSED FREEWRITING to get ideas on paper or onto your computer screen so that you can make connections that spring to mind as you write. Your discovery draft can serve as a first draft or as one more part of your notes when you write a more structured first draft.

- **Work from your notes.** Sort your notes from planning and shaping into groups of subtopics. When you start writing, you can systematically concentrate on each subtopic without having to search repeatedly through your pile of notes. Arrange the subtopics in what seems to be a sensible sequence, knowing you can always go back later and re-sequence the subtopics. Now, write a first draft by working through your notes on each subtopic. Draft either the entire essay or chunks of a few paragraphs at one time.

- **Use a combination of approaches.** When you know the shape of your material, write according to that structure. When you feel "stuck" and don't know what to say next, switch to writing as you would for a discovery draft.

---

**2t** **How can I overcome writer's block?**

If you're afraid or otherwise feel unable to start writing, perhaps you're being stopped by **writer's block**. You want to get started but somehow can't. Often, writer's block occurs because the writer harbors a fear of being wrong. To overcome that fear, or any other cause of your block, first admit it to yourself. Face it honestly so that you can understand whatever is holding you back. Writer's block can strike professional as well as student writers, and a variety of techniques to overcome it have become popular.

The most common cause of writer's block involves a writer's belief in myths about writing.

| | |
|---|---|
| **MYTH** | Writers are born, not made. |
| **TRUTH** | Everyone can write. Writers don't expect to "get it right" the first time. Being a good writer means being a patient rewriter. |
| **MYTH** | Writers have to be "in the mood" to write. |
| **TRUTH** | If writers always waited for "the mood" to occur, few would write at all. News reporters and other professional writers have deadlines to meet, whether or not they're in the mood to write. |
| **MYTH** | Writers have to be really good at grammar and spelling. |
| **TRUTH** | Writers don't let spelling and grammar block them. They write, and when they hear that quiet inner voice saying that a word or sentence isn't quite right, they mark the spot with a symbol or word in all capitals. After they're finished drafting, they return to those spots and work on them, perhaps using this handbook or a dictionary or thesaurus to check themselves. |
| **MYTH** | Writers don't have to revise. |
| **TRUTH** | Writers expect to revise—several times. Once words are on paper, writers can see what readers will see. This "revision" helps writers revise. |
| **MYTH** | Writing can be done at the last minute. |
| **TRUTH** | Drafting and revising take time. Ideas don't leap onto paper in final, polished form. |

Box 2.7 (p. 56) lists reliable strategies writers have developed to overcome writer's block. If you feel blocked, experiment to discover which works best for you. Also, add your own ideas about how to get started. As you use the list in Box 2.7, suspend judgment of your writing. Let things flow. Don't find fault with what you're keyboarding or writing. Your goal is to get yourself under way. You can evaluate and improve your writing when you're revising it. According to research, premature revision stops many writers cold—and leads to writer's block. Your reward for waiting to revise until after you finish your first draft is the comfort of having a springboard for the revision work in front of you.

## Ways to overcome writer's block

- **Check that one of the myths about writing discussed in section 2t, or one of your own, isn't stopping you.**

- **Avoid staring at a blank page.** Relax and move your hand across the keyboard or page. Write words, scribble, or draw while you think about your topic. The physical act of getting anything on paper can stir up ideas and lead you to begin drafting.

- **Visualize yourself writing.** Many professional writers say that they write more easily if they first picture themselves doing it. Before getting out of bed in the morning or while waiting for a bus or walking to classes, mentally construct a visual image of yourself in the place where you usually write, with the materials you need, busy at work.

- **Picture an image or a scene, or imagine a sound that relates to your topic.** Start writing by describing what you see or hear.

- **Write about your topic in a letter or e-mail to a friend.** This technique helps you relax and makes drafting nothing more than a chat on paper with someone you feel comfortable with.

- **Try writing your material as if you were someone else.** When they take on a role, many writers feel less inhibited about writing.

- **Start by writing the middle of your essay.** Skip the introduction and begin with a body paragraph, and write from the center of your essay out, instead of from beginning to end.

- **Use FREEWRITING or FOCUSED FREEWRITING.**

- **Change your method of writing.** If you usually use a computer, try writing by hand. When you write by hand, switch between pencil and pen or ink colors and treat yourself to good-quality paper so that you can enjoy the pleasure of writing on smooth, strong paper. Often that pleasure propels you to keep going.

- **Switch temporarily to writing about a topic that you care about passionately.** Write freely about that topic. Once writing starts to pour out of you, you can often use the momentum to switch back to the topic of your assignment.

### 2u How do I revise?

**Revising** is rewriting. When you see the word *revision,* break it down to *re-vision,* which means "to see again with fresh eyes." To revise, you evaluate, change, and reevaluate your draft to figure out ways to improve it. To do this, you need to read your writing honestly, without losing confidence or becoming defensive. After all, what's on the page is ink, not ego. As you work, look at whatever you change and evaluate the revision first on its own and then in the context of the surrounding material. Continue until you're satisfied that your essay is the best you can make it, in light of your specific WRITING SITUATION.

Whenever possible within your time frame, distance yourself from each draft. The best way is to leave a chunk of time between finishing a first draft and starting to revise. Doing so helps you develop an objective sense of your work. Student writers often want to hold on to their every word, especially if they had trouble getting started on a first draft. Resist such a feeling vigorously. Put away your draft and allow the rosy glow of authorial pride to dim a bit. The classical writer Horace recommended waiting nine years before revising! You might try to wait a few hours or even thirty minutes. Better yet, take a day or two before going back to look at your work with fresh eyes.

Also, as you're revising, don't start EDITING too soon. Editing comes after revising. Research shows that premature editing distracts writers from dealing with the larger issues that revision involves.

## 2u.1 Goals and activities during revision

Your goal during revision is to improve your draft at two levels: the *global level*, which involves the whole essay and paragraphs, and the *local level*, which involves sentences and words.

To revise successfully, you need first to expect to revise. The myth that good writers never have to revise is nonsense. Only the opposite is true: Writing is revising. Final drafts evolve from first drafts. Here's how to prepare your mind for revising:

- Shift mentally from suspending judgment (during idea gathering and drafting) to making judgments. Read your draft objectively with "a cold eye" to evaluate it.

- Decide whether to write an entirely new draft or to revise the one you have. Be critical as you evaluate your first draft, but don't be overly harsh. Many early drafts provide sufficient raw material for revision to get under way.

- Be systematic. Don't evaluate at random. Most writers work best when they concentrate on each element sequentially. Start with your draft's overall organization; next, move to its paragraphs, then to its sentences, and finally to its word choice. If you need practice in being systematic, try using a revision checklist, either one supplied by your instructor or the one in this handbook (2u.5).

You can engage in the activities of revision, listed in Box 2.8 (p. 58), by hand or on the computer, which allows you to make both large and small changes easily. Use "Cut" and "Paste" to reorder sentences or

**SUMMARY BOX** 2.8

## Major activities during revision

- **Add:** Insert needed words, sentences, and paragraphs. If your additions require new content, return to the structured techniques shown in sections 2e–2m.

- **Cut:** Get rid of whatever goes off the topic or repeats what has already been said.

- **Replace:** As needed, substitute new words, sentences, and paragraphs for what you have cut.

- **Move:** Change the sequence of paragraphs if the material isn't presented in logical order. Move sentences within paragraphs or to other paragraphs when your PARAGRAPH ARRANGEMENT does not allow the material to flow.

rearrange paragraphs. You might, for example, split up a paragraph, join two paragraphs, or otherwise shuffle them. Similarly, you might reorder the sequence of some sentences or interchange sentences between paragraphs. Sometimes, these experiments won't yield anything useful, but they might reveal a few surprises that help you "re-vision" your work.

As you try various revisions, use the "Save As" function on your computer to save drafts under slightly different names, such as "Animation Draft 1," "Animation Draft 2," and so on. By saving several drafts of your paper, you can always return to earlier versions if you later decide you prefer something in one of them. If you want to drop material, resist deleting it instantly. As handbook authors, we save almost everything. Doug, for instance, typically keeps a file named "Junk" for just this purpose. Lynn names her folder of discarded drafts of sentences, paragraphs, and whole essays "Discarded Stuff."

Beware of two temptations when writing with the computer. Because you can rearrange and otherwise revise endlessly, you may need to set limits, or you'll never finish the assignment. The opposite seduction is also possible: A neatly printed page may look like a final draft, but it definitely isn't one.

## 2u.2 The role of a thesis statement in revision

The THESIS STATEMENT of your essay has great organizing power because it controls and limits what your essay can cover. The thesis statement presents the TOPIC of your essay, your particular focus on that topic, and your PURPOSE for writing about that topic. Your first draft of a thesis statement is usually only an estimate of what you plan to cover in your essay. Therefore, as you revise, keep checking the accuracy of your thesis statement. Use the thesis statement's controlling power to bring it and your essay into line with each other. When your essay is finished, the thesis statement and what you say in your essay should match. If they don't, you need to revise either the thesis statement or the essay—or sometimes both.

Every writer's experience with revising a thesis statement varies from essay to essay. Sara Cardini, the student you met earlier in this chapter as she did her planning and shaping, wrote several versions of her thesis statement (shown in 2q) for her drafts. You can read Cardini's three complete drafts, along with comments, at the end of this chapter.

## 2u.3 The role of an essay title in revision

Your essay **title** can also show you what needs revising because it clarifies the overall point of the essay. An effective title sets you on your course and tells your readers what to expect. Some writers like to begin their first drafts with a title at the top of the page to focus their thinking. Then, as they revise drafts, they revise the title. If, however, no title springs to mind, don't be concerned. Often, a good title doesn't surface until after drafting, revising, and even editing. It can take that long to come up with one. Whatever you do, never tack on a title as an afterthought right before handing in your essay. A suitable title is essential for readers to think about as they begin focusing on your essay.

Titles can be direct or indirect. A **direct title** tells exactly what the essay will be about: for example, "The Characteristics of Japanese Animation." A direct title contains key words under which the essay could be cataloged in a library or an online database. A direct title shouldn't be too broad. For example, Cardini's first and second drafts of a title were "Japanese Videos" and "Japanese Anime" (2y.1 and 2y.2). By her final draft, Cardini had revised the title to "The Appeal of Japanese Animation for Adults" (2y.3). Conversely, a direct title should not be too narrow. "The Graphics of Anime" is too narrow a title for Cardini's essay, given what she discusses in it.

An **indirect title** only hints at the essay's topic. It tries to catch the reader's interest by presenting a puzzle that can be solved by reading the essay. When writing an indirect title, you don't want to be overly obscure or too cute. For example, a satisfactory indirect title for Cardini's final draft might be "More Than Simple Cartoons?" In contrast, the indirect title "Imagining That Walt Disney Had Been Japanese" wouldn't work because it's only remotely related to the point of the essay. Also, "Thanks, *Sailor Moon*" would probably be seen as overly cute for ACADEMIC WRITING.

> ◤ **ALERT:** When you write the title at the top of the page or on a title page, never enclose it in quotation marks or underline it. Let your

title stand on its own, without decoration. Where you place it will depend on which DOCUMENTATION STYLE you're using. ◆

Whether direct or indirect, your essay title stands on its own. It's never the opening sentence of your essay. For example, Cardini's essay, titled "The Appeal of Japanese Animation for Adults," would suffer a major blow if the first sentence were "It certainly does" or "I am the proof." Similarly, never does the first sentence of an essay refer to the essay's title. Rather, the first sentence starts the flow of the essay's content. Box 2.9 offers you guidelines for writing effective essay titles.

---

**SUMMARY BOX** 2.9

## Guidelines for writing essay titles

- Don't wait until the last minute to tack a title on your essay. Try writing a title before you begin drafting or while you're revising. Then double-check as you prepare your final draft to confirm that the title clearly relates to your essay's content.

- For a direct title, use key words that relate to your topic, but don't get overly specific and try to reveal your entire essay.

- For an indirect title, be sure that its meaning will become very clear when your readers have finished your essay. Be sure, also, that it isn't too cute.

- Don't use quotation marks with the title or underline it (unless your title includes another title; see section 30g).

- Don't consider your essay title as the first sentence of your essay.

---

### 2u.4 The role of unity and coherence in an essay

Chapter 3 in this handbook shows you many techniques for achieving unity and coherence in an essay, but here we need to preview the concepts because they're central concerns as you revise.

An essay has **unity** (3d) when all of its parts relate to the THESIS STATEMENT and to one another. You want to use two criteria to judge this. First, does the thesis statement clearly tie in to all TOPIC SENTENCES? Second, does each paragraph—especially each body paragraph—contain examples, reasons, facts, and details that relate directly to its topic sentence and, in turn, to the thesis statement? In a nutshell, as you revise make sure that nothing in the essay is off the topic.

An essay achieves **coherence** (3g) through closely built relationships among ideas and details that are built on word choice, use of

TRANSITIONAL EXPRESSIONS, clear use of PRONOUNS, and effective PARALLELISM.

## 2u.5 Using a revision checklist

A revision checklist can focus your attention as you evaluate and revise your writing. Use such a checklist, either one provided by your instructor or one that you compile on your own, based on Box 2.10.

---

CHECKLIST BOX **2.10**

**Revision**

Your goal is to answer yes to each question. If you answer no, you need to revise. The section numbers in parentheses tell you where to look in this handbook for help.

**THE GLOBAL VIEW: WHOLE ESSAY AND PARAGRAPHS**

1. Is your essay topic suitable and sufficiently narrow? (2d)

2. Does your thesis statement communicate your topic, focus, and purpose? (2q, Box 2.5)

3. Does your essay show that you are aware of your audience? (Box 1.4)

4. Is your essay arranged effectively? (3h)

5. Have you checked for material that strays off the topic? (3d)

6. Does your introduction prepare your reader for the rest of the essay? (3b)

7. Do your body paragraphs express main ideas in topic sentences as needed? (3c) Are your main ideas clearly related to your thesis statement? (3d)

8. Do your body paragraphs provide specific, concrete support for each main idea? (3c, 3f)

9. Do you use transitions and other techniques to connect ideas within and between paragraphs? (3j)

10. Does your conclusion give your essay a sense of completion? (3k)

**THE LOCAL VIEW: SENTENCES AND WORDS**

11. Are your sentences concise? (Chapter 16)

12. Do your sentences show clear relationships among ideas? (Chapter 17)

13. Do you use parallelism, variety, and emphasis correctly and to increase the impact of your writing? (Chapters 18 and 19)

➤

CHECKLIST BOX **2.10** *continued*

**Revision**

14. Have you eliminated sentence fragments? (Chapter 12) Have you eliminated comma splices and run-on sentences? (Chapter 13)

15. Have you eliminated confusing shifts? (Chapter 15)

16. Have you eliminated disjointed sentences? (Chapter 15)

17. Have you eliminated misplaced and dangling modifiers? (Chapter 14)

18. Have you used exact words? (21e, 21f)

19. Is your usage correct and your language appropriate? (Chapter 21)

20. Have you avoided sexist language? (21g)

---

**ESL TIP:** If you'd like information about issues of English grammar that often affect multilingual students, consult Part Seven in this handbook. Topics include those related to culture and education, as well as linguistic concerns, such as ARTICLES (Chapter 47); WORD ORDER (Chapter 48); PREPOSITIONS (Chapter 49); VERBALS (Chapter 50); and MODAL AUXILIARY VERBS (Chapter 51). ☻

## 2v How do I edit?

**Editing** means checking the technical correctness of your writing. You carefully examine your writing for correct grammar, spelling, punctuation, capitalization, and use of numbers, italics, and abbreviations. Some people use the terms *editing* and *revising* interchangeably, but these terms refer to very different steps in the writing process. In contrast to revising, editing involves looking at each word for its technical correctness. By editing, you fine-tune the surface features of your writing.

Editing is crucial in writing. No matter how much attention you've paid to planning, shaping, drafting, and revising, you need to edit carefully. Slapdash editing distracts and annoys your reader; lowers that reader's opinion of you and what you say in your essay; and, in a college assignment, usually earns a lower grade.

Our best advice to you about editing is this: Don't rush. Editing takes time. Inexperienced writers sometimes rush editing, eager to "get it over with." Resist any impulse to hurry. Be systematic and patient. Checking grammar and punctuation takes your full concentration, along with time to look up and apply the rules in this handbook.

When do you know you've finished revising and are ready to edit? Ask yourself, "Is there anything else I can do to improve the content, organization, development, and sentence structure of this draft?" If the answer is no, you're ready to edit.

Word processing programs include editing tools such as a spell-checker, style-checker, thesaurus, and readability analyzer. As we explained in Chapter 1, each tool has shortcomings serious enough to create new errors. Yet, if you use the tools intelligently with their shortcomings in mind, they can be useful.

Whenever possible, edit on a paper copy of your writing. It's much easier to spot editing errors on a printed page than on a computer screen. Double-space your paper before printing it for revising or editing. The extra space gives you room to write in your changes clearly so that you can read them easily later. After you finish editing, you can transfer your corrections to the computer. If you must edit onscreen, highlight every two or three sentences and read each slowly. By working in small segments, you reduce the tendency to read too quickly and miss errors.

An editing checklist helps you find errors. Using an editing checklist, either one provided by your instructor or one based on Box 2.11 that you tailor to your particular needs, can help you move through editing systematically.

A time-saving method for editing is to create a personal file of editing errors you tend to make repeatedly. For example, if the difference between *its* and *it's* always escapes you, or if you tend to misuse the colon, your personal file of editing errors can remind you to look over your draft for those problems.

---

**CHECKLIST BOX 2.11**

## Editing

Your goal is to answer yes to each question below. If you answer no, you need to edit. The numbers in parentheses tell you which chapters in this handbook to go to for more information.

1. Is your grammar correct? (Chapters 7–15)

2. Is your spelling, including hyphenation, correct? (Chapter 22)

3. Have you used commas correctly? (Chapter 24)

4. Have you used all other punctuation correctly? (Chapters 23 and 25–29)

5. Have you used capital letters, italics, abbreviations, and numbers correctly? (Chapter 30)

## 2w   How do I proofread?

To **proofread**, check your final draft for accuracy and neatness before handing it in. In contrast to editing, which is a check for technical correctness, proofreading is typographical. This is your last chance to catch typing (or handwriting) errors and to make sure what you hand in is a clean transcription of your final draft. No matter how hard you worked on earlier parts of the writing process, your final copy needs to be free of proofreading oversights. Shoddy proofreading distracts and annoys your reader; lowers that reader's opinion of you and what you say in your essay; and, if you're writing for college, usually earns a lower grade.

When proofreading, read your work carefully line by line, looking for typing errors, such as letters or words accidentally omitted, words typed twice in a row, wrong indents to start each paragraph, and similar typos or slips. Then, print out a complete fresh copy. Reprinting just one page is often difficult because of reflowing text. Never expect your instructor to make allowances for handwritten corrections.

Some techniques for proofreading include (1) using a ruler under each line as you read it to prevent yourself from looking beyond that line; (2) reading backwards, sentence by sentence, to prevent yourself from being distracted by the content of the paper; and (3) proofreading your final draft aloud, to yourself or to a friend, so that you can hear errors that have slipped past your eyes. As with revising and editing, whenever possible, print and proofread a double-spaced paper copy of your writing. Again, it's much easier to spot errors on a printed page than onscreen. If you must proofread onscreen, highlight every two or three sentences and read each slowly. Enlarging the type onscreen is another helpful trick to help you focus word by word.

## 2x   What is collaborative writing?

Some instructors use the term **collaborative writing** interchangeably with the term *peer-group writing*. In this handbook, we use the term *collaborate* to mean "students working together to write a paper." The underlying idea is that two (or more) heads are better than one.

Writing collaboratively enhances confidence, as writers support one another. Also important, the benefits of acquiring experience in collaborative writing extend beyond your college years. Many professions require participation in writing committees; members of the group must reach general agreement on how to proceed and contribute equally to a written report. Marketing managers, for example, head up teams who conduct consumer research and then—as a group—write up their findings. Box 2.12 provides guidelines for collaborative writing.

**SUMMARY BOX** 2.12

## Guidelines for collaborative writing

**STARTING**

1. Learn one another's names. If the group wishes, exchange e-mail addresses and/or phone numbers so that you can be in touch outside of class.

2. Participate actively in the group process. During discussions, help set a tone that encourages everyone to participate, including people who don't like to interrupt, who want time to think before they talk, or who are shy. Conversely, help the group set limits if someone dominates the discussions or makes all the decisions. If you lack experience contributing in a group setting, plan personal ways you'll take an active role.

3. As a group, assign work to be done between meetings. Distribute the responsibilities as fairly as possible. Also, decide whether to choose one discussion leader or to rotate leadership, unless your instructor assigns a particular procedure.

4. Make decisions regarding the technology you'll use. If everyone can use the same word processing program, for example, that will make sharing drafts or parts of drafts much easier. If not, you can use the "Save As" function in major word processing programs like Microsoft Word to save in a common format. Decide if you'll share materials via a floppy disk or CD-ROM or as an e-mail attachment. If any group members are unfamiliar with these processes, others need to help them learn. (Different areas and levels of expertise are an advantage of working in groups.)

5. Set a timeline and deadlines for the project. Agree on what to do in the event that someone misses a deadline.

**PLANNING THE WRITING**

6. After discussing the project, brainstorm as a group or use structured techniques for discovering and compiling ideas.

7. Together, agree on the ideas that seem best and allow for a period of INCUBATION, if time permits. Then, discuss your group choices again.

8. As a group, divide the project into parts and distribute assignments fairly. For example, if the project requires research, decide who will do it and how they'll share findings with others. If one person is going to be responsible for preparing drafts from pieces that others have written, make sure his or her other responsibilities are balanced.

9. As you work on your part of the project, take notes in preparation for giving your group a progress report.

## Guidelines for collaborative writing

10. As a group, OUTLINE or otherwise sketch an overview of the paper to get a preliminary idea of how best to use material contributed by individuals.

**DRAFTING THE WRITING**

11. Draft a THESIS STATEMENT. The thesis statement sets the direction for the rest of the paper. Each member of the group can draft a thesis statement and the group can discuss the advantages of each, but the group needs to agree on one version before getting too far into the rest of the draft. Your group might revise the thesis statement after the whole paper has been drafted, but using a preliminary version gets everyone started in the same direction.

12. Draft the rest of the paper. Decide whether each member of the group should write a complete draft or one part of the whole. For example, each group member might take one main idea and be responsible for drafting that section. Share draft materials among the group members using disks or e-mail attachments (see step 4). If this is impossible, make photocopies. For most group meetings, it will be important to have a paper copy of group materials, so print (or photocopy) copies for everyone.

**REVISING THE WRITING**

13. Read over the drafts. Are all the important points included?

14. Use the revision checklist (Box 2.10 in 2u.5) and work either as a group or by assigning portions to subgroups. If different people have drafted different sections, COHERENCE and UNITY should receive special attention in revision, as should your introduction and conclusion.

15. Agree on a final version. Assign someone to prepare the final draft and make sure every group member has a copy.

**EDITING AND PROOFREADING THE WRITING**

16. Use the editing checklist (Box 2.11 in 2v) to double-check for errors. If you find errors, correct and print out the page or the whole draft again. No matter how well the group has worked collaboratively, or how well the group has written the paper, a sloppy final version reflects negatively on the entire group.

17. As a group, review printouts or photocopies of the final draft. Don't leave the last stages to a subgroup. Draw on everyone's knowledge of grammar, spelling, and punctuation. Use everyone's eyes for proofreading.

18. If your instructor asks, be prepared to describe your personal contribution to the project and/or to describe or evaluate the contributions of others.

## 2y    A student essay in three drafts

The following sections observe Sara Cardini, a student, planning to write on the topic of Japanese animation. You'll find her writing assignment (2c), how she used an entry in her journal (2f), mapped her ideas (2j), wrote her THESIS STATEMENT (2q), and outlined (2r). During these activities, Cardini chose an informative writing purpose (1b.2).

### 2y.1  The first draft of a student essay

Here's Cardini's first draft showing her own notes to herself about revisions to make in the second draft. The notes resulted from comments of her PEER-RESPONSE GROUP and from her personal rereading of her draft.

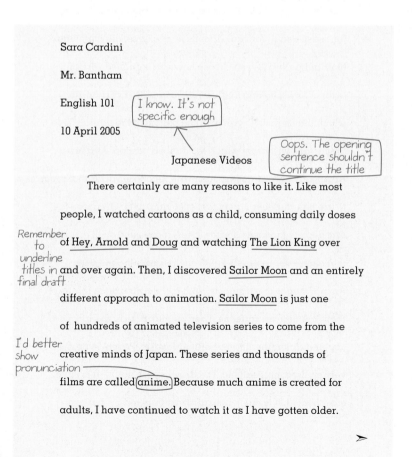

Sara Cardini

Mr. Bantham

English 101

*I know. It's not specific enough*

10 April 2005

Japanese Videos

*Oops. The opening sentence shouldn't continue the title*

There certainly are many reasons to like it. Like most

people, I watched cartoons as a child, consuming daily doses

*Remember to underline titles in final draft*

of Hey, Arnold and Doug and watching The Lion King over

and over again. Then, I discovered Sailor Moon and an entirely

different approach to animation. Sailor Moon is just one

of hundreds of animated television series to come from the

*I'd better show pronunciation*

creative minds of Japan. These series and thousands of

films are called anime. Because much anime is created for

adults, I have continued to watch it as I have gotten older.

Figure 2.9  Sara Cardini's first draft, with notes

*in my interest*

I am not alone. In recent years, [anime rocks] Still, people   Tone
appropriate?

who are unfamiliar with anime may wonder why adults

would waste their time watching cartoons. (Some careful

analysis makes the answer clear.) Anime is a sophisticated

Japanese cartoon style.    *Need to add thesis concept that
anime differs from American cartoons.*

     Someone watching [animes] for the first time notices several

*Check
plural*   distinctive qualities: ~~The most obvious difference between~~

~~Japanese and American cartoons is, of course, the language.~~

~~Most anime will let you choose between a dubbed version~~

~~(with actors speaking English) and a subtitled version (in~~

*I think
I'm
going
off
track
here.
Are
these
points
important
to my
comparison?* ~~which the English is written at the bottom of the screen). True~~

~~anime fans will never watch the dubbed version. As a result,~~

~~American viewers are barraged with Japanese voices that seem~~

~~to use a high-pitched, very fast speaking style.~~ Of course, the

film depicts Japanese houses, trees, rooms, and such in a way

~~that shows the contrasts between their country and ours.~~   *Keep
verb
tenses
consistent.*

Anime images move quickly, with a style often more frantic

than in American cartoons. Their soundtracks frequently [used]

*symphonic*

*Too
itsy
bitsy.
Make
into
one
sentence*   jazz and rock rather than ~~traditional~~ music. People in anime are

very stylized, not realistic. The drawing is colorful. It is more

complicated. It is often more abstract than most American

                                       ➤

*For example,*

cartoons. ~~E.G.~~ (take) a TV series called <u>Samurai X</u>, the most

*"take" isn't the right verb—fix*

popular anime cartoons with both American and Japanese

audiences. <u>Samurai X</u> is set in the nineteenth century and

tells the story of one warrior's life. It is drawn beautifully in

[wordy] → a way that looks both like older Japanese art prints and like

more contemporary movies such as <u>Crouching Tiger, Hidden</u>

<u>Dragon.</u>

*Bet this is a fragment. Check Chapter 12.*

*Whereas*

~~While~~ Americans considered animation entertainment

for children. The Japanese viewed it as ~~entertaining primarily~~

*mainly*

for adults. Since the beginning of print, cartooning in Japan

has been aimed at adults, so anime was a natural step.

*in this tradition*

It's

interesting how graphic novels were important in Japan long

before they were here, but lately you see more and more

graphic novels. In America, aside from editorial cartoons

and newspaper funny pages, comics were (aimed) primarily

*Used same word twice. Get out my thesaurus.*

*adolescent males*

at ~~boys~~. American animation in the 1940s and 1950s was

different. Think of Walt Disney. Japanese cartoons were

developed for both kids and old people, male and female

audiences. In Japan, animated cartoons take on adult subjects

often absent from American cartoons. ←

*Examples needed*

[There must be a better word]

The (special) style of anime comes largely from the films

➤

69

being produced for ⟨narrow⟩ audiences. The animators were    *Right word?*

creating works only for a Japanese market, at least until

quite recently. Therefore, they did not take into account the

traditions of other cultures. Indeed, US animation was

produced for an international audience, which called for

recognizable themes that came out of familiar European

*uninitiated*
traditions. For ~~rookie~~ viewers, then, anime provides a crash

*an Eastern*
course in ~~a~~ culture quite different from their own. Nearly
   ∧

all serious anime fans own guides that explain such things   *Add more detail here*

as Japanese social hierarchies. For instance, several anime

feature a *hagoromo* or feathered cloak worn by a mythological

figure known as the *tennyo*. Knowing that this figure has a

*symbolic*
certain meaning for a Japanese viewer and is not just a
   ∧

random decoration or character adds to the depth of a scene

in which it appears. Decoding some of these cultural

references is undoubtedly some of the fun and challenge for

the true *otakon*, or anime fan.

     Japanese television has many daily animated series

that vary in terms of sophistication and audience. Some of

*complex*
these have extremely ~~complicated~~ scripts, while others are
   ∧

bad by nearly any standard. Several of these television series

                                               ➤

*Add examples*

now appear in the United States. A wide range of anime

feature films is readily available on DVD, and many have

even found their way into American theaters. For instance,

Akira is a film about life thirty years after a nuclear war.

Probably the most famous theatrical anime in the United

*Better look at this sentence again!*

States is Spirited Away. Directed by Hayao Miyasaki, in

which a young girl, Chihiro, is able to free her parents from

a spell after many magical adventures. The movie will become
*probably*
^

a ~~probably~~ classic. Anime appears in all kinds of types and

genres, from childish works like Pokémon to dark science

fiction like Ghost in the Shell.

*I think I should move this up as the topic sentence for this paragraph.*

*Best word?*

One reason grown-ups enjoy anime is because they

missed a form they loved as children. Anime gives them

*Verb tense ok?*

*of design, creativity, sophistication, and content*

animated art but adds an adult level. While there have
^

been a few American cartoons aimed at adults (The Simpsons,

South Park), the animation is less detailed and the tone is

usually satiric. There are no such barriers in anime.

By studying anime, I also learned more about Japan.

I met people who took Japanese language classes and had

traveled to cities such as Tokyo and Osaka. I found out about

Japanese popular culture and how much fashion, music, etc.,

the Japanese borrow from Americans and how much we

borrow from them. I discovered that while the Japanese are

very different in some traditions, they are very much like us

in terms of their love of movies, TV, and music. For the first

time, I became very interested in how people in another *Does this para relate directly to my thesis?*

country live. Now I am considering traveling to Japan.

As Americans come to embrace anime, the form may

change. Some fans fear that the art of anime will be ~~wasted~~ *watered down*

in the bid for popularity and profits. Others celebrate the

combination of styles as some American animators borrow

from the Japanese. In this essay I have explained Japanese

animation. ← *I shoudn't declare what I have done. My ending needs work.*

## 2y.2 The second draft of a student essay

For her second draft, Cardini revised by working systematically through the notes she had written on the draft. The notes came from her own thinking as well as from the comments of the PEER-RESPONSE GROUP with which she had shared her paper.

From the assignment (2c), Cardini knew that her instructor would consider this second draft an "essay in progress." Her instructor's responses would help her write a final draft. She expected two types of comments: questions to help her clarify and expand on some of her ideas, and references to some of this handbook's section codes (number-letter combinations) to point out errors. Here is her second draft.

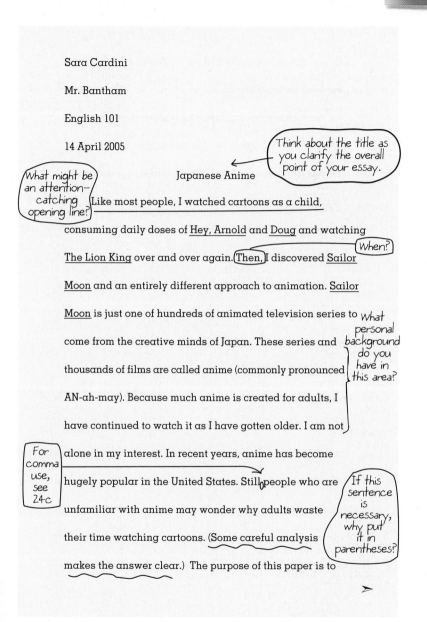

Sara Cardini

Mr. Bantham

English 101

14 April 2005

*Think about the title as you clarify the overall point of your essay.*

Japanese Anime

*What might be an attention-catching opening line?*

Like most people, I watched cartoons as a child, consuming daily doses of Hey, Arnold and Doug and watching The Lion King over and over again. Then, I discovered Sailor *When?*

Moon and an entirely different approach to animation. Sailor

Moon is just one of hundreds of animated television series to *What personal background do you have in this area?*

come from the creative minds of Japan. These series and

thousands of films are called anime (commonly pronounced

AN-ah-may). Because much anime is created for adults, I

have continued to watch it as I have gotten older. I am not

*For comma use, see 24c*

alone in my interest. In recent years, anime has become

hugely popular in the United States. Still, people who are *If this sentence is necessary, why put it in parentheses?*

unfamiliar with anime may wonder why adults waste

their time watching cartoons. (Some careful analysis

makes the answer clear.) The purpose of this paper is to

**Figure 2.10** Sara Cardini's second draft, with her instructor's responses

*Indicate the purpose of your paper without announcing it.* explain Japanese anime and how it differs from the style of American cartoons.

*Should this para come after the background information?*

Someone watching anime for the first time notices

several distinctive qualities. Anime images move quickly,

*Think about a stronger link between paragraphs.* with a style often more frantic than in American cartoons.

Their soundtracks frequently use jazz and rock rather *Interesting, but I'd like to know more detail*

than symphonic music. People in anime are very stylized,

not realistic. The drawing is more colorful, more complicated,

and often more abstract than in most American cartoons. For

example, a TV series called <u>Samurai X</u> is one of the most

popular anime cartoons with both American and Japanese

audiences. <u>Samurai X</u> is set in the nineteenth century and

*Since this para gives background information, does it belong here?* tells the story of one warrior's life. ← *Why is it popular?*

Whereas Americans considered animation entertainment

for children, the Japanese viewed it as mainly for adults. Since

the beginning of print, cartooning in Japan has targeted adults,

*This para needs a stronger topic sentence.* so anime was a natural step in this tradition. It's interesting

how graphic novels were important in Japan long before they

*Off topic?* were here, but lately you see more and more graphic novels.

➤

In the United States, aside from editorial cartoons and

newspaper funny pages, comics were aimed primarily at [*A little more guidance, please.*]

[*From what?*] adolescent males. American animation in the 1940s and

[*Off topic?*] 1950s was [different.] Think of Walt Disney. Japanese cartoons

were developed for both kids and old people, male and female

audiences. In Japan, animated cartoons take on adult

subjects often absent from American cartoons. These subjects

include war, death, sacrifice, love, Japan's historical past [*A link to the next para would be welcome here.*]

and future, and even occasionally sex and violence.

    The unique style of anime comes largely from the

[*Right word?*] films being produced for [narrow] audiences. The animators

were creating works only for a Japanese market, at least [*What does it refer to? See 9p*]

until quite recently. Therefore, [it] did not take into account

the traditions of other cultures. [Indeed,] American animation [*Right word?*]

was produced for an international audience, which called

for recognizable themes that came out of familiar European

traditions. For uninitiated viewers, then, anime provides a crash

course in an Eastern culture quite different from their own.

Nearly all serious anime fans own guides that explain such

➤

things as Japanese social hierarchies, clothing, dining habits,

traditions, rituals, and mythology. For instance, several anime *See next page.*

feature a *hagoromo*, or feathered cloak, worn by a mythological

figure known as the *tennyo*. Knowing that this figure has a

symbolic meaning for a Japanese viewer and is not just a

random decoration or character adds to the depth of a scene

in which it appears. Decoding some of these cultural references

*Excellent point!* is undoubtedly some of the fun and challenge for the true

*otakon*, or anime fan.

Anime appears in all kinds of types and genres, from

*Do you really mean childish?* childish works like Pokémon to dark science fiction like Ghost

in the Shell. Japanese televison has many daily animated series

that vary in terms of sophistication and audience. Some of *Meaning what?*

these have extremely complex scripts, while others are bad

by nearly any standard. Several of these television series

now appear in the United States, with some of the best known

including Inuyasha and Evangelion. A wide range of anime

feature films are readily available on DVD, and many have

even found their way into American theaters.

*See previous page.*

(For instance,) Akira is a film about life thirty years after a

nuclear war. Probably the most famous theatrical anime

video in the United States is Spirited Away, directed by

*More detail would make this vivid.*

Hayao Miyasaki, in which a young girl, Chihiro, is able to

free her parents from a spell after many magical adventures.

The movie will probably become a classic.

One reason American adults enjoy anime is because

they miss a form they loved as children. Anime gives them

animated art but adds an adult level of design, creativity,

sophistication, and content. While there have been a few

American cartoons aimed at adults (The Simpsons, South Park).

the animation is less detailed and the tone is usually satiric.

There are no such barriers in anime.

*Interesting concluding thoughts*

As Americans come to embrace anime, the form may

change. Some fans fear that the art of anime will be watered

down in the bid for popularity and profits. Others celebrate

*Bringing in your voice again makes for an effective ending.*

the combination of styles as some American animators

borrow from the Japanese. In this essay I have proved that

anime deserves our attention.

*But avoid making an absolute claim like this.*

Dear Sara,

You've done yourself proud. And you've inspired me to look up the fascinating subject of Japanese anime.

As you revise for your final draft, I'd urge you to acquire a little more personal voice. Think about how you feel on this subject and put that in words. Also, think about my questions and the codes that refer you to sections of the Troyka handbook.

I will enjoy reading your final draft.

RB

## 2y.3 A student's final draft

For her final draft, Cardini worked systematically through her second draft with an eye on her instructor's responses. Also, she revised in places where her instructor hadn't commented. As another check, Cardini referred to the revision checklist (Box 2.10 in 2u.5).

Next, to edit her final draft, Cardini looked up the handbook codes (number-letter combinations) her instructor wrote on her second draft. She also consulted the editing checklist (Box 2.11 in 2v). Then, before she started to proofread, she took a break from writing so she could refresh her ability to see typing errors. Distance from her work, she knew, would also help her see it more objectively.

Cardini's final draft appears on the following pages with notes in the margins to point out elements that help the essay succeed. These notes are for you only; don't write any notes on your final drafts.

## Sara Cardini's final draft

Sara Cardini

Mr. Bantham

English 101

28 April 2005

*Includes name, course information, and date, double-spaced and flush left*

*Header at top right has name and page number*

The Appeal of Japanese Animation for Adults

*Centers title*

I confess that I am an animation addict. Like most people, I watched cartoons as a child, consuming daily doses of Hey, Arnold and Doug and watching The Lion King over and over again. Then in junior high, just about the time I was getting tired of cartoons, I discovered Sailor Moon and an entirely different approach to animation. Sailor Moon is just one of hundreds of animated television series to come from the creative minds of Japan. These series and thousands of films are called anime (commonly pronounced AN-ah-may). Because much anime is created for adults, I have continued to watch it as I have gotten older. In fact, my interest has grown so strong that I have studied Japanese, have attended anime conferences, and am now studying filmmaking. I am not alone in my interest. In recent years, anime has become hugely popular in the United States. Still, people who are unfamiliar with anime may wonder why adults would waste their time watching cartoons. Some careful analysis makes the answer clear. Anime has traditions and features that distinguish it from American cartoons and make it sophisticated enough to appeal to adults.

*Includes attention-getting first line*

*Provides her credentials on this topic*

*Introduces a question*

*Offers a thesis*

*continued* ➤

(Proportions shown in this paper are adjusted to fit space limitations of this book. Follow actual dimensions shown in this book and your instructor's directions.)

Cardini 2

**Provides background on topic**

Animation developed differently in Japan and America after World War II. Whereas Americans considered animation entertainment for children, the Japanese viewed it as mainly **Uses comparison and contrast to develop paragraph** for adults. Since the beginning of print, cartooning in Japan has targeted adults, so anime was a natural step in this tradition. In America, aside from editorial cartoons and newspaper funny pages, comics were aimed primarily at adolescent males. Therefore, American animation in the 1940s and 1950s was different from the type developed in Japan. The early work of Walt Disney, for example, came from fairy tales, or it featured cute animal characters. In Japan, animated cartoons take on adult subjects often absent from American cartoons. These subjects include war, death, sacrifice, love, Japan's historical past and future, and even occasionally sex and violence. The plot lines are often extremely complex. Stories that would be kept simple in a Disney film to avoid viewer confusion have no such restrictions in Japan.

**Uses specific details to explain anime**

Complex plots are but one of the distinctive features of anime. Anime images move quickly, with a style often more frantic than in American cartoons. Their soundtracks frequently use jazz and rock rather than symphonic music. However, perhaps most striking are the large eyes and sharp

*continued* ➤

Cardini 3

features of the characters. People in anime are very stylized, not realistic. The drawing is more colorful, more complicated, and often more abstract than most American cartoons. For example, a TV series called <u>Samurai X</u> is one of the most popular anime cartoons with both American and Japanese audiences. <u>Samurai X</u> is set in the nineteenth century and tells the story of one warrior's life. It is drawn beautifully in a way that looks both like older Japanese art prints and like more contemporary movies such as <u>Crouching Tiger, Hidden Dragon</u>.

*Provides a concrete example*

The unique style of anime comes largely from the films being produced for specific audiences. The animators were creating works only for a Japanese market, at least until quite recently. Therefore, they did not take into account the traditions of other cultures. In contrast, American animation was produced for an international audience, which called for recognizable themes that came out of familiar European traditions. For uninitiated viewers, then, anime provides a crash course in an Eastern culture quite different from their own. Nearly all serious anime fans own guides that explain such things as Japanese social hierarchies, clothing, dining habits, traditions, rituals, and mythology. To cite one small example, several anime feature a *hagoromo,* or feathered cloak, worn by a mythological figure known as the *tennyo.* Knowing that this figure has a symbolic meaning for a Japanese viewer and is not just a random decoration or character adds to the depth of a scene in which it appears. Decoding some of these cultural references

*Uses cause and effect to explain differences*

*Cites a very specific example*

*continued* ➤

81

Cardini 4

is undoubtedly some of the fun and challenge for the true

*otakon*, or anime fan.

**Uses classification to explain types**   Anime appears in all kinds of types and genres, from children's works like Pokémon to dark science fiction like Ghost in the Shell. Japanese television has many daily animated series that vary in terms of sophistication and audience. Some of these have extremely complex scripts, while others are painfully simplistic. Several of these television series now appear in America, with some of the

**Provides specific titles as examples**   best known including Inuyasha and Evangelion. A wide range of anime feature films are readily available on DVD in America, and many have even found their way into theaters. For example, Akira is a film about life thirty years after a

**Focuses at length on one prominent example**   nuclear war. A misfit boy, Tetsuo, accidentally discovers the government experiments that led to that war and then learns that scientists are starting similar experiments once again. Probably the most famous theatrical anime film in the United States is Spirited Away, directed by Hayao Miyasaki, in which a young girl, Chihiro, is able to free her parents from a spell after many magical adventures. The movie will probably become a classic.

**States a reason in the topic sentence**   One reason American adults enjoy anime is because they miss a form they loved as children. Anime gives them animated art but adds an adult level of design, creativity, sophistication, and content. While there have been a few

**Contrasts American cartoons with anime**   American cartoons aimed at adults (The Simpsons, South Park), the animation is not very detailed and the tone is usually satiric. There are no such barriers in anime.

*continued* ➤

Cardini 5

As Americans come to embrace anime, the form may change. Some fans fear that the art of anime will be watered down in the bid for popularity and profits. Others celebrate the combination of styles as some American animators borrow from the Japanese. As an animation addict, I welcome more American animation for adults. Still, I would be disappointed if the distinctive qualities of anime disappeared. I fervently hope the Japanese animators will maintain their exotic creativity.

Speculates about the future in concluding strategy

Uses final comment to return to her opening idea

# Chapter 3

## WRITING PARAGRAPHS

### 3a   What is a paragraph?

A **paragraph** is a group of sentences that work together to develop a unit of thought. Paragraphing permits writers to divide material into manageable parts. When a group of paragraphs works together in logical sequence, the result is a complete essay or other whole piece of writing.

To signal the start of a new paragraph, indent the first line about one-half inch. Skip no extra lines between paragraphs. Business writing (Chapter 40) is an exception: It calls for BLOCK STYLE for paragraphs, which means you do not indent the first line but rather leave a double space between paragraphs. If you're already double-spacing, then leave two double lines for a total of four lines.

We explain later in this chapter the rich variety of paragraph arrangements (3h) and rhetorical strategies (3i) at your disposal for writing paragraphs. Types of arrangements and rhetorical strategies reflect patterns of thought in Western cultures. But first, let's look at characteristics of paragraphs in general. We start by discussing introductory paragraphs (3b); then, body paragraphs (3c through 3j); and last, concluding paragraphs (3k).

### 3b   How can I write effective introductory paragraphs?

An **introductory paragraph** leads the reader to sense what's ahead. It sets the stage. It also, if possible, attempts to arouse a reader's interest in the topic.

A THESIS STATEMENT can be an important component in an introduction. Many instructors require students to place the thesis statement at the end of the opening paragraph. Doing so disciplines students to state early the central point of the essay. If an introduction points in one direction, and the rest of the essay goes off in another, the essay isn't communicating a clear message. Professional writers don't necessarily include a thesis statement in their introductory paragraphs. Most have the skill to maintain a line of thought without overtly stating a main idea.

Introductory paragraphs, as well as concluding paragraphs (3k), are usually shorter than body paragraphs (3c).

Be careful not to tack on a sloppy introduction at the last minute. The introductory paragraph plays too important a role to be tossed off with merely a few shallow lines. While many writers prefer to write only a thesis statement as an introduction in an early draft, they always return to write a complete introductory paragraph after the body—the main part—of the writing is finished. For a list of specific strategies to use and pitfalls to avoid for introductory paragraphs, see Box 3.1.

---

**SUMMARY BOX** 3.1

## Introductory paragraphs

**STRATEGIES TO USE**

- Providing relevant background information
- Relating briefly an interesting story or anecdote
- Giving one or more pertinent—perhaps surprising—statistics
- Asking one or more provocative questions
- Using an appropriate quotation
- Defining a KEY TERM (5d)
- Presenting one or more brief examples (3i)
- Drawing an ANALOGY (3i)

**STRATEGIES TO AVOID**

- Don't write statements about your purpose, such as "I am going to discuss the causes of falling oil prices."
- Don't apologize, as in "I am not sure this is right, but this is my opinion."
- Don't use overworked expressions, such as "Haste makes waste, as I recently discovered" or "Love is grand."

---

Always integrate an introductory device into the paragraph so that it leads smoothly into the thesis statement. Some examples follow. In this chapter, each example paragraph has a number to its left for your easy reference. Here's an introductory paragraph that uses two brief examples to lead into the thesis statement at the end of the paragraph.

On seeing another child fall and hurt himself, Hope, just nine months old, stared, tears welling up in her eyes, and crawled to her mother to be comforted—as though she had been hurt, not her friend.

When 15-month-old Michael saw his friend Paul crying, Michael fetched his own teddy bear and offered it to Paul; when that didn't stop Paul's tears, Michael brought Paul's security blanket from another room.
**1**  Such small acts of sympathy and caring, observed in scientific studies, are leading researchers to trace the roots of empathy—the ability to share another's emotions—to infancy, contradicting a long-standing assumption that infants and toddlers were incapable of these feelings.

—Daniel Goleman, "Researchers Trace Empathy's Roots to Infancy"

In paragraph 2, the opening quotation sets up a dramatic contrast with the thesis statement.

**2**  "Alone one is never lonely," says May Sarton in her essay "The Rewards of Living a Solitary Life." Most people, however, don't share Sarton's opinion: They're terrified of living alone. They're used to living with others—children with parents, roommates with roommates, friends with friends, spouses with spouses. When the statistics catch up with them, therefore, they're rarely prepared. Chances are high that most adult men and women will need to know how to live alone, briefly or longer, at some time in their lives.

—Tara Foster, student

In paragraph 3, the writer asks a direct question, and next puts the reader in a dramatic situation to arouse interest in the topic.

**3**  What should you do? You're out riding your bike, playing golf, or in the middle of a long run when you look up and suddenly see a jagged streak of light shoot across the sky, followed by a deafening clap of thunder. Unfortunately, most outdoor exercisers don't know whether to stay put or make a dash for shelter when a thunderstorm approaches, and sometimes the consequences are tragic.

—Gerald Secor Couzens, "If Lightning Strikes"

**EXERCISE 3-1**  Write an introduction for each of the three essays informally outlined below. Then, for more practice, write one alternative introduction for each. If you have a peer-response group, share the various written introductions and decide which are most effective. For help, see 3b.

1.  Reading for fun
    *Thesis statement:* People read many kinds of books for pleasure.
    Body paragraph 1: murder mysteries and thrillers
    Body paragraph 2: romances and westerns
    Body paragraph 3: science fiction

2.  Cell phones
    *Thesis statement:* Cell phones have changed how some people behave in public.

Body paragraph 1: driving
Body paragraph 2: restaurants
Body paragraph 3: movies and concerts
Body paragraph 4: sidewalks, parks, and other casual spaces

3. Using credit cards

*Thesis statement:* Although credit cards can help people manage their finances wisely, they also offer too much temptation.

Body paragraph 1: convenience and safety
Body paragraph 2: tracking of purchases
Body paragraph 3: overspending dangers

## 3c   What are body paragraphs?

Each **body paragraph**, which belongs between an introductory paragraph (3b) and a concluding paragraph (3k), consists of a main idea and support for that idea. To be effective, a body paragraph needs three characteristics: unity (3d and 3e), development (3f), and coherence (3g). The sections shown in parentheses explain how you can achieve each characteristic. Box 3.2 gives an overview of all three characteristics.

---

**SUMMARY BOX** 3.2

### Characteristics of effective body paragraphs

- **Unity:** Have you made a clear connection between the main idea of the paragraph and the sentences that support the main idea? (3d and 3e)

- **Development:** Have you included detailed and sufficient support for the main idea of the paragraph? (3f)

- **Coherence:** Have you progressed from one sentence to the next in the paragraph smoothly and logically? (3g)

---

Paragraph 4 is an example of an effective body paragraph.

**4**   The Miss Plastic Surgery contest, trumpeted by Chinese promoters as "the world's first pageant for artificial beauties," shows the power of cosmetic surgery in a country that has swung from one extreme to another when it comes to the feminine ideal. In the 10th century, Emperor Li Yu ordered

Figure 3.1

his consort to bind her feet; women practiced the painful ritual for more than 900 years in the belief that small feet were more alluring. In contrast, at the height of the Cultural Revolution in the 1960s and 1970s, Maoist officials condemned any form of personal grooming or beautification as "unrevolutionary" and regularly beat women for owning hairbrushes, wearing blush, or painting their nails.

—Abigail Haworth, "Nothing About These Women Is Real"

Paragraph 4 has UNITY (3d) in that the main idea—the feminine ideal in China has swung from one extreme to another—stated in the TOPIC SENTENCE (3e) is supported by detailed examples. It has COHERENCE (3g) in that the content of every sentence ties into the content of the other sentences. Also, the paragraph *coheres*—sticks together—because of the use of transitional phrases ("In the 10th century" and "In contrast," for example). It has PARAGRAPH DEVELOPMENT (3f and 3i) in that the details provide support for the main idea.

## 3d How can I create unity in paragraphs?

A paragraph has **unity** when the connection between the main idea and its supporting sentences is clear.

Unity is ruined when any sentence in a paragraph "goes off the topic," which means its content doesn't relate to the main idea or to the other sentences in the paragraph. To show you broken unity, in paragraph 5 we've deliberately inserted two sentences (the fourth and the next to last) that go off the topic and ruin a perfectly good paragraph, shown as paragraph 6. (Neither a personal complaint about stress nor hormones produced by men and women during exercise belong in a paragraph defining different kinds of stress.)

**NO**   Stress has long been the subject of psychological and physiological speculation. In fact, more often than not, the word itself is ill defined and overused, meaning different things to different people. Emotional stress, for example, can come about as the result of a family argument or the death of a loved one. Everyone says, "Don't get stressed," but I have no idea **5** how to do that. Environmental stress, such as exposure to excessive heat or cold, is an entirely different phenomenon. Physiologic stress has been described as the outpouring of the steroid hormones from the adrenal glands. During exercise, such as weightlifting, males and females produce different hormones. Whatever its guise, a lack of a firm definition of stress has seriously impeded past research.

YES    Stress has long been the subject of psychological and physiological speculation. In fact, more often than not, the word itself is ill defined and overused, meaning different things to different people. Emotional stress, for example, can come about as the result of a family argument or the death of a loved one. Environmental stress, such as exposure to excessive heat or cold, is an entirely different phenomenon. Physiologic stress has been described as the outpouring of the steroid hormones from the adrenal glands. Whatever its guise, a lack of a firm definition of stress has seriously impeded past research.

**6**

—Herbert Benson, MD, *The Relaxation Response*

## 3e  How can topic sentences create paragraph unity?

A **topic sentence** contains the main idea of a paragraph and controls its content. Often, the topic sentence comes at the beginning of a paragraph, though not always. Professional essay writers, because they have the skill to carry the reader along without explicit signposts, sometimes decide not to use topic sentences. However, instructors often require students to use topic sentences. As apprentice writers, students might have more difficulty writing unified paragraphs.

### TOPIC SENTENCE STARTING A PARAGRAPH

In ACADEMIC WRITING, most paragraphs begin with a topic sentence so that readers know immediately what to expect. Paragraph 7 is an example.

Music patronage was at a turning point when Mozart went to Vienna in the last part of the eighteenth century. Many patrons of music continued to be wealthy aristocrats. Haydn's entire career was funded by a rich prince. Mozart's father and, for a time, Mozart himself were in the employ of another prince. But when Mozart went to Vienna in 1781, he contrived to make a living from a variety of sources. In addition to performances at aristocratic houses and commissions for particular works, Mozart gave piano and composition lessons, put on operas, and gave many public concerts of his own music.

**7**

—Jeremy Yudkin, "Composers and Patrons in the Classic Era"

Sometimes, a topic sentence both starts a paragraph and, in different wording, ends the paragraph. Paragraph 8 is an example.

Burnout is a potential problem for hardworking and persevering students to fight. A preliminary step for preventing student burnout is for students to work in moderation. Students can concentrate on school every day, if they don't overtax themselves. One method students can

**8**   use is to avoid concentrating on a single project for an extended period. For example, if students have to read two books for a midterm history test, they should do other assignments at intervals so that the two books will not get boring. Another means to moderate a workload is to regulate how many extracurricular projects to take on. When a workload is manageable, a student's immunity to burnout is strengthened.

—Bradley Howard, student

## TOPIC SENTENCE ENDING A PARAGRAPH

Some paragraphs give supporting details first and wait to state the topic sentence at the paragraph's end. This approach is particularly effective for building suspense or for creating a bit of drama. Paragraph 9 is an example.

**9**   Once the Romans had left, the political situation in Britain deteriorated rapidly. Softened by their dependence on the Roman legions, the Romanized Britons were ill-equipped to defend themselves from renewed attacks by the Picts in the north. Then, even as the Britons were trying to cope with their fiercer northern neighbors, a much more calamitous series of events took place: waves of Germanic-speaking people from the Continent began to invade the island. The "English" were coming to England.

—C. M. Millward, "The Arrival of the English"

## TOPIC SENTENCE IMPLIED, NOT STATED

Some paragraphs are a unified whole even without a single sentence that readers can point to as the topic sentence. Yet, most readers can catch the main idea anyway. Paragraph 10 is an example. What do you think might be a straightforward topic sentence for it?

**10**   It is easy to identify with the quest for a secret document, somewhat harder to do so with a heroine whose goal is identifying and understanding the element radium, which is why in dramatic biography writers and directors end up reverting to fiction. To be effective, the dramatic elements must, and finally will, take precedence over any "real" biographical facts. We viewers do not care—if we wanted to know about the element radium, we would read a book on the element radium. When we go to the movies to see *The Story of Marie Curie* we want to find out how her little dog Skipper died.

—David Mamet, *Three Uses of the Knife: On the Nature and Purpose of Drama*

**EXERCISE 3-2**   Working individually or with a peer-response group, identify the topic sentences in the following paragraphs. If the topic sentence is implied, write the point the paragraph conveys. For help, consult section 3e.

A.   A good college program should stress the development of high-level reading, writing, and mathematical skills and should provide you with

11    a broad historical, social, and cultural perspective, no matter what subject you choose as your major. The program should teach you not only the most current knowledge in your field but also—just as important—prepare you to keep learning throughout your life. After all, you'll probably change jobs, and possibly even careers, at least six times, and you'll have other responsibilities, too—perhaps as a spouse and as a parent and certainly as a member of a community whose bounds extend beyond the workplace.

           —Frank T. Rhodes, "Let the Student Decide"

B.    The once majestic oak tree crashes to the ground amid the destructive flames, as its panic-stricken inhabitants attempt to flee the fiery tomb. Undergrowth that formerly flourished smolders in ashes. A family of deer darts furiously from one wall of flame

12 to the other, without an emergency exit. On the outskirts of the inferno, firefighters try desperately to stop the destruction. Somewhere at the source of this chaos lies a former campsite containing the cause of this destruction—an untended campfire. This scene is one of many that illustrate how human apathy and carelessness destroy nature.

           —Anne Bryson, student

C.    Rudeness isn't a distinctive quality of our own time. People today would be shocked by how rudely our ancestors behaved. In the colonial period, a French traveler marveled that "Virginians don't use napkins, but they wear silk cravats, and instead of carrying white handkerchiefs,

13 they blow their noses either with their fingers or with a silk handkerchief that also serves as a cravat, a napkin, and so on." In the 19th century, up to about the 1830s, even very distinguished people routinely put their knives in their mouths. And when people went to the theater, they would not just applaud politely—they would chant, jeer, and shout. So, the notion that there's been a downhill slide in manners ever since time began is just not so.

           —"Horizons," *U.S. News & World Report*

## 3f   How can I develop my body paragraphs?

You develop a **body paragraph** by supplying detailed support for the main idea of the paragraph communicated by your TOPIC SENTENCE (3e), whether stated or implied. **Paragraph development** is not merely a repetition, using other words, of the main idea. When this happens, you're merely going around in circles. We've deliberately manipulated paragraph 4 (in 3c) to create paragraph 14 on the following page. It is an example of a poorly developed paragraph. It goes nowhere; rather, it restates one idea three times in different words.

**NO**      The Miss Plastic Surgery contest, trumpeted by Chinese
**14**    promoters as "the world's first pageant for artificial beauties,"
shows the power of cosmetic surgery in a country that has
swung from one extreme to another when it comes to the feminine ideal. In past decades, China did not promote personal
grooming. Beautification is a recent development.

**What separates most good writing from bad is the writer's
ability to move back and forth between main ideas and specific
details.** To check whether you are providing sufficient detail in a body
paragraph, use the RENNS Test. Each letter in the made-up word
*RENNS* cues you to remember a different kind of supporting detail at
your disposal, as listed in Box 3.3.

---

**SUMMARY BOX 3.3**

## The RENNS Test: Checking for supporting details

**R** = **Reasons** provide support.

**E** = **Examples** provide support.

**N** = **Names** provide support.

**N** = **Numbers** provide support.

**S** = **Senses**—sight, sound, smell, taste, touch—provide support.

---

Use the RENNS Test to check the quality of your paragraph development. Of course, not every paragraph needs all five kinds of RENNS
details, nor do the supporting details need to occur in the order of the
letters in *RENNS*. Paragraph 15 contains three of the five types of
RENNS details. Identify the topic sentence and as many RENNS as you
can before reading the analysis that follows the paragraph.

U.S. shores are also being inundated by waves of plastic debris. On
the sands of the Texas Gulf Coast one day last September, volunteers
collected 307 tons of litter, two-thirds of which was plastic, including
**15**   31,733 bags, 30,295 bottles, and 15,631 six-pack yokes. Plastic trash is
being found far out to sea. On a four-day trip from Maryland to Florida
that ranged 100 miles offshore, John Hardy, an Oregon State University
marine biologist, spotted "Styrofoam and other plastic on the surface,
most of the whole cruise."

—"The Dirty Seas," *Time*

In paragraph 15, the first sentence serves as the topic sentence. Supporting details for that main idea include examples, names, and numbers.

The writer provides examples of the kinds of litter found washed up on the beach and floating offshore. The writer names many specific things: Texas Gulf Coast, September, bags, bottles, six-pack yokes, Maryland, Florida, John Hardy, Oregon State University, marine biologist, and Styrofoam. And the writer uses specific numbers to describe the volume of litter collected (307 tons), to give counts of specific items (such as 31,733 bags), and to tell how far from shore (100 miles) the litter had traveled.

Paragraph 16 contains four of the five types of RENNS. Identify the topic sentence and as many RENNS as you can before you read the analysis that follows the paragraph.

**16** Where he lives, the air is so clean that sunsets are never red, not even purple. There's simply not enough dust in the atmosphere to break up the light. Instead, the purple evening sky is tinged with green from the forests below. Where he lives, the mountain slopes tumble downward from the sky, picking up trees as they go along and ending in the rush of a clear and unpolluted river. Eagles soar high above on the swirling air currents. Bighorn sheep bounce with sure hooves along the mountain peaks. Bears, deer, elk and mountain lions roam the lower slopes. Where he lives is America, as it existed long before the coming of white settlers. He lives where Five Mile Creek flows into The River of No Return in a country named Light on the Mountains. He is one-sixteenth Apache, but most of his forebearers came to America 300 years ago and kept moving westward in a search for freedom and elbow room. Even his name is appropriate— Sylvan Hart. Sylvan comes from a Latin root meaning "forest," and a hart is one of nature's most elusive creatures, the male red deer.

—from *Read Magazine*

In paragraph 16, the eighth sentence is the topic sentence. Supporting details for the main idea include examples (mountain slopes tumble downward from the sky, clear and unpolluted river, Eagles soar high above); the writer also uses names (Five Mile Creek, River of No Return, Apache, Sylvan Hart) and numbers (300 years ago). Sensory details, given in images, provide more support (dust in the atmosphere, swirling air currents, sky is tinged with green).

**EXERCISE 3-3** Working individually or with a peer-response group, look again at the paragraphs in Exercise 3-2. Identify the RENNS in each paragraph. For help, consult 3f.

## 3g How can I write coherent paragraphs?

A paragraph has **coherence** when its sentences relate to each other, not only in content but also in choice of words and grammatical structures. A coherent paragraph conveys continuity because the sentences follow naturally from one to the next. Techniques for achieving coherence are listed in Box 3.4; refer to the sections shown in parentheses for complete explanations.

---

**SUMMARY BOX** 3.4

### Techniques for achieving coherence

- Using appropriate transitional expressions (3g.1)
- Using pronouns when possible (3g.2)
- Using deliberate repetition of a key word (3g.3)
- Using parallel structures (3g.4)
- Using coherence techniques to create connections among paragraphs (3g.5)

---

### 3g.1 Using transitional expressions for coherence

**Transitional expressions** are words and phrases that signal connections among ideas. **Transitions** are bridges that lead your reader along your line of thought. They offer cues about what follows. Commonly used transitional expressions are listed in Box 3.5.

---

**SUMMARY BOX** 3.5

### Transitional expressions and the relationships they signal

| | |
|---|---|
| **ADDITION** | also, in addition, too, moreover, and, besides, furthermore, equally important, then, finally |
| **EXAMPLE** | for example, for instance, thus, as an illustration, namely, specifically |
| **CONTRAST** | but, yet, however, nevertheless, nonetheless, conversely, in contrast, still, at the same time, on the one hand, on the other hand |
| **COMPARISON** | similarly, likewise, in the same way |
| **CONCESSION** | of course, to be sure, certainly, granted |
| **RESULT** | therefore, thus, as a result, so, accordingly, consequently |
| **SUMMARY** | hence, in short, in brief, in summary, in conclusion, finally |
| **TIME** | first, second, third, next, then, finally, afterward, before, soon, later, meanwhile, subsequently, immediately, eventually, currently |
| **PLACE** | in the front, in the foreground, in the back, in the background, at the side, adjacent, nearby, in the distance, here, there |

◢◤ **ALERT:** In ACADEMIC WRITING, set off a transitional expression with a comma, unless the expression is one short word (24c and 24g). ◆

Vary your choices of transitional words. For example, instead of always using *for example,* try *for instance.* Also, when choosing a transitional word, make sure it correctly says what you mean. For instance, don't use *however* in the sense of *on the other hand* if you mean *therefore* in the sense of *as a result.* The three brief examples below demonstrate how to use transitional expressions for each context.

### COHERENCE BY ADDITION

Woodpeckers use their beaks to find food and to chisel out nests. *In addition,* they claim their territory and signal their desire to mate by using their beaks to drum on trees.

### COHERENCE BY CONTRAST

Most birds communicate by singing. Woodpeckers, *however,* communicate by the duration and rhythm of the drumming of their beaks.

### COHERENCE BY RESULT

The woodpecker's strong beak enables it to communicate by drumming on dry branches and tree trunks. *As a result,* woodpeckers can communicate across greater distances than songbirds can.

Paragraph 17 demonstrates how transitional expressions (shown in bold) enhance a paragraph's COHERENCE. The TOPIC SENTENCE is the final sentence.

**17** Before the days of television, people were entertained by exciting radio shows such as *Superman, Batman,* and "War of the Worlds." **Of course**, the listener was required to pay careful attention to the story if all details were to be comprehended. **Better yet**, while listening to the stories, listeners would form their own images of the actions taking place. When the broadcaster would give brief descriptions of the Martian space ships invading earth, **for example**, every member of the audience would imagine a different space ship. **In contrast**, television's version of "War of the Worlds" will not stir the imagination at all, for everyone can clearly see the actions taking place. All viewers see the same space ship with the same features. Each aspect is clearly defined, and **therefore**, no one will imagine anything different from what is seen. **Thus**, television can't be considered an effective tool for stimulating the imagination.

—Tom Paradis, "A Child's Other World"

## 3g.2 Using pronouns for coherence

**Pronouns**—words that refer to nouns or other pronouns—allow readers to follow your train of thought from one sentence to the next without boring repetition. Without pronouns, you would have to repeat nouns over and over. For example, this sentence uses no pronouns and therefore has needless repetition: *The woodpecker scratched the woodpecker's head with the woodpecker's foot.* In contrast, with pronouns the sentence can be *The woodpecker scratched **its** head with **its** foot.* Paragraph 18 illustrates how pronouns (shown in bold) contribute to COHERENCE.

**18**
> After Gary Hanson, now 56, got laid off from **his** corporate position in 2003, **he**, **his** wife, Susan, and **his** son, John, now 54 and 27, respectively, wanted to do a spot of cleaning. Though **they** are hard at work, **they** are not scrubbing floors or washing windows. **They** are running **their** very own house-cleaning franchise, *The Maids Home Services,* which **they** opened in February.
>
> —Sara Wilson, "Clean House: Getting Laid Off from His Corporate Job Gave This Franchisee a Fresh Start"

## 3g.3 Using deliberate repetition for coherence

A key word or phrase is central to the main idea of the paragraph. **Repetition** of key words or phrases is a useful way to achieve COHERENCE in a paragraph. The word or phrase usually appears first in the paragraph's TOPIC SENTENCE (3e) and then again throughout the paragraph. The idea of repetition is to keep a concept in front of the reader.

Use this technique sparingly to avoid being monotonous. The shorter a paragraph, the more likely a repeated key word or phrase will seem repetitious, and the less likely it is to be effective. In a longer paragraph, however, the repetition of a key word or phrase can be effective. Paragraph 19 contains repeated words and phrases (shown in bold) closely tied to the concept of anthropology that make the paragraph more coherent.

**19**
> **Anthropology**, broadly defined, is the study of **humanity**, from its evolutionary origins millions of years ago to its present great numbers and worldwide diversity. Many other disciplines, of course, share with **anthropology** a focus on one aspect or another of **humanity**. **Like** sociology, economics, political science, psychology, and other behavioral and social sciences, **anthropology** is concerned with the way people organize their lives and relate to one another in interacting, interconnected groups—societies—that share basic beliefs and practices. **Like** economists, **anthropologists are interested in** society's material foundations—in how people produce and distribute food and other valued goods. **Like** sociologists, **anthropologists are interested in** the way

people structure their relations in society—in families, at work, in institutions. **Like** political scientists, **anthropologists are interested in** power and authority: who has them and how they are allocated. And, **like** psychologists, **anthropologists are interested in** individual development and the interaction between society and individual people.

—Nancy Bonvillain, "The Study of Humanity"

## 3g.4 Using parallel structures for coherence

**Parallel structures** are created when grammatically equivalent forms are used in series, usually of three or more items, but sometimes only two (see PARALLELISM, Chapter 18). Using parallel structures helps to give a paragraph coherence. The repeated parallel structures reinforce connections among ideas, and they add both tempo and sound to the sentence.

In paragraph 20, the authors use several parallel structures (shown in bold): a parallel series of words (*the sacred, the secular, the scientific*); parallel phrases (*sometimes smiled at, sometimes frowned upon*); and six parallel clauses (the first being *banish danger with a gesture*).

20  Superstitions are **sometimes smiled at** and **sometimes frowned upon** as observances characteristic of **the old-fashioned**, **the unenlightened**, children, peasants, servants, immigrants, foreigners, or backwoods people. Nevertheless, they give all of us ways of moving back and forth among the different worlds in which we live—**the sacred**, **the secular**, and **the scientific**. They allow us to keep a private world also, where, smiling a little, we can **banish danger with a gesture** and **summon luck with a rhyme**, **make the sun shine in spite of storm clouds**, **force the stranger to do our bidding**, **keep an enemy at bay**, and **straighten the paths of those we love**.

—Margaret Mead and Rhoda Metraux, "New Superstitions for Old"

## 3g.5 Creating coherence among paragraphs

The same techniques for achieving COHERENCE in a paragraph apply to showing connections among paragraphs in a piece of writing. All four techniques help: transitional expressions (3g.1), pronouns (3g.2), deliberate repetition (3g.3), and parallel structures (3g.4). To see them in action, look over this handbook's student papers (2y, 5n, 34e, 35h, and 38j).

Example 21 shows two short paragraphs and the start of a third. The writer achieves coherence among the paragraphs by repeating the key word *gratitude* and the related words *grateful, thankful,* and *thank* and by using them as a transition into the next paragraph. The writer also uses PARALLELISM within the paragraphs in this example.

To me, gratitude and inner peace go hand in hand. The more genuinely grateful I feel for the gift of my life, the more peaceful I feel. Gratitude, then, is worthy of a little practice.

**21** If you're anything like me, you probably have many people to be thankful for: friends, family members, people from your past, teachers, gurus, people from work, someone who gave you a break, as well as countless others. You may want to thank a higher power for the gift of life itself, or for the beauty of nature.

As you think of people to be grateful for, remember that it can be anyone—someone who held a door open for you, or a physician who saved your life. . . .

**EXERCISE 3-4**    Working individually or with a peer-response group, locate the coherence techniques in each paragraph. Look for transitional expressions, pronouns, deliberate repetition, and parallel structures. For help, consult 3g.

A.    Kathy sat with her legs dangling over the edge of the side of the hood. The band of her earphones held back strands of straight copper hair that had come loose from two thick braids that hung down her back. She swayed with the music that only she could hear. Her shoulders raised, making circles in the warm air. Her arms reached out to her side; her open hands reached for the air; her closed hands brought the air back to her. Her arms reached over her head; her opened hands reached for a cloud; her closed hands brought the cloud back to her. Her head moved from side to side; her eyes opened and closed to the tempo of the tunes. Kathy was motion.

**22**

—Claire Burke, student

B.    Newton's law may have wider application than just the physical world. In the social world, racism, once set into motion, will remain in motion unless acted upon by an outside force. The collective "we" must be the outside force. We must fight racism through education. We must make sure every school has the resources to do its job. We must present to our children a culturally diverse curriculum that reflects our pluralistic society. This can help students understand that prejudice is learned through contact with prejudiced people, rather than with the people toward whom the prejudice is directed.

**23**

—Randolph H. Manning, "Fighting Racism with Inclusion"

C.    The snow geese are first, rising off the ponds to breakfast in the sorghum fields up the river. Twenty thousand of them, perhaps more, great white birds with black wing tips rising out of the darkness into the rosy reflected light of dawn. They make a sweeping turn, a cloud of wings rising above the cottonwoods. But cloud is the wrong word. They don't form a disorderly blackbird rabble but a kaleidoscope of goose formations, always shifting, but always orderly. The light catches them—white against the tan velvet of the hills. Then they're overhead, line after line, layer above layer of formations, and the sky is filled with the clamor of an infinity of geese.

**24**

—Tony Hillerman, *Hillerman Country*

**EXERCISE 3-5** Working individually or with a peer-response group, use RENNS (3f) and techniques for achieving coherence (3g) to develop three of the following topic sentences into paragraphs. When finished, list the RENNS and the coherence techniques you used in each paragraph.

1. Newspaper comic strips reflect current concerns in our culture.
2. The contents of trash in the United States says a great deal about US culture.
3. Dramas on television tend to have several common elements.
4. Part-time jobs can be very unappealing.
5. Time management is a lifesaver for college students.

## 3h  How can I arrange a paragraph?

When you choose a **paragraph arrangement** during DRAFTING, you order its sentences to communicate the paragraph's message most clearly and effectively. Later, during REVISION, experiment with other arrangements to see how else your sentences might be arranged for greatest impact. You may find sometimes that only one possible arrangement can work. For example, if you're explaining how to bake a cake, you want to give the directions in a particular order. At other times, you may find that more than one arrangement is possible. For example, if you're writing about solving a problem and therefore using the problem-to-solution arrangement, you might also use the technique of ordering from least to most important—or its reverse. Box 3.6 lists the most common ways to arrange a paragraph. More about each arrangement follows in this section.

**SUMMARY BOX** **3.6**

### Ways to arrange sentences in a paragraph

- By time
- By location
- From general to specific
- From specific to general
- From least to most important
- From problem to solution

### ARRANGING BY TIME

In a paragraph arranged according to time, or **chronological order**, events are presented in whatever order they took place. For example, when you tell a story, you write what happened first, then second, then

99

third, and so on. Using a time sequence is a very natural and easy way to organize a paragraph. Paragraph 25 is an example.

**25** In 1924, The Dawes Plan renegotiated the sums mandated from Germany as reparations and smoothed debt repayments to the United States. The private American capital that then began to flow to Europe (especially to Germany) created a short burst of prosperity for Europeans. In 1928, however, the booming New York stock market began to siphon money away from European investments, and virtually unregulated financial speculation led to Wall Street's crash in October 1929. The crash produced a banking crisis, for U.S. banks had lent their customers large amounts of money to invest in the stock market. The crash made repayments of these loans impossible and caused banks to fail. Little American capital remained for investment in Europe or elsewhere. Credit of all kinds grew scarce, and renewal of loans already made to Europeans became difficult.

—Donald Kagan, "American Investments"

## ARRANGING BY LOCATION

A paragraph arranged according to location, or **spatial order**, leads the reader's attention from one place to another. The movement can be in any direction—from top to bottom, left to right, inside to outside, and so on. Paragraph 26 traces natural disasters across the United States from west to east.

**26** In the United States, most natural disasters are confined to specific geographical areas. For example, the West Coast can be hit by damaging earthquakes at any time. Most Southern and Midwestern states can be swept by devastating tornadoes, especially in the spring, summer, and early fall. The Gulf of Mexico and the Atlantic Ocean can experience violent hurricanes in late summer and fall. These different natural disasters, and others as dangerous, teach people one common lesson—advance preparation can mean survival.

—Dawn Seaford, student

## ARRANGING FROM GENERAL TO SPECIFIC

The most common pattern for arranging information is from **general to specific**. Typically, the general statement is the TOPIC SENTENCE, and the supporting details (see RENNS, 3f) explain the specifics. Paragraph 27 is an example.

**27** Memory is something we all know intimately. It is a central and unambiguous part of our commonsense world, its presence as indisputable, if unsteady, as the weather. But when we begin to talk about memory, ambiguities and complexities rapidly emerge. How can we grasp memory itself? It is virtually impossible to imagine memory—what it is, how it works, where it lies—without recourse to metaphor. Is memory a storehouse, a computer, a filing system, an encyclopedia, or a landscape, a cathedral, a city? If it is a kind of narrative, is our model to be Proust or Joyce, Virginia Woolf or Christa Wolf?

—Michael Lambek and Paul Antze, "Forecasting Memory"

## ARRANGING FROM SPECIFIC TO GENERAL

A less common paragraph arrangement moves from **specific to general**. Paragraph 28 is an example. To achieve the greatest impact, the paragraph starts with details that support the topic sentence, which ends the paragraph.

**28** Replacing the spark plugs is probably the first thing most home auto mechanics do. But too often, the problem lies elsewhere. In the ignition system, the plug wires, distributor unit, coil, and ignition control unit play just as vital a role as the spark plugs. Moreover, performance problems are by no means limited to the ignition system. The fuel system and emissions control system also contain several components that equal the spark plug in importance. The do-it-yourself mechanic who wants to provide basic care for a car must be able to do more than change the spark plugs.

—Danny Witt, student

## ARRANGING FROM LEAST TO MOST IMPORTANT

A paragraph arranged from **least to most important** uses **climactic order**, which means that the high point—the climax—comes at the end. For a paragraph to be arranged from least to most important, it has to have at least three items: least, more, most. And remember that the last item always packs the greatest impact and is the most memorable. Paragraph 29 is an example.

**29** For a year, Hal and I worked diligently on that boat. At times, it was a real struggle for me to stay on course: as an 11-year-old, my attentions often wandered and the work was not always exciting. But Hal's dedication profoundly influenced me. By his own example, he taught me important lessons about how to be organized, how to set priorities, and how to be responsible. He also, through working with me on the design of the boat's electronics, played a pivotal role in developing my passion for science.

—Patrick Regan Buckley, "Lessons in Boat-Building—and Life"

## ARRANGING FROM PROBLEM TO SOLUTION

In some cases, an effective arrangement for a paragraph is **problem to solution**. Usually, the topic sentence presents the problem. The very next sentence presents the main idea of the solution. Then, the rest of the paragraph covers the specifics of the solution. Paragraph 30 is an example.

When I first met them, Sara and Michael were a two-career couple with a home of their own, and a large boat bought with a large loan. What interested them in a concept called voluntary simplicity was the birth of their daughter and a powerful desire to raise her themselves. Neither one of them, it turned out, was willing to restrict what they considered their "real life" into the brief time before work and the tired hours afterward. "A lot of people think that as they have children and things get more expensive, the only answer is to work harder in order to earn more money. It's not the only answer," insists Michael. The couple's decision was to trade two full-time careers for two half-time careers, and to curtail consumption. They decided to spend their money only on things that contributed to their major goal, the construction of a world where family and friendship, work and play, were all of a piece, a world, moreover, which did not make wasteful use of the earth's resources.

— Linda Weltner, "Stripping Down to Bare Happiness"

**EXERCISE 3-6**   Working individually or with a peer-response group, rearrange the sentences in each paragraph below so that it flows logically. To begin, identify the topic sentence, use it as the paragraph's first sentence, and continue from there. For help, consult 3h.

**PARAGRAPH A**

1. Remember, many people who worry about offending others wind up living according to other people's priorities.

2. Learn to decline, tactfully but firmly, every request that doesn't contribute to your goals.

3. Of all the timesaving techniques ever developed, perhaps the most effective is the frequent use of the word *no*.

4. If you point out that your motivation isn't to get out of work but to save your time to do a better job on the really important things, you'll have a good chance of avoiding unproductive tasks.

— Edwin Bliss, "Getting Things Done:
The ABC's of Time Management"

**PARAGRAPH B**

1. After a busy day, lens wearers often don't feel like taking time out to clean and disinfect their lenses, and many wearers skip the chore.

2. When buying a pair of glasses, a person deals with just the expense of the glasses themselves.

3. Although contact lenses make the wearer more attractive, glasses are easier and less expensive to care for.

4. However, in addition to the cost of the lenses themselves, contact lens wearers must shoulder the extra expense of cleaning supplies.

5. This inattention creates a danger of infection.

6. In contrast, contact lenses require daily cleaning and weekly enzyming that inconvenience lens wearers.

7. Glasses can be cleaned quickly with water and tissue at the wearer's convenience.

—Heather Martin, student

**PARAGRAPH C**

1. The researchers found that the participation of women in sport was a significant indicator of the health and living standards of a country.

2. Today, gradually, women have begun to enter sport with more social acceptance and individual pride.

3. In 1952, researchers from the Finnish Institute of Occupational Health who conducted an intensive study of the athletes participating in the Olympics in Helsinki predicted, "Women are able to shake off civil disabilities which millennia of prejudice and ignorance have imposed upon them."

4. Myths die hard, but they do die.

—Marie Hart, "Sport: Women Sit in the Back of the Bus"

**EXERCISE 3-7**  Working individually or with a peer-response group, determine the arrangements in these paragraphs. Choose from time, location, general to specific, specific to general, least to most important, and problem to solution. For help, consult 3h.

A.　　A combination of cries from exotic animals and laughter and gasps from children fills the air along with the aroma of popcorn and peanuts. A hungry lion bellows for dinner, his roar breaking through the confusing chatter of other animals. Birds of all kinds chirp endlessly at curious children. Monkeys swing from limb to limb, performing
**31** gymnastics for gawking onlookers. A comedy routine by orangutans employing old shoes and garments incites squeals of amusement. Reptiles sleep peacefully behind glass windows, yet they send shivers down the spines of those who remember the quick death many of these reptiles can induce. The sights and sounds and smells of the zoo inform and entertain children of all ages.

—Deborah Harris, student

B.　　No one even agrees anymore on what "old" is. Not long ago, 30 was middle-aged and 60 was old. Now, more and more people are living into their 70s, 80s and beyond—and many of them are living
**32** well, without any incapacitating mental or physical decline. Today, old age is defined not simply by chronological years, but by degree of health and well-being.

—Carol Tavris, "Old Age Isn't What It Used to Be"

C.    Lately, bee researchers have been distracted by a new challenge
from abroad. It's, of course, the so-called "killer bee" that was
imported into Brazil from Africa in the mid-1950s and has been
heading our way ever since. The Africanized bee looks like the Italian
bee but is more defensive and more inclined to attack in force. It

**33**  consumes much of the honey that it produces, leaving relatively little
for anyone who attempts to work with it. It travels fast, competes with
local bees and, worse, mates with them. It has ruined the honey
industry in Venezuela and now the big question is: Will the same thing
happen here?

—Jim Doherty, "The Hobby That Challenges You
to Think Like a Bee"

**EXERCISE 3-8**    Working individually or with a peer-response group, decide
what would be the best arrangement for a paragraph on each topic listed
here. Choose one or a combination of time, location, general to specific,
specific to general, least to most important, and problem to solution. For
help, consult 3h.

1. Ways to make friends
2. Automobile accidents
3. How to combine work and college
4. Teaching children table manners

## 3i    How can rhetorical strategies help me write paragraphs?

**Rhetorical strategies** are techniques for presenting ideas clearly and
effectively. Rhetorical strategies reflect patterns of thought long in use
in Western cultures. You choose a specific rhetorical strategy according
to what you want to accomplish. Box 3.7 lists the common rhetorical
strategies at your disposal.

**SUMMARY BOX** 3.7

### Common rhetorical strategies (patterns of thought) for paragraphs

- Narrative
- Description
- Process
- Examples
- Definition

- Analysis
- Classification
- Comparison and contrast
- Analogy
- Cause-and-effect analysis

Often, your TOPIC SENTENCE will steer you toward a particular pattern. For example, if a topic sentence is "Grilling a great hot dog is easy," the implied pattern—or rhetorical strategy—is to explain the process of how to grill a hot dog. Or if a topic sentence is "To see many different styles of architecture in one US city, visit Chicago," the implied pattern—or rhetorical strategy—is to give examples.

Sometimes, you need to use a combination of rhetorical strategies. For example, in a paragraph on types of color blindness, you might use a combination of definition and classification. A paragraph explaining why one brand of house paint is superior to another might call for comparison and contrast combined with description—and, perhaps, also definition and examples.

## WRITING A NARRATIVE

**Narrative** writing is a rhetorical strategy that tells a story. A *narration* relates what is happening or what has happened. Paragraph 34 is an example.

**34** Gordon Parks speculates that he might have spent his life as a waiter on the North Coast Limited train if he hadn't strolled into one particular movie house during a stopover in Chicago. It was shortly before World War II began, and on the screen was a hair-raising newsreel of Japanese planes attacking a gunboat. When it was over the camera operator came out on stage and the audience cheered. From that moment on Parks was determined to become a photographer. During his next stopover, in Seattle, he went into a pawnshop and purchased his first camera for $7.50. With that small sum, Parks later proclaimed, "I had bought what was to become my weapon against poverty and racism." Eleven years later, he became the first black photographer at *Life* magazine.

—Susan Howard, "Depth of Field"

## WRITING A DESCRIPTION

Writing a **description** is a rhetorical strategy that appeals to a reader's senses—sight, sound, smell, taste, and touch. *Descriptive writing* paints a picture in words. Paragraph 35 is an example.

**35** Walking to the ranch house from the shed, we saw the Northern Lights. They looked like talcum powder fallen from a woman's face. Rouge and blue eye shadow streaked the spires of a white light which exploded, then pulsated, shaking the colors down—like lives—until they faded from sight.

—Gretel Ehrlich, "Other Lives"

## WRITING ABOUT A PROCESS

Writing about a **process** is a rhetorical strategy that reports a sequence of actions by which something is done or made. A process usually proceeds chronologically—first do this, then do that. A process's complexity dictates the level of detail in the writing. For example, paragraph 36 provides an overview of a complicated process. Paragraph 37, on the other hand, gives explicit step-by-step directions.

**36**
Making chocolate isn't as simple as grinding a bag of beans. The machinery in a chocolate factory towers over you, rumbling and whirring. A huge cleaner first blows the beans away from their accompanying debris— sticks and stones, coins and even bullets can fall among cocoa beans being bagged. Then they go into another machine for roasting. Next comes separation in a winnower, shells sliding out one side, beans falling from the other. Grinding follows, resulting in chocolate liquor. Fermentation, roasting, and "conching" all influence the flavor of chocolate. Chocolate is "conched"—rolled over and over against itself like pebbles in the sea—in enormous circular machines named conches for the shells they once resembled. Climbing a flight of steps to peer into this huge, slow-moving glacier, I was expecting something like molten mud but found myself forced to conclude it resembled nothing so much as chocolate.

—Ruth Mehrtens Galvin, "Sybaritic to Some, Sinful to Others"

**37**
Traditionally, oil was extracted by pressing the olives between granite millstones. Many non-industrial mills now use a modern continuous-cycle system. The olives are conveyed up a belt, washed, and cut into pulp. The resulting paste is kneaded and centrifugally "decanted" to separate it into solids, water, and oil.

—Lori de Mori, "Making Olive Oil"

**WRITING USING EXAMPLES**

A paragraph developed by **examples** presents particular instances of a larger category. For instance, examples of the category "endangered animals" could include the black rhinoceros, South China tiger, Bulmer's fruit bat, and silvery gibbon. Paragraph 38 is an example of this strategy. On the other hand, sometimes one **extended example**, often called an *illustration*, is useful. Paragraph 39 is an example of this technique.

The current revolution in zoo design—the landscape revolution—is driven by three kinds of change that have occurred during this century.

**38** First are great leaps in animal ecology, veterinary medicine, landscape design, and exhibit technology, making possible unprecedented realism in zoo exhibits. Second is the progressive disappearance of wilderness—the very subject of zoos—from the earth. Third is knowledge derived from market research and from environmental psychology, making possible a sophisticated focus on the zoo-goer.

—Melissa Greene, "No Rms, Jungle Vu"

**39** He was one of the greatest scientists the world has ever known, yet if I had to convey the essence of Albert Einstein in a single word, I would choose *simplicity*. Perhaps an anecdote will help. Once, caught in a downpour, he took off his hat and held it under his coat. Asked why, he explained, with admirable logic, that the rain would damage the hat, but his hair would be none the worse for its wetting. This knack of going instinctively to the heart of the matter was the secret of his major scientific discoveries—this and his extraordinary feeling for beauty.

—Banesh Hoffman, "My Friend, Albert Einstein"

## WRITING USING DEFINITION

When you define something, you give its meaning. **Definition** is often used together with other rhetorical strategies. If, for example, you were explaining how to organize a seashell collection, you'd probably want to define the two main types of shells: bivalve and univalve. You can also develop an entire paragraph by definition, called an **extended definition**. An extended definition discusses the meaning of a word or concept in more detail than a dictionary definition. If the topic is very abstract, the writer tries to put the definition in concrete terms. Sometimes a definition tells what something is not, as well as what it is, as in paragraph 40.

**40** Chemistry is that branch of science that has the task of investigating the materials out of which the universe is made. It is not concerned with the forms into which they may be fashioned. Such objects as chairs, tables, vases, bottles, or wires are of no significance in chemistry; but such substances as glass, wool, iron, sulfur, and clay, as the materials out of which they are made, are what it studies. Chemistry is concerned not only with the composition of such substances, but also with their inner structure.

—John Arrend Timm, *General Chemistry*

## WRITING USING ANALYSIS

**Analysis**, sometimes called *division*, divides things up into their parts. It usually starts, often in its topic sentence, by identifying one subject and continues by explaining the subject's distinct parts, as in paragraph 41.

Jazz is by its very nature inexact, and thus difficult to define
with much precision: humble in its
roots, yet an avenue to wealth and
fame for its stars; improvised anew
with each performance, but following a handful of tried-and-true formulas; done by everybody but
**41** mastered by an elite few; made by
African Americans, but made the
definition of its age by white
bands—and predominantly white
audiences. Jazz is primarily an in-
strumental idiom, but nearly all jazz
is based on songs with words, and
there are great jazz singers. "If you
have to ask what jazz is," said Louis
Armstrong, "you'll never know."

—D. Kern Holoman, "Jazz"

### WRITING USING CLASSIFICATION

**Classification** groups items according to an underlying, shared characteristic. Paragraph 42 groups—classifies—interior violations of building-
safety codes.

A public health student, Marian Glaser, did a detailed analysis of
180 cases of building code violation. Each case represented a single
building, almost all of which were multiple-unit dwellings. In these 180
buildings, there were an incredible total of 1,244 different recorded violations—about seven per building. What did the violations consist of?
First of all, over one-third of the violations were exterior defects: broken
doors and stairways, holes in the walls, sagging roofs, broken chimneys,
**42** damaged porches, and so on. Another one-third were interior violations
that could scarcely be attributed to the most ingeniously destructive
rural southern migrant in America. There were, for example, a total of
160 instances of defective wiring or other electrical hazards, a very common cause of the excessive number of fires and needless tragic deaths in
the slums. There were 125 instances of inadequate, defective, or inoper-
able plumbing or heating. There were 34 instances of serious infestation
by rats and roaches.

—William Ryan, "Blaming the Victim"

### WRITING USING COMPARISON AND CONTRAST

A paragraph developed by *comparison* deals with similarities; a paragraph developed by *contrast* deals with differences. **Comparison and
contrast** writing is usually organized one of two ways: You can use

*point-by-point organization,* which moves back and forth between the items being compared; or you can use *block organization,* which discusses one item completely before discussing the other. Box 3.8 lays out the two patterns visually.

---

PATTERN BOX **3.8**

## Comparison and contrast

**POINT-BY-POINT STRUCTURE**

*Student body:* college A, college B

*Curriculum:* college A, college B

*Location:* college A, college B

**BLOCK STRUCTURE**

*College A:* student body, curriculum, location

*College B:* student body, curriculum, location

---

Paragraph 43 is structured point by point, going back and forth between the two children (whose names are in boldface) being compared.

**43** My husband and I constantly marvel at the fact that our two sons, born of the same parents and only two years apart in age, are such completely different human beings. The most obvious differences became apparent at their births. Our firstborn, **Mark**, was big and bold—his intense, already wise eyes, broad shoulders, huge and heavy hands, and powerful, chunky legs gave us the impression he could have walked out of the delivery room on his own. Our second son, **Wayne**, was delightfully different. Rather than having the football physique that **Mark** was born with, **Wayne** came into the world with a long, slim, wiry body more suited to running, jumping, and contorting. **Wayne's** eyes, rather than being intense like **Mark's**, were impish and innocent. When **Mark** was delivered, he cried only momentarily, and then seemed to settle into a state of intense concentration, as if trying to absorb everything he could about the strange, new environment he found himself in. Conversely, **Wayne** screamed from the moment he first appeared. There was nothing helpless or pathetic about his cry either—he was darn angry!

—Rosanne Labonte, student

Paragraph 44 uses the block pattern for comparison and contrast. The writer first discusses games and then business (each key word is in boldface).

**Games** are of limited duration, take place on or in fixed and finite sites, and are governed by openly promulgated rules that are enforced on the spot by neutral professionals. Moreover, they're performed by relatively evenly matched teams that are counseled and led through every move by seasoned hands. Scores are kept, and at the end of the game, a winner is declared. **Business** is usually a little different. In fact, **44** if there is anyone out there who can say that the business is of limited duration, takes place on a fixed site, is governed by openly promulgated rules that are enforced on the spot by neutral professionals, competes only on relatively even terms, and performs in a way that can be measured in runs or points, then that person is either extraordinarily lucky or seriously deluded.

—Warren Bennis, "Time to Hang Up the Old Sports Clichés"

## WRITING USING ANALOGY

An **analogy** is an extended comparison between objects or ideas from different classes—things not normally associated. Analogy is particularly effective in explaining unfamiliar or abstract concepts because a comparison can be drawn between what is familiar and what is not. An analogy often begins with a SIMILE or METAPHOR (21d), as in paragraph 45.

Casual dress, like casual speech, tends to be loose, relaxed, and colorful. It often contains what might be called "slang words": blue jeans, sneakers, baseball caps, aprons, flowered cotton housedresses, and the like. These garments could not be worn on a formal occasion without causing disapproval, but in ordinary circumstances, they pass without remark. "Vulgar words" in dress, on the other hand, give emphasis and get immediate attention in almost any circumstances, just as they do in **45** speech. Only the skillful can employ them without some loss of face, and even then, they must be used in the right way. A torn, unbuttoned shirt or wildly uncombed hair can signify strong emotions: passion, grief, rage, despair. They're most effective if people already think of you as being neatly dressed, just as the curses of well-spoken persons count for more than those of the customarily foul-mouthed do.

—Alison Lurie, *The Language of Clothes*

## WRITING USING CAUSE-AND-EFFECT ANALYSIS

**Cause-and-effect analysis** examines outcomes and the reasons for those outcomes. Causes lead to an event or an effect, and effects result from causes. (For a discussion of correct logic for assessing CAUSE AND EFFECT, see 4h.) Paragraph 46 discusses how television (the cause) becomes indispensable (the effect) to parents of young children.

Because television is so wonderfully available as child amuser and child defuser, capable of rendering a volatile three-year-old harmless at the flick of a switch, parents grow to depend upon it in the course of their daily lives. And as they continue to utilize television day after day, its importance in their children's lives increases. From a simple source of entertainment provided by parents when they need a break from childcare, television gradually changes into a powerful and disruptive **46** presence in family life. But despite their increasing resentment of television's intrusions into their family life, and despite their considerable guilt at not being able to control their children's viewing, parents don't take steps to extricate themselves from television's domination. They can no longer cope without it.

—Marie Winn, *The Plug-In Drug*

**EXERCISE 3-9** Working individually or with a peer-response group, decide what rhetorical strategies are used in each paragraph. Choose from any one or a combination of narrative, description, process, examples, definition, analysis, classification, comparison and contrast, analogy, and cause and effect. For help, consult 3i.

A.    Another way to think about metamessages is that they frame a conversation, much as a picture frame provides a context for the images in the picture. Metamessages let you know how to interpret **47** what someone is saying by identifying the activity that is going on. Is this an argument or a chat? Is it helping, advising, or scolding? At the same time, they let you know what position the speaker is assuming in the activity, and what position you are being assigned.

—Deborah Tannen, *You Just Don't Understand*

B.    I retain only one confused impression from my earliest years: it's all red, and black, and warm. Our apartment was red: the upholstery was of red moquette, the Renaissance dining-room was red, the figured silk hangings over the stained-glass doors were red, and the velvet curtains in Papa's study were red too. The furniture in this awful sanctum was **48** made of black pear wood; I used to creep into the kneehole under the desk and envelop myself in its dusty glooms; it was dark and warm, and the red of the carpet rejoiced my eyes. That is how I seem to have passed the early days of infancy. Safely ensconced, I watched, I touched, I took stock of the world.

—Simone de Beauvoir, *Memoirs of a Dutiful Daughter*

C.    In the case of wool, very hot water can actually cause some structural changes within the fiber, but the resulting shrinkage is minor. The fundamental cause of shrinkage in wool is felting, in which **49** the fibers scrunch together in a tighter bunch, and the yarn, fabric, and garment follow suit. Wool fibers are curly and rough-surfaced, and when squished together under the lubricating influence of water, the fibers wind around each other, like two springs interlocking. Because of their rough surfaces, they stick together and can't be pulled apart.

—James Gorman, "Gadgets"

D.    After our lunch, we drove to the Liverpool public library, where I was scheduled to read. By then, we were forty-five minutes late, and on arrival we saw five middle-aged white women heading away toward an old car across the street. When they recognized me, the women came over and apologized: They were really sorry, they said, but they had to leave or they'd get in trouble on the job. I looked at them. Every one

50  of them was wearing an inexpensive, faded housedress and, over that, a cheap and shapeless cardigan sweater. I felt honored by their open-mindedness in having wanted to come and listen to my poetry. I thought and I said that it was I who should apologize: I was late. It was I who felt, moreover, unprepared: What in my work, to date, deserves the open-minded attention of blue-collar white women terrified by the prospect of overstaying a union-guaranteed hour for lunch?

    —June Jordan, "Waiting for a Taxi"

E.    Lacking access to a year-round supermarket, the many species—from ants to wolves—that in the course of evolution have learned the advantages of hoarding must devote a lot of energy and ingenuity to protecting their stashes from marauders. Creatures like beavers and honeybees, for example, hoard food to get them through cold winters. Others, like desert rodents that face food scarcities throughout the year,

51  must take advantage of the short-lived harvests that follow occasional rains. For animals like burying beetles that dine on mice hundreds of times their size, a habit of biting off more than they can chew at the moment forces them to store their leftovers. Still others, like the male MacGregor's bowerbird, stockpile goodies during mating season so they can concentrate on wooing females and defending their arena d'amour.

    —Jane Brody, "A Hoarder's Life: Filling the Cache—and Finding It"

**EXERCISE 3-10**    Working individually or with a peer-response group, reread the paragraphs in Exercise 3-7 and determine the rhetorical strategy (or strategies) being used in each.

## 3j    What is a transitional paragraph?

**Transitional paragraphs** are found in long essays. These paragraphs form a bridge between one long discussion on a single topic that requires a number of paragraphs and another discussion, usually lengthy, of another topic. Paragraph 52 is an example of a transitional paragraph that allows the writer to move from a long discussion of people's gestures to a long discussion of people's eating habits.

    Like gestures, eating habits are personality indicators, and even food preferences and attitudes toward food reveal the inner self. Food plays

52  an important role in the lives of most people beyond its obvious one as a necessity.

    —Jean Rosenbaum, MD, *Is Your Volkswagen a Sex Symbol?*

## 3k  What are effective concluding paragraphs?

A **concluding paragraph** ends the discussion smoothly by following logically from the essay's introductory paragraph (3b) and the essay's body paragraphs (3c). Always integrate a concluding device into the final paragraph so that the discussion does not end abruptly. A conclusion that is hurriedly tacked on is a missed opportunity to provide a sense of completion and a finishing touch that adds to the whole essay. Box 3.9 lists strategies for concluding your essay as well as strategies to avoid.

---

**SUMMARY BOX** 3.9

### Strategies for concluding paragraphs

**STRATEGIES TO TRY**

- A strategy adapted from those used for introductory paragraphs (3b)—but be careful to choose a different strategy for your introduction and conclusion:
  - Relating a brief concluding interesting story or anecdote
  - Giving one or more pertinent—perhaps surprising—concluding statistics
  - Asking one or more provocative questions for further thought
  - Using an appropriate quotation to sum up the THESIS STATEMENT
  - Redefining a key term for emphasis
- An ANALOGY that summarizes the thesis statement
- A SUMMARY of the main points, but only if the piece of writing is longer than three to four pages
- A statement that urges awareness by the readers
- A statement that looks ahead to the future
- A call to readers

**STRATEGIES TO AVOID**

- Introducing new ideas or facts that belong in the body of the essay
- Rewording your introduction
- Announcing what you've discussed, as in "In this paper, I have explained why oil prices have dropped."
- Making absolute claims, as in "I have proved that oil prices don't always affect gasoline prices."
- Apologizing, as in "Even though I'm not an expert, I feel my position is correct."

The same writers who wait to write their introductory paragraph until they've drafted their body paragraphs often also wait to write their concluding paragraph until they've drafted their introduction. They do this to coordinate the beginning and end so that they can make sure they don't repeat the same strategy in both places.

Paragraph 53 is a concluding paragraph that summarizes the main points of the essay.

**53** Now the equivalent to molecule fingerprints, DNA profiles have indeed proven to be valuable investigative tools. As the FBI Laboratory continues to develop innovative technologies and share its expertise with criminal justice professionals worldwide, it takes great strides in bringing offenders to swift and sure justice, while clearing innocent individuals and protecting crime victims.

—"DNA Profiling Advancement: The Use of DNA Profiles in Solving Crimes," *The FBI Law Enforcement Bulletin*

Paragraph 54 is a concluding paragraph from an essay on the potential collapse of public schools. It looks ahead to the future and calls for action that involves taking control of them.

**54** Our schools provide a key to the future of society. We must take control of them, watch over them, and nurture them if they are to be set right again. To do less is to invite disaster upon ourselves, our children, and our nation.

—John C. Sawhill, "The Collapse of Public Schools"

**EXERCISE 3-11**    Working individually or in a peer-response group, return to Exercise 3-1, in which you wrote introductory paragraphs for three informally outlined essays. Now, write a concluding paragraph for each.

# Chapter 4

## THINKING, READING, AND WRITING CRITICALLY

Getting a college education and living a reflective life mean participating in a world of ideas and opinions. Your success with these activities depends largely on your level of comfort with **critical thinking** as a concept (4a) and as an activity (4b); **critical reading** as a concept (4c) and as an activity (4d and 4e); **critical writing** (4f); and **critical reasoning** (4g through 4j). The word *critical* here has a neutral meaning. It doesn't mean taking a negative view or finding fault, as when someone criticizes another person for doing something incorrectly. Rather, the term applies to a mental stance of examining ideas thoroughly and deeply, refusing to accept ideas merely because they seem sensible at first glance, and tolerating questions that often lack definitive answers.

### 4a   What is critical thinking?

Thinking isn't something you choose to do, any more than a fish chooses to live in water. To be human is to think. But while thinking may come naturally, awareness of how you think doesn't. Thinking about thinking is the key to critical thinking.

**Critical thinking** means taking control of your conscious thought processes. If you don't take control of those processes, you risk being controlled by the ideas of others. In fact, critical thinking is an attitude as much as an activity. If you face life with curiosity and a desire to dig beneath the surface, you're a critical thinker. The essence of critical thinking is thinking beyond the obvious—beyond the flash of visual images on a television screen, the alluring promises of glossy advertisements, the evasive statements by some people in the news, the half-truths of propaganda, the manipulations of SLANTED LANGUAGE and faulty reasoning. As an example of how critical thinking works, consider how the various elements of Figure 4.1 (p. 116) shape our response to the image.

A look at the obvious, surface content of the photograph simply shows a number of people standing in line. A closer look shows the deeper message that the photographer seeks to convey. The details in the photograph combine to lead viewers to a negative "close reading" of the scene.

Figure 4.1

Several elements of the photograph convey the idea that these people aren't gathered for a pleasant experience, such as going to a concert. Their body language is slumped and tired. Some people have crossed arms, and others (for example, the man in the striped shirt) have shifted their weight to one leg. It seems as though they've been in this line a long time, and in fact, it's hard to tell from the picture's angle just how long the line stretches. People stare ahead or blankly into space, not interacting with others around them. They aren't here for fun or socializing.

The setting of the image contributes to the sense of unpleasantness. Although it seems to be a very large room, the ceiling appears quite low. Although the ceiling has numerous lights (indeed, the stretch of lights makes you perceive the room as vast), the image is fairly dark. Both of these qualities contribute to a vague sense that the environment is oppressive or controlled. The physical surroundings echo the collective mood.

There are commonalities and differences among the people. There are men as well as women, of different races. People are dressed in jeans and in shorts, in shirts and in jackets. However, notice what people have in common. While there's some difference in clothing, nothing is very dressy and nothing is very flashy. Everyone wears fairly casual clothes, with sneakers being the most common footwear. Furthermore, the general age range is comparatively narrow. Are there any children, youths, or elderly? Finally, several people are carrying sheets of paper. Perhaps they're turning in a test, an application, or a form.

In fact, this photograph depicts an unemployment line. Someone who wanted to depict waiting on an unemployment line as an optimistic or pleasant event would have created quite a different image. We're not saying that losing a job is ever pleasant—far from it. However, a different image would have shaped a different response. We imagine that a state unemployment agency that wanted to convey its work as efficient and friendly wouldn't be very happy with this image.

Chapter 6 contains detailed advice for applying critical thinking to images.

## 4b How do I engage in critical thinking?

To engage in CRITICAL THINKING, you become fully aware of an idea or an action, reflect on it, and ultimately react to it. Actually, you already engage in this process numerous times every day. For example, you're thinking critically when you meet someone new and decide whether you like the person; when you read a book and form an opinion of it based on reasonable analysis; or when you interview for a job and then evaluate its requirements and your ability to fulfill them.

Box 4.1 describes the general process of critical thinking in academic settings. This same process applies as well to reading critically (4c and 4d) and writing critically (4f).

### SUMMARY BOX 4.1

### Steps in the critical thinking process

1. **Summarize.** Extract and restate the material's main message or central point. Use only what you see on the page. Add nothing.

2. **Analyze.** Examine the material by breaking it into its component parts. By seeing each part of the whole as a distinct unit, you discover how the parts interrelate. Consider the line of reasoning as shown by the EVIDENCE offered (4g) and logic used (4j). Read "between the lines" to draw INFERENCES (4c.2), gaining information that's implied but not stated. When reading or listening, notice how the reading or speaking style and the choice of words work together to create a TONE (1d).

3. **Synthesize.** Pull together what you've summarized and analyzed by connecting it to your own experiences, such as reading, talking with others, watching television and films, using the Internet, and so on. In this way, you create a new whole that reflects your newly acquired knowledge and insights combined with your prior knowledge.

4. **Evaluate.** Judge the quality of the material now that you've become informed through the activities of SUMMARY, ANALYSIS, and SYNTHESIS. Resist the very common urge to evaluate before you summarize, analyze, and synthesize.

The steps in the critical thinking process are somewhat fluid, just as the steps in the WRITING PROCESS are. Expect sometimes to combine steps, reverse their order, and return to parts of the process you thought you had completed. As you do so, remember that synthesis and evaluation are two different mental activities: *Synthesis* calls for making connections; *evaluation* calls for making judgments.

## 4c    What is the reading process?

Reading is an active process—a dynamic, meaning-making interaction between the page and your brain. Understanding the **reading process** helps people become critical thinkers.

Making **predictions** is a major activity in the reading process. Your mind is constantly guessing what's coming next. When it sees what comes next, it either confirms or revises its prediction and moves on. For example, suppose you're glancing through a magazine and come across the title "The Heartbeat." Your mind begins guessing: Is this a love story? Is this about how the heart pumps blood? Maybe, you say to yourself, it's a story about someone who had a heart attack. Then, as you read the first few sentences, your mind confirms which guess was correct. If you see words like *electrical impulse, muscle fibers,* and *contraction,* you know instantly that you're in the realm of physiology. In a few more sentences, you narrow your prediction to either "the heart as pump" or "the heart suffering an attack."

To make predictions efficiently, consciously decide your purpose for reading the material. People generally read for two reasons—for relaxation or for learning. Reading a popular novel helps you relax. Reading for college courses calls for you to understand material and remember it. When you read to learn, you usually have to reread. One encounter with new material is rarely enough to understand it fully.

The speed at which you read depends on your purpose for reading. When you're hunting for a particular fact, you can skim the page until you come to what you want. When you read about a subject you know well, you might read somewhat rapidly, slowing down when you come to new material. When you're unfamiliar with the subject, you need to work slowly because your mind needs time to absorb the new material.

The reading process involves your thinking on three levels, which is another reason why college work calls for much rereading, as described in Box 4.2.

### 4c.1  Reading for literal meaning

Reading for **literal meaning** is reading for comprehension. Your goal is to discover the main ideas, the supporting details, or, in a work of fiction, the central details of plot and character.

Reading for literal meaning is not as easy as it might sound. When you come across a new concept, think it through. Rushing through material to

---

**SUMMARY BOX** 4.2

## Steps in the reading process

1. **Reading for literal meaning:** Read "on the lines" to see what's stated (4c.1).

2. **Reading to draw inferences:** Read "between the lines" to see what's not stated but implied (4c.2).

3. **Reading to evaluate:** Read "beyond the lines" to form your own opinion about the material (4c.3).

---

"cover" it rather than to understand it takes more time in the end. If the author's writing style is complex, "unpack" the sentences: Break them into smaller units or reword them in a simpler style. Also, see Box 4.3 for specific suggestions about ways to improve your reading comprehension.

---

**SUMMARY BOX** 4.3

## Ways to help your reading comprehension

- **Make associations.** Link new material to what you already know, especially when you're reading about an unfamiliar subject. You may even find it helpful to read an easier book on the subject first in order to build your knowledge base.

- **Make it easy for you to focus.** If your mind wanders, be fiercely determined to concentrate. Do whatever it takes: Arrange for silence or music, for being alone or in the library with others who are studying. Try to read at your best time of day (some people concentrate better in the morning, others in the evening).

- **Allot the time you need.** To comprehend new material, you must allow sufficient time to read, reflect, reread, and study. Discipline yourself to balance classes, working, socializing, and family activities. Reading and studying take time. Nothing prevents success in college as much as poor time management.

- **Master the vocabulary.** If you don't understand the key terms in your reading, you can't fully understand the concepts. As you encounter new words, first try to figure out their meanings from context clues (21e). Also, many textbooks list key terms and their definitions (called a *glossary*) at the end of each chapter or of the book. Of course, nothing replaces having a good dictionary at hand.

## 4c.2 Reading to draw inferences

When you read for **inferences**, you're reading to understand what's suggested or implied but not stated. This is similar to the kind of critical thinking discussed in 4b. Here's an example.

> How to tell the difference between modern art and junk puzzles many people, although few are willing to admit it. The owner of an art gallery in Chicago had a prospective buyer for two sculptures made of discarded metal and put them outside his warehouse to clean them up. Unfortunately, some junk dealers, who apparently didn't recognize abstract expressionism when they saw it, hauled the two 300-pound pieces away.
>
> —Ora Gygi, "Things Are Seldom What They Seem"

The literal meaning of the Gygi paragraph is that some people can't tell the difference between art and junk. A summary is that two abstract metal sculptures were carted away as junk when an art dealer set them outside a warehouse to clean them. The inferential meaning is that people often don't want to appear uneducated or show themselves lacking in good taste because something called "art" looks like "junk" to them. The word *apparently*—a good word for inferences—uses IRONY (21d) to seem tactful but is just the opposite. Therefore, the art dealer doesn't end up feeling embarrassed because he left the sculptures outdoors unattended. If we are laughing, it is at the junk dealers—although the ultimate joke is on the whole art world.

Drawing inferences takes practice. Box 4.4 lists questions to help you read "between the lines." A discussion of each point follows the box.

---

**CHECKLIST BOX 4.4**

### Drawing inferences during reading

- Is the **tone** of the material appropriate?
- Can I detect **bias** in the material?
- Is the separation of **fact** and **opinion** clear or muddy?
- What is the **writer's position**, even if he or she doesn't outright state it?

---

### TONE

**Tone** in writing emerges from many aspects of what you write, but mostly from your word choice. Tone in writing is like tone in speaking: It can be formal, informal, pompous, sarcastic, and so on. If you read exclusively for literal meaning (4c.1), you're likely to miss the tone and possibly the point of the whole piece.

For example, as a critical reader, be suspicious of a highly emotional tone in writing. If you find it, chances are the writer is trying to manipulate the audience. Resist this. Also as a writer, if you find your tone growing emotional, step back and rethink the situation. No matter what point you want to make, your chance of communicating successfully to an audience depends on your using a moderate, reasonable tone. For instance, the exaggerations below in the NO example (*robbing treasures, politicians are murderers*) might hint at the truth of a few cases, but they're too extreme to be taken seriously. The language of the YES version is far more likely to deliver its intended message.

**NO**   Urban renewal must be stopped. Urban redevelopment is ruining this country, and money-hungry capitalists are robbing treasures from law-abiding citizens. Corrupt politicians are murderers, caring nothing about people being thrown out of their homes into the streets.

**YES**   Urban renewal is revitalizing our cities, but it has caused some serious problems. While investors are trying to replace slums with decent housing, they must also remember that they're displacing people who don't want to leave their familiar neighborhoods. Surely, a cooperative effort between government and the private sector can lead to creative solutions.

## BIAS

For inferential reading, you want to detect **bias**, also known as **prejudice**. This concept goes further than the idea that most writers try to influence readers to accept their points of view. When writing is distorted by hatred or dislike of individuals, groups of people, or ideas, you as a critical reader want to suspect the accuracy and fairness of the material. Bias can be worded in positive language, but critical readers aren't deceived by such tactics. Similarly, writers can merely imply their bias rather than state it outright. For example, suppose you read, "Poor people like living in crowded conditions because they're used to such surroundings" or "Women are so wonderfully nurturing that they can't succeed in business." As a critical reader, you will immediately detect the bias. Always, therefore, question material that rests on a weak foundation of discrimination and narrow-mindedness.

## FACT VERSUS OPINION

Another skill in reading inferentially is the ability to differentiate **fact** from **opinion**. *Facts* are statements that can be verified. *Opinions* are statements of personal beliefs. Facts can be verified by observation, research, or experimentation, but opinions are open to debate. A problem arises when a writer intentionally blurs the distinction between fact and opinion. Critical readers will know the difference.

For example, here are two statements, one of which is a fact and one of which is an opinion.

1. Women can never make good mathematicians.
2. Although fear of math isn't purely a female phenomenon, girls tend to drop out of math classes sooner than boys, and some adult women have an aversion to math and math-related activity that is akin to anxiety.

Reading inferentially, you can see that statement 1 is clearly an opinion. Is it worthy of consideration? Perhaps it could be open to debate, but the word *never* implies that the writer is unwilling to allow for even one exception. Conversely, statement 2 at least seems to be factual, though research would be necessary to confirm or deny the position.

## WRITER'S POSITION

As a reader, when you can "consider the source"—that is, find out who exactly made a statement—you hold an advantage. For example, you would probably read an essay for or against capital punishment differently if you knew the writer was an inmate on death row rather than a non-inmate who wished to express an opinion. To illustrate, statement 1 above is from a male Russian mathematician, as reported by David K. Shipler, a well-respected veteran reporter on Russian affairs for the *New York Times*. Statement 2 is from the book *Overcoming Math Anxiety* by Sheila Tobias, a university professor who has extensively studied why many people dislike math. Her credentials can help readers accept her statement as true. If, however, someone known for belittling women had made statement 2, a critical reader's reaction would probably be dismissive of the author's words.

**EXERCISE 4-1**   Working individually or with a peer-response group, decide which statements are facts and which are opinions. When the author and source are provided, explain how that information influenced your judgment. For help, consult 4c.2.

1. The life of people on earth is better now than it has ever been— certainly much better than it was 500 years ago.
   —Peggy Noonan, "Why Are We So Unhappy When We Have It So Good?"

2. The fast food industry pays the minimum wage to a higher proportion of its workers than any other American industry.
   —Eric Schlosser, *Fast Food Nation*

3. Every journey into the past is complicated by delusions, false memories, false naming of real events.
   —Adrienne Rich, poet, *Of Woman Born*

4. A mind is a terrible thing to waste.
   —United Negro College Fund

5. History is the branch of knowledge that deals systematically with the past.
   —*Webster's New World College Dictionary,* Fourth Edition

6. In 1927, F. E. Tylcote, an English physician, reported in the medical journal *Lancet* that in almost every case of lung cancer he had seen or known about, the patient smoked.
   —William Ecenbarger, "The Strange History of Tobacco"

7. At present, carbon emissions are about 6.5 billion metric tons each year worldwide—that works out to 22 billion tons of $CO_2$, which is created when carbon is burned. . . . Now, with climate worries on the rise, many scientists believe these emissions are doing damage to the planet.
   —"Surviving the Greenhouse,"
   <http://www.msnbc.com/news/291336.asp>

8. You can, Honest Abe notwithstanding, fool most of the people all of the time.
   —Stephen Jay Gould, "The Creation Myths of Cooperstown"

9. You change laws by changing lawmakers.
   —Sissy Farenthold, political activist, *Bakersfield Californian*

10. A critical task for all of the world's religions and spiritual traditions is to enrich the vision—and the reality—of the sense of community among us.
    —Joel D. Beversluis,
    *A Sourcebook for Earth's Community of Religions*

**EXERCISE 4-2**   Read the following passages, then (1) list all literal information, (2) list all implied information, and (3) list the opinions stated. Refer to sections 4c.1 and 4c.2 for help.

EXAMPLE   The study found many complaints against the lawyers were not investigated, seemingly out of a "desire to avoid difficult cases."
   —Norman F. Dacey

**Literal information:** Few complaints against lawyers are investigated.

**Implied information:** The term *difficult cases* implies a cover-up: Lawyers, or others in power, hesitate to criticize lawyers for fear of being sued or for fear of a public outcry if the truth about abuses and errors were revealed.

**Opinions:** No opinions. It reports on a study.

A.    It is the first of February, and everyone is talking about starlings. Starlings came to this country on a passenger liner from Europe. One hundred of them were deliberately released in Central Park, and from those hundred descended all of our countless millions of starlings today. According to Edwin Way Teale, "Their coming was the result of one man's fancy. That man was Eugene Schieffelin, a wealthy New York drug manufacturer. His curious hobby was the introduction into America of all the birds mentioned in William Shakespeare." The birds adapted to their new country splendidly.

                                —Annie Dillard, "Terror at Tinker Creek"

B.    In the misty past, before Bill Gates joined the company of the world's richest men, before the mass-marketed personal computer, before the metaphor of an information superhighway had been worn down to a cliché, I heard Roger Schank interviewed on National Public Radio. Then a computer science professor at Yale, Schank was already well known in artificial intelligence circles. Because those circles did not include me, a new programmer at Sperry Univac, I hadn't heard of him. Though I've forgotten the details of the conversation, I have never forgotten Schank's insistence that most people do not need to own computers.

     That view, of course, has not prevailed. Either we own a personal computer and fret about upgrades, or we are scheming to own one and fret about the technical marvel yet to come that will render our purchase obsolete. Well, there are worse ways to spend money, I suppose. For all I know, even Schank owns a personal computer. They're fiendishly clever machines, after all, and they've helped keep the wolf from my door for a long time.

                                  —Paul De Palma,
                   <http://www.when_is_enough_enough?.com>

## 4c.3   Reading to evaluate

When you read to evaluate, you're judging the writer's work. **Evaluative reading** comes after you've summarized, analyzed, and synthesized the material (Box 4.1). Reading "between the lines" is usually concerned with recognizing tone, detecting prejudice, differentiating fact from opinion, and determining the writer's position. Reading to evaluate, "beyond the lines," requires an overall assessment of the soundness of the writer's reasoning, evidence, or observations and the fairness and perceptiveness the writer shows, from accuracy of word choice and tone to the writer's respect for the reader.

## 4d  How do I engage in critical reading?

**Critical reading** is a process parallel to CRITICAL THINKING (4a and 4b). To read critically is to think about what you're reading while you're reading it. This means that words don't merely drift by as your eyes scan the lines. To prevent that from happening, use approaches such as reading systematically (4d.1) and reading closely and actively (4d.2).

### 4d.1  Reading systematically

To **read systematically** is to use a structured plan: **P**review, **R**ead, and **R**eview. Reading systematically closely parallels the writing process. Like PLANNING in writing, *previewing* gets you ready and keeps you from reading inefficiently. Like DRAFTING in writing, *reading* means moving through the material so that you come to understand and remember it. Like REVISION in writing, *reviewing* takes you back over the material to clarify, fine-tune, and make it thoroughly your own. Here are techniques for reading systematically.

1. **Preview:** Before you begin reading, look ahead. Glance at the pages you intend to read so that your mind can start making predictions (4c). As you look over the material, ask yourself questions. Don't expect to answer all the questions at this point; their purpose is to focus your thoughts.

   - To preview a chapter in a textbook, first look at the table of contents. How does this chapter fit into the whole book? What topics come before? Which come after? Now turn to the chapter you're assigned and read all the headings, large and small. Note the boldfaced words (in darker print), and all visuals and their captions, including photographs, drawings, figures, tables, and boxes. If there's a glossary at the end of the chapter, scan it for words you do and do not know.

   - To preview a book or material in a book that has few or no headings, again, begin with the table of contents and ask questions about the chapter titles. If the book has a preface or introduction, skim it. Check for introductory notes about the author and head notes, which often precede individual works in collections of essays or short stories. Read pivotal paragraphs, such as the opening paragraphs and (unless you're reading for suspense) the last few paragraphs.

2. **Read:** Read the material closely and actively (4d.2). Seek the full meaning at all three levels of reading: *literal, inferential,* and *evaluative* (4c). Most of all, expect to reread. Rarely can anyone fully understand and absorb college-level material in one reading. When you read, always set aside time to allow for more than one rereading.

3. **Review:** Go back to the spots you looked at when you previewed the material. Also, go back to other important places you discovered as you were reading. Ask yourself the same sorts of questions as when you previewed, this time answering as fully as possible. If you can't come up with answers, reread. For best success, review in *chunks*—small sections that you can capture comfortably. Don't try to cover too much material at one time.

- To help you concentrate as you read, keep in mind that you intend to review—and then do it: Review immediately after you read. Review again the next day and again about a week later. Each time you review, add new knowledge to refine your understanding of the material. As much as time permits, review at intervals during a course. The more reinforcement, the better.

- Collaborative learning can reinforce what you learn from reading. Ask a friend or classmate to discuss the material with you and quiz you. Conversely, offer to teach the material to someone; you'll quickly discover whether you've mastered it well enough to communicate it.

## 4d.2 Reading closely and actively

The secret to **reading closely and actively** is to annotate as you read. Annotating means writing notes to yourself in a book's margins and using asterisks and other codes to alert you to special material. Some readers start annotating right away, while others wait to annotate after they've previewed the material and read it once. Experiment to find what works best for you. We recommend your using two different ink colors, one for close reading (blue in the example on the facing page) and one for active reading (black in the example).

**Close reading** means annotating for content. You might, for example, number and briefly list the steps in a process or summarize major points in the margin. When you review, your marginal notes help you glance over the material and quickly recall what it's about.

**Active reading** means annotating to make connections between the material and what you already know or have experienced. This is your chance to converse on paper with the writer. Consider yourself a partner in the making of meaning, a full participant in the exchange of ideas that characterizes a college education.

If you feel uncomfortable writing in a book—even though the practice of annotating texts dates back to the Middle Ages—create a *double-entry notebook*. Draw a line down the center of your notebook page. On one side, write content notes (close reading). On the other, write synthesis notes (active reading). Be sure to write down exactly where in the reading you're referring to. Illustrated on page 128 is a short example from a double-entry notebook (the symbol ¶ stands for "paragraph").

Although I like to play, and sometimes like to watch, I cannot see what possible difference it makes which team beats which. The tactics are sometimes interesting, and certainly the prowess of the players deserves applause—but most men seem to use commercial sports as a kind of narcotic, shutting out reality, rather than heightening it.

There is nothing more boring, in my view, than a prolonged discussion by laymen of yesterday's game. These dreary conversations are a form of social alcoholism, enabling them to achieve a dubious rapport without ever once having to come to grips with a subject worthy of a grown man's concern.

It is easy to see the opiate quality of sports in our society when tens of millions of men will spend a splendid Saturday or Sunday fall afternoon sitting stupefied in front of the TV, watching a "big game," when they might be out exercising their own flaccid muscles and stimulating their lethargic corpuscles.

*Annotations:*
- Doesn't matter who wins, but tactics and prowess can be admired.
- Sports talk is boring.
- Other examples include soap operas and sitcoms.
- When my son and husband watch together, the rapport is very real.
- Instead of watching, men should exercise.

Annotations of an excerpt from the essay shown in Exercise 4-3, using blue for content (close reading) and black for synthesis (active reading).

**EXERCISE 4-3**   The following essay was published as a newspaper column. Annotate the entire essay, using one color of ink for your notes about content and another for your notes that synthesize as you connect the material to your knowledge and experience. Use the annotated excerpt above as a model.

### Sports Only Exercise Our Eyes
*by Sydney J. Harris*

Before I proceed a line further, let me make it clear that I enjoy physical exercise and sport as much as any man. I like to bat a

S. Harris essay. "Sports Only"

| content | connections I make |
|---|---|
| #1 H. likes sports and exercise. He even built a tennis court for his summer home. | H. isn't "everyman." It takes big bucks to build one's own tennis court. |
| #2 H. thinks the average American male is obsessed with sports. | That "average" (if there is such a thing) male sounds a lot like my husband. |
| #3 Athletics/Sports are one strand, not the web, of society. | It's worth thinking _why_ sports have such a major hold on men. And why not women, on "average"? (This might be a topic for a paper someday.) |

**Double-entry notebook excerpt, based on the first three paragraphs of the essay in Exercise 4-3. The left column deals with content (close reading), and the right covers synthesis (active reading).**

baseball, dribble a basketball, kick a soccer ball and, most of all, swat a tennis ball. A man who scorned physical activity would hardly build a tennis court on his summerhouse grounds, or use it every day.

Having made this obeisance, let me now confess that I am puzzled and upset—and have been for many years—by the almost obsessive interest in sports taken by the average American male.

Athletics is one strand in life, and even the ancient Greek philosophers recognized its importance. But it is by no means the whole web, as it seems to be in our society. If American men are not talking business, they're talking sports, or they're not talking at all.

This strikes me as an enormously adolescent, not to say retarded, attitude on the part of presumed adults. Especially when most of the passion and enthusiasm center on professional teams, which bear no indigenous relation to the city they play for, and consist of mercenaries who will wear any town's insignia if the price is right.

Although I like to play, and sometimes like to watch, I cannot see what possible difference it makes which team beats which. The tactics are sometimes interesting, and certainly the prowess of the players deserves applause—but most men seem to use commercial sports as a kind of narcotic, shutting out reality, rather than heightening it.

There is nothing more boring, in my view, than a prolonged discussion by laymen of yesterday's game. These dreary conversations are a form of social alcoholism, enabling them to achieve a dubious rapport without ever once having to come to grips with a subject worthy of a grown man's concern.

It is easy to see the opiate quality of sports in our society when tens of millions of men will spend a splendid Saturday or Sunday fall afternoon sitting stupefied in front of the TV, watching a "big game," when they might be out exercising their own flaccid muscles and stimulating their lethargic corpuscles.

Ironically, our obsession with professional athletics not only makes us mentally limited and conversationally dull, it also keeps us physically inert—thus violating the very reason men began engaging in athletic competitions. Isn't it tempting to call this national malaise of "spectatoritis" childish? Except children have more sense, and would rather run out and play themselves.

## 4e  How do I tell the difference between summary and synthesis?

Distinguishing between summary and synthesis is crucial in critical thinking, critical reading, and critical writing. **Summary** comes before synthesis (Box 4.1) in the critical thinking process. To *summarize* is to extract the main message or central point and restate it in a sentence or two. A summary doesn't include supporting evidence or details. It's the gist, the hub, the seed of what the author is saying. Also, it isn't your personal reaction to what the author says. (For help in writing a summary, see section 33j.)

**Synthesis** comes after summary in the critical thinking process (Box 4.1). To *synthesize* is to weave together material from several sources, including your personal prior knowledge, to create a new whole. Unsynthesized ideas and information are like separate spools of thread, neatly lined up, possibly coordinated but not integrated. Synthesized ideas and information are threads woven into a tapestry—a new whole that shows relationships.

People synthesize unconsciously all the time—interpreting and combining ideas from various sources to create new patterns. These thought processes are mirrored in the RHETORICAL STRATEGIES used in writing (3i). To synthesize, consciously apply those strategies. For instance, compare ideas in sources, contrast ideas in sources, create definitions that combine and extend definitions in individual sources, apply examples or descriptions from one source to illustrate ideas in another, and find causes and effects described in one source that explain another.

Now, let's examine two different examples of synthesis. Their sources are the essay by Sydney J. Harris in Exercise 4-3 and the following excerpt from a long essay by Robert Lipsyte. (Lipsyte, at the time a sports columnist for the *New York Times*, is writing in the spring of 1995, at the end of a nine-month US baseball strike. Lipsyte argues that commercial interests have invaded sports and, therefore, that sports no longer inspire loyalty, teach good sportsmanship, or provide young people with admirable role models.)

> Baseball has done us a favor. It's about time we understood that staged competitive sports events—and baseball can stand for all the games—are no longer the testing ground of our country's manhood and the theater of its once seemingly limitless energy and power.
>
> As a mirror of our culture, sports now show us spoiled fools as role models, cities and colleges held hostage and games that exist only to hawk products.
>
> The pathetic posturing of in-your-face macho has replaced a once self-confident masculinity.
>
> —Robert Lipsyte, "The Emasculation of Sports"

#### SYNTHESIS BY COMPARISON AND CONTRAST

Both Harris and Lipsyte criticize professional sports, but for different reasons. In part, Harris thinks that people who passively watch sports on TV and rarely exercise are ruining their health. Lipsyte sees a less obvious but potentially more sinister effect of sports: the destruction of traditional values by athletes who are puppets of "big business."

#### SYNTHESIS BY DEFINITION

The omission of women from each writer's discussion seems a very loud silence. Considered together, these essays define sports only in terms of males. Harris criticizes men for their inability to think and talk beyond sports and business, an insulting and exaggerated description made even less valid by the absence of women. Lipsyte, despite the numbers of women excelling both in team and individual sports, claims that sports have lost a "once self-confident masculinity." An extended definition would include women, even though they might prefer to avoid the negative portraits of Harris and Lipsyte.

Each synthesis belongs to the person who made the connections. Another person might make entirely different connections.

Here are techniques to help you recall prior knowledge and synthesize several sources. (The CRITICAL RESPONSE essay by a student, Anna Lozanov, in section 4f, is an excellent example of making connections between reading and personal experience.)

- Use MAPPING to discover relationships between sources and your prior knowledge.

- Use your powers of play. Mentally toss ideas around, even if you make connections that seem outrageous. Try opposites (for example, read about athletes and think about the most non-athletic person you know). Try turning an idea upside down (for example, list the benefits of being a bad sport). Try visualizing what you're reading about, and then tinker with the mental picture (for example, picture two people playing tennis and substitute dogs playing Frisbee or seals playing table tennis). The possibilities are endless— make word associations, think up song lyrics, draft a TV advertisement. The goal is to jump-start your thinking so that you can see ideas in new ways.

- Discuss your reading with someone else. Summarize its content, and elicit the other person's opinions and ideas. Deliberately debate that opinion or challenge those ideas. Discussions and debates are good ways to get your mind moving.

**EXERCISE 4-4**    Here is another excerpt from the essay by Robert Lipsyte quoted earlier. First, summarize the excerpt. Then, annotate it for its content and for the connections you make between Lipsyte's ideas and your prior knowledge. Finally, write a synthesis of this excerpt and the Sydney J. Harris essay in Exercise 4-3. Words in brackets supply background information some readers might need.

> We have come to see that [basketball star] Michael Jordan, [football star] Troy Aikman and [baseball star] Ken Griffey have nothing to offer us beyond the gorgeous, breathtaking mechanics of what they do. And it's not enough, now that there's no longer a dependable emotional return beyond the sensation of the moment itself. The changes in sports—the moving of franchises, free agency—have made it impossible to count on a player, a team, and an entire league still being around for next year's comeback. The connection between player and fan has been irrevocably destabilized, for love and loyalty demand a future. Along the way, those many virtues of self-discipline, responsibility, altruism, and dedication seem to have been deleted from the athletic contract with America.
> —Robert Lipsyte, "The Emasculation of Sports"

## 4f    How do I write a critical response?

A **critical response** essay has two missions: to provide a SUMMARY of a source's main idea and to respond to the main idea based on your SYNTHESIS (4b and 4e).

A well-written critical response accomplishes these two missions with style and grace. That is, it doesn't say, "My summary is . . ." or "Now, here's what I think. . . ." Instead, you want the two missions to blend together as seamlessly as possible. A critical response essay may be short or somewhat long, depending on whether you're asked to respond to a single passage or to an entire work. Box 4.5 gives general guidelines for writing a critical response.

---

**SUMMARY BOX** **4.5**

## Guidelines for writing a critical response

1. Write a SUMMARY of the main idea or central point of the material you're responding to.

2. Write a smooth TRANSITION between that summary and what comes next: your response. This transitional statement, which bridges the two parts, need not be a formal THESIS STATEMENT (2q), but it needs to signal clearly the beginning of your response.

3. Respond to the source based on your prior knowledge and experience.

4. Fulfill all DOCUMENTATION requirements. See Chapters 34–36 for coverage of four DOCUMENTATION STYLES (MLA, APA, CM, and CSE). Ask your instructor which to use.

---

Here's a student essay written as a critical response. The assignment was to read and respond to "Sports Only Exercise Our Eyes" by Sydney J. Harris, shown in Exercise 4-3. Anna Lozanov's transition from summary to response comes at the beginning of her third paragraph.

---

Lozanov 1

Anna Lozanov

Professor Dawson

English 102

24 September 2005

Critical Response to "Sports Only Exercise

Our Eyes" by Sydney J. Harris

Except for a brief period in high school when I was wild

about a certain basketball player, I never gave sports much

thought. I went to games because my friends went, not because

---

*continued* ➤

I cared about football or baseball or track. I certainly never expected to defend sports, and when I first read Sydney Harris's essay "Sports Only Exercise Our Eyes," I thoroughly agreed with him. Like Harris, I believed that men who live and breathe sports are "mentally limited and conversationally dull" (111).

For the entire thirteen years of my marriage, I have complained about the amount of time my husband, John, spends watching televised sports. Of course, I've tried to get him to take an interest in something else. There was the time as a newlywed when I flamboyantly interrupted the sixth game of the World Series--wearing only a transparent nightie. Then, one year, I had the further audacity to go into labor with our first child--right in the middle of the Super Bowl.

Even the child tried to help me cure my husband of what Harris calls an "obsession" (111). Some months after the fateful Super Bowl, the kid thoroughly soaked his father, who was concentrating so intently on the struggle for the American League pennant that he didn't even notice! Only a commercial brought the dazed sports fan back into the living room from the baseball stadium.

Just this weekend, however, I had an occasion to reconsider the value of sports. Having just read the Harris essay, I found myself paying closer attention to my husband and sons' weekend afternoon television routine. I was surprised to discover that they didn't just "vegetate" in front of the TV; during the course of the afternoon, they actually discussed ethics, priorities, commitments, and

continued ➤

Lozanov 3

the consequences of abusing one's body. When one of the commentators raised issues like point shaving and using steroids, John and the kids talked about cheating and using steroids. When another commentator brought up the issue of skipping one's senior year to go straight to the pros, John explained the importance of a college education and discussed the short career of most professional football players.

Then, I started to think about all the times I've gone to the basement and found my husband and sons performing exercise routines as they watched a game on TV. Even our seven-year-old, who loathes exercise, pedals vigorously on the exercise bike while the others do sit-ups and curls. Believe it or not, there are times when they're all exercising more than just their eyes.

I still agree with Harris that many people spend too much time watching televised sports, but after this weekend, I certainly can't say that all of that time is wasted--at least not at my house. Anything that can turn my couch potatoes into thinking, talking, active human beings can't be all bad. Next weekend, instead of putting on a nightie, I think I'll join my family on the couch.

Lozanov 4

Work Cited

Harris, Sydney J. "Sports Only Exercise Our Eyes." The Best of Sydney J. Harris. Boston: Houghton, 1975. 111-12.

## 4g   How do I assess evidence critically?

The cornerstone of all reasoning is evidence. **Evidence** consists of facts, statistical information, examples, and opinions of experts. As a reader, you expect writers to provide solid evidence for any claim made or conclusion reached. As a writer, you want to use evidence well to support your claims and conclusions. To assess evidence, you want to know how to evaluate it (4g.1) and how to tell the differences between primary and secondary sources (4g.2).

### 4g.1  Evaluating evidence

You can evaluate evidence by asking the following questions to guide your judgment.

- **Is the evidence sufficient?** To be sufficient, evidence can't be skimpy. As a rule, the more evidence, the better. Readers have more confidence in the results of a survey that draws on a hundred respondents rather than on ten. As a writer, you may convince your reader that violence is a serious problem in high schools on the basis of only two examples, but you'll be more convincing with additional examples.

- **Is the evidence representative?** Evidence is representative if it is typical. As a reader, assess the objectivity and fairness of evidence. Don't trust a claim or conclusion about a group based on only a few members rather than on a truly typical sample. A pollster surveying national political views would not get representative evidence by interviewing people only in Austin, Texas, because that group doesn't represent the regional, racial, political, and ethnic makeup of the entire US electorate. As a writer, the evidence you offer should represent your claim fairly; don't base your point on an exception.

- **Is the evidence relevant?** Relevant evidence is directly related to the conclusion you're drawing. Determining relevance often demands subtle thinking. Suppose you read that one hundred students who had watched television for more than two hours a day throughout high school earned significantly lower scores on a college entrance exam than one hundred students who had not. Can you conclude that students who watch less television perform better on college entrance exams? Not necessarily. Other differences between the two groups could account for the different scores: geographical region, family background, socioeconomic group, or the quality of schools attended.

- **Is the evidence accurate?** Accurate evidence is correct and complete. Inaccurate evidence is useless. Evidence must come from a reliable source, whether it is primary or secondary (4g.2). Equally important, evidence must be presented honestly, not misrepresented or distorted.

- **Is the evidence qualified?** Reasonable evidence doesn't make extreme claims. Claims that use words such as *all, always, never,* and *certainly* are disqualified if even one exception is found. Conclusions are more sensible and believable when qualified with words such as *some, many, may, possibly, often,* and *usually.* Remember that today's "facts" may be revised as time passes and knowledge grows.

## 4g.2 Recognizing primary versus secondary sources as evidence

**Primary sources** are firsthand evidence. They're based on your own or someone else's original work or direct observation. Because there's no one to distort the meaning of the original work, firsthand evidence has the greatest impact on a reader. For example, here's an eyewitness account that is a solid example of a primary source.

> Poverty is dirt. . . . Let me explain about housekeeping with no money. For breakfast, I give my children grits with no oleo or cornbread without eggs and oleo. This doesn't use up many dishes. What dishes there are, I wash in cold water and with no soap. Even the cheapest soap has to be saved for the baby's diapers. Look at my hands, so cracked and red. Once I saved for two months to buy a jar of Vaseline for my hands and the baby's diaper rash. When I had saved enough, I went to buy it and the price had gone up two cents. The baby and I suffered on.
>
> —Jo Goodwin Parker, "What's Poverty?"

What in Parker's account makes the reader trust what she says? She is specific, and she is authoritative. She is therefore reliable.

Of course, not all eyewitnesses are reliable, so you must judge which ones to believe. Few people will ever see the top of Mount Everest. People rely, therefore, on the firsthand observation of mountain climbers who've been there. Indeed, much of what we learn of history depends on letters, diaries, and journals—the reports of eyewitnesses who have seen events unfold.

Surveys, polls, and experiments—if the data are carefully controlled and measured—extend everyone's powers of observation. The outcomes of such work are considered primary sources. What can one individual know about the attitude of the US public toward marriage, or a presidential candidate, or inflation? For evidence on such matters, polls or surveys constitute primary evidence.

**Secondary sources** report, describe, comment on, or analyze the experiences or work of others. As evidence, a secondary source is at least once removed from the primary source. It reports on the original work, the direct observation, or the firsthand experience. Still, secondary evidence can have great value and impact if it meets the evaluation criteria listed in 4g.1. Here's a secondhand report of an observation:

> The immediate causes of death from nuclear attack are the blast wave, which can flatten heavily reinforced buildings many kilometers away, the firestorm, the gamma rays, and the neutrons, which effectively

fry the insides of passersby. A schoolgirl who survived the American nuclear attack on Hiroshima, the event that ended the Second World War, wrote this firsthand account:

> Through a darkness like the bottom of hell, I could hear the voices of the other students calling for their mothers. And at the base of the bridge, inside a big cistern that had been dug out there, was a mother weeping, holding above her head a naked baby that was burned bright red all over its body. . . . But every single person who passed was wounded, all of them, and there was no one, there was no one to turn to for help. And the singed hair on the heads of the people was frizzled and whitish and covered with dust. They did not appear to be human, not creatures of this world.

—Carl Sagan, *Cosmos*

The value of a secondhand account hinges on the reliability of the reporter. And that reliability comes from how specific, accurate, and authoritative the observations are. An expert's reputation comes from some special experience (the parents of children) or special training (an accountant could be an expert on taxes). Carl Sagan, the author of the sample paragraph above, was a respected scientist, scholar, and writer; therefore, readers can be quite confident that he has fully and fairly represented what the schoolgirl said. Still, of course, no one can be sure of that without seeing her original account. Box 4.6 gives guidelines for evaluating a secondary source.

---

**CHECKLIST BOX 4.6**

## Evaluating a secondary source

- **Is the source authoritative?** Did an expert or a person you can expect to write credibly on the subject write it?

- **Is the source reliable?** Does the material appear in a reputable publication—a book published by an established publisher, a respected journal or magazine—or on a reliable Internet site?

- **Is the source well known?** Is the source cited elsewhere as you read about the subject? (If so, the authority of the source is probably widely accepted.)

- **Is the information well supported?** Is the source based on primary evidence? If the source is based on secondary evidence, is the evidence authoritative and reliable?

- **Is the tone balanced?** Is the language relatively objective (and therefore more likely to be reliable), or is it slanted (probably not reliable)?

CHECKLIST BOX   **4.6** *continued*

**Evaluating a secondary source**

- **Is the source current?** Is the material up-to-date and therefore more likely to be reliable, or has later authoritative and reliable research made it outdated? ("Old" isn't necessarily unreliable. In many fields, classic works of research remain authoritative for decades or even centuries.)

**EXERCISE 4-5**   Indicate for each passage whether it constitutes primary or secondary evidence. Then, decide whether the evidence is reliable or not, and explain why or why not. Refer to section 4g for help.

A.   I went one morning to a place along the banks of the Madeira River where the railroad ran, alongside rapids impassable to river traffic, and I searched for any marks it may have left on the land. But there was nothing except a clearing where swarms of insects hovered over the dead black hen and other items spread out on a red cloth as an offering to the gods of macumba, or black magic. This strain of African origins in Brazil's ethnic character is strong in the Northwest Region.
—William S. Ellis, "Brazil's Imperiled Rain Forest"

B.   Most climatologists believe that the world will eventually slip back into an ice age in 10,000 to 20,000 years. The Earth has been unusually cold for the last two to three million years, and we are just lucky to be living during one of the warm spells. But the concern of most weather watchers looking at the next century is with fire rather than ice. By burning fossil fuels and chopping down forests, humans have measurably increased the amount of carbon dioxide in the atmosphere. From somewhere around 300 parts per million at the turn of the century, this level has risen to 340 parts per million today. If the use of fossil fuels continues to increase, carbon dioxide could reach 600 parts per million during the next century.
—Steve Olson, "Computing Climate"

C.   Marriages on the frontier were often made before a girl was half through her adolescent years, and some diaries record casualness in the manner such decisions were reached. Mrs. John Kirkwood recounts:

The night before Christmas, John Kirkwood . . . the pathfinder, stayed at our house over night. I had met him before and when he heard the discussion about my brother Jasper's wedding, he suggested that he and I also get married. I was nearly fifteen years old and I thought it was high time that I got married so I consented.
—Lillian Schlissel, *Women's Diaries of the Westward Journey*

**EXERCISE 4-6**  Individually or with a peer-response group, choose one of the following thesis statements and list the kinds of primary and secondary sources you might consult to support the thesis (you can guess intelligently, rather than being sure that the sources exist). Then, decide which sources in your list would be primary and which secondary.

> Thesis statement 1: Public schools in this area receive adequate funding.
>
> Thesis statement 2: Public schools in this area do not receive adequate funding.

## 4h  How do I assess cause and effect critically?

Some evidence has to rely on the accuracy of a cause-and-effect relationship. **Cause and effect** describes the relationship between one event (cause) and another event that happens as a result (effect). The relationship also works in reverse: One event (effect) results from another event (cause). Whether you begin with a cause or with an effect, you're using the same basic pattern.

Cause A ⎯⎯→ produces ⎯⎯→ effect B

You may seek to understand the effects of a known cause:

More studying ⎯⎯→ produces ⎯⎯→ ?

Or you may seek to determine the cause or causes of a known effect:

? ⎯⎯→ produces ⎯⎯→ recurrent headaches

Be careful not to take cause-and-effect statements at face value. Think through the relationship between cause A and effect B. Sometimes, the relationship is exactly the opposite of what's being claimed. Consult the guidelines in Box 4.7.

**CHECKLIST BOX 4.7**

## Assessing cause and effect

- **Is there a clear relationship between events?** Related causes and effects happen in sequence: A cause occurs before an effect. First the wind blows; then a door slams; then a pane of glass in the door breaks. But CHRONOLOGICAL ORDER merely implies a cause-and-effect relationship. Perhaps someone slammed the door shut. Perhaps someone threw a baseball through the glass pane. A cause-and-effect relationship must be linked by more than chronological sequence. The fact that B happens after A doesn't prove that A causes B.

CHECKLIST BOX    **4.7** *continued*

## Assessing cause and effect

- **Is there a pattern of repetition?** Scientific proof depends on a pattern of repetition. To establish that A causes B, every time A is present, B must occur. Or, put another way, B never occurs unless A is present. The need for repetition explains why the US Food and Drug Administration (FDA) runs thousands of clinical trials before approving a new medicine.

- **Are there multiple causes and/or effects?** Avoid oversimplification. The basic pattern of cause and effect—single cause, single effect (A causes B)—rarely represents the full picture. Multiple causes and/or effects are more typical of real life. For example, it would be oversimplification to assume that a lower crime rate is strictly due to high employment rates. Similarly, one cause can produce multiple effects. For example, advertisements for a liquid diet drink focus on the drink's most appealing effect, rapid weight loss, ignoring less desirable effects such as lost nutrients and a tendency to regain the weight.

### 4i   How do I assess reasoning processes critically?

To think, read, and write critically, you need to distinguish *sound reasoning* from *faulty reasoning*. **Induction** and **deduction** are the two basic reasoning processes. They're natural thought patterns people use every day to help them think through ideas and make decisions. The two processes are summarized in Box 4.8.

SUMMARY BOX   **4.8**

## Comparison of inductive and deductive reasoning

| | INDUCTIVE REASONING | DEDUCTIVE REASONING |
|---|---|---|
| Argument begins | with specific evidence | with a general claim |
| Argument concludes | with a general statement | with a specific statement |
| Conclusion is | reliable or unreliable | true or false |
| Purpose is | to discover something new | to apply what's known |

## RECOGNIZING AND USING INDUCTIVE REASONING

**Inductive reasoning** moves from particular facts or instances to general principles. Suppose you go to the Registry of Motor Vehicles to renew your driver's license and have to stand in line for two hours. A few months later you return to get new license plates, and once again you have to stand in line for two hours. You mention your annoyance to a couple of friends who say they had exactly the same experience. You conclude that the registry is inefficient and indifferent to the needs of its patrons. You've arrived at this conclusion by means of induction. Box 4.9 shows the features of inductive reasoning.

**SUMMARY BOX** 4.9

### Inductive reasoning

- **Inductive reasoning moves from the specific to the general.** It begins with specific evidence—facts, observations, or experiences—and moves to a general conclusion.

- **Inductive conclusions are considered reliable or unreliable, not true or false.** Because inductive thinking is based on a sampling of facts, an inductive conclusion indicates probability—the degree to which the conclusion is likely to be true—not certainty.

- **An inductive conclusion is held to be reliable or unreliable in relation to the quantity and quality of the evidence** (4g) on which it's based.

- **Induction leads to new "truths."** It can support statements about the unknown based on what's known.

## RECOGNIZING AND USING DEDUCTIVE REASONING

**Deductive reasoning** is the process of reasoning from general claims to a specific instance. Suppose you know that students who don't study for Professor Sanchez's history tests tend to do poorly. If your friend tells you she didn't study, you can make a reasonable conclusion about her grade. Your reasoning might go something like this:

PREMISE 1   Students who don't study do poorly on Professor Sanchez's exams.

PREMISE 2   My friend didn't study.

CONCLUSION   Therefore, my friend probably did poorly on the exam.

Deductive arguments have three parts: two **premises** and a conclusion. This three-part structure is known as a **syllogism**. The first and

141

second premises of a deductive argument may be statements of fact or assumptions. They lead to a conclusion, which is the point at which you want to think as precisely as possible because you're into the realm of *validity*.

Whether or not an argument is **valid** has to do with its form or structure. Here, the word *valid* isn't the general term people use in conversation to mean "acceptable" or "well grounded." In the context of reading and writing logical arguments, the word *valid* has a very specific meaning. A deductive argument is *valid* when the conclusion logically follows from the premises; a deductive argument is *invalid* when the conclusion doesn't logically follow from the premises. For example:

**VALID DEDUCTIVE ARGUMENT**

| | |
|---|---|
| PREMISE 1 | When it snows, the streets get wet. [fact] |
| PREMISE 2 | It is snowing. [fact] |
| CONCLUSION | Therefore, the streets are getting wet. |

**INVALID DEDUCTIVE ARGUMENT**

| | |
|---|---|
| PREMISE 1 | When it snows, the streets get wet. [fact] |
| PREMISE 2 | The streets are getting wet. [fact] |
| CONCLUSION | Therefore, it is snowing. |

Here's the problem with the invalid deductive argument: It has acceptable premises because they are facts. However, the argument's conclusion is wrong because it ignores other reasons why the streets might be wet. For example, the street could be wet from rain, from street-cleaning trucks that spray water, or from people washing their cars. Therefore, because the conclusion doesn't follow logically from the premises, the argument is invalid.

Another problem in a deductive argument can occur when the premises are implied but not stated—called **unstated assumptions**. An argument can be logically valid even though it is based on wrong assumptions. To show that such an argument is invalid, you need to attack the assumptions, not the conclusion, as wrong. For example, suppose a corporation argues that it can't install pollution-control devices because the cost would cut deeply into its profits. This argument rests on the unstated assumption that no corporation should do something that would lower its profits. That assumption is wrong, and so is the argument. To show that both are wrong, you need to challenge the assumptions.

Similarly, if a person says that certain information is correct because it's written in the newspaper, that person's deductive reasoning is flawed. The unstated assumption is that everything in a newspaper is correct—which isn't true. Whenever there's an unstated assumption, you need to state it outright and then check that it's true. Box 4.10 summarizes deductive reasoning.

---

**SUMMARY BOX** 4.10

## Deductive reasoning

- **Deductive reasoning moves from the general to the specific.** The three-part structure that makes up a deductive argument, or SYLLOGISM, includes two premises and a conclusion drawn from them.

- **A deductive argument is valid if the conclusion logically follows from the premises.**

- **A deductive conclusion may be judged true or false.** If both premises are true, the conclusion is true. If the argument contains an assumption, the writer must prove the truth of the assumption to establish the truth of the argument.

- **Deductive reasoning applies what the writer already knows.** Though it doesn't yield new information, it builds stronger arguments than inductive reasoning because it offers the certainty that a conclusion is either true or false.

---

**EXERCISE 4-7** Working individually or with a peer-response group, determine whether each conclusion here is valid or invalid. Be ready to explain your answers. For help, consult 4i.

1. Faddish clothes are expensive.
   This shirt is expensive.
   This shirt must be part of a fad.

2. When a storm is threatening, small-craft warnings are issued.
   A storm is threatening.
   Small-craft warnings will be issued.

3. The Pulitzer Prize is awarded to outstanding literary works.
   *The Great Gatsby* never won a Pulitzer Prize.
   *The Great Gatsby* isn't an outstanding literary work.

4. All states send representatives to the United States Congress.
   Puerto Rico sends a representative to the United States Congress.
   Puerto Rico is a state.

5. Finding a good job requires patience.
   Sherrill is patient.
   Sherrill will find a good job.

## 4j    How can I recognize and avoid logical fallacies?

**Logical fallacies** are flaws in reasoning that lead to illogical statements. Though logical fallacies tend to occur when ideas are argued, they can be found in all types of writing. Interestingly, most logical fallacies masquerade as reasonable statements, but in fact, they're attempts to manipulate readers by appealing to their emotions instead of their intellects, their hearts rather than their heads. The name for each logical fallacy indicates the way that thinking has gone wrong.

### HASTY GENERALIZATION

A **hasty generalization** draws conclusions from inadequate evidence. Suppose someone says, "My hometown is the best place in the state to live," and gives only two examples to support the opinion. That's not enough. And others might not feel the same way, perhaps for many reasons. Therefore, the person who makes such a statement is indulging in a hasty generalization. **Stereotyping** is another kind of hasty generalization. It happens, for example, when someone says, "Everyone from country X is dishonest." Such a sweeping claim about all members of a particular ethnic, religious, racial, or political group is stereotyping. Yet another kind of stereotyping is **sexism**, which occurs when someone discriminates against another person on the basis of GENDER. For example, when an observer of a minor traffic accident involving women makes negative comments about all "women drivers," the person is guilty of a combination of stereotyping and sexism—both components of hasty generalization.

### FALSE ANALOGY

A **false analogy** draws a comparison in which the differences outweigh the similarities or the similarities are irrelevant. For example, "Old Joe Smith would never make a good president because an old dog can't learn new tricks" is a false analogy. Joe Smith isn't a dog. Also, learning the role of a president bears no comparison to a dog's learning tricks. Homespun analogies like this have an air of wisdom about them, but they tend to fall apart when examined closely.

### BEGGING THE QUESTION

**Begging the question**, also called *circular reasoning*, tries to offer proof by simply using another version of the argument itself. For example, the statement "Wrestling is a dangerous sport because it is unsafe" begs the question. Because *unsafe* is a synonym for *dangerous*, the statement goes around in a circle, getting nowhere. Here's another example of circular reasoning but with a different twist: "Wrestling is a dangerous sport because wrestlers get injured." Here, the support for the second part of the statement "wrestlers get injured" is the argument made in the first part of the statement. Obviously, since wrestling is a popular sport, it can be safe when undertaken with proper training and practice.

### IRRELEVANT ARGUMENT

An **irrelevant argument** reaches a conclusion that doesn't follow from the premises. Irrelevant argument is also called *non sequitur* (Latin for "it does not follow"). An argument is irrelevant when a conclusion doesn't follow from the premises. Here's an example: "Jane Jones is a forceful speaker, so she'll make a good mayor." You'd be on target if you asked, "What does speaking ability have to do with being a good mayor?"

### FALSE CAUSE

A **false cause** assumes that because two events are related in time, the first caused the second. False cause is also known as *post hoc, ergo propter hoc* (Latin for "after this, therefore because of this"). For example, if someone claims that a new weather satellite launched last week has caused the rain that's been falling ever since, that person is connecting two events that, while related in time, have no causal relationship to each other. The launching didn't cause the rain.

### SELF-CONTRADICTION

**Self-contradiction** uses two premises that can't both be true at the same time. Here's an example: "Only when nuclear weapons have finally destroyed us will we be convinced of the need to control them." This is self-contradictory because no one would be around to be convinced if everyone has been destroyed.

### RED HERRING

A **red herring**, also called *ignoring the question,* tries to distract attention from one issue by introducing a second that's unrelated to the first. Here's an example: "Why worry about pandas becoming extinct when we haven't solved the plight of the homeless?" You'd be on target if you asked, "What do homeless people have to do with pandas?" If the argument were to focus on proposing that the money spent to prevent the extinction of pandas should go instead to the homeless, the argument would be logical; however, the original statement is a fallacy. By using an irrelevant issue, a person hopes to distract the audience, just as putting a herring in the path of a bloodhound would distract it from the scent it's been following.

### ARGUMENT TO THE PERSON

An **argument to the person** means attacking the person making the argument rather than the argument itself. It's also known as the *ad hominem* (Latin for "to the man") attack. When someone criticizes a person's appearance, habits, or character instead of the merits of that person's argument, the attack is a fallacy. Here's an example: "We'd take her position on child abuse seriously if she were not so nasty to her husband." You'd be on target if you were to ask, "What does nastiness to an adult, though not at all nice, have to do with child abuse?"

### GUILT BY ASSOCIATION

**Guilt by association** means that a person's arguments, ideas, or opinions lack merit because of that person's activities, interests, or companions. Here's an example: "Jack belongs to the International Hill Climbers Association, which declared bankruptcy last month. This makes him unfit to be mayor of our city." That Jack is a member of a group that declared bankruptcy has nothing to do with Jack's ability to be mayor.

### JUMPING ON THE BANDWAGON

**Jumping on the bandwagon** means something is right or permissible because "everyone does it." It's also called *ad populum* (Latin for "to the people"). This fallacy operates in a statement such as "How could bungee jumping be unhealthy if thousands of people have done it?" Following the crowd doesn't work because research shows that many people who bungee-jump suffer serious sight impairments later in life.

### FALSE OR IRRELEVANT AUTHORITY

Using **false** or **irrelevant authority** means citing the opinion of someone who has no expertise in the subject at hand. This fallacy attempts to transfer prestige from one area to another. Many television commercials rely on this tactic—a famous golf player praising a brand of motor oil or a popular movie star lauding a brand of cheese.

### CARD-STACKING

**Card-stacking**, also known as *special pleading*, ignores evidence on the other side of a question. From all available facts, people choose only those facts that show the best (or worst) possible case. Many television commercials use this strategy. When three slim, happy consumers praise a diet plan, only at the very end of the ad does the announcer say—in a very low and speedy voice—that results vary. Indeed, even that statement is vague and uninformative.

### THE EITHER-OR FALLACY

The **either-or fallacy**, also called *false dilemma*, offers only two alternatives when more exist. Such fallacies tend to touch on emotional issues, so many people accept them until they analyze the statement. Here's an example: "Either go to college or forget about getting a job." This rigid, two-sided statement ignores the truth that many jobs don't require a college education.

### TAKING SOMETHING OUT OF CONTEXT

**Taking something out of context** deliberately distorts an idea or a fact by removing it from its previously surrounding material. Here's an example: Suppose that a newspaper movie critic writes, "The plot was predictable and boring, but the music was sparkling." The next day, an advertisement for the movie claims "critics call it 'sparkling.'" Clearly, the ad has taken the critic's words out of context (only the music was called "sparkling") and thereby distorts the original.

## APPEAL TO IGNORANCE

**Appeal to ignorance** tries to make an incorrect argument based on something never having been shown to be false—or, the reverse, never having been shown to be true. Here's an example: "Because it hasn't been proven that eating food X doesn't cause cancer, we can assume that it does." The statement is a fallacy because the absence of opposing evidence proves nothing. Such appeals can be very persuasive because they prey on people's superstitions or lack of knowledge. Often, they're stated in the fuzzy language of DOUBLE NEGATIVES.

## AMBIGUITY AND EQUIVOCATION

**Ambiguity** and **equivocation** are statements open to more than one interpretation, thus concealing the truth. Here's an example: Suppose a person is asked, "Is she doing a good job?" and the person answers, "She's performing as expected." The answer is a fallacy because it's open to positive or negative interpretation.

**EXERCISE 4-8**   Following are letters to the editor of a newspaper. Working alone or with a peer-response group, do a critical analysis of each, paying special attention to logical fallacies.

1. To the Editor:
   I am writing to oppose the plan to convert the abandoned railroad tracks into a bicycle trail. Everyone knows that the only reason the mayor wants to do this is so that she and her wealthy friends can have a new place to play. No one I know likes this plan, and if they did, it would probably be because they're part of the wine and cheese set, too. The next thing you know, the mayor will be proposing that we turn the schools into art museums or the park into a golf course. If you're working hard to support a family, you don't have time for this bike trail nonsense. And if you're not working hard, I don't have time for you.

   Russell Shields

2. To the Editor:
   I encourage everyone to support the bicycle trail project. Good recreation facilities are the key to the success of any community. Since the bike trail will add more recreation opportunities, it will guarantee the success of our town. Remember that several years ago our neighbors over in Springfield decided not to build a new park, and look what happened to their economy, especially that city's high unemployment rate. We can't afford to let the same thing happen to us. People who oppose this plan are narrow-minded, selfish, and

almost unpatriotic. As that great patriot John Paul Jones said, "I have not yet begun to fight."

Susan Thompson

3. To the Editor:
   I'm tired of all this nonsense about pollution and global warming. We had plenty of cold days last winter, and as my dentist said, "If this is global warming, then I'd sure hate to see global cooling." Plus, there were lots of days this summer when I haven't had to turn on my air conditioner. I know there are statistics that some people say show the climate is changing, but you can't trust numbers, especially when they come from liberal scientists. These people just aren't happy unless they're giving us something to feel guilty about, whether it's smoking, drinking, or driving SUVs. Maybe if they stopped wasting their time worrying about pollution, they could do something useful, like find a cure for cancer.

Marcus Johnson

# Chapter 5

## WRITING ARGUMENTS

 **5a** **What is a written argument?**

When you write an **argument**, you attempt to convince a reader to agree with you on a topic open to debate. You support your position, proposal, or interpretation with EVIDENCE, reasons, and examples. Some people use the terms *argumentative writing* and *persuasive writing* interchangeably. When people distinguish between them, *persuasive writing* is the broader term. It includes advertisements, letters to editors, and emotional speeches, as well as the kind of formal written arguments expected in college courses and other formal situations.

A written argument consists of two main elements:

- The **claim** states the issue and then takes a position on a debatable topic (the position can be written as a THESIS STATEMENT).
- Facts and logical reasoning provide **support** for the claim (the support needs to be in the form of evidence, reasons, and examples).

In daily life, you might think of an argument as a personal conflict or disagreement, begun in anger and involving emotional confrontations. Many radio programs, Web sites, and BLOGS reinforce this impression by featuring people who seem more interested in pushing their own agendas than in trying to persuade reasonably. For academic writing, as well as business and public writing, however, arguments are ways of demonstrating CRITICAL THINKING, calmly and respectfully. On difficult issues, your goal is to persuade an audience to consider your ideas with an open mind, which means that your audience's viewpoints and values need to influence your decisions about content, organization, and style. The passion that underlies a writer's position comes not from angry words but from the force of a balanced, well-developed, clearly written presentation.

In this chapter, you'll learn how to develop an effective claim, or thesis, how to generate support, and how to organize your argument using two strategies: the classical pattern and the Rogerian pattern. In addition, you'll find information about how to analyze and refute opposing arguments. If you take a few minutes to review Chapters 1 through 4 of this handbook, you'll have a richer context for understanding this chapter.

**How do I choose a topic for an argument?**

When you choose a topic for written argument, be sure that it's open to debate. Don't confuse matters of information (facts) with matters of debate. An essay becomes an argument when it makes a claim—that is, *takes a position*—about a debatable topic. An effective way to develop a position is to ask two (or more) opposing questions about a topic.

| | |
|---|---|
| FACT | Students at Calhoon College must study a foreign language. |
| DEBATABLE | Should Calhoon College require students to study a foreign language? |
| ONE SIDE | Calhoon College should not require students to study a foreign language. |
| OTHER SIDE | Calhoon College should require students to study a foreign language. |

Though you need to select one side of a debatable question to defend in your essay, always keep the other side (or sides) in mind. Devoting some space to state and counter the opposing viewpoint shows readers that you're well informed and fair-minded. This effect is even stronger if you always maintain a respectful tone by avoiding insults, abstaining from exaggerations, and resisting sarcasm. If you neglect to mention opposing views, your readers could justifiably assume you're not well informed, fair-minded, or disciplined as a thinker. When multiple alternative viewpoints exist, choose the major opposing one, unless otherwise directed by your instructor.

Instructors sometimes assign students a topic and even the position to take. In such cases, you need to fulfill the assignment even if you disagree with the point of view. Readers expect you to reason logically about the assigned position. Indeed, experienced debate teams practice arguing all sides of an issue. Being assigned topics or positions is common beyond college, especially in work settings. Perhaps a manager asks you to develop a persuasive marketing campaign or to negotiate a price break from a supplier. Perhaps you'll be told to convince other workers that a new process will save them time and effort.

If you choose your own topic and position, select one that has sufficient substance for college writing. Readers expect you to take an intelligent, defensible position and to support it reasonably and convincingly. For example, "Book censorship in public libraries" is worthy of a college-level essay; "The color of baseball caps" is not. Also, so that you choose a claim sufficiently narrow to be practical, consider the length and time specified in your assignment.

Even if you think that all sides of a debatable topic have merit, you need to choose one of them anyway. Don't become paralyzed from indecision. You're not making a lifetime commitment. Concentrate on the merits of one position, and argue that position as effectively as possible, reserving some space to counter objections. Of course, the more thoroughly you think through all sides of the topic, the broader the perspective you'll bring to your writing, and the more likely it is that your writing will be effective. Finally, however, take a position.

## 5c    How do I develop a claim and a thesis statement for my argument?

A CLAIM is a statement that expresses a point of view on a debatable topic. It can be supported by evidence, reasons, and examples (including facts, statistics, names, experiences, and expert testimony). The exact wording of the claim rarely finds its way into the essay, but the claim serves as a focus for your thinking. Later, it serves as the basis for developing your THESIS STATEMENT.

| | |
|---|---|
| TOPIC | Wild animals as domestic pets |
| CLAIM | People should not be allowed to own wild animals. |
| CLAIM | People should be allowed to own wild animals. |

Before you decide on a claim, explore the topic. Don't rush. Consider all sides. **Remember that what mainly separates most good writing from bad is the writer's ability to move back and forth between general statements and specific details.** Therefore, before you start drafting, use the RENNS formula (3f) to check whether you can marshal sufficient details to support your generalizations.

To stimulate your thinking about the topic and decide the claim you'll argue, work with the PLANNING techniques discussed in Chapter 2. Another well-favored strategy is to create a two-column list, labeling one column *Pro* or *For*, the other *Con* or *Against*. If there are more than two opposing sides, label the columns accordingly. The columned list displays the quantity and quality of your material so that you can decide whether you're ready to start DRAFTING.

Lacie Juris, the student who wrote the argument essay that appears in section 5n, chose her own topic for a written argument in a first-year college writing class. Lacie was thinking about a career as a zookeeper, which led to her interest in issues concerning wild animals. In her career research, especially using the Web, she discovered a major controversy: the issue of private ownership of wild animals. Her curiosity aroused, Lacie read a number of sources and discovered a topic appropriate for her assignment. She worked on developing a claim about that topic that then evolved into a thesis statement. Here's how Lacie progressed from topic to claim to thesis statement.

| | |
|---|---|
| **TOPIC** | Private ownership of wild animals |
| **MY POSITION** | I think private ownership of wild animals should not be allowed. |
| **THESIS STATEMENT (FIRST DRAFT)** | It is bad for private citizens to own wild animals as pets. [This is a preliminary thesis statement. It clearly states the writer's position, but the word *bad* is vague, and the writer doesn't address how to stop private ownership of wild animals.] |
| **THESIS STATEMENT (SECOND DRAFT)** | To eliminate what few people realize are increasingly dangerous situations for people and animals alike, ownership of wild animals as pets by ordinary people needs to be made completely illegal. [This revised thesis statement is better because it states not only the writer's claim but also a reason for the claim. However, it suffers from a lack of conciseness and from the unnecessary passive construction "needs to be made."] |
| **THESIS STATEMENT (FINAL DRAFT)** | To eliminate dangerous situations for both people and animals alike, policymakers need to ban private ownership of wild animals as pets. [This final version works well because it states the writer's claim clearly and its language is concise, with verbs all in the active voice. The writer now has a thesis statement suitable for the time and length given in her assignment. Also, it meets the requirements for a thesis statement given in Box 2.5.] |

**EXERCISE 5-1**    Working individually or with a peer-response group, develop a claim and a thesis statement for each of the topics listed at the end of the exercise. You may choose any defensible position. For help, consult 5a through 5c.

**EXAMPLE**    **Topic:** Book censorship in high school

**Claim:** Books should not be censored in high school.

**Thesis statement:** When books are taken off high school library shelves or are dropped from high school curricula because they are considered inappropriate to read, students are denied an open exchange of ideas.

1. Commercials for alcoholic beverages on television
2. The commercialization of religious and/or patriotic holidays
3. Taking body-building supplements
4. Requiring students to undertake volunteer or community service

## 5d    Why might I need to define key terms?

**Key terms** in an essay are the words central to its topic and message. While the meaning of some key terms might be readily evident in your writing, others may be open to interpretation. For example, abstract words such as *love, freedom,* and *democracy* have different meanings in different contexts. Therefore, if you want to argue that "Justice demands capital punishment in the case of murder," the definition of *justice* would be crucial to your argument.

Many students ask whether they can use dictionary definitions in their college writing. While you always want to look up words in a dictionary to understand their precise meanings, you want to avoid quoting directly from a dictionary, which is often seen as lacking in grace or SYNTHESIS. Avoid also the unappealing, inexact expression "according to Webster's" to introduce a definition. However, if the meaning of a word is complex, highly unfamiliar to most readers, or easily misinterpreted, you can indeed decide that a quoted dictionary definition would serve well. If you do, include the complete title of the dictionary you're citing: for example, *Webster's New World College Dictionary,* Fourth Edition.

## 5e    What is the structure of a classical argument?

No single method is best for organizing all arguments, but a frequently used structure is the **classical argument**. The ancient Greeks and Romans developed this six-part structure, which is described in Box 5.1.

**SUMMARY BOX** 5.1

### The structure of a classical argument

1. **Introductory paragraph:** Sets the stage for the position argued in the essay. It gains the reader's interest and respect (3b).

2. **Thesis statement:** States the topic and position you want to argue (2q).

3. **Background information:** Gives readers the basic information they need for understanding your thesis and its support. As appropriate, you might include definitions of key terms (5d), historical or social context, prior scholarship, and other related material. You can include this as part of your introductory paragraph, or it can appear in its own paragraph placed immediately after the introduction.

4. **Evidence and reasons:** Supports the position you're arguing on the topic. This is the core of the essay. Each reason or piece of evidence usually consists of a general statement backed up with specific details,

➤

## The structure of a classical argument

including examples and other RENNS (3f). Evidence needs to meet the standards for critical thinking (4g) and reasoning (4h through 4j) to be logical. Depending on the length of the essay, you might devote one or two paragraphs to each reason or type of evidence. For organization, you might choose to present the most familiar reasons and evidence first, saving the most unfamiliar for last. Alternatively, you might proceed from the least important to the most important point so that your essay builds to a climax, leaving the most powerful impact for the end. (For alternative ways to arrange paragraphs, consult 3h and 3i.)

5. **Response to opposing position:** Sometimes referred to as the *rebuttal* or *refutation.* This material mentions and defends against an opposite point of view. Often this refutation, which can be lengthy or brief according to the overall length of the essay, appears in its own paragraph or paragraphs, usually immediately before the concluding paragraph or immediately following the introductory paragraph, as a bridge to the rest of the essay. If you use the latter structure, you can choose to place your thesis statement either at the end of the introductory paragraph or at the end of the rebuttal paragraph. Yet another choice for structure consists of each paragraph's presenting one type of evidence or reason and then immediately stating and responding to the opposing position. (See 5l for advice on handling opposing arguments.)

6. **Concluding paragraph:** Ends the essay logically and gracefully—never abruptly. It often summarizes the argument, elaborates its significance, or calls readers to action (3k).

## 5f How do I support my argument?

Use reasons, examples, and evidence to support an argument's claim. (See RENNS, Box 3.3.) One good method for developing reasons for an argument is to ask yourself *why* you believe your claim. When you respond "Because . . . ," you offer reasons for your claim. Another method to find reasons is to list pros and cons about your claim. The lists usually contain reasons. Evidence needs to be sufficient, representative, relevant, accurate, reasonable, and current. Specifically, evidence consists of facts, statistics, expert testimony, personal experience, and so on.

If you consult SOURCES to find supporting evidence, reasons, or examples, be sure to use correct DOCUMENTATION within the text of your essay and in your WORKS CITED or REFERENCES list at the end of your paper (Chapters 34–36). By doing this, you avoid engaging in PLAGIARISM, adopting someone else's ideas and trying to pass them off as your own. Plagiarism is a serious offense that can result in your failing a course or even being dismissed from college (Chapter 33).

## 5g   What types of appeals can provide support?

An effective argument relies on three types of **persuasive appeals**: logical appeals, emotional appeals, and ethical appeals. The ancient Greeks called these appeals *logos, pathos,* and *ethos.* Box 5.2 summarizes how to use the appeals.

---

**SUMMARY BOX** **5.2**

### Guidelines for persuasive appeals

- **Be logical:** Use sound reasoning (*logos*).
- **Enlist the emotions of the reader:** Appeal to the values and beliefs of the reader by arousing the reader's "better self" (*pathos*).
- **Establish credibility:** Show that you as the writer can be relied on as a knowledgeable person with good sense (*ethos*).

---

The **logical appeal** (*logos*) is the most widely used and intellectually solid and sound appeal in arguments. Sound reasoning involves using effective evidence and reasons. When the student writer Lacie Juris argues that owning pets is dangerous, for example, she provides facts about deaths, injuries, and property damage (5n). Logical writers analyze CAUSE AND EFFECT correctly. Also, they use appropriate patterns of INDUCTIVE REASONING and DEDUCTIVE REASONING, and they distinguish clearly between fact and opinion. Finally, sound reasoning means avoiding LOGICAL FALLACIES. One strategy for generating logical appeals is the **Toulmin model**, developed by the philosopher Stephen Toulmin, discussed in 5h.

When you use **emotional appeals** (*pathos*), you try to persuade your readers by appealing to their hearts more than their minds. Such appeals are generally more effective when you combine them with logical appeals. If an employee asks for a raise and gives reasons like "I have a family to support" or "I need to pay medical bills," that person probably won't get very far. The employee needs in addition to prove how his or her contributions have gone well beyond the job description, dramatically increased sales, or created other advantages.

Emotional appeals can use descriptive language and concrete details or examples to create a mental picture for readers, which is an approach that leads them to feel or understand the importance of your claim. Figure 5.1 (p. 156) provides an example of emotional appeals. You want to appeal to your audience's values and beliefs through honest examples and descriptions that add a sense of humanity and reality to the issue you're arguing.

# Sleeping Sickness
## Untreated, It Inevitably Kills

Spread by tsetse flies, this dreaded tropical disease claims more than 66,000 lives a year in 36 African nations. Doctors Without Borders volunteer Rebecca Golden returned from Angola, where a desperate battle against sleeping sickness is being waged after years of war have wrecked that nation's health care system.

"The treatment is a form of arsenic and is extremely painful," says Rebecca. "I was visiting some children receiving their medicine and was amazed at their courage and strength. **When the arsenic entered their bloodstream, they curled their toes, turned their heads, and closed their eyes tightly.** Their choice was to die or take the treatment. They accepted it with such calm. After 20 years of war and lost family members, they seem to accept this as just another part of the survival process."

Your support helps Doctors Without Borders save lives. **In our battle against sleeping sickness and other diseases, your gift can make a vital difference.**

---

## *Every Dollar Counts*

**$35** – Supplies a basic suture kit to repair minor shrapnel wounds.

**$75** – Provides 1,500 patients with clean water for a week.

**$100** – Provides infection-fighting antibiotics to treat nearly 40 wounded children.

**$200** – Supplies 40 malnourished children with special high-protein food for a day.

---

### Visit www.doctorswithoutborders.org

Figure 5.1 An argument that appeals to emotions

You want, however, to avoid manipulating your readers with biased, SLANTED LANGUAGE. Readers see through such tactics and resent them.

In her essay, Lacie Juris uses an emotional appeal well in her sixth paragraph. By referring to baby wild animals whose "capture robs [them] of the chance to learn skills necessary for survival," Lacie invokes the image of young and helpless creatures. At one point she writes, "Sadly, these animals never learned how to survive on their own." But she doesn't overdo *pathos* in her choice of language. Suppose she had written instead, "Picture these poor, innocent, forlorn animal babies racked with life-threatening hunger and viciously stalked by cruel beasts of the wild." Such words would be excessively dramatic, and most audience members would probably resent being manipulated.

When you use **ethical appeals**, or *ethos*, you establish your personal credibility with your audience. Audiences don't trust a writer who states opinions as fact, distorts evidence, or makes claims that can't be supported. They do trust a writer who comes across as honest, knowledgeable, and fair. Ethical appeals can't take the place of logical appeals, but the two work well together. One effective way to make an ethical appeal is to draw on your personal experience. (Some college instructors don't want students to write in the first person, so check with your instructor before you try this technique.) For example, suppose you want to argue that prisoners should have access to education in jail. If you yourself have been the victim of a crime, or know someone serving a prison sentence, you would have strong personal credibility for your position. Just be sure that any personal experience relates directly to the generalization you're supporting. Considering a variety of perspectives, using reliable SOURCES, and using a reasonable TONE all communicate that you're being fair-minded.

## 5h    What is the Toulmin model for argument?

One powerful method for generating logical appeals and for analyzing the arguments of others is the Toulmin model. For example, identifying the **warrants** (assumptions that are often unstated) is a good critical thinking strategy. The Toulmin model defines three essential elements in an effective argument: the claim, the support, and the warrants. They describe concepts that you've encountered before, as Box 5.3 explains.

**SUMMARY BOX** 5.3

### The Toulmin model for argument

- **Claim:** A variation of a thesis statement. If needed, the claim is qualified or limited.

  Lacie Juris makes the following claim in her argument: Policymakers need to ban private ownership of wild animals as pets.

- **Support:** REASONS and EVIDENCE, moving from broad reasons to specific data and details, support the claim.

  Lacie offers two main reasons: (1) Wild animals are dangerous to humans; and (2) Domestication is hazardous to the animals themselves. She then provides evidence for each of those reasons, drawing on source materials.

- **Warrants:** The writer's underlying assumptions, which are often implied rather than stated. Warrants may also need support (also called *backing*).

  Lacie's essay has two warrants: (1) We should outlaw situations that are dangerous to people; and (2) We should outlaw situations that are dangerous to animals. (Notice that these warrants are debatable. For example, driving a car is dangerous to people, but we don't outlaw that activity. Raising cattle for food is ultimately highly dangerous to animals, but we don't outlaw hamburgers.)

The concept of *warrant* is similar to the concept of *inferences*, a key component of reading critically (4d). Inferences are not stated outright but are implied "between the lines" of the writing. Similarly, warrants are unspoken underlying assumptions in an argument. Consider the following simple argument: "Johnson should not be elected mayor. She was recently divorced." The *claim* is that Johnson shouldn't be elected. The *support* is that Johnson has been divorced. The unstated *warrant* is "divorced people are not qualified to be mayor." Before they can accept the claim that Johnson shouldn't be elected, readers have to accept this warrant. Of course, a majority of readers would reject the warrant. Thus, this argument is weak. To identify the warrants in an argument, ask "What do I need to assume so that the support is sufficient for establishing each claim?"

The concepts in the Toulmin model can help you write arguments with a critical eye. They can be quite useful on their own as well as applied to the CLASSICAL ARGUMENT structure (Box 5.1). As you read and revise your own arguments, identify the claim, support, and warrants. If you don't have a clear claim or support, you'll probably have to assume that your argument is weak. Furthermore, make sure that all of your warrants will be convincing to readers. If they aren't, you need to provide backing, or reasons why the warrants are reasonable. For example, consider the following argument: "People should not receive a driver's license until the age of 25 because the accident rate for younger drivers is much higher than for older ones." One of the warrants here is that reducing the number of accidents should have highest priority. Obviously, many 18-to-24-year-old readers will not find that warrant convincing.

**EXERCISE 5-2**    Individually or with a peer-response group, discuss these simple arguments. Identify the claim, support, and warrants for each.

> EXAMPLE    The college should establish an honor code. Last semester more than fifty students were caught cheating on exams.
>
> **Claim:** The college should establish an honor code.
>
> **Support:** Last semester, more than fifty students were caught cheating on exams.
>
> **Warrants:**
> A. Enough students cheat on exams that the college should address the problem.
> B. Cheating should be prevented.
> C. Students would not have cheated if there had been an honor code.

1. The college should raise student tuition and fees. The football stadium is in such poor repair that the coach is having trouble recruiting players.

2. Vote against raising our taxes. In the past two years, we have already had a 2 percent tax increase.

3. The college should require all students to own laptop computers. Most students will have to use computers in their jobs after graduation.

## 5i    What part does audience play in my argument?

The PURPOSE of written argument is to convince your AUDIENCE either to agree with you or to be open to your position. In writing an argument, you want to consider what your readers already know or believe about your topic. Will the audience be hostile or open-minded to your position? Will it resist or adopt your point of view? What values, viewpoints, and assumptions will your audience hold?

Unfortunately, some members of some audiences can be persuaded by purely sensational or one-sided claims. Witness the effects on some readers of highly charged advertising or of narrowly one-sided ultra-conservative or ultraliberal claims. However, such arguments rarely change the minds of people who don't already agree with them. Critical thinking quickly reveals the weaknesses of such arguments, including a frequent use of LOGICAL FALLACIES (4j). That's why academic audiences expect a higher standard and value, above all, logical appeals and appropriate, adequate support. Topics such as the best responses to air pollution or bans on loud radios in recreation areas are usually less emotionally loaded. The more emotionally charged a topic is, the greater the chance that any position will elicit either strong agreement or strong disagreement. For example, abortion, school prayer, and gun control touch on matters of personal belief, including individual rights and religion.

In many instances, of course, you can't actually expect to change your reader's mind, which means your goal is to demonstrate that your point of view has its own merit. If you think that your audience is likely to read your point of view with hostility, you might consider using Rogerian argument.

## 5j    How can Rogerian argument help me reach opposing audiences?

**Rogerian argument** seeks common ground between points of view. The Rogerian approach is based on the principles of communication developed by the psychologist Carl Rogers. According to Rogers, communication is eased when people find common ground in their points of view. For example, the common ground in a debate over capital punishment might be that serious crimes are increasing in numbers and viciousness. Once both sides agree that this is the problem, they might be more willing to consider opposing opinions. Box 5.4 explains the structure of a Rogerian argument, which can be an effective alternative to CLASSICAL ARGUMENT structure.

---

## The structure of a Rogerian argument

1. **Introduction:** Sets the stage for the position that is argued in the essay. It gains the reader's interest and respect (3b).

2. **Thesis statement:** States the topic and position you want to argue (2q and 5c).

3. **Common ground:** Explains the issue, acknowledging that your readers probably don't agree with you. Speculates about and respectfully gives attention to the points of agreement you and your readers might share, especially concerning underlying problems or issues. For example, people on both sides of the gun control issue can share the desire for fewer violent crimes with guns. You might even acknowledge situations in which your reader's position may be desirable. This may take one paragraph or several, depending on the complexity of the issue.

4. **Discussion of your position:** Gives evidence and reasons for your stand on the topic, as in classical argument (Box 5.1).

5. **Concluding paragraph:** Summarizes why your position is preferable to your opponent's (3k). You might, for example, explain why a particular situation makes your position desirable.

---

When it comes to argument, people often "agree to disagree" in the best spirit of intellectual exchange. As you write a Rogerian argument, remember that your audience wants to see how effectively you've reasoned and presented your position. This stance approaches that of a formal oral debate in which all sides are explored with similar intellectual rigor.

## 5k   What is a reasonable tone in an argument?

A reasonable TONE tells your audience that you're being fair-minded. When you anticipate opposing positions and refute them with balanced language and emphasis, you demonstrate that you respect the other side. No matter how strongly you disagree with opposing arguments, never insult the other side. Name-calling reflects poor judgment and a lack of self-control. The saying "It's not what you say but how you say it" needs to be on your mind at all times as you write an argument. Avoid exaggerating, and never show anger. The more emotionally loaded a topic (for example, abortion or capital punishment), the more tempted you might be to use careless, harsh words. For instance, calling the opposing position "stupid" would say more about you as the writer than it would about the issue.

**EXERCISE 5-3**  Here is the text of a notorious e-mail fraud that has been sent to many people. Hundreds of variations of this e-mail exist, but usually the writer claims to have a large amount of money that he or she wants to transfer to an American bank. The writer wants the recipient's help in making the transfer. This is a complete lie. The writer has no money and is trying to trick people into revealing their bank account numbers to steal their money.

Either alone or in a small group, examine the ways this writer tries to establish emotional and ethical appeals. *Note:* We've reproduced the e-mail with the often incorrect original wording, grammar, and punctuation.

Good day,

It is my humble pleasure to write this letter irrespective of the fact that you do not know me. However, I came to know of you in my private search for a reliable and trustworthy person that can handle a confidential transaction of this nature in respect of this, I got your contact through an uprooted search on the internet. Though I know that a transaction of this magnitude will make any one apprehensive and worried, but I am assuring you that all will be well at the end of the day.

I am Ruth Malcasa, daughter of late Mr James Malcasa of Somalia, who was killed by the Somalian rebel forces on the 24th of December, 1999 in my country Somalia. When he was still alive, he deposited one trunk box containing the sum of USD$10 million dollars in cash (Ten Million dollars). with a private security and safe deposit company here in Lagos Nigeria. This money was made from the sell of Gold and Diamond by my mother and she has already decided to use this money for future investment of the family.

My father instructed me that in the case of his death, that I should look for a trusted foreigner who can assist me to move out this money from Nigeria immediately for investment. Based on this, I solicit for your assistance to transfer this fund into your Account, but I will demand for the following requirement: (1) Could you provide for me a safe Bank Account where this fund will be transferred to in your country after retrieving the box containing the money from the custody of the security company. (2) Could you be able to introduce me to a profitable business venture that would not require much technical expertise in your country where part of this fund will be invested?

I am a Christian and I want you to handle this transaction based on the trust I have established on you. For your assistance in this transaction, I have decided to compensate you with 10 percent of the total amount at the end of this business. The security of this business is very important to me and as such, I would like you to keep this business very confidential. I shall expect an early response from you. Thank you and God bless. Yours sincerely, Ruth Malcasa.

## How do I handle opposing arguments?

Dealing with opposing positions is crucial to writing an effective argument. If you don't acknowledge arguments that your opponents might raise, and explain why they are faulty or inferior, you create doubts that you have thoroughly explored the issue. You risk seeming narrow-minded.

The next to last paragraph in Lacie Juris's paper (5n), which summarizes opposing arguments, strengthens both her *ethos* (credibility) and her *logos* (logic). She's so confident in her own position that she can state the possible opponents' argument that owners will be able to control their wild pets. Then she provides reasons why that argument is wrong. Lacie had encountered this counterargument while doing her research. When you do research for your own arguments, look for essays, articles, and opinions that oppose your position, not only ones that agree with yours.

If your research doesn't generate opposing arguments, you need to develop them yourself. Imagine that you're debating someone who disagrees with you; what positions would that person take and why? Note that you can ask a classmate or friend to perform this role. Another strategy is to take the opposite side of the argument and try to develop the best reasons you can for that position. (In some formal debating situations, people are expected to prepare both sides of an issue and only learn immediately before the debate which position they are to argue.)

Once you have generated opposing arguments, you need to refute them, which means you want to show why they're weak or undesirable. Imagine that you're writing about national security and individual rights. You believe that the government shouldn't be allowed to monitor a private citizen's e-mail without a court order, and you have developed a number of reasons for your position. To strengthen your paper, you also generate some opposing arguments, including "People will be safer from terrorism if police can monitor e-mail," "Only people who have something to hide have anything to fear," and "It is unpatriotic to oppose the government's plans." How might you refute these claims? Following are some suggestions.

- **Examine the evidence for each opposing argument** (4g). Look especially for missing or contradictory facts (4j). In the given example, you might question the evidence that people would be safer from terrorism if police could monitor e-mail.
- **Use the Toulmin model to analyze the opposing argument** (5h). What are the claims, support, and warrants? Often, it's possible to show

that the warrants are questionable or weak. For example, a warrant in the counterarguments above is that the promise of increased safety is worth the price of privacy or individual rights. You might show why this warrant is undesirable.

- **Demonstrate that an opposing argument depends on emotion rather than reasoning.** The assertion that it's unpatriotic to oppose the government is primarily an emotional one.
- **Redefine key terms.** The term *patriotism* can be defined in various ways. You might point out, for example, that at the time of the American Revolution, "patriots" were the people who were opposing the British government then in power.
- **Explain the negative consequences of the opposing position.** Imagine that the opposing position actually won out, and explain how the results would be damaging. For example, if everyone knew that government officials might monitor their computer use, consider how this might affect free speech.
- **Concede an opposing point, but explain that doing so doesn't destroy your own argument.** For example, you might decide to concede that governmental monitoring of e-mails could reduce terrorism. However, you might argue that the increase in safety is not worth the threat to privacy and personal freedom.
- **Explain that the costs of the other position are not worth the benefits.**

**EXERCISE 5-4**  Individually or with a peer-response group, practice developing objections to specific arguments and responses to those objections. To do this, choose a debatable topic and brainstorm a list of points on that topic, some on one side of the topic, some on another. Following are some arguments to get you started. If you're part of a group, work together to assign the different positions for each topic to different sets of students. Then, conduct a brief debate on which side has more merit, with each side taking turns. At the end, your group can vote for the side that is more convincing.

1. It should be legal/illegal to ride motorcycles without a helmet.
2. Women should/should not expect pay equal to men's for the same work.
3. Students should/should not be required to take certain courses in order to graduate.

---

**5m**  **How did one student draft and revise her argument essay?**

Lacie Juris chose the topic of the essay shown in section 5n because of her career interest in being a zookeeper. Her preliminary reading on the Internet about keeping wild animals as pets led her to develop a thesis statement (5c). In a first draft, Lacie focused on why it was unfair to wild animals to be kept as pets, but she realized that she would need to be more precise. That led to her argument that being kept as a pet could be harmful to the animal. In a second draft, she realized that harm to animals might not by itself be convincing to members of her audience. She then developed a second main point, that pet wild animals could be dangerous to people. Knowing that this claim required evidence, Lacie did further research in databases and on the Internet to find the support she needed.

In a third draft, Lacie considered some opposing arguments to her position. She also looked carefully at her use of *pathos* and *ethos.* At one point, she realized that she was relying on excessively emotional language, which she knew could turn off some readers, so she revised several sentences. Also, she consulted the revision checklist (Box 2.10). Finally, she referred to the special checklist for revising written arguments in Box 5.5.

---

CHECKLIST BOX **5.5**

## Revising written arguments

- Is the thesis statement about a debatable topic? (5b and 5c)
- Do the reasons or evidence support the thesis statement? Are the generalizations supported by specific details? (5c)
- Does the argument deal with reader needs and concerns? (5i)
- Does the argument appeal chiefly to reason? Is it supported by an ethical appeal? If it uses an emotional appeal, is the appeal restrained? (5g)
- Is the tone reasonable? (5k)
- Is the opposing position stated and refuted? (5l)

---

**EXERCISE 5-5** Working individually or with a peer-response group, choose a topic from this list. Then, plan an essay that argues a debatable position on the topic. Apply all the principles you've learned in this chapter.

1. Animal experimentation
2. Luxury taxes for sport utility vehicles
3. Cloning of human beings
4. Taxpayer support for public colleges
5. Value of space exploration
6. Laws requiring seat belt use

Juris 1

Lacie Juris

Professor Calhoun-Dillahunt

English 101

28 April 2005

Lions, Tigers, and Bears, Oh My!

Fuzzy orange-and-white tiger cubs playfully fight over a chew toy while baby chimps hang precariously in front of the nursery window, looking almost human with their big ears and adorable expressions. They look so cute at the zoo. Wouldn't it be exciting to have one for your very own, to play with in your living room and show off to your neighbors? It would be a childhood fantasy come true--and for many people living in the United States, it is true. Tigers, for example, cost the same amount as purebred puppies. Animal rights advocates estimate that as many tigers are kept as pets in the United States as exist in the wild worldwide (Boehm). Unfortunately, these exotic dreams-come-true can turn deadly

at any moment. Because regulation of wild animal ownership varies from county to county in the United States, laws are difficult to enforce ("Wild Animals Are Not Pets"). To eliminate dangerous situations for both people and

*continued* ➤

165

animals alike, policymakers need to ban private ownership of wild animals as pets.

Wild animals are dangerous to humans, both owners and nearby residents. Wild animals have inborn behavior patterns and instincts, such as stalking prey, attacking when threatened, and acting in self-defense. Such patterns remain no matter where or how the animals grow up, no matter how well the owners train them for domesticated living. This is what makes the animals truly wild. Humans cannot influence, change, or even predict such animals' wild behaviors. An attack can occur without warning at any time when an animal's wild instincts take over ("Wild Animals Are Not Pets"). In fact, authorities blame pet tigers for at least seven deaths and thirty-one injuries between 2000 and 2002 (Davenport). In addition, wild pets can cause tremendous property damage, as illustrated by the case of Stoli, a tiger who caused $20,000 worth of damage to his owner's Mercedes in less than five minutes ("Lil").

Many animal owners teach their young exotic pets little games and tricks. Owners do not realize, however, that when the wild animals have grown to three or four times the strength of most people, the "pets" still expect to take part in the same games and tricks. Take, for example, the story of a pet African serval named Kenya. Servals are known as "leaping cats," with the capacity to jump twelve feet straight up and run forty-five miles an hour. Kenya belonged to a woman who purchased him at a pet store. Because Kenya was small, he seemed like the perfect exotic pet. However,

*continued* ➤

no one told the woman about servals' amazing jumping abilities--or about their becoming extremely territorial as adults. At home, the woman taught the baby Kenya to leap onto her shoulder, without realizing that she was actually teaching him to leap onto people in general. In addition, as he grew, he became so territorial that he attacked anyone who came to her house ("Kenya").

Another little-realized fact is that wild animals greatly endanger owners and people in the surrounding areas by transmitting diseases. When people purchase exotic animals, no one tells them if the animals are carrying diseases. Wild animals can host internal parasites, such as ascarid worms, tapeworms, flukes, and protozoa, all of which can be debilitating or even fatal to their human caretakers-- especially their small children. The animals can also carry external parasites that cause spotted fever and bubonic plague ("Questions," par. 3). In addition, no known vaccination can protect wild animals from rabies ("Rabies").

While the risk to humans of exotic pet ownership is very high, domestication is hazardous to the animals themselves. After all, wild animals need specific and natural environments to survive. Such settings do not include humans' houses or backyard kennels. Owners of wild animals usually lack the knowledge and funds to re-create the animal's environment

*continued* ➤

Juris 4

or to provide proper nutrition, let alone care for the animals if they become sick or injured (Boehm). Very few professional veterinarians are trained or willing to work on wild animals.

Usually, infant wild animals are stolen from their parents at only a few weeks, or even days, of life. Their capture robs the babies of the chance to learn skills necessary for survival if they are ever abandoned or rereleased into the wild. These animals often develop stress and behavior disorders because they have never experienced social interaction with their own species ("Wild Animals Are Not Pets"). Eventually, many owners become frightened or confused by sudden behavior problems with their "little babies," and they decide to leave the animals in remote places to fend for themselves. Sadly, these animals never learned how to survive on their own. As a result, they starve to death, or they seek out human habitation for food, an act that frequently ends in their death at the hands of frightened people ("Wild Animals Do Not").

Some people may argue for the benefits of personal ownership of wild animals. It allows ordinary people to enjoy exotic pets in their own homes. These people insist that they can safely restrict their wild animals' movements to their own property. Further, defenders of the private possession of wild animals argue that owners can help preserve endangered species. Increasingly, however, exotic pet owners' fantasies turn into nightmares as the wild animals become adults controlled by their basic instincts and inbred behaviors. Owners often expect local animal control agencies or animal

*continued* ➤

sanctuaries to deal with their problems, even though such facilities are already over capacity or are staffed by people unequipped to deal with undomesticated animals (Milloy).

Keeping wild animals as pets must be outlawed. Though exotic creatures may look like Simba or Tigger, they are still completely wild, and it is in the wild that they belong. "Wild Animals Are Not Pets" points out, "The only ones who benefit from the practice of sales of exotic animals as pets are the breeders and sellers. These people make an enormous amount of money by exploiting these animals once they are sold." Poachers also profit when they capture baby wild animals from their native habitats and sell them as pets to the highest bidder. The best way for humans to see and experience wild animals in safe environments is to visit and support zoos and wildlife parks that specialize in providing professionally constructed natural habitats for animals. In such settings, people can enjoy the beauty and behaviors of wild animals without putting humans and the animals at risk.

*continued* ➣

Works Cited

Boehm, Ted. "A New Local Worry: Exotic Cats--Lion and Tiger Prices Fall, and Once Rare Pets Become a Costly Menace." Wall Street Journal 30 June 2000: B1.

Davenport, Christian. "Fighting the Lure of the Wild: Danger of Exotic Animals as Pets Spurs Quest for Regulation." Washington Post 11 Mar. 2002: B1.

"Kenya." Cat Tales Zoological Park. 1999. 19 Apr. 2005 <http://cattales.org/kenya.html>.

"Lil." Cat Tales Zoological Park. 1999. 19 Apr. 2005 <http://cattales.org/Lil.html>.

Milloy, Ross E. "Banning Lions and Other Large Pets." New York Times 10 Dec. 2001: A19.

"Questions and Answers about Captive Exotic and Wild Animals as Pets." Humane Society of the United States. 2002. 11 Apr. 2005 <http://www.hsus.org/wildlife/issues_facing_wildlife/captive_exotics_and_wild_animals_as_pets/index.html>.

"Rabies and Animal Bites." York County Virginia. 11 Apr. 2005. <http://www.yorkcounty.gov/fls/ac/rabies.htm>.

"Wild Animals Are Not Pets." Wild Animal Orphanage. 2004. 19 Apr. 2005 <http://www.wildanimalorphanage.org/notpets.html>.

"Wild Animals Do Not Make Good Pets." Cat Tales Zoological Park. 1999. 19 Apr. 2005 <http://cattales.org/notapet.html>.

# Chapter 6

## CRITICALLY ANALYZING IMAGES AND USING THEM

### 6a    How can I view images with a critical eye?

Our digital age surrounds us with images in publications, on computers, on television, on cell phones. These images shape attitudes and beliefs, often in subtle ways. Consider, for example, how our notions of beauty have been shaped through the years by countless pictures of certain shapes and sizes of people. As a result—and as we suggested in the beginning of Chapter 4—you need to use critical thinking to analyze images as well as words. Doing so heightens your sensitivity to how others use images and equips you to use them effectively yourself.

You can view images critically in the same way that you can read texts critically by using summary, analysis, synthesis, and evaluation (Box 4.1) and by using literal, inferential, and evaluative reading (Box 4.2). For example, look at Figure 6.1 with a critical eye.

Figure 6.1

- *Summarizing* the picture, as well as viewing it literally, you can see—at a minimum—a street full of older houses with modern skyscrapers in the distance.

- *Analyzing* the picture, as well as viewing it inferentially, you can "read between the lines" to see that it's fairly rich with layers of meaning. You can think about the meanings conveyed by the condition of the houses versus those of the modern buildings or about the lives of the people who live and work in each place. You can focus on the message of the comparative sizes of the houses and skyscrapers; on the contrast between this street and those you imagine at the base of the skyscrapers; on why the photographer chose this perspective; on how different captions might give the picture different meanings. For example, consider the differences among three different captions: "Progress," "Inequality," or

---

### SUMMARY BOX 6.1

## Some helpful questions for analyzing visual images

- What does the image show?

- What are its parts? Do the parts belong together (like a lake, trees, and mountains), or do they contrast with one another (like a woman in a fancy dress sitting on a tractor)? What might be the significance of the relationships among the parts?

- If there is a foreground and a background in the image, what is in each and why?

- If the image is a scene, what seems to be going on? What might be its message? If the image seems to be part of a story, what might have happened before or after?

- How do the people, if any, seem to be related? For example, do they appear to be friends, acquaintances, or strangers?

- If the image has a variety of shadings, colorings, and focuses, what's sharply in focus, blurry, bright, in shadows, colorful, or drab? How do such differences, or lack of them, call attention to various parts of the image?

- Can you think of any connections between the image and things you've experienced or learned from school, work, or reading; visits to museums or other cultural sites; watching movies, plays, and television; or other aspects of your life?

- From your observations, what is your evaluation of the image?

"The Neighborhood." Many possible ideas can come to mind as you study the picture critically.

- *Synthesizing* the picture, you can connect what you've analyzed and inferred to what you associate with ideas you've learned from various life experiences.

- *Evaluating* the picture is the last step in viewing it critically. Resist evaluating prematurely because after you go through the earlier steps of thinking and reading critically, your evaluation becomes informed by more than a noncritical personal reaction such as "I do/don't like the picture." In evaluating a visual critically, you can speak of how the visual "struck" you at first glance; how it did or didn't gain depth of meaning as you analyzed it, looking at what could be inferred and/or imagined; and how it lent itself to synthesis within the realms of your personal experience and education.

**EXERCISE 6-1** Working individually or with a peer-response group, use critical thinking to consider one or both of the following photographs: Figure 6.2 below and Figure 6.3 on page 174. Write either informal notes or a mini-essay, according to what your instructor requires. Use the questions in Box 6.1 to generate your summary, analysis, synthesis, and evaluation of the photograph(s).

Figure 6.2

Figure 6.3

## 6b    How can images persuade?

Because they convey lots of information in a short space, and because they can generate powerful emotional responses (*pathos*), images play a strong role in persuasion. (Just think about advertising!) Sometimes persuasion comes through a single well-chosen image: a picture of a bruised child's face demonstrates the cruelty of child abuse; a picture of a grateful civilian hugging a soldier seeks to show that a military action is just and good. In their campaign ads, politicians frequently choose highly unflattering photographs of their opponents, hoping to make them look foolish, incompetent, or unpleasant.

Figure 6.4 is a photograph of a pile of rusted barrels in a beautiful natural setting. The contrast between the barrels and the snow-covered mountains in the background, the lake, and the blue sky is stark and alarming. The barrels stand between viewers and the stunning scenery; people can't ignore or look around them. The photographer has created this contrastive image to persuade you—but to what purpose? Perhaps this photo is an argument against pollution. Perhaps it's an argument against industrial development. Perhaps it's an argument saying that people can act carelessly. While images can be powerful, they're often more ambiguous than words; images can't state what they mean, although they can move viewers in certain fairly predictable directions. In Figure 6.4, you know that the photographer intends to disturb you.

Frequently, people use a series of images to persuade. Some magazines use photo essays, two or more pictures meant to be viewed in a

Figure 6.4

specific order to achieve a desired effect. An editorial cartoon might include two or more panels to make its point. More often than not, photo essays and editorials include captions or other words along with the images themselves.

## 6c How can I analyze words combined with images?

Many texts—from Web pages to advertisements, posters, brochures, and so on—are **multimodal** in that they combine words and images. These texts can take advantage of *logos* and *ethos*, in addition to the *pathos* (5g) readily created by pictures alone. Critically analyzing multimodal texts means considering the images (Box 6.1) and the words separately, and then analyzing how the two elements combine to create a single effect.

Ask yourself, "What is the relationship between the words and the image(s)?" and "Why did the writer choose this particular image for these particular words?"

- Sometimes words and images reinforce one another. A poster with several sentences about poverty, for example, may have a picture of an obviously malnourished person.
- Other times, words and images contrast with one another for effect. Think of a picture of a belching smokestack accompanied by a caption that says, "Everyone deserves fresh air."
- Occasionally, a text might contain images simply to add visual interest. A little decoration is sometimes fine, but always be wary of images that

seem simply to be thrown in for the sake of including an image. If there isn't a good reason for a particular combination of words and images, chances are that the document or message is weak.

Document design is the name given to the overall arrangement of words and visuals in a text. Chapters 42 and 43 explain several principles of document design.

**EXERCISE 6-2** Working individually or with a peer-response group, use critical thinking to analyze either or both of the visual arguments that follow. Write either informal notes or a mini-essay, according to what your instructor requires.

## 6d   What can images add to my writing?

Occasionally, you might be tempted to add images to your writing because you want to add visual interest. That is a laudable goal, as long as the images support or enhance the message your writing is trying to deliver. Always, however, be wary of throwing in one or more images merely for the sake of including an image. Your readers will rightly assume your images are communicating a message related to the text, and if none emerges, your entire document loses credibility. The best rule for inserting a photograph or other type of illustration into an essay is "When in doubt, leave it out."

For example, look at the student source-based essay "Lions, Tigers, and Bears, Oh My!" that ends Chapter 5 of this book. Notice the photograph

177

of a tiger roaring in the wild. Does where the student placed it in the essay reinforce the idea that people shouldn't raise wild exotic animals as pets? Now looking at the photo of an African serval (leaping cat), read the paragraph that starts with the topic sentence "Many animal owners teach their young exotic pets little games and tricks." What if anything do you think this photograph adds to the student's paper? Finally, suppose the student had inserted into her essay the photograph of a lion in a cage in a zoo. Would you have thought that image appropriate?

Another example of an essay to think about for images is the MLA-style research paper in Chapter 34. What sorts of images might you think appropriate to enhance the content of that essay?

As you think about whether to include images in your papers, consult Chapter 42, which discusses DOCUMENT DESIGN, the overall, well-planned arrangement of words and visuals in a text. The chapter explains several principles of document design that will help you if you do want to consider using images in your essays.

# Understanding Grammar and Writing Correct Sentences

# Chapter 7

## PARTS OF SPEECH AND SENTENCE STRUCTURES

### PARTS OF SPEECH

#### 7a  Why learn the parts of speech?

Knowing the names and definitions of parts of speech gives you a vocabulary for identifying words and understanding how language works to create meaning. No part of speech exists in a vacuum. To identify a word's part of speech correctly, you need to see how the word functions in a sentence. Sometimes the same word functions differently in different sentences, so check the part of speech used in each instance.

> We ate **fish**. [*Fish* is a noun. It names a thing.]
>
> We **fish** on weekends. [*Fish* is a verb. It names an action.]

#### 7b  What is a noun?

A **noun** names a person, place, thing, or idea: *student, college, textbook, education.* Box 7.1 lists different kinds of nouns.

 **ESL TIPS:** Here are some useful tips for working with nouns.

- Nouns often appear with words that tell how much or how many, whose, which one, and similar information. These words include ARTICLES* (*a, an, the*) and other determiners or limiting adjectives; see 7f and Chapter 46.
- Nouns sometimes serve as ADJECTIVES. For example, in the term *police officer,* the word *police* serves as an adjective to describe *officer.*

---

*Words printed in SMALL CAPITAL LETTERS are discussed elsewhere in the text and are defined in the Terms Glossary at the back of this book.

- Nouns in many languages other than English are inflected. This means they change form, usually with a special ending, to communicate gender (male, female, neuter); number (singular, plural); and case (see 9a through 9k).
- Words with these suffixes (word endings) are usually nouns: *-ness, -ence, -ance, -ty,* and *-ment.*

---

**SUMMARY BOX** **7.1**

## Nouns

| | | |
|---|---|---|
| **PROPER** | names specific people, places, or things (first letter is always capitalized) | *Garth Brooks, Paris, Buick* |
| **COMMON** | names general groups, places, people, or things | *singer, city, automobile* |
| **CONCRETE** | names things experienced through the senses: sight, hearing, taste, smell, and touch | *landscape, pizza, thunder* |
| **ABSTRACT** | names things not knowable through the senses | *freedom, shyness* |
| **COLLECTIVE** | names groups | *family, team* |
| **NONCOUNT OR MASS** | names "uncountable" things | *water, time* |
| **COUNT** | names countable items | *lake, minute* |

---

## 7c What is a pronoun?

A **pronoun** takes the place of a NOUN. The words or word that a pronoun replaces is called the pronoun's ANTECEDENT. See Box 7.2 (p. 182) for a list of different kinds of pronouns. For information on how to use pronouns correctly, see Chapters 9 and 10.

**David** is an accountant. [The noun *David* names a person.]

**He** is an accountant. [The pronoun *he* refers to its antecedent, *David.*]

The finance committee needs to consult **him**. [The pronoun *him* refers to its antecedent, *David.*]

**SUMMARY BOX** 7.2

## Pronouns

| | | |
|---|---|---|
| **PERSONAL** <br> *I, you, its, her,* <br> *they, ours,* <br> and others | refers to people or things | *I saw **her** take a book to **them**.* |
| **RELATIVE** <br> *who, which, that* | introduces certain <br> NOUN CLAUSES and <br> ADJECTIVE CLAUSES | *The book **that** I lost was valuable.* |
| **INTERROGATIVE** <br> *which, who,* <br> *whose,* and others | introduces a question | ***Who** called?* |
| **DEMONSTRATIVE** <br> *this, that, these,* <br> *those* | points out the antecedent | *Whose books are **these**?* |
| **REFLEXIVE** <br> **OR INTENSIVE** <br> *myself, themselves,* <br> and other *-self* or <br> *-selves* words | reflects back to the <br> antecedent; intensifies <br> the antecedent | *They claim to support **themselves**. **I myself** doubt it.* |
| **RECIPROCAL** <br> *each other,* <br> *one another* | refers to individual parts of <br> a plural antecedent | *We respect **each other**.* |
| **INDEFINITE** <br> *all, anyone, each,* <br> and others | refers to nonspecific <br> persons or things | ***Everyone** is welcome here.* |

**EXERCISE 7-1**    Underline and label all nouns (N) and pronouns (P). Refer to 7a through 7c for help.

EXAMPLE
<pre>
       P    N                    P          N            N
My mother celebrated her eightieth birthday this summer with
 P    N           N      P                    N
her family and friends; she greatly enjoyed the festivities.
</pre>

1. More and more people live into their eighties and nineties because they get better health benefits and they take better care of themselves.

2. Many elderly people now live busy lives, continuing in businesses or volunteering at various agencies.

3. My mother, Elizabeth, for example, spends four hours each morning as a volunteer for the Red Cross, where she takes histories from blood donors.

4. My neighbors, George and Sandra, who are eighty-six years old, still own and run a card and candy shop.

5. Age has become no obstacle for active seniors as evidenced by the activities they pursue today.

## 7d   What is a verb?

**Main verbs** express action, occurrence, or state of being. For information on how to use verbs correctly, see Chapter 8.

I **dance**. [action]

The audience **became** silent. [occurrence]

Your dancing **was** excellent. [state of being]

**ALERT:** If you're not sure whether a word is a verb, try substituting a different TENSE for the word. If the sentence still makes sense, the word is a verb.

**NO**   He is a **changed** man. He is a **will change** man. [*Changed* isn't a verb because the sentence doesn't make sense when *will change* is substituted.]

**YES**   The man **changed** his profession. The man **will change** his profession. [*Changed* is a verb because the sentence makes sense when the verb *will change* is substituted.] ◆

**EXERCISE 7-2**   Underline all main verbs. Refer to 7d for help.

**EXAMPLE**   The study of bats <u>produces</u> some surprising information.

1. Most bats developed many years ago from a shrew-like mammal.
2. One thousand different types of bats exist.
3. Bats comprise almost one quarter of all mammal species.
4. The smallest bat in the world measures only one inch long, while the biggest is sixteen inches long.
5. Bats survive in widely varied surroundings, from deserts to cities.

## 7e What is a verbal?

**Verbals** are verb parts functioning as NOUNS, ADJECTIVES, or ADVERBS. Box 7.3 lists the three different kinds of verbals.

---

**SUMMARY BOX 7.3**

### Verbals and their functions

| | | |
|---|---|---|
| **INFINITIVE**<br>*to* + verb | 1. noun<br>2. adjective or adverb | ***To eat** now is inconvenient.*<br>*Still, we have far **to go**.* |
| **PAST PARTICIPLE**<br>*-ed* form of REGULAR VERB or equivalent in IRREGULAR VERB | adjective | ***Boiled**, **filtered** water is safe.* |
| **PRESENT PARTICIPLE**<br>*-ing* form of verb | 1. noun (called a GERUND)<br>2. adjective | ***Eating** in diners on the road is an adventure.*<br>***Running** water may not be safe.* |

---

**ESL TIP:** For information about correctly using the verbals called *infinitives* and *gerunds* as objects, see Chapter 50.

## 7f What is an adjective?

**Adjectives** modify—that is, they describe or limit—NOUNS, PRONOUNS, and word groups that function as nouns. For information on how to use adjectives correctly, see Chapter 11.

I saw a **green** tree. [*Green* modifies the noun *tree*.]

It was **leafy**. [*Leafy* modifies the pronoun *it*.]

The flowering trees were **beautiful**. [*Beautiful* modifies the noun phrase *the flowering trees*.]

**ESL TIP:** You can identify some kinds of adjectives by looking at their endings. Usually, words with the SUFFIXES *-ful*, *-ish*, *-less*, and *-like* are adjectives.

**Determiners**, frequently called **limiting adjectives**, tell whether a noun is general (*a* tree) or specific (*the* tree). Determiners also tell which one (*this* tree), how many (*twelve* trees), whose (*our* tree), and similar information.

The determiners *a, an,* and *the* are almost always called **articles**. *The* is a **definite article**. Before a noun, *the* conveys that the noun refers to a specific item (*the* plan). *A* and *an* are **indefinite articles**. They convey that a noun refers to an item in a nonspecific or general way (*a* plan).

**ALERT:** Use *a* when the word following it starts with a consonant: *a carrot, a broken egg, a hip.* Also, use *a* when the word following starts with an *h* that is sounded: *a historical event, a home.* Use *an* when the word following starts with a vowel sound: *an honor, an old bag, an egg.* ◆

**ESL TIP:** For information about using articles with COUNT and NONCOUNT NOUNS, and about articles with PROPER NOUNS and GERUNDS, see Chapter 47. 🌐

Box 7.4 lists kinds of determiners. Notice, however, that some words in Box 7.4 function also as pronouns. To identify a word's part of speech, always check to see how it functions in each particular sentence.

**That** car belongs to Harold. [*That* is a limiting adjective.]

**That** is Harold's car. [*That* is a demonstrative pronoun.]

---

**SUMMARY BOX** 7.4

### Determiners (or limiting adjectives)

| | |
|---|---|
| **ARTICLES**<br>*a, an, the* | *The news reporter used **a** cell phone to report **an** assignment.* |
| **DEMONSTRATIVE**<br>*this, these, that, those* | *Those students rent that house.* |
| **INDEFINITE**<br>*any, each, few, other,*<br>*some,* and others | *Few films today have complex plots.* |
| **INTERROGATIVE**<br>*what, which, whose* | *What answer did you give?* |
| **NUMERICAL**<br>*one, first, two, second,*<br>and others | *The fifth question was tricky.* |
| **POSSESSIVE**<br>*my, your, their,* and others | *My violin is older than your cello.* |
| **RELATIVE**<br>*what, which, whose,*<br>*whatever,* and others | *We do not know which road to take.* |

## 7g What is an adverb?

**Adverbs** modify—that is, adverbs describe or limit—VERBS, ADJECTIVES, other adverbs, and CLAUSES. For information on how to use adverbs correctly, see Chapter 11.

Chefs plan meals **carefully**. [*Carefully* modifies the verb *plan*.]

Vegetables provide **very** important vitamins. [*Very* modifies the adjective *important*.]

Those potato chips are **too** heavily salted. [*Too* modifies the adverb *heavily*.]

**Fortunately**, people are learning that overuse of salt is harmful. [*Fortunately* modifies the rest of the sentence, an independent clause.]

**Descriptive adverbs** show levels of intensity, usually by adding *more* (or *less*) and *most* (or *least*): *more* happily, *least* clearly (11e). Many descriptive adverbs are formed by adding -*ly* to adjectives: *sadly, loudly, normally*. But many adverbs do not end in -*ly*: *very, always, not, yesterday*, and *well* are a few. Some adjectives look like adverbs but are not: *brotherly, lonely, lovely*.

**Relative adverbs** are words such as *where, why,* and *when*. They are used to introduce ADJECTIVE CLAUSES.

**Conjunctive adverbs** modify—that is, conjunctive adverbs describe or limit—by creating logical connections to give words meaning. Conjunctive adverbs can appear anywhere in a sentence: at the start, in the middle, or at the end.

**However**, we consider Isaac Newton an even more important scientist.

We consider Isaac Newton, **however**, an even more important scientist.

We consider Isaac Newton an even more important scientist, **however**.

Box 7.5 lists the kinds of relationships that conjunctive adverbs can show.

**SUMMARY BOX** 7.5

### Conjunctive adverbs and relationships they express

| RELATIONSHIP | WORDS |
|---|---|
| ADDITION | *also, furthermore, moreover, besides* |
| CONTRAST | *however, still, nevertheless, conversely, nonetheless, instead, otherwise* |
| COMPARISON | *similarly, likewise* |
| RESULT OR SUMMARY | *therefore, thus, consequently, accordingly, hence, then* |
| TIME | *next, then, meanwhile, finally, subsequently* |
| EMPHASIS | *indeed, certainly* |

**EXERCISE 7-3**    Underline and label all adjectives (ADJ) and adverbs (ADV). For help, consult 7e through 7g.

ADJ                                          ADJ
**EXAMPLE**    Scientific evidence shows that massage therapy can
                        ADV                         ADJ
                dramatically improve people's health.

1. Premature babies who are massaged gently gain 47 percent more weight than babies who do not receive touch treatment.

2. Frequently, massaged premature babies go home from the hospital sooner, saving an average of $10,000 per baby.

3. Also, daily massage helps many people with stomach problems digest their food easily because important hormones are released during the rubdown.

4. People with the HIV virus find their weakened immune system significantly improved by targeted massage.

5. In addition, massage treatments have helped people with asthma breathe more freely.

## 7h    What is a preposition?

**Prepositions** are words that convey relationships, usually in time or space. Common prepositions include *in, under, by, after, to, on, over,* and *since.* A PREPOSITIONAL PHRASE consists of a preposition and the words it modifies. For information about prepositions and commas, see 24k.2.

> **In the fall**, we will hear a concert **by our favorite tenor**.
>
> **After the concert**, he will fly **to San Francisco**.

**ESL TIP:** For a list of prepositions and the IDIOMS they create, see Chapter 49.

## 7i    What is a conjunction?

A **conjunction** connects words, PHRASES, or CLAUSES. **Coordinating conjunctions** join two or more grammatically equal words, phrases, or clauses. Box 7.6 (p. 188) lists the coordinating conjunctions and the relationships they express.

> We hike **and** camp every summer. [*And* joins two words.]
>
> We hike along scenic trails **or** in the wilderness. [*Or* joins two phrases.]
>
> I love the outdoors, **but** my family does not. [*But* joins two independent clauses.]

**SUMMARY BOX 7.6**

### Coordinating conjunctions and relationships they express

| RELATIONSHIP | WORDS |
|---|---|
| ADDITION | *and* |
| CONTRAST | *but, yet* |
| RESULT OR EFFECT | *so* |
| REASON OR CAUSE | *for* |
| CHOICE | *or* |
| NEGATIVE CHOICE | *nor* |

**Correlative conjunctions** are two conjunctions that work as a pair: *both . . . and; either . . . or; neither . . . nor; not only . . . but (also); whether . . . or;* and *not . . . so much as.*

**Both** English **and** Spanish are spoken in many homes in the United States.

**Not only** students **but also** businesspeople should study a second language.

**Subordinating conjunctions** introduce DEPENDENT CLAUSES. Subordinating conjunctions express relationships making the dependent clause in a sentence grammatically less important than the INDEPENDENT CLAUSE in the sentence. Box 7.7 lists the most common subordinating conjunctions. For information about how to use them correctly, see 17e through 17h.

**SUMMARY BOX 7.7**

### Subordinating conjunctions and relationships they express

| RELATIONSHIP | WORDS |
|---|---|
| TIME | *after, before, once, since, until, when, whenever, while* |
| REASON OR CAUSE | *as, because, since* |
| RESULT OR EFFECT | *in order that, so, so that, that* |
| CONDITION | *if, even if, provided that, unless* |
| CONTRAST | *although, even though, though, whereas* |
| LOCATION | *where, wherever* |
| CHOICE | *than, whether* |

**Because** it snowed, school was canceled.

Many people were happy **after** they heard the news.

## 7j   What is an interjection?

An **interjection** is a word or expression that conveys surprise or a strong emotion. Alone, an interjection is usually punctuated with an exclamation point (!). As part of a sentence, an interjection is usually set off by one or more commas.

**Hooray!** I won the race.

**Oh**, my friends missed seeing the finish.

**EXERCISE 7-4**   Identify the part of speech of each numbered and under-lined word. Choose from noun, pronoun, verb, adjective, adverb, preposi-tion, coordinating conjunction, correlative conjunction, and subordinating conjunction. For help, consult 7b through 7i.

The geneticist Barbara McClintock was a nonconformist[1]. She

preferred[2] the company of[3] the corn plants that she[4] eagerly studied to

the companionship[5] of many of the people she knew. When she won

the Nobel Prize in 1983, she learned of it over the radio because[6] she

had no telephone.

McClintock worked alone[7] throughout her fifty-year career at the

Cold Spring Harbor Laboratory in[8] New York. In the 1940s and[9] 1950s,

McClintock discovered[10] that parts of chromosomes break off and

recombine[11] with neighboring[12] chromosomes to create unique[13] genetic

combinations. This process, known as[14] crossing over, amazed

scientists and demonstrated that chromosomes formed the basis

of genetics. Still, scientists resisted McClintock's findings and did not

recognize the importance of[15] her research for many years[16]. Only after[17]

geneticists found[18] crossing over genes in both[19] plants and animals was the great value of McClintock's discovery acknowledged. Thirty to forty

years later, she won[20] the 1983 Nobel Prize for her groundbreaking

achievement.

Overall, McClintock's life was lonely[21], but her career was very[22]

productive. By the time of her death in 1992, her colleagues had

finally[23] come[24] to realize that Barbara McClintock was one[25] of the

towering giants of genetics.

## SENTENCE STRUCTURES

### 7k How is a sentence defined?

A **sentence** is defined in several ways: On a strictly mechanical level, a sentence starts with a capital letter and finishes with a period, question mark, or exclamation point. Grammatically, a sentence consists of an INDEPENDENT CLAUSE: *Skydiving is dangerous.* You might hear a sentence described as a "complete thought," but that definition is too vague to help much. From the perspective of its purpose, a sentence is defined as listed in Box 7.8.

---

**SUMMARY BOX 7.8**

**Sentences and their purposes**

- A **declarative sentence**
  makes a statement:           *Skydiving is dangerous.*

- An **interrogative sentence**
  asks a question:             *Is skydiving dangerous?*

- An **imperative sentence**
  gives a command:             *Be careful when you skydive.*

- An **exclamatory sentence**
  expresses strong feeling:    *How I love skydiving!*

---

### 7l What are a subject and a predicate in a sentence?

The **subject** and **predicate** of a sentence are its two essential parts. Without both, a group of words isn't a sentence. Box 7.9 shows the sentence pattern with both. Terms used in the box are defined after it.

## Sentence pattern I: Subjects and predicates

- Complete Subject     +     Complete Predicate

  The red telephone        rang loudly.

  ↑    SIMPLE SUBJECT       ↑ SIMPLE PREDICATE (VERB)

- Complete Subject     +     Complete Predicate

  The telephone and the doorbell     rang loudly.

  COMPOUND SUBJECT

- Complete Subject     +     Complete Predicate

  The red telephone     rang and startled everyone in the room.

  COMPOUND PREDICATE

The **simple subject** is the word or group of words that acts, is described, or is acted upon.

The **telephone** rang. [Simple subject, *telephone*, acts.]

The **telephone** is red. [Simple subject, *telephone*, is described.]

The **telephone** was being connected. [Simple subject, *telephone*, is acted upon.]

The **complete subject** is the simple subject and its MODIFIERS.

**The red telephone** rang.

A **complete compound subject** consists of two or more NOUNS or PRONOUNS and their modifiers.

**The telephone and the doorbell** rang.

The **predicate** contains the VERB in the sentence. The predicate tells what the subject is doing or experiencing or what is being done to the subject.

The telephone **rang**. [*Rang* tells what the subject, *telephone*, did.]

The telephone **is** red. [*Is* tells what the subject, *telephone*, experiences.]

The telephone **was being connected**. [*Was being connected* tells what was being done to the subject, *telephone*.]

A **simple predicate** contains only the verb.

> The lawyer **listened**.

A **complete predicate** contains the verb and its modifiers.

> The lawyer **listened carefully**.

A **compound predicate** contains two or more verbs.

> The lawyer **listened and waited**.

**ESL TIPS:** (1) The subject of a declarative sentence usually comes before the predicate, but there are exceptions (19e). In sentences that ask a question, part of the predicate usually comes before the subject. For more information about word order in English sentences, see Chapter 48. (2) In English, don't add a PERSONAL PRONOUN to repeat the stated noun.

> **NO** My **grandfather he** lived to be eighty-seven. [The personal pronoun, *he,* mistakenly repeats the stated noun, *grandfather.*]
>
> **YES** My **grandfather** lived to be eighty-seven.
>
> **NO** **Winter storms** that bring ice, sleet, and snow **they** can cause traffic problems. [The personal pronoun, *they,* mistakenly repeats the stated noun, *winter storms.*]
>
> **YES** **Winter storms** that bring ice, sleet, and snow can cause traffic problems. 🌐

**EXERCISE 7-5**  Use a slash to separate the complete subject from the complete predicate. For help, consult 7I.

> **EXAMPLE**  A smart shopper / is an intelligent, well-informed consumer.

1. Wise consumers use the Internet to compare prices to discover the best values available.
2. Smart clothing shoppers keep their eyes on the sale racks.
3. They buy summer clothes in the winter and winter clothes in the summer.
4. The financial savings make them content to wait a few months to wear their new clothes.
5. Another good way to earn money for clothing is for people to sell their good used clothing to a resale store.

## 7m   What are direct and indirect objects?

A **direct object** is a noun, pronoun, or group of words acting as a noun that receives the action of a TRANSITIVE VERB. To check for a direct object, make up a *whom?* or *what?* question about the verb.

An **indirect object** is a noun, pronoun, or group of words acting as a noun that tells *to whom* or *for whom* the action expressed by a transitive verb was done. To check for an indirect object, make up a *to whom? for whom? to what?* or *for what?* question about the verb.

Direct objects and indirect objects always fall in the PREDICATE of a sentence. Box 7.10 shows how direct and indirect objects function in sentences.

---

**PATTERN BOX 7.10**

### Sentence pattern II: Direct and indirect objects

- Complete Subject        +        Complete Predicate

  The caller                                   offered    money.
                                                  ↑           ↑
                                                VERB    DIRECT OBJECT

- Complete Subject        +        Complete Predicate

  The caller                        offered the lawyer money.
                                          ↑         ↑        ↑
                                        VERB   INDIRECT  DIRECT
                                                OBJECT   OBJECT

- Complete Subject        +        Complete Predicate

  The client                        sent a retainer to the lawyer.
                                        ↑       ↑              ↑
                                      VERB   DIRECT       INDIRECT
                                             OBJECT        OBJECT

---

**ESL TIPS:** (1) In sentences with indirect objects that follow the word *to* or *for,* always put the direct object before the indirect object.

**NO**   Will you please give **to John** this letter?

**YES**   Will you please give this letter **to John**?

(2) When a PRONOUN is used as an indirect object, some verbs require *to* or *for* before the pronoun, and others do not. Consult the *Dictionary of American English* (Heinle and Heinle) about each verb when you're unsure.

| **NO** | Please explain **me** the rule. [*Explain* requires *to* before an indirect object.] |
| **YES** | Please explain the rule **to me**. |
| **YES** | Please give **me** that book. Please give that book **to me**. [*Give* uses both patterns.] |

(3) When both the direct object and the indirect object are pronouns, put the direct object first and use *to* with the indirect object.

| **NO** | He gave **me it**. |
| **YES** | He gave **it to me**. |
| **YES** | Please give **me the letter**. [*Give* does not require *to* before an indirect object.] |

(4) Even if a verb does not require *to* before an indirect object, you may use *to* if you prefer. If you do use *to,* be sure to put the direct object before the indirect object.

| **YES** | Our daughter sent **our son** a gift. |
| **YES** | Our daughter sent a gift **to our son**. 🌐 |

**EXERCISE 7-6**   Draw a single line under all direct objects and a double line under all indirect objects. For help, consult 7m.

**EXAMPLE**   Toni Morrison's award-winning novels give <u><u>readers</u></u> the <u>gifts</u> of wisdom, inspiration, and pleasure.

1. Literary critics gave high praise to Toni Morrison for her first novel, *The Bluest Eye,* but the general public showed little interest.

2. *Song of Solomon* won Morrison the National Book Critics Circle Award in 1977, and *Beloved* won her the Pulitzer Prize in 1988.

3. A literary panel awarded Toni Morrison the 1993 Nobel Prize in Literature, the highest honor a writer can receive.

4. Her 1998 novel, *Paradise,* traces for readers the tragic lives of a rejected group of former slaves.

5. Twenty-five years after *The Bluest Eye* was published, Oprah Winfrey selected it for her reader's list, and it immediately became a bestseller.

## 7n   What are complements, modifiers, and appositives?

### COMPLEMENTS

A **complement** renames or describes a SUBJECT or an OBJECT. It appears in the PREDICATE of a sentence.

A **subject complement** is a NOUN, PRONOUN, or ADJECTIVE that follows a LINKING VERB. **Predicate nominative** is another term for a noun used as a subject complement, and **predicate adjective** is another term for an adjective used as a subject complement.

An **object complement** follows a DIRECT OBJECT and either describes or renames the direct object. Box 7.11 shows how subject and object complements function in a sentence.

---

**PATTERN BOX** 7.11

## Sentence pattern III: Complements

- Complete Subject     +      Complete Predicate

  The caller        was a student.

         ↑    ↑

         LINKING   SUBJECT
         VERB   COMPLEMENT

- Complete Subject     +      Complete Predicate

  The student        called himself a victim.

         ↑    ↑    ↑

         VERB   DIRECT   OBJECT
            OBJECT   COMPLEMENT

---

**EXERCISE 7-7**   Underline all complements and identify each as a subject complement (SUB) or an object complement (OB).

**EXAMPLE**   Many of the most familiar North American wildflowers are

              SUB
      actually nonnative <u>plants</u>.

1. The dainty Queen Anne's lace is a native of Europe.
2. The daisies and cornflowers that decorate our roadsides all summer were originally inhabitants of Europe as well.
3. The common purple loosestrife, originally from Asia, came to the North American continent as a garden plant.
4. Many scientists call these plants "alien invasives."
5. Many ecologists consider them threats to the forests, meadows, and wetlands of North America.

## MODIFIERS

A **modifier** is a word or group of words that describes or limits other words. Modifiers appear in the SUBJECT or the PREDICATE of a sentence.

195

The **large red** telephone rang. [The adjectives *large* and *red* modify the noun *telephone*.]

The lawyer answered **quickly**. [The adverb *quickly* modifies the verb *answered*.]

The person **on the telephone** was **extremely** upset. [The prepositional phrase *on the telephone* modifies the noun *person;* the adverb *extremely* modifies the adjective *upset*.]

**Therefore**, the lawyer spoke **gently**. [The adverb *therefore* modifies the independent clause *the lawyer spoke gently;* the adverb *gently* modifies the verb *spoke*.]

**Because the lawyer's voice was calm**, the caller felt reassured. [The adverb clause *because the lawyer's voice was calm* modifies the independent clause *the caller felt reassured*.]

## APPOSITIVES

An **appositive** is a word or group of words that renames the NOUN or PRONOUN preceding it.

The student's story, **a tale of broken promises**, was complicated. [The appositive *a tale of broken promises* renames the noun *story*.]

The lawyer consulted an expert, **her law professor**. [The appositive *her law professor* renames the noun *expert*.]

The student, **Joe Jones**, asked to speak to his lawyer. [The appositive *Joe Jones* renames the noun *student*.]

**ALERT:** When an appositive is not essential for identifying what it renames (that is, when it is NONRESTRICTIVE), use a comma or commas to set off the appositive from the rest of the sentence; see 24f. ◆

## 70   What is a phrase?

A **phrase** is a group of words that does not contain both a SUBJECT and a PREDICATE and therefore cannot stand alone as an independent unit.

### NOUN PHRASE

A **noun phrase** functions as a NOUN in a sentence.

The **modern census** dates back to the seventeenth century.

### VERB PHRASE

A **verb phrase** functions as a VERB in a sentence.

Two military censuses **are mentioned** in the Bible.

## PREPOSITIONAL PHRASE

A **prepositional phrase** always starts with a PREPOSITION and functions as a MODIFIER.

> William the Conqueror conducted a census **of landowners in newly conquered England in 1086**. [three prepositional phrases in a row, beginning with *of, in, in*]

## ABSOLUTE PHRASE

An **absolute phrase** usually contains a noun or PRONOUN and a PRESENT or PAST PARTICIPLE. An absolute phrase modifies the entire sentence that it's in.

> **Censuses being the fashion**, Quebec and Nova Scotia took sixteen counts between 1665 and 1754.

> Eighteenth-century Sweden and Denmark had complete records of their populations, **each adult and child having been counted**.

## VERBAL PHRASE

A **verbal phrase** contains a verb part that functions not as a verb, but as a noun or an ADJECTIVE. Such cases are INFINITIVES, present participles, and past participles.

> In 1624, Virginia began **to count its citizens** in a census. [*To count its citizens* is an infinitive phrase.]

> **Going from door to door**, census takers interview millions of people. [*Going from door to door* is a present participial phrase.]

> **Amazed by some people's answers**, census takers always listen carefully. [*Amazed by some people's answers* is a past participial phrase.]

## GERUND PHRASE

A **gerund phrase** functions as a noun. Telling the difference between a gerund phrase and a present participial phrase can be tricky because both use the *-ing* verb form. The key is to determine how the phrase functions in the sentence: A gerund phrase functions only as a noun, and a participial phrase functions only as a modifier.

> **Including each person in the census** was important. [This is a gerund phrase because it functions as a noun, which is the subject of the sentence.]

> **Including each person in the census**, Abby spent many hours on the crowded city block. [This is a present participial phrase because it functions as a modifier, namely, an adjective describing Abby.]

**EXERCISE 7-8** Combine each set of sentences into a single sentence by converting one sentence into a phrase—a noun phrase, verb phrase, prepositional phrase, absolute phrase, verbal phrase, or gerund phrase. You can omit, add, or change words. Identify which type of phrase you created.

You can combine most sets in several correct ways, but make sure the meaning of your finished sentence is clear. For help, consult 7o.

EXAMPLE    Large chain stores often pose threats to local independent retailers. Smaller store owners must find innovative ways to stay in business.

*With large chains posing threats to local independent retailers,* smaller store owners must find innovative ways to stay in business. (prepositional phrase)

1. Independent stores develop creative marketing strategies to compete with chain stores. Independent stores figure out ways to offer special features.

2. One independent children's bookstore attracted new customers. It did that by bringing live animals into the store.

3. Animals are popular with children. The store purchased two pet chickens, plus tarantulas, rats, cats, and fish.

4. This children's bookstore did not need to lower prices to draw customers. The store could survive by owning animals that appeal to youngsters.

5. Other sorts of independent stores sometimes take a slightly different approach. They compete by offering better service than the large chain stores can.

6. For example, independent hardware and housewares stores can be service-oriented and customer friendly. They sometimes can thrive financially doing this.

7. Many independent hardware and housewares store owners have begun to offer home-repair and decorating advice as well as to recommend house calls from staff members. They do this to attract and hold customers.

8. These store owners also feature high-end items that chains do not carry. They feature in-store displays and advertise heavily about their high-end items.

9. Independent hardware and housewares stores often stock fine items such as expensive lawn ornaments, costly brand-name paints, and rare Italian tiles. These stores tend to attract wealthier customers.

### 7p    What is a clause?

A **clause** is a group of words with both a SUBJECT and a PREDICATE. Clauses can be either *independent clauses,* also called *main clauses,* or *dependent clauses,* also called *subordinate clauses.*

## INDEPENDENT CLAUSES

An **independent clause** contains a subject and a predicate and can stand alone as a sentence. Box 7.12 shows the basic pattern.

---

**PATTERN BOX 7.12**

### Sentence pattern IV: Independent clauses

Independent Clause

| • Complete Subject | + | Complete Predicate |
|---|---|---|
| The telephone | | rang. |

---

## DEPENDENT CLAUSES

A **dependent clause** contains a subject and a predicate but can't stand alone as a sentence. To be part of a complete sentence, a dependent clause must be joined to an independent clause. Dependent clauses are either *adverb clauses* or *adjective clauses.*

## ADVERB CLAUSES

An **adverb clause**, also called a *subordinate clause,* starts with a SUB-ORDINATING CONJUNCTION, such as *although, because, when,* or *until.* A subordinating conjunction expresses a relationship between a dependent clause and an independent clause; see Box 7.7 in section 7i. Adverb clauses usually answer some question about the independent clause: *How? Why? When? Under what circumstances?*

> **If the bond issue passes**, the city will install sewers. [The adverb clause modifies the verb phrase *will install;* it explains under what circumstances.]

> They are drawing up plans **as quickly as they can**. [The adverb clause modifies the verb phrase *drawing up;* it explains how.]

> The homeowners feel happier **because they know the flooding will soon be better controlled**. [The adverb clause modifies the entire independent clause; it explains why.]

**ALERT:** When you write an adverb clause before an independent clause, separate the clauses with a comma; see 24c. ◆

## ADJECTIVE CLAUSES

An **adjective clause**, also called a *relative clause,* starts with a RELATIVE PRONOUN, such as *who, which,* or *that.* Or an adjective clause can start with a RELATIVE ADVERB, such as *when* or *where.* An adjective clause

---

**PATTERN BOX** **7.13**

## Sentence pattern V: Dependent clauses

- Dependent (Adverb) Clause    +    Independent Clause

| **Although** | the hour | was quite late, | the telephone | rang. |

↑ SUBORDINATING CONJUNCTION    ↑ COMPLETE SUBJECT    ↑ COMPLETE PREDICATE    ↑ COMPLETE SUBJECT    ↑ COMPLETE PREDICATE

- First Part of Independent Clause  +  Dependent (Adjective) Clause  +  Second Part of Independent Clause

The red telephone,  **which** belonged to Ms. Smythe,  rang loudly.

↑ COMPLETE SUBJECT    ↑ RELATIVE PRONOUN    ↑ COMPLETE PREDICATE

---

modifies the NOUN or PRONOUN that it follows. Box 7.13 shows how adverb and adjective clauses function in sentences.

The car **that Jack bought** is practical. [The adjective clause describes the noun *car; that* is a relative pronoun referring to *car.*]

The day **when I can buy my own car** is getting closer. [The adjective clause modifies the noun *day; when* is a relative adverb referring to *day.*]

Use *who, whom, whoever, whomever,* and *whose* when an adjective clause refers to a person or to an animal with a name.

The Smythes, **who collect cars**, are wealthy.

Their dog Bowser, **who is large and loud**, has been spoiled.

Use *which* or *that* when an adjective clause refers to a thing or to an animal that isn't a pet. Sometimes, writers omit *that* from an adjective clause. For grammatical analysis, however, consider the omitted *that* to be implied and, therefore, present.

For help in deciding whether to use *that* or *which,* see Box 9.4 in section 9s.

⚐ **ALERT:** When an adjective clause is NONRESTRICTIVE, use *which* and set it off from the independent clause with commas. Don't use commas with *that* in a RESTRICTIVE CLAUSE.

My car, **which** I bought used, needs major repairs. [The adjective clause is nonrestrictive, so it begins with *which* and is set off with commas.]

The car **that** I want to buy has a CD player. [The adjective clause uses *that* and is restrictive, so it is not set off with commas.] ◆

**EXERCISE 7-9**  Underline the dependent clause in each sentence, and label it an ADJ or an ADV clause. For help, consult 7p.

ADV
**EXAMPLE**   When umbrellas were invented, people used them
for sun protection.

1. Eighteenth-century ladies carried fancy umbrellas as a fashion statement while strolling down the street.
2. Although umbrellas are mostly used today in the rain, they have many other uses.
3. Gentlemen in England carry sturdy umbrellas, which make convenient walking sticks.
4. One company makes a "sporting umbrella" that unfolds into a seat.
5. Marketing consultants, who receive requests for moveable advertising, suggest umbrellas can be mini-billboards when they are decorated with a company's name and logo.

## NOUN CLAUSES

**Noun clauses** function as nouns. Noun clauses can begin with many of the same words that begin adjective clauses: *that, who, which,* and their derivatives, as well as *when, where, whether, why,* and *how.*

**Promises** are not always dependable. [noun]

**What politicians promise** is not always dependable. [noun clause]

The electorate often cannot figure out the **truth**. [noun]

The electorate often cannot know **that the truth is being manipulated**. [noun clause]

Because they start with similar words, noun clauses and adjective clauses are sometimes confused with each other. The way to tell them apart is that the word starting an adjective clause has an ANTECEDENT, while the word starting a noun clause doesn't.

Good politicians understand **whom they must please**. [Noun clause; *whom* does not have an antecedent.]

Good politicians **who make promises** know all cannot be kept. [Adjective clause modifies *politicians,* which is the antecedent of *who.*]

**ESL TIP:** Noun clauses in INDIRECT QUESTIONS are phrased as statements, not questions: *Kara asked why we needed the purple dye.* Don't phrase a noun clause this way: *Kara asked why* **did** [or **do**] *we need the purple dye?* If you prefer to change to a DIRECT QUESTION, usually VERB TENSE, PRONOUN, and other changes are necessary; see 15e.

## ELLIPTICAL CLAUSES

In an **elliptical clause**, one or more words are deliberately left out for CONCISENESS. For an elliptical clause to be correct, the one or more words you leave out need to be identical to those already appearing in the clause.

> Engineering is one of the majors [**that**] **she considered**. [*that*, functioning as a relative pronoun, omitted from adjective clause]

> She decided [**that**] **she would rather major in management**. [*that*, functioning as a conjunction, omitted between clauses]

> **After** [**he takes**] **a refresher course**, he will be eligible for a raise. [subject and verb omitted from adverb clause]

> Broiled fish tastes better **than boiled fish** [**tastes**]. [second half of the comparison omitted]

**EXERCISE 7-10** Use subordinate conjunctions and relative pronouns from the list below to combine each pair of sentences. You may use words more than once, but try to use as many different ones as possible. Some sentence pairs may be combined in several ways. Create at least one elliptical construction.

since which if after when as that although so that unless because

> **EXAMPLE** Reports of flying snakes have been around for hundreds of years. Scientists have never believed these findings.
>
> *Even though reports of flying snakes have been around for hundreds of years,* scientists have never believed these findings.

1. The idea that snakes can fly or even glide from treetops seems impossible. They lack wings, feathers, or any other kind of flying or gliding apparatus.

2. Yet, what seems impossible is not so for the paradise tree snake. This snake possesses many adaptations to allow it to soar long distances through the air.

3. The paradise tree snake has evolved into an animal of amazing agility. This allows it both to escape from predators and to catch its prey.

4. The paradise tree snake can land as far as sixty-nine feet from its launch point. People who visit the jungles of Southeast Asia can see this.

5. The snake dangles like the letter J from a tree branch. It throws itself upward and away from the branch, giving the impression of leaping in midair.

6. Immediately, it begins to fall at a steep angle. It then takes on an S-shape, ripples through the air, and appears to be crawling.

7. The snake changes to an S-shape. Its fall becomes much less steep, enabling the snake to soar outward from its launch point.

8. A special characteristic permits the snake to change its shape and begin to glide. This characteristic permits the snake to flatten its body.

9. Most snakes cannot glide through the air. The paradise tree snake most certainly can.

10. The paradise tree snake must maintain its ability to glide effortlessly through the treetops. Otherwise, birds and mammals may eat it into extinction.

## 7q    What are the four sentence types?

English uses four **sentence types**: simple, compound, complex, and compound-complex. A **simple sentence** is composed of a single INDEPENDENT CLAUSE and no DEPENDENT CLAUSES.

> Charlie Chaplin was born in London on April 16, 1889.

A **compound sentence** is composed of two or more independent clauses. These clauses may be connected by a COORDINATING CONJUNCTION (*and, but, for, or, nor, yet, so*), a semicolon alone, or a semicolon and a CONJUNCTIVE ADVERB.

Figure 7.4

> His father died early, **and** his mother spent time in mental hospitals.

> Many people enjoy Chaplin films**;** others do not.

> Many people enjoy Chaplin films**; however**, others do not.

A **complex sentence** is composed of one independent clause and one or more dependent clauses.

> **When times were bad**, Chaplin lived in the streets. [dependent clause starting *when;* independent clause starting *Chaplin*]

**When Chaplin was performing with a troupe that was touring the United States**, he was hired by Mack Sennett, **who owned the Keystone Company**. [dependent clause starting *when;* dependent clause starting *that;* independent clause starting *he;* dependent clause starting *who*]

A **compound-complex sentence** integrates a compound sentence and a complex sentence. It contains two or more independent clauses and one or more dependent clauses.

Chaplin's comedies were immediately successful, and he became rich **because he was enormously popular for playing the Little Tramp, who was loved for his tiny mustache, baggy trousers, big shoes, and trick derby**. [independent clause starting *Chaplin's;* independent clause starting *he;* dependent clause starting *because;* dependent clause starting *who*]

**When studios could no longer afford him**, Chaplin cofounded United Artists, and then he produced and distributed his own films. [dependent clause starting *when;* independent clause starting *Chaplin;* independent clause starting *then*]

**ALERTS:** (1) Use a comma before a coordinating conjunction connecting two independent clauses; see 24b. (2) When independent clauses are long or contain commas, use a subordinating conjunction—or use a semicolon to connect the sentences; see 25d. ◆

**EXERCISE 7-11**   Decide whether each of the following sentences is simple, compound, complex, or compound-complex. For help, consult 7q.

EXAMPLE   Many people would love to eat a healthy meal at a fast-food restaurant or a food concession at the movies. (*simple*)

1. Fast-food restaurants and healthy meals rarely go together.
2. A fried-chicken sandwich packs an enormous number of calories and fat, and a fried-fish sandwich is no better.
3. A double cheeseburger with bacon at a fast-food restaurant can contain over 1,000 calories and 80 grams of fat, but a plain burger reduces the unhealthy overload considerably.
4. You can purchase other relatively healthy meals at a fast-food restaurant, if you first get to know the chart of nutritional values provided for customers.
5. Even though US government regulations require that nutritional charts be posted on the wall in the public areas of every fast-food restaurant, consumers often ignore the information, and they choose main meals and side dishes with the most flavor, calories, and fat.

6. A healthy meal available at many fast-food restaurants is a salad with low-fat dressing, along with bottled water.

7. The temptations of high fat and calories also entice people at the food concessions in movie theaters.

8. Because calories from sugar have zero nutritional value, health experts use the expression "empty calories" for all sugar products, yet sales of colossal sugar-laden sodas at the movies continue to increase yearly.

9. The silent ingredient in a serving of chips with melted cheese, or nachos, is artery-clogging fat, and the culprits in extra-large candy bars are not only fat but also "empty calories."

10. In truth, many people need to stay away from fast-food restaurants and food concessions at the movies and thereby avoid the tasty temptations of high-calorie foods.

# Chapter 8

## VERBS

### 8a What do verbs do?

A **verb** expresses an action, an occurrence, or a state of being.

> Many people **overeat** on Thanksgiving. [action]
>
> Mother's Day **fell** early this year. [occurrence]
>
> Memorial Day **is** tomorrow. [state of being]

Verbs also reveal when something occurs—in the present, the past, or the future. Verbs convey other information as well; see Box 8.1. For types of verbs, see Box 8.2 on the next page.

---

**SUMMARY BOX** 8.1

### Information that verbs convey

**PERSON**    First person (the speaker: *I* dance), second person (the one spoken to: *you* dance), or third person (the one spoken about: *the man* dances).

**NUMBER**    Singular (one) or plural (more than one).

**TENSE**    Past (*we* **danced**), present (*we* **dance**), or future (*we* **will dance**); see 8g through 8k.

**MOOD**    Moods are indicative (*we* dance), imperative (commands and polite requests: *Dance*), or conditional (speculation, wishes: *if we were dancing . . .*); see 8l and 8m.

**VOICE**    Active voice or passive voice; see 8n through 8p.

---

**SUMMARY BOX 8.2**

## Types of verbs

**MAIN VERB**
The word in a PREDICATE that says something about the SUBJECT: *She **danced** for the group.*

**AUXILIARY VERB**
A verb that combines with a main verb to convey information about TENSE, MOOD, or VOICE (8e). The verbs *be, do,* and *have* can be auxiliary verbs or main verbs. The verbs *can, could, may, might, should, would, must,* and others are MODAL AUXILIARY VERBS. They add shades of meaning such as ability or possibility to verbs: *She **might dance** again.*

**LINKING VERB**
The verb that links a subject to a COMPLEMENT, a word or words that rename or describe the subject: *She **was** happy dancing. Be* is the most common linking verb; sometimes sense verbs (*smell, taste*) or verbs of perception (*seem, feel*) function as linking verbs. See also Box 8.3.

**TRANSITIVE VERB**
The verb followed by a DIRECT OBJECT that completes the verb's message: *They **sent** her a fan letter.*

**INTRANSITIVE VERB**
A verb that does not require a direct object: *Yesterday she **danced**.*

### LINKING VERBS

**Linking verbs** are main verbs that indicate a state of being or a condition. They link a SUBJECT with one or more words that rename or describe the subject, called a SUBJECT COMPLEMENT. A linking verb is like an equal sign between a subject and its complement. Box 8.3 shows how linking verbs function in sentences.

**PATTERN BOX 8.3**

## Linking verbs

- Linking verbs may be forms of the verb *be* (*am, is, was, were;* see 8e for a complete list).

| George Washington | **was** | president. |
|---|---|---|
| SUBJECT | LINKING VERB | COMPLEMENT (PREDICATE NOMINATIVE: RENAMES SUBJECT) |

---

**PATTERN BOX**  **8.3** *continued*

### Linking verbs

- Linking verbs may deal with the senses (*look, smell, taste, sound, feel*).

George Washington     **sounded**     confident.

SUBJECT       LINKING       COMPLEMENT (PREDICATE
                  VERB          ADJECTIVE DESCRIBES SUBJECT)

- Linking verbs can be verbs that convey a sense of existing or becoming—*appear, seem, become, get, grow, turn, remain, stay,* and *prove,* for example.

George Washington     **grew**     old.

SUBJECT       LINKING       COMPLEMENT (PREDICATE
                  VERB          ADJECTIVE DESCRIBES SUBJECT)

- To test whether a verb other than a form of *be* is functioning as a linking verb, substitute *was* (for a singular subject) or *were* (for a plural subject) for the original verb. If the sentence makes sense, the original verb is functioning as a linking verb.

  **NO**    George Washington **grew** a beard ⟶ George Washington **was** a beard. [*Grew* is not functioning as a linking verb.]

  **YES**   George Washington **grew** old ⟶ George Washington **was** old. [*Grew* is functioning as a linking verb.]

---

## VERB FORMS

### 8b   What are the forms of main verbs?

A **main verb** names an action (*People **dance***), an occurrence (*Christmas **comes** once a year*), or a state of being (*It **will be** warm tomorrow*). Every main verb has five forms.

- The **simple form** conveys an action, occurrence, or state of being taking place in the present (*I **laugh***) or, with an AUXILIARY VERB, in the future (*I **will laugh***).
- The **past-tense form** conveys an action, occurrence, or state completed in the past (*I **laughed***). REGULAR VERBS add *-ed* or *-d* to the simple form. IRREGULAR VERBS vary (see Box 8.4 for a list of common irregular verbs).
- The **past participle form** in regular verbs uses the same form as the past tense. Irregular verbs vary; see Box 8.4. To function as a verb, a past participle must combine with a SUBJECT and one or more auxiliary verbs (*I **have laughed***). Otherwise, past participles function as ADJECTIVES (***crumbled** cookies*).

- The **present participle form** adds *-ing* to the simple form (*laughing*). To function as a verb, a present participle combines with a subject and one or more auxiliary verbs (*I **was laughing***). Otherwise, present participles function as adjectives (*my **laughing** friends*) or as NOUNS (***Laughing** is healthy*).

- The **infinitive** usually consists of *to* and the simple form following *to* (*I started **to laugh** at his joke*); see 9i. The infinitive functions as a noun or an adjective, not a verb.

**ESL TIP:** When verbs function as other parts of speech, they're called VERBALS. Verbals are INFINITIVES, PRESENT PARTICIPLES, and PAST PARTICIPLES. When present participles function as nouns, they're called GERUNDS. For information about using gerunds and infinitives as OBJECTS after certain verbs, see Chapter 50. 🌐

## 8c   What is the *-s*, or *-es*, form of a verb?

The **-s form of a verb** is the third-person singular in the PRESENT TENSE. The ending *-s* (or *-es*) is added to the verb's SIMPLE FORM (*smell* becomes *smells,* as in *The bread **smells** delicious*).

*Be* and *have* are irregular verbs. For the third-person singular, present tense, *be* uses *is* and *have* uses *has.*

The cheesecake **is** popular.

The éclair **has** chocolate icing.

Even if you tend to drop the *-s* or *-es* ending when you speak, always use it when you write. Proofread carefully to make sure you haven't omitted any *-s* forms.

**ALERT:** In informal speech, the LINKING, or *copula,* VERB *to be* sometimes doesn't change forms in the present tense. However, ACADEMIC WRITING requires you to use standard third-person singular forms in the present tense.

He **is** [not *be*] hungry.

The bakery **has** [not *have*] fresh bread. ◆

**EXERCISE 8-1**   Rewrite each sentence, changing the subjects to the word or words given in parentheses. Change the form of the verbs shown in italics to match the new subject. Keep all sentences in the present tense. For help, consult 8c.

EXAMPLE   The Oregon giant earthworm *escapes* all attempts at detection. (Oregon giant earthworms)

*Oregon giant earthworms escape* all attempts at detection.

1. Before declaring the Oregon giant earthworm a protected species, US government agencies *require* concrete proof that it *is* not extinct. (a government agency) (they)

2. A scientist who *finds* one alive will demonstrate that Oregon giant earthworms *do* still exist, in spite of no one's having seen any for over twenty years. (Scientists) (the Oregon giant earthworm)

3. Last seen in the Willamette Valley near Portland, Oregon, the earthworms *are* white, and they *smell* like lilies. (the earthworm) (it)

4. Oregon giant earthworms *grow* up to three feet long. (The Oregon giant earthworm)

5. A clump of soil with a strange shape *indicates* that the giant creatures *continue* to live, but to demonstrate that they *are* not extinct, only a real specimen will do. (clumps of soil) (creature) (it)

## **8d** What is the difference between regular and irregular verbs?

A **regular verb** forms its PAST TENSE and PAST PARTICIPLE by adding -*ed* or -*d* to the SIMPLE FORM: *type, typed; cook, cooked; work, worked.* Most verbs in English are regular.

In informal speech, some people skip over the -*ed* sound, pronouncing it softly or not at all. In ACADEMIC WRITING, however, you're required to use it. If you're not used to hearing or pronouncing this sound, proofread carefully to see that you have all the needed -*ed* endings in your writing.

> **NO** The cake was **suppose** to be tasty.
>
> **YES** The cake was **supposed** to be tasty.

**Irregular verbs**, in contrast, don't consistently add -*ed* or -*d* to form the past tense and past participle. Some irregular verbs change an internal vowel to make the past tense and past participle: *sing, sang, sung.* Some change an internal vowel and add an ending other than -*ed* or -*d*: *grow, grew, grown.* Some use the simple form throughout: *cost, cost, cost.* Unfortunately, a verb's simple form doesn't provide a clue about whether the verb is irregular or regular.

Although you can always look up the principal parts of any verb, memorizing any you don't know solidly is much more efficient in the long run. About two hundred verbs in English are irregular. Box 8.4 lists the most frequently used irregular verbs.

**ALERT:** For information about changing *y* to *i*, or doubling a final consonant before adding the -*ed* ending, see 22d. ◆

SUMMARY BOX 8.4

## Common irregular verbs

| SIMPLE FORM | PAST TENSE | PAST PARTICIPLE |
| --- | --- | --- |
| arise | arose | arisen |
| awake | awoke *or* awaked | awaked *or* awoken |
| be (is, am, are) | was, were | been |
| bear | bore | borne *or* born |
| beat | beat | beaten |
| become | became | become |
| begin | began | begun |
| bend | bent | bent |
| bet | bet | bet |
| bid ("to offer") | bid | bid |
| bid ("to command") | bade | bidden |
| bind | bound | bound |
| bite | bit | bitten *or* bit |
| blow | blew | blown |
| break | broke | broken |
| bring | brought | brought |
| build | built | built |
| burst | burst | burst |
| buy | bought | bought |
| cast | cast | cast |
| catch | caught | caught |
| choose | chose | chosen |
| cling | clung | clung |
| come | came | come |
| cost | cost | cost |
| creep | crept | crept |
| cut | cut | cut |
| deal | dealt | dealt |
| dig | dug | dug |
| dive | dived *or* dove | dived |
| do | did | done |
| draw | drew | drawn |
| drink | drank | drunk |
| drive | drove | driven |
| eat | ate | eaten |
| fall | fell | fallen |
| feed | fed | fed |
| feel | felt | felt |
| fight | fought | fought |
| find | found | found |

## Common irregular verbs

| SIMPLE FORM | PAST TENSE | PAST PARTICIPLE |
|---|---|---|
| flee | fled | fled |
| fling | flung | flung |
| fly | flew | flown |
| forbid | forbade *or* forbad | forbidden |
| forget | forgot | forgotten *or* forgot |
| forgive | forgave | forgiven |
| forsake | forsook | forsaken |
| freeze | froze | frozen |
| get | got | got *or* gotten |
| give | gave | given |
| go | went | gone |
| grow | grew | grown |
| hang ("to suspend")* | hung | hung |
| have | had | had |
| hear | heard | heard |
| hide | hid | hidden |
| hit | hit | hit |
| hurt | hurt | hurt |
| keep | kept | kept |
| know | knew | known |
| lay | laid | laid |
| lead | led | led |
| leave | left | left |
| lend | lent | lent |
| let | let | let |
| lie | lay | lain |
| light | lighted *or* lit | lighted *or* lit |
| lose | lost | lost |
| make | made | made |
| mean | meant | meant |
| pay | paid | paid |
| prove | proved | proved *or* proven |
| quit | quit | quit |
| read | read | read |
| rid | rid | rid |
| ride | rode | ridden |
| ring | rang | rung |
| rise | rose | risen |
| run | ran | run |
| say | said | said |

*When it means "to execute by hanging," *hang* is a regular verb: *In wartime, some armies routinely **hanged** deserters.*

## Common irregular verbs

| SIMPLE FORM | PAST TENSE | PAST PARTICIPLE |
|---|---|---|
| see | saw | seen |
| seek | sought | sought |
| send | sent | sent |
| set | set | set |
| shake | shook | shaken |
| shine ("to glow")* | shone | shone |
| shoot | shot | shot |
| show | showed | shown *or* showed |
| shrink | shrank | shrunk |
| sing | sang | sung |
| sink | sank *or* sunk | sunk |
| sit | sat | sat |
| slay | slew | slain |
| sleep | slept | slept |
| sling | slung | slung |
| speak | spoke | spoken |
| spend | spent | spent |
| spin | spun | spun |
| spring | sprang *or* sprung | sprung |
| stand | stood | stood |
| steal | stole | stolen |
| sting | stung | stung |
| stink | stank *or* stunk | stunk |
| stride | strode | stridden |
| strike | struck | struck |
| strive | strove | striven |
| swear | swore | sworn |
| sweep | swept | swept |
| swim | swam | swum |
| swing | swung | swung |
| take | took | taken |
| teach | taught | taught |
| tear | tore | torn |
| tell | told | told |
| think | thought | thought |
| throw | threw | thrown |
| understand | understood | understood |
| wake | woke *or* waked | waked *or* woken |
| wear | wore | worn |
| wring | wrung | wrung |
| write | wrote | written |

*When it means "to polish," *shine* is a regular verb: We **shined** our shoes.

**EXERCISE 8-2** Write the correct past-tense form of the regular verbs given in parentheses. For help, consult 8d.

EXAMPLE The Stanford University football team (uses) <u>used</u> an innovative system to cool down after workouts.

(1) Many athletes (need) _____ a way to lower their body temperatures quickly. (2) They normally just (dump) _____ ice on themselves, but this method (lack) _____ efficiency and sometimes even (cause) _____ collapse. (3) To solve the problem, scientists (develop) _____ the Rapid Thermal Exchange system, which (cool) _____ an athlete from inside. (4) To test the new device, a football player (place) _____ his hand on a cool metal plate inside an airtight chamber, where a mild vacuum pressure (increase) _____ blood flow. (5) This (result) _____ in lowered body temperature as the cooled-down blood (flow) _____ throughout the body and (reduce) _____ the discomfort of being overly hot.

**EXERCISE 8-3** Write the correct past-tense form of the irregular verbs given in parentheses. For help, consult Box 8.4 in 8d.

EXAMPLE On October 24, 2005, the third annual "Take Back Your Time Day" (draw) <u>drew</u> a number of participants; promoters (choose) <u>chose</u> the date for the celebration deliberately because Time Day (fall) <u>fell</u> exactly nine weeks before the end of the year.

(1) This date struck a chord; people in the United States, on average, (spend) _____ nine more weeks than Europeans (spend) _____ at work. (2) The interest group (teach) _____ US workers, individuals, families, and friends to "Take Four Windows of Time." (3) Appropriating four windows of time (mean) _____ that between Labor Day and Take Back Your Time Day, workers in the United States (choose) _____ four periods of time to spend in deliberate, reflective, "life-renewing" pursuits. (4) People (dive) _____ into the commitment individually or with family and friends. (5) In addition, the event (be) _____ entirely flexible. (6) Participants (find) _____ four particular days, such as four Mondays or any other four periods of time, that (feel) _____ right for the person's schedule. (7) The celebration of "Take Back Your Time Day" (make) _____ people recognize how much time US workers (spend) _____ at their labor during the year. (8) The

celebration (draw) _____ attention to people's need to adjust their work world, adding free time and reflection to their lives. (9) "Take Back Your Time Day," in fact, (deal) _____ with a renewal of life. (10) In addition, promoters (seek) _____ responses about how participants (spend) _____ the time they (cut) _____ out of their work world. (11) Interestingly, The Simplicity Forum (lead) _____ the impetus of "Take Back Your Time Day." (12) The Simplicity Forum (take) _____ its major tenets from Henry David Thoreau, a nineteenth-century American author, who (teach) _____ people to "simplify, simplify."

## 8e  What are auxiliary verbs?

**Auxiliary verbs**, also called *helping verbs,* combine with MAIN VERBS to make VERB PHRASES. Box 8.5 shows how auxiliary verbs work.

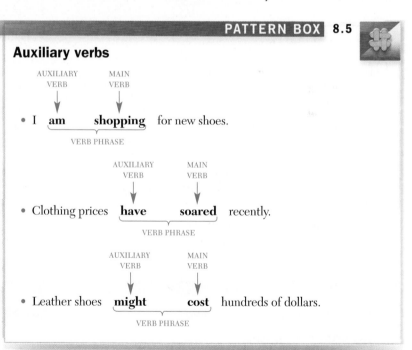

**PATTERN BOX 8.5**

**Auxiliary verbs**

- I **am shopping** for new shoes.
  - AUXILIARY VERB → am
  - MAIN VERB → shopping
  - VERB PHRASE

- Clothing prices **have soared** recently.
  - AUXILIARY VERB → have
  - MAIN VERB → soared
  - VERB PHRASE

- Leather shoes **might cost** hundreds of dollars.
  - AUXILIARY VERB → might
  - MAIN VERB → cost
  - VERB PHRASE

## USING *BE, DO, HAVE*

The three most common auxiliary verbs are *be, do,* and *have.* These three verbs can also be main verbs. Their forms vary more than most irregular verbs, as Boxes 8.6 and 8.7 (p. 216) show.

**SUMMARY BOX** 8.6

## Forms of the verb *be*

| SIMPLE FORM | be |
|---|---|
| *-S* FORM | is |
| PAST TENSE | was, were |
| PRESENT PARTICIPLE | being |
| PAST PARTICIPLE | been |

| PERSON | PRESENT TENSE | PAST TENSE |
|---|---|---|
| I | am | was |
| you (singular) | are | were |
| he, she, it | is | was |
| we | are | were |
| you (plural) | are | were |
| they | are | were |

**ALERT:** In ACADEMIC WRITING, always use the standard forms for *be, do,* and *have,* as shown in Boxes 8.6 and 8.7.

The gym **is** [not *be*] a busy place.

The gym **is** [not *be*] filling with spectators. ◆

**ESL TIP:** When *be, do,* and *have* function as auxiliary verbs, change their form to agree with a third-person singular subject—and don't add -s to the main verb.

**NO** **Does** the library **closes** at 6:00?

**YES** **Does** the library **close** at 6:00? ☺

**SUMMARY BOX** 8.7

## Forms of the verbs *do* and *have*

| SIMPLE FORM | do | have |
|---|---|---|
| *-S* FORM | does | has |
| PAST TENSE | did | had |
| PRESENT PARTICIPLE | doing | having |
| PAST PARTICIPLE | done | had |

## MODAL AUXILIARY VERBS

*Can, could, shall, should, will, would, may, might,* and *must* are the nine modal auxiliary verbs. **Modal auxiliary verbs** communicate ability, permission, obligation, advisability, necessity, or possibility. They never change form.

> Exercise **can lengthen** lives. [possibility]
>
> She **can jog** for five miles. [ability]
>
> The exercise **must occur** regularly. [necessity, obligation]
>
> People **should protect** their bodies. [advisability]
>
> **May** I **exercise?** [permission]

**ESL TIP:** For more about modal auxiliary verbs and the meanings they communicate, see Chapter 51.

**EXERCISE 8-4**  Using the auxiliary verbs in the list below, fill in the blanks in the following passage. Use each auxiliary word only once, even if a listed word can fit into more than one blank. For help, consult 8e.

| are | have | may | will | might | can | has |

**EXAMPLE**  Psychologists <u>have</u> discovered that most personal memories focus on recent events.

(1) Most adults _____ recall recent events more readily than distant ones when they _____ presented with a standard test of memory. (2) However, an important exception _____ been found among older adults, those age 50 and above. (3) People in this older age group _____ most readily recall events that happened in their late teens and early adulthood. (4) Researchers _____ concluded that because many significant life events, such as getting married and choosing a career, occur during this period, older adults _____ prefer to look back on this highly memorable period. (5) Similarly, younger adults _____ tend to focus on those same memorable events, which means that they summon more recent memories.

## 8f  What are intransitive and transitive verbs?

A verb is **intransitive** when an OBJECT isn't required to complete the verb's meaning: *I sing*. A verb is **transitive** when an object is necessary to complete the verb's meaning: *I need a guitar.* Many verbs have both transitive and intransitive meanings. Some verbs are only transitive: *need, have, like, owe, remember.* Only transitive verbs function in the PASSIVE VOICE. Dictionaries label verbs as transitive (*vt*) or intransitive (*vi*). Box 8.8 (p. 218) shows how transitive and intransitive verbs operate in sentences.

**SUMMARY BOX** 8.8

## Comparing intransitive and transitive verbs

### INTRANSITIVE (OBJECT NOT NEEDED)

They **sat** together quietly. [*Together* and *quietly* are not direct objects; they are modifiers.]

The cat **sees** in the dark. [*In the dark* is not a direct object; it is a modifier.]

I can **hear** well. [*Well* is not a direct object; it is a modifier.]

### TRANSITIVE (OBJECT NEEDED)

They **sent** a birthday card to me. [*Birthday card* is a direct object.]

The cat **sees** the dog. [*Dog* is a direct object.]

I can **hear** you. [*You* is a direct object.]

The verbs *lie* and *lay* are particularly confusing. *Lie* means "to recline, to place oneself down, or to remain." *Lie* is intransitive (it cannot be followed by an object). *Lay* means "to put something down." *Lay* is transitive (it must be followed by an object). As you can see in Box 8.9, the word *lay* is both the past tense of *lie* and the present-tense simple

**SUMMARY BOX** 8.9

## Using *lie* and *lay*

|  | lie | lay |
|---|---|---|
| **SIMPLE FORM** | lie | lay |
| **-S FORM** | lies | lays |
| **PAST TENSE** | lay | laid |
| **PRESENT PARTICIPLE** | lying | laying |
| **PAST PARTICIPLE** | lain | laid |

### Intransitive Forms

| **PRESENT TENSE** | The hikers **lie** down to rest. |
|---|---|
| **PAST TENSE** | The hikers **lay** down to rest. |

### Transitive Forms

| **PRESENT TENSE** | The hikers **lay** their backpacks on a rock. [*Backpacks* is a direct object.] |
|---|---|
| **PAST TENSE** | The hikers **laid** their backpacks on a rock. [*Backpacks* is a direct object.] |

form of *lay.* That makes things difficult. Our best advice is memorize them. Yet truthfully, each time we use *lie* and *lay,* we need to pause, think, and recite the list to ourselves.

Two other verb pairs tend to confuse people because of their intransitive and transitive forms: *raise* and *rise* and *set* and *sit.*

*Raise* and *set* are transitive (they must be followed by an object). *Rise* and *sit* are intransitive (they cannot be followed by an object). Fortunately, although each word has a meaning different from the other words, they don't share forms: *raise, raised, raised; rise, rose, risen;* and *set, set, set; sit, sat, sat.*

**EXERCISE 8-5**  Underline the correct word of each pair in parentheses. For help, consult 8f.

EXAMPLE  Whenever I come home, I always check to see where my cat is (laying, <u>lying</u>).

(1) Coming home from jogging one morning, I (laid, lay) my keys on the counter and saw my cat, Andy, (laying, lying) in a patch of sunlight on the living room floor. (2) When I (sat, set) down beside him, he (raised, rose) up on his toes, stretched, and then (laid, lay) down a few feet away. (3) (Sitting, Setting) there, I reached out to Andy, and my contrary cat jumped up onto the couch. As he landed, I heard a clinking noise. (4) I (raised, rose) the bottom of the slipcover, and there (laid, lay) my favorite earrings, the ones I thought I had lost last week. Deciding he had earned a special privilege, Andy curled up on a red silk pillow in the corner of the couch. (5) Since the earrings now (laid, lay) safely in my pocket, I let him (lay, lie) there undisturbed.

# VERB TENSE

## 8g  What is verb tense?

**Verb tense** conveys time. Verbs show tense (time) by changing form. English has six verb tenses, divided into simple and perfect groups. The three **simple tenses** divide time into present, past, and future. The simple **present tense** describes what happens regularly, what takes place in the present, and what is consistently or generally true. The simple **past tense** tells of an action completed or a condition ended. The simple **future tense** indicates action yet to be taken or a condition not yet experienced.

Rick **wants** to speak Spanish fluently. [simple present tense]

Rick **wanted** to improve rapidly. [simple past tense]

Rick **will want** to progress even further next year. [simple future tense]

The three **perfect tenses** also divide time into present, past, and future. They show more complex time relationships than the simple tenses. For information on using the perfect tenses, see section 8i.

The three simple tenses and the three perfect tenses also have **progressive forms**. These forms indicate that the verb describes what is ongoing or continuing. For information on using progressive forms, see section 8j. Box 8.10 summarizes verb tenses and progressive forms.

---

**SUMMARY BOX** 8.10

## Simple, perfect, and progressive tenses

**Simple Tenses**

| | REGULAR VERB | IRREGULAR VERB | PROGRESSIVE FORM |
|---|---|---|---|
| **PRESENT** | I talk | I eat<br>I am eating | I am talking; |
| **PAST** | I talked | I ate<br>I was eating | I was talking; |
| **FUTURE** | I will talk | I will eat<br>I will be eating | I will be talking; |

**Perfect Tenses**

| | REGULAR VERB | IRREGULAR VERB | PROGRESSIVE FORM |
|---|---|---|---|
| **PRESENT PERFECT** | I have talked | I have eaten | I have been talking;<br>I have been eating |
| **PAST PERFECT** | I had talked | I had eaten | I had been talking;<br>I had been eating |
| **FUTURE PERFECT** | I will have talked | I will have eaten | I will have been talking;<br>I will have been eating |

---

**ESL TIP:** Box 8.10 shows that most verb tenses are formed by combining one or more AUXILIARY VERBS with the SIMPLE FORM, the PRESENT PARTICIPLE, or the PAST PARTICIPLE of a MAIN VERB. Auxiliary verbs are necessary in the formation of most tenses, so never omit them.

> **NO** I **talking** to you.
>
> **YES** I **am talking** to you. 🌐

## 8h  How do I use the simple present tense?

The **simple present tense** uses the SIMPLE FORM of the verb (8b). It describes what happens regularly, what takes place in the present, and what is generally or consistently true. Also, it can convey a future occurrence with verbs like *start, stop, begin, end, arrive,* and *depart.*

Calculus class **meets** every morning. [regularly occurring action]

Mastering calculus **takes** time. [general truth]

The course **ends** in eight weeks. [specific future event]

**ALERT:** For a work of literature, always describe or discuss the action in the present tense. This holds true no matter how old the work.

In Shakespeare's *Romeo and Juliet,* Juliet's father **wants** her to marry Paris, but Juliet **loves** Romeo. ◆

## 8i  How do I form and use the perfect tenses?

The **perfect tenses** generally describe actions or occurrences that are still having an effect at the present time or are having an effect until a specified time. The perfect tenses are composed of an AUXILIARY VERB and a main verb's PAST PARTICIPLE (8b).

For the **present perfect tense** (see Box 8.10), use *has* only for the third-person singular subjects and *have* for all other subjects. For the **past perfect**, use *had* with the past participle. For the **future perfect**, use *will have* with the past participle.

PRESENT PERFECT   Our government **has offered** to help. [having effect now]

PRESENT PERFECT   The drought **has created** terrible hardship. [having effect until a specified time—when the rains come]

PAST PERFECT   As soon as the tornado **had passed**, the heavy rain started. [Both events occurred in the past; the tornado occurred before the rain, so the earlier event uses *had.*]

FUTURE PERFECT   Our chickens' egg production **will have reached** five hundred per day by next year. [The event will occur before a specified time.]

## 8j  How do I form and use progressive forms?

**Progressive forms** describe an ongoing event, action, or condition. They also express habitual or recurring actions or conditions. The **present progressive** uses the present-tense form of *be* that agrees with the subject in PERSON and NUMBER, plus the *-ing* form (PRESENT PARTICIPLE) of the main verb. The **past progressive** uses *was* or *were* to agree with the subject in person and number, and it uses the present participle of the main verb. The **future progressive** uses *will be* and the present participle. The **present perfect progressive** uses *have been* or *has been* to agree with the subject, plus the *-ing* form of the main verb. The **past perfect progressive** uses *had been* and the *-ing* form of the main verb. The **future perfect progressive** uses *will have been* plus the PRESENT PARTICIPLE.

| | |
|---|---|
| PRESENT PROGRESSIVE | The smog **is stinging** everyone's eyes. [event taking place now] |
| PAST PROGRESSIVE | Eye drops **were selling** well last week. [event ongoing in the past within stated limits] |
| FUTURE PROGRESSIVE | We **will be ordering** more eye drops than usual this month. [recurring event that will take place in the future] |
| PRESENT PERFECT PROGRESSIVE | Scientists **have been warning** us about air pollution for years. [recurring event that took place in the past and may still take place] |
| PAST PERFECT PROGRESSIVE | We **had been ordering** three cases of eye drops a month until the smog worsened. [recurring past event that has now ended] |
| FUTURE PERFECT PROGRESSIVE | By May, we **will have been selling** eye drops for eight months. [ongoing condition to be completed at a specific time in the future] |

**EXERCISE 8-6**   Underline the correct verb in each pair of parentheses. If more than one answer is possible, be prepared to explain the differences in meaning between the two choices. For help, consult 8g through 8j.

EXAMPLE   According to an article in *National Geographic News,* weird plants (are taking root, would have taken root) in ordinary backyards.

1. Some, smelling like spoiled meat, (will have ruined, are ruining) people's appetites.
2. Stalks similar to male anatomy (typify, are typifying) other examples.
3. *Shockingly large, black, carnivorous,* and *volatile* (describe, is describing) additional unusual plants.
4. Indeed, many unusual plants (live, lived) in places the world over today.
5. Many people now (are planting, planted) these weird items in their backyards.

6. In 1999, in East Lothian, Scotland, Diane Halligan (founded, had founded) The Weird and Wonderful Plant Company because she (was, is) disappointed with the plant selection at her local garden centers.

7. Halligan (chose, is choosing) to open an extraordinary plant store because she (wanted, is wanting) to provide a source of unusual plants for others as well as herself.

8. Marty Harper in Staunton, Virginia, like Halligan in Scotland, (contends, are contending) that his company (fills, would have filled) a niche for himself and others.

9. Harper, after much study on the subject of strange plants, (is indicating, indicates) that Madagascar holds the record for the most weird plants on the planet.

10. Isolated from the rest of the world, Madagascar (has provided, will have provided) a haven for unusual plants to develop undisturbed.

11. *Rafflesia arnoldii* (is, are) the oddest plant Harper (has encountered, will have encountered).

12. Harper, in an interview with *National Geographic*'s John Roach, (reveals, is revealing) that *Rafflesia arnoldii,* a parasitic plant, (has, have) the world's largest bloom, stinks, and (held, holds) in its center six or seven quarts of water.

13. According to Harper, procreation (remains, has remained) the primary reason for the development of the ostensibly outlandish shapes, sizes, odors, and actions of these unusual plants the world over.

14. Douglas Justice, another weird-plant aficionado like Halligan and Harper, (says, is saying) he (wonders, is wondering) what (motivates, motivated) people to choose the odd plants.

15. Harper, however, (exclaims, is exclaiming), "Such plants (make, were making) me smile."

## 8k    How do I use tense sequences accurately?

Verb **tense sequences** communicate time relationships. They help deliver messages about actions, occurrences, or states that take place at different times. Box 8.11 shows how tenses in the same sentence can vary depending on the timing of actions (or occurrences or states).

## Tense sequences

If your independent clause contains a simple-present-tense verb, then in your dependent clause you can

- use PRESENT TENSE to show same-time action:

    I **avoid** shellfish because I **am** allergic to it.

- use PAST TENSE to show earlier action:

    I **am** sure that I **deposited** the check.

- use the PRESENT PERFECT TENSE to show (1) a period of time extending from some point in the past to the present or (2) an indefinite past time:

    They **claim** that they **have visited** the planet Venus.

    I **believe** that I **have seen** that movie before.

- use the FUTURE TENSE for action to come:

    The book **is** open because I **will be reading** it later.

If your independent clause contains a past-tense verb, then in your dependent clause you can

- use the past tense to show another completed past action:

    I **closed** the door because you **told** me to.

- use the PAST PERFECT TENSE to show earlier action:

    The sprinter **knew** that she **had broken** the record.

- use the present tense to state a general truth:

    Christopher Columbus **determined** that the world is round.

If your independent clause contains a present-perfect-tense or past-perfect-tense verb, then in your dependent clause you can

- use the past tense:

    The bread **has become** moldy since I **purchased** it.

    Sugar prices **had** already **declined** when artificial sweeteners first **appeared**.

If your independent clause contains a future-tense verb, then in your dependent clause you can

- use the present tense to show action happening at the same time:

    You **will be** rich if you **win** the prize.

- use the past tense to show earlier action:

    You **will** surely **win** the prize if you **remembered** to mail the entry form.

**SUMMARY BOX** | **8.11** *continued*

**Tense sequences**

- use the present perfect tense to show future action earlier than the action of the independent-clause verb:

    The river **will flood** again next year unless we **have built** a better dam by then.

If your independent clause contains a future-perfect-tense verb, then in your dependent clause you can

- use either the present tense or the present perfect tense:

    Dr. Chang **will have delivered** five thousand babies by the time she **retires**.

    Dr. Chang **will have delivered** five thousand babies by the time she **has retired**.

---

**ALERT:** Never use a future-tense verb in a dependent clause when the verb in the independent clause is in the future tense. Instead, use a present-tense verb or present-perfect-tense verb in the dependent clause.

**NO**   The river **will flood** us unless we **will prepare** our defense.

**YES**   The river **will flood** us unless we **prepare** our defense.
[*Prepare* is a present-tense verb.]

**YES**   The river **will flood** us unless we **have prepared** our defense. [*Have prepared* is a present perfect verb.] ◆

Tense sequences may include INFINITIVES and PARTICIPLES. To name or describe an activity or occurrence coming either at the same time as the time expressed in the MAIN VERB or after, use the **present infinitive**.

I **hope to buy** a used car. [*To buy* comes at a future time. *Hope* is the main verb, and its action is now.]

I **hoped to buy** a used car. [*Hoped* is the main verb, and its action is over.]

I **had hoped to buy** a used car. [*Had hoped* is the main verb, and its action is over.]

The PRESENT PARTICIPLE (a verb's -*ing* form) can describe action happening at the same time.

**Driving** his new car, the man **smiled**. [The driving and the smiling happened at the same time.]

To describe an action that occurs before the action in the main verb, use the **perfect infinitive** (*to have gone, to have smiled*), the PAST PARTICIPLE, or the **present perfect participle** (*having gone, having smiled*).

Candida **claimed to have written** fifty short stories in college.
[*Claimed* is the main verb, and *to have written* happened first.]

**Pleased** with the short story, Candida **mailed** it to several magazines. [*Mailed* is the main verb, and *pleased* happened first.]

**Having sold** one short story, Candida **invested** in a computer.
[*Invested* is the main verb, and *having sold* happened first.]

**EXERCISE 8-7**  Underline the correct verb in each pair of parentheses that best suits the sequence of tenses. Be ready to explain your choices. For help, consult 8k.

> **EXAMPLE**  When he (is, <u>was</u>) seven years old, Yo-Yo Ma, possibly the world's greatest living cellist, (moves, <u>moved</u>) to the United States with his family.

1. Yo-Yo Ma, who (had been born, was born) in France to Chinese parents, (lived, lives) in Boston, Massachusetts, today and (toured, tours) as one of the world's greatest cellists.
2. Years from now, after Mr. Ma has given his last concert, music lovers still (treasure, will treasure) his many fine recordings.
3. Mr. Ma's older sister, Dr. Yeou-Cheng Ma, was nearly the person with the concert career. She had been training to become a concert violinist when her brother's musical genius (began, had begun) to be noticed.
4. Even though Dr. Ma eventually (becomes, became) a physician, she still (had been playing, plays) the violin.
5. The family interest in music (continues, was continuing), for Mr. Ma's children (take, had taken) piano lessons.
6. Although most people today (knew, know) Mr. Ma as a brilliant cellist, he (was making, has made) films as well.
7. One year, while he (had been traveling, was traveling) in the Kalahari Desert, he (films, filmed) dances of southern Africa's Bush people.
8. Mr. Ma first (becomes, became) interested in the Kalahari people when he (had studied, studied) anthropology as an undergraduate at Harvard University.
9. When he shows visitors around Boston now, Mr. Ma has been known to point out the Harvard University library where, he claims, he (fell asleep, was falling asleep) in the stacks when he (had been, was) a student.
10. Indicating another building, Mr. Ma admits that in one of its classrooms he almost (failed, had failed) German.

# MOOD

## 8l What is "mood" in verbs?

**Mood** in verbs conveys an attitude toward the action in a sentence. English has three moods: *indicative, imperative,* and *subjunctive.* Use the **indicative mood** to make statements about real things, about highly likely things, and for questions about fact.

INDICATIVE   The door to the tutoring center opened. [real]

She seemed to be looking for someone. [highly likely]

Do you want to see a tutor? [question about a fact]

The **imperative mood** expresses commands and direct requests. Often, the subject is omitted in an imperative sentence, but nevertheless the subject is implied to be either *you* or one of the indefinite pronouns such as *anybody, somebody,* or *everybody.*

**ALERT:** Use an exclamation point after a strong command; use a period after a mild command or a request (23e, 23a).

IMPERATIVE   Please shut the door.

Watch out! That screw is loose. ◆

The **subjunctive mood** expresses speculation, other unreal conditions, conjectures, wishes, recommendations, indirect requests, and demands. Often, the words that signal the subjunctive mood are *if, as if, as though,* and *unless.* In speaking, subjunctive verb forms were once used frequently in English, but they're heard far less today. Nevertheless, in ACADEMIC WRITING, you need to use the subjunctive mood.

SUBJUNCTIVE   If I **were** you, I would ask for a tutor.

## 8m What are subjunctive forms?

For the **present subjunctive**, always use the SIMPLE FORM of the verb for all PERSONS and NUMBERS.

The prosecutor asks that she **testify** [not *testifies*] again.

It is important that they **be** [not *are*] allowed to testify.

For the **past subjunctive**, use the simple past tense: *I wish that I* ***had*** *a car.* The one exception is for the past subjunctive of *be:* Use *were* for all forms.

I wish that I **were** [not *was*] leaving on vacation today.

They asked if she **were** [not *was*] leaving on vacation today.

227

**USING THE SUBJUNCTIVE IN *IF, AS IF, AS THOUGH,* AND *UNLESS* CLAUSES**

In dependent clauses introduced by *if, as if, as though,* and sometimes *unless,* the subjunctive describes speculations or conditions contrary to fact.

> If it **were** [not *was*] to rain, attendance at the race would be disappointing. [speculation]

> The runner looked as if he **were** [not *was*] winded, but he said he wasn't. [a condition contrary to fact]

In an *unless* clause, the subjunctive signals that what the clause says is highly unlikely.

> Unless rain **were** [not *was*] to create floods, the race will be held this Sunday. [Floods are highly unlikely.]

Not every clause introduced by *if, unless, as if,* or *as though* requires the subjunctive. Use the subjunctive only when the dependent clause describes speculation or a condition contrary to fact.

INDICATIVE    If she **is** going to leave late, I will drive her to the race. [Her leaving late is highly likely.]

SUBJUNCTIVE   If she **were** going to leave late, I would drive her to the race. [Her leaving late is a speculation.]

**USING THE SUBJUNCTIVE IN *THAT* CLAUSES**

When *that* clauses describe wishes, requests, demands, or recommendations, the subjunctive can convey the message.

> I wish that this race **were** [not *was*] over. [a wish about something happening now]

> He wishes that he **had seen** [not *saw*] the race. [a wish about something that is past]

> The judges are demanding that the doctor **examine** [not *examines*] the runners. [a demand for something to happen in the future]

Also, MODAL AUXILIARY VERBS *would, could, might,* and *should* can convey speculations and conditions contrary to fact.

> If the runner **were** [not *was*] faster, we **would** see a better race. [*Would* is a modal auxiliary verb.]

The issue here is that when an INDEPENDENT CLAUSE expresses a conditional statement using a modal auxiliary verb, you want to be sure that in the DEPENDENT CLAUSE you don't use another modal auxiliary verb.

NO    If I **would have trained** for the race, I **might have won**.

YES   If I **had trained** for the race, I **might have** won.

**EXERCISE 8-8**   Fill in each blank with the correct form of the verb given in parentheses. For help, consult 8l and 8m.

EXAMPLE   Imagining the possibility of brain transplants requires that we (to be) <u>be</u> open-minded.

(1) If almost any organ other than the brain (to be) _____ the candidate for a swap, we would probably give our consent. (2) If the brain (to be) _____ to hold whatever impulses form our personalities, few people would want to risk a transplant. (3) Many popular movies have asked that we (to suspend) _____ disbelief and imagine the consequences should a personality actually (to be) _____ transferred to another body. (4) In real life, however, the complexities of a successful brain transplant require that not-yet-developed surgical techniques (to be) _____ used. (5) For example, it would be essential that during the actual transplant each one of the 500 trillion nerve connections within the brain (to continue) _____ to function as though the brain (to be) _____ lying undisturbed in a living human body.

# VOICE

## 8n   What is "voice" in verbs?

**Voice** in a verb tells whether a SUBJECT acts or is acted upon. English has two voices, *active* and *passive*. A subject in the **active voice** performs the action.

Most clams **live** in salt water. [The subject *clams* does the acting: Clams *live.*]

They **burrow** into the sandy bottoms of shallow waters. [The subject *they* does the acting: They *burrow.*]

A subject in the **passive voice** is acted upon. The person or thing doing the acting often appears in a PHRASE that starts with *by*. Verbs in the passive voice use forms of *be, have,* and *will* as AUXILIARY VERBS with the PAST PARTICIPLE of the MAIN VERB.

Clams **are considered** a delicacy by many people. [The subject *clams* is acted upon *by many people.*]

Some types of clams **are** highly **valued** by seashell collectors. [The subject *types* is acted upon *by seashell collectors.*]

## 8o How do I write in the active, not passive, voice?

Because the ACTIVE VOICE emphasizes the doer of an action, active constructions are more direct and dramatic. Active constructions usually require fewer words than passive constructions, which makes for greater conciseness (16c). Most sentences in the PASSIVE VOICE can be converted to active voice.

PASSIVE African tribal masks are often imitated by Western sculptors.

ACTIVE Western sculptors often imitate African tribal masks.

## 8p What are proper uses of the passive voice?

Although the active voice is usually best, in special circumstances you need to use the passive voice.

When no one knows who or what did something or when the doer of an action isn't important, writers use the passive voice.

The lock **was broken** sometime after four o'clock. [Who broke the lock is unknown.]

In 1899, the year I was born, a peace conference **was held** at The Hague. [The doers of the action—holders of the conference—aren't important.]

—E. B. White, "Unity"

Sometimes the action in the sentence is more important than the doer of the action. For example, if you want to focus on historical discoveries in a narrative, use the passive voice. Conversely, if you want to emphasize the people making the discoveries, use the active voice.

ACTIVE Joseph Priestley **discovered** oxygen in 1774. [*Joseph Priestley* is the subject.]

PASSIVE Oxygen **was discovered** in 1774 by Joseph Priestley. [*Oxygen* is the subject.]

ACTIVE The postal clerk **sent** the unsigned letter before I **could retrieve** it from the mailroom. [The emphasis is on the doers of the action, *the postal clerk* and *I*, rather than on the events, *sent* and *could retreive*.]

PASSIVE The unsigned letter **was sent** before it **could be retrieved** from the postal clerk. [The emphasis is on the events, *was sent* and *could be retrieved*, not on the doers of the action, the unknown sender and *the postal clerk*.]

In former years, the social sciences and natural sciences preferred the passive voice. Recently, style manuals for these disciplines have been advising writers to use the active voice whenever possible. "Verbs are vigorous, direct communicators," point out the editors of the *Publication Manual of the American Psychological Association.* "Use the active rather than the passive voice," they say.*

**EXERCISE 8-9**    First, determine which sentences are in the active voice and which the passive voice. Second, rewrite each sentence in the other voice, and then decide which voice better suits the meaning. Be ready to explain your choice. For help, consult 8n through 8p.

EXAMPLE    In the West African country of Ghana, a few woodcarvers are creating coffins that reflect their occupants' special interests. (*active; change to passive*)

In the West African country of Ghana, *coffins that reflect their occupants' special interests are being created by a few woodcarvers.*

1. A coffin in the shape of a green onion was chosen by a farmer.
2. A hunter's family buried him in a wooden coffin shaped like a leopard.
3. A dead chief was carried through his fishing village by friends and relatives bearing his body in a large pink wooden replica of a fish.
4. The family of a wealthy man who greatly admired cars buried him in a coffin shaped like a Mercedes car.
5. Although a few of these fantasy coffins have been displayed in museums, most of them end up buried in the ground.

*American Psychological Association, *Publication Manual of the American Psychological Association,* 5th ed. (Washington: APA, 2001) 41.

# Chapter 9

## PRONOUNS: CASE AND REFERENCE

### PRONOUN CASE

#### 9a  What does "case" mean?

**Case** applies in different ways to PRONOUNS and to NOUNS. For pronouns, case refers to three pronoun forms: the **subjective** (pronoun as a SUBJECT), the **objective** (pronoun as an OBJECT), and the **possessive** (pronouns used in possessive constructions). For nouns, case refers to only one noun form: the possessive. (For help in using apostrophes in the possessive case, see Chapter 27.)

#### 9b  What are personal pronouns?

**Personal pronouns** refer to persons or things. Box 9.1 shows the case forms of personal pronouns (subjective, objective, and possessive), in both the singular and the plural.

Many of the most difficult questions about pronoun case concern *who/whom* and *whoever/whomever.* For a full discussion of how to choose between them, see 9g.

---

**SUMMARY BOX** 9.1

**Case forms of personal pronouns**

|  | SUBJECTIVE | OBJECTIVE | POSSESSIVE |
|---|---|---|---|
| **SINGULAR** | I, you, he, she, it | me, you, him, her, it | my, mine, your, yours, his, her, hers, its |
| **PLURAL** | we, you, they | us, you, them | our, ours, your, yours, their, theirs |

---

#### 9c  How do pronouns work in case?

In the subjective case, pronouns function as SUBJECTS.

**We** were going to get married. [*We* is the subject.]

John and **I** wanted an inexpensive band for our wedding. [*I* is part of the compound subject *John and I*.]

**He and I** found an affordable one-person band. [*He and I* is the compound subject.]

In the objective case, pronouns function as OBJECTS.

We saw **him** perform in a public park. [*Him* is the direct object.]

We showed **him** our budget. [*Him* is the indirect object.]

He wrote down what we wanted and shook hands with **us**. [*Us* is the object of the preposition *with*.]

In the possessive case, nouns and pronouns usually indicate ownership or imply a relationship.

The **musician's contract** was very fair. [The possessive noun *musician's* implies a type of ownership.]

**His contract** was very fair. [The possessive pronoun *his* implies a type of ownership.]

The **musicians' problems** stem from playing cheap instruments. [The possessive noun *musicians'* implies a type of relationship.]

**Their problems** stem from playing with cheap instruments. [The possessive pronoun *their* implies a type of relationship.]

Sometimes, however, the notion of ownership or relationship calls for a major stretch of the imagination in possessive constructions. In such cases, look for the following pattern: noun + the *s* sound + noun. This means that two nouns work together, one of which does the possessing and the other of which is possessed.

The **musician's arrival** was eagerly anticipated. [The musician neither owns the arrival nor has a relationship with the arrival. Instead, the pattern noun + the *s* sound + noun is operating.]

**ALERT:** Never use an apostrophe in personal pronouns: *ours, yours, its, his, hers, theirs* (27c). ◆

## 9d  Which case is correct when *and* connects pronouns?

When *and* connects pronouns, or nouns and pronouns, the result is a **compound construction**. Compounding, which means "putting parts together in a whole," has no effect on case. Always use pronouns in the subjective case when they serve as the subjects of a sentence; also, always use pronouns in the objective case when they serve as objects in a sentence. Never mix cases.

**COMPOUND PRONOUN SUBJECT** — **He and I** saw the solar eclipse. [*He and I* is a compound subject.]

**COMPOUND PRONOUN OBJECT** — That eclipse astonished **him and me**. [*Him and me* is a compound object.]

When you're unsure of the case of a pronoun, use the "Troyka test for case" in Box 9.2. In this four-step test, you drop some of the words from your sentence so that you can tell which case sounds correct.

When pronouns are in a PREPOSITIONAL PHRASE, they are always in the objective case. (That is, a pronoun is always the OBJECT of the preposition.) This rule holds whether the pronouns are singular or plural.

---

### SUMMARY BOX 9.2

## Troyka test for case

**SUBJECTIVE CASE**

**STEP 1:** Write the sentence twice, once using the subjective case, and once using the objective case.

**STEP 2:** Cross out enough words to isolate the element you are questioning.

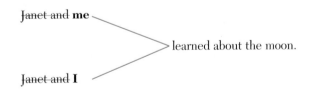

~~Janet and~~ **me** learned about the moon.

~~Janet and~~ **I** learned about the moon.

**STEP 3:** Omit the crossed-out words and read each sentence aloud to determine which one sounds right.

> **NO**   **Me** learned about the moon. [This doesn't sound right.]
>
> **YES**   **I** learned about the moon. [This sounds right, so the subjective case is correct.]

**STEP 4:** Select the correct version and restore the words you crossed out.

**Janet and I** learned about the moon.

---

**SUMMARY BOX**    **9.2** *continued*

### Troyka test for case

**OBJECTIVE CASE**

**STEP 1:**    Write the sentence twice, once using the subjective case, and once using the objective case.

**STEP 2:**    Cross out enough words to isolate the element you are questioning.

> The astronomer taught ~~Janet and~~ **I**
>
>                                      about the moon.
>
> The astronomer taught ~~Janet and~~ **me**

**STEP 3:**    Omit the crossed-out words and read each sentence aloud to determine which one sounds right.

> **NO**    The astronomer taught **I** about the moon. [This doesn't sound right.]

> **YES**    The astronomer taught **me** about the moon. [This sounds right, so the objective case is correct.]

**STEP 4:**    Select the correct version and restore the words you crossed out.

> The astronomer taught **Janet and me** about the moon.

---

> **NO**    Ms. Lester gave an assignment *to* **Sam and I**. [The prepositional phrase, which starts with the preposition *to*, cannot use the subjective-case pronoun *I*.]

> **YES**    Ms. Lester gave an assignment *to* **Sam and me**. [The prepositional phrase, which starts with the preposition *to*, calls for the objective-case pronoun *me*.]

Be especially careful when one or more pronouns follow the preposition *between*.

> **NO**    The dispute is *between* **Thomas and I**. [The prepositional phrase, which starts with the preposition *between*, cannot use the subjective-case pronoun *I*.]

> **YES**    The dispute is *between* **Thomas and me**. [The prepositional phrase, which starts with the preposition *between*, calls for the objective-case pronoun *me*.]

**EXERCISE 9-1** Underline the correct pronoun of each pair in parentheses. For help, consult 9c and 9d.

EXAMPLE    Bill and (I, me) noticed two young swimmers being pulled out to sea.

(1) The two teenagers caught in the rip current waved and hollered at Bill and (I, me). (2) The harder (they, them) both swam toward shore, the further away the undercurrent pulled them from the beach. (3) The yellow banners had warned Bill and (I, me) that a dangerous rip current ran beneath the water. (4) I yelled at Bill, "Between you and (I, me), (we, us) have to save them!" (5) (He and I, Him and me) both ran and dove into the crashing waves. (6) As former lifeguards, Bill and (I, me) knew what to do. (7) (We, Us) two remembered that the rule for surviving a rip current is to swim across the current. (8) Only when swimmers are safely away from the current should (they, them) swim toward shore. (9) I reached the teenage girl, who cried, "My boyfriend and (I, me) are drowning." (10) Bill rescued the frightened teenage boy, and when they were safely on shore, the boy looked at (he and I, him and me) and gasped, "Thanks. The two of (we, us) know you saved our lives."

## 9e    How do I match cases with appositives?

You can match cases with APPOSITIVES by putting pronouns and nouns in the same case as the word or words the appositive is renaming. Whenever you're unsure about whether to use the subjective or objective case, use the "Troyka test for case" in Box 9.2 to get the answer.

**We** [not *Us*] tennis players practice hard. [Here, the subjective-case pronoun *we* matches the noun phrase *tennis players*, which is the subject of this sentence.]

The winners, **she and I** [not *her and me*], advanced to the finals. [The subjective-case pronoun phrase *she and I* matches the noun *winners*, which is the subject of this sentence.]

The coach tells **us** [not *we*] tennis players to practice hard. [The objective-case pronoun *us* matches the noun phrase *tennis players*, which is the object in this sentence.]

The crowd cheered the winners, **her and me** [not *she and I*]. [The objective-case pronoun phrase *her and me* matches the noun *winners*, which is the object in this sentence.]

## 9f    How does case work after linking verbs?

A pronoun that comes after a LINKING VERB either renames the SUBJECT or shows possession. In both constructions, always use a pronoun in the subjective case. If you're unsure about how to identify a pronoun's case, use the "Troyka test for case" in Box 9.2.

The contest winner was **I** [not *me*]. [*Was* is a linking verb. *I* renames the subject, which is the noun phrase *contest winner,* so the subjective-case pronoun *I* is correct.]

The prize is **mine**. [*Is* is a linking verb. *Mine* shows possession, so the possessive-case pronoun *mine* is correct.]

**EXERCISE 9-2**  Underline the correct pronoun of each pair in parentheses. For help, consult 9c through 9f.

EXAMPLE  My college roommate and (I, me) have been interested in the Harlem Renaissance since (we, us) took an American literature survey course as sophomores.

(1) My roommate and (I, me) discovered (we, us) did not know much about the Harlem Renaissance. (2) (We, Us) two began reading the history and literature of the movement and wanted to know more about it. (3) Between (her and me, she and I), (we, us) divided the authors of the Harlem Renaissance into two groups. (4) However, learning about the movement meant more than reading works by the authors, (we, us) found. (5). It also meant (her and me, she and I) needed to study the background that created the movement. (6) (We, Us) learned that many African Americans moved from the South to large industrial cities in the North, a fact that directed (we, us) to other matters. (7) For example, a black middle class arose because (they, them) had industrial jobs, which earned (they, them) more opportunities for education. (8) (They, them) had a thirst for reading magazines and books by other African Americans. (9) Slowly, a radical group developed a "new consciousness," with the educated writers of the Harlem Renaissance being the most outspoken among (they, them). (10) (We, us), my roommate and (I, me), became even more interested in the Harlem Renaissance then because (she and I, her and me) remembered our parents talking about their participation in the civil rights movement of the 1960s.

## 9g  When should I use *who, whoever, whom,* and *whomever?*

The pronouns *who* and *whoever* are in the SUBJECTIVE CASE. The pronouns *whom* and *whomever* are in the OBJECTIVE CASE.

Informal spoken English tends to blur distinctions between *who* and *whom,* so with these words some people can't rely entirely on what "sounds right." Whenever you're unsure of whether to use *who* or *whoever* or to use *whom* or *whomever,* apply the "Troyka test for case" in Box 9.2. If you see *who* or *whoever,* test by temporarily substituting *he, she,* or *they.* If you see *whom* or *whomever,* test by temporarily substituting *him, her,* or *them.*

My father tells the same story to **whoever/whomever** he meets.

My father tells the same story to ~~she~~/**her**. [*Note:* When substituting, stop at *she/her*. The objective case *whomever* is correct because the sentence works when you substitute ***her*** for *whoever/whomever*. In contrast, the subjective case *whoever* is wrong because the sentence doesn't work when you substitute ***she*** for *whoever/whomever*.]

My father tells the same story to **whomever** he meets.

The most reliable variation of the test for *who, whom, whoever, whomever* calls for you to add a word before the substituted word set. In this example, the word *if* is added:

I wondered **who/whom** would vote for Ms. Wallace.

I wondered **if he**/~~if him~~ would vote for Ms. Wallace. [The subjective case *who* is correct because the sentence works when you substitute ***if he*** for *who/whom*. In contrast, the objective case *whom* is wrong because the sentence doesn't work when you substitute ***if him*** for *who/whom*.]

I wondered **who** would vote for Ms. Wallace.

Another variation of the test for *who, whom, whoever, whomever* calls for you to invert the word order in the test sentence.

Babies **who/whom** mothers cuddle grow faster and feel happier.

Mothers cuddle ~~they~~/**them**. [*Note:* When substituting, stop at *they/them*. By inverting the word order in the sentence—that is, by temporarily using *mothers* as the subject of the sentence—and substituting *they/them* for *who/whom,* you see that *them* is correct. Therefore, the objective case *whom* is correct.]

Babies **whom** mothers cuddle grow faster and feel happier.

At the beginning or end of a question, use *who* if the question is about the subject and *whom* if the question is about the object. To determine which case to use, recast the question into a statement, substituting *he* or *him* (or *she* or *her*).

**Who** watched the space shuttle liftoff? [*He* (not *Him*) *watched the space shuttle liftoff* uses the subjective case, so *who* is correct.]

Ted admires **whom**? [*Ted admires him* (not *he*) uses the objective case, so *whom* is correct.]

**Whom** does Ted admire? [*Ted admires him* (not *he*) uses the objective case, so *whom* is correct.]

To **whom** does Ted speak about becoming an astronaut? [*Ted speaks to them* (not *they*) uses the objective case, so *whom* is correct.]

**EXERCISE 9-3**  Underline the correct pronoun of each pair in parentheses. For help, consult 9g.

> EXAMPLE  Women (<u>who</u>, whom) both hold jobs outside the home and are mothers serve a "double shift."

(1) Women (who, whom) raise families do as much work at home as at their jobs. (2) In North American society, it is still mainly women (who, whom) cook dinner, clean the house, check the children's homework, read to them, and put them to bed. (3) Nevertheless, self-esteem runs high, some researchers have found, in many women on (who, whom) families depend for both wage earning and child rearing. (4) Compared with women (who, whom) pursue careers but have no children, those (who, whom) handle a double shift experience less anxiety and depression, according to the research. (5) Perhaps the reason for this finding is that those for (who, whom) the extra paycheck helps pay the bills feel pride and accomplishment when they rise to the challenge. (6) However, other studies note that women (who, whom) have both jobs and children experience tremendous stress. (7) Those (who, whom) feel unable both to support and to nurture their children despite their maximum efforts are the women for (who, whom) the dual responsibility is an almost unbearable burden.

## 9h   What pronoun case comes after *than* or *as*?

When *than* or *as* is part of a sentence of comparison, the sentence sometimes doesn't include words to complete the comparison outright. Rather, by omitting certain words, the sentence implies the comparison. For example, *My two-month-old Saint Bernard is larger **than** most full-grown dogs [are]* doesn't need the final word *are*.

When a pronoun follows *than* or *as*, the meaning of the sentence depends entirely on whether the pronoun is in the subjective case or the objective case. Here are two sentences that convey two very different messages, depending on whether the subjective case (*I*) or the objective case (*me*) is used.

1. My sister loved that dog more ***than* I**.
2. My sister loved that dog more ***than* me**.

In sentence 1, because *I* is in the subjective case, the sentence means *My sister loved that dog more than **I** [loved it]*. In sentence 2, because *me* is in the objective case, the sentence means *My sister loved that dog more than [she loved] **me***. In both situations, you can check whether you're using the correct case by supplying the implied words to see if they make sense.

239

## 9i   How do pronouns work before infinitives?

Most INFINITIVES consist of the SIMPLE FORMS of verbs that follow *to:* for example, *to laugh, to sing, to jump, to dance.* (A few exceptions occur when the *to* is optional: *My aunt helped the elderly man [to] cross the street;* and when the *to* is awkward: *My aunt watched the elderly man [to] get on the bus.*) For both the SUBJECTS of infinitives and the OBJECTS of infinitives, use the objective case.

> Our tennis coach expects **me *to serve***. [Because the word *me* is the subject of the infinitive *to serve,* the objective-case pronoun is correct.]

> Our tennis coach expects **him *to beat*** me. [Because the word *him* is the subject of the infinitive *to beat,* and *me* is the object of the infinitive, the objective-case pronoun is correct.]

## 9j   How do pronouns work with *-ing* words?

When a verb's *-ing* form functions as a NOUN, it's called a GERUND: *Brisk **walking** is excellent exercise.* When a noun or PRONOUN comes before a gerund, the POSSESSIVE CASE is required: ***His** brisk **walking** built up his stamina.* In contrast, when a verb's *-ing* form functions as a MODIFIER, it requires the subjective case for the pronoun, not the possessive case: ***He**, **walking** briskly, caught up to me.*

Here are two sentences that convey different messages, depending entirely on whether a possessive comes before the *-ing* word.

1. The detective noticed the **man *staggering***.
2. The detective noticed the **man's *staggering***.

Sentence 1 means that the detective noticed the *man;* sentence 2 means that the detective noticed the *staggering.* The same distinction applies to pronouns: When *the man* is replaced by *him* or *the man's* by *his,* the meaning is the same as in sentences 1 and 2.

1. The detective noticed **him *staggering***.
2. The detective noticed **his *staggering***.

In conversation, such distinctions are often ignored, but use them in ACADEMIC WRITING.

**EXERCISE 9-4**   Underline the correct pronoun of each pair in parentheses. For help, consult 9h through 9j.

**EXAMPLE**   Few contemporaries of the most famous novelist of the Victorian era had careers as productive as (<u>he</u>, him).

(1) The reading public wanted (him, his) to continue spinning new tales for their enjoyment, and he managed to write forty-seven novels

over a thirty-year career. (2) In his *Autobiography,* published near the end of his life, Anthony Trollope boasted that few people had led so full a life as (he, him). (3) His story begins with (him, his) landing a low-level civil service job that took him from his native England to Ireland and allowed (him, he) to view firsthand the terrible hardships facing the Irish people in the 1850s. (4) He absorbed what he saw so well that few people could depict Ireland better than (he, him). (5) Trollope's keen observations inspired (him, he) to write a series of novels about the Irish poor, each of which made him more popular as a writer. (6) After receiving a promotion and a transfer to London, Trollope became a keen observer of the English upper class and commented satirically in his novels on (their, them) hunting, shooting, and gambling. (7) Later in his life, his growing fame led to (him, his) mixing with the same rich and famous people he had earlier satirized in what some consider his greatest works, the massive six-novel Palliser series. (8) Indeed, no group of people is more realistically depicted than (they, them), although Trollope never lost his early fascination with the lives of the poor.

## 9k  What case should I use for *-self* pronouns?

Two types of pronouns end in *-self:* reflexive pronouns and intensive pronouns.

A **reflexive pronoun** reflects back on the subject, so it needs a subject in the sentence to be reflected back on. Without a subject, the reflexive pronoun cannot operate correctly.

The **detective** disguised **_himself_**. [The reflexive pronoun *himself* reflects back on the subject *detective.*]

Never use a reflexive pronoun to replace a personal pronoun in the subjective case.

**NO**  My teammates and **myself** will vote for a team captain.

**YES**  My teammates and **I** will vote for a team captain.

Also, never use a reflexive pronoun to replace a personal pronoun in the objective case. The only exception is when the object restates the subject.

**NO**  That decision is up to my teammates and **myself**.

**YES**  That decision is up to my teammates and **me**.

**Intensive pronouns,** which reflect back in the same way as reflexive pronouns, provide emphasis by making the message of the sentence more intense in meaning.

The detective felt that **his career _itself_** was at risk. [*Itself* intensifies the idea that the detective's career was at risk.]

## PRONOUN REFERENCE

**9l**     What is pronoun reference?

The word or group of words that a pronoun replaces is called its **antecedent**. In order for your writing to communicate its message clearly, each pronoun must relate precisely to an antecedent.

> I knew a **woman**, lovely in **her** bones / When small **birds** sighed, **she** would sigh back at **them**.
> —Theodore Roethke, "I Knew a Woman"

**9m**     What makes pronoun reference clear?

**Pronoun reference** is clear when your readers know immediately to whom or what each pronoun refers. Box 9.3 lists guidelines for using pronouns clearly, and the section in parentheses is where each is explained.

---

**SUMMARY BOX** 9.3

### Guidelines for clear pronoun reference

- Place pronouns close to their ANTECEDENTS (9n).
- Make a pronoun refer to a specific antecedent (9n).
- Do not overuse *it* (9q).
- Reserve *you* only for DIRECT ADDRESS (9r).
- Use *that, which,* and *who* correctly (9s).

---

**9n**     How can I avoid unclear pronoun reference?

Every pronoun needs to refer to a specific, nearby ANTECEDENT. If the same pronoun in your writing has to refer to more than one antecedent, replace some pronouns with nouns.

**NO**    In 1911, **Roald Amundsen** reached the South Pole just thirty-five days before **Robert F. Scott** arrived. **He** [who? Amundsen or Scott?] had told people that **he** [who? Amundsen or Scott?] was going to sail for the Arctic, but **he** [who? Amundsen or Scott?] was concealing **his** [whose? Amundsen's or Scott's?] plan. Soon, **he** [who? Amundsen or Scott?] turned south for the Antarctic. On the journey home, **he** [who? Amundsen or Scott?] and **his** [whose? Amundsen's or Scott's?] party froze to death just a few miles from safety.

**YES** In 1911, **Roald Amundsen** reached the South Pole just thirty-five days before **Robert F. Scott** arrived. **Amundsen** had told people that **he** was going to sail for the Arctic, but **he** was concealing **his** plan. Soon, **Amundsen** turned south for the Antarctic. Meanwhile, on **their** journey home, **Scott** and **his party** froze to death just a few miles from safety.

**ALERT:** Be careful with the VERBS *said* and *told* in sentences that contain pronoun reference. To maintain clarity, use quotation marks and slightly reword each sentence to make the meaning clear.

**NO** **Her** mother told **her she** was going to visit **her** grandmother.

**YES** **Her** mother told **her,** "**You** are going to visit your grandmother."

**YES** **Her** mother told **her,** "**I** am going to visit your grandmother." ◆

Further, if too much material comes between a pronoun and its antecedent, readers can lose track of the meaning.

Alfred Wegener, a German meteorologist and professor of geophysics

at the University of Graz in Austria, was the first to suggest that all

the continents on earth were originally part of one large landmass.

According to this theory, the supercontinent broke up long ago  and the

fragments drifted apart. <sub>Wegener</sub> He named this supercontinent Pangaea.

[*He* can refer only to Wegener, but material about Wegener's theory intervenes, so using *Wegener* again instead of *he* jogs the reader's memory and makes reading easier.]

When you start a new paragraph, be cautious about beginning it with a pronoun whose antecedent is in a prior paragraph. You're better off repeating the word.

**ESL TIP:** Many languages omit a pronoun as a subject because the verb delivers the needed information. English requires the use of the pronoun as a subject. For example, never omit *it* in the following: *Political science is an important academic subject.* **It** *is studied all over the world.* ☺

**EXERCISE 9-5**   Revise so that each pronoun refers clearly to its antecedent. Either replace pronouns with nouns or restructure the material to clarify pronoun reference. For help, consult 9n.

EXAMPLE    People who return to work after years away from the corporate world often discover that business practices have changed. They may find fiercer competition in the workplace, but they may also discover that they are more flexible than before.

Here is one possible revision: *People who return to work after years away from the corporate world often discover that business practices have changed. Those people may find fiercer competition in the workplace, but they may also discover that business practices are more flexible than before.*

Most companies used to frown on employees who became involved in office romances. They often considered them to be using company time for their own enjoyment. Now, however, managers realize that happy employees are productive employees. With more women than ever before in the workforce and with people working longer hours, they have begun to see that male and female employees want and need to socialize. They are also dropping their opposition to having married couples on the payroll. They no longer automatically believe that they will bring family matters into the workplace or stick up for each other at the company's expense.

One departmental manager had doubts when a systems analyst for research named Laura announced that she had become engaged to Peter, who worked as a technician in the same department. She told her that either one or the other might have to transfer out of the research department. After listening to her plea that they be allowed to work together on a trial basis, the manager reconsidered. She decided to give Laura and Peter a chance to prove that their relationship would not affect their work. The decision paid off. They demonstrated that they could work as an effective research team, right through their engagement and subsequent marriage. Two years later, when Laura was promoted to assistant manager for product development and after he asked to move also, she enthusiastically recommended that Peter follow Laura to her new department.

## 9o   How do pronouns work with *it, that, this,* and *which*?

When you use *it, that, this,* and *which,* be sure that your readers can easily understand what each word refers to.

NO    Comets usually fly by the earth at 100,000 mph, whereas asteroids sometimes collide with the earth. **This** interests scientists. [Does *this* refer to the speed of the comets, to comets flying by the earth, or to asteroids colliding with the earth?]

**YES** Comets usually fly by the earth at 100,000 mph, whereas asteroids sometimes collide with the earth. **This difference** interests scientists. [Adding a noun after *this* or *that* clarifies the meaning.]

**NO** I told my friends that I was going to major in geology, **which** made my parents happy. [Does *which* refer to telling your friends or to majoring in geology?]

**YES** My parents were happy **because I discussed my major with my friends.**

**YES** My parents were happy **because I chose to major in geology.**

Also, the title of any piece of writing stands on its own. Therefore, in your introductory paragraph, never refer to your title with *this* or *that*. For example, if an essay's title is "Geophysics as a Major," the following holds for the first sentence:

**NO** **This subject** unites the sciences of physics, biology, and paleontology.

**YES** **Geophysics** unites the sciences of physics, biology, and paleontology.

## 9p  How do I use *they* and *it* precisely?

The expression *they say* can't take the place of stating precisely who is doing the saying. Your credibility as a writer depends on your mentioning a source precisely.

**NO** **They say** that earthquakes are becoming more frequent.
[*They* doesn't identify the authority who made the statement.]

**YES** **Seismologists** say that earthquakes are becoming more frequent.

The expressions *it said* and *it is said that* reflect imprecise thinking. Also, they're wordy. Revising such expressions improves your writing.

**NO** **It said** in the newspaper that California has minor earthquakes almost daily. [*It said in the newspaper that* is wordy.]

**YES** **The newspaper reported** that California has minor earthquakes almost daily.

## 9q How do I use *it* to suit the situation?

The word *it* has three different uses in English. Here are examples of correct uses of *it*.

1. PERSONAL PRONOUN: Ryan wants to visit the 18-inch Schmidt telescope, but **it** is on Mount Palomar.
2. EXPLETIVE (sometimes called a *subject filler*, it delays the subject): **It** is interesting to observe the stars.
3. IDIOMATIC EXPRESSION (words that depart from normal use, such as using *it* as the sentence subject when writing about weather, time, distance, and environmental conditions): **It** is sunny. **It** is midnight. **It** is not far to the hotel. **It** is very hilly.

All three uses listed above are correct, but avoid combining them in the same sentence. The result can be an unclear and confusing sentence.

> **NO** Because our car was overheating, **it** came as no surprise that **it** broke down just as **it** began to rain. [*It* is overused here, even though all three uses—2, 1, and 3 on the above list, respectively—are acceptable.]

> **YES** **It** came as no surprise that our overheating car broke down just as the rain began. [The word order is revised so that *it* is used once.]

**ESL TIP:** In some languages, *it* is not used as an expletive. In English, it is.

> **NO** Is a lovely day.

> **YES** **It** is a lovely day.

## 9r When should I use *you* for direct address?

Reserve *you* for **direct address**, writing that addresses the reader directly. For example, we use *you* in this handbook to address you, the student. *You* is not a suitable substitute for specific words that refer to people, situations, or occurrences.

> **NO** Prison uprisings often happen **when you allow** overcrowding. [The reader, *you*, did not allow the overcrowding.]

> **YES** Prison uprisings often happen **when prisons are** overcrowded.

> **NO** In Russia, **you** usually have to stand in long lines to buy groceries. [Are *you*, the reader, planning to do your grocery shopping in Russia?]

> **YES** **Russian consumers** usually have to stand in long lines to buy groceries.

**EXERCISE 9-6** Revise these sentences so that all pronoun references are clear. If a sentence is correct, circle its number. For help, consult 9o through 9r.

EXAMPLE By collecting data on animal species around the world, you gain insight into the ways animals communicate.

*By collecting data on animal species around the world, researchers gain insight into the ways animals communicate.* [Revision changes person from *you* not used for direct address to third person, the noun *researchers.*]

1. Researchers find that animal communication is more complex and more varied than you might expect.
2. Throughout the animal kingdom, they use low-pitched noises to convey aggression and high-pitched noises to convey fear.
3. They say that dogs bark for many reasons: to ask for food, to alert a family to danger, to convey excitement.
4. Elephants send messages to herds three miles away using sounds too low for you to hear.
5. In the water, damselfish emit squeaks and dolphins send out clicks and whistles. This interests marine biologists.
6. Elk males have rutting contests to prove which male is stronger, with the one that ruts louder and longer proving his dominance.
7. They do not communicate only by using sounds: lobsters use chemical signals, lizards use head bobs, fireflies use light signals.
8. You can teach chimps to use sign language to communicate in simple sentences, such as "Give JoJo banana."

**9s** **When should I use *that, which,* and *who*?**

To use the pronouns *that* and *which* correctly, you want to check the context of the sentence you're writing. *Which* and *that* refer to animals and things. Only sometimes do they refer to anonymous or collective groups of people. Box 9.4 (p. 248) shows how to choose between *that* and *which*. For information about the role of commas with *that* and *which*, see 24f.

*Who* refers to people and to animals mentioned by name.

**John Polanyi, who** was awarded the Nobel Prize in Chemistry, speaks passionately in favor of nuclear disarmament. [*John Polanyi* is a person.]

**Lassie, who** was known for her intelligence and courage, was actually played by a series of male collies. [*Lassie* is the name of an animal.]

Many professional writers reserve *which* for nonrestrictive clauses and *that* for restrictive clauses. Other writers use *that* and *which* interchangeably for restrictive clauses. Current practice allows the use of either as long

**SUMMARY BOX 9.4**

## Choosing between *that* and *which*

**Choice:** Some instructors and style guides use either *that* or *which* to introduce a RESTRICTIVE CLAUSE (a DEPENDENT CLAUSE that is essential to the meaning of the sentence or part of the sentence). Others may advise you to use only *that* so that your writing distinguishes clearly between restrictive and NONRESTRICTIVE CLAUSES. Whichever style you use, be consistent in each piece of writing:

- The zoos **that** (or **which**) **most children like** display newborn and baby animals. [The point in this sentence concerns children's preferences. Therefore, the words *most children like* are essential for delivering the meaning and make up a restrictive clause.]

**No choice:** You are required to use *which* to introduce a nonrestrictive clause (a dependent clause that isn't essential to the meaning of the sentence or part of the sentence).

- Zoos, **which most children like**, attract more visitors if they display newborn and baby animals. [The point in this sentence concerns attracting more visitors to zoos. Therefore, the words *most children like* are not essential to the meaning of the sentence and make up a nonrestrictive clause.]

as you're consistent in each piece of writing. However, for ACADEMIC WRITING, your instructor might expect you to maintain the distinction.

**ALERT:** Use commas before and after a nonrestrictive clause. Don't use commas before and after a restrictive clause; see 24k.4. ◆

**EXERCISE 9-7**  Fill in the blanks with *that, which,* or *who.* For help, consult 9s.

EXAMPLE    For years, consumers <u>who</u> want the very latest electronic gadgets have had to travel to Japan to buy them.

1. In Japan, consumers can buy a set of tiny clip-on headphones _____ have enough memory for an hour's worth of music.

2. These headphones, _____ are a popular item in Japan, are unlikely to reach foreign markets, because manufacturers don't export them.

3. People from outside Japan _____ crave innovative Japanese products now have an alternative way of buying them _____ is less expensive than traveling to Japan.

4. Web-based businesses, _____ are springing up every day, now specialize in exporting products _____ are trend-setting in Japan.

5. These companies, _____ offer extra advantages such as English-language warranties and manuals, are finding a ready market among English-speaking technophiles.

# Chapter 10

## AGREEMENT

### 10a  What is agreement?

In everyday speech, agreement indicates that people hold the same ideas. Grammatical **agreement** is also based on sameness. Specifically, you need to match SUBJECTS and VERBS; see 10b through 10n. You also need to match PRONOUNS and ANTECEDENTS; see 10o through 10t.

## SUBJECT-VERB AGREEMENT

### 10b  What is subject-verb agreement?

**Subject-verb agreement** means that a SUBJECT and its VERB match in NUMBER (singular or plural) and PERSON (first, second, or third person). Box 10.1 presents these major concepts in grammatical agreement.

> The **firefly glows**. [*Firefly* is a singular subject in the third person; *glows* is a singular verb in the third person.]

> **Fireflies glow**. [*Fireflies* is a plural subject in the third person; *glow* is a plural verb in the third person.]

---

### SUMMARY BOX 10.1

## Major concepts in grammatical agreement

- **Number**, as a concept in grammar, refers to *singular* (one) and *plural* (more than one).
- The **first person** is the speaker or writer. *I* (singular) and *we* (plural) are the only subjects that occur in the first person.

  | SINGULAR | **I see** a field of fireflies. |
  | PLURAL | **We see** a field of fireflies. |

---

---

**Major concepts in grammatical agreement**

- The **second person** is the person spoken or written to. *You* (for both singular and plural) is the only subject that occurs in the second person.

  **SINGULAR** **You see** a shower of sparks.

  **PLURAL** **You see** a shower of sparks.

- The **third person** is the person or thing being spoken or written about. *He, she, it* (singular) and *they* (plural) are the third-person subject forms. Most rules for subject-verb agreement involve the third person.

  **SINGULAR** The **scientist sees** a cloud of cosmic dust.

  **PLURAL** The **scientists see** a cloud of cosmic dust.

---

## **10c** Why is a final *-s* or *-es* in a subject or verb so important?

SUBJECT-VERB AGREEMENT often involves one letter: *s* (or *es* for words that end in *-s*). For verbs in the present tense, you form the SIMPLE FORM of third-person singular by adding *-s* or *-es*: *laugh, laughs; kiss, kisses.* Major exceptions are the verbs *be (is), have (has),* and *do (does);* see 8c.

> That **student agrees** that **young teenagers watch** too much television.
>
> Those **young teenagers are** taking valuable time away from studying.
>
> That **student has** a part-time job for ten hours a week.
>
> Still, that **student does** well in college.

For a subject to become plural, you add *-s* or *-es* to its end: *lip, lips; princess, princesses.* Major exceptions include most pronouns (*they, it*) and a few nouns that for singular and plural either don't change (*deer, deer*) or change internally (*mouse, mice*). Box 10.2 shows you how to visualize the basic pattern for agreement using *-s* or *-es*.

---

**PATTERN BOX** 10.2

**Basic subject-verb agreement**

The **student works** long hours.   The **students work** long hours.

| SINGULAR SUBJECT | SINGULAR VERB | | PLURAL SUBJECT | PLURAL VERB |

Here's a device for remembering how agreement works for most subject-verb agreement. Note that the final -*s* or -*es* can take only one path at a time—to the end of the verb or to the end of the subject.

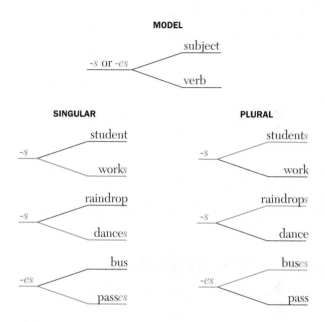

**ALERT:** When you use an AUXILIARY VERB with a main verb, never add -*s* or -*es* to the main verb: *The coach **can walk*** [not *can walks*] *to campus. The coach **does like*** [not *does likes*] *his job.* ◆

**EXERCISE 10-1**  Use the subject and verb in each set to write two complete sentences—one with a singular subject and one with a plural subject. Keep all verbs in the present tense. For help, consult 10c.

EXAMPLE    climber, increase

**Singular subject:** Without proper equipment, a mountain *climber increases* the risk of falling.

**Plural subject:** Without proper equipment, mountain *climbers increase* the risk of falling.

1. dog, bark
2. flower, bloom
3. team, compete
4. planet, rotate
5. author, write
6. tornado, demolish
7. jet, depart
8. professor, might quiz

## 10d Can I ignore words between a subject and its verb?

You can ignore all words between a subject and its verb. Focus strictly on the subject and its verb. Box 10.3 shows you this pattern.

**NO**   **Winners** of the state contest **goes** to the national finals.
[*Winners* is the subject; the verb must agree with it. Ignore the words *of the state contest.*]

**YES**   **Winners** of the state contest **go** to the national finals.

The words *one of the . . .* often require a second look. Use a singular verb to agree with the word *one*. Don't be distracted by the plural noun that comes after *of the.* (For information on the phrase *one of the . . . who,* see 10l.)

**NO**   **One** of the problems **are** the funds needed for traveling to the national finals.

**YES**   **One** of the problems **is** the funds needed for traveling to the national finals.

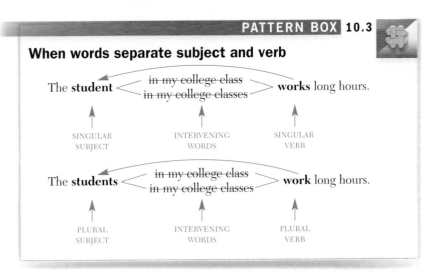

**PATTERN BOX 10.3**

### When words separate subject and verb

The **student** ⟨ in my college class / in my college classes ⟩ **works** long hours.

SINGULAR SUBJECT — INTERVENING WORDS — SINGULAR VERB

The **students** ⟨ in my college class / in my college classes ⟩ **work** long hours.

PLURAL SUBJECT — INTERVENING WORDS — PLURAL VERB

Similarly, eliminate all word groups between the subject and the verb, starting with *including, together with, along with, accompanied by, in addition to, except,* and *as well as.*

**NO**   The **moon**, *as well as* the planet Venus, **are** visible in the night sky. [*Moon* is the subject. The verb must agree with it. Ignore the words *as well as the planet Venus.*]

**YES** The **moon**, as well as the planet Venus, **is** visible in the night sky.

## 10e How do verbs work when subjects are connected by *and*?

When two SUBJECTS are connected by *and*, they create a single COMPOUND SUBJECT. A compound subject calls for a plural verb. Box 10.4 shows you this pattern. (For related material on PRONOUNS and ANTECEDENTS, see 10p.)

**The Cascade Diner *and* the Wayside Diner *have*** [not *has*] fried catfish today. [These are two different diners.]

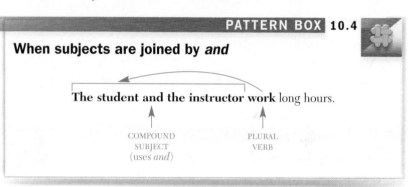

**PATTERN BOX 10.4**

**When subjects are joined by *and***

**The student and the instructor work** long hours.

COMPOUND SUBJECT (uses *and*)

PLURAL VERB

One exception occurs when *and* joins subjects that refer to a single thing or person.

**My friend *and* neighbor *makes*** [not *make*] excellent chili. [In this sentence, the friend is the same person as the neighbor. If they were two different people, *makes* would become *make*.]

**Macaroni *and* cheese *contains*** [not *contain*] carbohydrates, protein, and many calories. [*Macaroni and cheese* is one dish, not two separate dishes, so it requires a singular verb.]

## 10f How do verbs work with *each* and *every*?

The words *each* and *every* are singular even if they refer to a compound subject. Therefore, they take a singular verb.

***Each* human hand and foot *makes*** [not *make*] a distinctive print.

To identify lawbreakers, ***every* police chief, sheriff, and federal marshal *depends*** [not *depend*] on such prints.

**ALERT:** Use one word, either *each* or *every*, not both at the same time: **Each** [not *Each and every*] *robber has been caught*. (For more information about pronoun agreement for *each* and *every*, see 10i, 10p, and 10r.) ◆

## 10g How do verbs work when subjects are connected by *or*?

As Box 10.5 shows, when SUBJECTS are joined by *or*—or by the sets *either . . . or, neither . . . nor, not only . . . but (also)*—the verb agrees with the subject closest to it. Ignore everything before the last-mentioned noun or pronoun. Box 10.5 shows this pattern with *either . . . or*. (For related material on pronouns and antecedents, see 10q.)

~~Neither~~ spiders ~~nor~~ **flies upset** me.

~~Not only~~ spiders ~~but also~~ ~~all other~~ **arachnids have** four pairs of legs.

~~A dinner of six clam fritters, four blue crabs,~~ ***or*** ~~one steamed~~ **lobster sounds** good.

---

**PATTERN BOX** 10.5

### When subjects are joined by *or*

- ~~Either~~ the instructor ~~or~~
  ~~Either~~ the instructors ~~or~~ the **student knows** the answer.

SINGULAR SINGULAR
SUBJECT VERB

- ~~Either~~ the instructor ~~or~~
  ~~Either~~ the instructors ~~or~~ the **students know** the answer.

PLURAL PLURAL
SUBJECT VERB

---

## 10h How do verbs work with inverted word order?

In English sentences, the SUBJECT normally comes before its VERB: **Astronomy is** *interesting*. **Inverted word order** reverses the typical subject-verb pattern by putting the verb first. Most questions use inverted

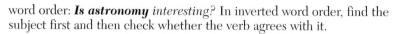

word order: *Is astronomy interesting?* In inverted word order, find the subject first and then check whether the verb agrees with it.

Into deep space **shoot** probing **satellites**. [The plural verb *shoot* agrees with the inverted plural subject *satellites*.]

On the television screen **appears** an **image** of Saturn. [The singular verb *appears* agrees with the inverted singular subject *image*.]

**ALERT:** When you start a sentence with *there*, check whether the subject is singular or plural, and then choose the right form of *be* to agree with the subject. If your sentence begins with *it*, always use the singular form of *be* (*is, was*) no matter whether the subject is singular or plural.

**There *are*** nine **planets** in our solar system. [The verb *are* agrees with the subject *planets*.]

**There *is*** probably no **life** on eight of them. [The verb *is* agrees with the subject *life*.]

**It *is*** astronomers who explore this theory daily. [The verb *is* agrees with *it*, not with *astronomers*.] ◆

**EXERCISE 10-2**   Supply the correct present-tense form of the verb in parentheses. For help, consult 10c through 10h.

EXAMPLE   Detectives and teachers (to know) <u>know</u> experienced liars can fool almost anybody, but a new computer can tell who is telling the truth.

1. Police officers and teachers often (to wish) _____ they could "read" people's facial expressions.
2. Trained police officers or a smart teacher (to know) _____ facial tics and nervous mannerisms (to show) _____ someone is lying.
3. However, a truly gifted liar, along with well-coached eyewitnesses, (to reveal) _____ very little through expressions or behavior.
4. There (to be) _____ forty-six muscle movements that create all facial expressions in the human face.
5. Neuroscientist Terrence Seinowski, accompanied by a team of researchers, (to be) _____ developing a computer program to recognize even slight facial movements made by the most expert liars.

## 10i   How do verbs work with indefinite pronouns?

**Indefinite pronouns** usually refer to nonspecific persons, things, quantities, or ideas. The nonspecific aspect is the reason these pronouns are labeled "indefinite." As part of a sentence, however, the indefinite pronoun is usually clear from the meaning.

Most indefinite pronouns are singular and require a singular verb for agreement. Yet, others are always plural, and a few can be singular *or* plural. Box 10.6 clarifies this situation by listing indefinite pronouns according to what verb form they require. (For related material on pronouns and antecedents, see 10r.)

---

**SUMMARY BOX** 10.6

## Common indefinite pronouns

**ALWAYS PLURAL**

both                     many

**ALWAYS SINGULAR**

| | | |
|---|---|---|
| another | every | no one |
| anybody | everybody | nothing |
| anyone | everyone | one |
| anything | everything | somebody |
| each | neither | someone |
| either | nobody | something |

**SINGULAR *OR* PLURAL, DEPENDING ON CONTEXT**

| | | |
|---|---|---|
| all | more | none |
| any | most | some |

---

Here are sample sentences:

**SINGULAR INDEFINITE PRONOUNS**

**Everything** about that intersection **is** dangerous.

But whenever **anyone says** anything, **nothing is** done.

**Each** of us **has** [not *have*] to shovel snow; **each is** [not *are*] expected to help.

**Every** snowstorm of the past two years **has** [not *have*] been severe.

**Every** one of them **has** [not *have*] caused massive traffic jams.

**SINGULAR OR PLURAL INDEFINITE PRONOUNS (DEPENDING ON MEANING)**

**Some** of our streams **are** polluted. [*Some* refers to the plural noun *streams*, so the plural verb *are* is correct.]

**Some** pollution **is** reversible, but **all** pollution **threatens** the balance of nature. [*Some* and *all* refer to the singular noun *pollution*, so the singular verbs *is* and *threatens* are correct.]

**All** that environmentalists ask **is** to give nature a chance. [*All* has the meaning here of "everything" or "the only thing," so the singular verb *is* is correct.]

Winter has driven the birds south; **all have** left. [*All* refers to the plural noun *birds,* so the plural verb *have* is correct.]

**ALERTS:** (1) Don't mix singular and plural with *this, that, these,* and *those* used with *kind* and *type. This* and *that* are singular, as are *kind* and *type; these* and *those* are plural, as are *kinds* and *types:* **This** [not *These*] **kind** of rainwear is waterproof. **These** [not *This*] **kinds** of sweaters keep me warm. (2) The rules for indefinite pronouns often collide with practices of avoiding SEXIST LANGUAGE. For suggestions, see 10s and 21g. ◆

## 10j How do verbs work with collective nouns?

A **collective noun** names a group of people or things: *family, audience, class, number, committee, team, group,* and the like. When the group of people or things is acting as one unit, use a singular verb. When members of the group are acting individually, use a plural verb. As you're writing, be careful not to shift back and forth between a singular and a plural verb for the same noun.

The senior **class** nervously ***awaits*** final exams. [The *class* is acting as a single unit, so the verb is singular.]

The senior **class *were fitted*** for their graduation robes today. [The members (of the class) were fitted as individuals, so the verb is plural.]

## 10k Why does the linking verb agree with the subject, not the subject complement?

Even though a LINKING VERB connects a sentence's SUBJECT to its SUBJECT COMPLEMENT, the linking verb agrees with the subject. It does not agree with the subject complement.

**NO** The worst **part** of owning a car ***are*** the bills. [The subject is the singular *part,* so the plural verb *are* is wrong. The subject complement is the plural *bills* and doesn't affect agreement.]

**YES** The worst **part** of owning a car ***is*** the bills. [The singular subject *part* agrees with the singular verb *is.* The subject complement doesn't affect agreement.]

257

## 10l What verbs agree with *who, which,* and *that*?

If the ANTECEDENT of *who, which,* or *that* is singular, use a singular verb. If the antecedent is plural, use a plural verb.

The scientist will share the prize with the **researchers *who* work** with her. [*Who* refers to *researchers*, so the plural verb *work* is used.]

George Jones is the **student *who* works** in the science lab. [*Who* refers to *student*, so the singular verb *works* is used.]

If you use phrases including *one of the* or *the only one of the* immediately before *who, which,* or *that* in a sentence, be careful about the verb you use. *Who, which,* or *that* always refers to the plural word immediately following *one of the*, so the verb must be plural. Although *the only one of* is also always followed by a plural word, *who, which,* or *that* must be singular to agree with the singular *one*.

Tracy is **one of the** students ***who* talk** in class. [*Who* refers to *students*, so the verb *talk* is plural. *Tracy* is pointed out, but the talking is still done by all of the students.]

Jim is **the only one of the** students ***who* talks** in class. [*Who* refers to *one*, so the verb *talks* is singular. *Jim* is the single person who is talking.]

**EXERCISE 10-3**   Supply the correct present-tense form of the verb in parentheses. For help, consult 10i through 10l.

EXAMPLE   Everybody on a class trip to the coastal waters of the Pacific Ocean (to enjoy) <u>enjoys</u> an opportunity to study dolphins in their natural habitat.

1. A class of college students in marine biology (to take) _____ notes individually while watching dolphins feed off the California coast.

2. Everyone in the class (to listen) _____ as a team of dolphin experts (to explain) _____ some of the mammals' characteristics.

3. A group of dolphins, called a pod, usually (to consist) _____ of 10,000 to 30,000 members.

4. One unique characteristic of dolphins' brains (to be) _____ the sleep patterns that (to keep) _____ one-half of the brain awake at all times.

5. All (to need) _____ to stay awake to breathe, or else they would drown.

## 10m How do verbs work with amounts, fields of study, and other special nouns?

**AMOUNTS**

SUBJECTS that refer to time, sums of money, distance, or measurement are singular. They take singular verbs.

**Two hours *is*** not enough time to finish. [time]

**Three hundred dollars *is*** what we must pay. [sum of money]

**Two miles *is*** a short sprint for some serious joggers. [distance]

**Three-quarters of an inch *is*** needed for a perfect fit.
[measurement]

## FIELDS OF STUDY

The name for a field of study is singular even if it appears to be plural: *economics, mathematics, physics,* and *statistics.*

> ***Statistics* is** required of science majors. [*Statistics* is a course of study, so the singular verb *is* is correct.]

> ***Statistics* show** that a teacher shortage is coming. [*Statistics* isn't used here as a field of study, so the plural verb *show* is correct.]

## SPECIAL NOUNS

*Athletics, news, ethics,* and *measles* are singular despite their plural appearance. Also, *United States of America* is singular: It is one nation. However, *politics* and *sports* take singular or plural verbs, depending on the meaning of the sentence.

> The ***news* gets** better each day. [*News* is a singular noun, so the singular verb *gets* is correct.]

> ***Sports* is** a good way to build physical stamina. [*Sports* is one general activity, so the singular verb *is* is correct.]

> Three ***sports* are** offered at the recreation center. [*Sports* are separate activities, so the plural verb *are* is correct.]

*Jeans, pants, scissors, clippers, tweezers, eyeglasses, thanks,* and *riches* are some of the words that require a plural verb, even though they refer to one thing. However, if you use *pair* with *jeans, pants, scissors, clippers, tweezers,* or *eyeglasses,* use a singular verb for agreement.

> Those ***slacks* need** pressing. [plural]

> That ***pair*** of slacks **needs** pressing. [singular]

*Series* and *means* can be singular or plural, according to the meaning you intend.

> Two new TV ***series* are** big hits. [*Series* refers to individual items (two different series), so the plural verb *are* is correct.]

> A ***series*** of disasters **is** plaguing our production. [*Series* refers to a whole group (the whole series of disasters), so the singular verb *is* is correct.]

**10n** **How do verbs work with titles, company names, and words as themselves?**

## TITLES

A title itself refers to one work or entity (even when plural and compound NOUNS are in the title), so a singular verb is correct.

*Breathing Lessons* by Anne Tyler **is** a prize-winning novel.

## COMPANY NAMES

Many companies have plural words in their names. However, a company should always be treated as a singular unit, requiring a singular verb.

*Cohn Brothers* **boxes** and **delivers** fine art.

## WORDS AS THEMSELVES

Whenever you write about words as themselves to call attention to those words, use a singular verb, even if more than one word is involved.

*We* **implies** that everyone is included.

During the Vietnam War, *protective reaction strikes* **was** a euphemism for *bombing.*

**EXERCISE 10-4**  Supply the correct present-tense form of the verb in parentheses. For help, consult 10i through 10n.

> EXAMPLE   In a fast-growing trend, some of the people who (to live) <u>live</u> on college campuses and (to participate) <u>participate</u> in campus life today are not students but retired persons.

1. *College-linked retirement communities* (to be) _____ the general term for retirement homes based on or near colleges and universities.

2. These communities, which (to gratify) _____ a retiree's desire for an active life and lifelong learning, are springing up on many campuses.

3. Many college-linked communities (to require) _____ their residents to have been formerly linked to the affiliated university, in a role such as a faculty or staff member, but some (to open) _____ their doors to all interested retirees.

4. To the residents of such retirement communities, the major advantage (to be) _____ opportunities for ongoing cultural, intellectual, and social growth.

5. However, the younger student body often (to benefit) _____ when retirees take part in courses and activities and thereby bring decades of wisdom and experience to their studies.

**EXERCISE 10-5**   This exercise covers all of subject-verb agreement (10b through 10n). Supply the correct form of the verb in parentheses.

EXAMPLE    Of the thirty thousand plant species on earth, the rose (to be) <u>is</u> the most universally known.

1. Each plant species (to invite) _____ much discussion about origins and meanings, and when talk turns to flowers, the rose is usually the first mentioned.

2. More fragrant and colorful (to be) _____ other types of flowers, yet roses (to remain) _____ the most popular worldwide.

3. Each of the types of roses (to symbolize) _____ beauty, love, romance, and secrecy.

4. There (to be) _____ more than two hundred pure species of roses and thousands of mixed species, thirty-five of which (to flourish) _____ in the soil of North America.

5. It's impossible to determine exactly where or when the first rose (to be) _____ domesticated, because roses have existed for so many centuries; one of the earliest references dates back to 3000 BC.

6. One myth from Greek mythology (to suggest) _____ that the rose first appeared with the birth of the goddess Aphrodite.

7. Another myth, which focuses on the rose's thorns, (to say) _____ that an angry god shot arrows into the stem to curse the rose forever with arrow-shaped thorns.

8. While theories of this kind (to explain) _____ the significance and evolution of the rose, few people can explain the flower's enduring popularity.

9. Even today, a couple (to demonstrate) _____ love by purchasing red roses.

10. Of all flowers, the best seller (to remain) _____ the rose.

## PRONOUN-ANTECEDENT AGREEMENT

### 10o   What is pronoun-antecedent agreement?

**Pronoun-antecedent agreement** means that a PRONOUN matches its ANTECEDENT in NUMBER (singular or plural) and PERSON (first, second, or third person). Box 10.7 (p. 262) shows you how to visualize this pattern of grammatical agreement. You might also want to consult Box 10.1 in 10b for explanations and examples of the concepts *number* and *person*.

The **firefly** glows when **it** emerges from **its** nest at night. [The singular pronouns *it* and *its* match their singular antecedent, *firefly*.]

**Fireflies** glow when **they** emerge from **their** nests at night. [The plural pronouns *they* and *their* match their plural antecedent, *fireflies*.]

## Pronoun-antecedent agreement

- Loud **music** has **its** harmful side effects.

THIRD-PERSON    THIRD-PERSON
SINGULAR      SINGULAR
ANTECEDENT    PRONOUN

- The **musicians** damaged **their** hearing.

THIRD-PERSON    THIRD-PERSON
PLURAL      PLURAL
ANTECEDENT    PRONOUN

### 10p   How do pronouns work when *and* connects antecedents?

When *and* connects two or more ANTECEDENTS, they require a plural pronoun. This rule applies even if each separate antecedent is singular. (For related material on subjects and verbs, see 10e.)

**The Cascade Diner *and* the Wayside Diner** closed for New Year's Eve to give **their** [not *its*] employees the night off. [Two separate diners require a plural pronoun.]

When *and* joins singular nouns that nevertheless refer to a single person or thing, use a singular pronoun.

**My friend *and* neighbor** makes **his** [not *their*] excellent chili every Saturday. [The friend is the same person as the neighbor, so the singular *his* (or *her*) is correct. If two different people were involved, the correct pronoun would be *their*, and *make* would be the correct verb.]

#### EACH, EVERY

The words *each* and *every* are singular, even when they refer to two or more antecedents joined by *and*. The same rule applies when *each* or *every* is used alone (10i). (For related material on subjects and verbs, see 10f.)

***Each* human hand *and* foot** leaves **its** [not *their*] distinctive print.

The rule still applies when the construction *one of the* follows *each* or *every*.

***Each one of the* robbers** left **his** [not *their*] fingerprints at the scene.

## 10q How do pronouns work when *or* connects antecedents?

When ANTECEDENTS are joined by *or*—or by CORRELATIVE CONJUNCTIONS such as *either . . . or, neither . . . nor,* or *not only . . . but (also)*—the antecedents might mix singulars and plurals. For the purposes of agreement, ignore everything before the final antecedent. Box 10.8 shows you how to visualize this pattern. (For related material on subjects and verbs, see 10g.)

After the restaurant closes, *either* the resident mice *or* **the owner's cat** gets **itself** a meal.

After the restaurant closes, *either* the owner's cat *or* **the resident mice** get **themselves** a meal.

---

**PATTERN BOX** 10.8

## When antecedents are joined by *or*

- **Either** the loudspeakers **or the microphone** needs **its** electric cord repaired.

  SINGULAR ANTECEDENT     SINGULAR PRONOUN

- **Either** the microphone **or the loudspeakers** need **their** electric cords repaired.

  PLURAL ANTECEDENT     PLURAL PRONOUN

---

## 10r How do pronouns work when antecedents are indefinite pronouns?

INDEFINITE PRONOUNS usually refer to unknown persons, things, quantities, or ideas. The unknown aspect is the reason these pronouns are labeled "indefinite." But in a sentence, context gives an indefinite pronoun a clear meaning, even if the pronoun doesn't have a specific antecedent. Most indefinite pronouns are singular. Two indefinite pronouns, *both* and *many,* are plural. A few indefinite pronouns can be singular or plural, depending on the meaning of the sentence.

For a list of indefinite pronouns, grouped as singular or plural, see Box 10.6 in 10i. For more information about avoiding sexist language, especially when using indefinite pronouns, see 10s and 21g. (For related material on subjects and verbs, see 10i.)

**SINGULAR INDEFINITE PRONOUNS**

**Everyone** taking this course hopes to get **his or her** [not *their*] college degree within a year.

**Anybody** wanting to wear a cap and gown at graduation must have **his or her** [not *their*] measurements taken.

**Each** of the students handed in **his or her** [not *their*] final term paper.

**SINGULAR *OR* PLURAL INDEFINITE PRONOUNS**

When winter break arrives for students, **most** leave **their** dormitories for home. [*Most* refers to *students,* so the plural pronoun *their* is correct.]

As for the luggage, **most** is already on **its** way to the airport. [*Most* refers to *luggage,* so the singular pronoun *its* is correct.]

**None** thinks that **he or she** will miss graduation. [*None* is singular as used in this sentence, so the singular pronoun phrase *he or she* is correct.]

**None** of the students has paid **his or her** [not *their*] graduation fee yet. [*None* is singular as used in this sentence, so the singular pronoun phrase *his or her* is correct.]

**None** are so proud as **they** who graduate. [*None* is plural as used in this sentence, so the plural pronoun *they* is correct.]

## 10s How do I use nonsexist pronouns?

A word is **nonsexist** when it carries neither male nor female gender. Each PRONOUN in English carries one of three genders: male (*he, him, his*); female (*she, her, hers*); or neutral (*you, your, yours, we, our, ours, them, they, their, theirs, it, its*). Usage today favors nonsexist terms in all word choices. You therefore want to use gender-free pronouns whenever possible. In the past, it was grammatically correct to use only masculine pronouns to refer to INDEFINITE PRONOUNS: "***Everyone*** open **his** *book.*" Today, however, people feel that the pronouns *he, his, him,* and *himself* exclude women, who make up over half the population. Box 10.9 shows three ways to avoid using masculine pronouns when referring to males and females together. For more information on gender-neutral language, see 21g.

Questions often arise concerning the use of *he or she* and *his or her.* In general, writers find these gender-free pronoun constructions awkward. To avoid them, many writers make the antecedents plural. Doing this becomes problematic when the subject is a SINGULAR INDEFINITE PRONOUN (Box 10.6 in section 10i). In the popular press (such as newspapers and magazines), the use of the plural pronoun *they* or *them* with a singular antecedent has been gaining favor. Indeed, some experts find that the history of English supports this use. In ACADEMIC WRITING,

**SUMMARY BOX** 10.9

## Avoiding the masculine pronoun when referring to males and females together

- **Solution 1:** Use a pair of pronouns—as in the phrase *he or she.* However, avoid using a pair more than once in a sentence or in many sentences in a row. A *he or she* construction acts as a singular pronoun.

  **Everyone** hopes that **he or she** will win a scholarship.

  A **doctor** usually has time to keep up to date only in **his or her** specialty.

- **Solution 2:** Revise into the plural.

  **Many students** hope that **they** will win a scholarship.

  **Most doctors** have time to keep up to date only in **their** specialties.

- **Solution 3:** Recast the sentence.

  Everyone hopes to win a scholarship.

  Few specialists have time for general reading.

however, it is better for you not to follow the practice of the popular press. Language practice changes, however, so what we say here is our best advice as we write this book.

## 10t    How do pronouns work when antecedents are collective nouns?

A COLLECTIVE NOUN names a group of people or things, such as *family, group, audience, class, number, committee,* and *team.* When the group acts as one unit, use a singular pronoun to refer to it. When the members of the group act individually, use a plural pronoun. In the latter case, if the sentence is awkward, substitute a plural noun for the collective noun. (For related material on subjects and verbs, see 10j.)

The **audience** was cheering as **it** stood to applaud the performers.
[The *audience* was acting as one unit, so the singular pronoun *it* is correct.]

The **audience** put on **their** coats and walked out. [The members of the audience were acting as individuals, so all actions become plural; therefore, the plural pronoun *their* is correct.]

The **family** is spending **its** vacation in Rockport, Maine. [All the family members went to one place together.]

The parallel sentence to the last example above would be *The **family** are spending **their** vacations in Maine, Hawaii, and Rome,* which might mean that each family member is going to a different place. But such a sentence is awkward. Therefore, revise the sentence.

> The **family members** are spending **their** vacations in Maine, Hawaii, and Rome. [Substituting a plural noun phrase *family members* for the collective noun *family* sounds more natural.]

**EXERCISE 10-6**   Underline the correct pronoun in parentheses. For help, consult 10o through 10t.

> **EXAMPLE**   Many people wonder what gives certain leaders (his or her, <u>their</u>) spark and magnetic personal appeal.

1. The cluster of personal traits that produces star quality is called *charisma,* a state that bestows special power on (its, their) bearers.

2. Charisma is the quality that allows an individual to empower (himself, herself, himself or herself, themselves) and others.

3. Power and authority alone don't guarantee charisma; (it, they) must be combined with passion and strong purpose.

4. A charismatic leader has the ability to draw other people into (his, her, his or her, their) dream or vision.

5. (He, She, He or she, They) can inspire followers to believe that the leader's goals are the same as (his, her, his or her, their) own.

6. Not all leaders who possess charisma enjoy having this ability to attract and influence (his, his or her, their) followers.

7. Charismatic leaders are often creative, especially in (his, her, his or her, their) capacity for solving problems in original ways.

8. Today, a number of major corporations offer (its, their) employees charisma-training courses to enhance leadership qualities.

9. Usually, it's not the quiet, low-profile manager but rather the charismatic manager with strong leadership qualities who convinces others that (his, her, his or her, their) best interests are served by the course of action (he, she, he or she, they) is/are proposing.

10. Charisma trainers advise would-be leaders to start by bringing order to (his, her, his or her, their) activities; in stressful times, anyone who appears to have some part of (his, her, his or her, their) life under control makes others relax and perform (his, her, his or her, their) responsibilities better.

# Chapter *11*

## ADJECTIVES AND ADVERBS

### 11a What are the differences between adjectives and adverbs?

The differences between adjectives and adverbs relate to how they function. **Adjectives** modify NOUNS and PRONOUNS. **Adverbs** modify VERBS, adjectives, and other adverbs. What's the same about adjectives and adverbs is that they're both MODIFIERS—that is, words or groups of words that describe other words. Box 11.1 compares adjectives and adverbs in action.

**ADJECTIVE**  The **brisk** *wind* blew. [Adjective *brisk* modifies noun *wind*.]

**ADVERB**  The wind *blew* **briskly**. [Adverb *briskly* modifies verb *blew*.]

---

**SUMMARY BOX** 11.1

### Differences between adjectives and adverbs

| WHAT ADJECTIVES MODIFY | EXAMPLES |
|---|---|
| nouns | The **concerned** *lawyer* took a **quick** *look* at the jury members. |
| pronouns | *She* felt **triumphant**, for *they* were **attentive**. |

| WHAT ADVERBS MODIFY | EXAMPLES |
|---|---|
| verbs | The lawyer *spoke* **quickly** and **well**. |
| adverbs | The lawyer spoke **very** *quickly*. |
| adjectives | The lawyer was **extremely** *busy*. |
| independent clauses | **Therefore**, *the lawyer rested*. |

---

Some people think that all adverbs end in *-ly*. But this isn't correct. While many adverbs do end in *-ly* (eat *swiftly*, eat *frequently*, eat *hungrily*), some do not (eat *fast*, eat *often*, eat *seldom*). To complicate matters further, some adjectives end in *-ly* (*lovely* flower, *friendly* dog). Use meaning, not an *-ly* ending, to identify adverbs.

267

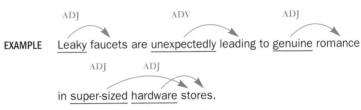

**ESL TIPS:** (1) In English, the adjective is always singular, even if its noun is plural: *The **hot*** [not *hots*] *drinks warmed us up.* (2) Word order in English calls for special attention to the placement of adjectives and adverbs. Here is an example using the adverb *carefully: Thomas closed* [don't place *carefully* here] *the window **carefully*** (see 48b and 48c).

**EXERCISE 11-1**  Underline and label all adjectives (ADJ) and adverbs (ADV). Then, draw an arrow from each adjective and adverb to the word or words it modifies. Ignore *a, an,* and *the* as adjectives. For help, consult 11a.

EXAMPLE
ADJ — Leaky faucets are ADV — unexpectedly leading to ADJ — genuine romance

ADJ  ADJ
in super-sized hardware stores.

1. Today's singles carefully look for possible mates at discount home improvement stores across the country.

2. Understandably, many people find these stores a healthy alternative to dark bars and blind dates.

3. Recently, an employee in the flooring department quietly confided that the best nights for singles are Wednesdays and Thursdays, while weekends generally attract families.

4. A young single mom returns home excitedly because a quick trip to the lumber department for a new door resulted in a date for Saturday night.

5. A lonely widower in his fifties jokingly says he wishes he had developed earlier an interest in wallpapering and gardening.

## 11b  When should I use adverbs—not adjectives—as modifiers?

Adverbs MODIFY verbs, adjectives, and other adverbs. Don't use adjectives as adverbs.

> **NO**  The candidate inspired us **great**. [Adjective *great* cannot modify verb *inspired*.]

> **YES**  The candidate inspired us **greatly**. [Adverb *greatly* can modify verb *inspired*.]

> **NO**  The candidate felt **unusual** energetic. [Adjective *unusual* cannot modify adjective *energetic*.]

> **YES**  The candidate felt **unusually** energetic. [Adverb *unusually* can modify adjective *energetic*.]

| NO | The candidate spoke **exceptional** forcefully. [Adjective *exceptional* cannot modify adverb *forcefully*.] |
|----|----|
| YES | The candidate spoke **exceptionally** forcefully. [Adverb *exceptionally* modifies adverb *forcefully*.] |

## 11c  What is wrong with double negatives?

A **double negative** is a nonstandard form. It is a statement with two negative MODIFIERS, the second of which repeats the message of the first. Negative modifiers include *no, never, not, none, nothing, hardly, scarcely,* and *barely.*

| NO | The factory workers will **never** vote for **no** strike. |
|----|----|
| YES | The factory workers will **never** vote for **a** strike. |
| NO | The union members did **not** have **no** money in reserve. |
| YES | The union members did **not** have **any** money in reserve. |
| YES | The union members had **no** money in reserve. |

Take special care to avoid double negatives with contractions of *not: isn't, don't, didn't, haven't,* and the like (27d). The contraction containing *not* serves as the only negative in a sentence. Don't add a second negative.

| NO | He **didn't** hear **nothing**. |
|----|----|
| YES | He **didn't** hear **anything**. |
| NO | They **haven't** had **no** meetings. |
| YES | They **haven't** had **any** meetings. |

Similarly, be careful to avoid double negatives when you use *nor.* The word *nor* is correct only after *neither* (7i). Use the word *or* after any other negative.

| NO | Stewart **didn't** eat dinner **nor** watch television last night. |
|----|----|
| YES | Stewart **didn't** eat dinner **or** watch television last night. |
| YES | Stewart **neither** ate dinner **nor** watched television last night. |

## 11d  Do adjectives or adverbs come after linking verbs?

LINKING VERBS connect a SUBJECT to a COMPLEMENT. Always use an adjective, not an adverb, as the complement.

The *guests looked* **happy**. [Verb *looked* links subject *guests* to adjective *happy*.]

The words *look, feel, smell, taste, sound,* and *grow* are usually linking verbs, but sometimes they're simply verbs. Check how any of these verbs is functioning in a sentence.

> Zora *looks* **happy**. [*Looks* functions as a linking verb, so the adjective *happy* is correct.]

> Zora *looks* **happily** at the sunset. [*Looks* doesn't function as a linking verb, so the adverb *happily* is correct.]

### BAD, BADLY

The words *bad* (adjective) and *badly* (adverb) are particularly prone to misuse with linking verbs.

> **NO**    The students felt **badly**. [This means the students used their fingers badly.]

> **YES**    The student felt **bad**. [This means the student had a bad feeling about something.]

> **NO**    The food smelled **badly**. [This means the food had a bad ability to smell.]

> **YES**    The food smelled **bad**. [This means the food had a bad smell to it.]

### GOOD, WELL

When the word *well* refers to health, it is an adjective; at all other times, *well* is an adverb. The word *good* is always an adjective.

> Evander looks **well**. [This means that Evander seems to be in good health, so the adjective *well* is correct.]

> Evander writes **well**. [This means that Evander writes skillfully, so the adverb *well* is correct.]

Use *good* as an adjective, except when you refer to health.

> **NO**    She sings **good**. [*Sings* isn't a linking verb, so it calls for an adverb, not the adjective *good*.]

> **YES**    She sings **well**. [*Sings* isn't a linking verb, so the adverb *well* is correct.]

**EXERCISE 11-2**    Underline the correct uses of negatives, adjectives, and adverbs by selecting between the choices in parentheses. For help, consult 11a through 11d.

> **EXAMPLE**    Because she was only five when her father died, Bernice King, Martin Luther King's youngest child, (<u>barely</u>, bare) remembers the details of her father's (solemnly, <u>solemn</u>) funeral, yet her father's image lives (strong, <u>strongly</u>) within her.

1. Although she did feel (badly, bad) about her father's death when she was younger, King's daughter has managed to put his influence on her to good use by speaking (passionately, passionate) about issues her father first introduced.

2. In her (widely, wide) acclaimed book of sermons and speeches, titled *Hard Questions, Hard Answers,* Bernice King strives to deal with the (intensely, intense) topic of race relations.

3. Bernice King believes, as did her father, that all people must connect (genuinely, genuine), or they won't (never, ever) manage to coexist.

4. Bernice King decided to enter the ministry after she heard a (deeply, deep) voice within her directing her to this (extremely, extreme) (spiritually, spiritual) profession.

5. Bernice King entered the public eye in 1993, when she gave a (locally, local) televised Martin Luther King Day sermon at her father's church, and since then she has lived (happily, happy) in her home in Atlanta with memories of her father that are (peacefully, peaceful) recollections.

## 11e   What are comparative and superlative forms?

When you write about comparisons, ADJECTIVES and ADVERBS often carry the message. The adjectives and adverbs also communicate degrees of intensity. When a comparison is made between two things, a **comparative** form is used. When a comparison is made about three or more things, a **superlative** form is used.

### REGULAR FORMS OF COMPARISON

Most adjectives and adverbs are regular. They communicate degrees of intensity in one of two ways: either by adding *-er* and *-est* endings or by adding the words *more, most, less,* and *least* (see Box 11.2 on p. 272).

The number of syllables in the adjective or adverb usually determines whether to use *-er, -est* or *more, most* and *less, least.*

* **One-syllable words** usually take *-er* and *-est* endings: *large, larger, largest* (adjectives); *far, farther, farthest* (adverbs).
* **Adjectives of two syllables** vary. If the word ends in *-y,* change the *y* to *i* and add *-er, -est* endings: *pretty, prettier, prettiest.* Otherwise, some two-syllable adjectives take *-er, -est* endings: *yellow, yellower, yellowest.* Others take *more, most* and *less, least: tangled, more tangled, most tangled; less tangled, least tangled.*
* **Adverbs of two syllables** take *more, most* and *less, least: quickly, more quickly, most quickly; less quickly, least quickly.*
* **Three-syllable words** take *more, most* and *less, least: dignified, more/most dignified, less/least dignified* (adjective); *carefully, more/most carefully, less/least carefully* (adverb).

271

## Regular forms of comparison for adjectives and adverbs

| | |
|---|---|
| **POSITIVE** | Use when nothing is being compared. |
| **COMPARATIVE** | Use when two things are being compared. Add the ending *-er* or the word *more* or *less*. |
| **SUPERLATIVE** | Use to compare three or more things. Add the ending *-est* or the word *most* or *least*. |

| POSITIVE [1] | COMPARATIVE [2] | SUPERLATIVE [3+] |
|---|---|---|
| green | greener | greenest |
| happy | happier | happiest |
| selfish | less selfish | least selfish |
| beautiful | more beautiful | most beautiful |

That tree is **green**.

That tree is **greener** than this tree.

That tree is the **greenest** tree on the block.

**ALERT:** Be careful not to use a double comparative or double superlative. Use either the *-er* and *-est* endings or *more*, *most* or *less*, *least*.

He was **younger** [not *more younger*] than his brother.

Her music was the **loudest** [not *most loudest*] on the stereo. ◆

## IRREGULAR FORMS OF COMPARISON

A few comparative and superlative forms are irregular. Box 11.3 gives you the list. We suggest that you memorize them so they come to mind easily.

**ALERTS:** (1) Be aware of the difference between *less* and *fewer*. They aren't interchangeable. Use *less* with NONCOUNT NOUNS, either items or values: *The sugar substitute has less **aftertaste**.* Use *fewer* with numbers or COUNT NOUNS: *The sugar substitute has fewer **calories**.* (2) Don't use *more*, *most* or *less*, *least* with **absolute adjectives**, that is, adjectives that communicate a noncomparable quality or state, such as *unique* or *perfect*. Something either *is*, or *is not*, one of a kind. No degrees of intensity are involved: *This teapot is **unique** [not the most unique]; The artisanship is **perfect** [not the most perfect].* ◆

SUMMARY BOX **11.3**

## Irregular forms of comparison for adjectives and adverbs

| POSITIVE [1] | COMPARATIVE [2] | SUPERLATIVE [3+] |
|---|---|---|
| good (*adjective*) | better | best |
| well (*adjective* and *adverb*) | better | best |
| bad (*adjective*) | worse | worst |
| badly (*adverb*) | worse | worst |
| many | more | most |
| much | more | most |
| some | more | most |
| little* | less | least |

The Wallaces saw a **good** movie.

The Wallaces saw a **better** movie than the Pascals did.

The Wallaces saw the **best** movie they had ever seen.

The Millers had **little** trouble finding jobs.

The Millers had **less** trouble finding jobs than the Smiths did.

The Millers had the **least** trouble finding jobs of everyone.

*When you're using *little* for items that can be counted (e.g., pickles), use the regular forms *little, littler, littlest*.

**EXERCISE 11-3**　Complete the chart that follows. Then, write a sentence for each word in the completed chart. For help, consult 11e.

EXAMPLE　*funny, funnier, funniest:* My brother has a *funny* laugh; he thinks Mom has a *funnier* laugh; the person who has the *funniest* laugh in our family is Uncle Dominic.

| POSITIVE | COMPARATIVE | SUPERLATIVE |
|---|---|---|
| small | _____ | _____ |
| _____ | greedier | _____ |
| _____ | _____ | most complete |
| gladly | _____ | _____ |
| _____ | _____ | fewest |
| _____ | thicker | _____ |
| some | _____ | _____ |

## **11f**   Why avoid a long string of nouns as modifiers?

NOUNS sometimes MODIFY other nouns: *truck driver, train track, security system*. Usually, these terms create no problems. However, avoid using several nouns in a row as modifiers. A string of too many nouns makes it difficult for your reader to figure out which nouns are being modified and which nouns are doing the modifying. You can revise such sentences in several ways.

**REWRITE THE SENTENCE**

> **NO**    I asked my adviser to write **two college recommendation letters** for me.

> **YES**    I asked my adviser to write *letters of recommendation to two colleges* for me.

**CHANGE ONE NOUN TO A POSSESSIVE AND ANOTHER TO AN ADJECTIVE**

> **NO**    He will take the **United States Navy examination** for **navy engineer training**.

> **YES**    He will take the *United States **Navy's** examination* for ***naval** engineer training*.

**CHANGE ONE NOUN TO A PREPOSITIONAL PHRASE**

> **NO**    Our **student adviser training program** has won many awards.

> **YES**    Our *training program **for student advisers*** has won many awards. [This change requires a change from the singular *adviser* to the plural *advisers*.]

**EXERCISE 11-4**    Underline the better choice in parentheses. For help, consult this entire chapter.

**EXAMPLE**    Alexis, a huge and powerful six-year-old Siberian tiger, (curious, <u>curiously</u>) explores her new zoo home together with five other tigers.

1. The new tiger home at the world-famous Bronx Zoo is a (special, specially) designed habitat, planted with (dense, denser) undergrowth so that it (close, closely) imitates the tigers' natural wilderness.

2. Like tigers in the wild, the six tigers in this habitat, which (more, many) experts consider the (more authentic, most authentic) of all artificial tiger environments in the world, will face some of the physical challenges and sensory experiences that keep them happy and (healthy, healthier).

3. Research shows that tigers feel (bad, badly) and fail to thrive in zoos without enrichment features placed in (good, well) locations to inspire tigers to stalk (stealthy, stealthily) through underbrush, loll (lazy, lazily) on heated rocks, or tug (vigorous, vigorously) on massive pull toys.

4. Wildlife zoologists think that the new Tiger Mountain exhibit will also serve zoo visitors (good, well) by allowing them to observe and admire the amazing strength, agility, and intelligence of a (rapid, rapidly) dwindling species.

5. Today, (fewer, less) than 5,000 Siberian tigers remain in the wild, which makes it imperative for zoos to raise people's awareness of the (great, greatest) need to prevent the extinction of these big cats that are considered among the (more, most) powerful, beautiful animals in the world.

# Chapter 12

## SENTENCE FRAGMENTS

### 12a  What is a sentence fragment?

A **sentence fragment** looks like a sentence, but it's actually only part of a sentence. That is, even though a sentence fragment begins with a capital letter and ends with a period (or question mark or exclamation point), it doesn't contain an INDEPENDENT CLAUSE. Fragments are merely unattached PHRASES or DEPENDENT CLAUSES.

| | |
|---|---|
| **FRAGMENT** | The telephone with redial capacity. [no verb] |
| **CORRECT** | The telephone has redial capacity. |
| **FRAGMENT** | Rang loudly for ten minutes. [no subject] |
| **CORRECT** | The telephone rang loudly for ten minutes. |
| **FRAGMENT** | At midnight. [a phrase without a verb or subject] |
| **CORRECT** | The telephone rang at midnight. |
| **FRAGMENT** | Because the telephone rang loudly. [dependent clause starting with subordinating conjunction *because*] |
| **CORRECT** | Because the telephone rang loudly, the family was awakened in the middle of the night. |
| **FRAGMENT** | Which really annoyed me. [dependent clause starting with relative pronoun *which*] |
| **CORRECT** | The telephone call was a wrong number, which really annoyed me. |

Sentence fragments can ruin the clarity of your writing. Moreover, in ACADEMIC WRITING and BUSINESS WRITING, sentence fragments imply that you don't know basic sentence structure or that you're a careless proofreader.

| | |
|---|---|
| **NO** | The lawyer was angry. When she returned from court. She found the key witness waiting in her office. [Was the lawyer angry when she returned from court, or when she found the witness in her office?] |

| YES | The lawyer was angry when she returned from court. She found the key witness waiting in her office. |
|-----|---|
| YES | The lawyer was angry. When she returned from court, she found the key witness waiting in her office. |

Let's go beyond the grammatical terms to a more practical approach to recognizing sentence fragments, so that you can avoid them in your writing. To learn to recognize sentence fragments, see 12b; to learn several ways to correct sentence fragments, see 12c and 12d.

Many writers wait until the REVISING and EDITING stages of the WRITING PROCESS to check for sentence fragments. During DRAFTING, the goal is to get ideas down on paper or disk. As you draft, if you suspect that you've written a sentence fragment, simply underline or highlight it in boldface or italics and move on. Later, you can easily find it to check and correct.

## 12b  How can I recognize a sentence fragment?

If you tend to write SENTENCE FRAGMENTS, you want a system for recognizing them. Box 12.1 shows you a Sentence Test for checking that you haven't written a sentence fragment. Following this box, we discuss each question in more detail in 12b.1 through 12b.3.

---

**SUMMARY BOX** 12.1

### Sentence test to identify sentence fragments

**QUESTION 1: IS THE WORD GROUP A DEPENDENT CLAUSE?**

A DEPENDENT CLAUSE is a word group that has a subject and a verb but starts with a word that creates dependence—either a SUBORDINATING CONJUNCTION or a RELATIVE PRONOUN.

| FRAGMENT | **When** winter comes early. [starts with *when,* a word that creates dependence] |
|----------|---|
| CORRECT | **When** winter comes early, **ships often rescue the stranded whales**. [adds an independent clause to create a sentence] |
| FRAGMENT | **Which** can happen quickly. [starts with *which,* a word that creates dependence] |
| CORRECT | **Whales cannot breathe through the ice and will drown, which** can happen quickly. [adds an independent clause to create a sentence] |

> **SUMMARY BOX** 12.1 *continued*
>
> ## Sentence test to identify sentence fragments
>
> **QUESTION 2: IS THERE A VERB?**
>
> **FRAGMENT** Thousands of whales in the Arctic Ocean. [Because a verb is missing, this is a phrase, not a sentence.]
>
> **CORRECT** Thousands of whales **live** in the Arctic Ocean. [adds a verb to create a sentence]
>
> **QUESTION 3: IS THERE A SUBJECT?**
>
> **FRAGMENT** Stranded in the Arctic Ocean. [Because a subject is missing, this is a phrase, not a sentence.]
>
> **CORRECT** **Many whales *were*** stranded in the Arctic Ocean. [adds a subject (and the verb *were* to *stranded*) to create a sentence]

## 12b.1 Question 1: Is the word group a dependent clause?

If you answer yes to question 1, you're looking at a sentence fragment. A DEPENDENT CLAUSE is a word group that has a subject and a verb but starts with a word that creates dependence. The only words that create dependence are SUBORDINATING CONJUNCTIONS and RELATIVE PRONOUNS. Such a word before an INDEPENDENT CLAUSE creates a dependent clause, which can't stand alone as a sentence and is therefore a sentence fragment. To become a complete sentence, the fragment needs either to be joined to an independent clause or to be rewritten.

### FRAGMENTS WITH SUBORDINATING CONJUNCTIONS

A complete list of subordinating conjunctions appears in Box 7.7 in 7i. Some frequently used ones are *after, although, because, before, if, unless,* and *when.*

**FRAGMENT** **Because** she returned my books. [*Because,* a subordinating conjunction, creates a dependent clause.]

**CORRECT** **Because** she returned my books, ***I can study***. [A comma and the independent clause *I can study* are added, and the sentence becomes complete.]

**FRAGMENT** **Unless** I study. [*Unless,* a subordinating conjunction, creates a dependent clause.]

**CORRECT** ***I won't pass the test*** **unless** I study. [The independent clause *I won't pass the test* is added, and the sentence becomes complete.]

⚡ **ALERT:** When a dependent clause starts with a subordinating conjunction and comes before its independent clause, use a comma to separate the clauses (24c). ◆

## FRAGMENTS WITH RELATIVE PRONOUNS

Relative pronouns are *that, which, who, whom,* and *whose.*

**FRAGMENT**    **That** we had studied for all week. [*That,* a relative pronoun, creates a dependent clause here.]

**CORRECT**    ***We passed the exam*** **that** we had studied for all week. [The independent clause *We passed the exam* is added, and the sentence becomes complete.]

When *which, who,* and *whose* begin questions, they function as INTERROGATIVE PRONOUNS, not relative pronouns. Questions are complete sentences, not fragments: *Which* class are you taking? *Who* is your professor? *Whose* book is that?

## 12b.2   Question 2: Is there a verb?

If you answer no to question 2, you're looking at a sentence fragment. When a VERB is missing from a word group, the result is a PHRASE, not a sentence. You can figure out if a word is a verb by seeing if it can change in TENSE. Verbs have tenses to tell what *is* happening, what *has* happened, or what *will* happen.

Now the telephone **rings**. [present tense]

Yesterday, the telephone **rang**. [past tense]

When you check for verbs, remember that VERBALS (7e) are not verbs. Verbals might look like verbs, but they don't function as verbs.

**FRAGMENT**    Yesterday, the students **registering** for classes. [*Registering* is a verbal called a present participle, not a verb.]

**CORRECT**    Yesterday, the students **were registering** for classes. [Adding the auxiliary verb *were* to the present participle *registering* creates a verb.]

**FRAGMENT**    Now the students **to register** for classes. [*To register* is a verbal called an infinitive, not a verb.]

**CORRECT**    Now the students **want to register** for classes. [Adding the verb *want* to the infinitive *to register* creates a verb.]

## 12b.3 Question 3: Is there a subject?

If you answer no to question 3, you're looking at a sentence fragment. When a SUBJECT is missing from a word group, the result is a PHRASE, not a sentence. To see if a word is a subject, ask, "Who (or What) performs the action?"

**FRAGMENT**    Studied hard for class. [*Who* studied hard for class? unknown]

`CORRECT`    The students studied hard for class. [*Who* studied hard for class? *The students* is the answer, so a subject makes the sentence complete.]

**FRAGMENT**    Contained some difficult questions. [*What* contained some difficult questions? unknown]

`CORRECT`    The test contained some difficult questions. [*What* contained some difficult questions? *The test* is the answer, so a subject makes the sentence complete.]

Be especially careful with COMPOUND PREDICATES—for example, *We **took** the bus to the movie **and walked** home.* If you were to place a period after *movie*, the second part of the compound predicate would be a sentence fragment. Every sentence needs its own subject. To check for this kind of sentence fragment, ask the question "Who?" or "What?" of each verb.

**NO**    A few students organized a study group to prepare for midterm exams. **Decided to study together for the rest of the course**. [*Who* decided to study together? The answer is *The students* (who formed the group), but this subject is missing.]

`YES`    A few students organized a study group to prepare for midterm exams. ***The students* decided to study together for the rest of the course.**

IMPERATIVE SENTENCES—commands and some requests—may appear at first glance to be fragments caused by missing subjects. They're not fragments, however. Imperative sentences are complete sentences because their subjects are implied. An implied subject can be *you, anybody, somebody, everybody,* or another INDEFINITE PRONOUN.

Run! [This sentence implies the pronoun *you*. The complete sentence would be *You run!*]

Return all library books to the front desk. [This sentence implies the indefinite pronoun *everyone*. The complete sentence would be *Everyone (should) return all library books to the front desk.*]

**EXERCISE 12-1**    Identify each word group as either a complete sentence or a fragment. If the word group is a sentence, circle its number. If it's a fragment, tell why it's incomplete. For help, see Box 12.1 in 12b and sections 12b.1 through 12b.3.

**EXAMPLE** Although antibacterial soaps have become popular. [Starts with a subordinating conjunction (*although*), which creates dependence, and lacks an independent clause to complete the thought; see Box 12.1 and section 12c.1]

1. Because antibacterial soaps do not provide protection against viruses.
2. Viruses responsible for a variety of common health problems.
3. Regular soap often successfully eliminates bacteria, viruses, and dirt.
4. Indicate that antibacterial soaps may wash away useful bacteria.
5. Eliminates most of the harmful bacteria as effectively as regular soap.
6. Careful hand washing cannot be stressed enough.
7. To work efficiently, antibacterial soaps, even those purchased in health food stores.

8. Most studies show that antibacterial soaps do not lead to resistant bacteria.
9. Although many people still believe they should not use antibacterial soaps.
10. Bacteria from overuse of antibiotics.

## 12c  What are major ways of correcting fragments?

Once you've identified a SENTENCE FRAGMENT (12b), you're ready to correct it. You can do this in one of two ways: by joining it to an independent clause (12c.1) or by rewriting it (12c.2).

### 12c.1  Correcting a sentence fragment by joining it to an independent clause

One way you can correct a sentence fragment is by joining it to an INDEPENDENT CLAUSE—that is, to a complete sentence. The first two examples on page 282 deal with dependent-clause fragments; the examples following the ALERT examine fragments with missing subjects and/or verbs.

**FRAGMENT**  **Because** the ice was thick. [Although this word group has a subject (*ice*) and verb (*was*), it starts with the subordinating conjunction *because*.]

**CORRECT**  **Because** the ice was thick, *icebreakers were required to serve as rescue ships*. [Adding a comma and joining the fragment to the independent clause *icebreakers were required to serve as rescue ships* creates a complete sentence.]

**CORRECT**  *Icebreakers were required to serve as rescue ships* **because** the ice was thick. [Joining the fragment to the independent clause *Icebreakers were required to serve as rescue ships* creates a complete sentence.]

**FRAGMENT**  **Who** feared the whales would panic. [This fragment starts with the relative pronoun *who*.]

**CORRECT**  *The noisy motors of the ships worried the crews,* **who** feared the whales would panic. [Joining the fragment to the independent clause *The noisy motors of the ships worried the crews* creates a complete sentence.]

**ALERT:** Be careful with all words that indicate time, such as *after, before, since,* and *until*. They aren't always subordinating conjunctions. Sometimes they function as ADVERBS—especially if they begin a complete sentence. At other times, they function as PREPOSITIONS. When you see one of these words that indicate time, realize that you aren't necessarily looking at a dependent-clause fragment.

**Before**, the whales had responded to classical music. [This is a complete sentence in which *Before* is an adverb that modifies the independent clause *the whales had responded to classical music*.]

**Before the whales had responded to classical music**, some crew members tried rock and roll music. [If the word group before the comma stood on its own, it would be a sentence fragment because it starts with *Before* functioning as a subordinating conjunction.] ◆

**FRAGMENT**  **To announce new programs for crime prevention.** [*To announce* starts an infinitive phrase, not a sentence.]

**CORRECT**  *The mayor called a news conference last week* **to announce** new programs for crime prevention. [The infinitive phrase starting with *to announce* is joined with an independent clause.]

**FRAGMENT**  **Hoping for strong public support.** [*Hoping* starts a present-participle phrase, not a sentence.]

**CORRECT**  **Hoping** for strong public support, *she gave examples of problems throughout the city*. [The present-participle phrase starting with *Hoping* is joined with an independent clause.]

| FRAGMENT | **Introduced by her assistant.** [*Introduced* starts a past-participle phrase, not a sentence.] |
|---|---|
| CORRECT | **Introduced** by her assistant, ***the mayor began with an opening statement.*** [The past-participle phrase starting with *Introduced* is joined with an independent clause.] |
| FRAGMENT | **During the long news conference.** [*During* functions as a preposition—starting a prepositional phrase, not a sentence.] |
| CORRECT | ***Cigarette smoke made the conference room seem airless*** **during** the long news conference. [The prepositional phrase starting with *during* is joined with an independent clause.] |
| FRAGMENT | **A politician with fresh ideas.** [*A politician* starts an appositive phrase, not a sentence.] |
| CORRECT | ***Most people respected the mayor,*** **a politician** with fresh ideas. [The appositive phrase starting with *a politician* is joined with an independent clause.] |

**EXERCISE 12-2**  Find and correct any sentence fragments. If a sentence is correct, circle its number. For help, consult 12a through 12c.

EXAMPLE  Many communities prohibit the building of cell phone transmission towers. Which they consider to be unsightly.

Many communities prohibit the building of cell phone transmission towers, *which* they consider to be unsightly.

1. Although telephone companies always need to build more towers to fulfill the increasing demand for cell phone service.
2. The companies are hard-pressed to find suitable locations, especially on the densely populated east and west coasts of the United States.
3. Because cell phone use has expanded rapidly. One telecommunications analyst predicts that the number of cell phone towers, which now is well over 100,000, will triple over five years.
4. Companies have built the towers inside tall structures such as flagpoles, silos, water towers, even smokestacks. To disguise the ugly structures.
5. The best hiding places of all are church steeples. Which are often the tallest structures in a community.
6. While the equipment that runs the towers usually fits out of sight in the church basement. The tall antenna is concealed inside the steeple.
7. Strapped for funds. Churches are often eager to rent space to telecommunications companies.
8. In one case, a church whose steeple had burned down was unable to rebuild it without payments provided by a cellular company.

283

9. Even though the steeple is a historic structure that appears on the town's seal.

10. The reconstruction preserved the historic architecture, hid the tower, and even left room for the bats and pigeons. That traditionally inhabited the original steeple.

## 12c.2 Correcting a sentence fragment by rewriting it

A second way you can correct a sentence fragment is by rewriting it as an INDEPENDENT CLAUSE—that is, as a complete sentence. The first two examples below deal with dependent-clause fragments; the others examine fragments with missing subjects and/or verbs.

| | |
|---|---|
| **FRAGMENT** | **Because** the ice was thick. [Although this word group has a subject (*ice*) and verb (*was*), it starts with the subordinating conjunction *because*.] |
| **CORRECT** | The ice was thick. [The fragment starting with *Because* is rewritten to become a complete sentence.] |
| **FRAGMENT** | **Who** feared the whales would panic. [This fragment starts with the relative pronoun *who*.] |
| **CORRECT** | ***The crew*** feared the whales would panic. [The fragment starting with *Who* is rewritten to become a complete sentence.] |
| **FRAGMENT** | **To announce** new programs for crime prevention. [*To announce* starts an infinitive phrase, not a sentence.] |
| **CORRECT** | ***The mayor called a news conference last week because she wanted* to announce** new programs for crime prevention. [The infinitive phrase starting with *To announce* is rewritten to become a complete sentence.] |
| **FRAGMENT** | **Hoping** for strong public support. [*Hoping* starts a present-participle phrase, not a sentence.] |
| **CORRECT** | ***She was* hoping** for strong public support. [The present-participle phrase starting with *Hoping* is rewritten to become a complete sentence.] |
| **FRAGMENT** | **Introduced** by her assistant. [*Introduced* starts a past-participle phrase, not a sentence.] |
| **CORRECT** | **Introduced** by her assistant, ***the mayor began with an opening statement***. [The past-participle phrase starting with *Introduced* is rewritten to become a complete sentence.] |
| **FRAGMENT** | **During** the long news conference. [*During* functions as a preposition that starts a prepositional phrase, not a sentence.] |

CORRECT **It was hard to breathe** during the long news conference. [The prepositional phrase starting with *During* is rewritten to become a complete sentence.]

FRAGMENT **A politician** with fresh ideas. [*A politician* starts an appositive phrase, not a sentence.]

CORRECT **She seemed to be** a politician with fresh ideas. [The appositive phrase is rewritten to become a complete sentence.]

## 12d How can I fix a fragment that is part of a compound predicate?

A COMPOUND PREDICATE contains two or more VERBS. When the second part of a compound predicate is punctuated as a separate sentence, it becomes a sentence fragment.

FRAGMENT The reporters asked the mayor many questions about the new program. **And then discussed her answers among themselves.** [*And then discussed* starts a compound predicate fragment, not a sentence.]

CORRECT The reporters asked the mayor many questions about the new program and then discussed her answers among themselves. [The compound predicate fragment starting with *And then discussed* is joined to the independent clause.]

CORRECT The reporters asked the mayor many questions about the new program. **Then the reporters discussed** her answers among themselves. [The compound predicate fragment starting with *And then discussed* is rewritten as a complete sentence.]

**EXERCISE 12-3** Go back to Exercise 12-1 (pp. 280–281) and revise the sentence fragments into complete sentences. In some cases, you may be able to combine two fragments into one complete sentence.

## 12e What are the two special fragment problems?

Two special fragment problems sometimes involve lists and examples. Lists and examples must be part of a complete sentence, unless they are formatted as a column.

You can connect a list fragment by attaching it to the preceding independent clause using a colon or a dash. You can correct an example fragment by attaching to an independent clause (with or without punctuation, depending on the meaning) or by rewriting it as a complete sentence.

**FRAGMENT** You have a choice of desserts. **Carrot cake, chocolate silk pie, apple pie, or peppermint ice cream.** [The list cannot stand on its own as a sentence.]

CORRECT You have a choice of desserts: carrot cake, chocolate silk pie, apple pie, or peppermint ice cream. [A colon joins the sentence and the list.]

CORRECT You have a choice of desserts—carrot cake, chocolate silk pie, apple pie, or peppermint ice cream. [A dash joins the sentence and the list.]

**FRAGMENT** Several good places offer brunch. **For example, the restaurants Sign of the Dove and Blue Yonder.** [Examples can't stand on their own as a sentence.]

CORRECT Several good places offer brunch—**for example**, the restaurants Sign of the Dove and Blue Yonder.

CORRECT Several good places offer brunch. **For example,** *there are* the restaurants Sign of the Dove and Blue Yonder.

## 12f How can I recognize intentional fragments?

Professional writers sometimes intentionally use fragments for emphasis and effect.

> But in the main, I feel like a brown bag of miscellany propped against a wall. Pour out the contents, and there is discovered a jumble of small things priceless and worthless. **A first-water diamond, an empty spool, bits of broken glass, lengths of string, a key to a door long since crumbled away, a rusty knife-blade, old shoes saved for a road that never was and never will be, a nail bent under the weight of things too heavy for any nail, a dried flower or two still a little fragrant.**
>
> —Zora Neale Hurston, *How It Feels to Be Colored Me*

Being able to judge the difference between an acceptable and unacceptable sentence fragment comes from years of reading the work of skilled writers. For ACADEMIC WRITING, most instructors don't accept sentence fragments in student writing until a student demonstrates a consistent ability to write well-constructed, complete sentences. As a rule, avoid sentence fragments in academic writing.

**EXERCISE 12-4** Revise this paragraph to eliminate all sentence fragments. In some cases, you can combine word groups to create complete sentences; in other cases, you must supply missing elements to rewrite. Some sentences may not require revision. In your final version, check not only the individual sentences but also the clarity of the whole paragraph. For help, consult 12a through 12d.

EXAMPLE  Although many people considered him crazy. George Ferris decided to build a "Great Wheel" in 1892.

Although many people considered him *crazy, George* Ferris decided to build a "Great Wheel" in 1892.

(1) The 1893 World's Columbian Exposition Committee contacted George Ferris. Because the members knew he was a creative designer. (2) The World's Columbian Exposition received its name from Christopher Columbus. Who had discovered what he called the "New World" 400 years earlier. (3) The Chicago exposition committee wanted a more dramatic structure than the Eiffel Tower. Which the French had built for the Paris Exposition of 1889. (4) George Ferris, who was an architect and bridge-builder with a vision, proposed a gigantic rotating wheel that people could ride on safely. (5) Since he designed a wheel that was 250 feet in diameter and held 36 cars, each 27 feet long and 13 feet wide. (6) Many people, including the exposition director Daniel Burnham, doubted that Ferris could build a large steel structure. That could carry 2,160 passengers each ride. (7) Ferris built his giant wheel, and people paid fifty cents for a twenty-minute ride. Even though most other rides cost only five cents. (8) At night, 3,000 incandescent bulbs lit the rotating wheel. Which fascinated the people who stared in amazement. (9) William Sullivan, who was also a bridge-builder, later designed a smaller, more practical wheel. Sullivan's company has made over 1,300 Ferris Wheels since 1906. (10) George Ferris, the "crackpot" with wheels in his head, built an extraordinarily creative moving structure. That remains today a sentimental favorite at carnivals and amusement parks.

**EXERCISE 12-5**  Revise this paragraph to eliminate all sentence fragments. In some cases, you can combine word groups to create complete sentences; in other cases, you must supply missing elements to revise word groups. Some sentences may not require revision. In your final version, check not only the individual sentences but also the clarity of the whole paragraph. Refer to 12a through 12e for help.

(1) Some teenagers and young adults. (2) Are continually on instant messaging almost every moment that they are using their computers. (3) Which are rarely turned off. (4) According to America Online (AOL), the most popular instant-messaging service. (5) 195 million people use its instant-messaging service. (6) Creating more than 1.6 billion messages per day. (7) Becoming an integral part of

the social fabric of our world. (8) Instant messaging has replaced the telephone, and even some e-mail. (9) For millions of young adults. (10) As a result, AOL and its main rivals, Microsoft and Yahoo. (11) Continue to add new features to their instant-messaging services. (12) Such as tiny video images embedded in messages or interface between messaging and cell phones. (13) All these companies acknowledge, however. (14) That instant messaging, while a wildly popular communications tool, does not make money for them. (15) Now provided as a free service. (16) Instant messaging may eventually become a way for these companies to increase their income. (17) Perhaps the companies could sell the software that manages multitudes of instant messages. (18) That are sent within large corporations for the business-related use of their employees.

# Chapter 13

## COMMA SPLICES AND RUN-ON SENTENCES

### 13a  What are comma splices and run-on sentences?

Comma splices and run-on sentences are somewhat similar errors: One has a comma by itself between two complete sentences, and one has no punctuation at all between two complete sentences.

A **comma splice**, also called a *comma fault,* occurs when a comma, rather than a period, is used incorrectly between complete sentences. The word *splice* means "to fasten ends together," which is a handy procedure, except when splicing has anything to do with sentences.

A **run-on sentence**, also called a *fused sentence* and a *run-together sentence,* occurs when two complete sentences run into each other without any punctuation. Comma splices and run-on sentences create confusion because readers can't tell where one thought ends and another begins.

> **COMMA SPLICE**  The icebergs broke off from the **glacier, they** drifted into the sea.
>
> **RUN-ON SENTENCE**  The icebergs broke off from the **glacier they** drifted into the sea.
>
> **CORRECT**  The icebergs broke off from the **glacier. They** drifted into the sea.

There is one exception. You can use a comma between two independent clauses, but only if the comma is followed by one of the seven coordinating conjunctions: *and, but, for, or, nor, yet, so.* A comma in such a construction is correct; see Chapter 24.

> **CORRECT**  The icebergs broke off from the glacier**, and** they drifted into the sea.

**ALERT:** Occasionally, when your meaning allows it, you can use a colon or a dash to join two independent clauses. ◆

Many writers wait until the REVISING and EDITING stages of the WRITING PROCESS to check for comma splices and run-on sentences.

During DRAFTING, the goal is to put ideas down on paper or disk. As you draft, if you suspect that you've written a comma splice or a run-on sentence, simply underline or highlight it in boldface or italics, and move on. Later, you can easily find it to check and correct.

## 13b   How can I recognize comma splices and run-on sentences?

When you know how to recognize an INDEPENDENT CLAUSE, you'll know how to recognize COMMA SPLICES and RUN-ON SENTENCES. An independent clause can stand alone as a complete sentence. An independent clause contains a SUBJECT and a PREDICATE. Also, an independent clause doesn't begin with a word that creates dependence—that is, it doesn't begin with a SUBORDINATING CONJUNCTION or a RELATIVE PRONOUN.

Interestingly, almost all comma splices and run-on sentences are caused by only four patterns. If you become familiar with these four patterns, listed in Box 13.1, you'll more easily locate them in your writing.

**ALERT:** To proofread for comma splices, cover all words on one side of the comma and see if the words remaining form an independent clause. If they do, next cover all words you left uncovered, on the other side of the comma. If the second side of the comma is also an independent clause, you're looking at a comma splice. (This technique doesn't work for run-on sentences because a comma isn't present.) ◆

---

**PATTERN BOX 13.1**

### Detecting comma splices and run-on sentences

- Watch out for a PRONOUN starting the second independent clause.

    **NO**   The physicist Marie Curie discovered **radium, she** won two Nobel Prizes.

    **YES**   The physicist Marie Curie discovered **radium. She** won two Nobel Prizes.

- Watch out for a CONJUNCTIVE ADVERB (such as *furthermore, however, similarly, therefore,* and *then;* see Box 7.5, section 7g, for a complete list) starting the second independent clause.

    **NO**   Marie Curie and her husband, Pierre, worked together at **first, however**, he died tragically at age forty-seven.

    **YES**   Marie Curie and her husband, Pierre, worked together at **first. However**, he died tragically at age forty-seven.

---

---

**PATTERN BOX** **13.1** *continued*

## Detecting comma splices and run-on sentences

- Watch out for a TRANSITIONAL EXPRESSION (such as *in addition, for example, in contrast, of course,* and *meanwhile;* see Box 3.5, section 3g.1, for a reference list) starting the second independent clause.

  **NO**　Marie Curie and her husband won a Nobel Prize for the discovery of **radium, in addition, Marie** herself won another Nobel Prize for her work on the atomic weight of radium.

  **YES**　Marie Curie and her husband won a Nobel Prize for the discovery of **radium; in addition, Marie** herself won another Nobel Prize for her work on the atomic weight of radium.

- Watch out for a second independent clause that explains, says more about, contrasts with, or gives an example of what's said in the first independent clause.

  **NO**　Marie Curie died of leukemia in **1934, exposure** to radioactivity killed her.

  **YES**　Marie Curie died of leukemia in **1934. Exposure** to radioactivity killed her.

---

Experienced writers sometimes use a comma to join very short independent clauses, especially if one independent clause is negative and the other is positive: *Mosquitoes don't **bite, they** stab.* In ACADEMIC WRITING, however, many instructors consider this an error, so you'll be safe if you use a period. (Another option is a semicolon, if the two independent clauses are closely related in meaning: *Mosquitoes don't **bite; they** stab.*)

## 13c　How can I correct comma splices and run-on sentences?

Once you have identified a COMMA SPLICE or a RUN-ON SENTENCE, you're ready to correct it. You can do this in one of four ways, as shown in Box 13.2 (p. 292) and discussed further sections 13c.1 through 13c.4.

### 13c.1 Using a period to correct comma splices and run-on sentences

You can use a period to correct comma splices and run-on sentences by placing the period between the two sentences. For the sake of sentence variety and emphasis (Chapter 19), however, you want to choose other

## Ways to correct comma splices and run-on sentences

- Use a period between the INDEPENDENT CLAUSES (13c.1).
- Use a semicolon between the independent clauses (13c.2).
- Use a comma together with a COORDINATING CONJUNCTION (13c.3).
- Revise one independent clause into a DEPENDENT CLAUSE (13c.4).

options as well, such as those shown in 13c.3 and 13c.4. Strings of short sentences rarely establish relationships and levels of importance among ideas.

| | |
|---|---|
| **COMMA SPLICE** | A shark is all **cartilage, it** doesn't have a bone in its body. |
| **RUN-ON SENTENCE** | A shark is all **cartilage it** doesn't have a bone in its body. |
| **CORRECT** | A shark is all **cartilage. It** doesn't have a bone in its body.<br>[A period separates the independent clauses.] |
| **COMMA SPLICE** | Sharks can smell blood from a quarter mile **away, they** then swim toward the source like a guided missile. |
| **RUN-ON SENTENCE** | Sharks can smell blood from a quarter mile **away they** then swim toward the source like a guided missile. |
| **CORRECT** | Sharks can smell blood from a quarter mile **away. They** then swim toward the source like a guided missile. [A period separates the independent clauses.] |

### 13c.2 Using a semicolon to correct comma splices and run-on sentences

You can use a semicolon to correct comma splices and run-on sentences by placing the semicolon between the two sentences. Use a semicolon only when the separate sentences are closely related in meaning. For the sake of sentence variety and emphasis, however, you'll want to choose other options, such as those shown in 13c.1, 13c.3, and 13c.4; for correct semicolon use, see Chapter 25.

| | |
|---|---|
| **COMMA SPLICE** | The great white shark supposedly eats **humans, research** shows that most white sharks spit them out after the first bite. |

| | |
|---|---|
| **RUN-ON SENTENCE** | The great white shark supposedly eats **humans research** shows that most white sharks spit them out after the first bite. |
| **CORRECT** | The great white shark supposedly eats **humans; research** shows that most white sharks spit them out after the first bite. [A semicolon separates two independent clauses that are close in meaning.] |

## 13c.3 Using a comma together with a coordinating conjunction to correct comma splices and run-on sentences

You can connect independent clauses with a comma together with a co-ordinating conjunction (*and, but, for, or, nor, yet, so*) to correct a comma splice. You can also correct a run-on sentence by inserting a comma followed by a coordinating conjunction.

✒ **ALERT:** Use a comma before a coordinating conjunction that links independent clauses (24b). ◆

When you use a coordinating conjunction, be sure that your choice fits the meaning of the material. *And* signals addition; *but* and *yet* signal contrast; *for* and *so* signal cause; and *or* and *nor* signal alternatives.

| | |
|---|---|
| **COMMA SPLICE** | All living creatures give off weak electrical charges in the **water, special** pores on a shark's skin can detect these signals. |
| **RUN-ON SENTENCE** | All living creatures give off weak electrical charges in the **water special** pores on a shark's skin can detect these signals. |
| **CORRECT** | All living creatures give off weak electrical charges in the **water, *and* special** pores on a shark's skin can detect these signals. |

**EXERCISE 13-1** Revise the comma splices and run-on sentences by using a period, a semicolon, or a comma and coordinating conjunction. For help, consult sections 13c.1 through 13c.3.

| | |
|---|---|
| EXAMPLE | Every two years, a very popular "Celebration of Books" takes place at Oklahoma State University at Tulsa writers from across the United States gather along with readers to discuss the art of writing. |
| | Every two years, a very popular "Celebration of Books" takes place at Oklahoma State University at *Tulsa. Writers* from across the United States gather along with readers to discuss the art of writing. |

293

1. During the "Celebration of Books," aspiring writers can ask published authors questions about writing, for example, many people wish to know how to find an agent.

2. Besides asking about agents, would-be writers also query published authors about writing techniques many questions deal with whether to write using a computer, a typewriter, or longhand.

3. The "Celebration of Books" offers panel discussions on a variety of topics, including memoir writing, poetry development, and techniques of plotting short stories other panels cover writing the western novel and true crime stories.

4. The "Celebration of Books" appeals to readers, many of whom can see their favorite authors in person speaking on panels and in more informal settings such as receptions and book signings fans of authors greatly enjoy such opportunities.

5. In addition to writers, many well-known artists and musicians are honored at the "Celebration of Books," its Advisory Board recommended this expansion years ago to widen the conference's appeal.

## 13c.4 Revising one independent clause into a dependent clause to correct comma splices and run-on sentences

You can correct a comma splice or run-on sentence by revising one of the two independent clauses into a dependent clause. This method is suitable only when one idea can logically be subordinated (17e) to the other. Also, be careful never to end the dependent clause with a period or semicolon. If you do, you've created the error of a SENTENCE FRAGMENT.

### CREATE DEPENDENT CLAUSES WITH SUBORDINATING CONJUNCTIONS

One way to create a dependent clause is to insert a SUBORDINATING CONJUNCTION (such as *because, although, when,* and *if*—see Box 7.7, section 7i, for a complete list). Always choose a subordinating conjunction that fits the meaning of each particular sentence: *because* and *since* signal cause; *although* signals contrast; *when* signals time; and *if* signals condition. Dependent clauses that begin with a subordinating conjunction are called ADVERB CLAUSES.

| | |
|---|---|
| **COMMA SPLICE** | Homer and Langley Collyer had packed their house from top to bottom with **junk, police** could not open the front door to investigate a reported smell. |
| **RUN-ON SENTENCE** | Homer and Langley Collyer had packed their house from top to bottom with **junk police** could not open the front door to investigate a reported smell. |
| **CORRECT** | **Because** Homer and Langley Collyer had packed their house from top to bottom with **junk, police** could not |

open the front door to investigate a reported smell.
[*Because* starts a dependent clause that is joined by a comma with the independent clause starting with *police.*]

| | |
|---|---|
| **COMMA SPLICE** | Old newspapers and car parts filled every room to the **ceiling, enough** space remained for fourteen pianos. |
| **RUN-ON SENTENCE** | Old newspapers and car parts filled every room to the **ceiling enough** space remained for fourteen pianos. |
| **CORRECT** | **Although** old newspapers and car parts filled every room to the **ceiling, enough** space remained for fourteen pianos. [The subordinating conjunction *although* starts a dependent clause that is joined by a comma with the independent clause starting with *enough.*] |

◢◤ **ALERT:** Place a comma between an introductory dependent clause and the independent clause that follows (24c). ◆

## CREATE DEPENDENT CLAUSES WITH RELATIVE PRONOUNS

You can create a dependent clause with a RELATIVE PRONOUN (*who, whom, whose, which, that*). Dependent clauses with a relative pronoun are called ADJECTIVE CLAUSES.

| | |
|---|---|
| **COMMA SPLICE** | The Collyers had been crushed under a pile of **newspapers, the newspapers** had toppled onto the brothers. |
| **RUN-ON SENTENCE** | The Collyers had been crushed under a pile of **newspapers the newspapers** had toppled onto the brothers. |
| **CORRECT** | The Collyers had been crushed under a pile of **newspapers *that* had toppled** onto the brothers. [The relative pronoun *that* starts a dependent clause and is joined with the independent clause starting with *The Collyers*, after deletion of *the newspapers.*] |

◢◤ **ALERT:** Sometimes you need commas to set off an adjective clause from the rest of the sentence. This happens only when the adjective is NONRESTRICTIVE (nonessential), so check carefully (24f). ◆

**EXERCISE 13-2** Working individually or with your peer-response group, identify and then revise the comma splices and run-on sentences. Circle the numbers of correct sentences. For help, consult 13b through 13c.4.

EXAMPLE

| | |
|---|---|
| **COMMA SPLICE** | Artists occasionally need a catalyst to set them on the road to their careers, for B. B. King, a tractor acted as that catalyst. |

| | |
|---|---|
| **RUN-ON SENTENCE** | Artists occasionally need a catalyst to set them on the road to their careers for B. B. King, a tractor acted as that catalyst. |
| **CORRECT** | Artists occasionally need a catalyst to set them on the road to their **careers; for** B. B. King, a tractor acted as that catalyst. |

(1) B. B. King, the great blues guitarist and singer, born Riley B. King in Itta Bena, Mississippi, began his working life as a sharecropper and tractor driver, he earned one dollar a day at a plantation owned by Johnson Barrett in Indianola, Mississippi. (2) As a side venture to his farm work, King sang with the excellent St. John's Gospel Singers he wanted the group to leave Mississippi to find riches and recognition in the music world. (3) In 1946, King left the group, he had tried very hard to urge to take the chance to go with him. (4) King was working hard all day in Mr. Barrett's fields, driving a tractor, he always returned to the barn at the end of the day, jumping off the tractor to the ground. (5) One day, the sudden movement made the tractor charge ahead and break off its exhaust stack King had already turned off the engine. (6) A terrified young King, fearing his boss's anger over the damaged tractor, ran away to Memphis with his guitar and $2.50, his fear kept him there for many months. (7) After a year of unsuccessfully pursuing a music career, King became discouraged and returned to Indianola he went back to work for Johnson Barrett. (8) By 1948, King had saved enough money as a tractor driver, sharecropper, and street musician to try his luck again making a living as a musician and singer, he returned to Memphis and finally found recognition and fortune, not only in that city but internationally. (9) By 1999, B. B. King had been nominated for twenty Grammy Awards, he won his ninth in that year for *Blues on the Bayou,* in the category of the Best Traditional Blues Recording. (10) In 1998, B. B. King was installed in the Grammy Hall of Fame, after having received the Grammy Lifetime Achievement Award in 1987, among his most dramatic honors were honorary PhDs granted by Yale University and the University of Mississippi.

## 13d How can I correctly use a conjunctive adverb or other transitional expression between independent clauses?

CONJUNCTIVE ADVERBS and other TRANSITIONAL EXPRESSIONS link ideas between sentences. When these words fall between sentences, a period or semicolon must immediately precede them—and a comma usually immediately follows them.

Conjunctive adverbs include such words as *however, therefore, also, next, then, thus, furthermore,* and *nevertheless* (see Box 7.5, section 7g, for a complete list). Be careful to remember that conjunctive adverbs are not COORDINATING CONJUNCTIONS (*and, but*, and so on; see 13c.3).

| | |
|---|---|
| **COMMA SPLICE** | Buying or leasing a car is a matter of individual preference**, however,** it's wise to consider several points before making a decision. |
| **RUN-ON SENTENCE** | Buying or leasing a car is a matter of individual preference **however** it's wise to consider several points before making a decision. |
| CORRECT | Buying or leasing a car is a matter of individual preference**. However,** it's wise to consider several points before making a decision. |
| CORRECT | Buying or leasing a car is a matter of individual preference**; however,** it's wise to consider several points before making a decision. |

Transitional expressions include *for example, for instance, in addition, in fact, of course,* and *on the one hand/on the other hand* (see Box 3.5 section 3g.1, for a complete list).

| | |
|---|---|
| **COMMA SPLICE** | Car leasing requires a smaller down payment**, for example,** in many cases, you need only $1,000 or $2,000 and the first monthly payment. |
| **RUN-ON SENTENCE** | Car leasing requires a smaller down payment **for example** in many cases, you need only $1,000 or $2,000 and the first monthly payment. |
| CORRECT | Car leasing requires a smaller down payment**. For example,** in many cases, you need only $1,000 or $2,000 and the first monthly payment. |
| CORRECT | Car leasing requires a smaller down payment**; for example,** in many cases, you need only $1,000 or $2,000 and the first monthly payment. |

**ALERT:** A conjunctive adverb or a transitional expression is usually followed by a comma when it starts a sentence (24c). ◆

**EXERCISE 13-3**    Revise comma splices or run-on sentences caused by incorrectly punctuated conjunctive adverbs or other transitional expressions. If a sentence is correct, circle its number. For help, consult 13d.

EXAMPLE    Yearly, the US National Aeronautics and Space Administration (NASA) requests federal funding for space exploration, however, many US citizens wonder what practical value the space program offers.

Yearly, the U.S. National Aeronautics and Space Administration
(NASA) requests federal funding for space *exploration.*
*However,* many US citizens wonder what practical value the
space program offers. [comma splice; corrected by inserting
a period before a conjunctive adverb]

1. US citizens may not realize products developed by NASA directly affect
   their lives. For example, NASA has developed or improved a number of
   goods and services now available to the general public.

2. People may be surprised to learn that bar coding on products grew out
   of NASA's need to keep track of thousands of spacecraft components,
   indeed, bar codes allow merchants to track what they sell and to
   record items for reordering.

3. Methods of medical imaging today are based on NASA's developing
   ways to process signals for sending images from space, in addition,
   the ear thermometer, popular for use with adults and children,
   developed out of NASA technology to identify the birth of stars.

4. Firefighters now wear fire-resistant suits because of space technology
   furthermore, NASA research created protective lenses that now save
   welders' eyes from harmful radiation.

5. Not all items coming from NASA's experiments result in medical
   advances or safety for workers, for instance, thermal gloves, ski
   boots, and failsafe flashlights are now available to the general
   public as a direct result of NASA's work.

**EXERCISE 13-4**   Revise all comma splices and run-on sentences, using as
many different methods of correction as you can.

(1) Energy psychology represents fairly new methods joining
Eastern lines of thought to the mind and body and Western psychology
and psychotherapy, according to an article by Leonard Holmes, PhD,
proponents of energy psychology contend that striking acupuncture
points and at the same time recalling an anxiety-producing incident
can alleviate anxiety and phobias. (2) Holmes inquires whether this
idea is true in fact, he goes on to question the connection the
acupuncture points have to anxiety. (3) In the early 1980s, Roger
Callahan, PhD, popularized procedures utilizing energy psychology,
he called the procedures "The Callahan Technique" or "Thought Field
Therapy." (4) In the beginning, Callahan's training programs were
costly, generally hundreds of dollars, now, on the other hand, they are
moderately priced. (5) Other therapists such as clinical psychologist
David Feinstein, PhD, have joined the ranks promoting energy
psychology, interestingly, Feinstein sells an interactive CD-ROM that
presents guidance in energy psychology/psychotherapy. (6) A qualified

therapist can use the CD-ROM laypersons should not experiment with the contents of the CD-ROM. (7) Today, proponents of energy psychology contend it results in the successful handling of problems such as trauma, abuse, depression, and addictive cravings, other uses for energy psychology, or "Emotional Freedom Techniques" (EFT), as Gary Craig calls them on his Web site, include treatment for medical conditions such as headaches and breathing difficulties. (8) Craig, not a licensed health professional, contends the "missing piece to the healing puzzle" is EFT he quotes from supposedly scientific clinical trials indicating that patients have seen dramatic results in their conditions because of EFT. (9) Holmes thinks energy psychotherapy is still too early in its development to be widely applied he cautions the general public to avoid trying it on their own. (10) Holmes advises extreme caution for psychologists about continuing to use EFT more needs to be known from research.

# Chapter 14

---

## MISPLACED AND DANGLING MODIFIERS

### MISPLACED MODIFIERS

#### 14a  What is a misplaced modifier?

A **modifier** is a word or group of words that describes or limits another word or group of words. A **misplaced modifier** is positioned incorrectly in a sentence, which means, therefore, that it describes the wrong word and changes the writer's meaning. Always place a modifier as close as possible to what it describes.

#### AVOIDING SQUINTING MODIFIERS

A **squinting modifier** is misplaced because it modifies both the word that comes before it and the word that follows it. Check that your modifiers are placed so that they communicate the meaning you intend.

> **NO**  The football player being recruited **eagerly** believed each successive offer would be better. [What was *eager*? The recruitment or the player's belief?]

> **YES**  The football player being recruited believed **eagerly** that each successive offer would be better.

> **YES**  The football player being **eagerly** recruited believed that each successive offer would be better.

#### PLACING LIMITING WORDS CAREFULLY

Words such as *only, not only, just, not just, almost, hardly, nearly, even, exactly, merely, scarcely,* and *simply* serve to limit the meaning of a word according to where they are placed. When you use such words, position them precisely. Consider how moving the placement of the word *only* changes the meaning of this sentence: *Professional coaches say that high salaries motivate players.*

> **Only** professional coaches say that high salaries motivate players.
> [No one else says this.]

> Professional coaches **only** say that high salaries motivate players.
> [The coaches probably do not mean what they say.]

Professional coaches say **only** that high salaries motivate players.
[The coaches say nothing else.]

Professional coaches say that **only** high salaries motivate players.
[Nothing except high salaries motivates players.]

Professional coaches say that high salaries **only** motivate players.
[High salaries do nothing other than motivate players.]

Professional coaches say that high salaries motivate **only** players.
[High salaries do motivate the players but not the coaches and managers.]

## 14b   How can I avoid split infinitives?

An INFINITIVE is a VERB form that starts with *to: to motivate, to convince, to create* are examples (7e). A **split infinitive** occurs when words are placed between the word *to* and its verb. The effect is awkward.

**NO**   Orson Welles's radio drama "War of the Worlds" managed **to, in October 1938, convince** listeners that they were hearing an invasion by Martians. [*In October 1938* is misplaced because the words come between *to* and *convince*.]

**YES**   **In October 1938**, Orson Welles's radio drama "War of the Worlds" managed **to convince** listeners that they were hearing an invasion by Martians.

Often, the word that splits an infinitive is an ADVERB ending in *-ly*. In general, place adverbs either before or after the infinitive.

**NO**   People feared that they would no longer be able **to happily live** in peace.

**YES**   People feared that they would no longer be able **to live happily** in peace.

The rule about split infinitives has changed recently. Current usage says that when the best placement for a single adverb is actually between *to* and the verb, use that structure freely.

Welles wanted **to realistically portray** a Martian invasion for the radio audience.

If you want to avoid splitting infinitives in your ACADEMIC WRITING, revise to avoid the split:

Welles wanted his "Martian invasion" **to sound realistic** for the radio audience. [The adverb *realistically* was changed to the adjective *realistic*.]

**14c** **How can I avoid other splits in my sentences?**

When too many words split—that is, come between—a SUBJECT and its VERB or between a verb and its OBJECT, the result is a sentence that lurches rather than flows from beginning to end.

**NO** The **announcer**, because the script, which Welles himself wrote, called for perfect imitations of emergency announcements, **opened** with a warning that included a description of the "invasion." [The subject *announcer* is placed too far away from the verb *opened,* so this split is too large.]

**YES** Because the script, which Welles himself wrote, called for perfect imitations of emergency announcements, the **announcer opened** with a warning that included a description of the "invasion." [The subject and verb, *announcer opened,* aren't split.]

**NO** Many churches **held** for their frightened communities **"end of the world" prayer services**. [The verb *held* is placed too far away from the object *"end of the world" prayer services,* so this split is too large.]

**YES** Many churches **held "end of the world" prayer services** for their frightened communities. [The verb and object, *held "end of the world" prayer services,* aren't split.]

**EXERCISE 14-1** Revise these ten sentences to correct misplaced modifiers, split infinitives, and other splits. If a sentence is correct, circle its number. For help, consult 14a through 14c.

**EXAMPLE** Barrow, Alaska, is closer to the North Pole <u>located on the Arctic Ocean</u> than any other US city.

*Located on the Arctic Ocean,* Barrow, Alaska, is closer to the North Pole than any other US city.

1. The 4,400 residents of Barrow, Alaska, in a region where wind chills can go down to 100 degrees below zero Fahrenheit not only survive but thrive.

2. These hardy residents adjust their lives to 24-hour nights in winter and 24-hour days in summer, 64 percent of whom are original natives.

3. The mayor of Barrow rides over the hard-packed snow his bike to work every day.

4. Businesses provide electric plug-in stations so customers while they shop can keep their cars running and heated.

5. Fran Tate runs Pepe's North of the Border, the Mexican restaurant closest to the North Pole, and she asks customers to every time they visit sign her guest book.

6. Fran nearly sends Christmas cards and a personal note to the 7,000 people on her list, including the psychologist Dr. Joyce Brothers and the basketball legend Karl Malone.

7. At Ipalook Elementary School's enormous indoor playground, students who are playing happily go outside whenever the weather is above 20 degrees below zero Fahrenheit.

8. Barrow has no roads connecting it with the outside world, which means the residents rely on airplanes for supplies and mail.

9. The airport for one of Alaska's largest corporations, which is a fuel and construction business owned by the Inupiat natives, is essential.

10. Residents, because they have no mall or movie theater, read, talk with friends in town, chat on the Internet, and enjoy the peace and quiet of the open tundra.

**EXERCISE 14-2**  Using each list of words and phrases, create all the possible logical sentences. Insert commas as needed. Explain differences in meaning among the alternatives you create. For help, consult 14a through 14c.

EXAMPLE    exchange students
           learned to speak French
           while in Paris
           last summer

A. Last summer, / exchange students / learned to speak French / while in Paris.

B. While in Paris, / exchange students / learned to speak French / last summer.

C. Exchange students / learned to speak French / while in Paris / last summer.

D. Exchange students / learned to speak French / last summer / while in Paris.

1. chicken soup
   according to folklore
   helps
   cure colds

2. tadpoles
   instinctively
   swim
   toward
   their genetic relatives

3. the young driver
   while driving
   in the snow
   skidded
   carelessly

4. climbed
   the limber teenager
   a tall palm tree
   to pick a ripe coconut
   quickly

5. and cause mini-avalanches
   ski patrollers
   set explosives
   often
   to prevent big avalanches

## DANGLING MODIFIERS

### 14d    How can I avoid dangling modifiers?

A **dangling modifier** describes or limits a word or words that never actually appear in the sentence. Aware of the intended meaning, the writer
unconsciously supplies the missing words, but the reader gets confused.
To correct a dangling modifier, state clearly your intended SUBJECT in the
sentence.

**NO**    **Having read Faulkner's short story "A Rose for
Emily," *the ending*** surprised us. [This sentence says *the
ending* was *reading the story,* which is impossible.]

**YES**    Having read Faulkner's short story "A Rose for Emily," **we
were surprised by the ending**. [Second half of sentence is
rewritten to include the subject *we.*]

**YES**    **We** read Faulkner's short story "A Rose for Emily" **and
were surprised by the ending**. [Sentence is rewritten to
include the subject *We.*]

**NO**    **When courting Emily, *the townspeople*** gossiped about
her. [This sentence says *the townspeople* were *courting Emily,* which
isn't true.]

**YES**    **When Emily was being courted *by Homer Barron***, the
townspeople gossiped about her. [First half of sentence is
rewritten to include the name of the person doing the courting: *Homer
Barron.*]

A major cause of dangling modifiers is the unnecessary use of the
PASSIVE VOICE. Whenever possible, use the ACTIVE VOICE.

**NO**    **To earn money, china-painting lessons** were offered by
Emily to wealthy young women. [*China-painting lessons* cannot
*earn money. Were offered by Emily* is in the passive voice.]

**YES**    **To earn money, Emily** offered china-painting lessons to
wealthy young women. [Change to the active voice; *Emily offered*
corrects the problem.]

**EXERCISE 14-3**    Identify and correct any dangling modifiers in these sentences. If a sentence is correct, circle its number. For help, consult 14d.

**EXAMPLE**    To succeed as scientists, obstacles must be overcome by
women.

*To succeed as scientists, women* must overcome obstacles.

1. In the past, few high-status science awards were won by women, a situation that failed to give many outstanding women scientists the recognition they deserve.
2. Having entered many fields of science in large numbers since the 1970s, numerous low-level and mid-level jobs are now held by women.
3. Attaining the highest achievements and awards has been beyond the grasp of even the most gifted women scientists.
4. When the announcement of the newly elected members of the prestigious National Academy of Sciences was made in 2003, major advances by women was suddenly realized.
5. Having selected seventy-two new members in 2003, seventeen were women, a larger number than ever before.
6. When selecting new members, important scientific discoveries are the major decisive factor.
7. Having discovered the relationship between telomeres (the tips of chromosomes) and aging, an obvious choice for membership was Dr. Carol Grieder of Johns Hopkins School of Medicine.
8. By discovering that a surprisingly large number of human genes control the sense of smell, Dr. Linda Buck earned her Academy membership.
9. To make the study of primates less subjective and more scientifically organized, the Academy recognized Dr. Jeanne Altmann.
10. Having risen from 12 percent in the mid-1980s to 20 percent today, an increasingly greater membership for women in the National Academy of Sciences is expected.

## 14e How can I proofread successfully for misplaced and dangling modifiers?

Sentence errors like MISPLACED MODIFIERS and DANGLING MODIFIERS are hard to spot because of the way the human brain works. Writers know what they mean to say when they write. When they PROOFREAD, however, they often misread what they've written for what they intended to write. The mind unconsciously adjusts for the error. In contrast, readers see only what's on the paper or screen. We suggest that you read your writing aloud, or have someone else read it to you, to proofread it for these kinds of problems.

# Chapter 15

## SHIFTING AND MIXED SENTENCES

### SHIFTING SENTENCES

#### 15a What is a shifting sentence?

A **shift** within a sentence is an unnecessary, abrupt change in PERSON, NUMBER, SUBJECT, VOICE, TENSE, MOOD, or DIRECT or INDIRECT DISCOURSE. These shifts blur meaning. Sometimes a shift occurs between two or more sentences in a paragraph. If you set out on one track (writing in FIRST PERSON, for example), your readers expect you to stay on that same track (and not unnecessarily shift to THIRD PERSON, for example). When you go off track, you have written a shifting sentence or paragraph.

#### 15b How can I avoid shifts in person and number?

Who or what performs or receives an action is defined by the term *person*. FIRST PERSON (*I, we*) is the speaker or writer; SECOND PERSON (*you*) is the one being spoken or written *to;* and THIRD PERSON (*he, she, it, they*) is the person or thing being spoken or written *about.*

The essential point is that shifts are incorrect unless the meaning in a particular context makes them necessary.

> **NO** I enjoy reading financial forecasts of the future, but **you** wonder which will turn out to be correct. [The first person *I* shifts to the second person *you*.]

> **YES** I enjoy reading financial forecasts of the future, but **I** wonder which will turn out to be correct.

NUMBER refers to whether words are *singular* (one) or *plural* (more than one) in meaning. Do not start to write in one number and then shift for no reason to the other number.

| **NO** | Because **people** are living longer, **an employee** now retires later. [The plural *people* shifts to the singular *employee*.] |
| **YES** | Because **people** are living longer, **employees** now retire later. |

In ACADEMIC WRITING, reserve *you* for addressing the reader directly. Use the third person for general statements.

| **NO** | **I** like my job in customer service because **you** get to solve people's problems. [*I* is in the first person, so a shift to the second person *you* is incorrect.] |
| **YES** | **I** like my job in customer service because **I** get to solve people's problems. |

| **NO** | **People** enjoy feeling productive, so when a job is unsatisfying, **you** usually become depressed. [*People* is in the third person, so a shift to the second person *you* is incorrect.] |
| **YES** | **People** enjoy feeling productive, so when a job is unsatisfying, **they** usually become depressed. |

Be careful with words in the singular (usually NOUNS) used in a general sense, such as *employee, student, consumer, neighbor,* and *someone.* These words are always third-person singular. The only pronouns for these ANTECEDENTS in the third-person singular are *he, she,* and *it.* Remember that *they* is plural, so the word *they* can't be used with singular nouns.

| **NO** | When **an employee** is treated with respect, **they** are more motivated to do a good job. [*Employee* is third-person singular, so the shift to the third-person plural *they* is incorrect.] |
| **YES** | When **an employee** is treated with respect, **he or she** is more motivated to do a good job. |
| **YES** | When **employees** are treated with respect, **they** are more motivated to do a good job. |
| **YES** | **An employee** who is treated with respect is more motivated to do a good job. |
| **YES** | **Employees** who are treated with respect are more motivated to do a good job. |

**ALERT:** When you use INDEFINITE PRONOUNS (such as *someone, everyone,* or *anyone*), you want to use GENDER-NEUTRAL LANGUAGE. For advice, see 10s and 21g. ◆

**EXERCISE 15-1** Eliminate shifts in person and number between, as well as within, sentences. Some sentences may not need revision. For help, consult 15b.

(1) In Agra, India, millions of visitors to the Taj Mahal see a glorious white-marble building that serves as a tribute to undying love, but you also see pollution and serious deterioration of the property. (2) The tourist arrives in horse-drawn carts or electric cars because they may not travel in vehicles that burn fossil fuel in the vicinity of the monument. (3) Government officials have closed down polluting factories in the immediate area, but it allows a petrochemical plant owned by people who have political connections to remain open, darkening the air and the monument. (4) Huge crowds arrive daily to see the gorgeous Taj Mahal, which is perfect in its architectural proportions and is topped with beautiful minarets. (5) But he or she also sees terrible neglect, such as huge beehives hanging from archways, litter on the lawns and in the gardens, and canals choked with trash. (6) The whole place smells of pigeon droppings, decorative panels are faded and destroyed, and many sections are off limits to sightseers. (7) However, recently a large Indian corporation has begun managing the monument, and they are starting to make improvements. (8) Soon visitors will enter through a new, clean tourist center, complete with a café and computerized ticketing, and you will find a tour of the cleansed, restored monument to eternal love a very pleasant experience.

## 15c  How can I avoid shifts in subject and voice?

A SHIFT in SUBJECT is rarely justified when it is accompanied by a shift in VOICE. The voice of a sentence is either *active* (*People expect changes*) or *passive* (*Changes are expected*). Some subject shifts, however, are justified by the meaning of a passage: for example, *People look forward to the future, but the future holds many secrets.*

> **NO** Most **people expect** major improvements in the future, but some **hardships are** also **anticipated**. [The subject shifts from *people* to *hardships,* and the voice shifts from active to passive.]

> **YES** Most **people expect** major improvements in the future, but **they** also **anticipate** some hardships.

> **YES** Most **people expect** major improvements in the future but also **anticipate** some hardships.

## 15d  How can I avoid shifts in tense and mood?

TENSE refers to the time in which the action of a VERB takes place—past, present, or future: *We **will go** to the movies after we **finish** dinner.* An unnecessary tense SHIFT within or between sentences can make the statement confusing or illogical.

**NO**    A campaign to clean up movies in the United States **began** in the 1920s as civic and religious groups **try** to ban sex and violence from the screen. [The tense incorrectly shifts from the past *began* to the present *try*.]

**YES**    A campaign to clean up movies in the United States **began** in the 1920s as civic and religious groups **tried** to ban sex and violence from the screen.

**NO**    Film producers and distributors **created** the Production Code in the 1930s. At first, violating its guidelines **carried** no penalty. Eventually, however, films that **fail** to get the board's seal of approval **do not receive** wide distribution. [This shift occurs between sentences—the past tense *created* and *carried* shift to the present tense *fail* and *do not receive*.]

**YES**    Film producers and distributors **created** the Production Code in the 1930s. At first, violating its guidelines **carried** no penalty. Eventually, however, films that **failed** to get the board's seal of approval **did not receive** wide distribution.

MOOD indicates whether a sentence is a statement or a question (INDICATIVE MOOD), a command or request (IMPERATIVE MOOD), or a conditional or other-than-real statement (SUBJUNCTIVE MOOD). A shift in mood creates an awkward construction and can cause confusion.

**NO**    The Production Code included two guidelines on violence: **Do not show** the details of brutal killings, and movies **should not be** explicit about how to commit crimes. [The verbs shift from the imperative mood *do not show* to the indicative mood *movies should not be*.]

**YES**    The Production Code included two guidelines on violence: **Do not show** the details of brutal killings, and **do not show** explicitly how to commit crimes. [This revision uses the imperative mood for both guidelines.]

**YES**    The Production Code included two guidelines on violence: Movies **were not to show** the details of brutal killings or explicit ways to commit crimes.

**NO**    The code's writers worried that **if a crime were to be** accurately **depicted** in a movie, **copycat crimes will follow**. [The sentence shifts from the subjunctive mood *if a crime were to be depicted* to the indicative mood *copycat crimes will follow*.]

**YES**    The code's writers worried that **if a crime were to be** accurately **depicted** in a movie, **copycat crimes would follow**.

**15e**   **How can I avoid shifts between indirect and direct discourse?**

**Indirect discourse** is not enclosed in quotation marks because it reports, rather than quotes, something that someone said. In contrast, **direct discourse** is enclosed in quotation marks because it quotes exactly the words that someone said. It's incorrect to write direct discourse and omit the quotation marks. Also, it's incorrect to write sentences that mix indirect and direct discourse. Such SHIFT errors confuse readers, who can't tell what was said and what is being merely reported.

> **NO**   A critic said that board members were acting as censors and **what you are doing is unconstitutional**. [*Said that* sets up indirect discourse, but *what you are doing is unconstitutional* is direct discourse; it also lacks quotation marks and the changes in language that distinguish spoken words from reported words.]

> **YES**   A critic said that board members were acting as censors and **that what they were doing was unconstitutional**. [This revision uses indirect discourse consistently.]

> **YES**   A critic, in stating that board members were acting as censors, added, **"What you are doing is unconstitutional."** [This revision uses discourse correctly, with quotation marks and other changes in language to distinguish spoken words from reported words.]

Whenever you change your writing from direct discourse to indirect discourse (when you decide to paraphrase rather than quote someone directly, for example), you need to make changes in VERB TENSE and other grammatical features for your writing to make sense. Simply removing the quotation marks is not enough.

> **NO**   He asked **did we enjoy the movie**? [This version has the verb form needed for direct discourse, but the pronoun *we* is wrong and quotation punctuation is missing.]

> **YES**   He asked **whether we enjoyed the movie**. [This version is entirely indirect discourse, and the verb has changed from *enjoy* to *enjoyed*.]

> **YES**   He asked, **"Did you enjoy the movie?"** [This version is direct discourse. It repeats the original speech exactly, with correct quotation punctuation.]

**EXERCISE 15-2**   Revise these sentences to eliminate incorrect shifts within sentences. Some sentences can be revised in several ways. For help, consult 15b through 15e.

EXAMPLE    In 1942, the US government is faced with arresting five million people for not paying their federal income taxes.

In 1942, the US government *was faced* with arresting five million people for not paying their federal income taxes.

1. Congress needed money to pay for US participation in World War II, so a new tax system was proposed.
2. Tax payments were due on March 15, not April 15 as it is today.
3. For the first time, Congress taxed millions of lower-income citizens. Most people do not save enough to pay the amount of taxes due.
4. When a scientific poll showed lawmakers that only one in seven Americans had saved enough money, he became worried.

**EXERCISE 15-3**    Revise this paragraph to eliminate incorrect shifts between sentences and within sentences. For help, consult 15b through 15e.

(1) According to sociologists, people experience role conflict when we find ourselves trying to juggle too many different social roles. (2) When people reach overload, he or she decided, "to cut back somewhere." (3) For example, a well-known politician might decide not to run for reelection because family life would be interfered with by the demands of the campaign. (4) In other cases, you may delay having children so they can achieve early career success. (5) A person might say to themselves that I can't do this right now and focus instead on career goals. (6) In yet another example, a plant manager might enjoy social interaction with employees but consequently find themselves unable to evaluate him or her objectively. (7) In short, sociologists find that although not all role conflicts cause problems, great hardships are suffered by some individuals faced with handling difficult balancing acts. (8) People can minimize role conflicts, however, if we learn to compartmentalize our lives. (9) A good example of this is people saying that I'm going to stop thinking about my job before I head home to my family.

# MIXED SENTENCES

## 15f   What is a mixed sentence?

A mixed sentence has two or more parts, with the first part starting in one direction and the rest of the parts going off in another. This mixing of sentence parts leads to unclear meaning. To avoid this error, as you write each sentence, remember how you started it and make sure that whatever comes next in the sentence relates grammatically and logically to that beginning.

**NO** Because our side lost the contest eventually motivated us to do better. [*Because our side lost the contest* starts the sentence in one direction, but *eventually motivated us to do better* goes off in another direction.]

**YES** Because our side lost the contest, **we** eventually became motivated to do better.

**YES** Our side lost the contest, **which** eventually motivated us to do better.

**NO** Because television's first transmissions in the 1920s included news programs became popular with the public. [The opening dependent clause starts off on one track (and is not correctly punctuated), but the independent clause goes off in another direction. What does the writer want to emphasize, the first transmissions or the popularity of news programs?]

**YES** Because television's first transmissions in the 1920s included news, programs became popular with the public. [The revision helps but is partial: the dependent clause talks about the news, but the independent clause goes off in another direction by talking about the popularity of the programs in general.]

**YES** Television's first transmissions in the 1920s included news programs, **which were** popular with the public. [Dropping *because* and adding *which were* solves the problem by keeping the focus on news programs throughout.]

**NO** By increasing the time for network news to thirty minutes increased the prestige of network news programs. [A prepositional phrase, such as *by increasing,* can't be the subject of a sentence.]

**YES** Increasing the time for network news to thirty minutes increased the prestige of network news programs. [Dropping the preposition *by* clears up the problem.]

**YES** By increasing the time for network news to thirty minutes, **the network executives** increased the prestige of network news programs. [Inserting a logical subject, *the network executives,* clears up the problem.]

The phrase *the fact that* lacks CONCISENESS, and it also tends to cause a mixed sentence.

**NO** The fact that quiz show scandals in the 1950s prompted the networks to produce even more news shows.

**YES** The fact **is** that quiz show scandals in the 1950s prompted the networks to produce even more news shows. [Adding *is* clarifies the meaning.]

YES   Quiz show scandals in the 1950s prompted the networks to produce even more news shows. [Dropping *the fact that* clarifies the meaning.]

## 15g   How can I correct a mixed sentence due to faulty predication?

**Faulty predication**, sometimes called *illogical predication*, occurs when a SUBJECT and its PREDICATE don't make sense together.

NO   The purpose of television was invented to entertain people. [A *purpose* cannot be *invented.*]

YES   The purpose of television was to entertain people.

YES   Television was invented to entertain people.

Faulty predication often results from a lost connection between a subject and its SUBJECT COMPLEMENT.

NO   Walter Cronkite's outstanding **characteristic** as a newscaster **was credible**. [The subject complement *credible* could logically describe *Walter Cronkite,* but *Walter Cronkite* is not the sentence's subject. Rather, the sentence's subject is his *characteristic.* Therefore, the sentence lacks a subject complement that would name a *characteristic* of *Walter Cronkite as a newscaster.*]

YES   Walter Cronkite's outstanding **characteristic** as a newscaster **was credibility**. [When *credibility* is substituted for *credible,* the sentence is correct.]

YES   Walter Cronkite was credible as a newscaster. [When *Walter Cronkite* becomes the sentence's subject, *credible* is correct,]

In ACADEMIC WRITING, avoid nonstandard constructions such as *is when* and *is where*. They should be avoided not only because they are nonstandard, but also because they usually lead to faulty predication.

NO   A disaster **is when** TV news shows get some of their highest ratings.

YES   TV news shows get some of their highest ratings during a disaster.

In academic writing, avoid constructions such as *the reason . . . is because*. Using both *reason* and *because* makes the construction redundant (it says the same thing twice). Instead, use either *the reason . . . is that* or *because* alone.

313

| NO | One **reason** that TV news captured national attention in the 1960s **is because** it covered the Vietnam War thoroughly. |

| YES | One **reason** TV news captured national attention in the 1960s **is that** it covered the Vietnam War thoroughly. |

| YES | TV news captured national attention in the 1960s **because** it covered the Vietnam War thoroughly. |

**EXERCISE 15-4**    Revise the mixed sentences so that the beginning of each sentence fits logically with its end. If a sentence is correct, circle its number. For help, consult 15f and 15g.

EXAMPLE    The reason women and men sometimes behave differently is because their brains operate differently.

*Women and men sometimes behave differently* because their brains operate differently.

1. By studying brain scans has provided researchers with pictures of neuron activity in the human brain.

2. The reason that a man's brain is 10 to 15 percent larger than a woman's brain is because men's bodies are generally 10 to 15 percent larger than women's.

3. The fact that women use both sides of the brain and more readily see relationships among objects or ideas.

4. One theory focuses on whether women have more brain neurons that control difficult intellectual functions such as language is being studied.

5. Whether walking or doing complicated math, women activate neurons in several areas of the brain at the same time.

6. The reason most men are able to focus more intently on an activity is because their neural action stays only in one area of the brain.

7. Because of a woman's ability to think simultaneously about a variety of topics enables her to read or sew while watching television.

8. While reading a map is usually when differences in men's and women's brain activity show up on the scans.

9. Neurologists are interested in men's ability to look at maps and mentally rotate positions on them.

10. Even though women perform better on a memory test are three times as likely as men to develop Alzheimer's disease.

## 15h    What are correct elliptical constructions?

An **elliptical construction** deliberately leaves out one or more words in a sentence for CONCISENESS.

Victor has his book and Joan's. [This means *Victor has his book and Joan's book*. The second *book* is left out deliberately.]

For an elliptical construction to be correct, the one or more words you leave out need to be identical to those already appearing in the sentence. For instance, the sample sentence above about Victor and Joan would have an incorrect elliptical construction if the writer's intended meaning were *Victor has his book, and Joan has her own book.*

**NO** During the 1920s in Chicago, the cornetist Manuel Perez **was leading** one outstanding jazz group, and Tommy and Jimmy Dorsey another. [The words *was leading* cannot take the place of *were leading,* which is required after *Tommy and Jimmy Dorsey.*]

**YES** During the 1920s in Chicago, the cornetist Manuel Perez **was leading** one outstanding jazz group, and Tommy and Jimmy Dorsey **were leading** another.

**YES** During the 1920s in Chicago, the cornetist Manuel Perez **led** one outstanding jazz group, and Tommy and Jimmy Dorsey another. [*Led* is correct with both *Manuel Perez* and *Tommy and Jimmy Dorsey,* so *led* can be omitted after *Dorsey.*]

## 15i  What are correct comparisons?

When you write a sentence in which you want to compare two or more things, make sure that no important words are omitted.

**NO** Individuals driven to achieve make **better** business executives. [*Better* is a word of comparison (11e), but no comparison is stated.]

**YES** Individuals driven to achieve make **better** business executives **than do people not interested in personal accomplishments**.

**NO** Most personnel officers value high achievers **more than risk takers**. [*More* is a word of comparison, but it's unclear whether the sentence says *personnel officers value high achievers over risk takers* or *personnel officers value high achievers more than risk takers value them.*]

**YES** Most personnel officers value high achievers **more than they value** risk takers.

**YES** Most personnel officers value high achievers **more than** risk takers **do**.

**15j** **How can I proofread successfully for little words I forget to use?**

If you're rushing or distracted as you write, you might unintentionally omit little words, such as ARTICLES, PRONOUNS, CONJUNCTIONS, and PREPOSITIONS. Lynn does, unfortunately. She solves this by reading her writing aloud, word by word; or, better still, she asks someone else to read it aloud because she tends to fill in mentally any missing words in her own work.

> **NO** On May 2, 1808, citizens Madrid rioted against French soldiers and were shot.

> **YES** On May 2, 1808, citizens **of** Madrid rioted against French soldiers and were shot.

> **NO** The Spanish painter Francisco Goya recorded both the riot the execution in a pair of pictures painted 1814.

> **YES** The Spanish painter Francisco Goya recorded both the riot **and** the execution in a pair of pictures painted **in** 1814.

**EXERCISE 15-5**  Revise this paragraph to create correct elliptical constructions, to complete comparisons, and to insert any missing words. For help, see 15h through 15j.

(1) A giant tsunami is as destructive and even larger than a tidal wave. (2) The word *tsunami* is Japanese for "harbor wave," for this kind wave appears suddenly in harbor or bay. (3) A tsunami begins with rapid shift in ocean floor caused by an undersea earthquake or volcano. (4) The wave this produces in the open sea is less than three feet high, but it can grow to a height of a hundred feet as it rushes and strikes against the shore. (5) For this reason, tsunamis are much more dangerous to seaside towns than ships on the open sea. (6) In 1960, a huge tsunami that struck coasts of Chile, Hawaii, and Japan killed total of 590 people. (7) In 2004, a huge tsunami that struck coasts of Indonesia, Thailand, Malaysia, and other countries killed total 275,000 people.

# Chapter 16

---

## CONCISENESS

### 16a    What is conciseness?

**Conciseness** requires you to craft sentences that are direct and to the point. Its opposite, **wordiness**, means you are filling sentences with empty words and phrases that increase the word count but contribute nothing to meaning. Wordy writing is padded with deadwood, forcing readers to clear away the branches and overgrowth—an annoying waste of time that implies the writer isn't skilled. Usually, the best time to work on making your writing more concise is while you're REVISING.*

**WORDY**    ~~As a matter of fact, t~~he television station ~~which is situated~~  
       <sub>T</sub>  <sub>local</sub>

       ~~in the local area~~ wins ~~a great~~ many awards ~~in the final~~

       ~~analysis~~ because of its ~~type of~~ coverage of ~~all kinds of~~

       controversial issues.

**CONCISE**    The local television station wins many awards for its  
       coverage of controversial issues.

### 16b    What common expressions are not concise?

Many common expressions we use in informal speech are not concise. Box 16.1 lists some and shows you how to eliminate them.

---

*Words printed in SMALL CAPITAL LETTERS are discussed elsewhere in the text and are defined in the Terms Glossary at the back of the book.

**SUMMARY BOX** 16.1

# Cutting unnecessary words and phrases

| EMPTY WORD OR PHRASE | WORDY EXAMPLE REVISED |
|---|---|
| as a matter of fact | Many marriages, ~~as a matter of fact~~, end in divorce. |
| at the present time | The revised proposal for outdoor lighting angers many villagers ^now^ ~~at the present time~~. |
| because of the fact that, in light of the fact that, due to the fact that | Because ~~of the fact that~~ the museum has a special exhibit, it stays open late. |
| by means of | We traveled by ~~means of a~~ car. |
| factor | The project's final cost was ~~the~~ essential ~~factor~~ to consider. |
| for the purpose of | Work crews arrived ~~for the purpose of~~ ^to^ fixing the potholes. |
| have a tendency to | The team ~~has a tendency~~ ^tends^ to lose home games. |
| in a very real sense | ~~In a very real sense,~~ ^A^ all firefighters are heroes. |
| in the case of | ~~In the case of~~ ^T^ he election~~, it~~ will be close. |
| in the event that | ~~In the event that~~ ^If^ you're late, I will buy our tickets. |
| in the final analysis | ~~In the final analysis, no~~ ^N^ o two eyewitnesses agreed on what they saw. |
| in the process of | We are ~~in the process of~~ reviewing the proposal. |
| it seems that | ~~It seems that~~ ^T^ he union went on strike over health benefits. |
| manner | The child spoke ~~in a reluctant manner~~. ^reluctantly.^ |
| nature | The movie review was ~~of a~~ sarcastic ~~nature~~. |

**SUMMARY BOX** 16.1 *continued*

## Cutting unnecessary words and phrases

| EMPTY WORD OR PHRASE | WORDY EXAMPLE REVISED |
|---|---|
| that exists | The crime rate ~~that exists~~ is unacceptable. |
| the point I am trying to make | ~~The point I am trying to make is~~ television reporters invade our privacy. |
| type of, kind of | Gordon took a relaxing ~~type of~~ vacation. |
| What I mean to say is | ~~What I mean to say is~~ I love you. |

**EXERCISE 16-1**   Working individually or with a group, revise this paragraph in two steps. First, underline all words that interfere with conciseness. Second, revise each sentence to make it more concise. (You'll need to drop words and replace or rearrange others.)

EXAMPLE   It seems that most North Americans think of motor scooters as vehicles that exist only in European countries.

It seems that most North Americans think of motor scooters as vehicles that exist only in European countries.

Most North Americans think of motor scooters as only European vehicles.

1. As a matter of fact, in the popular imagination, motor scooters are the very essence of European style.

2. Today, over one million scooters are purchased by people in Europe each year, compared with a number that amounts to only 70,000 buyers in the United States.

3. In fact, Europeans have long used fuel-efficient, clean-running scooters for the purpose of getting around in a manner that is relatively easy in congested cities.

4. The use of these brightly colored, maneuverable scooters allows city dwellers to zip through traffic jams and thereby to save time and to save gas.

5. However, sales of scooters, it might interest you to know, are in the process of increasing in North America.

6. What I am trying to say is that motor scooters use much less gasoline than cars, and that as a matter of fact the cost factor is about one-fourth that of an inexpensive new car.

7. In addition, some motor scooters, it is pleasing to note, now run on electricity, which in fact makes them noise and emission free.

8. A scooter running by means of electrical power amounts to a cost in the neighborhood of 25 cents to travel 50 miles at 30 miles per hour.
9. Members of many different population groups, from college students to retired persons, have begun to be finding this type of vehicle to be of a useful nature in a very real sense.
10. Traveling by means of an agile, snappy scooter makes getting around a college campus or doing errands in a city neighborhood quick and easy.

## 16c  What sentence structures usually work against conciseness?

Two sentence structures, although appropriate in some contexts, often work against CONCISENESS because they can lead to WORDINESS: writing EXPLETIVE constructions and writing in the PASSIVE VOICE.

### AVOIDING EXPLETIVE CONSTRUCTIONS

An expletive construction starts with *it* or *there* followed by a form of the VERB *be*. When you cut the expletive construction and revise, the sentence becomes more direct.

~~It is necessary for~~ students ^S^ ~~to~~ *must* fill in both questionnaires.

~~There are~~ eight instructors ^E^ ~~who~~ teach in the Computer Science Department.

**ESL TIPS:** (1) *It* in an expletive construction is not a PRONOUN referring to a specific ANTECEDENT. *It* is an "empty" word that fills the SUBJECT position in the sentence but does not function as the subject. The actual subject appears after the expletive construction: ***It was the teacher*** *who answered the question.* If concise, the sentence would be *The teacher answered the question.* (2) *There* in an expletive construction does not indicate a place. Rather, *there* is an "empty" word that fills the subject position in the sentence but does not function as the subject. The actual subject appears after the expletive construction: ***There are many teachers*** *who can answer the question.* If concise, the sentence would be *Many teachers can answer the question.* ☻

### AVOIDING THE PASSIVE VOICE

In general, the passive voice is less concise—as well as less lively—than the ACTIVE VOICE. In the active voice, the subject of a sentence does the action named by the verb.

ACTIVE  Professor Higgins teaches public speaking. [*Professor Higgins* is the subject, and he does the action: He *teaches.*]

In the passive voice, the subject of a sentence receives the action named by the verb.

> **PASSIVE** Public speaking is taught by Professor Higgins. [*Public speaking* is the subject, and it receives the action *taught*.]

Unless your meaning justifies using the passive voice, choose the active voice. (For more information, see 8n through 8p.)

> **PASSIVE** Volunteer work was done by students for credit in sociology. [The passive phrase *was done by students* is unnecessary for the intended meaning. *Students*, not *volunteer work*, are doing the action and should get the action of the verb.]

> **ACTIVE** **The students did** volunteer work for credit in sociology.

> **ACTIVE** **Volunteer work earned** students credit in sociology. [Since the verb has changed to *earned*, *volunteer work* performs the action of the verb.]

In mistakenly believing the passive voice sounds "mature" or "academic," student writers sometimes deliberately use it. Wordy, overblown sentences suggest that a writer hasn't carefully revised.

> **NO** One very important quality that can be developed during a first job is self-reliance. This strength was gained by me when I was allowed by my supervisor to set up and conduct a survey project on my own.

> **YES** Many individuals develop the important quality of self-reliance during their first job. I gained this strength when my supervisor allowed me to set up and conduct my own survey project.

> **YES** During their first job, many people develop self-reliance, as I did when my supervisor let me set up and conduct my own survey project.

## 16d How else can I revise for conciseness?

Four other techniques can help you achieve CONCISENESS: eliminating unplanned repetition (16d.1); combining sentences (16d.2); shortening CLAUSES (16d.3); and shortening PHRASES and cutting words (16d.4). These techniques involve matters of judgment.

### 16d.1 Eliminating unplanned repetition

Unplanned repetition lacks conciseness because it delivers the same message more than once, usually in slightly different words. Unplanned repetition, or redundancy, implies that the writer lacks focus and judgment.

The opposite—planned repetition—reflects both focus and judgment, as it creates a powerful rhythmic effect; see 19e. As you revise, check that every word is necessary for delivering your message.

**NO**  Bringing **the project** to **final completion** three weeks early, the supervisor of **the project** earned our **respectful regard**. [*Completion* implies *bringing to final*; *project* is used twice in one sentence; and *regard* implies *respect*.]

**YES**  Completing the project three weeks early, the supervisor earned our respect. [eighteen words reduced to eleven by cutting all redundancies]

**NO**  **Astonished**, the architect **circled around** the building **in amazement**. [*Circled* means "went around," and *astonished* and *in amazement* have the same meaning.]

**YES**  **Astonished,** the architect **circled** the building. [nine words reduced to six]

**YES**  The architect **circled** the building **in amazement**. [nine words reduced to seven]

**ESL TIP:** In all languages, words often carry an unspoken message, and native speakers understand the implied meanings of those words. In English, some implied meanings can cause redundancy in writing. For example, *I sent an e-mail by computer* is redundant. In American English, *to send an e-mail* implies *by computer*. As you become more familiar with American English, you'll begin to notice such redundancies. 🌐

## 16d.2  Combining sentences

Look at sets of sentences in your writing to see if you can fit information contained in one sentence into another sentence. (For more about combining sentences, see Chapter 17, particularly 17i.)

**TWO SENTENCES**  The *Titanic* hit an iceberg and sank. Seventy-three years later, a team of French and American scientists located the ship's resting site.

**SENTENCES COMBINED**  Seventy-three years after the *Titanic* hit an iceberg and sank, a team of French and American scientists located the ship's resting site.

**TWO SENTENCES**  Cameras revealed that the stern of the ship was missing and showed external damage to the ship's hull. Otherwise, the *Titanic* was in excellent condition.

**SENTENCES COMBINED**  Aside from a missing stern and external damage to the ship's hull, the *Titanic* was in excellent condition.

## 16d.3 Shortening clauses

Look at clauses in your writing to see if you can more concisely convey the same information. For example, sometimes you can cut a RELATIVE PRONOUN and its verb.

**WORDY** The *Titanic,* **which was** a huge ocean liner, sank in 1912.

**CONCISE** The Titanic, a huge ocean liner, sank in 1912.

Sometimes you can reduce a clause to a word.

**WORDY** The scientists held a memorial service for the passengers and crew **who had drowned**.

**CONCISE** The scientists held a memorial service for the **drowned** passengers and crew.

Sometimes an ELLIPTICAL CONSTRUCTION (7p and 15h) can shorten a clause. If you use this technique, be sure that any omitted word is implied clearly.

**WORDY** **When they were** confronted with disaster, some passengers behaved heroically, **while** others **behaved** selfishly.

**CONCISE** Confronted with disaster, some passengers behaved heroically, others selfishly.

## 16d.4 Shortening phrases and cutting words

Sometimes you can reduce a phrase or redundant word pair to a single word. Redundant word pairs and phrases include *each and every, one and only, forever and ever, final and conclusive, perfectly clear, few* (or *many) in number, consensus of opinion,* and *reason . . . is because.*

**NO** **Each and every** person was hungry after the movie.

**YES** **Every** person was hungry after the movie.

**YES** **Each** person was hungry after the movie.

**NO** The **consensus of opinion** was that the movie was disappointing.

**YES** The **consensus** was that the movie was disappointing.

**YES** **Everyone agreed** that the movie was disappointing.

| WORDY | More than fifteen hundred **travelers on that voyage** died in the shipwreck. |
| CONCISE | More than fifteen hundred **passengers** died in the shipwreck. |

Sometimes you can rearrange words so that others can be deleted.

| WORDY | Objects **found** inside the ship included **unbroken** bottles of wine and expensive **undamaged** china. |
| CONCISE | **Undamaged** objects inside the ship included bottles of wine and expensive china. |

## 16e How do verbs affect conciseness?

ACTION VERBS are strong verbs. *Be* and *have* are weak verbs that often lead to wordy sentences. When you revise weak verbs to strong ones, you can both increase the impact of your writing and reduce the number of words in your sentences. Strong verbs come into play when you revise your writing to reduce PHRASES and to change NOUNS to verbs.

| WEAK VERB | The plan before the city council **has to do with** tax rebates. |
| STRONG VERB | The plan before the city council **proposes** tax rebates. |
| WEAK VERBS | The board members **were of the opinion** that the changes in the rules **were changes they would not accept**. |
| STRONG VERBS | The board members **said** that **they would not accept** the changes in the rules. |

### REPLACING A PHRASE WITH A VERB

Phrases such as *be aware of, be capable of, be supportive of* can often be replaced with one-word verbs.

I **envy** [not *am envious of*] your mathematical ability.

I **appreciate** [not *am appreciative of*] your modesty.

Your skill **illustrates** [not *is illustrative of*] how hard you studied.

### REVISING NOUNS INTO VERBS

Many nouns are derived from verbs. Such nouns usually end with *-ance*, *-ment*, and *-tion* (*tolerance, enforcement, narration*). When you turn such wordy nouns back into verbs, your writing is more concise.

| NO | The **accumulation of** paper lasted thirty years. |
| YES | The paper **accumulated** for thirty years. |

> **NO**    We **arranged for the establishment of** a student advisory committee.
>
> **YES**    We **established** a student advisory committee.
>
> **NO**    The building **had the appearance of** having been neglected.
>
> **YES**    The building **appeared** to have been neglected.

**EXERCISE 16-2**   Working individually or with a group, combine each set of sentences to eliminate wordy constructions. For help, consult 16c through 16e.

> **EXAMPLE**    In recent years, ranchers have tried to raise and market many exotic meats. These meats have included emu, ostrich, and bison. These attempts have failed.
>
> In recent years, ranchers have failed to raise and market many exotic meats, such as emu, ostrich, and bison.

1. Each new attempt of ranchers to raise exotic animals like emu, ostrich, and bison for the commercial value of their meat follows a pattern. There is a similar pattern to each new attempt. Each new attempt begins when a few people make the claim that some exotic animal tastes better than beef and is more nutritious.

2. Emus were discovered by ranchers. Emus are birds that look like small ostriches. Emus quickly became unprofitable to raise. Only a few consumers found emu meat tasty.

3. It was found by ostrich ranchers that there was an early, strong demand for the meat of ostriches. That strong demand soon fizzled out quite a bit, the ranchers found.

4. There is the American Ostrich Association. The membership of the American Ostrich Association once used to be 3,000. Today, the membership of the American Ostrich Association now has only 500 people belonging to it.

5. Bison, also known as buffalo, were a longer-lasting craze. Ranchers had a strong desire to own the mighty animals; however, the price of bison was increased greatly by the demand. It became uneconomical for ranchers to purchase young animals.

6. Also, bison are difficult to raise. They tend to need strong fences to hold them in. They cannot find enough food to eat. They eat by grazing. The land of some buffalo ranches consists of poor pasture land or is in mountainous terrain.

7. Recently, the yak has been discovered by ranchers. The yak is an animal from Central Asia. It is from rugged mountainous areas. For centuries, the yak has supported the people of the Himalayan region.

8. Yaks have the ability to forage more efficiently compared with bison or cows. Yaks are easier to care for than bison or cows. Yaks possess a better resistance to many diseases.

9. Chefs in a few gourmet restaurants are beginning to serve yak meat. They are devising fancy recipes for it. They are featuring it on their menus. The meat is mild-tasting and succulent. The meat is also low in fat.

10. Even though yaks are easy to raise and even are environmentally friendly, there is a problem. The ranchers must overcome that problem before they can raise yaks profitably. That problem is the fact that consumers lack familiarity with yaks. Consumers have a reluctance to try yak meat.

**EXERCISE 16-3** Working individually or with a group, revise this paragraph in two steps. First, underline all words that interfere with conciseness. Second, revise the paragraph to make it more concise. (You'll need to drop words and replace or rearrange others.)

EXAMPLE      Within a matter of minutes after the completion of a championship game, the winning team's players are enabled to put on caps that have been embroidered with their team's name, the year, as well as the word "champions."

Minutes after completing a championship game, the winning team's players receive caps embroidered with their team's name, the year, and the word "champions."

(1) At the present time, caps for sports teams are manufactured in factories located primarily in Asian countries such as China, Korea, and Taiwan. (2) Championship caps are quickly produced and shipped by factories wherever they are needed for both of the two teams playing in a final game or series. (3) The very moment the game ends, a trucking company delivers the caps to the winning team's locker room, and it then immediately and instantly burns the losing team's caps so as to prevent embarrassing anyone. (4) Companies that produce all types of sports apparel know that in most cases there is only a short period of time available for making and earning high profits from merchandise connected to a winning team. (5) Within barely a day or two, they flood the market with all sorts of every kind of t-shirts, jackets, caps, coffee mugs, in addition to banners showing and presenting the winning team's championship information.

# Chapter 17

## COORDINATION AND SUBORDINATION

Used well, **coordination** and **subordination** in sentences enhance writing style. These structuring methods reflect the relationships between ideas that a writer seeks to express. Some writers enlist coordination and subordination while they draft, but often writers wait until they revise to check for good opportunities to use these two techniques.

| | |
|---|---|
| TWO SENTENCES | The sky turned dark gray. The wind died down. |
| USING COORDINATION | The sky turned dark gray, **and** the wind died down. |
| USING SUBORDINATION 1 | **As** the sky turned dark gray, the wind died down. [Here, the wind is the focus.] |
| USING SUBORDINATION 2 | **As** the wind died down, the sky turned dark gray. [Here, the sky is the focus.] |

## COORDINATION

### 17a　What is coordination of sentences?

**Coordination** of sentences is a grammatical strategy to communicate that the ideas in two or more INDEPENDENT CLAUSES are equivalent or balanced. Coordination can produce harmony by bringing related elements together. Whenever you use the technique of coordination of sentences, make sure that it works well with the meaning you want to communicate.

The sky turned **brighter, and** people emerged happily from buildings.

The sky turned **brighter;** people emerged happily from buildings.

### 17b　What is the structure of a coordinate sentence?

A **coordinate sentence**, also known as a *compound sentence*, consists of two or more INDEPENDENT CLAUSES joined either by a semicolon or by a comma working in concert with a COORDINATING CONJUNCTION (*and, but, for, or, nor, yet, so*). Box 17.1 shows the pattern for coordination of sentences.

**PATTERN BOX 17.1**

## Coordinate (compound) sentences

Independent clause $\begin{Bmatrix} \textbf{, and} \\ \textbf{, but} \\ \textbf{, for} \\ \textbf{, or} \\ \textbf{, nor} \\ \textbf{, yet} \\ \textbf{, so} \\ \textbf{;} \end{Bmatrix}$ independent clause.

---

**17c** **What meaning does each coordinating conjunction convey?**

Each COORDINATING CONJUNCTION has its own meaning. When you choose one, be sure that its meaning accurately expresses the relationship between the equivalent ideas that you want to convey.

- **and** means addition
- **but** and **yet** mean contrast
- **for** means reason or choice
- **or** means choice
- **nor** means negative choice
- **so** means result or effect

**ALERT:** Always use a comma before a coordinating conjunction that joins two INDEPENDENT CLAUSES (24b). ◆

---

**17d** **How can I avoid misusing coordination?**

One major misuse of COORDINATION occurs when unrelated or non-equivalent ideas, each in its own INDEPENDENT CLAUSE, are coordinated. The result looks like a coordinated sentence, but the ideas are unrelated.

**NO**   Computers came into common use in the 1970s, and they sometimes make costly errors. [The statement in each independent clause is true, but the ideas are not related or equivalent.]

329

| | |
|---|---|
| **YES** | Computers came into common use in the 1970s, and now they are indispensable business tools. |

A second major misuse of coordination occurs when it's overused. Simply stringing sentences together with COORDINATING CONJUNCTIONS makes relationships among ideas unclear—and the resulting sentence lacks style.

| | |
|---|---|
| **NO** | Dinosaurs could have disappeared for many reasons, **and** one theory holds that a sudden shower of meteors and asteroids hit the earth, **so** the impact created a huge dust cloud that caused a false winter. The winter lasted for years, **and** the dinosaurs died. |
| **YES** | Dinosaurs could have disappeared for many reasons. One theory holds that a sudden shower of meteors and asteroids hit the earth. The impact created a huge dust cloud that caused a false winter. The winter lasted for years, killing the dinosaurs. |

**EXERCISE 17-1**  Working individually or with a group, revise these sentences to eliminate illogical or overused coordination. If you think a sentence needs no revision, explain why. For help, consult 17a through 17d.

| | |
|---|---|
| **EXAMPLE** | Fencing, once a form of combat, has become a competitive sport worldwide, and today's fencers disapprove of those who identify fencing with fighting. |
| | Fencing, once a form of combat, has become a competitive sport worldwide, *but* today's fencers disapprove of those who identify fencing with fighting. |

1. As depicted in movies, fencing sometimes appears to be reckless swordplay, and fencing requires precision, coordination, and strategy.
2. In the 1800s, fencing became very popular, and it was one of the few sports included in the first modern Olympic Games in 1896, and fencing has been part of the Olympics ever since.
3. Fencing equipment includes a mask, a padded jacket, a glove, and one of three weapons—a foil, épée, or saber—and a fencer's technique and targets differ depending on the weapon used and the fencer's experience.
4. Generally, a fencer specializes in one of the three weapons, but some competitors are equally skilled with all three.
5. The object of fencing is to be the first to touch the opponent five times, and a "president," who is sometimes assisted by a number of judges, officiates at competitions.

## SUBORDINATION

**17e**    ### What is subordination in sentences?

**Subordination** is a grammatical strategy to communicate that one idea in a sentence is more important than another idea in the same sentence. To use subordination, you place the more important idea in an INDEPENDENT CLAUSE and the less important—the subordinate—idea in a DEPENDENT CLAUSE. The information you choose to subordinate depends on the meaning you want to deliver.

INDEPENDENT CLAUSE                                                          DEPENDENT

Two cowboys fought a dangerous Colorado snowstorm **while they**

CLAUSE                                    DEPENDENT CLAUSE

**were looking for cattle. When they came to a canyon,**

INDEPENDENT CLAUSE

they saw outlines of buildings through the blizzard.

To illustrate the difference in writing style when you use subordination, here's a passage with the same message as the example above, but without subordination.

Two cowboys fought a dangerous Colorado snowstorm. They were looking for cattle. They came to a canyon. They saw outlines of buildings through the blizzard.

**17f**    ### What is the structure of a subordinate sentence?

A subordinate sentence starts the DEPENDENT CLAUSE with either a SUBORDINATING CONJUNCTION or a RELATIVE PRONOUN.

**If** they are very lucky, the passengers may glimpse dolphins breaking water playfully near the ship.

—Elizabeth Gray, student

Pandas are solitary animals, **which** means they are difficult to protect from extinction.

—Jose Santos, student

For patterns of subordination with dependent clauses, see Box 17.2 (p. 332). Dependent clauses are of two types: ADVERB CLAUSES and ADJECTIVE CLAUSES. An adverb clause starts with a subordinating conjunction. An adjective clause starts with a relative pronoun.

## Subordination

**SENTENCES WITH ADVERB CLAUSES**

- **Adverb clause,** independent clause.
  **After the sky grew dark,** the wind died suddenly.
- Independent clause, **adverb clause.**
  Birds stopped singing, **as they do during an eclipse.**
- Independent clause **adverb clause.**
  The stores closed **before the storm began.**

**SENTENCES WITH ADJECTIVE CLAUSES**

- Independent clause **restrictive (essential)\* adjective clause.**
  Weather forecasts warned of a storm **that might bring a thirty-inch snowfall.**
- Independent clause, **nonrestrictive (nonessential)\* adjective clause.**
  Spring is the season for tornadoes, **which may have wind speeds over 220 miles an hour.**
- Beginning of independent clause, **restrictive (essential)\* adjective clause** end of independent clause.
  Anyone **who lives through a tornado** remembers its power.
- Beginning of independent clause, **nonrestrictive (nonessential)\* adjective clause,** end of independent clause.
  The sky, **which had been clear,** turned greenish black.

\*For an explanation of RESTRICTIVE and NONRESTRICTIVE ELEMENTS, see 24f.

## 17g What meaning does each subordinating conjunction convey?

Each SUBORDINATING CONJUNCTION has its own meaning. When you choose one, be sure that its meaning accurately expresses the relationship between the ideas that you want to convey. Box 17.3 lists subordinating conjunctions according to their different meanings.

**SUMMARY BOX 17.3**

## Subordinating conjunctions and their meanings

**TIME**

*after, before, once, since, until, when, whenever, while*

**After** you have handed in your report, you cannot revise it.

**REASON OR CAUSE**

*as, because, since*

**Because** you have handed in your report, you cannot revise it.

**PURPOSE OR RESULT**

*in order that, so that, that*

I want to read your report **so that** I can evaluate it.

**CONDITION**

*even if, if, provided that, unless*

**Unless** you have handed in your report, you can revise it.

**CONTRAST**

*although, even though, though, whereas, while*

**Although** you have handed in your report, you can ask to revise it.

**CHOICE**

*than, whether*

You took more time to revise **than** I did before the lab report deadline.

**PLACE OR LOCATION**

*where, wherever*

**Wherever** you say, I'll come to hand in my report.

**EXERCISE 17-2**   Working individually or with a group, combine each pair of sentences, using an adverb clause to subordinate one idea. Then, revise each sentence so that the adverb clause becomes the independent clause. For help, see 17e through 17g, especially Box 17.2.

EXAMPLE   The US Mint produces new coins. The US Bureau of Engraving and Printing makes $1, $5, $10, $20, $50, and $100 bills.

a. While the US Mint produces new coins, the US Bureau of Engraving and Printing makes $1, $5, $10, $20, $50, and $100 bills.

b. While the US Bureau of Engraving and Printing makes $1, $5, $10, $20, $50, and $100 bills, the US Mint produces new coins.

1. The US Mint can produce more than 50 million coins a day. The US Bureau of Engraving and Printing can produce 20 million notes a day.

2. The Federal Reserve Banks are responsible for both destroying old money and ordering new coins and notes. They must keep the right amount of money in circulation.

3. Coins can stay in circulation for decades. People let them accumulate in jars and drawers in their homes.

4. A $1 bill lasts about fifteen to eighteen months. It reaches its average life span.

5. The US Federal Reserve Banks destroy dirty, worn, and torn bills. The Federal Reserve Banks are destroying more than $40 billion worth of money a year.

**EXERCISE 17-3** Working individually or with a group, combine each pair of sentences, using an adjective clause to subordinate one idea to the other. Then, revise each sentence so that the adjective clause becomes the independent clause. Use the relative pronoun given in parentheses. For help, consult 17e through 17g, especially Box 17.2 (p. 332).

EXAMPLE Aristides was an ancient Greek politician famous for his honesty and judgment. He was known as Aristides the Just. (who)

a. Aristides, *who* was an ancient Greek politician famous for his honesty and judgment, was known as Aristides the Just.

b. Aristides, *who* was known as Aristides the Just, was an ancient Greek politician famous for his honesty and judgment.

1. An ancient Greek law allowed voters to banish politicians from their city. It asked citizens to write the name of an unpopular politician on their ballots. (that)

2. A voter was filling out a ballot when Aristides the Just walked by. The voter needed help in spelling *Aristides*. (who)

3. Aristides knew the voter did not recognize him. He asked why the voter wanted to banish that particular politician. (who)

4. The voter said he resented hearing someone called "the Just" all the time. He handed Aristides his ballot. (who)

5. Aristides' reaction demonstrated that the nickname "the Just" was well deserved. His reaction was to write his own name on the voter's ballot even though that person's vote helped banish Aristides. (which)

## 17h  How can I avoid misusing subordination?

One major misuse of SUBORDINATION occurs when a SUBORDINATING CONJUNCTION doesn't communicate a sensible relationship between the INDEPENDENT CLAUSE and the DEPENDENT CLAUSE. See Box 17.3 in 17g for a list of subordinating conjunctions and their different meanings.

> **NO** **Because** Beethoven was deaf when he wrote them, his final symphonies were masterpieces. [*Because* is illogical here; it says the masterpieces resulted from the deafness.]

> **YES** **Although** Beethoven was deaf when he wrote them, his final symphonies were masterpieces. [*Although* is logical here; it says Beethoven wrote masterpieces in spite of his being deaf.]

A second major misuse of subordination occurs when it's overused, resulting in too many images or ideas crowded together in one sentence. This causes readers to lose track of the message. Whenever you write a sentence with two or more dependent clauses, check that your message is clear. If it isn't, you've probably overused subordination.

> **NO** A new technique for eye surgery, **which is supposed to correct nearsightedness, which previously could be corrected only by glasses,** has been developed, **although many eye doctors do not approve of the new technique because it can create unstable vision, which includes intense glare from headlights on cars and many other light sources.** [The base sentence *A new technique for eye surgery has been developed* is crowded with five dependent clauses attached to it.]

> **YES** A new technique for eye surgery, **which is supposed to correct nearsightedness,** has been developed. Previously, only glasses could correct nearsightedness. Many doctors do not approve of the new technique **because it can create unstable vision.** The problems include intense glare from car headlights and many other sources of light. [In this revision, one long sentence has been broken into four sentences, which makes the material easier to read and the relationships among ideas clearer. Two dependent clauses remain, which balance well with the other sentence constructions. Some words have been moved to new positions.]

**ESL TIP:** If your instructor, manager, or peer reviewers advise that your sentences are too long and complex, limit the number of words in each sentence. Many ESL instructors recommend that you revise any sentence that contains more than three independent and dependent clauses in any combination. ⊕

**EXERCISE 17-4**   Working individually or with a group, correct illogical or excessive subordination in this paragraph. As you revise according to the message you want to deliver, use some dependent clauses as well as some short sentences. (Also, if you wish, apply the principles of coordination discussed in sections 17a through 17d.) For help, consult 17h.

Although many people in the United States consider the hot dog an American invention, it actually originated in Germany in 1852 when butchers in Frankfurt, Germany, stuffed meat into a long casing, which, in honor of the town, they called a "frankfurter." Because one butcher noticed that the frankfurter resembled the shape of his dog, a dachshund, he decided to name the meat roll a "dachshund sausage," a name which caught on in Germany. When Germans brought dachshund sausages to the United States, peddlers sold them on the streets, although the dachshund sausages were so hot that people often burned their fingers because they had trouble holding the meat. When one clever peddler put the sausage in a bun, a *New York Times* cartoonist decided to draw a picture of hot dachshund sausages in buns, although he called them "hot dogs" because he didn't know how to spell *dachshund*.

## 17i   How can I effectively use coordination and subordination together?

Your writing style improves when you use a logical and pleasing variety of SENTENCE TYPES, utilizing COORDINATION and SUBORDINATION to improve the flow of ideas. Here's a paragraph that demonstrates a good balance in the use of coordination and subordination.

When I was growing up, I lived on a farm just across the field from my grandmother. My parents were busy trying to raise six children and to establish their struggling dairy farm. It was nice to have Grandma so close. While my parents were providing the necessities of life, my patient grandmother gave her time to her shy, young granddaughter. I always enjoyed going with Grandma and collecting the eggs that her chickens had just laid. Usually, she knew which chickens would peck, and she was careful to let me gather the eggs from the less hostile ones.

—Patricia Mapes, student

When you use both coordination and subordination, never use both a COORDINATE CONJUNCTION and a SUBORDINATE CONJUNCTION to express one relationship in one sentence.

> **NO**    **Although** the story was well written, **but** it was too illogical.
> [The subordinating conjunction *although* expresses the contrast, so also using *but* is incorrect.]

> **YES**    **Although** the story was well written, it was too illogical.

> **YES**    The story was well written, **but** it was too illogical.

**EXERCISE 17-5**    Working individually or in a group, use subordination and coordination to combine these sets of short, choppy sentences. For help, consult all sections of this chapter.

> **EXAMPLE**    Owls cannot digest the bones and fur of the mice and birds they eat. They cough up a furry pellet every day.
>
> *Because* owls cannot digest the bones and fur of the mice and birds they *eat, they* cough up a furry pellet every day.

1. Owl pellets are the latest teaching tool in biology classrooms around the country. The pellets provide an alternative to dissecting frogs and other animals.

2. Inside the pellet are the remains of the owl's nightly meal. They include beautifully cleaned hummingbird skulls, rat skeletons, and lots of bird feathers.

3. The owl-pellet market has been cornered by companies in New York, California, and Washington. These companies distribute pellets to thousands of biology classrooms all over the world.

4. Company workers scour barns and the ground under trees where owls nest to pick up the pellets. The pellets sell for $1 each.

5. The owl-pellet business may have a short future. The rural areas of the United States are vanishing. Old barns are being bulldozed. All the barns are torn down. The owls will be gone, too.

**EXERCISE 17-6**    Working individually or with a group, revise this paragraph to make it more effective by using coordination and subordination. For help, consult all sections of this chapter.

Thirst is the body's way of surviving. Every cell in the body needs water. People can die by losing as little as 15 to 20 percent of their water requirements. Blood contains 83 percent water. Blood provides indispensable nutrients for the cells. Blood carries water to the cells. Blood carries waste away from the cells. Insufficient water means cells cannot be fueled or cleaned. The body becomes sluggish. The body can survive eleven days without water. Bodily functions are seriously disrupted by a lack of water for more than one day. The body loses water. The blood thickens. The heart must pump harder. Thickened blood is harder to pump through the heart. Some drinks replace the body's need for fluids. Alcohol or caffeine in drinks leads to dehydration. People know they should drink water often. They can become moderately dehydrated before they even begin to develop a thirst.

# Chapter 18

## PARALLELISM

### 18a  What is parallelism?

When you write words, PHRASES, or CLAUSES within a sentence to match in their grammatical forms, the result is **parallelism**. Parallelism serves to emphasize information or ideas in writing. The technique relates to the concept of parallel lines in geometry, lines that run alongside each other and never meet. Parallelism delivers grace, rhythm, and impact.

> The deer often come to eat their grain, the wolves to destroy their sheep, the bears to kill their hogs, and the foxes to catch their poultry. [The message of the multiple, accumulating assaults is echoed by the parallel structures.]
>
> —J. Hector St. Jean de Crèvecoeur,
> *Letters from an American Farmer*

You gain several advantages in using parallel structures:

- You can express ideas of equal weight in your writing.
- You can emphasize important information or ideas.
- You can add rhythm and grace to your writing style.

Many writers attend to parallelism when they are REVISING. If you think while you're DRAFTING that your parallelism is faulty or that you can enhance your writing style by using parallelism, underline or highlight the material and keep moving forward. When you revise, you can return to the places you've marked.

### 18b  What is a balanced sentence?

A **balanced sentence** is a type of parallelism in which contrasting content is delivered. The two parallel structures are usually, but not always, INDEPENDENT CLAUSES. A balanced sentence uses COORDINATION. The two coordinate structures are characterized by opposites in meaning, sometimes with one structure cast in the negative.

By night, the litter and desperation disappeared as the city's glittering lights came on; by day, the filth and despair reappeared as the sun rose.

—Jennifer Kirk, student

**ALERT:** Authorities differ about using a comma, a semicolon, or nothing between the parts of a short balanced sentence. In ACADEMIC WRITING, to avoid appearing to make the error of a COMMA SPLICE, use a semicolon (or revise in some other way), as in the following sentence.

Mosquitoes don't bite; they stab. ◆

## 18c    How do words, phrases, and clauses work in parallel form?

When you put words, PHRASES, and CLAUSES into parallel form, you enhance your writing style with balance and grace.

| PARALLEL WORDS | Recommended exercise includes running, swimming, and cycling. |
|---|---|

PARALLEL WORDS

Recommended exercise includes running, swimming, and cycling.

PARALLEL PHRASES

Exercise helps people maintain healthy bodies and handle mental pressures.

PARALLEL CLAUSES

Many people exercise because they want to look healthy, because they need to increase stamina, and because they hope to live longer.

## 18d    How does parallelism deliver impact?

Parallel structures serve to emphasize the meaning that sentences deliver. Deliberate, rhythmic repetition of parallel forms creates an effect of balance, reinforcing the impact of a message.

Go back to Mississippi, go back to Alabama, go back to South Carolina, go back to Georgia, go back to Louisiana, go back to the slums and ghettos of our northern cities, knowing that somehow this situation can and will be changed.

—Martin Luther King Jr., "I Have a Dream"

If King had not used PARALLELISM, his message would have made less of an impact on his listeners. His structures reinforce the power of his message. A sentence without parallelism could have carried his message, but with far less effect: *Return to your homes in Mississippi, Alabama, South Carolina, Georgia, Louisiana, or the northern cities, and know that the situation will be changed.*

Here's a longer passage in which parallel structures, concepts, and rhythms operate. Together, they echo the intensity of the writer's message.

You ask me what is **poverty**? Listen to me. Here I am, dirty, **smelly**, and with no "proper" underwear on and with the stench of my rotting teeth near you. I will tell you. Listen to me. Listen without pity. I cannot use your pity. Listen with understanding. Put yourself in my dirty, worn-out, ill-fitting shoes, and hear me.

**Poverty** is getting up every morning from a dirt- and illness-stained mattress. The sheets have long since been used for diapers. **Poverty** is living in a **smell** that never leaves. This is a **smell** of urine, sour milk, and spoiling food sometimes joined with the strong **smell** of long-cooked onions. Onions are cheap. If you have **smelled** this **smell**, you did not know how it came. It is **the smell** of the outdoor privy. It is **the smell** of young children who cannot walk the long dark way in the night. It is **the smell** of the mattresses where years of "accidents" have happened. It is **the smell** of the milk that has gone sour because the refrigerator long has not worked, and it costs money to get it fixed. It is **the smell** of rotting garbage. I could bury it, but where is the shovel? Shovels cost money.

—Jo Goodwin Parker, "What Is Poverty?"

**EXERCISE 18-1** Working individually or with a group, highlight all parallel elements of the Jo Goodwin Parker passage above in addition to those shown in boldface.

## 18e How can I avoid faulty parallelism?

**Faulty parallelism** usually results when you join nonmatching grammatical forms.

### PARALLELISM WITH COORDINATING CONJUNCTIONS

The coordinating conjunctions are *and, but, for, or, nor, yet,* and *so.* To avoid faulty parallelism, write the words that accompany coordinating conjunctions in matching grammatical forms.

| NO | Love *and* being married go together. |
|---|---|
| YES | Love *and* marriage go together. |
| YES | Being in love *and* being married go together. |

## PARALLELISM WITH CORRELATIVE CONJUNCTIONS

Correlative conjunctions are paired words such as *not only . . . but (also)*, *either . . . or*, and *both . . . and*. To avoid faulty parallelism, write the words joined by correlative conjunctions in matching grammatical forms.

| NO | Differing expectations for marriage *not only* **can lead to disappointment** *but also* **makes the couple angry**. |
|---|---|
| YES | Differing expectations for marriage *not only* **can lead to disappointment** *but also* **can make the couple angry**. |

## PARALLELISM WITH *THAN* AND *AS*

To avoid faulty parallelism when you use *than* and *as* for comparisons, write the elements of comparison in matching grammatical forms.

| NO | **Having a solid marriage** can be more satisfying *than* **the acquisition of wealth**. |
|---|---|
| YES | **Having a solid marriage** can be more satisfying *than* **acquiring wealth**. |
| YES | **A solid marriage** can be more satisfying *than* **wealth**. |

## PARALLELISM WITH FUNCTION WORDS

**Function words** include ARTICLES (*the, a, an*); the *to* of the INFINITIVE (*to* love); PREPOSITIONS (for example, *of, in, about*); and sometimes RELATIVE PRONOUNS. When you write a series of parallel structures, be consistent in the second and successive structures about either repeating or omitting a function word. Generally, repeat function words only if you think that the repetition clarifies your meaning or highlights the parallelism that you intend.

| NO | **To assign** unanswered letters their proper weight, **free** us from the expectations of others, **to give** us back to ourselves—here lies the great, the singular power of self-respect. |
|---|---|
| YES | **To assign** unanswered letters their proper weight, **to free** us from the expectations of others, **to give** us back to ourselves—here lies the great, the singular power of self-respect. |

—Joan Didion, "On Self-Respect"

I have in my own life a precious friend, a woman of 65 **who has** lived very hard, **who is** wise, **who listens** well, **who has been** where I am and can help me understand it, and **who represents** not only an ultimate ideal mother to me but also the person I'd like to be when I grow up.

—Judith Viorst,
"Friends, Good Friends—and Such Good Friends"

We looked into the bus, which **was** painted blue with orange daisies, **had** picnic benches instead of seats, and **showed** yellow curtains billowing out its windows.

—Kerrie Falk, student

**EXERCISE 18-2** Working individually or with a group, revise these sentences by putting appropriate information in parallel structures. For help, consult 18a through 18e.

EXAMPLE    Difficult bosses affect not only their employees' performances but their private lives are affected as well.

Difficult bosses affect not only their employees' performances *but their private lives as well.*

1. According to the psychologist Harry Levinson, the five main types of bad boss are the workaholic, the kind of person you would describe as bullying, a person who communicates badly, the jellyfish type, and someone who insists on perfection.
2. As a way of getting ahead, to keep their self-respect, and for survival purposes, wise employees handle problem bosses with a variety of strategies.
3. To cope with a bad-tempered employer, workers can both stand up for themselves and reasoning with a bullying boss.
4. Often, bad bosses communicate poorly or fail to calculate the impact of their personality on others; being a careful listener and sensitivity to others' responses are qualities that good bosses possess.
5. Employees who take the trouble to understand what makes their bosses tick, engage in some self-analysis, and staying flexible are better prepared to cope with a difficult job environment than suffering in silence like some employees.

**EXERCISE 18-3** Working individually or with a group, combine the sentences in each numbered item, using techniques of parallelism. For help, consult 18a through 18e.

EXAMPLE    College scholarships are awarded not only for academic and athletic ability, but there are also scholarships that recognize unusual talents. Other scholarships even award accidents of birth, like left-handedness.

College scholarships are awarded not only for academic and athletic ability *but also for unusual talents and even for accidents of birth, like left-handedness.*

1. A married couple met at Juniata College in Huntingdon, Pennsylvania. They are both left-handed, and they have set up a scholarship for needy left-handed students attending Juniata.

2. Writers who specialize in humor bankroll a student humor writer at the University of Southern California in Los Angeles. A horse-racing association sponsors a student sportswriter. The student must attend Vanderbilt University in Nashville, Tennessee.

3. The Rochester Institute of Technology in New York State is choosing 150 students born on June 12, 1979. Each one is to receive a grant of $1,500 per year. These awards are to be given to select students to honor the school's 150th anniversary, which was celebrated on June 12, 1979.

4. The College of Wooster in Ohio grants generous scholarships to students if they play the bagpipes, a musical instrument native to Scotland. Students playing the traditional Scottish drums and those who excel in Scottish folk dancing also qualify.

5. In return for their scholarships, Wooster's bagpipers must pipe for the school's football team. The terms of the scholarships also require the drummers to drum for the team. The dancers have to cheer the athletes from the sidelines.

**EXERCISE 18-4** Working individually or with a group, underline the parallel elements in these three passages. Next, imitate the parallelism in the examples, using a different topic of your choice for each.

A. Our earth is but a small star in a great universe. Yet of it we can make, if we choose, a planet unvexed by war, untroubled by hunger or fear, undivided by senseless distinctions of race, color, or theory.
—Stephen Vincent Benét

B. Some would recover [from polio] almost entirely. Some would die. Some would come through unable to move their legs, or unable to move arms and legs; some could move nothing but an arm, or nothing but a few fingers and their eyes. Some would leave the hospital with a cane, some with crutches, crutches and steel leg braces, or in wheelchairs—white-faced, shrunken, with frightened eyes, light blankets over their legs. Some would remain in an iron lung—a great, eighteen-hundred-pound, casket-like contraption, like the one in which the woman in the magic show (her head and feet sticking out of either end) is sawed in half.
—Charles L. Mee Jr., "The Summer Before Salk"

C.     I am lonely only when I am overtired, when I have worked too long without a break, when for the time being I feel empty and need filling up. And I am lonely sometimes when I come back home after a lecture trip, when I have seen a lot of people and talked a lot, and am full to the brim with experience that needs to be sorted out.

—May Sarton, "The Rewards of a Solitary Life"

## 18f   How does parallelism work in outlines and lists?

All items in formal OUTLINES and lists must be parallel in grammar and structure. (For more about outline format and outline development, see 2r.)

**OUTLINES**

**NO**                       Reducing Traffic Fatalities
    I. Stricter laws
       A. Top speed should be 55 mph on highways.
       B. Higher fines
       C. Requiring jail sentences for repeat offenders
    II. The use of safety devices should be mandated by law.

**YES**                       Reducing Traffic Fatalities
    I. Passing stricter speed laws
       A. Making 55 mph the top speed on highways
       B. Raising fines for speeding
       C. Requiring jail sentences for repeat offenders
    II. Mandating by law the use of safety devices

**LISTS**

**NO** Workaholics share these characteristics:
1. They are intense and driven.
2. Strong self-doubters
3. Labor is preferred to leisure by workaholics.

**YES** Workaholics share these characteristics:
1. They are intense and driven.
2. They have strong self-doubts.
3. They prefer labor to leisure.

**EXERCISE 18-5**   Working individually or with a group, revise this outline so that all lines are complete sentences in parallel form. For help, consult 2r and 18f.

Improving Health

I.  Exercise
    A.  Aerobics
    B.  Stretching and strength training
    C.  Vary routine
II.  Better Eating Habits
    A.  Healthy food
    B.  Eat less
    C.  Eat more often

# Chapter 19

## VARIETY AND EMPHASIS

### 19a  What are variety and emphasis in writing?

When you write sentences of various lengths and structures within a paragraph or longer piece of writing, you create **sentence variety**. Working in concert with sentence variety, **emphasis** allows you to add weight to ideas of special importance.

Using techniques of variety and emphasis adds style and clarity to your writing. Usually, the best time to apply the principles of variety and emphasis is while you are REVISING.

### 19b  How do different sentence lengths create variety and emphasis?

To emphasize one idea among many others, you can express it in a sentence noticeably different in length from the sentences surrounding it. In the following example, a four-word sentence between two longer sentences carries the key message of the passage.

> Today is one of those excellent January partly cloudies in which light chooses an unexpected landscape to trick out in gilt, and then shadow sweeps it away. **You know you're alive.** You take huge steps, trying to feel the planet's roundness arc between your feet.
> —Annie Dillard, *Pilgrim at Tinker Creek*

Sometimes a string of short sentences creates impact and emphasis. Yet, at other times, a string of short sentences can be dull to read.

**NO**  There is a problem. It is widely known as sick-building syndrome. It comes from indoor air pollution. It causes office workers to suffer. They have trouble breathing. They have painful rashes. Their heads ache. Their eyes burn.

**YES**  Widely known as sick-building syndrome, indoor air pollution causes office workers to suffer. They have trouble breathing. They have painful rashes. Their heads ache. Their eyes burn. [Many revisions are possible. This uses a long sentence to mention indoor air pollution and its victims; next, this retains the series of short sentences to emphasize each problem. Also, the conciseness of the revised version reduces 37 words to 27.]

Similarly, a string of COMPOUND SENTENCES can be monotonous to read and may fail to communicate relationships among ideas.

**NO**     Science fiction writers are often thinkers, **and** they are often dreamers, **and** they let their imaginations wander. Jules Verne was such a writer, **and** he predicted spaceships, **and** he forecast atomic submarines, **but** most people did not believe airplanes were possible.

**YES**    Science fiction writers are often thinkers and dreamers who let their imaginations wander. One such writer, Jules Verne, predicted spaceships and atomic submarines before most people believed airplanes were possible.

**EXERCISE 19-1**  Working individually or with a group, revise these sets of sentences to vary the sentence lengths effectively. For help, consult 19a and 19b.

1.  *Don Quixote* is a book. Cervantes wrote the book in 1605. It is considered by many scholars to be the first modern novel. The book is about the adventures of a knight named Don Quixote. Don Quixote's squire is named Sancho Panza. Some people think Cervantes wrote the book to make fun of other books. The other books are called romances. The romances feature knights who are bold. Those knights are often able to achieve great deeds. The deeds are fantastic. Don Quixote is not the type of knight found in romances. He is old. He is also skinny. Sancho Panza is not the type of brave squire found in romances. He is afraid of almost everything.

2.  As a knight, Don Quixote is inspired by high ideals of chivalry, those ideals being gallantry, unselfishness, and faithfulness. Don Quixote is unaware, unlike those who know him, that his high ideals lead him to live in his own imaginary world that nobody else understands, and he is so idealistic and his behavior is so impractical that the word *quixotic* comes from his last name and means "resembling Don Quixote's lofty behavior that is also foolish."

## 19c How do occasional questions, commands, or exclamations create variety and emphasis?

The majority of sentences in English are DECLARATIVE—they tell something by making a statement. Declarative sentences offer an almost infinite variety of structures and patterns. For variety and emphasis, you might want to use three alternative types of sentences occasionally.

A sentence that asks a question is called INTERROGATIVE. Occasional questions, placed appropriately, tend to involve readers. A sentence that issues a mild or strong command is called IMPERATIVE. Occasional mild commands, appropriately used, gently urge a reader to think along with you. A sentence that makes an exclamation is called EXCLAMATORY. An occasional exclamatory sentence, appropriate to the context, can enliven writing, but you should use this sentence type only rarely in ACADEMIC WRITING.

**ALERT:** A declarative statement ends with a period (Chapter 23)—or semicolon (Chapter 25) or colon (Chapter 26). A mild command ends with a period. A strong command and an exclamation end with an exclamation point (Chapter 23). ◆

Here's a paragraph with declarative, interrogative, and imperative sentences.

> Imagine what people ate during the winter as little as seventy-five years ago. They ate food that was local, long-lasting, and dull, like acorn squash, turnips, and cabbage. Walk into an American supermarket in February and the world lies before you: grapes, melons, artichokes, fennel, lettuce, peppers, pistachios, dates, even strawberries, to say nothing of ice cream. Have you ever considered what a triumph of civilization it is to be able to buy a pound of chicken livers? If you lived on a farm and had to kill a chicken when you wanted to eat one, you wouldn't ever accumulate a pound of chicken livers.
>
> —Phyllis Rose, "Shopping and Other Spiritual Adventures in America Today"

**EXERCISE 19-2**  Working individually or with a group, write an imitation of the following paragraph. This paragraph varies sentence lengths and uses a question and a command effectively. The result emphasizes key points. Choose your own topic, but follow the style of the paragraph as closely as possible. For help, consult 19c.

> What do many American cities have in common? One answer is innovative solutions to problems. Consider the city of Portland,

Oregon. As a member of the only elected regional government in the United States, Portland works with surrounding communities on long-term planning. One decision of the regional government was to establish a growth boundary around the city of Portland. Inside the boundary, growth is allowed. Consequently, the urban area of Portland has been revitalized, and public transportation is easily available in the city. However, outside the boundary, instead of miles and miles of housing developments, an agricultural region has been preserved. Are innovative solutions available only to big cities? The answer is no, according to the citizens of the small city of Arcata, California. What began as a cost-effective and environmentally safe wastewater treatment solution is now the Arcata Marsh and Wildlife Sanctuary, over one hundred acres of wetlands that attract over two hundred bird species annually. To show their support for the wastewater/wetlands project, many automobile owners in Arcata have bumper stickers that read: Flush with pride!

## 19d    How can modifiers create variety and emphasis?

MODIFIERS can expand sentences to add richness to your writing and create a pleasing mixture of variety and emphasis. Your choice of where to place modifiers to expand your sentences depends on the focus you want each sentence to communicate, either on its own or in concert with its surrounding sentences. Be careful where you place modifiers because you don't want to introduce the error known as a MISPLACED MODIFIER.

| | |
|---|---|
| **BASIC SENTENCE** | The river rose. |
| **ADJECTIVE** | The **swollen** river rose. |
| **ADVERB** | The river rose **dangerously**. |
| **PREPOSITIONAL PHRASE** | The river rose **above its banks**. |
| **PARTICIPIAL PHRASE** | **Swelled by melting snow**, the river rose. |

| | |
|---|---|
| ABSOLUTE PHRASE | **Uprooted trees swirling away in the current**, the river rose. |
| ADVERB CLAUSE | **Because the snows had been heavy that winter**, the river rose. |
| ADJECTIVE CLAUSE | The river, **which runs through vital farmland**, rose. |

**EXERCISE 19-3**  Working individually or with a group, expand each sentence by adding each kind of modifier illustrated in 19d.

1. We bought a house.
2. The roof leaked.
3. I remodeled the kitchen.
4. Neighbors brought food.
5. Everyone enjoyed the barbeque.

## 19e  How does repetition affect variety and emphasis?

You can repeat one or more words that express a main idea when your message is suitable. This technique creates a rhythm that focuses attention on the main idea. Here's an example that uses deliberate repetition along with a variety of sentence lengths to deliver its meaning.

> Coal is **black** and it warms your house and cooks your food. The night is **black**, which has a moon, and a million stars, and is beautiful. Sleep is **black**, which gives you rest, so you wake up feeling **good**. I am **black**. I feel very **good** this evening.
> —Langston Hughes, "That Word *Black*"

At the same time, don't confuse deliberate repetition with a lack of vocabulary variety.

> **NO**  An insurance agent can be an excellent adviser when you want to buy a car. An insurance agent has complete records on most cars. An insurance agent knows which car models are prone to have accidents. An insurance agent can tell you which car models are the most expensive to repair if they are in a collision. An insurance agent can tell you which models are most likely to be stolen. [Although only a few synonyms exist for *insurance agent, car,* and *model,* some do and should be used. Also, the sentence structure here lacks variety.]

> **YES**  If you are thinking of buying a new car, an insurance agent, who usually has complete records on most cars, can be an

excellent adviser. Any professional insurance broker knows which automobile models are prone to have accidents. Did you know that some cars suffer more damage than others in a collision? If you want to know which vehicles crumple more than others and which are the most expensive to repair, ask an insurance agent. Similarly, some car models are more likely to be stolen, so find out from the person who specializes in dealing with car insurance claims.

## 19f How else can I create variety and emphasis?

### CHANGING WORD ORDER

**Standard word order** in English places the SUBJECT before the VERB.

The **mayor** *walked* into the room. [*Mayor,* the subject, comes before the verb *walked.*]

Any variation from standard word order creates emphasis. For example, **inverted word order** places the verb before the subject.

Into the room *walked* the **mayor**. [*Mayor,* the subject, comes after the verb *walked.*]

### CHANGING A SENTENCE'S SUBJECT

The subject of a sentence establishes the focus for that sentence. To create the emphasis you want, you can vary each sentence's subject. All the sample sentences below express the same information, but the focus changes in each according to the subject (and its corresponding verb).

**Our study** *showed* that 25 percent of college students' time is spent eating or sleeping. [Focus is on the study.]

**College students** *eat or sleep* 25 percent of the time, according to our study. [Focus is on the students.]

**Eating or sleeping** *occupies* 25 percent of college students' time, according to our study. [Focus is on eating and sleeping.]

**Twenty-five percent of college students' time** *is spent* eating or sleeping, according to our study. [Focus is on the percentage of time.]

### USING A PERIODIC SENTENCE AMONG CUMULATIVE SENTENCES

The **cumulative sentence** is the most common sentence structure in English. Its name reflects the way information accumulates in the sentence until it reaches a period. Its structure starts with a SUBJECT and VERB and continues with modifiers. Another term for a cumulative sentence is *loose sentence* because it lacks a tightly planned structure.

For greater impact, you might occasionally use a **periodic sentence**, also called a *climactic sentence*, which reserves the main idea for the end of the sentence. This structure tends to draw in the reader as it moves toward the period. If overused, however, periodic sentences lose their punch.

CUMULATIVE   A car hit a shoulder and turned over at midnight last night on the road from Las Vegas to Death Valley Junction.

PERIODIC   At midnight last night, on the road from Las Vegas to Death Valley Junction, a car hit a shoulder and turned over.

—Joan Didion, "On Morality"

# Chapter 20

## USAGE GLOSSARY

A usage glossary presents the customary manner of using particular words and phrases. "Customary manner," however, is not as firm in practice as the term implies. Usage standards change. If you think a word's usage might differ from what you read here, consult a dictionary published more recently than the current edition of this handbook.

The meaning of *informal* or *colloquial* in the definition of a word or phrase is that it's found in everyday or conversational speech, but it needs to be avoided in ACADEMIC WRITING. Another term, *nonstandard*, indicates that the word or phrase, although widely understood in speech and dialect writing, isn't suitable in standard spoken or written English.

Terms of grammar and writing in this Usage Glossary are defined in the Terms Glossary, which begins after the last chapter.

**a, an**   Use *a* before words that begin with a consonant (*a dog, a grade, a hole*) or a consonant sound (*a one-day sale, a European*). Use *an* before words or acronyms that begin with a vowel sound or a silent *h* (*an owl; an hour; an MRI*, because the *M* is sounded "em"). American English uses *a*, not *an*, before words starting with a pronounced *h*: *a* (not *an*) *historical event*.

**accept, except**   The verb *accept* means "agree to; receive." As a preposition, *except* means "leaving out." As a verb, *except* means "exclude; leave out."

The workers wanted to **accept** [verb] management's offer **except** [preposition] for one detail: They wanted the limit on overtime **excepted** [verb] from the contract.

**advice, advise**   *Advice*, a noun, means "recommendation." *Advise*, a verb, means "recommend; give advice."

I **advise** [verb] you to follow your car mechanic's **advice** [noun].

**affect, effect**   As a verb, *affect* means "cause a change in; influence." (*Affect* is a noun in psychology.) As a noun, *effect* means "result or conclusion"; as a verb, *effect* means "bring about."

Loud music **affects** people's hearing for life, so some bands have **effected** changes to lower the volume. Many fans, however, don't care about the harmful **effects** of high decibel levels.

**aggravate, irritate**   *Aggravate* is used colloquially to mean "irritate." In academic writing, use *aggravate* only to mean "intensify; make worse." Use *irritate* to mean "annoy; make impatient."

The coach was **irritated** by reduced time for practice, which **aggravated** the team's difficulties with concentration.

**ain't**   *Ain't* is a nonstandard contraction. Use *am not, is not,* or *are not* for standard spoken and written English.

**all ready, already**   *All ready* means "completely prepared." *Already* means "before; by this time."

The team was **all ready** to play, but it had **already** begun to rain.

**all right**   *All right* is always written as two words, never one (never *alright*).

**all together, altogether**   *All together* means "in a group; in unison." *Altogether* means "entirely; thoroughly."

The twelve jurors told the judge that it was **altogether** absurd for them to stay **all together** in a single hotel room.

**allude, elude**   *Allude* means "refer to indirectly." *Elude* means "escape notice."

The detectives **alluded** to budget cuts by saying, "Conditions beyond our control allowed the suspect to **elude** us."

**allusion, illusion**   An *allusion* is an indirect reference to something. An *illusion* is a false impression or idea.

The couple's casual **allusions** to European tourist sites created the **illusion** that they had visited them.

**a lot**   *A lot* is informal for *a great deal* or *a great many.* Avoid using it in academic writing. If you must use it, write it as two words (never *alot*).

**a.m., p.m.**   Use these abbreviations only with numbers, not as substitutes for the words *morning, afternoon,* and *evening.* Some editors consider capital letters wrong for these abbreviations, yet many editors and dictionaries allow both. Whichever you choose, be consistent in each piece of writing.

We will arrive in the **evening** [not *p.m.*], and we must leave by **8:00 a.m.**

**among, amongst, between**   Use *among* for three or more items. Use *between* for two items. American English prefers *among* to *amongst*.

> My three housemates discussed **among** [not *between* or *amongst*] themselves the choice **between** staying in college and getting full-time jobs.

**amoral, immoral**   *Amoral* means "neither moral (conforming to standards of rightness) nor immoral (the opposite of *moral*)." *Amoral* also means "without any sense of what's moral or immoral." *Immoral* means "morally wrong."

> Although many people consider birth control an **amoral** issue, some religions consider using birth control **immoral**.

**amount, number**   Use *amount* for noncountable things (wealth, work, happiness). Use *number* for countable items.

> The **amount** of rice to cook depends on the **number** of guests.

**an**   See *a, an*.

**and/or**   This term is appropriate in business and legal writing when either or both of the two items can apply: *We are planning to open additional offices in California **and/or** New York.* In the humanities, writers usually express the alternatives in words: *We are planning to open additional offices in California, New York, or both.*

**anymore**   Use *anymore* with the meaning "now, any longer" only in negations or questions. In positive statements, instead of *anymore*, use an adverb such as *now*.

> No one wants to live without air conditioning **anymore**. Summers are so hot **now** [not *anymore*] that more people than ever suffer from heatstroke.

**anyone, any one**   *Anyone* is a singular indefinite pronoun meaning "any person at all." *Any one* (two words), an adjective that modifies a pronoun, means "a member of a group."

> **Anyone** could test-drive **any one** of the display vehicles.

**anyplace**   *Anyplace* is informal. Use *any place* or *anywhere* instead.

**anyways, anywheres**   *Anyways* and *anywheres* are nonstandard for *anyway* and *anywhere*.

**apt, likely, liable**   *Apt* and *likely* are used interchangeably. Strictly, *apt* indicates a tendency or inclination. *Likely* indicates a reasonable expectation or greater certainty than *apt* does. *Liable* usually denotes legal responsibility or implies unpleasant consequences but usage today allows it to mean *likely*.

Evander is **apt** to run stop signs, so he is **likely** to get a ticket. That means he's **liable** for any consequences.

**as, as if, as though, like**   Use *as, as if,* or *as though,* but not *like,* when the words coming after include a verb.

This hamburger tastes good, **as** [not *like*] a hamburger should. It tastes **as if** [or *as though,* not *like*] it were barbequed over charcoal, not gas.

Both *as* and *like* can function as prepositions in comparisons. However, use *as* to indicate equivalence between two nouns or pronouns, and use *like* to indicate similarity but not equivalence.

My friend Roger served **as** [not *like*] mediator in a dispute about my neighbor's tree that dripped sap on my driveway **like** [not *as*] a leaky water faucet.

**assure, ensure, insure**   *Assure* means "promise; convince." *Ensure* and *insure* both mean "make certain or secure," but *insure* is reserved for financial or legal matters.

The insurance agent **assured** me that he could **insure** my car, but only I could **ensure** that I would drive safely.

**as to**   *As to* is nonstandard for *about*.

**awful, awfully**   *Awful* is an adjective meaning "inspiring awe" and "creating fear." *Awfully* is an adverb meaning "in a way to inspire awe" and "terrifying." Only colloquially are *awful* and *awfully* used to mean "very" or "extremely."

I was **extremely** [not *awfully*] tired yesterday.

**a while, awhile**   As two words, *a while* (an article and a noun) can function as a subject or object. As one word, *awhile* is an adverb. In a prepositional phrase, the correct form is *for a while, in a while,* or *after a while.*

It took **a while** [article and noun] to drive to the zoo, where we saw the seals bask **awhile** [adverb modifying verb *bask*] in the sun after romping **for a while** [prepositional phrase] in the water.

**backup, back up**   As a noun, *backup* means "a replacement, fill-in, surrogate; a copy of computer files." As an adjective, *backup* means "alternate; alternative." As a verb, *back up* (two words) means "to serve as a substitute or support"; "to accumulate, as from a stoppage"; and "to make a backup copy of a computer disk or hard drive."

I'll need a **backup** [noun] of your hard drive if I'm going to serve as your **backup** [adjective] computer consultant. I **back up** [verb] all computer disks and drives when I work with them.

**bad, badly**   *Bad* is an adjective only after linking verbs (*look, feel, smell, taste, sound*; these verbs can function as either linking verbs or action verbs depending on the context). *Badly* is an adverb; it's nonstandard after linking verbs.

Farmers feel **bad** [*feel* is a linking verb, so *bad* is the adjective] because a **bad** [adjective] drought is **badly** [adverb] damaging their crops.

**been, being**   *Been* and *being* cannot stand alone as main verbs. They work only with auxiliary verbs.

You **are being** [not *being*] honest to admit that you **have been** [not *been*] tempted to eat the whole pie.

**being as, being that**   *Being as* and *being that* are nonstandard for *because* or *since*.

We had to forfeit the game **because** [not *being as* or *being that*] our goalie was badly injured.

**beside, besides**   As prepositions, *beside* means "next to, by the side of," and *besides* means "other than, in addition to." As an adverb, *besides* means "also, moreover."

She stood **beside** the new car, insisting that she would drive. No one **besides** her had a driver's license. **Besides**, she owned the car.

**better, had better**   *Better* is informal for *had better*.

We **had better** [not *better* alone] be careful of the ice.

**between**   See *among, amongst, between.*

**bias, biased**   As a noun, *bias* means "a mental leaning for or against something or someone." As an adjective, *biased* means "prejudiced." As a verb, *bias* means "create prejudice." The past tense of this verb is *biased*.

Horace's **bias** [noun] against federal-level politicians grew from his disapproval of their **biased** [adjective] attitudes toward certain foreign countries. Eventually, Horace **biased** [verb] his wife's beliefs about politicians as well..

**breath, breathe**   *Breath* is a noun; *breathe* is a verb.

Take a deep **breath** [noun] before you start so that you can **breathe** [verb] normally afterward.

**bring, take**   *Bring* indicates movement from a distant place to a near place. *Take* indicates movement from a near to a distant place.

If you **bring** over sandwiches, we'll have time to **take** [not *bring*] the dog to the vet.

**but, however, yet**   Use *but, however,* or *yet* alone, not in combination with each other.

The economy is strong, **but** [not *but yet* or *but however*] unemployment is high.

**calculate, figure**   These are colloquial terms for *estimate, imagine, expect, think,* and the like.

**can, may**   *Can* signifies ability or capacity. *May* requests or grants permission. In negative expressions, *can* is acceptable for *may.*

When you **can** [not *may*] get here on time, you **may** [not *can*] be excused early. However, if you are *not* on time, you **cannot** [or *may not*] expect privileges.

**can't hardly, can't scarcely**   These double negatives are nonstandard for *can hardly* and *can scarcely.*

**capitol, capital**   *Capitol* means "a building in which legislators meet." *Capital* means a city (Denver, the *capital* of Colorado), wealth, or "most important" (a *capital* offense).

If the governor can find enough **capital**, the state legislature will agree to build a new **capitol** for our state.

**censor, censure**   The verb *censor* means "delete objectionable material; judge." The verb *censure* means "condemn or reprimand officially."

The town council **censured** the mayor for trying to **censor** a report.

**chairman, chairperson, chair**   Many writers and speakers prefer the gender-neutral terms *chairperson* and *chair* to *chairman.* In general, *chair* is used more than *chairperson.*

**choose, chose**   *Choose* is the simple form of the verb. *Chose* is the past-tense form of the verb.

I **chose** a movie last week, so you **choose** one tonight.

**cite, site**   The verb *cite* means "quote by way of example, authority, or proof." The noun *site* means "a particular place or location."

The private investigator **cited** evidence from the crime **site** and the defendant's Web **site**.

**cloth, clothe**   *Cloth* is a noun meaning "fabric." *Clothe* is a verb meaning "dress with garments or fabric."

"**Clothe** me in red velvet," proclaimed the king, and the royal tailors ran to gather samples of **cloth** to show him.

**complement, compliment**    As a noun, *complement* means "something that goes well with or completes." As a noun, *compliment* means "praise, flattery." As a verb, *complement* means "brings to perfection; goes well with, completes." As a verb, *compliment* means "praise, flatter."

> The dean's **compliment** was a perfect **complement** to the thrill of my graduating. My parents felt proud when she **complimented** me publicly, an honor that **complemented** their joy.

**comprise, include**    See *include, comprise.*

**conscience, conscious**    The noun *conscience* means "a sense of right and wrong." The adjective *conscious* means "being aware or awake."

> Always be **conscious** of what your **conscience** is telling you.

**consensus of opinion**    This phrase is redundant; use *consensus* only.

> The legislature reached **consensus** on the issue of campaign reform.

**continual(ly), continuous(ly)**    *Continual* means "occurring repeatedly." *Continuous* means "going on without interruption."

> Larry needed intravenous fluids **continuously** for days, so the nurses **continually** monitored him.

**could care less**    *Could care less* is nonstandard for *could not care less.*

**could of**    *Could of* is nonstandard for *could have.*

**couple, a couple of**    *Couple* means "two," but it can also be nonstandard for *a few* or *several.*

> Rest here for **a few** [not *a couple* or *a couple of*] minutes.

**criteria, criterion**    A *criterion* is "a standard of judgment." *Criteria* is the plural of *criterion.*

> A sense of history is an important **criterion** for judging political candidates, but voters must consider other **criteria** as well.

**data**    *Data* is the plural of *datum,* a word rarely used today. Informally, *data* is used as a singular noun that takes a singular verb. In academic or professional writing, *data* is considered plural and takes a plural verb (although this usage is currently viewed as overly formal by some).

> The **data** suggest [not *suggests*] some people are addicted to e-mail.

**different from, different than**  In academic and professional writing, use *different from* even though *different than* is common in informal speech.

> Please advise us if your research yields data **different from** past results.

**disinterested, uninterested**  The preferred use of *disinterested* means "impartial, unbiased." Colloquially, *disinterested* can mean "not interested, indifferent," but in more formal contexts, *uninterested* is preferred for "not interested, indifferent."

> Jurors need to be **disinterested** in hearing evidence, but never **uninterested**.

**don't**  *Don't* is a contraction for *do not,* never for *does not* (its contraction is *doesn't*).

> She **doesn't** [not *don't*] like crowds.

**effect**  See *affect, effect.*

**elicit, illicit**  The verb *elicit* means "draw forth or bring out." The adjective *illicit* means "illegal."

> The senator's **illicit** conduct **elicited** a mass outcry from her constituents.

**elude**  See *allude, elude.*

**emigrate (from), immigrate (to)**  *Emigrate* means "leave one country to live in another." *Immigrate* means "enter a country to live there."

> My great-grandmother **emigrated** from Kiev, Russia, to London, England, in 1890. Then, she **immigrated** to Toronto, Canada, in 1892.

**enclose, inclose; enclosure, inclosure**  In American English, *enclose* and *enclosure* are the preferred spellings.

**ensure**  See *assure, ensure, insure.*

**enthused**  *Enthused* is nonstandard for *enthusiastic.*

> Adam was **enthusiastic** [not *enthused*] about the college he chose.

**etc.**  *Etc.* is the abbreviation for the Latin *et cetera,* meaning "and the rest." For writing in the humanities, avoid using *etc.* Acceptable substitutes are *and the like, and so on,* or *and so forth.*

**everyday, every day**  The adjective *everyday* means "daily." *Every day* (two words) is an adjective with a noun.

Being late for work has become an **everyday** [adjective] occurrence for me. **Every day** [subject] brings me closer to being fired. I worry about it **every day** [object].

**everyone, every one**    *Everyone* is a singular, indefinite pronoun. *Every one* (two words) is an adjective and a pronoun, meaning "each member in a group."

**Everyone** enjoyed **every one** of the comedy skits.

**everywheres**    *Everywheres* is nonstandard for *everywhere*.

**except**    See *accept, except*.

**explicit, implicit**    *Explicit* means "directly stated or expressed." *Implicit* means "implied, suggested."

The warning on cigarette packs is **explicit**: "Smoking is dangerous to health." The **implicit** message is "Don't smoke."

**farther, further**    Although many writers reserve *farther* for geographical distances and *further* for all other cases, current usage treats them as interchangeable.

**fewer, less**    Use *fewer* for anything that can be counted (that is, with count nouns): *fewer* dollars, *fewer* fleas, *fewer* haircuts. Use *less* with collective nouns (or other noncount nouns): *less* money, *less* scratching, *less* hair.

**firstly, secondly, thirdly**    The terms *firstly, secondly,* and *thirdly* are from British English. In American English, use *first, second,* and *third*.

**former, latter**    When two items are referred to, *former* signifies the first item and *latter* signifies the second item. Never use *former* and *latter* when referring to more than two items.

Brazil and Ecuador are South American countries. Portuguese is the official language in the **former**, Spanish in the **latter**.

**go, say**    All forms of *go* are nonstandard when used in place of all forms of *say*.

While stepping on my hand, Frank **says** [not *goes*], "Your hand is in my way."

**gone, went**    *Gone* is the past participle of *go; went* is the past tense of *go*.

They **went** [not *gone*] to the concert after Ira **had gone** [not *had went*] home.

**good, well**   *Good* is an adjective. As an adverb, *good* is nonstandard. Instead, use *well.*

**Good** [adjective] maintenance helps cars run **well** [adverb; not *good*].

**good and**   *Good and* is a nonstandard intensifier. Instead, use more precise words.

They were **exhausted** [not *good and tired*].

**got, have**   *Got* is nonstandard for *have.*

What do we **have** [not *got*] for supper?

**hardly**   Use *hardly* with *can,* never with *can't.*

**have, of**   Use *have,* not *of,* after such verbs as *could, should, would, might,* and *must.*

You ***should*** **have** [not *should of* ] called first.

**have got, have to, have got to**   Avoid using *have got* when *have* alone delivers your meaning. Also, avoid using *have to* or *have got to* for *must.*

I **have** [not *have got*] several more sources to read. I **must** [not *have got to*] finish my reading today.

**he/she, s/he, his/her**   When using gender-neutral language, write out *he or she* or *his or her* instead of using and/or constructions. To be more concise, switch to plural pronouns and antecedents. (For more about gender-neutral language, see 21g.)

**Everyone** bowed ***his or her*** head. [***Everyone*** bowed **his** head is considered sexist language if women were present when the heads were bowed.]

The **people** bowed **their** heads.

**historic, historical**   The adjective *historic* means "important in history" or "highly memorable." The adjective *historical* means "relating to history." Use *a,* not *an,* before these words because they start with the consonant *h.*

**hopefully**   *Hopefully* is an adverb meaning "with hope, in a hopeful manner," so as an adverb, it can modify a verb, an adjective, or another adverb. However, *hopefully* is nonstandard as a sentence modifier meaning "we hope"; therefore, in academic writing, avoid this usage.

They waited **hopefully** [adverb] for the crippled airplane to land. **We hope** [not *Hopefully,*] it will land safely.

**humanity, humankind, humans, mankind**   To use gender-neutral language, choose *humanity, humankind,* or *humans* instead of *mankind.*

Some think that the computer has helped **humanity** more than any other twentieth-century invention.

**i.e.**    This abbreviation refers to the Latin term *id est*. In academic writing, use the English translation "that is."

**if, whether**    At the start of a noun clause that expresses speculation or unknown conditions, you can use either *if* or *whether*. However, in such conditional clauses use only *whether* (or *whether or not*) when alternatives are expressed or implied. In a conditional clause that does not express or imply alternatives, use only *if*.

**If** [not *whether*] you promise not to step on my feet, I might dance with you. Still, I'm not sure **if** [or *whether*] I want to dance with you. Once I decide, I'll dance with you **whether** [not *if*] I like the music or **whether** [not *if*] the next song is fast or slow.

**illicit**    See *elicit, illicit.*

**illusion**    See *allusion, illusion.*

**immigrate**    See *emigrate, immigrate.*

**immoral**    See *amoral, immoral.*

**imply, infer**    *Imply* means "hint at or suggest." *Infer* means "draw a conclusion." A writer or speaker *implies*; a reader or listener *infers*.

When the governor **implied** that she wouldn't seek reelection, reporters **inferred** that she was planning to run for vice president.

**include, comprise**    The verb *include* means "contain or regard as part of a whole." The verb *comprise* means "consist of or be composed of."

**incredible, incredulous**    *Incredible* means "extraordinary; not believable." *Incredulous* means "unable or unwilling to believe."

Listeners were **incredulous** as the freed hostages described the **incredible** hardships they had experienced.

**in regard to, with regard to, as regards, regarding**    Use *about, concerning,* and *for* in place of these wordy phrases. Also, avoid the nonstandard *as regards to.*

**Concerning** [not *in regard to, with regard to, as regards,* or *regarding*] your question, we can now confirm that your payment was received.

**inside of, outside of**    These phrases are nonstandard when used to mean *inside* or *outside*. When writing about time, never use *inside of* to mean "in less than."

She waited **outside** [not *outside of*] the apartment house. He changed to clothes that were more informal in **less than** [not *inside of*] ten minutes.

**insure**   See *assure, ensure, insure.*

**irregardless**   *Irregardless* is nonstandard for *regardless.*

**is when, is where**   Never use these constructions when you define something. Instead, use active verbs.

Defensive driving **involves staying** [not *is when you stay*] alert.

**its, it's**   *Its* is a personal pronoun in the possessive case. *It's* is a contraction of *it is.*

The dog buried **its** bone today. **It's** hot today, which makes the dog restless.

**kind, sort**   Combine *kind* and *sort* with *this* or *that* when referring to singular nouns. Combine *kinds* and *sorts* with *these* or *those* when referring to plural nouns. Also, never use *a* or *an* after *kind of* or *sort of.*

To stay cool, drink **these kinds** of fluids [not *this kind*] for **this sort of** day [not *this sort of a*].

**kind of, sort of**   These phrases are colloquial adverbs. In academic writing, use *somewhat.*

The campers were **somewhat** [not *kind of*] dehydrated after the hike.

**later, latter**   *Later* means "after some time; subsequently." *Latter* refers to the second of two items.

The college library stays open **later** than the town library; also, the **latter** is closed on weekends.

**lay, lie**   The verb *lay* (**lay**, *laid, laid, laying*) means "place or put something, usually on something else" and needs a direct object. The verb *lie* (**lie**, *lay, lain, lying*), meaning "recline," doesn't need a direct object. Substituting *lay* for *lie,* or the opposite, is nonstandard.

**Lay** [not *lie*] down the blanket [direct object], and then place the baby to **lie** [not *lay*] in the shade.

**leave, let**   *Leave* means "depart." *Leave* is nonstandard for *let.* *Let* means "allow, permit."

Could you **let** [not *leave*] me use your car tonight?

**less**   See *fewer, less.*

**lie**    See *lay, lie.*

**like**    See *as, as if, as though, like.*

**likely**    See *apt, likely, liable.*

**lots, lots of, a lot of**    These are colloquial constructions. Instead, use *many, much,* or *a great deal.*

**mankind**    See *humanity, humankind, humans, mankind.*

**may**    See *can, may.*

**maybe, may be**    *Maybe* is an adverb; *may be* (two words) is a verb phrase.
> **Maybe** [adverb] we can win, but our team **may be** [verb phrase] too tired.

**may of, might of**    *May of* and *might of* are nonstandard for *may have* and *might have.*

**media**    *Media* is the plural of *medium,* yet colloquial usage now pairs it with a singular verb (for example, *The **media saturates** us with information about every fire*).

**morale, moral**    *Morale* is a noun meaning "a mental state relating to courage, confidence, or enthusiasm." As a noun, *moral* means an "ethical lesson implied or taught by a story or event." As an adjective, *moral* means "ethical."
> One **moral** [noun] of the story is that many people who suffer from low **morale** [noun] still abide by high **moral** [adjective] standards.

**most**    *Most* is nonstandard for *almost.* Also, *most* is the superlative form of an adjective (*some* words, *more* words, ***most*** words) and of adverbs (***most*** suddenly).
> **Almost** [not *Most*] all writers agree that Shakespeare penned the **most** [adjective] brilliant plays ever written.

**Ms.**    *Ms.* is a woman's title free of reference to marital status, equivalent to *Mr.* for men. Generally, use *Ms.* unless a woman requests *Miss* or *Mrs.*

**must of**    *Must of* is nonstandard for *must have.*

**nowheres**    *Nowheres* is nonstandard for *nowhere.*

**number**    See *amount, number.*

**of**   Use *have,* not *of,* after modal auxiliary verbs (*could, may, might, must, should, would*). See also *could of; may of; might of; must of; should of; would of.*

**off of**   *Off of* is nonstandard for *off.*
Don't fall **off** [not *off of*] the stage.

**OK, O.K., okay**   These three forms are informal. In academic writing, choose words that express more specific meanings. If you must use the term, choose the full word *okay.*
The weather was **suitable** [not *okay*] for a picnic.

**on account of, owing to the fact that**   Use *because* or *because of* in place of these wordy phrases.
**Because of the rain** [not *On account of the rain* or *Owing to the fact that it rained*], the picnic was cancelled.

**oral, verbal**   The adjective *oral* means "spoken or being done by the mouth." The adjective *verbal* means "relating to language" (*verbal* skill) or to words rather than actions, facts, or ideas.

**outside of**   See *inside of, outside of.*

**percent, percentage**   Use *percent* with specific numbers: two *percent,* 95 *percent.* Use *percentage* to refer to portions of a whole in general terms.
Of the eligible US population, **35 percent** votes regularly in national elections. In local elections, **the percentage** [not *the percent*] is much lower.

**pixel, pixelation, pixilated**   *Pixel,* a relatively new word created from "picture/pix" and "element," is the name for a small dot on a video screen. *Pixelation* (with an *e,* as in *pixel*) is a noun meaning "a film technique that makes people appear to move faster than they are." *Pixilated* (with an *i*), a verb unrelated to *pixels,* derives from *pixie,* meaning "a mischievous elf," and now describes someone who is slightly drunk.

**plus**   *Plus* is nonstandard for *and, also, in addition,* and *moreover.*
The band booked three concerts in Hungary, **and** [not *plus*] it will tour Poland for a month. **In addition,** [not *Plus,*] it may perform once in Austria.

**precede, proceed**   *Precede* is a verb that means "go before." *Proceed* is a verb that means "to advance, go on, undertake, carry on."

**Preceded** by elephants and music, the ringmaster **proceeded** into the main tent.

**pretty**  *Pretty* is informal for *rather, quite, somewhat,* or *very.*
The flu epidemic was **quite** [not *pretty*] severe.

**principal, principle**  As a noun, *principal* means "chief person; main or original amount." As an adjective, *principal* means "most important." *Principle* is a noun that means "a basic truth or rule."
During the assembly, the **principal** [noun] said, "A **principal** [adjective] value in our democracy is the **principle** [noun] of free speech."

**proceed**  See *precede, proceed.*

**quotation, quote**  *Quotation* is a noun, and *quote* is a verb. Don't use *quote* as a noun.
One newspaper reporter **quoted** [verb] the US president, and soon the **quotations** [noun—not *quotes,* which is a verb] were widely broadcast.

**raise, rise**  *Raise* is a verb (**raise**, *raised, raised, raising*) that means "lift" or "construct" and needs a direct object. *Rise* (**rise**, *rose, risen, rising*) means "go upward" and doesn't need a direct object. Substituting *rise* for *raise,* or the opposite, is nonstandard.
When the soldiers **rise** [not *raise*] early, they **raise** [not *rise* or *rise up*] the flag of liberty.

**real, really**  These words are nonstandard for *very* and *extremely.*

**reason is because**  This phrase is redundant. To be concise and correct, use *reason is that.*
One **reason** we moved **is that** [not *is because*] our factory was relocated.

**reason why**  This phrase is redundant. To be concise and correct, use *reason* or *why.*
I don't know **why** [not *the reason why*] they left home.

**regarding**  See *in regard to, with regard to, as regards, regarding.*

**regardless**  See *irregardless.*

**respectful, respectfully**  As an adjective, *respectful* means "marked by respect, showing regard for, or giving honor to." *Respectfully* is the adverb form of *respectful.* Be careful not to confuse these words with *respective* and *respectively* (see next entry).
The child listened **respectfully** [adverb] to the lecture about **respectful** [adjective] behavior.

**respective, respectively**   *Respective,* a noun, refers to two or more individual persons or things. *Respectively,* an adverb, refers back to two or more individuals or things in the same sequence in which they were originally mentioned.

> After the fire drill, Dr. Daniel Eagle and Dr. Jessica Chess returned to their **respective** offices [that is, he returned to his office, and she returned to her office] on the second and third floors, **respectively** [his office is on the second floor, and her office is on the third floor].

**right**   *Right* is sometimes used colloquially for *quite, very, extremely,* or similar intensifiers.

> You did **very** [not *right*] well on the quiz.

**rise**   See *raise, rise.*

**scarcely**   Use *scarcely* with *can,* never with *can't.*

**secondly**   See *firstly, secondly, thirdly.*

**seen**   *Seen* is the past participle of the verb *see* (*see, saw,* **seen***, seeing*). *Seen* is nonstandard for *saw,* a verb in the past tense. Always use *seen* with an auxiliary verb.

> Last night, I **saw** [not *seen*] the movie that you **had seen** [not *seen*] last week.

**set, sit**   The verb *set* (**set***, set, setting*) means "put in place, position, put down" and needs a direct object. The verb *sit* (**sit***, sat, sitting*) means "be seated" and doesn't need a direct object. Substituting *set* for *sit,* or the opposite, is nonstandard.

> Susan **set** [not *sat*] the sandwiches beside the salad, made Spot **sit** [not *set*] down, and then **sat** [not *set*] on the sofa.

**shall, will, should**   *Shall* was once used with *I* and *we* for future-tense verbs, and *will* was used for all other persons. Today, *shall* is considered highly formal, and *will* is more widely used. Similarly, distinctions were once made between *shall* and *should,* but today *should* is preferred. However, in questions, *should* is used about as often as *shall.*

> We **will** [or *shall*] depart on Monday, but he **will** [never *shall*] wait until Thursday to depart. **Should** [or *Shall*] I telephone ahead to reserve a suite at the hotel?

**should of**   *Should of* is nonstandard for *should have.*

**sit**   See *set, sit.*

**site**   See *cite, site.*

**sometime, sometimes, some time**    The adverb *sometime* means "at an unspecified time." The adverb *sometimes* means "now and then." *Some time* (two words) is an adjective with a noun that means "an amount or span of time."

> **Sometime** [adverb for "at an unspecified time"] next year, I must take my qualifying exams. I **sometimes** [adverb for "now and then"] worry whether I'll find **some time** [adjective with a noun] to study for them.

**sort of**    See *kind of, sort of.*

**stationary, stationery**    *Stationary* means "not moving; unchanging." *Stationery* refers to paper and related writing products.

> Using our firm's **stationery**, I wrote to city officials about a **stationary** light pole that had been knocked over in a car accident.

**such**    *Such* is informal for intensifiers such as *very* and *extremely.* However, *such* is acceptable to mean "of the same or similar kind."

> The play got **very** [not *such*] bad reviews. The playwright was embarrassed by **such** strong criticism.

**supposed to, used to**    The final -*d* is essential in both phrases.

> We were **suppose*d*** to [not *suppose to*] leave early. I **use*d* to** [not *use to*] wake up before the alarm rang.

**sure**    *Sure* is nonstandard for *surely* or *certainly.*

> I was **certainly** [not *sure*] surprised at the results.

**sure and, try and**    Both phrases are nonstandard for *sure to* and *try to.*

> Please **try to** [not *try and*] reach my doctor.

**than, then**    *Than* indicates comparison; *then* relates to time.

> Please put on your gloves, and **then** your hat. It's colder outside **than** you think.

**that, which**    Use *that* with restrictive (essential) clauses only. You can use *which* with both restrictive and nonrestrictive (nonessential) clauses; however, many people reserve *which* to use only with nonrestrictive clauses.

> The house **that** [or *which*] Jack built is on Beanstalk Street, **which** [not *that*] runs past the reservoir.

**that there, them there, this here, these here**    These phrases are nonstandard for *that, them, this, these,* respectively.

**their, there, they're**   *Their* is a possessive pronoun. *There* means "in that place" or is part of an expletive construction. *They're* is a contraction of *they are.*

> **They're** going to **their** accounting class in the building over **there** near the library. Do you know that **there** are twelve sections of Accounting 101?

**theirself, theirselves, themself**   These words are nonstandard for *themselves.*

**them**   Use *them* as an object pronoun only. Do not use *them* in place of the adjectives *these* and *those.*

> Let's buy **those** [not *them*] delicious looking strawberries.

**then**   See *than, then.*

**thirdly**   See *firstly, secondly, thirdly.*

**thusly**   *Thusly* is nonstandard for *thus.*

**till, until**   Both are acceptable, although *until* is preferred for academic writing.

**to, too, two**   *To* is a preposition; it also is part of an infinitive verb. *Too* is an adverb meaning "also; more than enough." *Two* is a number.

> When you go **to** Chicago, visit the Art Institute. Try **to** visit Harry Caray's for dinner, **too**. It won't be **too** expensive because **two** people can share a meal.

**toward, towards**   Although both are acceptable, writers of American English generally prefer *toward.*

**try and, sure and**   See *sure and, try and.*

**type**   *Type* is nonstandard when used to mean *type of.*

> I recommend that you use only that **type of** [not *type*] glue on plastic.

**unique**   Never combine *unique* with *more, most,* or other qualifiers.

> Solar heating is **unique** [not *somewhat unique*] in the Northeast. One **unique** [not *very unique*] heating system in a Vermont house uses hydrogen for fuel.

**uninterested**   See *disinterested, uninterested.*

**used to**   See *supposed to, used to.*

**utilize**  *Utilize* is considered an overblown word for *use* in academic writing.

The team **used** [not *utilized*] all its players to win the game.

**verbal, oral**  See *oral, verbal*.

**wait on**  *Wait on* is an informal substitute for *wait for. Wait on* is appropriate only when people give service to others.

I had to **wait for** [not *wait on*] half an hour for the hotel desk clerk to **wait on** me.

**way, ways**  When referring to distance, use *way* rather than *ways*.

He is a long **way** [not *ways*] from home.

**Web site, website**  Usage at the time of this book's publication calls for two words and a capital *W*. Increasingly, the informal *website* is being used.

**well**  See *good, well*.

**where**  *Where* is nonstandard for *that* when *where* is used as a subordinating conjunction.

I read **that** [not *where*] salt raises blood pressure.

**where . . . at**  This phrase is redundant; use only *where*.

**Where** is your house? [not *Where is your house at?*]

**whether**  See *if, whether*.

**which**  See *that, which*.

**who, whom**  Use *who* as a subject or a subject complement; use *whom* as an object (see 9g).

**who's, whose**  *Who's* is the contraction of *who is. Whose* is a possessive pronoun.

**Who's** willing to drive? **Whose** truck should we take?

**will**  See *shall, will*.

**-wise**  The suffix *-wise* means "in a manner, direction, or position." Never attach *-wise* indiscriminately to create new words. Instead, choose words that already exist; when in doubt, consult a dictionary to see if the *-wise* word you have in mind is acceptable.

**World Wide Web**    Written out, the three words start with a capital W. Its abbreviation only in URLs is *www.* When you use only the word *Web,* start it with a capital W.

**would of**    *Would of* is nonstandard for *would have.*

**your, you're**    *Your* is a possessive. *You're* is the contraction of *you are.*
  **You're** kind to volunteer **your** time at the senior center.

# Chapter 21

# THE IMPACT OF WORDS

## 21a   What is American English?

Evolving over centuries into a rich language, **American English** is the variation of English spoken in the United States. It demonstrates that many cultures have created the US "melting pot" society. Food names are good examples: Africans brought the words *okra, gumbo,* and *goober* (peanut); Spanish and Latin American peoples contributed *tortilla, taco, burrito,* and *enchilada;* Greek speakers gave us *pita,* Cantonese speakers *chow,* Japanese speakers *sushi,* and so on.

In all languages, the meanings of some words change with time. For example, W. Nelson Francis points out in *The English Language* (New York: Norton, 1965) that the word *nice* "has been used at one time or another in its 700-year history to mean: *foolish, wanton, strange, lazy, coy, modest, fastidious, refined, precise, subtle, slender, critical, attentive, minutely accurate, dainty, appetizing, agreeable.*"

## 21b   What are levels of formality in language?

**Levels of formality** in DICTION and SENTENCE VARIETY can be divided into three levels: highly informal (an e-mail or a letter to a friend); highly formal (the language of ceremony, written and often spoken); and medium or semiformal (ACADEMIC WRITING). A medium or semiformal level is expected in academic writing because its TONE is reasonable and evenhanded, its writing style clear and efficient, and its word choice appropriate for an academic audience.

| | |
|---|---|
| INFORMAL | Stars? Wow! They're, like, made of gas! |
| MEDIUM OR SEMIFORMAL | Gas clouds slowly transformed into stars. |
| FORMAL | The condensations of gas spun their slow gravitational pirouettes, slowly transmogrifying gas cloud into star. |
| | —Carl Sagan, "Starfolk: A Fable" |

In the informal example, the writer's attitude toward the subject is playful and humorous, so it's appropriate when writing to a close friend, in a journal, or in a BLOG. In the medium or semiformal example, the writer's attitude toward the subject is straightforward, so it's appropriate for most academic and professional situations. In the formal example, the writer's words are appropriate for readers who know about scientific phenomena and understand FIGURATIVE LANGUAGE.

## 21c What is edited American English?

**Edited American English**, also known as STANDARD ENGLISH, reflects the standards of the written language expected of a textbook. These standards apply in magazines such as *U.S. News & World Report* and *National Geographic;* in newspapers such as the *Washington Post* and the *Wall Street Journal;* and in most nonfiction books. With edited American English, you can achieve the medium or semiformal language level required in ACADEMIC WRITING.

Edited American English isn't a special or fancy dialect for elite groups. Rather, it's a form of the language used by educated people to standardize communication in the larger world. Edited American English conforms to widely established rules of grammar, sentence structure, punctuation, and spelling—as covered in this handbook.

**Nonstandard English** is legitimately spoken by some groups in our society. With its own grammar and usage customs, it communicates clearly to other speakers of nonstandard English. Yet, one thing is certain: Speakers of nonstandard English often benefit when they can switch, either temporarily or permanently, to the medium or semiformal level of language (21b) required in academic writing. This means that speakers of nonstandard English never need to reject their preferred or home language. Indeed, it's the right of all individuals to decide what works for them in various situations in their lives, and the ability to "code switch" gives them options.

Also, advertising language and other writing intended for a large, diverse audience might ignore the conventions of edited American English. Such published, nonstandard departures from edited American English are not appropriate in academic writing.

## 21d What is figurative language?

**Figurative language** uses words for more than their literal meanings. Such words aren't merely decorative or pretentious (21h). Figurative language greatly enhances meaning. It makes comparisons and connections that draw on one idea or image to explain another. Box 21.1 (p. 376) explains the different types of figurative language and describes one type you should avoid, the **mixed metaphor**.

## Types of figurative language

- **Analogy:** Comparing similar traits shared by dissimilar things or ideas. Its length can vary from one sentence (which often takes the form of a simile or metaphor) to a paragraph.

  A **cheetah sprinting across the dry plains** after its prey, the **base runner dashed** for home plate, cleats kicking up dust.

- **Irony:** Using words to suggest the opposite of their usual sense.

  Told that a minor repair on her home would cost $2,000 and take two weeks, she said, **"Oh, how nice!"**

- **Metaphor:** Comparing otherwise dissimilar things. A metaphor doesn't use the word *like* or *as* to make a comparison. (See below about not using mixed metaphors.)

  Rush-hour **traffic** in the city **bled out through major arteries** to the suburbs.

- **Personification:** Assigning a human trait to something not human.

  The **book begged** to be read.

- **Overstatement** (also called *hyperbole*): Exaggerating deliberately for emphasis.

  If this paper is late, the professor will **kill** me.

- **Simile:** Comparing dissimilar things. A simile uses the word *like* or *as*.

  Langston Hughes observes that a deferred **dream dries up "like a raisin in the sun."**

- **Understatement:** Emphasizing by using deliberate restraint.

  It feels **warm** when the temperature reaches **105 degrees**.

- **Mixed metaphor:** Combining two or more inconsistent images in one sentence or expression. Never use a mixed metaphor.

  **NO** The violence of the hurricane reminded me of a train ride. [A train ride is not violent, stormy, or destructive.]

  **YES** The violence of the hurricane reminded me of a train's crashing into a huge tractor trailer.

**EXERCISE 21-1**   Working individually or with a group, identify each type of figurative language or figure of speech. Also revise any mixed metaphors. For help, consult 21d.

1. Good manners are the grease for the wheels of human interaction.
2. Without manners, people would be meaner than junkyard dogs.
3. Being rude is like tracking mud on a freshly mopped floor.
4. If you can't mind your business, at least mind your manners.
5. Good manners are the icing on the cake of human behavior.
6. Being rude should be a criminal offense.
7. Compliments are magicians wielding great power.
8. When you're rude to people, you're playing with fire and getting in over your head.
9. Being polite when you're frustrated, irritated, and exasperated is as difficult as staying awake while driving when you haven't had enough sleep.
10. He's so tactless that if speech were a weapon, his would be a blunt instrument.

## 21e   How can using exact diction enhance my writing?

**Diction**, the term for choice of words, affects the clarity and impact of any writing you do. Your best chance of delivering your intended message to your readers is to choose words that fit exactly with each piece of writing. To choose words correctly—that is, to have good diction—you need to understand the concepts of *denotation* and *connotation* in words.

### 21e.1   What is denotation in words?

The **denotation** of a word is its exact, literal meaning. It's the meaning you find when you look up the word in a dictionary. Readers expect you to use words according to their established meanings for their established functions.

#### USING DICTIONARIES

A dictionary is your ultimate authority for a word's denotation—that is, its definition. The reference section in most college libraries includes one or more kinds of dictionaries for general use and for specialized areas.

- An **unabridged dictionary** contains the most extensive, complete, and scholarly entries. *Unabridged* means "not shortened." Such dictionaries include all infrequently used words that abridged dictionaries often omit. The most comprehensive, authoritative unabridged dictionary of

English is the *Oxford English Dictionary* (OED), which traces each word's history and gives quotations to illustrate changes in meaning and spelling over the life of the word.

- An **abridged dictionary** contains most commonly used words. *Abridged* means "shortened." When an abridged dictionary serves the needs of most college students, the dictionaries are referred to as "college editions." Typical of these is *Merriam-Webster's Collegiate Dictionary* (at <http://www.m-w.com/netdict.htm> online and also in print) and *The New American Webster Handy College Dictionary*.

- A **specialized dictionary** focuses on a single area of language. You can find dictionaries of slang (for example, *Dictionary of Slang and Unconventional English*, ed. Eric Partridge); word origins (for example, *Dictionary of Word and Phrase Origins*, ed. William Morris and Mary Morris); synonyms (for example, *Roget's 21st Century Thesaurus*); usage (for example, *Modern American Usage: A Guide*, ed. Jacques Barzun); idioms (for example, *A Dictionary of American Idioms*, by Adam Makkai); regionalisms (for example, *Dictionary of American Regional English*, ed. Frederic Cassidy); and many others.

**ESL TIP:** *The Dictionary of American English* (Boston: Heinle & Heinle, distributed by Berlitz, 2000) is particularly useful for students who speak English as a second (or third, etc.) language.

## 21e.2 What is connotation in words?

**Connotation** refers to ideas implied by a word. Connotations are never completely fixed, for they can vary in differing contexts. Connotations involve associations and emotional overtones that go beyond a word's definition. For example, *home* usually evokes more emotion than its denotation "a dwelling place" or its synonym *house*. *Home* carries the connotation, for some, of the pleasures of warmth, security, and love of family. For others, however, *home* may carry unpleasant connotations, such as abusive experiences or the impersonal atmosphere of an institution to house the elderly.

### USING A THESAURUS

Sometimes a good college dictionary explains the small differences among synonyms, but a thesaurus is devoted entirely to providing synonyms for words. In distinguishing among **synonyms**—the other words close in meaning to a word—a thesaurus demonstrates connotation in operation. As you use a thesaurus, remain very alert to the subtle shades of meaning that create distinctions among words. For instance, using *notorious* to describe a person famous for praiseworthy achievements in public life is wrong. Although *notorious* means "well-known" and "publicly discussed"—which is true of famous people—the connotation of the word is "unfavorably known or talked about." George Washington is famous, not notorious. Al Capone, by contrast, is notorious.

Here's another example, with the word *obdurate,* which means "not easily moved to pity or sympathy." Its synonyms include *inflexible, obstinate, stubborn,* and *hardened.*

> **NO** Footprints showed in the **obdurate** concrete.
>
> **YES** The supervisor remained **obdurate** in refusing to accept excuses.
>
> **YES** My **obdurate** roommates won't let my pet boa constrictor live in the bathtub.

**ALERT:** Most word processing programs include a thesaurus. But be cautious in using it. Unless you know the exact meaning of an offered synonym, as well as its part of speech, you may choose a wrong word or introduce a grammatical error into your writing. For example, one word processing program's thesaurus offers these synonyms for *deep* in the sense of "low (down, inside)": *low, below, beneath,* and *subterranean.* None of these words could replace *deep* in a sentence such as *The crater is too deep* [not *too low, too below, too beneath,* or *too subterranean*] *to be filled with sand or rocks.* ◆

**EXERCISE 21-2** Working individually or with a group, look at each list of words and divide the words among three headings: "Positive" (good connotations); "Negative" (bad connotations); and "Neutral" (no connotations). If you think that a word belongs under more than one heading, you can assign it more than once, but be ready to explain your thinking. For help, consult a good dictionary and 21e.2.

**EXAMPLE**   grand, big, bulky, significant, oversized

> *Positive:* grand, significant; *Negative:* bulky, oversized; *Neutral:* big

1. harmony, sound, racket, shriek, melody, music, noise, pitch, voice
2. talkative, articulate, chattering, eloquent, vocal, verbose, gossipy, fluent, gabby
3. decorative, beautiful, modern, ornate, overelaborate, dazzling, flashy, elegant, sparkling
4. long, lingering, enduring, continued, drawn-out, stretched, never-ending, unbreakable, incessant
5. calculating, shrewd, crafty, ingenious, keen, sensible, sly, smooth, underhanded

21f ## How can using specific words enhance my writing?

**Specific words** identify individual items in a group (*Buick, Honda*). **General words** relate to an overall group (*car*). **Concrete words** identify what can be perceived by the senses, by being seen, heard, tasted, felt, smelled (*padded black leather dashboard*), and convey specific images and details. **Abstract words** denote qualities (*kind*), concepts (*speed*), relationships (*friends*), acts (*cooking*), conditions (*bad weather*), and ideas (*transportation*) and are more general.

Usually, specific and concrete words bring life to general and abstract words. Therefore, whenever you use general and abstract words, try to supply enough specific, concrete details and examples to illustrate them. Here are sentences with general words that come to life when revised with specific words.

GENERAL His car gets good gas mileage.

SPECIFIC His Slurpo gets about 35 mpg on the highway and 30 mpg in the city.

GENERAL Her car is comfortable and easy to drive.

SPECIFIC When she drives her new Cushia on a five-hour trip, she arrives refreshed and does not need a long nap to recover, as she did when she drove her ten-year-old Upushme.

What separates most good writing from bad is the writer's ability to move back and forth between the general and abstract and the specific and concrete. Consider these sentences that effectively use a combination of general and specific words to compare cars:

GENERAL    CONCRETE    ┌──── SPECIFIC────┐    ABSTRACT
My car, a midnight-black Corvette LS1 convertible, has a powerful

┌─ SPECIFIC ─┐    GENERAL    SPECIFIC    GENERAL
5.7-liter V8 engine with ride controls, the Tour for regular driving and

SPECIFIC    ┌── CONCRETE ──┐    GENERAL
the Sport for a close-to-the-road feel. In contrast, Harvey's automobile,

CONCRETE    ┌──── SPECIFIC────┐    ABSTRACT
a bright red Dodge Viper SRT-10 convertible, has a mighty

┌──────── SPECIFIC ────────┐
8.3-liter V10 engine with 6-speed manual transmission.

**EXERCISE 21-3** Revise this paragraph by providing specific and concrete words and phrases to explain and enliven the ideas presented here in general and abstract language. You may revise the sentences to accommodate your changes in language. For help, consult 21f.

I hope to get a job as an administrative assistant in the company. At the interview, the person who would be my supervisor was pleasant. We seemed to get along well. The other assistants in the division appeared to be nice. My college courses clearly have prepared me for the position. I think the job would teach me a great deal more. The salary is a bit less than I had hoped for, but the Human Resources representative promised me raises at regular intervals if my work is good. Also, my trip to work would not take too much time for me. If my interviewer calls to offer me the job, I will accept it.

## **21g** What is gender-neutral language?

**Gender-neutral language**, also referred to as gender-free or *nonsexist language,* relies on terms that don't communicate whether the person is male or female (for example, in replacing *policeman* with *police officer* or *doctors' wives* with *doctors' spouses*).

**Sexist language** assigns roles or characteristics to people based on their sex and gender. Many people today feel that sexist language unfairly discriminates against both sexes. For example, it inaccurately assumes that every nurse and homemaker is female (and therefore referred to as "she"), and that every physician and stockbroker is male (and therefore referred to as "he"). One common instance of sexist language occurs when the pronoun *he* is used to refer to someone whose sex is unknown or irrelevant. Although tradition holds that *he* is correct in such situations, many people find it offensive. They feel that using masculine pronouns to represent all humans excludes women and thereby distorts reality.

Gender-neutral language rejects demeaning STEREOTYPES or outdated assumptions, such as "women are bad drivers" and "men can't cook." In your writing, never describe women's looks, clothes, or age unless you do the same for men or doing so is important to the context. Never use a title for one spouse and the first name for the other spouse: *Phil Miller* (not *Mr. Miller*) and *his wife, Jeannette,* travel on separate planes; or *Jeannette and Phil Miller* live in Idaho. Box 21.2 (p. 382) gives you guidelines for using gender-neutral language.

**EXERCISE 21-4**  Working individually or with a group, revise these sentences by changing sexist language to gender-neutral language. For help, consult 21g.

1. Dogs were one of the first animals to be domesticated by mankind.
2. Traditionally, certain breeds of dogs have helped men in their work.
3. On their long shifts, firemen often kept Dalmatians as mascots and companions, whereas policemen preferred highly intelligent and easily trained German shepherds.

4. Another breed, the Newfoundland, accompanied many fishermen on their ocean voyages, and the Newfoundland has been credited with rescuing many a man overboard.

5. Breeds known as hunting dogs have served as the helpers and companions of sportsmen.

6. Maids and cleaning women didn't need dogs, so no breed of dog is associated with women's work.

7. Another group that dogs have not helped is postmen.

8. Everyone who owns a dog should be sure to spend some time exercising his dog and making sure his dog is in good health.

9. No man-made inventions, such as televisions or computers, can take the place of having a dog.

10. Now even though most dogs do not work, they are still man's best friend.

**SUMMARY BOX 21.2**

## How to avoid sexist language

- Avoid using only the masculine pronoun to refer to males and females together. The *he or she* and *his or hers* constructions act as singular PRONOUNS, and they therefore call for singular VERBS. Try to avoid using *he or she* constructions, especially more than once in a sentence or in consecutive sentences. A better solution is revising to the plural. You can also revise to omit the gender-specific pronoun.

  **NO** A **doctor** has little time to read outside **his** specialty.

  **YES** A **doctor** has little time to read outside **his or her** specialty.

  **NO** A successful **stockbroker** knows **he** has to work long hours.

  **YES** Successful **stockbrokers** know **they** have to work long hours.

  **NO** **Everyone** hopes that **he or she** will win the scholarship.

  **YES** **Everyone** hopes to win the scholarship.

- Avoid using *man* when referring to both men and women.

  **NO** **Man** is a social animal.

  **YES** **People** are social animals.

  **NO** The history of **mankind** is predominately violent.

  **YES** **Human** history is predominately violent.

  **NO** Dogs are **men's** best friends.

  **YES** Dogs are **people's** best friends.

> **SUMMARY BOX** **21.2** *continued*
>
> ## How to avoid sexist language
>
> * Avoid stereotyping jobs and roles by gender when referring to both men and women.
>
> | NO | YES |
> |---|---|
> | chairman | chair, chairperson |
> | policeman | police officer |
> | businessman | businessperson, business executive |
> | statesman | statesperson, diplomat |
> | teacher . . . she | teachers . . . they |
> | principal . . . he | principals . . . they |
>
> * Avoid expressions that seem to exclude one sex.
>
> | NO | YES |
> |---|---|
> | the common man | the average person |
> | man-sized sandwich | huge sandwich |
> | old wives' tale | superstition |
>
> * Avoid using demeaning and patronizing labels.
>
> | NO | YES |
> |---|---|
> | male nurse | nurse |
> | gal Friday | assistant |
> | coed | student |
> | My girl can help. | My secretary can help (*or better still,* Ida Morea can help). |

## 21h What other types of language do I want to avoid?

Language that distorts or tries to manipulate a reader needs to be avoided in ACADEMIC WRITING. These and other types of language to avoid in an academic LEVEL OF FORMALITY are listed, with examples, in Box 21.3 (p. 384).

## 21i What is regional language?

**Regional language**, also called *dialectal language,* is specific to certain geographical areas. For example, a *dragonfly* is a *snake feeder* in parts of Delaware, a *darning needle* in parts of Michigan, and a *snake doctor* or an *ear sewer* in parts of the southern United States. Using a dialect in writing for the general reading public tends to shut some people out of

383

**SUMMARY BOX 21.3**

## Language to avoid in academic writing

- Never use **slanted language**, also called *loaded language;* readers feel manipulated by the overly emotional TONE and DICTION.

  **NO** Our senator is a deceitful, crooked thug.

  **YES** Our senator lies to the public and demands bribes.

  **NO** Why do labs employ Frankensteins to maim helpless kittens and puppies?

  **YES** Why do labs employ uncaring technicians who harm kittens and puppies?

- Never use **pretentious language**; readers realize you're showing off.

  **NO** As I alighted from my vehicle, my clothing became besmirched with filth.

  **YES** My coat got muddy as I got out of my car.

  **NO** He has a penchant for ostentatiously flaunting recently acquired haberdashery accoutrements.

  **YES** He tends to show off his new clothes shamelessly.

- Never use **sarcastic language**; readers realize you're being nasty.

  **NO** He was a regular Albert Einstein with my questions. [This is sarcastic if you mean the opposite.]

  **YES** He had trouble understanding my questions.

- Never use **colloquial language**; readers sense you're being overly casual and conversational.

  **NO** Christina flunked chemistry.

  **YES** Christina failed chemistry.

- Never use **euphemisms**, also called *doublespeak;* readers realize you're hiding the truth (more in 21l).

  **NO** Our company will **downsize** to meet efficiency standards.

  **YES** Our company has to cut jobs to maintain our profits.

  **NO** We consider our hostages as **foreign guests** being guarded by **hosts**.

  **YES** We consider our hostages as enemies to be guarded closely.

➤

---

**SUMMARY BOX** 21.3 *continued*

## Language to avoid in academic writing

- Never use NONSTANDARD ENGLISH (more in 21c).
- Never use MIXED METAPHORS (more in 21d).
- Never use SEXIST LANGUAGE or STEREOTYPES (more in 21g and 4j).
- Never use regional language (more in 21i).
- Never use CLICHÉS (more in 21j).
- Never use unnecessary JARGON (more in 21k).
- Never use BUREAUCRATIC LANGUAGE (more in 21m).

the communication. Except when dialect is the topic of the writing, ACADEMIC WRITING rarely accommodates dialect well. Avoid it in academic assignments.

### 21j What are clichés?

A **cliché** is a worn-out expression that has lost its capacity to communicate effectively because of overuse. Many clichés are SIMILES or METAPHORS, once clever but now flat. For example, these are clichés: *dead as a doornail, gentle as a lamb,* and *straight as an arrow.*

If you've heard certain expressions repeatedly, so has your reader. Instead of a cliché, use descriptive language that isn't worn out. If you can't think of a way to rephrase a cliché, drop the words entirely.

Interestingly, however, English is full of frequently used word groups that aren't clichés: for example, *up and down* and *from place to place.* These common word groups aren't considered clichés, so you can use them freely. If you're not sure of how to tell the difference between a cliché and a common word group, remember that a cliché often—but not always—contains an image (*busy as a bee* and *strong as an ox*).

**EXERCISE 21-5** Working individually or with a group, revise these clichés. Use the idea in each cliché to write a sentence of your own in plain, clear English. For help, consult 21j.

1. The bottom line is that Carl either raises his grade point average or finds himself in hot water.

2. Carl's grandfather says, "When the going gets tough, the tough get going."

385

3. Carl may not be the most brilliant engineering major who ever came down the pike, but he has plenty of get-up-and-go.

4. When they were handing out persistence, Carl was first in line.

5. The $64,000 question: Will Carl make it safe and sound, or will the college drop him like a hot potato?

## 21k    When is jargon unnecessary?

**Jargon** is the specialized vocabulary of a particular group. Jargon uses words that people outside that group might not understand. Specialized language exists in every field: professions, academic disciplines, business, various industries, government departments, hobbies, and so on.

Reserve jargon for a specialist AUDIENCE. As you write, keep your audience in mind as you decide whether a word is jargon in the context of your material. For example, a football fan easily understands a sportswriter's use of words such as *punt* and *safety,* but they are jargon words to people unfamiliar with American-style football. Avoid using jargon unnecessarily. When you must use jargon for a nonspecialist audience, be sure to explain any special meanings.

The example below shows specialized language used appropriately; it's taken from a college textbook. The authors can assume that students know the meaning of *eutrophicates, terrestrial,* and *eutrophic.*

As the lake eutrophicates, it gradually fills until the entire lake will be converted into a terrestrial community. Eutrophic changes (or eutrophication) are the nutritional enrichment of the water, promoting the growth of aquatic plants.

—Davis and Solomon, *The World of Biology*

## 21l    What are euphemisms?

**Euphemisms** attempt to avoid the harsh reality of truth by using more pleasant, "tactful" words. Good manners dictate that euphemisms sometimes be used in social situations: For example, in US culture, *passed away* is, in some situations, thought to be gentler than *died.* Such uses of euphemisms are acceptable.

In other situations, however, euphemisms drain meaning from truthful writing. Unnecessary euphemisms might describe socially unacceptable behavior (for example, *Johnny has a wonderfully vivid imagination* instead of *Johnny lies*). They also might try to hide unpleasant facts (for example, *She is between assignments* instead of *She's lost her job*). Avoid unnecessary euphemisms.

## 21m   What is bureaucratic language?

**Bureaucratic language** uses words that are stuffy and overblown. Bureaucratic language (or *bureaucratese,* a word created to describe the style) is marked by unnecessary complexity. This kind of language can take on a formality that complicates the message and makes readers feel left out.

**NO**   In reference to the above captioned, you can include a page that additionally contains an Include instruction under the herein stated circumstances. The page including the Include instruction is included when you paginate the document, but the included text referred to in its Include instruction is not included. [This message is meaningless, but the writer seems to understand the message. Anyone who doesn't is clearly uninformed or unable to read intelligently!]

—From instructions for compiling a user's manual

In response to earlier editions of this handbook, we've been asked to give a YES alternative for this example. We regret that we can't understand enough of the NO example to do that. If you, gentle reader, can, please contact us at <troykalq@nyc.rr.com> or <ddhesse@ilstu.edu>.

**EXERCISE 21-6**   Working individually or with a group, revise these examples of pretentious language, jargon, euphemisms, and bureaucratic language. For help, consult 21h and 21k through 21m.

1. Allow me to express my humble gratitude to you two benefactors for your generous pledge of indispensable support on behalf of the activities of our Bay City's youngsters.

2. No lateral transfer applications will be processed before an employee's six-month probation period terminates.

3. She gave up the ghost shortly after her husband kicked the bucket.

4. Creating nouns in positions meant for verbs is to utter ostentatious verbalizations that will lead inexorably to further obfuscations of meaning.

5. After his operation, he would list to port when he stood up and list to starboard when he sat down.

6. The precious youths were joy riding in a temporarily displaced vehicle.

7. The forwarding of all electronic communiqués must be approved by a staff member in the upper echelon.

8. Coming to a parting of the ways is not as easy as pie.

# Chapter 22

---

## SPELLING

### 22a What makes a good speller?

You might be surprised to hear that good spellers don't know how to spell and hyphenate every word they write. What they do know, however, is to check if they're not sure of a word's spelling. If your inner voice questions a spelling, do what good spellers do—consult a dictionary.

What do you do if even the first few letters of a word seem mysterious? This is a common problem among writers. Our best advice is that you think of an easy-to-spell SYNONYM for the word you need; look up that synonym in a thesaurus; and among the synonyms, find the word you need to spell.

Many people, surveys show, incorrectly believe that only naturally skilled spellers can write well. The truth is that correct spelling matters a great deal in final drafts, but not in earlier drafts. The best time to check spellings you doubt is when you're EDITING.

The various origins and ways that English-speaking people around the world pronounce words make it almost impossible to rely solely on pronunciation to spell a word. What you can rely on, however, are the proofreading hints and spelling rules explained in this chapter.

**ALERT:** Word processing software usually includes a spell-check program, which claims to spot spelling errors because the words typed in don't match the spellings in the software's dictionary. Such programs have one major drawback. The programs can't detect that you've spelled a word incorrectly if what you've typed is a legitimate spelling of a legitimate word. For example, if you mean *top* but type *too,* or if you mean *from* and type *form,* no spell-check program "sees" a mistake. In these and similar cases, only the human eye (that is, a reader) can discover the errors. ◆

### 22b How can I proofread for errors in spelling and hyphen use?

Many spelling errors are the result of illegible handwriting, slips of the pen, or typographical mistakes. Catching these "typos" requires especially careful proofreading, using the techniques in Box 22.1.

**SUMMARY BOX** 22.1

## Proofreading for errors in spelling

- Slow down your reading speed to allow yourself to concentrate on the individual letters of words rather than on the meaning of the words.

- Stay within your "visual span," the number of letters you can identify with a single glance (for most people, about six letters).

- Put a ruler or large index card under each line as you proofread, to focus your vision and concentration.

- Read each paragraph in reverse, from the last sentence to the first. This method can keep you from being distracted by the meaning of the material.

---

### 22c   How are plurals spelled?

In American English, plurals take many forms. The most common form adds -*s* or -*es* at the end of the word. The following list covers all variations of creating plurals.

- **Adding -*s* or -*es*:** Plurals of most words are formed by adding -*s*, including words that end in "hard" -*ch* (sounding like *k*): *leg, legs*; *shoe, shoes*; *stomach, stomachs*. Words ending in -*s*, -*sh*, -*x*, -*z*, or "soft" -*ch* (as in *beach*) are formed by adding -*es* to the singular: *lens, lenses*; *tax, taxes*; *beach, beaches*.

- **Words ending in -*o*:** Add -*s* if the -*o* is preceded by a vowel: *radio, radios*; *cameo, cameos*. Add -*es* if the -*o* is preceded by a consonant: *potato, potatoes*. With a few words, you can choose the -*s* or -*es* plural form, but current practice generally supports adding -*es*: *cargo, cargoes*; *tornado, tornadoes*; *zero, zeros* or *zeroes*.

- **Words ending in -*f* or -*fe*:** Some words ending in -*f* and -*fe* are made plural by adding -*s*: *belief, beliefs*. Others require changing -*f* or -*fe* to -*ves*: *life, lives*; *leaf, leaves*. Words ending in -*ff* or -*ffe* simply add -*s*: *staff, staffs*; *giraffe, giraffes*.

- **Compound words:** For most compound words, add -*s* or -*es* at the end of the last word: *checkbooks, player-coaches*. In a few cases, the first word is made plural: *sister-in-law, sisters-in-law; miles per hour*. (For information about hyphens in compound words, see 22g.)

- **Internal changes and endings other than -*s*:** A few words change internally or add endings other than -*s* to become plural: *foot, feet; man, men; crisis, crises; child, children*.

389

- **Foreign words:** The best advice is to check your dictionary. In general, many Latin words ending in *-um* form the plural by changing *-um* to *-a*: *curricul**um**, curricul**a**; dat**um**, dat**a**; medi**um**, medi**a**.* Also, Latin words that end in *-us* usually form the plural by changing *-us* to *-i*: *alumn**us**, alumn**i**; syllab**us**, syllab**i**.* Additionally, Greek words that end in *-on* usually form the plural by changing *-on* to *-a*: *criteri**on**, criteri**a**; phenomen**on**, phenomen**a**.*

- **One-form words:** Some words have the same form in both the singular and the plural: *deer, elk, fish.* You need to use modifiers, as necessary, to indicate which form you mean: ***one** deer, **nine** deer.*

**EXERCISE 22-1**  Write the correct plural form of these words. For help, consult 22c.

| | | |
|---|---|---|
| 1. yourself | 6. millennium | 11. echo |
| 2. sheep | 7. lamp | 12. syllabus |
| 3. photo | 8. runner-up | 13. wife |
| 4. woman | 9. criterion | 14. get-together |
| 5. appendix | 10. lunch | 15. crisis |

## 22d  How are suffixes spelled?

A **suffix** is an ending added to a word that changes the word's meaning or its grammatical function. For example, adding the suffix *-able* to the VERB *depend* creates the ADJECTIVE *dependable*.

- ***-y* words:** If the letter before a final *-y* is a consonant, change the *-y* to *-i* and add the suffix: *try, tr**ies**, tr**ied**.* In the case of *trying* and similar words, the following rule applies: Keep the *-y* when the suffix begins with *-i* (*apply, apply**ing***). If the letter before the final *-y* is a vowel, keep the final *-y*: *employ, employ**ed**, employ**ing**.* These rules don't apply to IRREGULAR VERBS (see Box 8.4 in section 8d).

- ***-e* words:** Drop a final *-e* when the suffix begins with a vowel, unless doing this would cause confusion: for example, *be + ing* can't be written *bing*, but *require* does become *requiring; like* does become *liking.* Keep the final *-e* when the suffix begins with a consonant: *require, requir**ement**; like, like**ly**.* Exceptions include *argue, arg**ument**; judge, jud**gment**; true, tr**uly**.*

- **Words that double a final letter:** If the final letter is a consonant, double it *only* if it passes three tests: (1) Its last two letters are a vowel followed by a consonant; (2) it has one syllable or is accented on the last syllable; (3) the suffix begins with a vowel: *drop, drop**ped**; begin, begin**ning**; forget, forget**table**.*

- **-cede, -ceed, -sede words:** Only one word in the English language ends in *-sede: super***sede**. Only three words end in *-ceed: ex***ceed**, *pro***ceed**, *suc***ceed**. All other words with endings that sound like "seed" end in *-cede: con***cede**, *inter***cede**, *pre***cede**.

- **-ally and -ly words:** The suffixes *-ally* and *-ly* turn words into adverbs. For words ending in *-ic*, add *-ally: logic***ally**, *statistic***ally**. Otherwise, add *-ly: quick***ly**, *sharp***ly**.

- **-ance, -ence, and -ible, -able:** No consistent rules govern words with these suffixes. When in doubt, look up the word.

## 22e   What is the *ie, ei* rule?

The famous rhymed rule for using *ie* and *ei* is usually true:

*I* before *e* [bel**ie**ve, f**ie**ld, gr**ie**f],

Except after *c* [c**ei**ling, conc**ei**t],

Or when sounded like "ay"—

As in n**ei**ghbor and w**ei**gh [**ei**ght, v**ei**n].

There are major exceptions (sorry!) to the *ie, ei* rule, listed here. Our best advice is that you memorize them.

- **ie:** consc**ie**nce, financ**ie**r, sc**ie**nce, spec**ie**s
- **ei:** **ei**ther, n**ei**ther, l**ei**sure, s**ei**ze, counterf**ei**t, for**ei**gn, forf**ei**t, sl**ei**ght (as in *sleight of hand*), w**ei**rd

**EXERCISE 22-2**   Follow the directions for each group of words. For help, consult 22d and 22e.

1. Add *-able* or *-ible:* (a) profit; (b) reproduce; (c) control; (d) coerce; (e) recognize.
2. Add *-ance* or *-ence:* (a) luxuri_____; (b) prud_____; (c) devi_____; (d) resist_____; (e) independ_____.
3. Drop the final *-e* as needed: (a) true + ly; (b) joke + ing; (c) fortunate + ly; (d) appease + ing; (e) appease + ment.
4. Change the final *-y* to *-i* as needed: (a) happy + ness; (b) pry + ed; (c) pry + ing; (d) dry + ly; (e) beautify + ing.
5. Double the final consonant as needed: (a) commit + ed; (b) commit + ment; (c) drop + ed; (d) occur + ed; (e) regret + ful.
6. Insert *ie* or *ei* correctly: (a) rel_____f; (b) ach_____ve; (c) w_____rd; (d) n_____ce; (e) dec_____ve.

## 22f How are homonyms and other frequently confused words spelled?

**Homonyms** are words that sound exactly like other words: *to, too, two; no, know*. The different spellings of homonyms tend to confuse many writers. The same holds for words that sound almost alike (*accept, except; conscience, conscious*).

Another reason for spelling problems is so-called swallowed pronunciation, which means one or more letters at the end of a word aren't pronounced clearly. For example, the *-d* ending in *used to* or *prejudiced* or the *-ten* ending in *written* are often swallowed rather than pronounced. When writers spell as they mispronounce, spelling errors result.

For more information about word usage that affects spelling, see Chapter 20, "Usage Glossary." Box 22.2 lists homonyms and other words that can be confused and lead to misspellings.

---

### SUMMARY BOX 22.2

### Homonyms and other frequently confused words

| | |
|---|---|
| • ACCEPT | to receive |
| EXCEPT | with the exclusion of |
| • ADVICE | recommendation |
| ADVISE | to recommend |
| • AFFECT | to influence [verb]; emotion [noun] |
| EFFECT | result [noun]; to bring about or cause [verb] |
| • AISLE | space between rows |
| ISLE | island |
| • ALLUDE | to make indirect reference to |
| ELUDE | to avoid |
| • ALLUSION | indirect reference |
| ILLUSION | false idea, misleading appearance |
| • ALREADY | by this time |
| ALL READY | fully prepared |
| • ALTAR | sacred platform or place |
| ALTER | to change |
| • ALTOGETHER | thoroughly |
| ALL TOGETHER | everyone or everything in one place |
| • ARE | PLURAL form of *to be* |
| HOUR | sixty minutes |
| OUR | plural form of *my* |

## Homonyms and other frequently confused words

- ASCENT the act of rising or climbing
  ASSENT consent [noun]; to consent [verb]

- ASSISTANCE help
  ASSISTANTS helpers

- BARE nude, unadorned
  BEAR to carry; an animal

- BOARD piece of wood
  BORED uninterested

- BRAKE device for stopping
  BREAK to destroy, make into pieces

- BREATH air taken in
  BREATHE to take in air

- BUY to purchase
  BY next to, through the agency of

- CAPITAL major city; money
  CAPITOL government building

- CHOOSE to pick
  CHOSE PAST TENSE of *choose*

- CITE to point out
  SIGHT vision
  SITE a place

- CLOTHES garments
  CLOTHS pieces of fabric

- COARSE rough
  COURSE path; series of lectures

- COMPLEMENT something that completes
  COMPLIMENT praise, flattery

- CONSCIENCE sense of morality
  CONSCIOUS awake, aware

- COUNCIL governing body
  COUNSEL advice [noun]; to advise [verb]

- DAIRY place associated with milk production
  DIARY personal journal

- DESCENT downward movement
  DISSENT disagreement

**SUMMARY BOX** 22.2 *continued*

## Homonyms and other frequently confused words

- DESERT / DESSERT
  to abandon [verb]; dry, usually sandy area [noun]
  final, sweet course in a meal

- DEVICE / DEVISE
  a plan; an implement
  to create

- DIE / DYE
  to lose life (dying) [verb]; one of a pair of dice [noun]
  to change the color of something (dyeing)

- DOMINANT / DOMINATE
  commanding, controlling
  to control

- ELICIT / ILLICIT
  to draw out
  illegal

- EMINENT / IMMANENT / IMMINENT
  prominent
  living within; inherent
  about to happen

- ENVELOP / ENVELOPE
  to surround
  container for a letter or other papers

- FAIR / FARE
  light-skinned; just, honest
  money for transportation; food

- FORMALLY / FORMERLY
  conventionally, with ceremony
  previously

- FORTH / FOURTH
  forward
  number four in a series

- GORILLA / GUERRILLA
  animal in ape family
  fighter conducting surprise attacks

- HEAR / HERE
  to sense sound by ear
  in this place

- HOLE / WHOLE
  opening
  complete; an entire thing

- HUMAN / HUMANE
  relating to the species *Homo sapiens*
  compassionate

- INSURE / ENSURE
  to buy or give insurance
  to guarantee, protect

- ITS / IT'S
  POSSESSIVE form of *it*
  CONTRACTION for *it is*

- KNOW / NO
  to comprehend
  negative

## Homonyms and other frequently confused words

| | | |
|---|---|---|
| • | LATER | after a time |
| | LATTER | second one of two things |
| • | LEAD | heavy metal substance [noun]; to guide [verb] |
| | LED | past tense of *lead* |
| • | LIGHTNING | storm-related electricity |
| | LIGHTENING | making lighter |
| • | LOOSE | unbound, not tightly fastened |
| | LOSE | to misplace |
| • | MAYBE | perhaps [adverb] |
| | MAY BE | might be [verb] |
| • | MEAT | animal flesh |
| | MEET | to encounter |
| • | MINER | a person who works in a mine |
| | MINOR | underage; less important |
| • | MORAL | distinguishing right from wrong; the lesson of a fable, story, or event |
| | MORALE | attitude or outlook, usually of a group |
| • | OF | PREPOSITION indicating origin |
| | OFF | away from; not on |
| • | PASSED | past tense of *pass* |
| | PAST | at a previous time |
| • | PATIENCE | forbearance |
| | PATIENTS | people under medical care |
| • | PEACE | absence of fighting |
| | PIECE | part of a whole; musical arrangement |
| • | PERSONAL | intimate |
| | PERSONNEL | employees |
| • | PLAIN | simple, unadorned |
| | PLANE | to shave wood; aircraft |
| • | PRECEDE | to come before |
| | PROCEED | to continue |
| • | PRESENCE | being at hand; attendance at a place or in something |
| | PRESENTS | gifts |

**SUMMARY BOX** 22.2 *continued*

## Homonyms and other frequently confused words

- PRINCIPAL     foremost [adjective]; school head [noun]
  PRINCIPLE     moral conviction, basic truth

- QUIET     silent, calm
  QUITE     very

- RAIN     water that falls to earth [noun]; to fall like rain [verb]
  REIGN     to rule
  REIN     strap to guide or control an animal [noun]; to guide or control [verb]

- RAISE     to lift up
  RAZE     to tear down

- RESPECTFULLY     with respect
  RESPECTIVELY     in that order

- RIGHT     correct; opposite of *left*
  RITE     ritual
  WRITE     to put words on paper

- ROAD     path
  RODE     past tense of *ride*

- SCENE     place of an action; segment of a play
  SEEN     viewed

- SENSE     perception, understanding
  SINCE     measurement of past time; because

- STATIONARY     standing still
  STATIONERY     writing paper

- THAN     in comparison with; besides
  THEN     at that time; next; therefore

- THEIR     possessive form of *they*
  THERE     in that place
  THEY'RE     contraction of *they are*

- THROUGH     finished; into and out of
  THREW     past tense of *throw*
  THOROUGH     complete

- TO     toward
  TOO     also; indicates degree (*too much*)
  TWO     number following *one*

- WAIST     midsection of the body
  WASTE     discarded material [noun]; to squander, to fail to use up [verb]

---

**SUMMARY BOX** | **22.2** *continued*

**Homonyms and other frequently confused words**

- WEAK — not strong
  WEEK — seven days

- WEATHER — climatic condition
  WHETHER — if, when alternatives are expressed or implied

- WHERE — in which place
  WERE — past tense of *be*

- WHICH — one of a group
  WITCH — female sorcerer

- WHOSE — possessive form of *who*
  WHO'S — contraction for *who is*

- YOUR — possessive form of *you*
  YOU'RE — contraction for *you are*
  YORE — long past

---

**EXERCISE 22-3** Circle the correct homonym or commonly confused word of each group in parentheses.

Imagine that you (are, our) standing in the middle of a busy sidewalk, with a worried look on (your, you're, yore) face. In your hand (your, you're, yore) holding a map, (which, witch) you are puzzling over. If that happened in (real, reel) life, (its, it's) almost certain that within (to, too, two) or three minutes a passerby would ask if you (where, were) lost and would offer you (assistance, assistants). That helpful passerby, (buy, by) taking a (personal, personnel) interest in your problem, is displaying a quality known as empathy—the ability (to, too, two) put oneself in another person's place. Some researchers claim that empathy is an instinct that (human, humane) beings share with many other animals. Other scientists wonder (weather, whether) empathy is instead a (conscience, conscious) (moral, morale) choice that people make. Whatever explanation for the origin (of, off) empathy is (right, rite, write), such empathy generally has a positive (affect, effect)—especially if (your, you're, yore) a person who (maybe, may be) (to, too, two) lost to (know, no) (where, were) (to, too, two) turn.

## 22g    What are compound words?

A **compound word** puts together two or more words to express one concept.

> **Open compound words** remain as separate words, such as *decision making, problem solving,* and *editor in chief.*

> **Hyphenated compound words** use a hyphen between the words, such as *trade-in, fuel-efficient,* and *tax-sheltered.* For punctuation advice about hyphens, see 29i.

> **Closed compound words** appear as one word, such as *proofread, city-wide,* and *workweek.*

Single-word compounds usually start as open (two-word) compounds and then become hyphenated compounds before ending up as closed compounds. To check whether a compound term consists of closed, hyphenated, or open words, consult an up-to-date dictionary.

# PART 4

# Using Punctuation and Mechanics

# Chapter 23

## PERIODS, QUESTION MARKS, AND EXCLAMATION POINTS

**Periods**, **question marks**, and **exclamation points** are collectively called *end punctuation* because they occur at the ends of sentences.

I love you. Do you love me? I love you!

## PERIODS

### 23a    When does a period end a sentence?

A **period** ends a statement, a mild command, or an INDIRECT QUESTION.* Never use a period to end a DIRECT QUESTION, a strong command, or an emphatic declaration.

**END OF A STATEMENT**
A journey of a thousand miles must begin with a single step.
— Lao-tsu, *The Way of Lao-tsu*

**MILD COMMAND**
Put a gram of boldness into everything you do.
— Baltasar Gracian

**INDIRECT QUESTION**
I asked if they wanted to climb Mt. Everest. [As an indirect question, this sentence reports that a question was asked. If it were a direct question, it would end with a question mark: *I asked, "Do you want to climb Mt. Everest?"*]

### 23b    How do I use periods with abbreviations?

Most **abbreviations**, though not all, call for periods. Typical abbreviations with periods include *Mt., St., Dr., Mr., Ms., Mrs., Jr., Fri., Feb., a.m.,* and *p.m.* (For more about *a.m.* and *p.m.*, see Chapter 20, "Usage

---

*Words printed in SMALL CAPITAL LETTERS are discussed elsewhere in the text and are defined in the Terms Glossary at the back of the book.

Glossary," and section 30j; for more about abbreviations in general, see 30i through 30l.)

➤ **ALERT:** Spell out the word *professor* in ACADEMIC WRITING; never abbreviate it. ◆

Abbreviations without periods include the postal codes for states (for example, IL, CO) and the names of some organizations and government agencies (for example, CBS and NASA).

> **Ms.** Yuan, who works at **NASA,** lectured to **Dr.** Garcia's physics class at 9:30 **a.m.**

➤ **ALERT:** When the period of an abbreviation falls at the end of a sentence that calls for a period, the period of the abbreviation serves also to end the sentence. If, however, your sentence ends in a question mark or an exclamation point, put it after the period of the abbreviation.

> The phone rang at 4:00 **a.m.**
>
> It's upsetting to answer a wrong-number call at 4:00 **a.m.!**
>
> Who would call at 4:00 **a.m.?** ◆

## QUESTION MARKS

### 23c  When do I use a question mark?

A **question mark** ends a **direct question**, one that quotes the exact words the speaker used. (In contrast, an **indirect question** reports a question and ends with a period.)

> How many attempts have been made to climb Mt. Everest? [An indirect question would end with a period: *She wants to know how many attempts have been made to climb Mt. Everest.*]

➤ **ALERT:** Never use a question mark with a period, comma, semicolon, or colon.

> **NO**   She asked, "How are you**?.**"
>
> **YES**   She asked, "How are you**?**" ◆

Questions in a series are each followed by a question mark, whether or not each question is a complete sentence.

> After the fierce storm, the mountain climbers debated what to do next. Turn back**?** Move on**?** Rest for a while**?**

➤ **ALERT:** When questions in a series are not complete sentences (as in the preceding example), you can choose whether to capitalize the first letter, but be consistent within each piece of writing. ◆

Sometimes a statement or mild command is phrased as a question to be polite. In such cases, a question mark is optional, but be consistent in each piece of writing.

Would you please send me a copy**.**

## 23d When can I use a question mark in parentheses?

The only time to use a question mark in parentheses (?) is if a date or other number is unknown or doubtful. Never use (?) to communicate that you're unsure of information.

Mary Astell, a British writer of pamphlets on women's rights, was born in 1666 **(?)** and died in 1731.

The word *about* is often a more graceful substitute for (?): *Mary Astell was born **about** 1666.*

Also, never use (?) to communicate IRONY or sarcasm. Choose words to deliver your message.

**NO** Having altitude sickness is a pleasant **(?)** experience.

**YES** Having altitude sickness is **as** pleasant **as having a bad case of the flu**.

## EXCLAMATION POINTS

## 23e When do I use an exclamation point?

An **exclamation point** ends a strong command or an emphatic declaration. A strong command is a firm and direct order: *Look out behind you!* An emphatic declaration is a shocking or surprising statement: *There's been an accident!*

**ALERT:** Never combine an exclamation point with a period, comma, semicolon, or colon.

**NO** "There's been an accident**!,**" she shouted.

**YES** "There's been an accident**!**" she shouted.

**YES** "There's been an accident," she shouted. [Use this form if you prefer not to use an exclamation point.] ◆

## 23f What is considered overuse of exclamation points?

In ACADEMIC WRITING, words, not exclamation points, need to communicate the intensity of your message. Reserve exclamation points for an emphatic declaration within a longer passage.

When we were in Nepal, we tried each day to see Mt. Everest. But each day we failed. **Clouds defeated us!** The summit never emerged from a heavy overcast.

Also, using exclamation points too frequently suggests an exaggerated sense of urgency.

**NO** Mountain climbing can be dangerous. You must know correct procedures**!** You must have the proper equipment**!** Otherwise, you could die**!**

**YES** Mountain climbing can be dangerous. You must know correct procedures**.** You must have the proper equipment**.** Otherwise, you could die**!**

Never use (!) to communicate amazement or sarcasm. Choose words to deliver your message.

**NO** At 29,035 feet **(!)**, Mt. Everest is the world's highest mountain. Yet, Chris **(!)** wants to climb it.

**YES** At **a majestic** 29,035 feet, Mt. Everest is the world's highest mountain. Yet, Chris, **amazingly**, wants to climb it.

**EXERCISE 23-1** Insert any needed periods, question marks, and exclamation points and delete any unneeded ones. For help, consult all sections of this chapter.

EXAMPLE Dr Madan Kataria, who calls himself the Giggling Guru (!), established the world's first laughter club in 1995.

    Dr**.** Madan Kataria, who calls himself the Giggling Guru**,** established the world's first laughter club in 1995.

1. More than 1,000 (?) laughter clubs exist throughout the world, each seeking to promote health by reducing stress and strengthening the immune system!

2. Dr Madan Kataria, a physician in Bombay, India, developed a yoga-like (!) strategy based on group (!) laughter and then set up laughter clubs.

3. Laughter clubs say, "Yes!" when asked, "Is laughter the best medicine."

4. The clubs' activities include breathing and stretching exercises and playful (?) behaviors, such as performing the opera laugh (!), the chicken laugh (!), and the "Ho-Ho, Ha-Ha" (?) exercise.

5. According to the German psychologist Dr Michael Titze, "In the 1950s people used to laugh eighteen minutes a day (!), but today we laugh not more than six (?) minutes per day, despite huge rises in the standard of living."

**EXERCISE 23-2** Insert needed periods, question marks, and exclamation points. For help, consult all sections of this chapter.

In May 2003, the fiftieth anniversary of the first successful ascent of Mt Everest drew 500 climbers to the icy, treacherous peak A 15-year-old became the youngest person to scale Everest, and a 70-year-old became the oldest Can you imagine that some people broke speed records as well, several of which they broke on the same day One man climbed Everest for the thirteenth time When Edmund Hillary and Tenzing Norgay became the first people to reach the summit, on May 29, 1953, they did not have the advantage of oxygen tanks, thousands of yards of fixed rope, or 60 aluminum ladders set up across a perilous ice fall Today's climbers benefit from all these technological advances, in addition to ultralight equipment and thousands of local people organized to carry supplies and set up camp If the climb is no longer as difficult as it was for Hillary and Tenzing, what is the reason for Everest's continuing fascination Other Himalayan peaks are harder to climb, but none, of course, is taller Perhaps that is the reason for Everest's special lure: nowhere else can a climber actually sit on top of the world

# Chapter 24

## COMMAS

### 24a  What is the role of the comma?

Commas are the most frequently used marks of punctuation, occurring twice as often as all other punctuation marks combined. A comma must be used in certain places, it must not be used in other places, and it's optional in still other places. This chapter helps you sort through the various rules.

For quick access to most answers when you have a comma question, consult Box 24.1. The sections in parentheses indicate where you can find fuller explanations.

---

**SUMMARY BOX** 24.1

### Key uses of commas

**COMMAS WITH COORDINATING CONJUNCTIONS LINKING INDEPENDENT CLAUSES (24B)**

> Postcards are ideal for brief greetings**, and** they can also be miniature works of art. [*and* is a coordinating conjunction]

**COMMAS AFTER INTRODUCTORY ELEMENTS (24C)**

> **Although most postcards cost only a dime,** one recently sold for thousands of dollars. [clause]

> **On postcard racks,** several designs are usually available. [phrase]

> **For example,** animals are timeless favorites. [transitional expression]

> **However,** most cards show local landmarks. [word]

**COMMAS WITH ITEMS IN A SERIES (24D)**

> **Places, paintings, and people** appear on postcards. [*and* between last two items]

> **Places, paintings, people, animals** occupy dozens of display racks. [no *and* between last two items]

---

## Key uses of commas

**COMMAS WITH COORDINATE ADJECTIVES (24E)**

Some postcards feature **appealing, dramatic** scenes.

**NO COMMAS WITH CUMULATIVE ADJECTIVES (24E)**

Other postcards feature **famous historical** scenes.

**COMMAS WITH NONRESTRICTIVE ELEMENTS (24F)**

**Four years after the first postcard appeared,** the US government began to issue prestamped postcards. [nonrestrictive element introduces independent clause]

The Golden Age of postcards, **which lasted from about 1900 to 1929,** yielded many especially valuable cards. [nonrestrictive element interrupts independent clause]

Collectors attend postcard shows, **which are similar to baseball-card shows.** [nonrestrictive element ends independent clause]

**NO COMMAS WITH RESTRICTIVE ELEMENTS (24F)**

Collectors **who attend these shows** may specialize in a particular kind of postcard. [restrictive clause]

**COMMAS WITH QUOTED WORDS (24H)**

One collector told me, "Attending a show is like digging for buried treasure." [quoted words at end of sentence]

"I always expect to find a priceless postcard," he said. [quoted words at start of sentence]

"Everyone there," he joked, "believes a million-dollar card is hidden in the next stack." [quoted words interrupted mid-sentence]

## 24b   How do commas work with coordinating conjunctions?

Never use a comma when a coordinating conjunction links only two words, two PHRASES, or two DEPENDENT CLAUSES.

**NO**    Habitat for Humanity depends on volunteers for **labor, and donations** to help with its construction projects. [*Labor* and *donations* are two words; the conjunction explains their relationship. No comma is needed.]

**YES**    Habitat for Humanity depends on volunteers for **labor and donations** to help with its construction projects.

**NO** Each language has **a beauty of its own, and forms of expression** that are duplicated nowhere else. [A *beauty of its own* and *forms of expression* are only two phrases.]

**YES** Each language has **a beauty of its own and forms of expression** that are duplicated nowhere else.

—Margaret Mead, "Unispeak"

Do use a comma when a coordinating conjunction links two or more INDEPENDENT CLAUSES. Place the comma before the coordinating conjunction. Box 24.2 shows this pattern.

---

**PATTERN BOX 24.2**

## Commas before coordinating conjunctions that link independent clauses

$$\text{Independent clause,} \begin{cases} \text{and} \\ \text{but} \\ \text{for} \\ \text{or} \\ \text{nor} \\ \text{yet} \\ \text{so} \end{cases} \text{independent clause.}$$

---

The sky turned dark gray, **and** the wind died suddenly.

The November morning had just begun, **but** it looked like dusk.

Shopkeepers closed their stores early, **for** they wanted to get home.

Soon high winds would start, **or** thick snow would begin silently.

Farmers could not continue harvesting, **nor** could they round up their animals in distant fields.

People on the road tried to reach safety, **yet** a few unlucky ones were stranded.

The firehouse whistle blew four times, **so** everyone knew a blizzard was closing in.

### EXCEPTIONS

- When two independent clauses are very short and they contrast with each other, you can link them with a comma without using a coordinating conjunction: *Mosquitoes don't bite, they stab.* Some instructors consider this an error, so in ACADEMIC WRITING, you'll never be wrong if you use a period or semicolon (Chapter 25) instead of a comma.

- When one or both independent clauses linked by a coordinating conjunction happen to contain other commas, dropping the coordinating conjunction and using a semicolon instead of the comma can help clarify meaning.

> With temperatures below freezing, the snow did not melt; and **people** wondered, gazing at the white landscape, when they would see grass again.

**ALERTS:** (1) Never put a comma *after* a coordinating conjunction that joins independent clauses.

| NO | A house is renovated in two weeks **but,** an apartment takes a week. |
| --- | --- |
| YES | A house is renovated in two weeks**, but** an apartment takes a week. |

(2) Never use a comma alone between independent clauses, or you'll create the error known as a COMMA SPLICE (see Chapter 13).

| NO | Five inches of snow fell in two hours, driving was hazardous. |
| --- | --- |
| YES | Five inches of snow fell in two hours**, and** driving was hazardous. ◆ |

**EXERCISE 24-1** Working individually or in a group, combine each pair of sentences using the coordinating conjunction shown in parentheses. Rearrange words when necessary. For help, consult 24b.

EXAMPLE   Children spend less time playing outdoors than ever before. That has been found to be a significant problem. (and)

Children spend less time playing outdoors than ever before, **and** that has been found to be a significant problem.

1. If your parents ever said to you, "Go outside and burn off some energy," you should thank them. They did you a big favor. (for)
2. Spending time outside as children is good for people. Now there is scientific proof. (and)
3. As children play outside, their senses are stimulated. That helps them learn in numerous ways. (and)
4. For example, children's vision is fully stimulated by being outside. They should spend more time playing outdoors than reading or watching TV, which stimulates only a narrow part of their vision. (so)

5. When children spend time playing outside, they may engage in intense physical activity. They may be less active but still discover the magic of the natural world. (or)

6. The outdoors can be a child's greatest source of stimulation. Many parents don't realize this. (yet)

7. Sadly enough, recess at many schools has been reduced. Children miss out on an opportunity for what scientists now know is another form of education. (so)

8. But as people learn more about the many benefits of outdoor play for children, parents will not allow children to spend so much time on indoor activities. Schools will not continue to reduce recess time. (nor)

9. Instead, school leaders may heed renowned educators such as Maria Montessori, Rudolf Steiner, and Howard Gardner, who understood the close connection between movement and learning. Children will once again enjoy the benefits of a longer recess. (and)

10. Enjoying the natural world may be part of our genetic makeup. It only makes sense that children should be encouraged to get their vitamin D from sunlight and to use up some energy. (so)

## 24c How do commas work with introductory clauses, phrases, and words?

A comma follows any introductory element that comes before an INDEPENDENT CLAUSE. An introductory element can be a CLAUSE, PHRASE, or words. Because these elements are not sentences by themselves, you need to join them to independent clauses. Box 24.3 shows this pattern.

---

**PATTERN BOX 24.3**

### Commas with introductory clauses, phrases, and words

- Introductory clause,
- Introductory phrase, ⟶ independent clause.
- Introductory word,

---

**When the topic is dieting,** many people say sugar craving is their worst problem. [introductory dependent clause]

**Between 1544 and 1689,** sugar refineries appeared in London and New York. [introductory prepositional phrase]

**Beginning in infancy,** we develop lifelong tastes for sweet foods. [introductory participial phrase]

**Sweets being a temptation for many adults,** most parents avoid commercial baby foods that contain sugar. [introductory absolute phrase]

**For example,** fructose comes from fruit, but it's still sugar. [introductory transitional expression]

**Nevertheless,** many people think fructose isn't harmful. [introductory conjunctive adverb]

**To satisfy a craving for ice cream,** even timid people sometimes brave midnight streets. [introductory infinitive phrase]

### EXCEPTION

When an introductory element is short, and the sentence can be understood easily, some writers omit the comma. However, in ACADEMIC WRITING, you'll never be wrong if you use the comma.

> **YES** In 1992, the Americans with Disabilities Act was passed. [preferred]

> **YES** In 1992 the Americans with Disabilities Act was passed.

An **interjection** is an introductory word that conveys surprise or other emotions. Use a comma after an interjection at the beginning of a sentence: *Oh, we didn't realize that you're allergic to cats. Yes, your sneezing worries me.*

**ALERT:** Use a comma before and after a transitional expression that falls in the middle of a sentence. When the transitional expression starts a sentence, follow it with a comma. When the transitional expression ends a sentence, put a comma before it.

**By the way,** the parade begins at noon. [introductory transitional expression with comma after it]

The parade, **by the way,** begins at noon. [transitional expression with comma before and after it, in middle of sentence]

The parade begins at noon, **by the way.** [transitional expression with comma before it, at end of sentence]

**However,** our float isn't finished. [introductory conjunctive adverb with comma after it]

Our float, **however,** isn't finished. [conjunctive adverb with comma before and after it, in middle of sentence]

Our float isn't finished**, however**. [conjunctive adverb with comma before it, at end of sentence] ◆

**EXERCISE 24-2** Working individually or with a group, combine each set of sentences into one sentence according to the direction in parentheses. Use a comma after the introductory element. You can add, delete, and rearrange words as needed. For help, consult 24c.

EXAMPLE  People have known that humor is good for them. They have known this for a long time. (Begin with *for a long time.*)

**For a long time,** people have known that humor is good for them.

1. People laugh. Scientists study them to find out what actually happens. (Begin with *when.*)

2. Scientists track our physiological reactions. They discover the chemicals we produce while we are laughing. (Begin with *in fact.*)

3. Our brains use dopamine when we laugh. Dopamine is a chemical we produce that makes us feel good. (Begin with *produced.*)

4. We sometimes activate our tear ducts by laughing. That reduces stress. (Begin with *interestingly.*)

5. Scientists tested people's saliva immediately after they laughed. Scientists concluded that immune systems may benefit from laughter. (Begin with *immediately.*)

6. Blood pressure and heart rates tend to go below baseline after we laugh. People should be happy about this effect because that's what happens after we exercise well. (Begin with *although.*)

7. Laughter causes the inner lining of our blood vessels to expand. This expansion produces good chemicals in our bodies. (Begin with *in addition.*)

8. One of these good chemicals is nitric oxide. It reduces inflammation and clotting. (Begin with *in the human body.*)

9. Laughter may even help with pain management. Laughter seems to have an analgesic effect. (Begin with *seeming.*)

10. Humor has so many physical benefits, and it makes us feel better. Try to enjoy a few laughs every day. (Begin with *because.*)

## 24d How do commas work with items in a series?

A **series** is a group of three or more elements—words, PHRASES, or CLAUSES—that match in grammatical form and are of equal importance in a sentence. Box 24.4 shows this pattern.

---

**PATTERN BOX 24.4**

### Commas in a series

- word**,** word**, and** word
- phrase**,** phrase**, and** phrase
- clause**,** clause**, and** clause

- word**,** word**,** word
- phrase**,** phrase**,** phrase
- clause**,** clause**,** clause

---

Marriage requires **sexual, financial, and emotional** discipline.
— Anne Roiphe, "Why Marriages Fail"

Culture is a way of **thinking, feeling, believing**.
— Clyde Kluckhohn, *Mirror for Man*

My love of flying goes back to those early days **of roller skates, of swings, and of bicycles**.

— Tresa Wiggins, student

We have been taught **that children develop by ages and stages, that the steps are pretty much the same for everybody, and that to grow out of the limited behavior of childhood, we must climb them all**.

— Gail Sheehy, *Passages*

Many general publications omit the comma between the next to last item of a series and the coordinating conjunction. Recently, practice is changing even in ACADEMIC WRITING, which means that some instructors require the use of a comma here and others consider it an error. Check with your instructor.

> **NO** The sweater comes in **blue, green, pink and black.** [Do the sweaters come in three or four colors?]

> **YES** The sweater comes in **blue, green, pink, and black.** [The comma before *and* clarifies that the sweaters come in four colors.]

At all times, however, follow the "toast, juice, and ham and eggs rule." That is, when one of the items in a series contains *and,* don't use a comma in that item.

When items in a series contain commas or other punctuation, separate them with SEMICOLONS instead of commas (25e).

> If it's a bakery, they have to sell cake; if it's a photography shop, they have to develop film; and if it's a dry-goods store, they have to sell warm underwear.
>
> —Art Buchwald, "Birth Control for Banks"

Numbered or lettered lists within a sentence are considered items in a series. With three or more items, use commas (or semicolons if the items themselves contain commas) to separate them.

> To file your insurance claim, please enclose (1) a letter requesting payment, (2) a police report about the robbery, and (3) proof of purchase of the items you say are missing.

**ALERT:** In a series, never use a comma before the first item or after the last item, unless a different rule makes it necessary.

| NO | Many **artists, writers, and composers, have indulged** in daydreaming. |

| YES | Many artists, writers, and composers have indulged in daydreaming. |

| NO | Such dreamers include**,** Miró, Debussy, Dostoevsky, and Dickinson. |

| YES | Such dreamers include Miró, Debussy, Dostoevsky, and Dickinson. |

| YES | Such dreamers include, **of course,** Miró, Debussy, Dostoevsky, and Dickinson. [As a transitional expression, *of course* is set off from the rest of the sentence by commas before and after it (24c).] ◆ |

**EXERCISE 24-3** Insert commas to separate the items in a series. If a sentence needs no commas, explain why. For help, consult 24d.

EXAMPLE    Families from New York New Jersey and Pennsylvania raise the puppies that become Seeing Eye dogs.

Families from *New York, New Jersey, and Pennsylvania* raise the puppies that become Seeing Eye dogs.

1. To socialize future Seeing Eye dogs, families with children ages 9 to 14 care for specially bred German shepherds retrievers and mixed-breed puppies for up to 16 months.

2. One youngster in each family becomes the pup's primary caretaker and is responsible for feeding training and grooming the future Seeing Eye dog.

3. While living with their families, the pups learn basic obedience commands, such as sit stay come and down.

4. Groups of families get together frequently to take their Seeing Eye dogs-in-training on outings, so that the puppies become familiar with things that frighten some dogs, such as riding in cars being in crowds walking on slippery floors and hearing loud noises.

5. When the puppies grow up, the families have the pain of giving them up but the satisfaction of knowing that their dogs will lead happy and productive lives while improving the quality of life for their future owners.

## 24e How do commas work with coordinate adjectives?

**Coordinate adjectives** are two or more ADJECTIVES of equal weight that describe—that is, modify—a NOUN. In contrast, **cumulative adjectives** build meaning from word to word, as they move toward the noun. Box 24.5 shows the pattern for coordinate adjectives. The key to applying this rule is recognizing when adjectives are coordinate and when they aren't. Box 24.6 tells you how.

The audience cheered when the **pulsating, rhythmic** music filled the stadium. [*Pulsating* and *rhythmic* are coordinate adjectives.]

Each band had a **distinctive musical** style. [*Distinctive* and *musical* aren't coordinate adjectives.]

---

**PATTERN BOX 24.5**

### Commas with coordinate adjectives

**coordinate adjective, coordinate adjective** noun

---

**ALERT:** Don't put a comma between a final coordinate adjective and the noun it modifies.

**NO**   Hundreds of **roaring, cheering, yelling, fans** filled the stadium.

**YES**   Hundreds of **roaring, cheering, yelling fans** filled the stadium. ◆

## SUMMARY BOX 24.6

### Tests for coordinate and cumulative adjectives

If either one of these tests works, the adjectives are coordinate and require a comma between them.

- Can the order of the adjectives be reversed without changing the meaning or creating nonsense? If yes, use a comma.

  **NO**    The concert featured **new several** bands. [*New several* makes no sense.]

  **YES**    The **huge, restless** crowd waited for the concert to begin. [*Restless, huge* still carries the same meaning, so these are coordinate adjectives.]

- Can *and* be sensibly inserted between the adjectives? If yes, use a comma.

  **NO**    The concert featured **several and new** bands. [*Several and new* makes no sense.]

  **YES**    The **huge and restless** crowd waited. [Modifier *huge and restless* makes sense, so these are coordinate adjectives.]

---

**EXERCISE 24-4**    Insert commas to separate coordinate adjectives. If a sentence needs no commas, explain why. For help, consult 24e.

**EXAMPLE**    Only corn grown for popcorn pops consistently because all other kinds of corn lack tough enamel-like shells.

Only corn grown for popcorn pops consistently because all other kinds of corn lack *tough,* *enamel-like* shells.

1. The outside of an unpopped popcorn kernel is a hard plastic-like coating.

2. Inside an unpopped kernel is a soft starchy substance combined with water.

3. Applying heat causes the water molecules to expand until the pressure pops the dark yellow kernel.

4. The popped kernel turns itself inside out and absorbs air into its white pulpy matter.

5. The thinner softer shells of nonpopcorn corn don't allow water to heat to the high popping temperature.

415

## 24f How do commas work with nonrestrictive elements?

A **restrictive element** contains information (a descriptive word, clause, or phrase) that's essential for a sentence to deliver its message; thus, it is often called an *essential element*. A **nonrestrictive element** contains information that's not essential for a sentence to deliver its meaning, and therefore, it is often called a *nonessential element*. The key is in recognizing what's essential (restrictive) and what's nonessential (nonrestrictive) in a sentence. Box 24.7 defines and explains the differences in the meanings of these terms.

---

**SUMMARY BOX** 24.7

### Restrictive and nonrestrictive defined

**RESTRICTIVE**

A restrictive element contains information essential for the sentence to deliver its message. By being essential, the words in the element limit—that is, "restrict"—the meaning in some way. Don't use commas with restrictive elements.

> Many US states retest drivers **who are over sixty-five** to check their driving competency.

The information *who are over sixty-five* is essential to understanding the sentence because it limits or restricts the meaning of *drivers* to only those over the age of sixty-five. Drivers *under* sixty-five are not included. To check whether an element is essential, drop it and read the sentence. If the meaning of the sentence changes, then the information element is essential in delivering the message intended in the sentence. This means the element is restrictive (essential), and <u>commas are not used</u>.

**NONRESTRICTIVE**

A nonrestrictive element contains information that's *not* essential for the sentence to deliver its message. By being nonessential, the words in the element don't limit—or "restrict"—the meaning in some way. Use commas with nonrestrictive (nonessential) elements.

> My parents**, who are both over sixty-five,** took a defensive-driving course.

The information *who are both over sixty-five* is not essential because the words *my parents* carry the sentence's message so that we know who took a defensive driving course. (Information about their age is "extra" to this message, so <u>commas are required</u>.)

---

Box 24.8 shows the pattern for comma use with nonrestrictive elements. The pattern for restrictive elements calls for no commas.

**PATTERN BOX 24.8**

## Commas with nonrestrictive elements

**Nonrestrictive element,** independent clause.

Beginning of independent clause, **nonrestrictive element,** end of independent clause.

Independent clause, **nonrestrictive element.**

Restrictive and nonrestrictive elements can fall at the beginning, in the middle, or at the end of a sentence. To test whether an element is nonrestrictive, read the sentence without the element. If the meaning of the sentence does not change, the element is nonrestrictive.

### MORE EXAMPLES OF RESTRICTIVE ELEMENTS

Some people **in my neighborhood** enjoy jogging. [The reader needs the information *in my neighborhood* to know which people enjoy jogging. The information is essential, so no commas are used.]

Some people **who are in excellent physical condition** enjoy jogging. [The reader needs the information *who are in excellent physical condition* to know which people enjoy jogging. The information is essential, so no commas are used.]

The agricultural scientist **Wendy Singh** has developed a new fertilization technique. [*Wendy Singh* is essential to identify exactly which agricultural scientist developed the new technique, so no commas are used.]

### MORE EXAMPLES OF NONRESTRICTIVE ELEMENTS

**An energetic person,** Anna Hom enjoys jogging. [Without knowing that Anna Hom is *an energetic person*, the reader can understand that she enjoys jogging. The information is nonessential, so a comma is used.]

Anna Hom, **who is in excellent physical condition,** enjoys jogging. [Without knowing Anna Hom's *physical condition*, the reader can understand that Anna Hom enjoys jogging. The information is nonessential, so commas are used.]

Anna Hom enjoys jogging, **which is also Adam's favorite pastime**. [Without knowing about *Adam's favorite pastime*, the reader can understand that Anna Hom enjoys jogging. The information is nonessential, so commas are used.]

417

The agricultural scientist**, a new breed of farmer,** explains how to control a farming environment. [Without knowing that the scientist is *a new breed of farmer,* the reader can understand that the agricultural scientist explains how to control a farming environment. The information is nonessential, so commas are used.]

**EXERCISE 24-5** Using your knowledge of restrictive and nonrestrictive elements, insert commas as needed. If a sentence is correct, explain why. For help, consult 24f.

EXAMPLE  During the 1990s when Internet start-ups were proliferating computer science majors often received many job offers even before they graduated.

During the 1990s**,** *when Internet start-ups were proliferating***,** computer science majors often received many job offers even before they graduated.

1. In the fall of 2000 at the height of the Internet boom over 700 students packed a lecture hall for an introductory computer science course at the University of California at Berkeley.
2. Students who arrived late for class had to stand around the sides and back of the room.
3. A few years later when the boom began to turn to bust only 350 students registered for the introductory course.
4. Something similar occurred at Carnegie Mellon University where the number of students applying to the School of Computer Science fell by 36 percent.
5. These students who understood the US economic cycle switched to less specialized majors.
6. A typical student might change his or her major from computer science to business information technology which offers a wider variety of commercial skills.
7. Other business-related majors such as communications and advertising are becoming more popular.
8. Because educators and computer scientists know that the decrease in the number of computer science majors is only temporary they are not worried about the future.
9. Each time the US economy recovers increasing demands for advances in computer technology companies suddenly need programmers and systems analysts again.
10. Then students whose strongest interest is computer science will flock back to the courses that once more promise lucrative and interesting job possibilities.

## 24g How do commas set off parenthetical expressions, contrasts, words of direct address, and tag sentences?

**Parenthetical expressions** are "asides." They add information but aren't necessary for understanding the message of a sentence. Set them off with parentheses or commas.

American farmers **(according to US government figures)** export more wheat than they sell at home.

A major drought**, sad to say,** wiped out this year's wheat crop.

Expressions of **contrast** state what is *not* the case. Set them off with commas.

Feeding the world's population is a serious**, though not impossible,** problem.

We must work against world hunger continuously**, not only when famines strike**.

Words of **direct address** name the person or group being spoken to (addressed). Set them off with commas.

Join me**, brothers and sisters,** to end hunger.

Your contribution to the Relief Fund**, Steve,** will help us greatly.

A **tag sentence** is a normal sentence that ends with a "tag," an attached phrase or question. Set off a tag with a comma. When the tag is a question, the sentence ends with a question mark. This holds whether or not the **tag question** is formed with a CONTRACTION.

People will give blood regularly**, I hope.**

The response to the blood drive was impressive**, wasn't it?**

**EXERCISE 24-6**   Add commas to set off any parenthetical or contrasting elements, words of direct address, and tag sentences. Adjust end punctuation as necessary. For help, consult 24g.

EXAMPLE    Writer's block it seems to me is a misunderstood phenomenon.
           Writer's block*, it seems to me,* is a misunderstood phenomenon.

1. An inability to write some say stems from lack of discipline and a tendency to procrastinate.
2. In other words the only way to overcome writer's block is to exert more willpower.

3. But writer's block is a complex psychological event that happens to conscientious people not just procrastinators.

4. Such people strangely enough are often unconsciously rebelling against their own self-tyranny and rigid standards of perfection.

5. If I told you my fellow writer that all it takes to start writing again is to quit punishing yourself, you would think I was crazy wouldn't you?

## 24h How do commas work with quoted words?

**Explanatory words** are *said, stated, declared,* and other words that introduce DIRECT DISCOURSE. When they fall in the same sentence, quoted words are set off from explanatory words. Box 24.9 shows this pattern.

Speaking of ideal love, the poet William Blake wrote, "Love seeketh not itself to please."

"My love is a fever," said William Shakespeare about love's passion.

"I love no love," proclaimed the poet Mary Coleridge, "but thee."

---

**PATTERN BOX 24.9**

### Commas with quoted words

Explanatory words, "Quoted words."

"Quoted words," explanatory words.

"Quoted words begin," explanatory words, "quoted words continue."

---

### EXCEPTION

When the quoted words are blended into the grammatical structure of your sentence, don't use commas to set them off. These are instances of INDIRECT DISCOURSE, usually occurring with *as* and *that.*

The duke describes the duchess **as** "too soon made glad."

The duchess insists **that** "appearing glad often is but a deception."

**ALERT:** When the quoted words end with an exclamation point or a question mark, retain that original punctuation, even if explanatory words follow.

| | |
|---|---|
| **QUOTED WORDS** | *"O Romeo! Romeo!"* |
| **NO** | "O Romeo! Romeo!," whispered Juliet from her window. |
| **NO** | "O Romeo! Romeo," whispered Juliet from her window. |
| **YES** | "O Romeo! Romeo!" whispered Juliet from her window. |

| QUOTED WORDS | *"Wherefore art thou Romeo?"* |
|---|---|
| **NO** | "Wherefore art thou Romeo**?,**" Juliet urgently asked. |
| **NO** | "Wherefore art thou Romeo**,**" Juliet urgently asked. |
| **YES** | "Wherefore art thou Romeo**?"** Juliet urgently asked. ◆ |

**EXERCISE 24-7** Punctuate the following dialogue correctly. If a sentence is correct, explain why. For help, consult 24h.

EXAMPLE  "Can you tell me just one thing?," asked the tourist.
         "Can you tell me just one thing**?"** asked the tourist.

1. "I'm happy to answer any questions you have" said the rancher to the tourist.

2. "Well, then" said the tourist "I'd like to know how you make ends meet on such a tiny ranch."

3. "Do you see that man leaning against the shed over there?" asked the rancher.

4. The rancher continued "He works for me, but I don't pay him any money. Instead, I have promised him that after two years of work, he will own the ranch."

5. "Then, I'll work for him, and in two more years, the ranch will be mine again!," said the rancher with a smile.

---

**24i** **How do commas work in dates, names, addresses, correspondence, and numbers?**

When you write dates, names, addresses, correspondence, and numbers, use commas according to accepted practice. Boxes 24.10 through 24.13 provide some guidelines.

---

**SUMMARY BOX** 24.10

## Commas with dates

- Use a comma between the date and the year: *July 20, 1969.*
- Use a comma between the day and the date: *Sunday, July 20.*
- Within a sentence, use a comma on both sides of the year in a full date: *Everyone planned to be near a TV set on July 20, 1969, to watch the lunar landing.*

---

**SUMMARY BOX** 24.10 *continued*

## Commas with dates

- Never use a comma when only the month and year, or the month and day, are given. Also, never use a comma between the season and year.

  **YES**  People knew that one day in **July 1969** would change the world.

  **YES**  News coverage was especially heavy on **July 21**.

  **YES**  In **summer 1969** a man walked on the moon.

- Never use a comma in an inverted date, a form used in the US military and throughout the world except in the United States.

  **YES**  People stayed near their televisions on **20 July 1969** to watch the lunar landing.

---

**SUMMARY BOX** 24.11

## Commas with names, places, and addresses

- When an abbreviated academic degree (*MD, PhD*) comes after a person's name, use a comma between the name and the title (*Angie Eng, MD*), and also after the title if other words follow in the sentence: *The jury listened closely to the expert testimony of **Angie Eng, MD, last week***.

- When an indicator of birth order or succession (*Jr., Sr., III, IV*) follows a name, never use a comma: *Martin Luther **King Jr.*** or *Henry **Ford II***

- When you invert a person's name, use a comma to separate the last name from the first: ***Troyka, David***

- When city and state names are written together, use a comma to separate them: ***Philadelphia, Pennsylvania.*** If the city and state fall within a sentence, use a comma after the state as well: *My family settled in **Philadelphia, Pennsylvania,** before I was born.*

- When a complete address is part of a sentence, use a comma to separate all the items, except the state and ZIP code: *I wrote to **Shelly Kupperman, 1001 Rule Road, Upper Saddle River, NJ 07458,** for more information about the comma.*

**SUMMARY BOX** 24.12

## Commas in correspondence

- For the opening of an informal letter, use a comma: **Dear Betty,**
- For the opening of a business or formal letter, use a colon:
  **Dear Ms. Kiviat:**
- For the close of a letter, use a comma:
  **Sincerely yours,**     **Best regards,**     **Love,**

**SUMMARY BOX** 24.13

## Commas with numbers

- Counting from right to left, put a comma after every three digits in numbers with more than four digits.

  72,867                    156,567,066

- A comma is optional in most four-digit numbers. Be consistent within each piece of writing.

  $1776                     $1,776

  1776 miles                1,776 miles

  1776 potatoes             1,776 potatoes

- Never use a comma in a four-digit year: **1990** (*Note:* If the year has five digits or more, do use a comma: **25,000 BC**.)

- Never use a comma in an address of four digits or more:
  **12161 Dean Drive**

- Never use a comma in a page number of four digits or more:
  *see page 1338*

- Use a comma to separate related measurements written as words:
  *five feet, four inches*

- Use a comma to separate a scene from an act in a play:
  *act II, scene iv* (or *act 2, scene 4*)

- Use a comma to separate references to a page and a line:
  *page 10, line 6*

**EXERCISE 24-8** Insert commas where they are needed. For help, consult 24i.

EXAMPLE   On June 1 1984 the small German-French production company
released a feature film called *Paris Texas*.

On June 1, 1984, the small German-French production
company released a feature film called *Paris, Texas*.

1. Made by the noted German director Wim Wenders, *Paris Texas* was set
   in an actual town in Lamar County Texas with a population of 24699.

2. The movie's title was clearly intended to play off the slightly more
   famous Paris in France.

3. The custom of naming little towns in the United States after
   cosmopolitan urban centers in the Old World has resulted in such
   places as Athens Georgia and St. Petersburg Florida.

4. As of December 1 2005 the American St. Petersburg was estimated to
   have nearly 250000 citizens and the American Athens nearly 109000.

5. By comparison, St. Petersburg Russia and Athens Greece were estimated
   to have populations of 4 million and 1 million, respectively.

## 24j   How do commas clarify meaning?

A comma is sometimes needed to clarify the meaning of a sentence, even
though no rule calls for one. The best solution is to revise the sentence.

NO   Of the gymnastic team's twenty five were injured.

YES   Of the gymnastic team's **twenty, five** were injured.

YES   Of **twenty on** the gymnastic team, five were injured. [preferred]

NO   Those who can practice many hours a day.

YES   **Those who can,** practice many hours a day.

YES   **They** practice many hours a day **when they can**. [preferred]

NO   George dressed and performed for the sellout crowd.

YES   **George dressed,** and performed for the sellout crowd.

YES   **After** George dressed, **he** performed for the sellout crowd.
[preferred]

**EXERCISE 24-9** Working individually or with a group, insert commas to prevent misreading. For help, consult 24j.

EXAMPLE   For scientists tracking and measuring hurricanes is still an
inexact science.

For scientists, tracking and measuring hurricanes is still an
inexact science.

1. Lasting for thirteen days in August 1992 Hurricane Andrew after 2005's Katrina was the second most expensive hurricane.
2. Andrew was rated a category four smaller than 2005's Katrina when it made landfall in south Florida.
3. The highest gust officially recorded 164 miles per hour at 130 feet above the ground occurred before Andrew shut down the National Hurricane Center's measuring devices.

4. The thousands of vortexes within Andrew as with many high-intensity storms are what caused the worst damage.
5. Andrew difficult to measure accurately was upgraded from a category four to a category five hurricane ten years after it occurred.

## 24k    How can I avoid misusing commas?

Throughout this chapter, Alert notes remind you about comma misuses as they relate to each comma rule. Most of these misuses are overuses—inserting a comma where one is unnecessary. This section summarizes the Alert notes and lists other frequent misuses of the comma.

When advice against overusing a comma clashes with a rule requiring one, follow the rule that requires the comma.

> The town of Kitty Hawk, North Carolina, attracts thousands of tourists each year. [Even though the comma after *North Carolina* separates the subject and its verb (which it normally shouldn't), the comma is required here because of the rule that calls for a comma when the name of a state follows the name of a city within a sentence (24i).]

### 24k.1  Commas with coordinating conjunctions

Never use a comma after a COORDINATING CONJUNCTION that joins two INDEPENDENT CLAUSES, unless another rule makes it necessary (24b). Also, don't use a comma to separate two items joined with a coordinating conjunction—there must be at least three (24d).

> **NO**   The sky was dark gray **and,** it looked like dusk.
>
> **YES**   The sky was dark gray**,** **and** it looked like dusk.

| NO | **The moon, and the stars** were shining last night. |
|---|---|
| YES | **The moon and the stars** were shining last night. |

## 24k.2 Commas with subordinating conjunctions and prepositions

Never put a comma after a SUBORDINATING CONJUNCTION or a PREPOSITION, unless another rule makes it necessary.

| NO | **Although,** the storm brought high winds, it did no damage. |
|---|---|
| YES | **Although the storm brought high winds,** it did no damage. [comma follows full subordinated dependent clause, not the subordinate conjunction that begins it] |

| NO | The storm did no damage **although,** it brought high winds. |
|---|---|
| YES | The storm did no damage **although it brought high winds.** [no comma after a subordinating conjunction] |

| NO | People expected worse **between,** the high winds and the heavy downpour. |
|---|---|
| YES | People expected worse **between the high winds and the heavy downpour.** [preposition begins sentence element that needs no comma before or after] |

## 24k.3 Commas in a series

Never use a comma before the first, or after the last, item in a series, unless another rule makes it necessary (24d).

| NO | The gymnasium was decorated **with, red, white, and blue** ribbons for the Fourth of July. |
|---|---|
| NO | The gymnasium was decorated with **red, white, and blue, ribbons** for the Fourth of July. |
| YES | The gymnasium was decorated with **red, white, and blue** ribbons for the Fourth of July. |

Never put a comma between a final COORDINATE ADJECTIVE and the NOUN that the adjectives modify. Also, don't use a comma between adjectives that are not coordinate (24e).

| NO | He wore an **old, baggy, sweater.** |
|---|---|
| YES | He wore an **old, baggy sweater.** [coordinate adjectives] |

**NO**  He has **several, new sweaters.**

**YES**  He has **several new sweaters.** [noncoordinate, or cumulative, adjectives]

## 24k.4  Commas with restrictive elements

Never use a comma to set off a RESTRICTIVE (essential) element from the rest of a sentence (24f).

**NO**  **Vegetables, stir-fried in a wok,** are crisp and flavorful. [The words *stir-fried in a wok* are essential, so they are not set off with commas.]

**YES**  **Vegetables stir-fried in a wok** are crisp and flavorful.

## 24k.5  Commas with quotations

Never use a comma to set off INDIRECT DISCOURSE; use a comma only with DIRECT DISCOURSE (24h).

**NO**  Jon said **that, he likes** stir-fried vegetables.

**YES**  Jon said **that he likes** stir-fried vegetables.

**YES**  **Jon said, "I like** stir-fried vegetables."

## 24k.6  Commas that separate a subject from its verb, a verb from its object, or a preposition from its object

A comma does not make sense between these elements, though in some cases another comma rule might supersede this guideline (as in the first example in section (24k).

**NO**  **The brothers Wright, made** their first successful airplane flights on December 17, 1903. [As a rule, a comma doesn't separate a subject from its verb.]

**YES**  **The brothers Wright made** their first successful airplane flights on December 17, 1903.

**NO**  These inventors enthusiastically **tackled, the problems** of powered flight and aerodynamics. [As a rule, a comma doesn't separate a verb from its object.]

**YES**  These inventors enthusiastically **tackled the problems** of powered flight and aerodynamics.

**NO** Airplane hobbyists **from, all over the world** visit Kitty Hawk's flight museum. [As a rule, a comma doesn't separate a preposition from its object.]

**YES** Airplane hobbyists **from all over the world** visit Kitty Hawk's flight museum.

**EXERCISE 24-10** Some commas have been deliberately misused in these sentences. Delete misused commas. If a sentence is correct, explain why. For help, consult all parts of this chapter, especially 24j and 24k.

**EXAMPLE** People who live in earthquake-prone regions, have long looked forward to reliable means of forecasting tremblers.

People who live in earthquake-prone *regions have* long looked forward to reliable means of forecasting tremblers.

1. Since the 1970s, scientists have attempted to provide accurate predictions of, earthquake size and intensity.
2. The task has turned out to be harder than expected, for research geologists have yet to develop a clear understanding of the many complex forces, that cause earthquakes.
3. The earth's crust is made up of large, rigid, plates that slide over a semiliquid mantle, and stress builds up when two plates meet.
4. Scientists need to understand, exactly when the stress will become so great that a quake results, but that has proved difficult.
5. Although, geologists can accurately predict the local aftershocks that result from a large earthquake, they cannot precisely determine when a big quake will hit or, when distant aftershocks will occur.
6. Scientists use information about tensions, along major cracks in rock layers, to understand the general process of predicting, where a large tremor will hit.
7. For example, geologists have predicted that the next major earthquake along, the North Anatolian fault in Turkey, will strike near the city of Istanbul.
8. Unfortunately, scientists cannot save thousands of lives by determining, even the approximate date of the expected large quake.
9. Interestingly, scientists once had amazing success in predicting a 1975 earthquake in Haicheng, China, after, a sequence of small earthquakes, changes in groundwater level, and strange behavior by animals.
10. However, geologists say that, even these clues did not successfully reveal the magnitude, and timing of any other major earthquake.

## 241 How can I avoid comma errors?

You can avoid most comma errors with these two bits of advice:

- As you write or reread what you've written, never insert a comma simply because you happen to pause to think or take a breath before moving on. Pausing isn't a reliable guide for writers, although that myth continues to thrive. Throughout the United States, and indeed the world, people's breathing rhythms, accents, and thinking patterns vary greatly.

- As you're writing, if you're unsure about a comma, insert it and circle the spot. Later, when you're EDITING, check this handbook for the rule that applies.

# Chapter 25

## SEMICOLONS

### 25a | What are the uses of a semicolon?

While a period signals the complete separation of INDEPENDENT CLAUSES, a **semicolon** indicates only a partial ("semi") separation. Use a semicolon in only two situations. A semicolon can replace a period between sentences that are closely related in meaning (25b and 25c). Also, a semicolon belongs between sentence structures that already contain one or more commas (25d) and with certain lists (25e).

### 25b | When can I use a semicolon, instead of a period, between independent clauses?

The choice between a period and a semicolon for separating independent clauses depends on whether your meaning is better communicated by a complete separation (period) or a partial separation (semicolon). Box 25.1 shows this pattern for using semicolons.

---

**PATTERN BOX 25.1**

**Semicolon I**

Independent clause; independent clause.

---

The desert known as Death Valley became a US National Park in 1994; it used to be a US National Monument.

This is my husband's second marriage; it's the first for me.
— Ruth Sidel, "Marion Deluca"

**ALERT:** Never use a comma alone between independent clauses—this rule will prevent you from creating the error known as a COMMA SPLICE (Chapter 13). ◆

## 25c When else can I use a semicolon between independent clauses?

When the second of a set of independent clauses closely related in meaning starts with a CONJUNCTIVE ADVERB or with a TRANSITIONAL EXPRESSION, you can choose to separate the clauses with a semicolon instead of a period. Also, insert a comma following a conjunctive adverb or transitional expression that starts an independent clause. Although some professional writers today omit the comma after short words (*then, next, soon*), the rule remains for most ACADEMIC WRITING. Box 25.2 shows this pattern for using semicolons.

**PATTERN BOX 25.2**

### Semicolon II

Independent clause**;** conjunctive adverb, independent clause.

Independent clause**;** transitional expression, independent clause.

The average annual rainfall in Death Valley is about two inches**;** **nevertheless,** hundreds of plant and animal species survive and even thrive there. [conjunctive adverb]

Photographers have spent years recording desert life cycles**; as a result,** we can watch bare sand flower after a spring storm. [transitional expression]

**ALERT:** Never use only a comma between independent clauses that are connected by a conjunctive adverb or word of transition—this rule will prevent you from creating the error known as a COMMA SPLICE. ◆

## 25d How do semicolons work with coordinating conjunctions?

As a general rule, when INDEPENDENT CLAUSES are linked by a COORDINATING CONJUNCTION, good practice calls for a comma, not a period or semicolon, before the coordinating conjunction (24b). However, when one or more of the independent clauses already contain a comma, link the independent clauses by substituting a semicolon for the period. This can help your reader see the relationship between the ideas more clearly. Box 25.3 (p. 432) shows the various combinations of this pattern.

## Semicolon III

Independent clause, one that contains a comma; coordinating conjunction followed by independent clause.

Independent clause; coordinating conjunction followed by independent clause, one that contains a comma.

Independent clause, one that contains a comma; coordinating conjunction followed by independent clause, one that contains a comma.

When the peacock has presented his back, the spectator will usually begin to walk around him to get a front view; **but** the peacock will continue to turn so that no front view is possible.
> —Flannery O'Connor, "The King of the Birds"

Our Constitution is in actual operation; everything appears to promise that it will last; **but** in this world, nothing is certain but death and taxes.
> —Benjamin Franklin, in a 1789 letter

For anything worth having, one must pay the price; **and** the price is always work, patience, love, self-sacrifice.
> —John Burroughs

## 25e When should I use semicolons between items in a series?

When a sentence contains a series of items that are long or that already contain one or more commas, separate the items with semicolons. Punctuating this way groups the elements so that your reader can see where one item ends and the next begins. Box 25.4 shows this pattern.

## Semicolon IV

Independent clause containing a series of items, any of which contains a comma; another item in the series; and another item in the series.

The assistant chefs chopped onions, green peppers, and parsley; sliced chicken and duck breasts into strips; started a broth simmering; **and** filled a large, shallow copper pan with oil.

## 25f  How do I avoid misusing the semicolon?

### NOT USING A SEMICOLON AFTER AN INTRODUCTORY PHRASE

If you use a semicolon after an introductory PHRASE, you create the error known as a SENTENCE FRAGMENT (Chapter 12).

**NO**  **Open until midnight;** the computer lab is well used. [Using a semicolon turns an introductory phrase into a sentence fragment.]

**YES**  **Open until midnight,** the computer lab is well used.

### NOT USING A SEMICOLON WITH A DEPENDENT CLAUSE

If you use a semicolon with a DEPENDENT CLAUSE, you create the error known as a sentence fragment.

**NO**  **Although the new dorms have computer facilities;** many students still prefer to go to the computer lab. [Using a semicolon turns a dependent clause into a sentence fragment.]

**YES**  **Although the new dorms have computer facilities,** many students still prefer to go to the computer lab.

### NOT USING A SEMICOLON TO INTRODUCE A LIST

When the words that introduce a list form an independent clause, use a colon, never a semicolon (26b).

**NO**  **The newscast featured three major stories;** the latest pictures of Uranus, a speech by the president, and dangerous brush fires in Nevada. [*The newscast featured three major stories* is an independent clause, so the punctuation before the list should be a colon, not a semicolon.]

**YES**  **The newscast featured three major stories:** the latest pictures of Uranus, a speech by the president, and dangerous brush fires in Nevada.

**EXERCISE 25-1**  Insert semicolons as needed in these items. Also, fix any incorrectly used semicolons. If a sentence is correct, explain why. For help, consult all sections of this chapter.

**EXAMPLE**  Bicycle racing is as popular in Europe as baseball or basketball is in the United States, it is even more heavily commercialized.

Bicycle racing is as popular in Europe as baseball or basketball is in the United States; it is even more heavily commercialized.

1. The Tour de France is the world's best-known bicycle race, the 94-year-old Giro d'Italia runs a close second.

2. Both are grueling, three-week-long events that require cyclists to cover over 2,000 miles of difficult, mountainous terrain, and both are eagerly anticipated, draw enormous crowds along their routes, and receive extensive media coverage.

3. That media attention leads to marketing opportunities for the events' sponsors; which place ads along the race's route, in the nearby towns, and on the cyclists themselves.

4. Martin Hvastija, a participant in the 2003 Giro d'Italia, had no chance of winning the race, nevertheless, he drew extensive media attention for his sponsors.

5. His method was simple; he managed to ride out in front of the field for a few brief miles.

6. Although he had no chance of winning the race; newscasters beamed his image around the world during the short time he was a front-runner, during the same period; showing the world the brightly colored advertising logos on his jersey.

7. In addition to sponsoring individual athletes, corporations plaster ads all over the towns that the race goes through, they toss samples, coupons, and gadgets to spectators from promotional vehicles that ride the route an hour ahead of the cyclists, and they run ads during TV and radio coverage of the race.

8. In 2003, the organizers of the Giro took in over $8 million in fees from advertisers and $12 million in broadcast rights from the Italian state-owned TV network, RAI, however, these figures were down a bit from the previous year.

9. An additional source of revenues for race organizers is fees from the towns where the race starts and ends each day, as a result, organizers determine the actual course according to which cities are willing to pay the $120,000 charge.

10. Media watchers think the Giro d'Italia could become even more profitable and popular, especially among young adults, but only if it took a cue from the Tour de France by encouraging; more international press coverage, more star riders, and even heavier corporate sponsorship.

**EXERCISE 25-2**   Combine each set of sentences into one sentence so that it contains two independent clauses. Use a semicolon correctly between the two clauses. You may add, omit, revise, and rearrange words. Try to use all the patterns in this chapter, and explain the reasoning behind your decisions. More than one revision may be correct. For help, consult all sections of this chapter.

> **EXAMPLE**   Rosa Parks's refusal to move to the back of a bus in Montgomery, Alabama, in 1955 sparked the modern civil rights movement. Her action led to the greatest social revolution in US history.
>
> Rosa Parks's refusal to move to the back of a bus in Montgomery, Alabama, in 1955 sparked the modern civil rights movement; *her* action led to the greatest social revolution in US history.

1. Rosa Parks was a single African American woman who took a defiant stand against bigotry. She was one of the most respected civil rights leaders of the 1950s.

2. In October 2005, Rosa Parks died. Interestingly, she was the first woman in the history of the United States to be chosen to lie in state at the Rotunda, which is located in the US Capitol in Washington, DC.

3. During her lifetime, Parks remained active in the quest for improved race relations, traveling frequently to advocate for equality. Nevertheless, she devoted much of her time to an organization that she helped to found, and she wrote two autobiographical books.

4. Parks never expected the honors that her act of defiance brought her. In 1980, she won the Martin Luther King Jr. award. In 1984, she won the Eleanor Roosevelt Women of Courage Award. In 1999, she won the US Congressional Gold Medal of Honor Award.

5. Parks continued to spread her message to the people of the world, as she did when she embarked on a 381-day tour throughout the United States and many foreign countries in 1996. She advised her audiences to coexist peacefully, to live as one, and to make the world a better place for all people.

# Chapter 26

## COLONS

### 26a  What are the uses of a colon?

A **colon** is a full stop that draws attention to the words that follow. It can be placed only at the end of an INDEPENDENT CLAUSE. A colon introduces a list, an APPOSITIVE, or a QUOTATION.

### 26b  When can a colon introduce a list, an appositive, or a quotation?

When a complete sentence—that is, an INDEPENDENT CLAUSE—introduces a list, an APPOSITIVE, or a QUOTATION, place a colon before the words being introduced. These words don't have to form an independent clause themselves, but a complete sentence before the colon is essential. Box 26.1 shows this pattern for using a colon.

---

**SUMMARY BOX 26.1**

**Colon I**

> Independent clause: list.
>
> Independent clause: appositive.
>
> Independent clause: "Quoted words."

---

#### INTRODUCING LISTED ITEMS

When a complete sentence introduces a list, a colon is required, as demonstrated in the following example.

> **If you really want to lose weight, you must do three things:** eat smaller portions, exercise, and drink lots of water. [The required independent clause comes before the listed items, so a colon is correct.]

When the lead-in words at the end of an independent clause are *such as, including, like,* or *consists of,* never use a colon. In contrast, if the lead-in words at the end of an independent clause are *the following* or *as follows,* do use a colon.

**The students demanded improvements *such as*** an expanded menu in the cafeteria, improved janitorial services, and more up-to-date textbooks.

**The students demanded *the following*:** an expanded menu in the cafeteria, improved janitorial services, and more up-to-date textbooks.

## INTRODUCING APPOSITIVES

An APPOSITIVE is a word or words that rename a NOUN or PRONOUN. When an appositive is introduced by an independent clause, use a colon.

**Only cats are likely to approve of one old-fashioned remedy for cuts:** a lotion of catnip, butter, and sugar. [The required independent clause comes before the appositive: *a lotion of catnip, butter, and sugar* renames *old-fashioned remedy.*]

## INTRODUCING QUOTATIONS

When an independent clause introduces a quotation, use a colon after it. (If the words introducing a quotation don't form an independent clause, use a comma.)

**The little boy in *E.T.* did say something neat:** "How do you explain school to a higher intelligence?" [The required independent clause comes before the quotation.]

— George F. Will, "Well, I Don't Love You, E.T."

## 26c When can I use a colon between two independent clauses?

When a second INDEPENDENT CLAUSE explains or summarizes a first independent clause, you can use a colon to separate them. Box 26.2 (p. 438) shows this pattern for using a colon.

**ALERT:** You can choose to use a capital letter or a lowercase letter for the first word of an independent clause that follows a colon. Whichever you choose, be consistent within a piece of writing. We use a capital letter in this handbook.

We will never forget the first time we made dinner together: **He** got stomach poisoning and was too sick to go to work for four days.

—Lisa Baladendrum, student ◆

## Colon II

Independent clause: Independent clause that explains or summarizes the prior independent clause.

### 26d What standard formats require a colon?

A variety of standard formats in American English require a colon. Also, colons are used in many DOCUMENTATION STYLES, as shown in Chapters 34, 35, and 36.

**TITLE AND SUBTITLE**

*A Brief History of Time: From the Big Bang to Black Holes*

**HOURS, MINUTES, AND SECONDS**

The plane took off at 7:15 p.m.

The runner passed the halfway point at 1:23:02.

◢◢ **ALERT:** In the military, hours and minutes are written without colons and with four digits on a 24-hour clock: *The staff meeting originally scheduled for Tuesday at **0930** will be held Tuesday at **1430** instead.* ◆

**REFERENCES TO BIBLE CHAPTERS AND VERSES**

Psalms 23:1–3

Luke 3:13

**MEMOS**

Date:      January 9, 2006

To:        Dean Kristen Olivero

From:      Professor Daniel Black

Re:        Student Work-Study Program

**SALUTATION IN A BUSINESS LETTER**

Dear Dr. Jewell:

## 26e  When is a colon wrong?

### INDEPENDENT CLAUSES

A colon can introduce a list, an APPOSITIVE, or a QUOTATION, but only when an INDEPENDENT CLAUSE does the introducing. Similarly, a colon can be used between two independent clauses when the second summarizes or explains the first. In following these rules, be sure that you're dealing with independent clauses, not other word groups.

> **NO**  The cook bought: eggs, milk, cheese, and bread. [*The cook bought* isn't an independent clause.]

> **YES**  The cook bought eggs, milk, cheese, and bread.

Never use a colon to separate a PHRASE or DEPENDENT CLAUSE from an independent clause. Otherwise, you'll create the error known as a SENTENCE FRAGMENT.

> **NO**  Day after day: the drought dragged on. [*Day after day* is a phrase, not an independent clause.]

> **YES**  Day after day, the drought dragged on.

> **NO**  After the drought ended: the farmers celebrated. [*After the drought ended* is a dependent clause, not an independent clause.]

> **YES**  After the drought ended, the farmers celebrated.

### LEAD-IN WORDS

Never use a colon after the lead-in words *such as, including, like,* and *consists of.*

> **NO**  The health board discussed many problems **such as:** poor water quality, aging sewage treatment systems, and the lack of alternative water supplies. [A colon is incorrect after *such as.*]

> **YES**  The health board discussed poor water quality, aging sewage treatment systems, and the lack of alternative water supplies. [*Such as* is dropped and the sentence slightly revised so that the colon is not needed.]

> **YES**  The health board discussed many problems**, such as** poor water quality, an aging sewage treatment system, and the lack of alternative water supplies. [Comma before *such as* tells the reader that the list coming up is nonrestrictive (nonessential)—it illustrates *problems.*]

> **YES**  The health board discussed many problems: poor water quality, aging sewage treatment systems, and the lack of alternative water supplies. [If *such as* is dropped, a colon after the independent clause is correct.]

**EXERCISE 26-1**   Insert colons where needed and delete any not needed. If a sentence is correct, explain why. For help, consult all sections of this chapter.

EXAMPLE   The twentieth century saw a flowering of Irish literature, W. B. Yeats, G. B. Shaw, Samuel Beckett, and Seamus Heaney all won the Nobel Prize for Literature.

The twentieth century saw a flowering of Irish literature: W. B. Yeats, G. B. Shaw, Samuel Beckett, and Seamus Heaney all won the Nobel Prize for Literature.

1. People who work the night shift are typically deprived of essential sleep, an average of nine hours a week.

2. The Iroquois of the Great Lakes region lived in fortified villages and cultivated: corn, beans, and squash.

3. Five nations originally formed the Iroquois Confederacy: the Mohawk, the Oneida, the Onondaga, the Cayuga, and the Seneca.

4. Later, these five Iroquois nations were joined by: the Tuscarora.

5. Shouting: "Come back!" Adam watched the vehicle speed down the highway.

6. When a runner breaks through that unavoidable wall of exhaustion, a very different feeling sets in; an intense sense of well-being known as the "runner's high."

7. However: the "runner's high" soon disappears.

8. Two new nations were born on the same day in 1947, India and Pakistan achieved their independence from Britain at midnight on August 15.

9. Date     December 8, 2005
   To       English 101 Instructors
   From     Dean of Instruction
   Re       Classroom Assignments

10. Only a hurricane could have kept Lisa from meeting Nathaniel at 800 p.m.; unfortunately, that night a hurricane hit.

11. George's interests were typical of a sixteen-year-old's, cars, music videos, and dating.

12. Like many people who have never learned to read or write, the woman who told her life story in *Aman; The Story of a Somali Girl* was able to remember an astonishing number of events in precise detail.

13. The Greek philosopher Socrates took these words as his motto, "The unexamined life is not worth living."

14. Socrates was executed: after being found guilty of teaching young people new ideas.

15. The voice coming from the radio could belong to only one person; the great jazz singer Ella Fitzgerald.

# Chapter 27

## APOSTROPHES

### 27a  What is the role of the apostrophe?

The **apostrophe** plays four roles in writing: It creates the POSSESSIVE CASE of NOUNS, forms the possessive case of INDEFINITE PRONOUNS, stands for one or more omitted letters in a word (a CONTRACTION), and can help form plurals of letters and numerals.

In contrast, here are two roles the apostrophe doesn't play: It doesn't belong with plurals of nouns, and it doesn't form the plural of PERSONAL PRONOUNS in the possessive case.

### 27b  How do I use an apostrophe to show a possessive noun?

An apostrophe works with a NOUN to form the POSSESSIVE CASE, which shows ownership or a close relationship.

OWNERSHIP          The **writer's** pen ran out of ink.

CLOSE RELATIONSHIP          The **novel's** plot is complicated.

Possession in nouns can be communicated in two ways: by a PHRASE starting with *of* (comments **of** the instructor; comments **of** Professor Furman) or by an apostrophe and the letter *s* (the instructor**'s** comments; Professor Furman**'s** comments). Here's a list of specific rules governing the usage of *'s*.

- **Add 's to nouns not ending in -s:**

  She felt a **parent's** joy. [*Parent* is a singular noun not ending in -s.]
  They care about their **children's** education. [*Children* is a plural noun not ending in -s.]

- **Add 's to singular nouns ending in -s:**

  You can add *'s* or the apostrophe alone to show possession when a singular noun ends in -s. In this handbook, we use *'s* to clearly mark singular-noun possessives, no matter what letter ends the noun. Whichever rule variation you choose, be consistent within each piece of writing.

The **bus's** (or **bus'**) air conditioning is out of order.

**Chris's** (or **Chris'**) ordeal ended.

If you encounter a tongue-twisting pronunciation (*Charles* **Dickens's** *novel*), you may decide not to add the additional -*s* (*Charles* **Dickens'** *novel*). You must, however, be consistent in each piece of writing.

- **Add only an apostrophe to a plural noun ending in -*s*:**

  The **boys'** statements were taken seriously.

  Three **months'** maternity leave is in the **workers'** contract.

- **Add 's to the last word in compound words and phrases:**

  His **mother-in-law's** corporation has bought out a competitor.

  The **tennis player's** strategy was brilliant.

  We want to hear the **caseworker's** recommendation.

- **Add 's to each noun in individual possession:**

  **Shirley's** and **Kayla's** houses are next to each other. [Shirley and Kayla each own a house; they don't own the houses jointly.]

- **Add 's to only the last noun in joint or group possession:**

  **Kareem and Brina's** house has a screened porch. [Kareem and Brina own one house.]

  **Avram and Justin's** houses always have nice lawns. [Avram and Justin jointly own more than one house.]

## 27c How do I use an apostrophe with possessive pronouns?

When a POSSESSIVE PRONOUN ends with -*s* (*hers, his, its, ours, yours,* and *theirs*), never add an apostrophe. Below is a list of PERSONAL PRONOUNS and their possessive forms.

| PERSONAL PRONOUNS | POSSESSIVE FORMS |
|---|---|
| I | my, mine |
| you | your, yours |
| he | his |
| she | her, hers |
| it | its |
| we | our, ours |
| they | their, theirs |
| who | whose |

**27d** **How do I use an apostrophe with contractions?**

In a **contraction**, an apostrophe takes the place of one or more omitted letters. Be careful not to confuse a contraction with a POSSESSIVE PRO- NOUN. Doing so is a common spelling error, one that many people— including employers—consider evidence of a poor education. Whether or not that's fair, it's usually true.

**it's** (contraction for *it is*)          **its** (possessive pronoun)
**they're** (contraction for *they are*)   **their** (possessive pronoun)
**who's** (contraction for *who is*)       **whose** (possessive form of *who*)
**you're** (contraction for *you are*)     **your** (possessive pronoun)

> NO  The government has to balance **it's** budget.
> YES  The government has to balance **its** budget.

> NO  The professor **who's** class was canceled is ill.
> YES  The professor **whose** class was canceled is ill.

In choosing whether or not to use a contraction, consider that many instructors think contractions aren't appropriate in ACADEMIC WRITING. Nevertheless, the *MLA Handbook* accepts contractions, including *'90s* for *the 1990s*. In this handbook, we use contractions because we're ad- dressing you, the student. We suggest, however, that before you use con- tractions in your academic writing, you check with your instructor. Here's a list of common contractions.

**COMMON CONTRACTIONS**

| | |
|---|---|
| aren't = *are not* | she's = *she is* |
| can't = *cannot* | there's = *there is* |
| didn't = *did not* | they're = *they are* |
| don't = *do not* | wasn't = *was not* |
| he's = *he is* | we're = *we are* |
| I'd = *I would, I had* | weren't = *were not* |
| I'm = *I am* | we've = *we have* |
| isn't = *is not* | who's = *who is* |
| it's = *it is* | won't = *will not* |
| let's = *let us* | you're = *you are* |

**ALERT:** One contraction required in all writing is *o'clock* (which stands for *of the clock*, an expression used long ago). ◆

**27e** **How do I use an apostrophe with possessive indefinite pronouns?**

An apostrophe works with an INDEFINITE PRONOUN (see list in Box 10.6 in 10i) to form the POSSESSIVE CASE, which shows ownership or a close relationship.

> OWNERSHIP **Everyone's** dinner is ready.
>
> CLOSE RELATIONSHIP **Something's** aroma is appealing.

Possession in indefinite pronouns can be communicated in two ways: by a PHRASE starting with *of* (*comments of everyone*) or by an apostrophe and the letter *s* (*everyone's comments*).

**27f** **How do I form the plural of miscellaneous elements?**

Until recently, the plural of elements such as letters meant as letters, words meant as words, numerals, and symbols could be formed by adding either *'s* or *s*. The most current MLA guidelines endorse the use of *s* only, with the exception of adding *'s* to letters meant as letters. MLA requires underlining—never italics—for two elements only: (1) letters meant as letters and (2) words meant as words. Don't underline the *s* or *'s* that creates the plural for any of the elements discussed in this section. (For published books, any underlined words in a manuscript are printed in italics, as is done in this handbook.) The examples below reflect MLA practices.

| | |
|---|---|
| PLURAL OF LETTERS MEANT AS LETTERS | Printing **M's** and **N's** confuses young children. |
| | Printing **m's** and **n's** confuses young children. |
| PLURAL OF LETTERS MEANT AS WORDS | He was surprised to get all **Bs** in his courses. |
| PLURAL OF WORDS MEANT AS WORDS | Too many **ifs** in a contract make me suspicious. |
| PLURAL OF NUMBERS | Her e-mail address contains many **7s**. |
| PLURAL OF YEARS | I remember the **1990s** well. |
| PLURAL OF SYMBOLS | What do those **&s** mean? |

**27g** **When is an apostrophe wrong?**

If you're a writer who makes the same apostrophe errors repeatedly, memorize the rules you need (some you're likely to know almost without thought). Then, you won't be annoyed by "that crooked little mark," a nickname popular with students who wish the apostrophe would go away. Box 27.1 lists the major apostrophe errors.

**SUMMARY BOX** 27.1

## Leading causes of apostrophe errors

- Never use an apostrophe with the PRESENT-TENSE VERB.

  Cholesterol **plays** [not **play's**] an important role in how long we live.

- Always use an apostrophe after the -s in a POSSESSIVE plural of a noun.

  **Patients'** [not **Patients**] questions seek detailed answers.

- Never add an apostrophe at the end of a nonpossessive noun ending in -s.

  Medical **studies** [not **studies'** or **study's**] show this to be true.

- Never use an apostrophe to form a nonpossessive plural.

  **Teams** [not **Team's**] of doctors have studied the effects of cholesterol.

**EXERCISE 27-1**  Rewrite these sentences to insert 's or an apostrophe alone to make the words in parentheses show possession. (Delete the parentheses.) For help, consult 27b and 27e.

EXAMPLE   All boxes, cans, and bottles on a (supermarket) shelves are designed to appeal to (people) emotions.

All boxes, cans, and bottles on a *supermarket's* shelves are designed to appeal to *people's* emotions.

1. A (product) manufacturer designs packaging to appeal to (consumers) emotions through color and design.
2. Marketing specialists know that (people) beliefs about a (product) quality are influenced by their emotional response to the design of its package.
3. Circles and ovals appearing on a (box) design supposedly increase a (product user) feelings of comfort, while bold patterns and colors attract a (shopper) attention.
4. Using both circles and bold designs in (Arm & Hammer) and (Tide) packaging produces both effects in consumers.
5. (Heinz) ketchup bottle and (Coca-Cola) famous logo achieve the same effects by combining a bright color with an old-fashioned, "comfortable" design.
6. Often, a (company) marketing consultants will custom-design products to appeal to the supposedly "typical" (adult female) emotions or to (adult males), (children), or (teenagers) feelings.

7. One of the (marketing business) leading consultants, Stan Gross, tests (consumers) emotional reactions to (companies) products and their packages by asking consumers to associate products with well-known personalities.

8. Thus, (test takers) responses to (Gross) questions might reveal that a particular brand of laundry detergent has (Sylvester Stallone) toughness, (Oprah Winfrey) determination, or (someone else) sparkling personality.

9. Manufacturing (companies) products are not the only ones relying on (Gross) and other corporate (image makers) advice.

10. (Sports teams) owners also use marketing specialists to design their (teams) images, as anyone who has seen the angry bull logo of the Chicago Bulls basketball team will agree.

**EXERCISE 27-2**    Rewrite these sentences so that each contains a possessive noun. For help, consult 27b and 27e.

   EXAMPLE    Strangely, the weight of the kilogram seems to be decreasing.
               Strangely, the *kilogram's weight* seems to be decreasing.

1. The weight of a kilogram depends on precise measurements so that scientists of the world can assume international consistency of the mass of a kilogram in scientific reports.

2. For all measurement units except the kilogram, international standards that refer to natural phenomena such as the speed of light and electrical currents of magnetic fields are used.

3. A platinum-iridium bar created in 1889 in England became the standard of the world for the weight of a kilogram.

4. Because even the relatively stable metal of a platinum-iridium bar has been decaying slowly over time, the decrease in weight of the bar raises the possibility of imprecise results in the current research of scientists.

5. The efforts of the National Institute of Standards and Technology have captured the interest of everyone as it works to equate the weight of a kilogram to the mass of an electrical unit.

# Chapter 28

## QUOTATION MARKS

### 28a What is the role of quotation marks?

**Quotation marks** are used most often to enclose **direct quotations**— the exact spoken or written words of a speaker or writer. Quotation marks also set off some titles, and quotation marks can call attention to words used in a special sense.

Double quotation marks (" ") are standard. In most computer fonts, the opening marks differ slightly in appearance from the closing marks. The opening marks look like tiny 6s, the closing marks like tiny 9s. In some computer fonts, the opening and closing marks look the same (" "). Single quotation marks (' ' or ' ') are used for quotations within quotations: *Gregory said, "I heard the man shout 'Help me' but could not reach him in time."* Quotation marks operate only in pairs: to open and to close. When you proofread your writing, check carefully that you've inserted the closing mark.

Please note, before you continue reading this chapter, that we use MLA STYLE to format the examples here and in other chapters. This affects the documentation features and the lengths of "short" and "long" quotations. These factors vary with different documentation styles. For MLA style, used in most English courses, see Chapter 34. For APA STYLE, see Chapter 35.

### 28b How do I use quotation marks with short direct quotations?

DIRECT QUOTATIONS are exact words from print or nonprint sources. In MLA STYLE, a quotation is considered *short* if it occupies no more than four typed lines. Use double quotation marks at the start and finish of a short quotation. Give DOCUMENTATION information after a short quotation, before the sentence's ending period.

#### SHORT QUOTATIONS

Gardner has suggested the possibility of a ninth intelligence: existential, "the proclivity to pose (and ponder) questions about life, death, and ultimate realities" (72).

Susana Urbina, who surveyed many studies about intelligence, found that intelligence "is such a multifaceted concept that no single quality can define it . . ." (1130).

## 28c Are quotation marks used with long quotations?

No. With a long DIRECT QUOTATION, don't use quotation marks. In MLA STYLE, a quotation is *long* if it occupies more than four typed lines. Instead of using quotation marks with a long quotation, indent all its lines as a block (that is, the quotation is "set off" or "displayed"). This format makes quotation marks unnecessary. Give DOCUMENTA-TION information after the period that ends the quotation.

**LONG QUOTATIONS**

Gardner uses criteria by which to judge whether an ability deserves to be categorized as an "intelligence." Each must confer

> a set of skills of problem solving--enabling the individual
> to resolve genuine problems or difficulties [author's
> emphasis] that he or she encounters and laying the
> groundwork for the acquisition of new knowledge.
> (Frames 60-61)

In the Gardner example above, note that a capital letter is *not* used to start the quotation. The lead-in words (*Each must confer*) are an incomplete sentence, so they need the quotation to complete the sentence.

Goleman also emphasizes a close interaction of the emotional and rational states with the other intelligences that Gardner has identified:

> These two minds, the emotional and the rational, operate
> in tight harmony for the most part, intertwining their very
> different ways of knowing to guide us through the world.
> Ordinarily there is a balance between emotional and rational
> minds, with emotion feeding into and informing the operations
> of the rational mind, and the rational mind refining and
> sometimes vetoing the inputs of the emotions. (9)

In the Goleman example above, note that a capital letter starts the quotation because the lead-in words are a complete sentence. (A colon can—but isn't required to—end the lead-in sentence because it's an independent clause; see 26b.)

**ALERT:** Whether a quotation is one word or occupies many lines, always document its SOURCE. Also, when you quote material, be very careful to record the words exactly as they appear in the original. ◆

## 28d How do I use quotation marks for quotations within quotations?

In MLA STYLE, practice varies between short and long quotations when a quotation contains internal quotation marks. In short quotations of prose, use single quotation marks for any internal quotation marks, and use double quotation marks for the entire quotation. Give DOCUMENTATION information after the entire quotation, before the sentence's ending period. For other documentation styles, check each style's manual.

In long quotations of prose—those that are displayed (set off in a block) and not enclosed in quotation marks—keep the double quotation marks as they appear in the original. Give DOCUMENTATION information after the long quotation following any closing punctuation, and before the period that ends a short quotation.

### SHORT QUOTATIONS: USE SINGLE WITHIN DOUBLE QUOTATION MARKS (MLA STYLE)

With short quotations, the double quotation marks show the beginning and end of words taken from the source; the single quotation marks replace double marks used in the source.

#### ORIGINAL SOURCE

Most scientists concede that they don't really know what "intelligence" is. Whatever it might be, paper and pencil tests aren't the tenth of it.

—Brent Staples, "The IQ Cult," p. 293

#### STUDENT'S USE OF THE SOURCE

Brent Staples argues in his essay about IQ as object of reverence: "Most scientists concede that they don't really know what 'intelligence' is. Whatever it might be, paper and pencil tests aren't the tenth of it" (293).

### LONG QUOTATIONS: USE QUOTATION MARKS AS IN SOURCE

All long quotations must be set off (displayed) without being enclosed in quotation marks. Therefore, show any double and single quotation marks exactly as the source does.

## 28e How do I use quotation marks for quotations of poetry and dialogue?

### POETRY (MLA STYLE)

A quotation of poetry is *short* if it includes three lines or fewer of the poem. As with prose quotations (28d), use double quotation marks to enclose the material. If the poetry lines have internal double quotation marks, change them to single quotation marks. To show when a line of poetry breaks to the next line, use a slash (/) with one space on each side. Give DOCUMENTATION information after a short poetry quotation, before the period that ends the sentence (see also 29e).

> As Auden wittily defined personal space, "some thirty inches from my nose / The frontier of my person goes" (*Complete* 205).

A quotation of poetry is *long* if it includes more than three lines of the poem. As with prose quotations (28d), indent all lines as a block, without quotation marks to enclose the material. Start new lines exactly as they appear in your source. Give documentation information after the long quotation and after the period that ends the quotation.

**ALERT:** When you quote lines of poetry, follow the capitalization of your source. ◆

### DIALOGUE (MLA AND APA STYLES)

Dialogue, also called DIRECT DISCOURSE, presents a speaker's exact words. Enclose direct discourse in quotation marks. In contrast, INDIRECT DISCOURSE reports what a speaker said. Don't enclose indirect discourse in quotation marks. In addition to these differences in punctuation, PRONOUN use and VERB TENSES also differ for these two types of discourse.

DIRECT DISCOURSE    The mayor said**,** **"I** intend to veto that bill**."**

INDIRECT DISCOURSE    The mayor said **that he intended** to veto that bill.

Whether you're reporting the words of a real speaker or making up dialogue in a short story, use double quotation marks at the beginning and end of a speaker's words. This tells your reader which words are the speaker's. Also, start a new paragraph each time the speaker changes.

> "I don't know how you can see to drive," she said.
>
> "Maybe you should put on your glasses."
>
> "Putting on my glasses would help you to see?"
>
> "Not me; you," Macon said. "You're focused on the windshield instead of the road."
>
> —Anne Tyler, *The Accidental Tourist*

In American English, if two or more paragraphs present a single speaker's words, use double opening quotation marks at the start of each paragraph, but save the closing double quotation marks until the end of the last quoted paragraph.

**EXERCISE 28-1** Working individually or with a group, decide whether each sentence below is direct or indirect discourse and then rewrite each sentence in the other form. Make any changes needed for grammatical correctness.

With direct discourse, put the speaker's words wherever you think they belong in the sentence. For help, consult 28b through 28e.

> **EXAMPLE** A school counselor told Betty, a senior at Whatsamatta U, that she needed to take one more three-unit elective to graduate in May.
>
> A school counselor told Betty, a senior at Whatsamatta U, "You need to take one more three-unit elective to graduate in May."

1. "Betty, would you be interested in taking an introductory electronics course?" asked the counselor.
2. Betty asked why she would take such a course when she was a nursing major.
3. The counselor looked Betty straight in the eye and said, "Some knowledge of electronics may not be part of your major, but it's a very important modern subject, nevertheless."
4. Betty wondered whether it might give her a greater understanding of all the electronics used in medical diagnosis and treatment today. But she also asked if there wasn't another elective that might do more to enhance her nursing career.
5. The counselor was quiet for a moment and then declared, "And don't forget, electronics is something you can always fall back on, Betty. And the more you have to fall back on, the softer the landing."

## 28f  How do I use quotation marks with titles of short works?

When you refer to certain short works by their titles, enclose the titles in quotation marks (other works, usually longer, need to be in italics or underlined; see 30g). Short works include short stories, essays, poems, articles from periodicals, pamphlets, brochures, songs, and individual episodes of a series on television or radio.

> What is the rhyme scheme of Andrew Marvell's "Delight in Disorder"? [poem]
>
> Have you read "The Lottery"? [short story]
>
> The best source I found is "The Myth of Political Consultants." [magazine article]
>
> "Shooting an Elephant" describes George Orwell's experiences in Burma. [essay]

Titles of some other works are neither enclosed in quotation marks nor written in italics or underlined. For guidelines, see Box 30.1 in 30e and Box 30.2 in 30g.

⚐ **ALERT:** When placing the title of your own piece of writing on a title page or at the top of a page, never use quotation marks. ◆

**EXERCISE 28-2** Working individually or with a group, correct any misuses of quotation marks. For help, consult 28f.

1. The song America the Beautiful by Katharine Lee Bates celebrates the natural beauty and the ideals that many people associate with the United States.

2. Ralph Waldo Emerson's essay The American Scholar praises the ideals of independence and self-reliance in American education and was first heard as an oration delivered to the "Phi Beta Kappa Society."

3. However, not only the ideals, but also the harsh realities of life in America for Filipino immigrants form the basis of Carlos Bulosan's autobiography, America Is in the Heart.

4. A film that honestly and poignantly reveals the realities facing a family of Irish immigrants in New York City and their hopes for a better life is In America.

5. The poet Langston Hughes in his poem Let America Be America Again is fierce in his criticism of the way poor people and minorities are often treated in the United States.

## 28g How do I use quotation marks for words used as words?

When you refer to a word as a word, you can choose to either enclose it in quotation marks or put it in italics (or use underlining). Whichever you choose, be consistent throughout each piece of writing.

> **NO** Many people confuse affect and effect.
>
> **YES** Many people confuse "affect" and "effect."
>
> **YES** Many people confuse *affect* and *effect*.

Always put quotation marks around the English translation of a word or PHRASE. Also, use italics (or underlining) for the word or phrase in the other language.

> My grandfather usually ended arguments with *de gustibus non disputandum est* ("there is no disputing about tastes").

Many writers use quotation marks around words or phrases meant ironically or in other nonliteral ways.

> The proposed tax "reform" is actually a tax increase.

Some writers put technical terms in quotation marks and define them—but only the first time they appear. Never reuse quotation marks after a term has been introduced and defined.

"Plagiarism"—the undocumented use of another person's words or ideas—can result in expulsion. Plagiarism is a serious offense.

Some student writers put quotation marks around words that they sense might be inappropriate for ACADEMIC WRITING, such as a SLANG term or a CLICHÉ used intentionally to make a point. However, when possible, use different language—not quotation marks. Take time to think of accurate, appropriate, and fresh words instead. If you prefer to stick with the slang or cliché, use quotation marks.

They "eat like birds" in public, but they "stuff their faces" in private.

They **eat almost nothing** in public, but they **eat hefty heaps of food** in private.

A nickname doesn't call for quotation marks, unless you use the nickname along with the full name. When a person's nickname is widely known, you don't have to give both the nickname and the full name. For example, use *Senator Ted Kennedy* or *Senator Edward Kennedy*, whichever is appropriate in context. Because he's well known, don't use *Senator Edward "Ted" Kennedy*.

**EXERCISE 28-3**   Working individually or with a group, correct any misuses of quotation marks. If you think a sentence is correct, explain why. For help, consult 28g.

> EXAMPLE   The word asyndeton simply means that a conjunction has been omitted, as when Shakespeare writes, A woman mov'd is like a fountain troubled, / Muddy, ill seeming, thick, bereft of beauty.
>
> The word "asyndeton" simply means that a conjunction has been omitted, as when Shakespeare writes, "A woman mov'd is like a fountain troubled, / Muddy, ill seeming, thick, bereft of beauty."

1. Shakespeare's phrases such as the sound and the fury from *Macbeth* and pale fire from *The Tempest* have been used by authors such as William Faulkner and Vladimir Nabokov as titles for their books.

2. Shakespeare's understanding of human nature was "profound" and helped him become a "prolific" writer.

3. Many words used commonly today, such as "addiction" and "alligator," were first used in print by Shakespeare.

4. To understand the difference between the words sanguinary and
   *sanguine* is important for a reader of Shakespeare because the
   former means bloody and the latter means optimistic.

5. In the play *Romeo and Juliet,* one of Shakespeare's most famous
   quotations is What's in a name? That which we call a rose / By any
   other name would smell as sweet.

## 28h How do I use quotation marks with other punctuation?

### COMMAS AND PERIODS WITH QUOTATION MARKS

A comma or period that is grammatically necessary is always placed inside the closing quotation mark.

> Jessica enjoyed F. Scott Fitzgerald's story "The Freshest Boy," so
> she was eager to read his novels. [comma before closing quotation mark]

> Max said, "Don't stand so far away from me." [comma before opening
> quotation mark (24k.5); period before closing quotation mark]

> Edward T. Hall coined the word "proxemia." [period before closing
> quotation mark]

### SEMICOLONS AND COLONS WITH QUOTATION MARKS

A semicolon or colon is placed outside the closing quotation mark, unless it is part of the quotation.

> Computers offer businesses "opportunities that never existed
> before"; some workers disagree. [semicolon after closing quotation mark]

> We have to know each culture's standard for "how close is close":
> No one wants to offend. [colon after closing quotation mark]

### QUESTION MARKS, EXCLAMATION POINTS, AND DASHES
### WITH QUOTATION MARKS

If the punctuation marks belong to the words enclosed in quotation
marks, put them inside the quotation marks.

> "Did I Hear You Call My Name?" was the winning song.

> "I've won the lottery!" Arielle shouted.

> "Who's there? Why don't you ans—"

If a question mark, an exclamation point, or a dash doesn't belong to
the material being quoted, put the punctuation outside the quotation
marks.

Have you read Nikki Giovanni's poem "Knoxville, Tennessee"?

If only I could write a story like David Wallace's "Girl with Curious Hair"!

Weak excuses—a classic is "I have to visit my grandparents"—change little.

When you use quotation marks and want to know how they work with capital letters, see 30d; with brackets, 29c; with ellipsis points, 29d; and with the slash, 29e.

## 28i When are quotation marks wrong?

Never enclose a word in quotation marks to call attention to it, to intensify it, or to be sarcastic.

> **NO** I'm "very" happy about the news.
>
> **YES** I'm very happy about the news.

Never enclose the title of your paper in quotation marks (or underline it). However, if the title of your paper contains another title that requires quotation marks, use those marks only for the included title.

> **NO** "The Elderly in Nursing Homes: A Case Study"
>
> **YES** The Elderly in Nursing Homes: A Case Study
>
> **NO** Character Development in Shirley Jackson's Story The Lottery
>
> **YES** Character Development in Shirley Jackson's Story "The Lottery"

**EXERCISE 28-4** Correct any errors in the use of quotation marks and other punctuation with quotation marks. If you think a sentence is correct, explain why. For help, consult 28e through 28i.

1. Dying in a shabby hotel room, the witty writer Oscar Wilde supposedly said, "Either that wallpaper goes, or I do".

2. Was it the Russian novelist Tolstoy who wrote, "All happy families resemble one another, but each unhappy family is unhappy in its own way?"

3. In his poem A Supermarket in California, Allen Ginsberg addresses the dead poet Walt Whitman, asking, Where are we going, Walt Whitman? The doors close / in an hour. Which way does your beard point tonight?

4. Toni Morrison made this reply to the claim that "art that has a political message cannot be good art:" She said that "the best art is political" and that her aim was to create art that was "unquestionably political" and beautiful at the same time.

5. Benjamin Franklin's strange question—"What is the use of a newborn child?—" was his response to someone who doubted the usefulness of new inventions.

# Chapter 29

## OTHER PUNCTUATION MARKS

This chapter explains the uses of **dashes**, **parentheses**, **brackets**, **ellipsis points**, **slashes**, and **hyphens**. These punctuation marks aren't used often, but each serves a purpose and gives you options with your writing style.

## DASH

### 29a When can I use a dash in my writing?

The **dash**, or a pair of dashes, lets you interrupt a sentence to add information. Such interruptions can fall in the middle or at the end of a sentence. To make a dash, hit the hyphen key twice (--). Do not put a space before, between, or after the hyphens. Some word processing programs automatically convert two hyphens into a dash; either form is correct. In print, the dash appears as an unbroken line approximately the length of two hyphens joined together (—). If you handwrite, make the dash at least twice as long as a hyphen.

### USING DASHES FOR SPECIAL EMPHASIS

If you want to emphasize an example, a definition, an APPOSITIVE, or a contrast, you can use a dash or dashes. Some call a dash "a pregnant pause"—that is, take note, something special is coming. Use dashes sparingly so that you don't dilute their impact.

#### EXAMPLE

The caretakers—those who are helpers, nurturers, teachers, mothers—are still systematically devalued.
　　　　　　　　　　　　—Ellen Goodman, "Just Woman's Work?"

#### DEFINITION

Although the emphasis at the school was mainly language—speaking, reading, writing—the lessons always began with an exercise in politeness.
　　　　　　　　　　　　—Elizabeth Wong, *Fifth Chinese Daughter*

**APPOSITIVE**

Two of the strongest animals in the jungle are vegetarians—the elephant and the gorilla.

—Dick Gregory, *The Shadow That Scares Me*

**CONTRAST**

Fire cooks food—and burns down forests.

—Smokey the Bear

Place what you emphasize with dashes next to or nearby the material it refers to so that what you want to accomplish with your emphasis is not lost.

**NO** The current **argument is**—one that faculty, students, and coaches debate fiercely—whether to hold athletes to the same academic standards as others face.

**YES** The current **argument**—one that faculty, students, and coaches debate fiercely—**is** whether to hold athletes to the same academic standards as others face.

## USING DASHES TO EMPHASIZE AN ASIDE

An **aside** is a writer's comment, often the writer's personal views, on what's been written. Generally, this technique isn't appropriate for ACADEMIC WRITING, so before you insert an aside, carefully consider your writing PURPOSE and your AUDIENCE.

Television showed us the war. It showed us the war in a way that was—if you chose to watch television, at least—unavoidable.

—Nora Ephron, *Scribble Scribble*

**ALERTS:** (1) If the words within a pair of dashes require a question mark or an exclamation point, place it before the second dash.

A first date—do you remember?—stays in the memory forever.

(2) Never use commas, semicolons, or periods next to dashes. If such a need arises, revise your writing.

(3) Never enclose quotation marks in dashes except when the meaning requires them. These two examples show that, when required, the dash stops before or after the quotation marks; the two punctuation marks do not overlap.

Many of George Orwell's essays—"A Hanging," for example—draw on his experiences as a civil servant.

"Shooting an Elephant"—another Orwell essay—appears in many anthologies. ◆

**EXERCISE 29-1**  Write a sentence about each topic, shown in italics. Use dashes to set off what is asked for, shown in roman, in each sentence. For help, consult 29a.

EXAMPLE   *science,* a definition
*Ecology*—the study of the interactions among animals, plants, and the physical environment—is closely related to both biology and geology.

1. *movie,* a contrast
2. *singer,* an appositive
3. *hobby,* an example
4. *a fact,* an aside
5. *career,* a definition
6. *social science,* a contrast
7. *writing,* an example
8. *teacher,* an appositive
9. *business,* a definition
10. *technology,* an aside

## PARENTHESES

### 29b   When can I use parentheses in my writing?

**Parentheses** let you interrupt a sentence to add various kinds of information. Parentheses are like dashes (29a) in that they set off extra or interrupting words—but unlike dashes, which emphasize material, parentheses de-emphasize what they enclose. Use parentheses sparingly because overusing them can make your writing lurch, not flow.

#### USING PARENTHESES TO ENCLOSE INTERRUPTING WORDS
##### EXPLANATION
After they've finished with the pantry, the medicine cabinet, and the attic, they will throw out the red geranium (too many leaves), sell the dog (too many fleas), and send the children off to boarding school (too many scuffmarks on the hardwood floors).
—Suzanne Britt, "Neat People vs. Sloppy People"

##### EXAMPLE
Though other cities (Dresden, for instance) had been utterly destroyed in World War II, never before had a single weapon been responsible for such destruction.
—Laurence Behrens and Leonard J. Rosen, *Writing and Reading Across the Curriculum*

##### ASIDE
The older girls (non-graduates, of course) were assigned the task of making refreshments for the night's festivities.
—Maya Angelou, *I Know Why the Caged Bird Sings*

459

The sheer decibel level of the noise around us is not enough to make us cranky, irritable, or aggressive. (It can, however, affect our mental and physical health, which is another matter.)
—Carol Tavris, *Anger: The Misunderstood Emotion*

## USING PARENTHESES FOR LISTED ITEMS AND ALTERNATIVE NUMBERS

When you number listed items within a sentence, enclose the numbers (or letters) in parentheses. Never use closing parentheses to set off numbers in a displayed list; use periods.

Four items are on the agenda for tonight's meeting: (1) current treasury figures, (2) current membership figures, (3) the budget for renovations, and (4) the campaign for soliciting additional public contributions.

**ALERTS:** For listed items that fall within a sentence, (1) use a colon before a list only if an INDEPENDENT CLAUSE comes before the list, and (2) use commas or semicolons to separate three or more items, but be consistent within a piece of writing. If, however, any item contains punctuation itself, use a semicolon to separate the items. ◆

In legal writing and in some BUSINESS WRITING, you can use parentheses to enclose a numeral that repeats a spelled-out number.

The monthly rent is three hundred fifty dollars ($350).

Your order of fifteen (15) gross was shipped today.

In ACADEMIC WRITING, especially in subjects in which the use of figures or measurements is frequent, enclose alternative or comparative forms of the same number in parentheses: *2 mi (3.2 km).*

## USING OTHER PUNCTUATION WITH PARENTHESES

When a complete sentence enclosed in parentheses stands alone, start it with a capital letter and end it with a period. When a sentence in parentheses falls within another sentence, never start with a capital or end with a period.

**NO** Looking for his car keys (He had left them at my sister's house.) wasted an entire hour.

**YES** Looking for his car keys (he had left them at my sister's house) wasted an entire hour.

**YES** Looking for his car keys wasted an entire hour. (He had left them at my sister's house.)

If the material before the parenthetical material requires a comma, place that comma after the closing parenthesis unless you're using commas to set off numbers in a list.

**NO**     Although clearly different from my favorite film, (*The Wizard of Oz*) *Gone With the Wind* is also outstanding.

**YES**     Although clearly different from my favorite film (*The Wizard of Oz*), *Gone With the Wind* is also outstanding.

**YES**     Dorothy wore (1) a white blouse, (2) a blue pinafore, and (3) ruby slippers.

You can use a question mark or an exclamation point within parentheses that occur in a sentence.

Looking for clues (what did we expect to find?) wasted four days.

Place parentheses around quotation marks that come before or after any quoted words.

**NO**     Alberta Hunter "(Down Hearted Blues)" is known for singing jazz.

**YES**     Alberta Hunter ("Down Hearted Blues") is known for singing jazz.

## BRACKETS

## 29c   When do I need to use brackets in my writing?

Brackets allow you to enclose words that you want to insert into quotations, but only in the specific cases discussed below.

### ADJUSTING A QUOTATION WITH BRACKETS

When you use a quotation, you might need to change the form of a word (a verb's tense, for example), add a brief definition, or fit the quotation into the grammatical structure of your sentence. In such cases, enclose the material you have inserted into the quotation in brackets. (These examples use MLA STYLE for PARENTHETICAL REFERENCES; see 34b.)

#### ORIGINAL SOURCE

Current research shows that successful learning takes place in an active environment.

       —Deborah Moore, "Facilities and Learning Styles," p. 22

#### QUOTATION WITH BRACKETS

Deborah Moore supports a student-centered curriculum and agrees with "current research **[which]** shows that successful learning takes place in an active environment" (22).

**ORIGINAL SOURCE**

The logic of the mind is *associative;* it takes elements that symbolize a reality, or trigger a memory of it, to be the same as that reality.

　　　　　　　　　　—Daniel Goleman, *Emotional Intelligence,* p. 294

**QUOTATION WITH BRACKETS**

The kinds of intelligence are based in the way the mind functions: "The logic of the mind is *associative* [one idea connects with another]; it takes elements that symbolize a reality, or trigger a memory of it, to be the same as that reality" (Goleman 294).

## USING BRACKETS TO POINT OUT AN ERROR IN A SOURCE OR TO ADD INFORMATION WITHIN PARENTHESES

In words you want to quote, sometimes page-makeup technicians or authors make a mistake without realizing it—a wrong date, a misspelled word, or an error of fact. You fix that mistake by putting your correction in brackets, without changing the words you want to quote. This tells your readers that the error was in the original work and not made by you.

### USING [SIC] TO SHOW A SOURCE'S ERROR

Insert *sic* (without italics), enclosed in brackets, in your MLA-style essays and research papers to show your readers that you've quoted an error accurately. *Sic* is a Latin word that means "so," or "thus," which says "It is so (or thus) in the original."

**USE FOR ERROR**

A journalist wrote, "The judge accepted an **[sic]** plea of not guilty."

**USE FOR MISSPELLING**

The building inspector wrote about the consequence of doubling the apartment's floor space: "With that much extra room per person, the tennants **[sic]** would sublet."

### USING BRACKETS WITHIN PARENTHESES

Use brackets to insert information within parentheses.

That expression **(first used in *A Fable for Critics* [1848] by James R. Lowell)** was popularized in the early twentieth century by Ella Wheeler Wilcox.

## ELLIPSIS POINTS

### 29d　How do I use ellipsis points in my writing?

The word *ellipsis* means "omission." **Ellipsis points** in writing are a series of three spaced dots (use the period key on the keyboard). You're required to use ellipsis points to indicate you've intentionally omitted words—perhaps even a sentence or more—from the source you're quoting. These rules apply to both prose and poetry.

The *MLA Handbook* no longer recommends that ellipsis points you have inserted be enclosed in brackets to make it clear to your reader that the omission is yours. See Chapter 34 for more information.

## 29d.1 Using ellipsis points with prose

**ORIGINAL SOURCE**

These two minds, the emotional and the rational, operate in tight harmony for the most part, intertwining their very different ways of knowing to guide us through the world. Ordinarily, there is a balance between emotional and rational minds, with emotion feeding into and informing the operations of the rational mind, and the rational mind refining and sometimes vetoing the inputs of the emotions. Still, the emotional and rational minds are semi-independent faculties, each, as we shall see, reflecting the operation of distinct, but interconnected, circuitry in the brain.

—Daniel Goleman, *Emotional Intelligence*, p. 9

**QUOTATION OF SELECTED WORDS, NO ELLIPSIS NEEDED**

Goleman explains that the "two minds, the emotional and the rational" usually provide "a balance" in our daily observations and decision making (9).

**QUOTATION WITH ELLIPSIS MID-SENTENCE**

Goleman emphasizes the connections between parts of the mind: "Still, the emotional and rational minds are semi-independent faculties, each . . . reflecting the operation of distinct, but interconnected, circuitry in the brain (9).

**QUOTATION WITH ELLIPSIS AND PARENTHETICAL REFERENCE**

Goleman emphasizes that the "two minds, the emotional and the rational, operate in tight harmony for the most part . . ." (9). [*Note:* In MLA style, place a sentence-ending period after the parenthetical reference.]

**QUOTATION WITH ELLIPSIS ENDING THE SENTENCE**

On page 9, Goleman states: "These two minds, the emotional and the rational, operate in tight harmony for the most part. . . ." [*Note:* In MLA style, when all needed documentation information is written into a sentence—that is, not placed in parentheses at the end of the sentence—there's no space between the sentence-ending period and an ellipsis.]

**QUOTATION WITH SENTENCE OMITTED**

Goleman explains: "These two minds, the emotional and the rational, operate in tight harmony for the most part, intertwining their very different ways of knowing to guide us through the world. . . . Still, the emotional and rational minds are semi-independent faculties" (9).

**QUOTATION WITH WORDS OMITTED FROM THE MIDDLE OF ONE SENTENCE TO THE MIDDLE OF ANOTHER**

Goleman states: "Ordinarily, there is a balance between emotional and rational minds . . . reflecting the operation of distinct, but interconnected, circuitry in the brain" (9).

**QUOTATION WITH WORDS OMITTED FROM THE BEGINNING OF A SENTENCE AND FROM THE MIDDLE OF ONE SENTENCE TO A COMPLETE OTHER SENTENCE**

Goleman explains: ". . . there is a balance between emotional and rational minds. . . . Still, the emotional and rational minds are semi-independent faculties, each, as we shall see, reflecting the operation of distinct, but interconnected, circuitry in the brain" (9).

When you omit words from a quotation, you also omit punctuation related to those words, unless it's needed for the sentence to be correct.

Goleman explains: "These two minds . . . operate in tight harmony" (9). [comma in original source omitted after *minds*]

Goleman explains that the emotional and rational minds work together while, "still, . . . each, as we shall see, [reflects] the operation of distinct, but interconnected, circuitry in the brain" (9). [comma kept after *still* because it's an introductory word; *still* changed to begin with lowercase letter because now middle of sentence; form of *reflecting* changed for sense of sentence]

## 29d.2  Using ellipsis points with poetry

When you omit one or more words from a line of poetry, follow the rules stated above for prose. However, when you omit a full line or more from poetry, use a full line of spaced dots.

**ORIGINAL SOURCE**

### Little Boy Blue

Little boy blue, come blow your horn,
The sheep's in the meadow, the cow's in the corn
Where is the little boy who looks after the sheep?
He's under the haystack, fast asleep.

**QUOTATION WITH LINES OMITTED**

**Little Boy Blue**

Little boy blue, come blow your horn,

. . . . . . . . . . . . . . . . . . . . . . . . . . . . . . . . . . .

Where is the little boy who looks after the sheep?

He's under the haystack, fast asleep.

# SLASH

## 29e  When can I use a slash in my writing?

The **slash** (/), also called a *virgule* or *solidus,* is a diagonal line that separates or joins words in special circumstances.

### USING A SLASH TO SEPARATE QUOTED LINES OF POETRY

When you quote more than three lines of a poem, no slash is involved; you merely follow the rules in 28e. When you quote three lines or fewer, enclose them in quotation marks and run them into your sentence—and use a slash to divide one line from the next. Leave a space on each side of the slash.

> One of my mottoes comes from the beginning of Anne Sexton's poem "Words": "Be careful of words, / even the miraculous ones."

Capitalize and punctuate each line of poetry as in the original—but even if the quoted line of poetry doesn't have a period, use one to end your sentence. If your quotation ends before the line of poetry ends, use ellipsis points (29d).

### USING A SLASH FOR NUMERICAL FRACTIONS IN MANUSCRIPTS

To type numerical fractions, use a slash (with no space before or after the slash) to separate the numerator and denominator. In mixed numbers— that is, whole numbers with fractions—leave a space between the whole number and its fraction: 1 2/3, 3 7/8. Do not use a hyphen. (For information about using spelled-out and numerical forms of numbers, see 30m through 30o.)

### USING A SLASH FOR *AND/OR*

When writing in the humanities, try not to use word combinations connected with a slash, such as *and/or.* In academic disciplines in which such combinations are acceptable, separate the words with a slash. Leave no space before or after the slash. In the humanities, listing both alternatives in normal sentence structure is usually better than separating choices with a slash.

| **NO** | The best quality of reproduction comes from 35 mm slides/direct-positive films. |
|---|---|
| **YES** | The best quality of reproduction comes from 35 mm slides **or** direct-positive films. |

**EXERCISE 29-2**  Supply needed dashes, parentheses, brackets, ellipsis points, and slashes. If a sentence is correct as written, circle its number. In some sentences, when you can use either dashes or parentheses, explain your choice. For help, consult all sections of this chapter.

**EXAMPLE**  Two tiny islands in the English Channel Jersey and Guernsey have breeds of cows named after them.

Two tiny islands in the English Channel—Jersey and Guernsey—have breeds of cows named after them.

1. In *The Color Purple* a successful movie as well as a novel, Alice Walker explores the relationships between women and men in traditional African American culture.
2. W. C. Fields offered two pieces of advice on job hunting: 1 never show up for an interview in bare feet, and 2 don't read your prospective employer's mail while he is questioning you about your qualifications.
3. A series of resolutions was passed 11–0 with one council member abstaining calling on the mayor and the district attorney to improve safety conditions and step up law enforcement on city buses.
4. All the interesting desserts ice cream, chocolate fudge cake, pumpkin pie with whipped cream are fattening, unfortunately.
5. Thunder is caused when the flash of lightning heats the air around it to temperatures up to 30,000°F 16,666°C.
6. Christina Rossetti wonders if the end of a life also means the end of love in a poem that opens with these two lines: "When I am dead, my dearest, Sing no sad songs for me."
7. After the internationally famous racehorse Dan Patch died suddenly from a weak heart, his devoted owner, Will Savage, died of the same condition a mere 32 1/2 hours later.
8. In his famous letter from the Birmingham jail on April 16, 1963, Martin Luther King Jr. wrote: "You the eight clergymen who had urged him not to hold a protest deplore the demonstrations taking place in Birmingham."
9. The world's most expensive doll house sold for $256,000 at a London auction contains sixteen rooms, a working chamber organ, and a silver clothes press but no toilet.
10. The person renting this apartment agrees to pay seven hundred fifty dollars $750 per month in rent.

11. Railroad entrepreneur George Francis Train his real name! dreamed of creating a chain of great cities across the United States, all connected by his Union Pacific Railroad.

12. Patients who pretend to have ailments are known to doctors as "Munchausens" after Baron Karl Friedrich Hieronymus von Münchhausen he was a German army officer who had a reputation for wild and unbelievable tales.

**EXERCISE 29-3**  Follow the directions for each item. For help, consult all sections of this chapter.

> **EXAMPLE**  Write a sentence about getting something right using a dash.
> *I tried and failed, I tried and failed again—and then I did it.*

1. Write a sentence that quotes only three lines of the following sonnet by William Shakespeare:

   Let me not to the marriage of true minds
   Admit impediments. Love is not love
   Which alters when it alteration finds,
   Or bends with the remover to remove.
   O, no! it is an ever-fixèd mark
   That looks on tempests and is never shaken;
   It is the star to every wand'ring bark,
   Whose worth's unknown, although his height be taken.
   Love's not Time's fool, though rosy lips and cheeks
   Within his bending sickle's compass come;
   Love alters not with his brief hours and weeks,
   But bears it out even to the edge of doom.
   　　If this be error, and upon me proved,
   　　I never writ, nor no man ever loved.

2. Write a sentence using parentheses to enclose a brief example.
3. Write a sentence using dashes to set off a definition.
4. Write a sentence that includes four numbered items in a list.
5. Quote a few sentences from any source you choose. Omit words without losing meaning or use brackets to insert words to maintain meaning or grammatical structure. Use ellipsis points to indicate the omission, and place the parenthetical reference where it belongs.

## HYPHEN

### 29f   When do I need a hyphen in my writing?

A **hyphen** serves to divide words at the end of a line, to combine words into compounds, and to communicate numbers.

## 29g When do I use a hyphen at the end of a line?

Generally, try not to divide a word with a hyphen at the end of a line. (In printed books, hyphens are acceptable because of the limits on line length.) If you must divide a word, try hard not to divide the last word on the first line of a paper, the last word in a paragraph, or the last word on a page.

When you can't avoid using a hyphen at the end of a line, break the word only between syllables. If you aren't sure about the syllables in a word, consult a dictionary. Box 29.1 lists guidelines for end-of-line word breaks.

---

**SUMMARY BOX 29.1**

### Hyphens in end-of-line word breaks

- Divide words only between syllables.

    **NO**     ent-ertain     proc-eed

    **YES**    enter-tain     pro-ceed

- Never divide words that are short, of one syllable, or pronounced as one syllable.

    **NO**     we-alth     en-vy     scream-ed

    **YES**    wealth     envy     screamed

- Never divide a word when only one letter would be left or carried over, or when two letters would be carried over.

    **NO**     a-live     touch-y     helicopt-er

    **YES**    alive     touchy     helicop-ter

- Divide between two consonants according to pronunciation.

    **NO**     ful-lness     omitt-ing     punct-ure

    **YES**    full-ness     omit-ting     punc-ture

---

## 29h How do I use a hyphen with prefixes and suffixes?

**Prefixes** are syllables in front of a **root**—a word's core, which carries the origin or meaning. Prefixes modify meanings. **Suffixes** also have modifying power, but they follow roots. Some prefixes and suffixes are attached to root words with hyphens, but others are not. Box 29.2 shows you how to decide.

**SUMMARY BOX** 29.2

## Hyphens with prefixes and suffixes

- Use hyphens after the prefixes *all-*, *ex-*, *quasi-*, and *self-*.

  **YES**   all-inclusive   self-reliant

- Never use a hyphen when *self* is a root word, not a prefix.

  **NO**   self-ishness   self-less

  **YES**   selfishness   selfless

- Use a hyphen to avoid a distracting string of letters.

  **NO**   ant**ii**ntellectual   bel**ll**ike   pr**oo**utsourcing

  **YES**   ant**i-i**ntellectual   bel**l-l**ike   pr**o-o**utsourcing

- Use a hyphen to add a prefix or suffix to a numeral or a word that starts with a capital letter.

  **NO**   post1950s   proAmerican   Rembrandtlike

  **YES**   post-1950   pro-American   Rembrandt-like

- Use a hyphen before the suffix *-elect*.

  **NO**   presidentelect

  **YES**   president-elect

- Use a hyphen to prevent confusion in meaning or pronunciation.

  **YES**   re-dress (means *dress again*)   redress (means *set right*)

  **YES**   un-ionize (means *remove the ions*)   unionize (means *form a union*)

- Use a hyphen when two or more prefixes apply to one root word.

  **YES**   pre- and post-Renaissance

---

**29i**   **How do I use hyphens with compound words?**

A **compound word** puts two or more words together to express one concept. Compound words come in three forms: an open-compound word, as in *night shift;* hyphenated words, as in *tractor-trailer;* and a closed-compound word, as in *handbook.* Box 29.3 (p. 470) lists basic guidelines for positioning hyphens in compound words.

## Hyphens with compound words

- Divide a compound word already containing a hyphen only after that hyphen, if possible. Also, divide a closed-compound word only between the two complete words, if possible.

  **NO**   self-con-scious   sis-ter-in-law   mas-terpiece

  **YES**   self-conscious   sister-in-law   master-piece

- Use a hyphen between a prefix and an open-compound word.

  **NO**   antigun control [*gun control* is an open-compound word]

  **YES**   anti-gun control

- Use a hyphen for most compound words that precede a noun but not for most compound words that follow a noun.

  **YES**   well-researched report   report is well researched

- Use hyphens when a compound modifier includes a series.

  **YES**   two-, three-, or four-year program

- Never use a hyphen when a compound modifier starts with an *-ly* adverb.

  **NO**   happily-married couple   loosely-tied package

  **YES**   happily married couple   loosely tied package

- Use a hyphen with most COMPARATIVE (*-er*) and SUPERLATIVE (*-est*) compound forms, but not when the compound modifier includes *more/most* or *less/least.*

  **NO**   better fitting shoe

  **YES**   better-fitting shoe

  **NO**   least-significant factors

  **YES**   least significant factors

- Never use a hyphen when a compound modifier is a foreign phrase.

  **YES**   *post hoc* fallacies

- Never use a hyphen with a possessive compound.

  **NO**   a full-week's work   eight-hours' pay

  **YES**   a full week's work   eight hours' pay

**EXERCISE 29-4**   Provide the correct form of the words in parentheses, according to the rules in 29f through 29i. Explain your reasoning for each.

1. The tiger is (all powerful) _____ in the cat family.
2. (Comparison and contrast) _____ studies of tigers and lions show that the tiger is the (more agile) _____ and powerful.
3. Male tigers and lions look similar except for their hair length: Tigers have (ultra short) _____ hair and male lions have (extra long) _____ hair in their manes.
4. The tiger's body is a (boldly striped) _____ yellow, with a white (under body) _____.
5. The Bengal tiger, the largest of the family, is aggressive and (self confident) _____.
6. In India, where the Bengal tiger is called a (village destroyer) _____, it goes (in to) _____ villages to hunt for food.
7. Entire villages have been temporarily abandoned by (terror stricken) _____ people who have seen a Bengal tiger nearby.
8. Villagers seek to protect their homes by destroying tigers with traps, (spring loaded) _____ guns, and (poisoned arrows) _____.
9. Bengal tigers are also called (cattle killers) _____, although they attack domestic animals only when they cannot find wild ones.
10. Many people who do not live near a zoo get to see tigers only in (animal shows) _____, although (pro animal) _____ activists try to prevent tigers from being used this way.

# Chapter 30

## CAPITALS, ITALICS, ABBREVIATIONS, AND NUMBERS

### CAPITALS

### 30a When do I capitalize a "first" word?

**FIRST WORD IN A SENTENCE**

Always capitalize the first letter of the first word in a sentence.

**F**our inches of snow fell last winter.

**A SERIES OF QUESTIONS**

If questions in a series are complete sentences, start each with a capital letter. If, however, the questions aren't complete sentences, you can choose to capitalize or not. Whatever your choice, be consistent in each piece of writing. In this handbook, we use capitals for a series of questions.

What facial feature would most people like to change? **E**yes? **E**ars? **N**ose?

What facial feature would most people like to change? **e**yes? **e**ars? **n**ose?

**SMALL WORDS IN TITLES OR HEADINGS**

Capitalize small words (*the, a, an,* and short PREPOSITIONS such as *of, to*) in a title or heading only when they begin the title or when the source capitalizes these small words.

Always capitalize *I*, no matter where it falls in a sentence or group of words: *I love you now, although I didn't use to.* The same holds for *O,* the INTERJECTION: *You are, O my fair love, a burning fever; O my gentle love, embrace me.* In contrast, never capitalize the interjection *oh*, unless it starts a sentence or is capitalized in words you're quoting.

**AFTER A COLON**

When a complete sentence follows a colon, you can choose to start that sentence with either a capital or a lowercase letter, but be consistent in each piece of writing. When the words after a colon are not a complete sentence, do not capitalize.

She reacted instantly: **S**he picked up the ice cream and pushed it back into her cone.

She reacted instantly: **s**he picked up the ice cream and pushed it back into her cone.

She bought four pints of ice cream: **v**anilla, chocolate, strawberry, and butter pecan.

**ALERT:** A colon can follow only a complete sentence (an INDEPENDENT CLAUSE; see 26a). ◆

### FORMAL OUTLINE

In a formal outline (2r), start each item with a capital letter. Use a period only when the item is a complete sentence.

## 30b When do I use capitals with listed items?

### A LIST RUN INTO A SENTENCE

If run-in listed items are complete sentences, start each with a capital and end each with a period (or question mark or exclamation point). If the run-in listed items are incomplete sentences, start each with a lowercase letter and end each with a comma—unless the items already contain commas, in which case use semicolons. If you list three or more items that are incomplete sentences, use *and* before the last item.

> **YES** We found three reasons for the delay: (1) **B**ad weather held up delivery of materials. (2) **P**oor scheduling created confusion. (3) **I**mproper machine maintenance caused an equipment failure.

> **YES** The reasons for the delay were (1) **b**ad weather, (2) **p**oor scheduling, **and** (3) **e**quipment failure.

> **YES** The reasons for the delay were (1) **b**ad weather, which had been predicted; (2) **p**oor scheduling, which is the airline's responsibility; **and** (3) **e**quipment failure, which no one can predict.

### A DISPLAYED LIST

In a displayed list, each item starts on a new line. If the items are sentences, capitalize the first letter and end with a period (or question mark or exclamation point). If the items are not sentences, you can use a capital letter or not. Whichever you choose, be consistent in each piece of writing. Punctuate a displayed list as you would a run-in list.

> **YES** We found three reasons for the delay:
> 1. **B**ad weather held up delivery of materials.
> 2. **P**oor scheduling created confusion.
> 3. **I**mproper machine maintenance caused an equipment failure.

473

> **YES**  The reasons for the delay were
> 1. **b**ad weather**,**
> 2. **p**oor scheduling**, and**
> 3. **e**quipment failure**.**

**ALERTS:** (1) If a complete sentence leads into a displayed list, you can end the sentence with a colon. However, if an incomplete sentence leads into a displayed list, use no punctuation. (2) Use PARALLELISM for items in a list. For example, if one item is a sentence, use sentences for all the items (18f); or if one item starts with a VERB, start all items with a verb in the same TENSE; and so on. ◆

## 30c  When do I use capitals with sentences in parentheses?

When you write a complete sentence within parentheses that falls within another sentence, don't start with a capital or end with a period—but do use a question mark or exclamation point, if needed. When you write a sentence within parentheses that doesn't fall within another sentence, capitalize the first word and end with a period (or question mark or exclamation point).

> I did not know till years later that they called it the Cuban Missile Crisis. But I remember Castro. (**W**e called him Castor Oil and were awed by his beard**.**) We might not have worried so much (**w**hat would the communists want with our small New Hampshire town**?**) except we lived 10 miles from a U.S. air base.
> —Joyce Maynard, "An 18-Year-Old Looks Back on Life"

## 30d  When do I use capitals with quotations?

If a quotation within your sentence is itself less than a complete sentence, never capitalize the first quoted word. If the quotation you have used in your sentence is itself a complete sentence, capitalize the first word.

> Mrs. Enriquez says that students who are learning a new language should visit that country and "**a**bsorb a good accent with the food."

> Talking about students who live in a new country Mrs. Enriquez says, "**T**hey'll absorb a good accent with the food."

When you write DIRECT DISCOURSE—which you introduce with verbs such as *said, stated, reported,* and others (see 33k) followed by a comma, capitalize the first letter of the quoted words. However, never capitalize a partial quotation, and never capitalize the continuation of a one-sentence quotation within your sentence.

Mrs. Enriquez said, "Students who are learning a new language should visit that country. They'll absorb a good accent with the food." [complete sentence]

Mrs. Enriquez told me that the best way to "absorb a good accent" in a language is to visit the country and eat its food. [part of a quotation integrated in a sentence]

"Of course," she continued with a smile, "the accent lasts longer than the food." [continuation of a one-sentence quotation]

## 30e When do I capitalize nouns and adjectives?

Capitalize PROPER NOUNS (nouns that name specific people, places, and things): *Abraham Lincoln, Mexico, World Wide Web*. Also, capitalize **proper adjectives** (adjectives formed from proper nouns): *a Mexican entrepreneur, a Web address*. Don't capitalize ARTICLES (*the, a, an*) that accompany proper nouns and proper adjectives, unless they start a sentence.

When a proper noun or adjective loses its very specific "proper" association, it also loses its capital letter: *french fries, pasteurized*. When you turn a common noun (*lake*) into a proper noun (*Lake Mead*), capitalize all words.

Expect sometimes that you'll see capitalized words that this handbook says not to capitalize. For example, a corporation's written communications usually capitalize its own entities (*our Board of Directors or this Company*), even though the rule calls for lowercase (*the board of directors, the company*). Similarly, the administrators of your school might write *the Faculty* and *the College* (or *the University*), even though the rule calls for a lowercase *f, c,* and *u*. How writers capitalize can depend on AUDIENCE and PURPOSE in each specific context.

Box 30.1 is a capitalization guide. If you don't find what you need, locate an item in it (or in Box 30.2 on p. 480) that's close to what you want, and use it as a model.

**SUMMARY BOX 30.1**

## Capitalization

| | CAPITALS | LOWERCASE LETTERS |
|---|---|---|
| **NAMES** | Mother Teresa (*also, used as names:* Mother, Dad, Mom, Pa) | my mother [relationship] |
| | Doc Holliday | the doctor [role] |

## Capitalization

| | CAPITALS | LOWERCASE LETTERS |
|---|---|---|
| **TITLES** | President Truman | the president |
| | Democrat [party member] | a democrat [believer in democracy] |
| | Representative Harold Ford | the congressional representative |
| | Senator Edward M. Kennedy | a senator |
| | Queen Elizabeth II | the queen |
| **GROUPS OF PEOPLE** | Caucasian [race] | white, black [*also* White, Black] |
| | African American, Hispanic, [ethnic group] | |
| | Irish, Korean, Canadian [nationality] | |
| | Jewish, Catholic, Protestant, Buddhist [religious affiliation] | |
| **ORGANIZATIONS** | Congress | the legislative branch of the US government |
| | the Ohio State Supreme Court | the state supreme court |
| | the Republican Party | the party |
| | National Gypsum Company | the company |
| | Chicago Cubs | a baseball team |
| | American Medical Association | a professional group |
| | Sigma Chi | a fraternity |
| | Alcoholics Anonymous | a self-help group |
| **PLACES** | Los Angeles | the city |
| | the South [region] | turn south [direction] |
| | the West Coast | the US states along the western seaboard |
| | Main Street | the street |
| | Atlantic Ocean | the ocean |
| | the Black Hills | the hills |
| **BUILDINGS** | the Capitol [in Washington, DC] | the state capitol |
| | Ace High School | a high school |
| | Front Road Café | a restaurant |
| | Highland Hospital | a hospital |

➤

**SUMMARY BOX** 30.1 *continued*

## Capitalization

| | CAPITALS | LOWERCASE LETTERS |
|---|---|---|
| **SCIENTIFIC TERMS** | Earth [as one of nine planets] | the earth [otherwise] |
| | the Milky Way, the Galaxy [as name] | our galaxy, the moon, the sun |
| | *Streptococcus aureus* | a streptococcal infection |
| | Gresham's law | the theory of relativity |
| **LANGUAGES, SCHOOL COURSES** | Spanish, Chinese | |
| | Chemistry 342 | a chemistry course |
| | History 111 | my history class |
| | Introduction to Photography | a photography course |
| **NAMES OF SPECIFIC THINGS** | Black Parrot tulip | a climbing rose |
| | Purdue University | the university |
| | Heinz ketchup | ketchup, sauce |
| | a Toyota Camry | a car |
| | Twelfth Dynasty | the dynasty |
| | the *Boston Globe* | a newspaper |
| **TIMES, SEASONS, HOLIDAYS** | Monday, Fri. | today |
| | September, February | a month |
| | the Roaring Twenties | the decade |
| | the Christmas season | spring, summer, autumn, winter, the fall semester |
| | Kwanzaa, New Year's Day | a feast day, the holiday |
| | Passover, Ramadan | a religious holiday or observance |
| **HISTORICAL EVENTS AND DOCUMENTS** | World War II | the war |
| | Battle of the Bulge | the battle |
| | the Great Depression (of the 1930s) | the depression [any serious economic downturn] |
| | the Reformation | the eighteenth century |
| | Paleozoic | an era or age, prehistory |
| | the Bill of Rights | fifth-century manuscripts |
| **RELIGIOUS TERMS** | Athena, God | a goddess, a god |
| | Islam | a religion |
| | the Torah, the Koran (or Qur'an) | a holy book |
| | the Bible | biblical |

**SUMMARY BOX** **30.1** *continued*

## Capitalization

| | CAPITALS | LOWERCASE LETTERS |
|---|---|---|
| **LETTER PARTS** | Dear Ms. Schultz: <br> Sincerely, <br> Yours truly, | |
| **PUBLISHED AND RELEASED MATERIAL** | "The Lottery" <br> *A History of the United States to 1877* <br> *Jazz on Ice* <br> Nixon Papers <br> Mass in B Minor | [Capitalize first letter of first word and all other major words] <br> the show, a performance <br> the archives <br> the B minor mass |
| **ACRONYMS AND INITIALISMS** | NASA, NATO, UCLA, AFL-CIO, DNA | |
| **COMPUTER TERMS** | Gateway, Dell <br> Microsoft Word, WordPerfect <br> Netscape Navigator <br> the Internet <br> World Wide Web, the Web <br> Web site, Web page | a computer company <br> computer software <br><br> a browser <br> a computer network <br> www <br> a home page, a link |
| **PROPER ADJECTIVES** | Victorian <br> Midwestern <br> Indo-European | southern <br> transatlantic <br> alpine |

**EXERCISE 30-1**   Individually or with a group, add capital letters as needed. See 30a through 30e for help.

1. The state of california is best known as the golden state, but other nicknames include the land of milk and honey, the el dorado state, and the grape state.

2. Most people think of san Francisco as northern california, but the city of Eureka, from the greek word meaning "I have found it," is 280 miles north of san Francisco, and the state line is another 90 miles north of eureka.

3. South of san Francisco on the california coast is santa Barbara, which hosts the annual Dickens Universe, a weeklong series of studies and celebrations of the famous writer charles dickens.

4. The highest point in the continental United States is mt. Whitney at 14,495 feet high, and the lowest place in the continental United States is bad Water in death valley at 282 feet below sea level, both located in california.

5. Having approximately 500,000 detectable seismic tremors per year, california rocks, literally.

6. Because the tehema county fairgrounds are located in red bluff, california hosts the largest three-day rodeo in the united States.

7. Numerous songs have been written about california, including "california girls" by the beach boys and the theme of the tv show *the beverly hillbillies.*

8. san Bernardino county with almost three million acres is the largest county in the united states.

9. Hollywood and movie stars are what many people associate california with, and well they might because two of California's governors, ronald reagan and arnold schwarzenegger, were actors before they became governors.

10. When told all these fantastic facts about california, a typical valley girl would respond, "whatever."

## ITALICS

### 30f  What are italics?

**Italic typeface** slants to the right (*like this*); **roman typeface** does not (like this). If your word processing program doesn't give you the option of italics, underline instead. In fact, MLA STYLE requires underlining, not italics, in all documents.

| | |
|---|---|
| ROMAN | your writing |
| UNDERLINING | <u>your writing</u> |
| ITALICS | *your writing* |

### 30g  How do I choose between using italics and quotation marks?

As a rule, use italics for titles of long works (*The Matrix*, a movie) or for works that contain subsections (*Masterpiece Theater*, a television show). Generally, use quotation marks for titles of shorter works ("I Wanna Hold Your Hand," a song) and for titles of subsections within longer works such as books (Chapter 1, "Loomings").

Box 30.2 is a guide for using italics, quotation marks, or nothing. If you don't find what you need, locate an item that is as much like what you want as possible and use it as a model.

---

**SUMMARY BOX 30.2**

## Italics, quotation marks, or nothing

| ITALICS | QUOTATION MARKS OR NOTHING |
|---|---|
| **TITLES AND NAMES** | |
| *Sense and Sensibility* [a novel] | title of student essay |
| *Death of a Salesman* [a play] | act 2 [part of a play] |
| *A Beautiful Mind* [a film] | the Epilogue [a part of a film or book] |
| *Collected Works of O. Henry* [a book] | "The Last Leaf" [a story in a book] |
| *Simon & Schuster Handbook for Writers* [a textbook] | "Agreement" [a chapter in a book] |
| *The Prose Reader* [a collection of essays] | "Putting in a Good Word for Guilt" [an essay] |
| *Iliad* [a book-length poem] | "Nothing Gold Can Stay" [a short poem] |
| *Scientific American* [a magazine] | "The Molecules of Life" [an article in a magazine] |
| *Symphonie Fantastique* [a long musical work] | Violin Concerto No. 2 in B-flat Minor [a musical work identified by form, number, and key—neither quotation marks nor italics] |
| *The Best of Bob Dylan* [a CD] | "Mr. Tambourine Man" [a song] |
| *Twilight Zone* [a television series] | "Terror at 30,000 Feet" [an episode of a television series] |
| *Kids Count* [a Web site title] | Excel [a software program] |
| the *Los Angeles Times* [a newspaper]* | |
| **OTHER WORDS** | |
| *semper fidelis* [words in a language other than English] | burrito, chutzpah [widely understood non-English words] |
| What does *our* imply? [a word meant as a word] | |
| the *abc*'s; the letter *x* [letters meant as letters] | 6s and 7s; & [numerals and symbols] |

*When *The* is part of a newspaper's title, don't capitalize or italicize it in MLA-style or CM-style documentation. In APA-style and CSE-style documentation, capitalize and italicize *The*.

## 30h Can I use italics for special emphasis?

Some professional writers, especially writers of nonfiction and self-help material, occasionally use italics to clarify a meaning or stress a point. In ACADEMIC WRITING, however, you're expected to convey special emphasis through your choice of words and sentence structure, not with italics (or underlining). If your message absolutely calls for it, use italics sparingly—and only after you're sure nothing else will do.

> Many people we *think* are powerful turn out on closer examination to be merely frightened and anxious.
>
> —Michael Korda, *Power!*

**EXERCISE 30-2** Edit these sentences for correct use of italics (or underlining), quotation marks, and capitals. For help, consult 30a through 30h.

1. The article "the Banjo" in the Encyclopaedia Britannica calls the Banjo "America's only national instrument" because it combines the traditional mbanza (an instrument native to certain southern areas of africa) and some European stringed instruments.

2. The writer of a humor column at a newspaper called The "Globe and Mail" has described an imaginary newspaper called The mop and pail, where things are more ridiculous than in Real Life.

3. "Porgy and Bess," a Folk Opera by George and ira Gershwin and Du Bose Heyward, introduced the beautiful, haunting song *Summertime.*

4. Marlon Brando persuaded the Director of *The Godfather* to cast him as the Elderly don Corleone by auditioning with cotton-stuffed cheeks and mumbling hoarsely.

5. When the name of a Small Business begins with the letter a repeated many times, as in AAAAAbc "Auto Body," we know its marketing plan includes being listed First in the telephone directory.

## ABBREVIATIONS

## 30i What are standard practices for using abbreviations?

Some abbreviations are standard in all writing circumstances (*Mr.,* not *Mister,* in a name; *St.* Louis, the city, not *Saint* Louis). In some situations, you may have a choice whether to abbreviate or spell out a word. Choose what seems suited to your PURPOSE for writing and your AUDIENCE, and be consistent within each piece of writing.

> **NO** The great painter Vincent Van Gogh was **b.** in Holland in 1853, but he lived most of his life and died in **Fr.**
>
> **YES** The great painter Vincent Van Gogh was **born** in Holland in 1853, but he lived most of his life and died in **France**.

> **NO** Our field hockey team left after Casey's **psych** class on **Tues.**, **Oct.** 10, but the flight had to make an unexpected stop (in **Chi.**) before reaching **L.A.**

> **YES** Our field hockey team left after Casey's **psychology** class on **Tuesday**, **October** 10, but the flight had to make an unexpected stop (in **Chicago**) before reaching **Los Angeles**.

> **NO** Please confirm in writing your order for one **doz.** helmets in **lg** and **x-lg**.

> **YES** Please confirm in writing your order for one **dozen** helmets in **large** and **extra large**.

**ALERTS:** (1) Many abbreviations call for periods (*Mrs., Ms., Dr.*), but the practice is changing. The trend today is to drop the periods (*PS,* not *P.S.; MD,* not *M.D.; US,* not *U.S.*), yet firm rules are still evolving.

(2) **Acronyms** (pronounceable words formed from the initials of a name) generally have no periods: *NASA* (National Aeronautics and Space Administration) and *AIDS* (*a*cquired *i*mmune *d*eficiency *s*yndrome).

(3) **Initialisms** (names spoken as separate letters) usually have no periods (*IBM, ASPCA, UN*).

(4) Postal abbreviations for states have no periods (30k).

(5) When the final period of an abbreviation falls at the end of a sentence, that period serves also to end the sentence. ◆

## 30j How do I use abbreviations with months, time, eras, and symbols?

### MONTHS

According to MLA STYLE, abbreviations for months belong only in "Works Cited" lists, tables, charts, and the like. Write out the full spelling, never the abbreviation, in your ACADEMIC WRITING. Box 30.3 shows month abbreviations in MLA style.

**SUMMARY BOX** 30.3

### Month abbreviations—MLA style

| | | | | | |
|---|---|---|---|---|---|
| January | Jan. | May | (none) | September | Sept. |
| February | Feb. | June | (none) | October | Oct. |
| March | Mar. | July | (none) | November | Nov. |
| April | Apr. | August | Aug. | December | Dec. |

## TIMES

Use the abbreviations *a.m.* and *p.m.* only with exact times: *7:15 a.m.; 3:47 p.m.* Although some publication styles use the capitalized versions, *A.M.* and *P.M.*, MLA style calls for the use of lowercase letters.

*✎* **ALERT:** Never use *a.m.* and *p.m.* in place of the words *morning, evening,* and *night.*

**NO**  My hardest final exam is in the **a.m.** tomorrow, but by early **p.m.**, I'll be ready to study for the rest of my finals.

**YES**  My hardest final exam is in the **morning** tomorrow, but by early **evening**, I'll be ready to study for the rest of my finals. ◆

## ERAS

In MLA style, use capital letters, without periods, in abbreviations for eras. Some writers prefer using *CE* ("common era") in place of *AD* (Latin for *anno Domini,* "in the year of our Lord") as the more inclusive term. In addition, many writers prefer using *BCE* ("before the common era") in place of *BC* ("before Christ").

When writing the abbreviations for eras, place *AD* before the year (*AD 476*) and all the others after the year (*29 BC; 165 BCE; 1100 CE*).

## SYMBOLS

In MLA style, decide whether to use symbols or spelled-out words according to your topic and the focus of your document (see also 30m). However, never use a freestanding symbol, such as *$, %,* or *¢* in your sentences; always use it with a numeral. With many exceptions, spell out both the symbol and the numeral accompanying it (*twenty centimeters*), unless the number is more than one or two words (*345 centimeters,* not *three hundred forty-five centimeters*).

The exceptions include *$18; 7 lbs.; 24 KB; 6:34 a.m., 5"; 32°;* and numbers in addresses, dates, page references, and decimal fractions (*8.3*). In writing about money, the form *$25 million* is an acceptable combination of symbol, numeral, and spelled-out word.

In confined spaces, such as charts and tables, use symbols with numerals (*20¢*). In documents that focus on technical matters, use numerals but spell out the unit of measurement (*2,500 pounds*)—in MLA style. In other documentation styles, such as APA, CM, and CSE, the guidelines differ somewhat, so you need to check each style's manual.

## 30k  How do I use abbreviations for other elements?

### TITLES

Use either a title of address before a name (***Dr.** Daniel Klausner*) or an academic degree after a name (*Daniel Klausner, **PhD***), not both. However, because *Jr., Sr., II, III,* and so forth are part of a given name, you can use both titles of address and academic degree abbreviations: ***Dr. Martin Luther King Jr.***; *Gavin Alexander **II, MD***

**ALERTS:** (1) Insert a comma both before and after an academic degree that follows a person's name, unless it falls at the end of a sentence: *Joshua Coleman, **LLD,** is our guest speaker,* or *Our guest speaker is Joshua Coleman, **LLD**.* (2) Never put a comma before an abbreviation that is part of a given name: *Steven Elliott **Sr.**, Douglas Young **III**.* ◆

### NAMES AND TERMS

If you use a term frequently in a piece of writing, follow these guidelines: The first time you use the term, spell it out completely and then put its abbreviation in parentheses immediately after. In later references, use the abbreviation alone.

Spain voted to continue as a member of the **North Atlantic Treaty Organization** (**NATO**), to the surprise of other **NATO** members.

When referring to the United States, use the abbreviation *US* as a modifier before a noun (*the **US** ski team*), but spell out *United States* when you use it as a noun (*the ski team from the **United States.***)

### ADDRESSES

If you include a full address in a piece of writing, use the postal abbreviation for the state name, as listed in Box 30.4. For any other combination of a city and a state, or a state by itself, spell out the state name; never abbreviate it.

---

## SUMMARY BOX 30.4

### Postal abbreviations

**UNITED STATES**

| | | | |
|---|---|---|---|
| **AL** | Alabama | **ID** | Idaho |
| **AK** | Alaska | **IL** | Illinois |
| **AZ** | Arizona | **IN** | Indiana |
| **AR** | Arkansas | **IA** | Iowa |
| **CA** | California | **KS** | Kansas |
| **CO** | Colorado | **KY** | Kentucky |
| **CT** | Connecticut | **LA** | Louisiana |
| **DE** | Delaware | **ME** | Maine |
| **DC** | District of Columbia | **MD** | Maryland |
| **FL** | Florida | **MA** | Massachusetts |
| **GA** | Georgia | **MI** | Michigan |
| **HI** | Hawaii | **MN** | Minnesota |

**SUMMARY BOX** **30.4** *continued*

### Postal abbreviations

**UNITED STATES (*continued*)**

| | | | |
|---|---|---|---|
| **MS** | Mississippi | **PA** | Pennsylvania |
| **MO** | Missouri | **RI** | Rhode Island |
| **MT** | Montana | **SC** | South Carolina |
| **NE** | Nebraska | **SD** | South Dakota |
| **NV** | Nevada | **TN** | Tennessee |
| **NH** | New Hampshire | **TX** | Texas |
| **NJ** | New Jersey | **UT** | Utah |
| **NM** | New Mexico | **VT** | Vermont |
| **NY** | New York | **VA** | Virginia |
| **NC** | North Carolina | **WA** | Washington [state] |
| **ND** | North Dakota | **WV** | West Virginia |
| **OH** | Ohio | **WI** | Wisconsin |
| **OK** | Oklahoma | **WY** | Wyoming |
| **OR** | Oregon | | |

**CANADA**

| | | | |
|---|---|---|---|
| **AB** | Alberta | **NT** | Northwest Territories |
| **BC** | British Columbia | **NU** | Nunavut |
| **MB** | Manitoba | **ON** | Ontario |
| **NB** | New Brunswick | **PE** | Prince Edward Island |
| **NL** | Newfoundland and Labrador | **QC** | Quebec |
| | | **SK** | Saskatchewan |
| **NS** | Nova Scotia | **YT** | Yukon Territory |

**ALERT:** When you write the names of a US city and state within a sentence, use a comma before and after the state.

**NO** Portland, Oregon is much larger than Portland, Maine.

**YES** Portland, Oregon, is much larger than Portland, Maine.

If you include a ZIP code, however, don't use a comma after the state. Do place the comma after the ZIP code. ◆

### SCHOLARLY WRITING (MLA STYLE)

MLA style permits abbreviations for a selection of scholarly terms. These are listed in Box 30.5 (p. 486). Never use them in the body of your ACA-DEMIC WRITING. Reserve them for your "Works Cited" lists and for any notes you might write in a separate list at the end of your research paper.

## SUMMARY BOX 30.5

### Major scholarly abbreviations—MLA style

| | | | |
|---|---|---|---|
| **anon.** | anonymous | **i.e.** | that is |
| **b.** | born | **ms., mss.** | manuscript, manuscripts |
| **c.** *or* © | copyright | | |
| **c.** *or* **ca.** | circa *or* about [with dates] | **NB** | note well (*nota bene*) |
| | | **n.d.** | no date (of publication) |
| **cf.** | compare | | |
| **col., cols.** | column, columns | **p., pp.** | page, pages |
| **d.** | died | **par.** | paragraph |
| **ed., eds.** | edition, edited by, editor(s) | **pref.** | preface, preface by |
| | | **rept.** | report, reported by |
| **e.g.** | for example | **rev.** | review, reviewed by; revised, revised by |
| **esp.** | especially | | |
| **et al.** | and others | **sec., secs.** | section, sections |
| **ff.** | following pages, following lines, folios | **v.** *or* **vs.** | versus [*v.* in legal cases] |
| | | **vol., vols.** | volume, volumes |

## 30l   When can I use *etc.*?

The abbreviation *etc.* comes from the Latin *et cetera*, meaning "and the rest." In ACADEMIC WRITING, don't use *etc.* Accepted substitutes include *and the like, and so on, and so forth*, among others. Even better is a more concrete description. An acceptable use of *etc.* is in tables and charts.

> **NO**   We took paper plates, plastic forks, **etc.,** to the picnic.

> **YES**   We took paper plates, plastic forks, **and other disposable items** to the picnic.

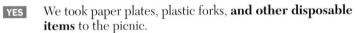 **ALERT:** If you do write *etc.,* always put a comma after the period if the abbreviation falls in the middle of a sentence. ◆

**EXERCISE 30-3**   Working individually or with a group, revise these sentences for correct use of abbreviations. For help, consult 30i through 30l.

1. Originally named the Geo. S. Parker Company, located in Salem, Mass., the toy co. changed its name to Parker Bros. when Chas. joined the business in 1888.

2. Sev. of their games have become quite famous, esp. Monopoly and Clue, both of which were released in the 20th cent.

3. The obj. of the game Monopoly (meaning "dominating the mkt.") is to get the most $ by purchasing, renting, & selling real est.

4. Clue, another pop. brd. game, is a murder mys. in which players move from 1 rm. to another, making accusations to reveal the i.d. of the murderer, the weapon used, and the room where the crime took place.

5. On a cold day in Jan., when the snow is 3 ft. deep and it's dark by early eve., passing the hrs. with your fam. and friends playing a board game is great fun.

## NUMBERS

### 30m  When do I use spelled-out numbers?

Your decision to write a number as a word or as a figure depends on what you're referring to and how often numbers occur in your piece of writing. The guidelines we give in this handbook are for MLA STYLE, which focuses on writing in the humanities. For other disciplines, follow the guidelines in their style manuals.

When you write numbers for more than one category in a piece of writing, reserve figures for some categories of numbers and spelled-out words for other categories. Never mix spelled-out numbers and figures for a particular category.

> **NO**  In **four** days, our volunteers increased from **five** to **eight** to **17** to **233**.

> **YES**  In **four** days, our volunteers increased from **5** to **8** to **17** to **233**. [Numbers referring to volunteers are in numerals, while *four* is spelled out because it refers to a different category: days.]

**ALERT:** When you write a two-word number, use a hyphen between the spelled-out words, starting with *twenty-one* and continuing through *ninety-nine*. ◆

If you use numbers infrequently in a document, spell out all numbers that call for no more than two words: *fifty-two cards, twelve hundred students.* If you use specific numbers often in a document (temperatures when writing about climate, percentages in an economics essay, or other specific measurements of time, distance, and other quantities), use figures: *36 inches, 11 nanoseconds.* If you give only an approximation, spell out the numbers: *About twelve inches of snow fell.*

In the humanities, the names of centuries are always spelled out: *the eighteenth century.*

When you write for courses in the humanities, never start a sentence with a figure. Spell out the number—or better still, revise the sentence so that the number doesn't need to fall at the beginning. For practices in other disciplines, consult their manuals.

**NO**    **$375 dollars** for each credit is the tuition rate for nonresidents.

**YES**    **Three hundred seventy-five dollars** for each credit is the tuition rate for nonresidents.

**YES**    The tuition rate for nonresidents is **$375** for each credit.

## 30n What are standard practices for writing numbers?

Box 30.6 shows standard practices for writing numbers. Consider it a basic guide, and rely on the manual of each documentation style for answers to other questions you may have.

**SUMMARY BOX** 30.6

### Specific numbers in writing

| | |
|---|---|
| **DATES** | August 6, 1941 |
| | 1732–1845 |
| | from 34 BC to AD 230 (*or* 34 BCE to 230 CE) |
| **ADDRESSES** | 10 Downing Street |
| | 237 North 8th Street |
| | Export Falls, MN 92025 |
| **TIMES** | 8:09 a.m., 6:00 p.m. |
| | six o'clock (*not* 6 o'clock) |
| | four in the afternoon *or* 4 p.m. (*not* four p.m.) |
| **DECIMALS** | 0.01 |
| **AND FRACTIONS** | 98.6 |
| | 3.1416 |
| | 7/8 |
| | 12 1/4 |
| | a sixth |
| | three-quarters (*not* 3-quarters) |
| | one-half |
| **CHAPTERS** | Chapter 27, page 2 |
| **AND PAGES** | p. 1023 *or* pp. 660–62 (MLA style) |

➤

**SUMMARY BOX** 30.6 *continued*

## Specific numbers in writing

| | |
|---|---|
| **SCORES AND STATISTICS** | a 6–0 score |
| | 29% (*or* twenty-nine percent) |
| | a 5 to 1 ratio (*and* a ratio of 5:1) |
| | a one percent change (*and* at the 1 percent level) |
| **IDENTIFICATION NUMBERS** | 94.4 on the FM dial |
| | please call (012) 345–6789 |
| **MEASUREMENTS** | 67.8 miles per hour |
| | 2 level teaspoons |
| | a 700-word essay |
| | 8-by-10-inch photograph |
| | 2 feet |
| | 1.5 gallons |
| | 14 liters |
| **ACT, SCENE, AND LINE** | act 2, scene 2 (*or* act II, scene ii) |
| | lines 75–79 |
| **TEMPERATURES** | 40°F *or* −5°F |
| | 20° Celsius |
| **MONEY** | $1.2 billion |
| | $3.41 |
| | 25¢ (*or* twenty-five cents) |
| | $10,000 |

**EXERCISE 30-4** Revise these sentences so that the numbers are in correct form, either spelled out or as figures. For help, consult 30m and 30n.

1. At five fifteen p.m., the nearly empty city streets filled with 1000's of commuters.

2. A tarantula spider can survive without food for about two years and 3 months.

3. By the end of act one, scene five, Romeo and Juliet are in love and at the mercy of their unhappy fate.

4. Sound travels through air at a speed of 1,089 feet per second, but in water it travels four hundred and fifty percent faster, at four thousand, eight hundred fifty-nine feet per second.

5. 21 years old and unhappily married, Cleopatra met middle-aged Julius Caesar in forty-eight BCE.

6. An adult blue whale, which can weigh one hundred tons—the combined weight of 30 elephants—has gained over seven-point-five pounds an hour since infancy.

7. On the morning of August thirteen, nineteen hundred thirty, 3 huge meteorites smashed into the Amazon jungle.

8. 2 out of every 5 people who have ever lived on earth are alive today, according to 1 estimate.

9. The house at six hundred and fifty-three Oak Street—the 1 that children think is haunted—has been empty for 8 years, waiting for a buyer willing to pay its price of $ six million, forty-nine thousand dollars.

10. The 1912 sinking of the *Titanic,* in which one thousand five hundred and three people drowned, is widely known, but few people remember that more than three thousand people lost their lives aboard the ferryboat *Doña Paz* when it hit an oil tanker in the Philippines in nineteen eighty-seven.

## 30o How do I use hyphens with spelled-out numbers?

A **spelled-out number** uses words, not figures. Box 30.7 gives you guidelines.

**ALERT:** Use figures rather than words for a fraction written in more than two words. If your context calls for figures, use hyphens only between the words of the numerator and only between the words of the denominator—but never between the numerator and the denominator: two one-hundredths (*2/100*), thirty-three ten-thousandths (*33/10,000*). ◆

---

**SUMMARY BOX 30.7**

### Hyphens with spelled-out numbers

• Use a hyphen between two-word numbers from *twenty-one* through *ninety-nine*, whether they stand alone or are part of a larger number.

  **YES**  thirty-five  two hundred thirty-five

• Use a hyphen in a COMPOUND-WORD modifier formed from a number and a word, whether the number is in words or figures.

  **YES**  fifty-minute class [*also* 50-minute class]

  **YES**  three-to-one odds [*also* 3-to-1 odds]

• Use a hyphen between the numerator and the denominator of two-word fractions.

  **YES**  one-half  two-fifths  seven-tenths

• Use a hyphen between compound nouns joining two units of measure.

  **YES**  light-years  kilowatt-hours

# Chapter 31

## RESEARCH WRITING AS A PROCESS

### 31a  What is research writing?

**Research** is a systematic process of gathering information to answer a question. You do this all the time. You're doing research when you're trying to decide which college to attend, which MP3 player to buy, or which travel arrangements will make the best vacation. Perhaps you talk to others. Perhaps you find facts or information, in print or online. Along the way you might write a few notes to yourself. You analyze and evaluate what you learn and then make a decision.

Other kinds of research are more formal, and we don't mean just the type conducted by scientists in white lab coats. People wanting to start small businesses usually have to research the local business climate and present their findings to lenders to get a loan. Citizens wanting to oppose a new construction project have to research the effects of the project and present their findings in a careful way to a group of elected officials.

Every research activity, formal or informal, involves two processes:

- Gathering information
- Analyzing, synthesizing, and evaluating what you've gathered

More formal research writing, including business and public reports and academic research papers, involves a third process:

- Writing an accurately documented paper based on your ANALYSIS,* SYNTHESIS, and EVALUATION of what you've gathered

This section explains all three phases of research writing, especially the kind of research papers (sometimes called *term papers*) you'll frequently encounter in college. We'd like to stress that researching can strengthen parts of many writing projects, both in college and beyond; it helps you make assertions based on studies and facts. However, some projects are more research-intensive throughout.

*Words printed in SMALL CAPITAL LETTERS are discussed elsewhere in the text and are defined in the Terms Glossary at the back of the book.

Some student researchers use information from **primary sources**—from direct observations, interviews, surveys, measurements, original documents and records, and so on. However, most students, especially when writing college research papers, use information from **secondary sources**—from reading, using analysis to discuss and review what people with respected credentials and authority have written.

Research is an absorbing, creative activity. It lets you come to know a subject deeply and leads to fresh insights. The entire process, especially when repeated in a number of courses and settings, helps to shape you into a self-reliant learner. Nevertheless, many researchers—inexperienced and experienced—feel intimidated at the beginning of a research writing project. We find that research writing goes most easily when you deliberately break it down into organized steps using a manageable research plan.

## 31b How do I schedule a research project?

Research takes time, so plan ahead and budget your time intelligently. As soon as you get an assignment for a research paper, plan your schedule, using Box 31.1 as a model. Because no two research paper projects are alike, adapt this schedule to your needs. You might, for example, need only one day for some steps but two weeks for others. So, while you need to stay flexible, you also want to keep your eye on the calendar.

---

**SUMMARY BOX 31.1**

### Sample schedule for a research project

Assignment received _____

Assignment due date _____

**PLANNING**

**FINISH BY (DATE)**

1. Start my research log (31c).
2. Choose a topic suitable for research (31d).  _____
3. Draft my research question (31e).  _____
4. Decide on my purpose and audience (31f).  _____
5. Take practical steps (31g):
   a. Gather equipment.
   b. Learn how to use my college library.  _____
6. Decide what documentation style I'll use (31h).  _____

➤

**SUMMARY BOX** 31.1 *continued*

## Sample schedule for a research project

| RESEARCHING | FINISH BY (DATE) |
|---|---|

7. Plan my "search strategy," but modify as necessary (32b). _____

8. Decide the kinds of research I need to do:
   a. Field research (32c). If yes, schedule tasks. _____
   b. Library and scholarly sources (32d). _____
   c. Web sources (32i). _____

9. Locate and evaluate sources (32d, 32j). _____

10. Compile a working bibliography (31i) or annotated bibliography (31j). _____

11. Take content notes from sources I find useful (31k). _____

### WRITING

12. Draft my thesis statement (31l). _____

13. Outline, as required (31m). _____

14. Draft my paper (31n). _____

15. Use correct parenthetical citations (34b–34c; 35b–35c; 36a, 36c). _____

16. Revise my paper (31o). _____

17. Compile my final bibliography (Works Cited or References), using the documentation style required (Chapters 34–36). _____

### EVALUATION OF THIS SCHEDULE

Have I planned realistically for my completion date?

If I haven't, what steps do I need to revise in my schedule?

## 31c What is a research log?

A **research log** is your diary of your research process. Use a separate notebook for the log, or create a new folder or file on the computer. Whichever format you rely on, make your research schedule one of the first entries.

Although much of your research log will never find its way into your research paper itself, what you write in it greatly increases your efficiency. A well-kept log traces your line of reasoning as your project evolves, tells where you've ended each work session, and suggests what your next steps might be. In your log, always record the date as well as the following elements:

- Your current step in your search for information; the search strategy you used to find that information; the name, location, and other details of exactly where you found the information; the main point of the information you found; and the exact file or folder name in which you've stored your detailed content notes.
- Your suggested next step for when you return to your research.
- Your evolving overall thoughts and insights as you move through the research and writing processes.
- Your awareness that you're becoming ready to move away from gathering material to organizing it; from organizing it to writing about it; and from drafting to revising.

Figure 31.1 shows a selection from the research log of Andrei Gurov, who wrote the MLA-style research paper shown in section 34e.

October 20: Because I'm not sure where online to start searching for sources about déjà vu, I've decided to use the "Research Navigator" our professor told us is available at <prenhall.com/troyka>. [Pause] Done—sure enough, when I clicked on the cover of this book, then on "research," and finally on the EBSCO database, I could navigate my way to a number of sources. I filed them in the folder offered and printed out what looked like the best ones. One problem I noted immediately: because the topic of déjà vu seems largely to be studied by psychologists and neuroscientists, the researchers use only the first initial of their first names. That's okay for APA style, but MLA requires the full first name. That's a problem I'll have to tackle.

Figure 31.1 A selection from the research log of Andrei Gurov, who wrote the MLA-style research paper shown in section 34e

### 31d How do I choose and narrow a research topic?

Sometimes, of course, you don't choose a research topic. Research in the workplace and many public arenas often emerges from specific situations. A doctor needs to decide the best way to treat a patient. An office manager needs to make a decision about purchasing new computers. An actor needs to research a time period to better portray a character.

Even in college, some instructors assign a specific topic for research (for example, "Are there scientific theories to explain false memory?"). Others leave more choice to you, assigning a general subject (for example, "memory") and expecting you to narrow it to a manageable topic. Still other instructors expect you to choose a topic on your own (for example, "Write a research paper on a topic of current interest or importance").

## 31d.1  Choosing a topic on your own

The freedom to choose any topic you want can sometimes lead to what is called "research topic block." Don't panic. Instead, use some of the strategies for generating ideas in Box 31.2.

---

**SUMMARY BOX 31.2**

## Finding general ideas for research

- **Get ready.** Carry a small notebook and a pen, a laptop, or a PDA (such as a Palm Pilot). Ideas have a way of popping into your mind when you least expect them. Jot down your thoughts on the spot so that they don't slip away.

- **Talk with others.** Ask instructors or other experts in your area of interest what issues currently seem "hot" to them. Ask them to recommend readings or the names of authorities on those issues.

- **Think actively.** Use the structured techniques for gathering ideas demonstrated in sections 2f through 2m.

- **Browse some textbooks.** Read the table of contents and major headings of textbooks for subjects that interest you. As you narrow your focus, note the names of important books and experts, often mentioned in reference lists at the end of chapters or in the final pages of the book.

- **Browse the Internet.** Many Web search engines provide topic directories. Click on some general categories and review subcategories until you locate specific topics that interest you. Then try further subject searches or KEYWORD searches (32d.1) to see where they lead.

- **Read encyclopedia articles about your interests.** General encyclopedias survey a wide range of topics, while specialized encyclopedias concentrate on a specific area. Never, however, stop with encyclopedias—they are too basic for college-level research.

- **Browse the library or a well-stocked bookstore.** Stroll through the **stacks** (the rows of shelves) to find subjects that interest you. Look at books as well as periodicals. Thumb through popular magazines, and browse academic journals in fields that interest you.

## 31d.2 Narrowing a general topic into a workable one

Whether you're working with a topic of your choice or an assigned one, you want to check that it's sufficiently narrow for the time frame and other requirements of your research paper. Also, you want to be sure that the narrowed topic is worthy of a college research project. Box 31.3 offers guidelines.

**SUMMARY BOX** 31.3

### Deciding on a specific, worthwhile research topic

- **Expect to consider various topics before making your final choice.** Give yourself time to think. Keep your mind open to flashes of insight and to alternative ideas. At the same time, be careful not to let indecision paralyze you.

- **Select a topic that interests you.** Your topic will be a companion for a while, sometimes for most of a semester. Select a topic that arouses your interest and allows you the pleasure of satisfying your intellectual curiosity.

- **Choose a sufficiently narrow topic.** You want to be successful within the time and length given by the assignment. Avoid topics that are too broad, such as "emotions." A better choice would be "how people perceive and respond to anger in others."

- **Choose a topic worth researching.** Avoid trivial topics that prevent you from doing what instructors and others expect of a student researcher: investigating ideas, analyzing them critically, and creating a synthesis of complex concepts.

  **NO**  The sizes of different kinds of cars

  **YES**  The effect of SUVs on the environment

- **Choose a topic that has a sufficient number of appropriate sources available.** If you can't find useful sources—ones that relate directly to your topic and ones that are credible, not simply plentiful—drop the topic.

- **Talk with a professor in your field of interest, if possible.** Before the meeting, read a little about your topic so that you can ask informed questions. Ask whether you've narrowed your topic sufficiently and productively. Also, ask for the titles of major books and names of major authorities on your topic.

A good academic topic allows you to demonstrate your critical thinking abilities. There are two broad ways of doing so. First, you might choose a topic on which intelligent people have formed different opinions.

Then, you might analyze your sources and draw on your own experiences to decide which position appears best. The purpose of such a paper would be to attempt to PERSUADE readers that you've considered the various positions and reached a reasonable conclusion.

Alternatively, you might choose to INFORM readers in a paper that synthesizes several sources related to a complex subject. Writing a SYNTHESIS means pulling together extensive information from varied sources to examine essential points that relate to a topic. For example, imagine you've been assigned to write the sample research paper about déjà vu in 34e. After you've read a dozen articles on the topic of déjà vu, you might try to identify three or four key points and then organize information from your reading around those points. Your goal is to clarify complicated or scattered information for your readers.

For a more detailed narrative of Andrei Gurov's research process and the final draft of his research paper, see 34e.1 and 34e.2.

## 31e What is a research question?

A **research question** about your topic is the controlling question that drives your research. Few research paper assignments are phrased as questions. Therefore, most research writing calls on you to ask a thought-provoking, underlying question and then to search for answers to it. Regarding research as a quest for an answer gives your work a specific focus: You can't know whether you've found useful source material unless you know what you're looking for.

Research questions, whether stated or implied, and the strategies needed to answer them vary widely. Your purpose might be to present and explain information: "How does penicillin destroy bacteria?" Or your purpose might be to argue one side of an issue: "Is Congress more important than the Supreme Court in setting social policy?" You can then consult various sources in an attempt to work toward an answer.

*Attempt* is an important word in relation to research. Some research questions lead to a final, definitive answer, but some do not. The previous question about penicillin leads to a reasonably definitive answer (you describe how the antibiotic penicillin destroys the cell walls of some bacteria); this means your writing has an informative purpose. The other question about social policy has no definitive answer, so you're asked to offer an informed opinion based on facts and authoritative viewpoints gathered from your research; this means your writing has a persuasive purpose.

To formulate a research question, begin by BRAINSTORMING a list of questions that come to mind about your topic. Write your list of ideas in your research log (31c).

Suppose, for example, the topic you want to write about is "homelessness." Here are some typical questions you might ask.

- Why can't a rich country like the United States eliminate homelessness?
- Who is homeless?
- How do people become homeless?
- Is it true that many families—not just adults—are homeless?
- Is the homelessness problem getting better or worse?
- What are we doing to solve the problem of homelessness?
- What is it like to be homeless?

Some questions will interest you more than others, so begin with one of those. If a question leads to a dead end, pursue another. Only when you find yourself accumulating answers—or in the case of questions without definitive answers, accumulating viewpoints—is it likely you're dealing with a usable research question. Once you have an explicitly stated research question, you can streamline your research by taking notes only from those sources that help you answer your research question.

Stay flexible as you work. The results of your research may lead you to modify the research question slightly. Actually, such modifying is part of the "moving ahead and circling back" that characterizes research writing. When you've finished researching and notetaking in response to your final research question, you have a starting place for formulating the preliminary THESIS STATEMENT for your research paper.

## 31f How do I determine the purpose and audience for my research paper?

To decide whether your paper will have an informative purpose or a persuasive purpose, see what your research question asks. If the answer to it involves giving facts, information, and explanation, your purpose is to inform. For example, "How have computers changed over time?" calls for INFORMATIVE WRITING. Conversely, if the answer involves offering an educated opinion based on contrasting views and supporting evidence, your purpose is to persuade. For example, "Why should people be aware of current developments in computers?" calls for PERSUASIVE WRITING. You may find that your purpose shifts during your research process.

AUDIENCES for research papers vary. In some situations, only your instructor will read your paper. More often, your audience starts with your peers, the other students in your class. Next, it moves on to a general public audience or to specialists on your topic, with your instructor as one among many readers. Your sense of these other readers' expertise in your topic can guide your decisions about content, level of detail, and DICTION. Section 1c provides advice for analyzing audience.

## 31g What practical steps can help me work efficiently?

To conduct your research with greatest efficiency, you need to do some footwork before you start researching. First, gather the materials listed in Box 31.4 so that they're organized and ready for use at a moment's notice. Second, become familiar with your college library (31g.1). Third, be sure to become skilled and comfortable with searching topics online, if you're not already (32j).

---

**SUMMARY BOX** 31.4

### Equipment you might need for research

1. A copy of your assignment.

2. This handbook, especially Part Five, or access to the Internet so that you can read the book online and use its guidelines.

3. Your research log (31c).

4. Index cards for taking notes (unless you use a laptop). If you use different colors of index cards, you might color-code the different categories of information you find. Also, you might use one size for bibliography cards and the other for content note cards. Another coding strategy is to use pens of different ink colors or self-sticking dots of various colors.

5. Coins (or dollar bills or a debit card) for copy machines or printers.

6. Disks, CDs, a thumb or keychain drive, or other means for storing downloaded source materials.

7. If you use index cards and other paper, a small stapler, paper clips, and rubber bands.

8. A separate bag or even a backpack with wheels to carry research-project materials and books you check out from the library. (Librarians joke about researchers with wheelbarrows.)

---

### 31g.1 Learning how to use library resources

When you learn how your college library functions, your research efficiency increases. Though almost all libraries in the United States and Canada are organized around the same principles for organizing information, physical layouts and procedures differ considerably. If you visit your college library for the sole purpose of figuring out what's located where, you'll feel comfortable and confident when you work there.

Some college libraries provide orientations through English courses; some offer individual training sessions; and most offer informative Web sites or handouts about their resources. Box 31.5 provides a checklist for familiarizing yourself with your library.

CHECKLIST BOX **31.5**

## Learning your library

- How do you get access to the library's catalog and databases, both from inside the library and, if possible, through the Internet? What are the log-in procedures?

- How does the library's catalog work?

- What periodical indexes or databases does your library have, online or in print? (*Indexes* and *databases* are lists of articles in journals and magazines, grouped by subject areas.)

- Where is the general reference collection? (You can't check out reference books, so when you need to use them, build extra time into your schedule to spend at the library.)

- Where is the special reference collection? (Same rules apply as for general reference books.)

- Are the book and journal stacks open (fully accessible shelves) or closed (request each item by filling out a form to hand to library personnel)? If the latter, become familiar with the required procedures not only for asking for a book or journal but also for picking it up when it's ready.

- Where are the library's physical collections of journals and magazines stored? Most libraries place periodicals published in the past year in open areas and older periodicals in bound volumes, on microfiche, on CDs, or online. Learn to use whatever system is in place at your library.

- What periodicals exist online in full-text formats (copies you can read online rather than only from a print copy)?

- What, if anything, is stored on microfilm or microfiche? If you think you'll use that material, take the time to learn how to use the machines. (We find that each library's machines work differently—and many of them have stumped us on occasion.)

- Does the library have special collections, such as local historical works or the writings of persons worthy of such an exclusive honor?

## 31g.2 Decide how you'll use the computer

How you use the computer in the research process is largely a matter of personal preference. Some students use a computer only for finding sources and for DRAFTING and REVISING the paper itself. These students

501

do the rest of their research steps by hand on index cards and sheets of paper: keeping their research log (31c), compiling their WORKING BIBLIOGRAPHY (31i), taking content notes (31k), and so forth.

Other students carry out their entire research process on computer. They set up folders for every phase of their project. To accumulate print sources for their working bibliography, these students download them onto a disk, a jump or keychain drive, a laptop, or a hard drive—always carefully recording the origin of the source in the documentation style they've selected (31h). They type their research log, working bibliography, and content notes directly into computer files.

## 31h   What documentation style should I use?

A **documentation style** is a system for providing information about each source you've used in your research paper. Documentation styles vary from one academic discipline to another. The humanities often use MLA (Modern Language Association) style (Chapter 34). The social sciences frequently use APA (American Psychological Association) style (Chapter 35). Biology and other natural sciences often use CSE (Council of Science Editors) style (Chapter 36). CM (*Chicago Manual*) style is used in various disciplines, generally in the humanities (Chapter 36). If you don't know which style to use, ask your instructor. Never mix documentation styles; use only one style in each piece of writing.

Determining the documentation style you need to follow when you're developing your SEARCH STRATEGY (32b) helps to guarantee that you'll write down the exact details you need to document your sources. You'll need to document all secondary sources. If you're doing primary research, decide what you must document before you begin. Your instructor may have special requirements, such as asking you to submit your research notes or results from observations, questionnaires, surveys, interviews, or anything else that produces primary data.

## 31i   What is a working bibliography?

A **working bibliography** is a preliminary list of the PRIMARY and SECONDARY SOURCES you gather in your research. It contains information about the source and where others might find it. Following is a list of basic elements to include (see more detailed information about documenting specific types of sources in Chapters 34–36).

| BOOKS | PERIODICAL ARTICLES | ONLINE SOURCES |
|---|---|---|
| Author(s) | Author(s) | Author (if available); editor or sponsor of site |
| Title | Title | Title of document and title of site |

| BOOKS | PERIODICAL ARTICLES | ONLINE SOURCES |
|---|---|---|
| Publisher and place of publication | Name of periodical, volume number, issue number | Name of database or online source |
| Year of publication | Date of issue | Date of electronic publication |
| Call number | Page numbers of article | Electronic address (URL) |
| | | Date you accessed the source |

Begin your working bibliography as soon as you start identifying sources. Compiling a working bibliography will help you find out what is available on a particular subject before you do extensive reading and notetaking. If your search turns up very few sources, you may want to change your topic. If it reveals a vast number of sources, you definitely want to narrow your topic or even choose a different one. At the outset, don't leave anything out; even an unpromising source may later prove useful. Expect to add and drop sources throughout the research writing process. As a rough estimate, your working bibliography needs to be about twice as long as the list of sources you end up using. You can record your working bibliography on note cards or on a computer.

On the one hand, note cards have the advantage of being easy to sift through and rearrange. You can also carry them with you when you do library research. At the end of your writing process, you can easily sort and alphabetize them to prepare your final bibliography. Write only one source on each card. Figure 31.2 displays a handwritten

Figure 31.2 Sample bibliography note card in MLA style

bibliography note card by Andrei Gurov for his MLA-style research paper in section 34e.

On the other hand, putting your working bibliography on a computer saves you from having to type your list of sources later. If you use a computer for this purpose, clearly separate one entry from another. You can organize the list alphabetically, by author, or according to your subtopics.

Whichever method you use, when you come across a potential source, immediately record the information exactly as you need it to fulfill the requirements of the DOCUMENTATION STYLE you need to use for your assignment (31h). Spending a few extra moments at this stage can save you hours of work and frustration later on.

## 31j What is an annotated bibliography?

An **annotated bibliography** includes not only publishing information about your sources but also your brief summary of each one, and perhaps a commentary. Figure 31.3 shows part of an annotated bibliography for sources used in the APA-style student paper in Chapter 35.

McKenna, K. Y., Green, A. S., & Gleason, M. E. (2003). Relationship formation on the Internet: What's the big attraction? *Journal of Social Issues, 58,* 9–31.

Two studies show that people who share "true selves" over the Internet often form closer relationships than when they meet face to face. One study surveyed Internet users. A second study found that students who meet first on the Internet tend to like each other better than students who meet first in person.

Miyake, K., & Zuckerman, M. (1993). Beyond personality impressions. *Journal of Personality, 61*(3), 411–436.

This research study examines how both physical and vocal attractiveness affect judges' responses to individuals. The researchers found that, for five different personality measures, judges rate more attractive people more highly.

Figure 31.3 Section from an annotated bibliography in APA style

## 31k  How do I take content notes?

When you write **content notes**, you record information from your sources. As with your working bibliography, you can make content notes either in a computer file or on index cards.

- If you're using index cards, put a heading on each card that gives a precise link to one of your bibliography items. Include the source's title and the numbers of the pages from which you're taking notes.

- On the computer, keep careful track of what ideas came from each source. One strategy is to open a new file for each. Later, after you've taken notes on many of your sources, you can determine what subtopics are important for your paper. You can then open a new file for each topic and use the "Cut" and "Paste" functions to gather notes from all of your sources under each topic.

- On every note card or every note in your computer, do one of three things: (1) Copy exact words from a source in a quotation, enclosing it in quotation marks; (2) write a paraphrase of the source; or (3) write a summary of the source. Keeping track of the kind of note you're taking will help you avoid PLAGIARISM. You might use the codes *Q* for QUOTATION, *P* for PARAPHRASE, and *S* for SUMMARY. Or you might use a different typeface or ink color.

- As you're taking notes, separately record your own reactions and ideas, but take care to differentiate your ideas from those found in your sources. You might write your own thoughts in a different colored ink (note card) or font (computer); you might use the back of your note cards or a computer's "Comment" feature. You can also record your thinking in your RESEARCH LOG.

Figure 31.4 shows one of Andrei Gurov's note cards for his paper in 34e.2.

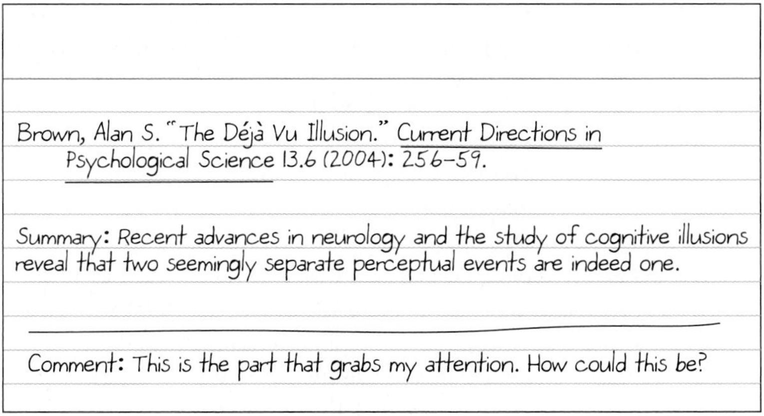

Brown, Alan S. "The Déjà Vu Illusion." *Current Directions in Psychological Science* 13.6 (2004): 256–59.

Summary: Recent advances in neurology and the study of cognitive illusions reveal that two seemingly separate perceptual events are indeed one.

Comment: This is the part that grabs my attention. How could this be?

**Figure 31.4  A handwritten content note card**

## 31l    How do I draft a thesis statement for a research paper?

Drafting a THESIS STATEMENT for a research paper marks the transition from the research process to the writing process. A thesis statement in a research paper sets out the central theme, which you need to sustain throughout the paper (see section 2q, especially Box 2.5). As with any piece of writing, your research paper must fulfill the promise of its thesis statement.

You might begin thinking of a preliminary thesis statement at some middle point in the research process, although it's perfectly acceptable to wait until you've completely finished researching. To start your thesis statement, you might try to convert your RESEARCH QUESTION into a preliminary thesis statement. Of course, because a question is not an assertion, you want to state your thesis as a DECLARATIVE SENTENCE, not as a question. Remember that a good thesis statement makes an assertion that conveys your point of view about your topic and foreshadows the content of your paper (again, see Box 2.5 in 2q). And not least, remember that your research needs to support your thesis statement. Ask yourself whether the material you've gathered from sources can effectively give support. If not, revise your thesis statement, conduct further research, or do both.

Here are examples of subjects narrowed to topics, focused into research questions, and then cast as thesis statements.

| | |
|---|---|
| SUBJECT | *rain forests* |
| TOPIC | The importance of rain forests |
| RESEARCH QUESTION | What is the importance of rain forests? |
| INFORMATIVE THESIS STATEMENT | Rain forests provide the human race with many irreplaceable resources. |
| PERSUASIVE THESIS STATEMENT | Rain forests must be preserved because they offer the human race many irreplaceable resources. |
| SUBJECT | *nonverbal communication* |
| TOPIC | Personal space |
| RESEARCH QUESTION | How do standards for personal space differ among cultures? |
| INFORMATIVE THESIS STATEMENT | Everyone has expectations concerning the use of personal space, but accepted distances for that space are determined by each person's culture. |
| PERSUASIVE THESIS STATEMENT | To prevent intercultural misunderstandings, people must be aware of cultural differences in standards for personal space. |

| | |
|---|---|
| SUBJECT | *computers* |
| TOPIC | artificial intelligence |
| RESEARCH QUESTION | How close are researchers to developing artificial intelligence in computers? |
| INFORMATIVE THESIS STATEMENT | Scientists disagree about whether computers need emotions to have artificial intelligence. |
| PERSUASIVE THESIS STATEMENT | Because emotions play a strong role in human intelligence, computers must have emotions before they can truly have artificial intelligence. |

Andrei Gurov (whose research paper appears in section 34e) revised his preliminary thesis statement twice before he felt that it expressed the point he wanted to make. Andrei also took the key step of checking that he would be able to support it sufficiently with sources throughout the paper.

### FIRST PRELIMINARY THESIS STATEMENT

Déjà vu can be explained by a variety of scientific theories. [Andrei realized that this draft thesis would lead to a paper that would merely list, paragraph by paragraph, each theory, and that the paper would lack synthesis.]

### SECOND PRELIMINARY THESIS STATEMENT

Many people believe feelings of déjà vu have mysterious origins, but science has shown this is not true. [Andrei liked this statement better because it began to get at the complexity of the topic, but he wanted to work on it more because he felt the second part was too general.]

### FINAL THESIS STATEMENT

Although a few people today still prefer to believe that feelings of déjà vu have mysterious or supernatural origins, recent research in cognitive psychology and the neurosciences has shed much rational light on the phenomenon.

## 31m  How do I outline a research paper?

Some instructors require an OUTLINE of your research paper, either before you hand in the paper or along with the paper. In such cases, your instructor is probably expecting you to be working from an outline as you write your drafts. Your research log often comes in handy when you group ideas, especially for a first draft of your paper—and as you make an *informal outline* for it. An outline can serve as a guide as you plan and write your paper. For directions on composing a *formal outline*, see section 2r. To see a topic outline of Andrei Gurov's research paper, turn to section 34e.

## **31n** How do I draft a research paper?

DRAFTING and REVISING a research paper is like drafting and revising any other piece of writing (Chapter 2). Yet to write a research paper, you need extra time for planning, drafting, thinking, redrafting, rethinking, and creating a final draft because you need to demonstrate all of the following:

- You've followed the steps of the research process presented in Chapters 31–33.
- You understand the information that you've located during your research.
- You've evaluated the SOURCES you've used in your research.
- You haven't PLAGIARIZED your material from someone else (33b).
- You've used sources well in your writing, correctly employing QUOTATIONS, PARAPHRASES, and SUMMARIES (33f–33k).
- You've moved beyond SUMMARY to SYNTHESIS so that your sources are interwoven with each other and with your own thinking, not merely listed one by one (4e).
- You've used DOCUMENTATION accurately. (For MLA STYLE, see Chapter 34; for APA STYLE, see Chapter 35; for other documentation styles, see Chapter 36.)

Expect to write a number of drafts of your research paper. The first draft is your chance to discover new insights and connections. Successive drafts help you master the information you've learned and add it authoritatively to the knowledge you already had about the topic. In the first draft, organize the broad categories of your paper. As many research writers do, you may move material around within a category or from one category to another. You'll do that because the act of writing will give you new insights and help you make fresh connections. Box 31.6 suggests some ways to write your first draft.

**SUMMARY BOX** 31.6

### Suggestions for drafting a research paper

- Some researchers categorize notes and write a section at a time. They organize the notes into broad categories by making a separate group for each topic. As patterns begin to emerge, these writers might move material from one category to another. Each category becomes a section of the first draft. This method not only assures researchers that their first draft will include all of the material from their research, but reveals any gaps in information that call for additional research. Of course, you may discover that some of your research doesn't fit your topic and thesis. Put it aside; it might be useful in a later draft.

**Suggestions for drafting a research paper**

- Some researchers finish their research and then slowly review half of the information they've gathered. Next, setting aside that information, they write a partial first draft by drawing on the information they remember from their reading. Then, they use the same process with the second half of the information that they've gathered. Finally, with their two partial drafts and all of their research notes in front of them, they write a complete first draft. Researchers who use this method say it gives them a broad overview of their material quickly and identifies any gaps in information that they need to fill in with further research.

- Some researchers stop at various points during their research and use FREEWRITING to get their ideas into words. Researchers who use this method say that it helps them recognize when they need to adjust their RESEARCH QUESTION or change the emphasis of their search. After a number of rounds of researching and freewriting, these researchers find that they can write their complete first draft relatively easily.

- Some writers review their sources and create an OUTLINE before drafting (2r). Some find a formal outline helpful, while others use a less formal approach.

## 31o How do I revise a research paper?

Before you write each new draft, read your previous draft with a sharp eye. For best results, take a break of a few days (or at least a few hours) before beginning this process. This gives you distance from your material, and a clearer vision of what you need to revise. For a more objective point of view, consider asking a few people you respect to read and react to your first, or perhaps your second, draft.

One key to REVISING any research paper is to examine carefully the evidence you have included. **Evidence** consists of facts, statistics, expert studies and opinions, examples, and stories. As a reader, you expect writers to provide solid evidence to back up their claims and conclusions. Similarly, when you write, readers expect you to provide evidence that clearly supports your claims and conclusions. Use RENNS (3f) to see if you can develop paragraphs more fully. Identify each of the points you have made in your paper, including your thesis and all your subpoints. Then ask the questions in Box 31.7 (p. 510).

Experienced writers know that writing is really *rewriting*. Research papers are among the most demanding composing assignments, and most writers revise several times. Once you've produced a *final draft*,

## Questions for evaluating your evidence

- **Is the evidence sufficient?** To be sufficient, evidence can't be thin or trivial. As a rule, the more evidence you present, the more convincing your thesis will be to readers.

- **Is the evidence representative?** Representative evidence is customary and normal, not based on exceptions. When evidence is representative, it provides a view of the issue that reflects the usual circumstances rather than rare ones.

- **Is the evidence relevant?** Relevant evidence relates directly to your thesis or topic sentence. It illustrates your reasons straightforwardly and never introduces unrelated material.

- **Is the evidence accurate?** Accurate evidence is correct, complete, and up to date. It comes from a reliable SOURCE. Equally important, you present it honestly, without distorting or misrepresenting it.

- **Is the evidence reasonable?** Reasonable evidence is not phrased in extreme language, such as *all, never,* or *certainly.* Reasonable evidence is well thought out and free of logical fallacies (4j).

you're ready to edit (2v), format (Chapter 42), and proofread (2w) your work. Check for correct grammar, punctuation, capitalization, and spelling. (No amount of careful research and good writing can make up for an incorrectly presented, sloppy, error-laden document.)

Consult Boxes 2.8 and 2.10 to remind yourself of the general principles of revising, and consult the research paper revision checklist in Box 31.8 to verify that you've remained aware of all aspects of research writing.

To see one example of the research writing process in action, turn to section 34e. There you'll see the final draft of an MLA-style research paper; a narrative of decisions that the student made during his research process; and commentary (on the text page facing each page of the student's paper) that gives you insight into specific aspects of his paper.

For an APA-style research paper, turn to section 35h. There you'll see the final draft of a student's paper and a narrative of the decisions that the student made during his research process.

# Revising a research paper

If the answer to any of the following questions is no, you need to revise. The section numbers in parentheses tell you where to find useful information.

## WRITING

- Does your introductory paragraph lead effectively into the material? (3b)

- Have you met the basic requirements for a written thesis statement? (2q and 31l)

- Do your thesis statement and the content of your paper address your research question(s)? (31e and 31l)

- Have you discussed the topic of each paragraph fully, using RENNS? (3e and 3f)

- Does the concluding paragraph end your paper effectively? (3k)

## RESEARCH

- Have you included appropriate and effective evidence? (3f and Box 31.7)

- Have you deleted irrelevant or insignificant information? (3g)

- Do your ideas follow sensibly and logically within each paragraph and from one paragraph to the next? (3j)

- Have you used quotations, paraphrases, and summaries well? (33f–33k)

- Have you integrated your source material well without plagiarizing? (33c)

## FORMAT AND DOCUMENTATION

- Have you used the correct format for your parenthetical citations or other documentation style? (Chapters 34–36)

- Does each citation tie into an item in your WORKS CITED (MLA style) or REFERENCES (APA style) list of sources at the end of your paper? (34d and 35f)

- Does the paper exactly match the format you've been assigned to follow? Check margins, spacing, title, headings, page number, font, and so on (Chapter 42).

# Chapter 32

FINDING AND EVALUATING SOURCES

## 32a What is a source?

A **source** is any form of information that provides ideas, examples, information, or evidence. For a research paper, sources can be books, articles, Web pages, Internet files, CD-ROMs, videos, lectures, and other types of communication. Sources can also be interviews; surveys; direct observations of situations, places, or people; performances or lectures; museums; and so on. Sources differ greatly in terms of quality. To be able to use sources responsibly for your research, you need to judge each source's trustworthiness and value. This chapter explains how to locate and evaluate sources.

A source is either primary or secondary. A **primary source** is original work—such as experiments or firsthand reports of experiments, observations, interviews, surveys, and FIELD RESEARCH that you carry out yourself—and documents like letters, diaries, novels, poems, short stories, autobiographies, and journals. When you use a primary source, no one comes between you and the material.

A **secondary source** reports, describes, comments on, or analyzes someone else's work. This information comes to you secondhand. That is, someone other than the primary source relays the information, which adds a layer between you and the original material. This doesn't mean secondary sources are inferior. Indeed, scholars and other experts are excellent secondary sources. However, you need to evaluate secondary sources carefully to make sure that what's being relayed to you isn't distorted or biased in the process.

Suppose you're researching student attitudes toward marriage. Surveying several students would be primary research. Consulting scholars' books and articles about students and marriage would be secondary research. Your decision to use primary or secondary sources depends on your RESEARCH QUESTION or the nature of your assignment.

As you locate, assemble, and evaluate sources related to your topic, expect to accumulate much more information than you'll actually use. Indeed, the quality of your paper depends partly on your ability to eliminate inadequate or repetitive sources and to recognize what is valuable material. Turn to 32h and 32k for detailed guidelines for evaluating sources.

**ESL TIP:** In the United States, PLAGIARISM is a major offense in academic writing. In some cultures, it's customary to take material from scholarly authorities on your topic. However, this practice is forbidden in the United States unless you use quotation marks around the exact words and then state the place where you found those words. For detailed information about how to avoid plagiarism, see Chapter 33. 🌐

## 32b What is a search strategy?

A **search strategy** is an organized procedure for locating and gathering information to answer your specific RESEARCH QUESTION. Using a search strategy guarantees that you'll work systematically rather than haphazardly and that you'll find what you're looking for more quickly.

Following are three frequently used search strategies. If no single one meets your requirements, create your own.

The **expert method** is useful when you know your specific topic. Begin by reading articles or books by an expert in the field. Of course, this means that you have to know who the experts are, and sometimes that's difficult. Talk with people who are generally knowledgeable about your topic, learn what you can from them, and ask them to refer you to work by experts on the topic. (For example, if you're interested in researching dating relationships, a psychology instructor may be able to tell you who are the leading experts on that topic.) Alternatively, or in addition, interview an expert in person, on the phone, or through e-mail. Turn to 32c for detailed advice about conducting effective interviews.

The **chaining method** is useful when your topic is a general one. Start with reference books and bibliographies in current articles or on Web sites; use them to link to additional sources. Keep following the links until you reach increasingly expert sources. Alternatively, talk with people who have some general knowledge of your topic and ask them to refer you to experts they might know.

The **layering method** is useful when you need to find your own topic. You layer information by first consulting general sources and then finding ones that are more specific. You try to relate the information you gather to other scholarly sources in the same subject area.

You may find yourself switching or combining methods. That's fine. "Flexibility with focus" is the guiding principle for experienced researchers. Discovering early in the process what sources are available allows you time to find those that are harder to locate; to use interlibrary loan if an item isn't available in your library or online; to wait for someone to return checked-out books you need; or to schedule interviews, arrange visits, or conduct surveys.

One more piece of advice: Avoid getting too far along in your search until you're reasonably certain you're going in a useful direction. Rather than spend endless hours simply gathering sources, read and analyze some of your materials to make sure your topic is a good one. Your RESEARCH LOG can be useful for this purpose.

## 32c What is field research?

**Field research** involves going into real-life situations to observe, survey, interview, or be part of some activity firsthand. A field researcher might, for example, go to a factory, a lecture, a day-care center, or a mall—anywhere that people engage in everyday activities. A field researcher might also conduct interviews of experts and other identified individuals. Because field research yields original data, it's a PRIMARY SOURCE.

Conducting field research takes careful planning. Be sure to allow time to gather the data you want, ANALYZE it, and then SYNTHESIZE it with other sources and with your own knowledge and experience. Field research often involves events that can't be revisited. Therefore, record as much information as possible during your research and decide later what information you can use. Afterwards, while your memory is fresh, go over your notes and highlight major types of information. Also, fill in any details you might not have written down.

### OBSERVING AND SURVEYING

For observations of behavior (for example, the audience at a sporting event or elementary school children at play during recess), you can take notes during the activity. Permission to videotape instead of taking notes is hard to get because of privacy concerns. Try to remain objective so that you can see things clearly. One strategy is to take notes in a two-column format. On the left, record only objective observations; on the right, record comments or possible interpretations. Figure 32.1 is an example of a double-column note strategy.

If you want to survey a group of people, allow time to write, reflect on, and revise a questionnaire. Test the questionnaire on a few people. Revise any questions that don't work well. For detailed advice on creating an effective questionnaire, see 39b.

### INTERVIEWING AN EXPERT

An expert can offer valuable information, a new point of view, and firsthand facts, statistics, and examples. Probably the best place to start is with the faculty at your college. Your instructors are also scholars and researchers with expertise in many areas. They may suggest good additional sources, as well as other experts to contact. Indeed, your family and friends might qualify as experts, if they've been involved with an issue you're researching. Corporations, institutions, and professional organizations often have public relations offices that can answer questions or put you in contact with experts.

Make every attempt to conduct interviews in person so that you can observe body language and facial expressions as you talk. However, if distance is a problem, you can conduct interviews over the phone or online. Box 32.1 provides specific suggestions for conducting interviews.

| Notes | Comment/Analyses |
|---|---|
| Small conference room; round table covered with papers | |
| JP suggests fundraising plan | JP seems nervous. Her normal behavior, or is it this situation? |
| AR and CT lean forward; SM leans back | |
| SM interrupts JP's plan, asks for more; CT silent | The fact that JP and AR are women might explain SM's response. Or is it that he's more senior? |
| JP continues proposal | |
| SM looks out window, taps pencil | Seems to have made up his mind. A power move? |

Figure 32.1 A double-column field research note

**SUMMARY BOX 32.1**

## Conducting research interviews

- Arrange the interview well in advance, conduct background research, prepare specific questions, and show up on time.
- Rehearse how to ask your questions without reading them (perhaps highlight the key word in colored ink). Looking your interviewee in the eye as you ask questions establishes ease and trust. If you're interviewing on the telephone, be organized and precise.
- Create a shortcut symbol or letter for key terms you expect to hear during the interview. This cuts down on your time needed to look away from your interviewee.
- Take careful notes, listening especially for key names, books, or other print or online sources.
- Use standard 8 1/2-by-11-inch paper so that you have room to write.
- Bring extra pens or pencils.
- Never depend on recording an interview. People have become very reluctant to permit anyone to record them, and many will cancel appointments on the spot if recording is even mentioned.

## 32d How do I find library-based sources?

In an age when the Web contains over nine billion pages of information, it might seem almost prehistoric to talk about libraries. After all, the **library** is where generations of college students have traditionally gone to find sources: books and periodicals organized by catalogs and indexes. However, notice that we've referred to "library-based" sources and not necessarily to the library itself. In many respects, the function that a library performs is even more important than its physical building. Librarians and scholars have systematically gathered and organized sources so that students and researchers can find the best ones efficiently and reliably. Many libraries give you remote access to their holdings via the Internet, so you might use library-based sources without ever setting foot in the building.

Still, the building itself continues to be a vital place for all research. One key advantage of going to the library is your chance to consult face-to-face with librarians. They train for their profession by learning how to advise students and other researchers about using library resources to greatest advantage. Never hesitate to ask questions about how to proceed or where to find a resource.

**Catalogs** list sources—usually books, but also films, recordings, and documents—that the library owns (32d.2). **Indexes** list articles in periodicals; each index covers a specific topic area (32d.3). Catalogs and indexes exist mainly in electronic format; less commonly, some catalogs and indexes are still in print format. **Databases** always exist electronically (32d.1). They consist of one or more indexes and contain extensive lists of articles, reports, and books. You can access and search electronic catalogs, indexes, and databases from computers in the library or by connecting to the library online. You can also subscribe to databases, but this can be expensive for students. Fortunately, at most colleges, your tuition pays for access to online library resources, so take advantage of that benefit. Public libraries also subscribe to databases.

If you're accessing a database by connecting to the library online, you need to use a **browser** (such as Mozilla Firefox or Microsoft Internet Explorer), a software program that gives you access to the Web and the search engines located there.

### 32d.1 Using databases

Sources that you identify through scholarly databases are almost always more reliable and appropriate than sources you find by simply browsing the Web. The reliability of scholarly databases stems from their origins: Only experts and professionals who recognize works of merit compile them.

The best way to access a database at your library is to go to your college library's Web site, whether you're online in the library, at home, or in a dormitory. Figure 32.2 shows an example of a college library Web site.

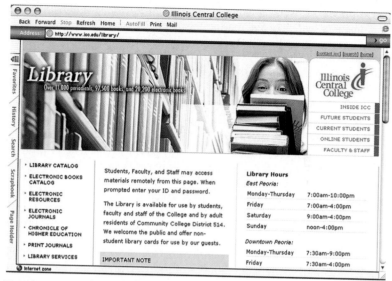

Figure 32.2 A college library Web site

Each home page of a library shows the resources available through that Web site, although more might be available in the library itself. Most college libraries subscribe to one or more database services, such as EBSCO, FirstSearch, and IBIS. Because the college pays for these services, you don't have to, but you'll need an ID or password to use them. Commonly, your student number serves as your ID, but check with a librarian to see what's required at your college.

Many businesses and corporations subscribe to databases, too, making them available to people associated with the company. A law firm, for example, likely subscribes to LexisNexis, which provides searchable access to legal cases and decisions.

Each entry in a database contains bibliographic information, including a title, author, date of publication, and publisher (in the case of books or reports) or periodical (in the case of articles). The entry might also provide an abstract, or summary, of the material. Once you locate an entry that seems promising, you need to find the complete article itself, through various methods. You might need to find a print copy of the source, or you might be able to use the database to connect freely to the full text of the source. The third option might be to purchase from the database full copies of the sources you find. If you're on a tight budget, try to purchase only what looks truly useful. You can request materials that are not in your library through interlibrary loan (32g).

**EXERCISE 32-1** Working either individually or as part of a group, access your library's Web site. You may do this either by going to the library itself or by connecting to the library online. List all of the types of information available. In particular, list the indexes and databases you can search and the subject areas each one covers. Note whether any of the databases have full-text versions of articles. Note if the library's Web site has any online "help" or "search suggestions."

## USING KEYWORDS

When you search library databases, **keywords**, also called *descriptors* or *identifiers*, are your lifeline to success. Keywords are the main words in a source's title or the words that the author or editor has identified as central. Without keywords, you'd have great difficulty accessing sources listed in online or electronic database book catalogs and periodical indexes. Similarly, to find information on the World Wide Web or on the Internet, keywords are essential.

When you search using keywords, chances are you'll come up with a large or even overwhelming number of sources. Much of what turns up won't be relevant to your topic. The two main ways to make keyword searches more efficient are using guided searches (answers to prompts) and using Boolean expressions (keyword combinations).

## USING GUIDED SEARCHES

**Guided searches**, also called *advanced searches*, allow you to look through a database or search engine by answering prompts provided in an onscreen form. A typical search involves selecting a range of dates of publication (for example, after 2004 or between 1990 and 1995) and specifying only a certain language (such as English) or a certain format (such as books). Figure 32.3 is an example of a search for sources that have the words *déjà vu* in their titles and sources that use *false memory* as another keyword but are not about *crime*.

## USING BOOLEAN EXPRESSIONS

Using **Boolean expressions** means that you search a database or search engine by typing keyword combinations that narrow and refine your search. To combine keywords, use the words *AND, OR,* and *NOT,* or the symbols that represent those words. Boolean expressions, generally placed between keywords, instruct the search engine to list only those Web sites in which your keywords appear in certain combinations and to ignore others. Box 32.2 explains a few ways to search with keywords more effectively, using the subject "relationships" as an example. Most databases or search engines explain other ways they handle expressions and formats in a "Help" or a "Search Tips" feature.

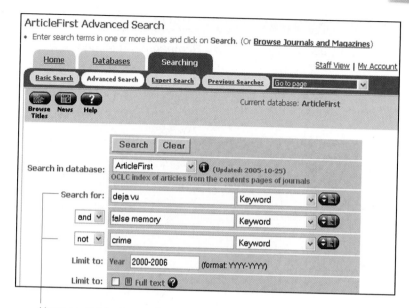

Users can list the keywords
they want to search for or
not to search for.

Figure 32.3  A guided or advanced search

**SUMMARY BOX 32.2**

## Refining keyword searches with Boolean expressions

**AND or the + ("plus") symbol:** Narrows the focus of your search
because both keywords must be found. For example, if you were
researching the topic of the APA paper in section 35h (the role of
physical attractiveness in new relationships over the Internet) you
would try the expression *relationships AND attractiveness AND
Internet.* Many search engines, such as Google.com, don't require the
word *AND* between terms. Figure 32.4 (p. 520) illustrates the results.

**NOT or the − ("minus") symbol:** Narrows a search by excluding
texts containing the specified word or phrase. If you want to eliminate
instant messaging from your search, type *relationships AND
attractiveness AND Internet NOT instant messaging.*

➤

**SUMMARY BOX** **32.2** *continued*

## Refining keyword searches with Boolean expressions

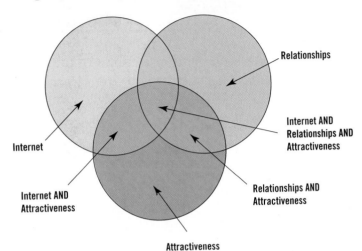

Figure 32.4 A Venn diagram showing overlaps among *relationships*, *attractiveness*, and *Internet*

**OR:** Expands a search's boundaries by including more than one keyword. If you want to expand your search to include sources about relationships begun through either instant messaging or chat rooms, try the expression *relationships AND attractiveness AND Internet AND Instant Messaging OR chat rooms.* You'll get pages mentioning relationships and attractiveness only if they also mention instant messaging or chat rooms.

**" ":** Quotation marks direct a search engine to match your exact word order on a Web page. For example, a search for "online relationships" will find pages that contain the exact phrase *online relationships*. However, it won't return pages with the the the phrase *relationships online*. If you search for *James Joyce* without using quotation marks, most engines will return all pages containing the words *James* and *Joyce* anywhere in the document; however, a search using "James Joyce" brings you closer to finding Web sites about the Irish writer.

### 32d.2 Finding books

A library's **book catalog**, which lists its holdings (its entire collection), exists as a computer database in almost every modern library. You can find a book by searching by **author**, by **title**, by **subject**, and by

KEYWORD. Figure 32.5 shows the home page for a typical type of catalog, this one at the Library of Congress. Note that it allows you to search by title, author, subject, call number, or keyword; to search particular indexes; or to search using BOOLEAN EXPRESSIONS.

URL for Library of Congress Catalog

Begin here for new search

Advanced search

General help areas

Links

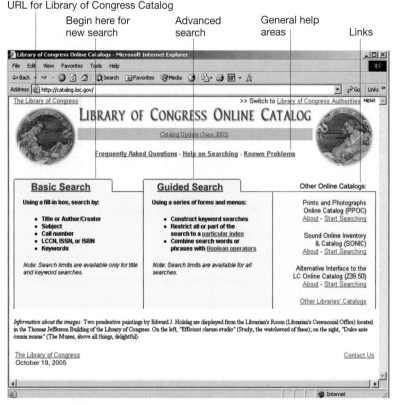

Figure 32.5  Library of Congress Online Catalog

Suppose a source recommends that you find a book by the **author** Thomas L. Friedman, but you don't know its title. You can search the catalog for books by this author. A screen on your library's computer will have a place for you to type "Friedman, Thomas" in a space for "author." (Usually, you enter last name, then first name, but check which system your library uses.) If your library owns any books by Thomas Friedman, the computer will display their titles and other bibliographic information, such as the library call number. Then you can use the call number to request the book or to find it yourself.

Keyword
search fields

Screen displaying
one of the results

**Figure 32.6 Catalog title and author search**

Among the books you might find when searching for "Friedman, Thomas" is *The World Is Flat: A Brief History of the Twenty-first Century* (New York: Farrar, Straus and Giroux, 2005). Suppose you know that book's **title**, but not its author, and want to see if your library owns a copy. A screen on your library's catalog will have a place for you to type in the title; some systems omit words like *the* or *a,* so that in this case, you would type in only "World Flat Brief History Twenty-first Century." Figure 32.6 is a sample title-author keyword search for a book catalog.

Suppose, however, you don't know an author's name or a book title. You have only a research topic, and you need to find sources. In this case, you need to search by **subject**, using the terms listed in the *Library of Congress Subject Headings (LCSH).* The *LCSH* is a multivolume catalog available, primarily in book form, in the reference section of every library. A version of the information in the *LCSH* is online at <http://authorities.loc.gov>. The *LCSH* lists only **subject headings**, which are organized from most general to most narrow. Suppose you're researching the topic of "globalization." If you enter that term into a space for subject searches in your own library's "Search" screen, *The World Is Flat:*

*A Brief History of the Twenty-first Century* by Thomas Friedman will be listed if the book is available.

Finally, you may wish to search by **keyword** in your library's holdings. If you were researching a paper on the future of jobs in the changing world economy, you could find Friedman's book using the keywords *economy, globalization, outsourcing, employment,* and so on.

An entry in the library's book catalog contains a great deal of useful information: a book's title, author, publisher, date and place of publication, and length, along with its location in the library. A full-record catalog entry (a complete set of information about the source rather than a brief listing that may have only author, title, and call number) lists additional subjects covered in that book. The list of additional subjects can provide valuable clues for further searching.

Many libraries allow you to print out this information, send it to your e-mail account, or download and save it. Whether you choose one of these options or copy the information yourself directly into your WORKING BIBLIOGRAPHY, it's crucial to record the **call number** exactly as it appears, with all numbers, letters, and decimal points. The call number tells where the book is located in the library's stacks (storage shelves). If you're researching in a library with *open stacks* (that is, you're permitted to go where books are shelved), the call number leads you to the area in the library where you can find all books on the same subject. Simply looking at what's on the shelves may yield useful sources. Keep in mind that in physically browsing the stacks, however, you're missing sources that other students have checked out or that are "on hold" at the library's reserve desk. The book catalog generally will contain information about whether a book is checked out or on reserve.

A call number is especially crucial in a library or special collection with *closed stacks* (that is, a library where you fill in a call slip, hand it in at the call desk, and wait for the book to arrive). Such libraries don't permit you to browse the stacks, so you have to rely entirely on the book catalog. If you fill in the wrong number or an incomplete number, your wait will be in vain.

## 32d.3 Finding periodicals

**Periodicals** are newspapers, magazines, and journals published at set intervals. To use periodicals efficiently, consult indexes to periodicals, which allow you to search by subject, title, keyword, or author. Most exist as online databases that are updated frequently. Your library very likely subscribes to several of the indexes that you'll need, and you can access them through the library's Web site. The URL for accessing each index online will vary from college to college. Find out how to log on by consulting the librarian in your college library. (A few indexes are published on CD-ROMs, and a few are published only in print.)

List of article indexes
available at this library

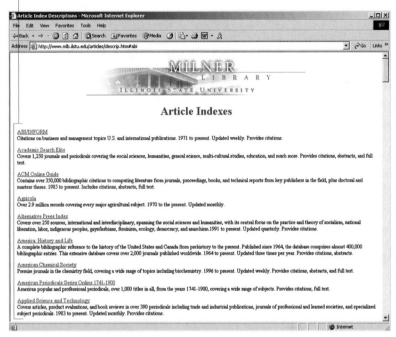

**Figure 32.7** Listing of indexes that include relevant articles

## USING INDEXES

Your library's home page generally provides different ways to access various indexes. Figure 32.7 shows one example. Users who select "Show Databases" under "By Subject" will see an alphabetical list of subject areas, beginning "General Indexes, Agriculture, Anthropology, Art, Biography," and so on. When you choose a subject area, you'll see a list of all the databases for that area, as shown in the same figure. It's important to choose the right index for your search because the wrong one may miss some of the best sources for your paper.

**General indexes** to periodicals list articles in journals, magazines, and newspapers. Large libraries have many general indexes. Among them are the following:

- The *Readers' Guide to Periodical Literature* (online at *Readers' Guide Abstracts*) is the most well-known index, though its uses are limited for college-level research because it doesn't include scholarly journals. Some libraries still have the print volumes. This index includes over two hundred magazines and journals for general readers. Nevertheless, you can use it to find topics, get a broad overview, and narrow a subject.

- *Periodical Abstracts* indexes general and academic journals in business, current affairs, psychology, religion, and many other areas.
- *NewsBank* covers over four hundred US newspapers. It has full-text coverage from 1993 on. *NewsBank* also offers reproductions of articles from 1980 to 1992, but these are stored on microfiche, not online, in some libraries.

**Specialized indexes** are more appropriate than general indexes for most college-level research. Specialized indexes list articles in journals published by and for expert, academic, or professional readers. Many specialized indexes include the abstract, or summary, that is printed at the beginning of each scholarly article. Box 32.3 provides examples of specialized indexes.

---

**SUMMARY BOX 32.3**

## Examples of specialized indexes

*Art Abstracts*

*Business Abstracts*

*Education Full Text*

*General Science Abstracts*

*Humanities Index*

*MLA International Bibliography of Books and Articles in the Modern Languages and Literatures*

*Music Index Online*

*PsycINFO*

*Social Sciences Abstracts*

---

You search periodical indexes by using KEYWORDS. Shown in Figure 32.8 (p. 526) are three screens from a keyword search of *PsycINFO* for Andrei Gurov's research paper that appears in section 34e.2.

### LOCATING THE ARTICLES THEMSELVES

Periodical indexes help you locate the titles of specific articles on your topic. Once you have the listing, though, how do you get your hands on the article itself? Sometimes you can find a full-text online version of the article to read, download, or print.

Frequently, however, you need to find a printed copy of the periodical. Begin by checking what periodicals your college library lists in its online catalogs. This list might be in the library's catalog, or the list might be available separately; ask how your library lists periodicals. In either

Keyword search

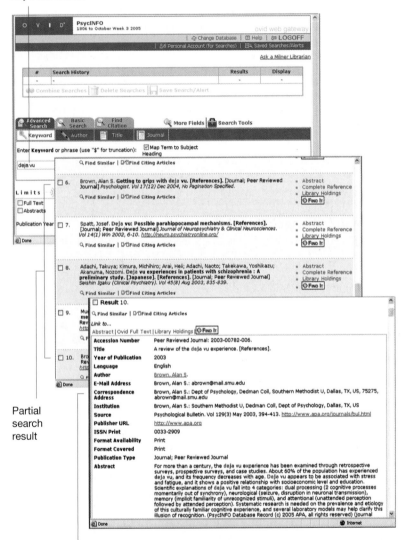

Partial
search
result

One article selected from database

**Figure 32.8  Keyword search of *PsycINFO***

case, search for the periodical name you want (for example, *American Literature* or *The Economist*), not for the article's author or title. If your library subscribes to that periodical, you use its call number to find its location in the library. You then need to find the specific article you want by looking for the issue in which the article you're looking for is printed.

Few libraries subscribe to all of the periodicals listed in specialized indexes. For advice on locating sources that your college doesn't own, see 32g.

**EXERCISE 32-2**   Use two databases that are available through your library to conduct two searches for one or more of the terms below. (Alternatively, your instructor may suggest a different term or have you pursue a topic of your own choosing.)

If possible, choose one general database (or index) such as *Readers' Guide Abstracts* and one specialized database or index. Compile a brief report that compares the sources you generate. You might address questions like these: How many sources did each search turn up? Is there any overlap? What kinds of periodicals are represented in each database? What access does your library provide to the several sources you find most interesting in each search? Note: If you're generating lots of hits, restrict your search to the past year or two.

Suggested terms for searching (with type of specialized database to consult in parentheses): *memory* (psychology); *globalization* (business, economics, sociology); *cloning* (biology); *global warming* (geology, geography); *obesity* (medicine).

## 32e   How do I use reference works?

**Reference works** include encyclopedias, almanacs, yearbooks, fact books, atlases, dictionaries, biographical reference works, and bibliographies. Some references are *general,* providing information on a vast number of subjects, but without any depth. Others are *specialized,* providing information on selected topics, often for more expert or professional audiences.

### 32e.1  General reference works

Reference works are the starting point for many college and other advanced researchers—but they're no more than a starting point. **General reference works** by themselves are insufficient for academic research. Still, they help researchers identify useful KEYWORDS, find examples, and verify facts. Most widely used reference works are available in electronic versions, usually online. Check your library's Web site to see if the reference work you want is available online through a subscription or license the library has purchased. Alternatively, you can search the Web by entering the work's name to see if it's available there. (For example, *Encyclopaedia Britannica* is at <http://www.britannica.com>.) Be aware that often you have to pay a fee for works you don't access through the library.

### GENERAL ENCYCLOPEDIAS

Articles in multivolume general encyclopedias, such as the *Encyclopaedia Britannica,* summarize information on a wide variety of subjects. The articles can give you helpful background information and the names of major figures and experts in the field. Best of all, many articles end with a brief bibliography of major works on the subject. General encyclopedias aren't the place to look for information on recent events or current research, although sometimes they cover a field's ongoing controversies up until the date that the reference was published.

## ALMANACS, YEARBOOKS, FACT BOOKS

Almanacs, yearbooks, and fact books are huge compilations of facts in many subject areas. They're often available both in print and online. They're excellent for verifying information from other sources and, in some cases, for finding supporting facts and figures. Almanacs, such as *The World Almanac,* present capsule accounts of a year's events and data about government, politics, economics, science and technology, sports, and many other categories. *Facts on File,* which is indexed online by LexisNexis, covers world events in a weekly digest and in an annual one-volume yearbook. The annual *Statistical Abstract of the United States* (accessed online through <http://www.census.gov>) contains a wealth of data on the United States. *Demographic Yearbook* and the *United Nations Statistical Yearbook* carry worldwide data.

## ATLASES AND GAZETTEERS

Atlases (such as *The Times Atlas of the World*) contain maps of our planet's continents, seas, and skies. Gazetteers (such as *The Columbia Gazetteer of the World,* available online for a fee at <http://www.columbiagazetteer.org>) provide comprehensive geographical information on topography, climates, populations, migrations, natural resources, crops, and so on.

## DICTIONARIES

**Dictionaries** define words and terms. In addition to general dictionaries, specialized dictionaries exist in many academic disciplines to define words and phrases specific to a field.

## BIOGRAPHICAL REFERENCE WORKS

Biographical reference books give brief factual information about famous people—their accomplishments along with pertinent events and dates in their lives. Biographical references include the *Who's Who* series, *The Dictionary of American Biography,* and many others. Specialized biographical references in various fields are also available.

## BIBLIOGRAPHIES

Bibliographies list books, articles, documents, films, and other resources and provide publication information so that you can find those sources. Some bibliographies are comprehensive and list sources on a wide range of topics. Others list only sources on a particular subject. Specialized bibliographies can be very helpful in your research process. Annotated or critical bibliographies describe and evaluate the works that they list. These resources are increasingly available online but require you either to access them through a library's paid subscription service or to pay a fee each time you use them.

## 32e.2 Specialized reference works

**Specialized reference works** provide more authoritative and specific information than do general reference works. Specialized reference works are usually appropriate for college-level research because the information is more advanced and detailed. They can be invaluable for introducing you to the controversies and KEYWORDS in a subject area. In particular, finding authors' names in such books can help you begin to accumulate a list of credible authors.

There are hundreds of specialized references. We've listed just a few examples here.

> *Encyclopedia of Banking and Finance*
> *Handbook of Modern Marketing*
> *New Grove Dictionary of Music and Musicians*
> *Oxford Companion to Art*
> *Dictionary of American Biography*
> *An Encyclopedia of World History*
> *A Dictionary of Literary Terms*
> *Oxford Companion to American Literature*
> *Encyclopedia of Philosophy*
> *Encyclopedia of Religion*
> *Political Science Bibliographies*
> *Encyclopedia of Chemistry*
> *Encyclopedia of the Biological Sciences*
> *Encyclopedia of Psychology*
> *International Encyclopedia of Film*
> *Oxford Companion to the Theatre*

Because hundreds of one-volume works are highly specific (for example, *Encyclopedia of Divorce*, *Encyclopedia of Aging*, and *Encyclopedia Dictionary of Psychology*), we haven't listed them here. Check what specialized reference books your college library has available that might help you in your search.

## 32f  How do I find government documents?

Government publications are available in astounding variety. You can find information on laws and legal decisions, regulations, population, weather patterns, agriculture, national parks, education, and health, to name just a few topics. Since the middle 1990s, most government documents have been available through the World Wide Web. The Government Printing Office (GPO) maintains the *Catalog of U.S. Government Publications* online at <http://www.gpoaccess.gov/index.html>. The GPO site has a searchable database. Information about legislation is also available at the Web site THOMAS, a service of the Library of Congress, which you can access at <http://thomas.loc.gov>. A directory of all federal government sites that provide statistical information is at <http://www.fedstats.gov>.

The LexisNexis database service provides access to a huge number of other governmental reports and documents. For example, it includes the *Congressional Information Service (CIS)*, which indexes all papers produced by US congressional panels and committees. These documents include the texts of hearings (for example, testimony about homelessness) and reports (for example, a comparative study of temporary shelters for homeless people).

## 32g What if my library doesn't have a source I need?

Almost no library owns every book or subscribes to every periodical. However, many libraries are connected electronically to other libraries' book catalogs and can give you access to additional holdings. Often you or a librarian can request materials from other libraries through interlibrary loan (generally free of charge). Alternatively, your college may have a different document delivery system (perhaps at a cost to you).

## 32h How do I evaluate sources?

Finding a source is only part of your effort. Your next step is to evaluate the quality of each source. Your critical thinking skills (Chapter 4) will be important in this effort. First, decide whether the information in the source relates to your topic in more than a vague, general sense. Then, ask how a source might help you answer your research question (31e). Finally, using the criteria in Box 32.4, evaluate each source with a cold, critical eye.

**ESL TIP:** The definition of *authority* can differ across cultures. However, in the United States, a source must meet specific criteria to be considered authoritative. A source is not reliable simply because the author or speaker is an important member of the community, claims to have knowledge about a topic, or publishes material in print or online. When considering whether to use a source for your research, ask yourself the questions in Box 32.4.

## Evaluating sources

1. **Is the source authoritative?** Generally, encyclopedias, textbooks, and academic journals (*The American Scholar, Journal of Counseling and Development*) are authoritative. Books published by university presses (Indiana University Press) and by publishers that specialize in scholarly books are also trustworthy. Material published in newspapers, in general-readership magazines (*Newsweek, U.S. News & World Report*), and by established commercial publishers (Prentice Hall) are usually reliable, but you want to apply the other criteria in this list with special care, cross-checking names and facts whenever possible. Web sites maintained by professional organizations, such as the National Council of Teachers of English at <http://www.ncte.org>, are authoritative.

2. **Is the author an expert?** Biographical material in the article or book may tell you if the author is an expert on the topic. Look up the author in a reputable, up-to-date biographical dictionary. Alternatively, enter the author's name in an Internet search engine. Look to see if the author has a degree in this field and whether he or she is affiliated with a reliable institution. Also, if an author is often cited by professionals in the field and published in journals, he or she is probably considered an expert.

3. **Is the source current?** Check the publication date. Research is ongoing in most fields, and information is often modified or replaced by new findings. Check databases and online subject directories to see if newer sources are available.

4. **Does the source support its information sufficiently?** Are its assertions or claims supported with sufficient evidence? If the author expresses a point of view but offers little evidence to back up that position or resorts to logical fallacies, reject the source. Use wise judgment and don't take chances.

5. **Is the author's tone balanced?** Use your critical thinking skills when you evaluate a source (Chapter 4). If the TONE is unbiased and the reasoning is logical, the source is probably useful. Some warning signs of biased tone are name calling, sarcasm, stereotyping, or absolute assertions about matters that are open to interpretation (using *always, everyone,* and similar words).

## 32i    What should I know about searching the Web?

Sources from the library or from library databases have the advantage of being selected by experts. While you still have to evaluate them, they have passed a screening process. On the other hand, anyone can put anything on the Web. This makes the Web a rich source of information, but it also makes finding what you need difficult, and it opens the possibility of encountering inaccurate or biased materials. Therefore, searching library databases remains a crucial method of finding many scholarly sources.

## 32j How do I search the Web?

The principles for searching the Web are much like those for searching databases (32d.1). You start with a broad subject and narrow it to arrive at a suitable topic for an academic research paper. Once you use a browser to get on the Web, you can search for sites by using a SEARCH ENGINE or by typing an address (called a **URL**, for "universal resource locator" or "uniform resource locator") into the search box. **Search engines** are programs designed to hunt the Internet for sources on specific topics that you identify by using keywords (32j.1) or through subject directories (32j.2). Box 32.5 lists some commonly used search engines.

---

**SUMMARY BOX** 32.5

### Addresses for some search engines

| | |
|---|---|
| AltaVista | http://altavista.com |
| Excite | http://www.excite.com |
| Lycos | http://www.lycos.com |
| Yahoo! | http://www.yahoo.com |
| Ask Jeeves | http://www.ask.com |
| Google | http://www.google.com |
| Metacrawler | http://www.metacrawler.com |
| Dogpile | http://www.dogpile.com |

---

As the Internet matures, search engines are constantly acquiring new features. A special page on the Google search engine, "Google Scholar" (shown in Figure 32.9), permits scholarly searches that have features in common with searches of library databases.

◢◢ **ALERT:** When you write a URL, such as <http://www.prenhall.com/ troyka>, the Modern Language Association (MLA) tells you to surround it with angle brackets so that readers can clearly distinguish the URL from the body text. However, don't use angle brackets when you type a URL in the locator box at the top of a Web page. ◆

Search Advanced Scholar Search
Scholar Preferences
Scholar Help

Stand on the shoulders of giants

Google Home - About Google - About Google Scholar

©2005 Google

| Google Scholar BETA | **Advanced Scholar Search** | |
|---|---|---|
| **Find articles** | with **all** of the words | |
| | with the **exact phrase** | |
| | with **at least one** of the words | |
| | **without** the words | |
| | where my words occur | anywhere in the article ◆ |
| **Author** | Return articles written by | |
| | | e.g., "PJ Hayes" or McCarthy |
| **Publication** | Return articles published in | |
| | | e.g., J Biol Chem or Nature |
| **Date** | Return articles published between | and |
| | | e.g., 1996 |
| **Subject Areas** | ⦿ Return articles in all subject areas. | |
| | ○ Return only articles in the following subject areas: | |
| | ☐ Biology, Life Sciences, and Environmental Science | |
| | ☐ Business, Administration, Finance, and Economics | |
| | ☐ Chemistry and Materials Science | |

Figure 32.9  An advanced search screen for the Google Scholar search engine

## 32j.1  Using keywords

In the same way you use KEYWORDS to find materials in library data-bases (32d.1), you use them to find information on the Internet. Type a word or group of words in the search box on the opening page of the search engine, and click on the "Search" or "Enter" button. The en-gine scans for your word(s) in Web pages, and then lists sites that con-tain them.

## 32j.2  Using subject directories

**Subject directories** provide a good alternative to keyword searches. These directories are lists of topics (education, computing, entertainment, and so on) or resources and services (shopping, travel, and so on), with links to Web sites on those topics and resources. Most search engines' home pages have one or more subject directories. In addition, there are some indepen-dent subject directories. Box 32.6 (p. 534) lists some examples.

Clicking on a general category within a subject directory will take you to lists of increasingly specific categories. Eventually, you'll get a list of

## Addresses for some independent subject directories

| | |
|---|---|
| *Educator's Reference Desk* | http://www.eduref.org |
| *Infomine* | http://infomine.ucr.edu |
| *Internet Public Library* | http://www.ipl.org |
| *Librarians' Index to the Internet* | http://lii.org |
| *Library of Congress* | http://lcweb.loc.gov |
| *Refdesk.com* | http://www.refdesk.com |

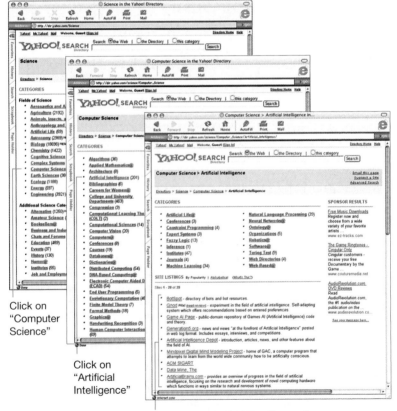

Click on "Computer Science"

Click on "Artificial Intelligence"

Sources on "Artificial Intelligence"

**Figure 32.10  A Yahoo! subject directory for "Artificial Intelligence"**
*Source:* Reproduced with permission of Yahoo! Inc. © 2003 by Yahoo! Inc. YAHOO
and the YAHOO! logo are trademarks of Yahoo! Inc. *Microsoft® Internet Explorer*
reprinted by permission from Microsoft® Corporation.

Web pages on the most specific subtopic you select. These search engines also allow you to click on a category and enter keywords for a search. For example, suppose that you are using Yahoo to search for information on artificial intelligence. As Figure 32.10 (p. 534) shows, you'll first go to Yahoo's general category of "Science." Under "Science" you'll find the category of "Computer Science," and within "Computer Science," you'll find a link to "Artificial Intelligence," a page that lists nineteen additional categories and dozens of sources.

Box 32.7 summarizes the information in this section by providing some general guidelines for using search engines and directories with keywords.

---

**SUMMARY BOX 32.7**

## Tips on using search engines and directories

- Use keyword combinations or BOOLEAN EXPRESSIONS (Box 32.2) unless you have a very specific, narrow topic with unique keywords. A search for even a moderately common topic may produce thousands of hits, many of which won't be relevant to your topic. You might also switch to a subject directory.

- Most search engines attempt to search as much of the Web as possible. But because the World Wide Web is vast and unorganized, different search engines will give different results for the same search. Try using more than one search engine, or use a **metasearch engine**, one that searches several search engines at once. (Dogpile is a metasearch engine.)

- Check the "Help" or "Search Tips" page of your search engine. Search engines add or change features frequently.

- Use the "Advanced Search" page, if one is available. It allows you to search or sort by date, language, file format, and domain type, as well as by various combinations of keywords.

- When you find a useful site, go to the toolbar at the top of the screen and click on "Bookmark" or "Favorites" and then click on "Add." Doing so allows you to return to a good source easily by opening "Bookmarks" or "Favorites" and clicking on the address.

- Use the "History" or "Go" function to track the sites you visit, in case you want to revisit one you previously thought was not helpful.

- Sources on the Web may come in various formats. Most common are Web pages in HTML (Hypertext Markup Language) format. However, you may also encounter Word or Excel documents, PowerPoint slides, or PDF (portable document format) files, each of which requires specific software. PDF files, which require the free Adobe Acrobat Reader that you can download from <http://www.adobe.com>, allow people to preserve documents in their original formats.

**EXERCISE 32-3**    Use a search engine of your choice to search for sources on "déjà vu." (To make the search easier, you may omit the accents.) For each option below, record how many hits occur.

1. Enter the phrase *"deja vu"*
2. Enter the word *"memory"*
3. Enter the phrase *"memory" AND "deja vu"*
4. Enter the phrase *"deja vu" AND "consciousness"*
5. To any of the searches above, add the word *"research"*
6. Repeat this exercise by searching another topic that interests you.

## 32k   How do I evaluate Web sources?

The same strategies for evaluating library sources, discussed in 32h, apply to evaluating Web sources. Ask if the Web source is well supported with evidence and free from fallacies or bias. Use strategies for critical thinking and analysis (Chapters 4 and 6).

However, you need to evaluate Web sources with additional care for two reasons. First, because anyone can post anything on the Web, some sources may very well be plagiarized. Second, many sources on the Web have been written by individuals posing as experts and, as a result, may offer false or misleading information.

You're always accountable for the sources you choose. Most sites also contain material that will help you assess their credibility, such as a bibliography, links to the author or editor, or a description of the sponsoring organization. You want to discard sites that do not contain such verifying information, however useful they may seem. Err on the side of caution.

An important question to ask about any Web site is why the information exists and why it was put on the Internet. What motives might the site's authors have? Are you asked to take action of any kind? If yes, take special care to judge the source's bias. For example, the World Wildlife Fund can ask for contributions and still maintain a Web site that contains reliable information. Conversely, a hate group or extreme political organization can't be trusted to be objective. Box 32.8 summarizes the questions to ask about Web sites.

**SUMMARY BOX** 32.8

## Judging the reliability of Web sources

**RELIABLE SOURCES ARE . . .**

**From educational, not-for-profit, or government organizations.** One sign is an Internet address ending in .*edu, .org, .gov*, or a country abbreviation such as .*us* or .*uk*. However, if any of these organizations fail to list their sources, don't use them. After all, many colleges and universities now host student Web sites, which also end in .*edu*.

**From expert authors.** Experts have degrees or credentials in their fields that you can check. See if their names appear in other reliable sources, in bibliographies on your topic, or in reference books in your college's library. Check whether the site's author gives an e-mail address for questions or comments.

**From reliable print sources.** Online versions of the *New York Times, Time* magazine, and other publications that are produced by the publisher are just as reliable as the print versions.

**Well supported with evidence.** The information is presented in a balanced, unbiased fashion.

**Current.** The site's information is updated.

**QUESTIONABLE SOURCES ARE . . .**

**From commercial organizations advertising to sell a product (.*com*); Web sites that are advertisements or personal pages; junk mail.** These sites may or may not list sources. If they fail to, don't use them. If they do, check that the sources are legitimate, not a front for some commercial enterprise.

**From anonymous authors or authors without identifiable credentials.** Chat rooms, Usenet, discussion groups, bulletin boards, and similar networks are questionable because they don't give credentials or other qualifying information.

**Secondhand excerpts and quotations.** Materials that appear on a site that is not the official site of the publisher (such as a quotation taken from the *New York Times*) may be edited in a biased or inaccurate manner. Such sources may be incomplete and inaccurate.

**Unsupported or biased.** These sites carry declarations and assertions that have little or no supporting evidence.

**Outdated.** The site's information hasn't been updated in a year or more.

# Chapter 33

## USING SOURCES AND AVOIDING PLAGIARISM

### 33a How do I use sources well?

When you turn from researching to writing your research paper, you combine your content notes into an extended new writing that answers your RESEARCH QUESTION (31e) about your topic (31d). Using sources well means using QUOTATIONS (33h), PARAPHRASES (33i), and SUMMARIES (33j) to create a synthesis of those materials and your own thoughts. It also means documenting your sources and avoiding PLAGIARISM. Generally, you'll begin this process after you've located most of your sources and evaluated them (Chapter 32), written a WORKING BIBLIOGRAPHY (31i), and taken content notes (31k). Of course, during the process of DRAFTING, you might discover the need to do some additional research, and that's fine. Be careful, though, to avoid a trap into which we see some writers fall—endlessly researching to put off the challenging work of drafting.

Pulling together a SYNTHESIS of your sources and your own thinking about the topic means

- Mastering the information from each source
- Finding relationships among the pieces of information from various sources
- Adding your own thinking to the mix

To write effectively, organize your paper around a logical sequence based on the main points in your synthesis. Further, support each main point and important subpoint with specific ideas or facts drawn from your sources. Once again, the RENNS formula, discussed in 3f, can help: Use **R**easons, **E**xamples, **N**ames, **N**umbers, and the five **S**enses. Also, if your PURPOSE is persuasive rather than informative, remember to present opposing viewpoints evenhandedly and then refute them reasonably (5l).

All SOURCE-BASED WRITING needs to be

- Accurate
- Effective
- Honest (the only way to avoid plagiarism)

A crucial part of honesty is using correct documentation (Chapters 34–36). **Documentation** means making two types of entries in your research paper each time you use a source:

1. Writing a parenthetical citation for each quotation, paraphrase, and summary you take from sources (for examples in MLA STYLE, see 34c; for APA, see 35c).

2. Composing a BIBLIOGRAPHY for the end of your paper. MLA calls this list of sources WORKS CITED, while APA calls it REFERENCES. This list needs to include full bibliographic information on each source from which you have quoted, paraphrased, and summarized in your paper (for examples, see 34d for MLA style, or 35f for APA).

Today's bibliographies differ from those of the past. The root word *biblio-* means "book," so traditionally, the bibliographic information referred to a book's title, author, publisher, and place and year of publication. Now that the age of digital technology is here, researchers include in their bibliographies sources not only from printed books but also from technological sources.

Documentation is vital for two reasons. It tells your readers where to find your sources in case they want to consult those sources in greater depth or want to verify that you've used them properly. Documentation also gives credit to others for their work. A **documentation style** refers to a specific system for providing information on sources used in a research paper. Documentation styles vary among the disciplines. This handbook presents four documentation styles in Chapters 34–36, as shown in Box 33.1.

---

**SUMMARY BOX 33.1**

## Where to find MLA, APA, CM, and CSE information

**MLA STYLE: CHAPTER 34**

- MLA parenthetical citations (34b–34c)
- Guidelines for compiling an MLA-style Works Cited list (Box 34.1)
- Models for an MLA Works Cited list (34d.1)
- Content or other notes with MLA parenthetical documentation (34d.2)

**APA STYLE: CHAPTER 35**

- APA in-text citations (35b–35c)
- Guidelines for compiling an APA-style References list (Box 35.1)
- Models for an APA References list (35f)
- Abstracts and content notes (35d–35e)

**SUMMARY BOX** 33.1 *continued*

**Where to find MLA, APA, CM, and CSE information**

**CM STYLE: CHAPTER 36**

- Guidelines for compiling CM-style bibliographic notes (Box 36.1)
- Directory of CM-style bibliographic note models (36b)

**CSE STYLE: CHAPTER 36**

- Guidelines for compiling a CSE-style Cited References list (Box 36.2)
- Directory of CSE-style list of references models (36d)

## 33b   What is plagiarism?

**Plagiarism** is presenting another person's words, ideas, or visual images as if they were your own. Plagiarizing is like stealing: It is a form of academic dishonesty or cheating. Plagiarism is a serious offense that can be grounds for a failing grade or expulsion from a college. Beyond that, you're hurting yourself. If you're plagiarizing, you're not learning.

Plagiarism isn't something that just college instructors get fussy about. In the workplace, it can get you fired and hinder your being hired elsewhere. Plagiarism at work also has legal implications; words, ideas, and images, especially those that describe or influence business practices and decisions, are *intellectual property.* Using someone else's intellectual property without permission or credit is a form of theft that may land you in court. Furthermore, plagiarism in any setting—academic, business, or civic—hurts your credibility and reputation. Box 33.2 lists the major types of plagiarism.

**SUMMARY BOX** 33.2

**Types of plagiarism**

You're plagiarizing if you . . .

- Buy a paper from an Internet site, another student or writer, or any other source and pass it off as your own.

- Turn in any paper that someone else has written, whether the person has given it to you, you've downloaded it from the Internet, or you've copied it from any other source.

- Change selected parts of an existing paper and claim the paper as your own.

**Types of plagiarism**

- Neglect to put quotation marks around words that you quote directly from a source, even if you document the source.

- Copy or paste into your paper any *key terms, phrases, sentences,* or *longer passages* from another source without using documentation to tell precisely where the material came from.

- Use *ideas* from another source without correctly citing and documenting that source, even if you put the ideas into your own words.

- Combine ideas from many sources and pass them off as your own without correctly citing and documenting the sources.

- Take language, ideas, or visual images from anyone (colleagues, companies, organizations, and so on) without obtaining permission or crediting them.

**ESL TIP:** Perhaps you come from a country or culture that considers it acceptable for students to copy the writing of experts and authorities. Some cultures, in fact, believe that using another's words, even without citing them, is a sign of respect or learning. However, this practice is considered unacceptable in American and most Western settings. It is plagiarism, and you need to avoid it by using the strategies we discuss in this chapter. ✇

## 33c How do I avoid plagiarism?

You can avoid plagiarism two ways. First, be very systematic and careful when you take content notes and when you quote, paraphrase, or summarize materials. Second, become comfortable with the concept of DOCUMENTATION, which you need each time you use a source. Box 33.3 (p. 542) describes the main strategies you can use to avoid plagiarism.

Another important way to avoid plagiarism is to dive willingly into any interim tasks your instructors build into research assignments. For example, many instructors set interim deadlines such as a date for handing in a WORKING BIBLIOGRAPHY (31i) or an ANNOTATED BIBLIOGRAPHY. Further, some instructors want to read and coach you about how to improve one or more of your research paper drafts. In some cases, they might want to look over your research log (31c), content notes (31k), and/or photocopies of your sources.

Never assume that your instructor can't detect plagiarism. Instructors have keen eyes for writing styles that are different from the ones students generally produce and from your own style in particular. They recognize professionally drawn visuals and charts. Instructors can access Web sites that electronically check your submitted work against all material available online. Further, Internet sites such as <http://www.turnitin.com> allow instructors to check your writing against hundreds of thousands of papers

**SUMMARY BOX 33.3**

## Strategies for avoiding plagiarism

- Use DOCUMENTATION to acknowledge your use of the ideas or phrasings of others, taken from the sources you've compiled on your topic.
- Become thoroughly familiar with the documentation style that your instructor tells you to use for your research paper (Chapters 34–36). To work efficiently, make a master list of the information required to document all sources that you quote, paraphrase, or summarize according to your required documentation style.
- Write down absolutely all the documentation facts that you'll need for your paper, keeping careful records as you search for sources. Otherwise, you'll waste much time trying to retrace your steps to get a documentation detail you missed.
- Use a consistent system for taking CONTENT NOTES, making sure to maintain the distinction between your own thinking and the ideas that come directly from a source. Perhaps use different colors of ink or another coding system to keep these three uses of sources separate:
  1. Quotations from a source (documentation required)
  2. Material paraphrased or summarized from a source (documentation required)
  3. Thoughts of your own triggered by what you've read or experienced in life (no documentation required)
- Write clear, perhaps oversized, quotation marks when you're directly quoting a passage. Make them so distinct that you can't miss seeing them later.
- Consult with your instructor if you're unsure about any phase of the documentation process.

for free or for sale on the World Wide Web and the Internet. (Also, that site adds your paper to its huge database of student papers so that no one can plagiarize your work.) Moreover, when instructors receive papers that they suspect contain plagiarized passages, they can check with other professors to see whether a student paper looks familiar.

## 33d How do I work with Internet sources to avoid plagiarism?

Online sources can both greatly help researchers and create new possible problems. Because it's so easy to download source materials, it's potentially easy to misrepresent someone else's work as your own, even if you don't intend to be dishonest.

You might be tempted to download a completed research paper from the Internet. *Don't.* That's intellectual dishonesty, which can get you into real trouble. Or you might be tempted to borrow wording from what you wrongly consider an "obscure" Internet source. *Don't.* Not only is this intellectual dishonesty, but instructors will easily detect it. Even if you have absolutely no intention of plagiarizing, being careless, especially with cutting and pasting, can easily lead to trouble. Box 33.4 suggests ways to avoid plagiarism when you're working with digital or online sources.

**SUMMARY BOX 33.4**

## Guidelines for avoiding plagiarizing online sources

- Never cut material from an online source and paste it directly in your paper. You can too easily lose track of which language is your own and which comes from a source.

- Keep material that you downloaded or printed from the Internet separate from your own writing, whether you intend to QUOTE, SUMMARIZE, or PARAPHRASE the material. Be careful how you manage copied files. Use another color or a much larger font as a visual reminder that this isn't your work. Just as important, make sure that you type in all of the information you need to identify each source, according to the documentation style you need to use.

- Copy or paste downloaded or printed material into your paper only when you intend to use it as a direct quotation or visual. Immediately place quotation marks around the material, or set off a long passage as a block quotation. Be sure to document the source at the same time as you copy or paste the quotation into your paper. Don't put off documenting the passage until later because you may forget to do it or do it incorrectly.

- Summarize or paraphrase materials *before* you include them in your paper. If you have printed or downloaded Internet sources to separate files, don't copy directly from those files into your paper. Summarize or paraphrase the sources in a different file, and then paste the summaries or paraphrases into your paper. Document the source of each passage at the same time as you insert it in your paper. If you put off this task until later, you may forget to do it or get it wrong.

- Use an Internet service to check a passage you're not sure about. If you're concerned that you may have plagiarized material by mistake, try submitting one or two sentences that concern you to <http://www.google.com>. To make this work, always place quotation marks around the sentences you want to check when you type them into the search window.

## 33e What don't I have to document?

You don't have to document common knowledge or your own thinking. **Common knowledge** is information that most educated people know, although they may need to remind themselves of certain facts by looking up information in a reference book. For example, here are a few facts of common knowledge that you don't need to document.

- Bill Clinton was the US president before George W. Bush.
- Mercury is the planet closest to the sun.
- Normal human body temperature is 98.6 degrees Fahrenheit.
- All the oceans on our planet contain salt water.

Sometimes, of course, a research paper doesn't contain common knowledge. For example, Andrei Gurov, whose research paper appears in 34e.2, had only very general common knowledge about the topic of déjà vu. Most of his paper consists of ideas and information that he quotes, paraphrases, and summarizes from sources.

A very important component of a research paper that doesn't need documentation is **your own thinking**, which is based on what you've learned as you built on what you already knew about your topic. It consists of your ANALYSIS, SYNTHESIS, and interpretation of new material as you read or observe it. You don't have to document your own thinking. Your own thinking helps you formulate a THESIS STATEMENT and organize your research paper by composing TOPIC SENTENCES that carry along your presentation of information. For example, suppose that you're drawing on an article about the connections between emotions and logic in people. While reading the article, you come to a personal conclusion that computers can't have emotions. This idea is not stated anywhere in the article you are reading or in any other source you use. Certainly, you need to cite the ideas from the article that led to your conclusion, but you don't need to cite your own thinking. On the other hand, if you find a source that states this very idea, you must cite it.

## 33f What must I document?

You must document everything that you learn from a source. This includes ideas as well as specific language. Expressing the ideas of others in your own words doesn't release you from the obligation to tell exactly where you got those ideas—you need to use complete, correct documentation. Here's an example in action.

### SOURCE

Park, Robert L. "Welcome to Planet Earth." The Best American Science Writing 2001. Ed. Jesse Cohen. New York: Ecco/ HarperCollins, 2001. 302-08. [This source information is arranged in MLA documentation style.]

### ORIGINAL (PARK'S EXACT WORDS)

The widespread belief in alien abductions is just one example of the growing influence of pseudoscience. Two hundred years ago, educated people imagined that the greatest contribution of science would be to free the world from superstition and humbug. It has not happened. (304)

### PLAGIARISM EXAMPLE

Belief in alien kidnappings illustrates the <u>influence of pseudoscience</u>. In the nineteenth century, educated people imagined that science would <u>free the world from superstition</u>, but they were wrong.

Even though the student changed some wording in the example above, the ideas aren't original to her. To avoid plagiarism she's required to document the source. The underlined phrases are especially problematic examples of plagiarism because they're Park's exact wording.

### CORRECT EXAMPLE (USING QUOTATION, PARAPHRASE, AND DOCUMENTATION)

Robert Park calls people's beliefs in alien kidnapping proof of "the growing influence of pseudoscience" (304). Centuries of expectation that science would conquer "superstition and humbug" are still unfulfilled (304). [This citation is arranged in MLA documentation style.]

The writer of the correct example above has used Park's ideas properly through a combination of quotation and paraphrase and documentation. For example, she correctly quotes the phrase "the growing influence of pseudoscience," and she paraphrases the statement "Two hundred years ago, educated people imagined that the greatest contribution of science would be to free the world," rephrasing it as "Centuries of expectation that science would conquer." She also gives the author's name in the sentence and twice includes parenthetical citations, which would lead the reader to find the source on the Works Cited page. Sections 33g through 33j explain exactly how to use sources effectively and document correctly.

## 33g How can I effectively integrate sources into my writing?

**Integrating sources** means blending information and ideas from others with your own writing. Before trying to integrate sources into your writing, you need to ANALYZE and SYNTHESIZE your material. Analysis requires you to break ideas down into their component parts so that you can think them through separately. Do this while reading your sources and reviewing your notes. Synthesis requires you to make connections among different ideas, seeking relationships and links that tie them together.

**How can I use quotations effectively?**

A **quotation** is the exact words of a source enclosed in quotation marks. Well-chosen quotations can lend a note of authority and enliven a document with someone else's voice. Think, for example, of a good marketing campaign. A company can incorporate real-life quotes to help support its claim that a product or service works effectively. In academic writing, you achieve some of the same benefits by supporting your work with quotations.

You face conflicting demands when you use quotations in your writing. Although quotations provide support, you can lose coherence in your paper if you use too many of them. If more than a quarter of your paper consists of quotations, you've probably written what some people call a "cut and paste special"—merely stringing together a bunch of someone else's words. Doing so gives your readers—including instructors—the impression that you've not bothered to develop your own thinking and you're letting other people do your talking.

In addition to avoiding too many quotations, you also want to avoid using quotations that are too long. Readers tend to skip over long quotations and lose the drift of the paper. Also, your instructor might assume that you just didn't take the time required to PARAPHRASE or SUMMARIZE the material. Generally, summaries and paraphrases are more effective for reconstructing someone else's argument. If you do need to quote a long passage, make absolutely sure every word in the quotation counts. Edit out irrelevant parts, using ellipsis points to indicate deleted material (29d and 33h.1). Box 33.5 provides guidelines for using quotations. Sections 33h.1 and 33h.2 give examples of acceptable and unacceptable quotations.

### 33h.1 Making quotations fit smoothly with your sentences

When you use quotations, the greatest risk you take is that you'll end up with incoherent, choppy sentences. You can avoid this problem by making the words you quote fit smoothly with three aspects of your writing: grammar, style, and logic. Here are some examples of sentences that don't mesh well with quotations, followed by revised versions.

#### SOURCE

Goleman, Daniel. Emotional Intelligence. New York: Bantam, 1995. 9.
[This source information is arranged in MLA documentation style.]

#### ORIGINAL (GOLEMAN'S EXACT WORDS)

These two minds, the emotional and the rational, operate in tight harmony for the most part, intertwining their very different ways of knowing to guide us through the world.

## Guidelines for using quotations

1. Use quotations from authorities on your subject to support or refute what you write in your paper.
2. Never use a quotation to present your THESIS STATEMENT or a TOPIC SENTENCE.
3. Select quotations that fit your message. Choose a quotation for these reasons:
   * Its language is particularly appropriate or distinctive.
   * Its idea is particularly hard to paraphrase accurately.
   * The source's authority is especially important to support your thesis or main point.
   * The source's words are open to interpretation.
4. Never allow quotations to make up more than a quarter of your paper. Instead, rely on paraphrases (33i) and summaries (33j).
5. Quote accurately. Always check each quotation against the original source—and then recheck it.
6. Integrate quotations smoothly into your writing.
7. Avoid PLAGIARISM (33b–33d).
8. Document quotations carefully.

**INCOHERENT GRAMMAR PROBLEM**

Goleman explains how the emotional and rational minds "intertwining their very different ways of knowing to guide us through the world" (9). [Corrected: Goleman explains how emotional and rational minds mix "their very different ways of knowing to guide us through the world" (9).]

**INCOHERENT STYLE PROBLEM**

Goleman explains how the emotional minds based on reason work together by "intertwining their very different ways of knowing to guide us through the world" (9). [Corrected: Goleman explains how the emotional and rational minds work together by "intertwining their very different ways of knowing to guide us through the world" (9).]

**INCOHERENT LOGIC PROBLEM**

Goleman explains how the emotional and rational minds work together by "their very different ways of knowing to guide us through the world" (9). [Corrected: Coleman explains how the emotional and rational minds work

547

together by combining "their very different ways of knowing to guide us through the world" (9).]

### CORRECT USE OF THE QUOTATION

Goleman explains how the emotional and rational minds work together by "intertwining their very different ways of knowing to guide us through the world" (9). [This citation is arranged in MLA documentation style.]

After writing sentences that contain quotations, read the material aloud and listen to whether the language flows smoothly and gracefully. Perhaps you need to add a word or two placed in brackets (29c) within the quotation so that the wording works grammatically and effortlessly with the rest of your sentence. Of course, make sure your bracketed additions don't distort the meaning of the quotation. For example, the following quotation comes from the same page of the source quoted above. The bracketed material explains what the phrase *these minds* refers to in the original quotation—this helps the reader understand what was clear in the context of the original source but isn't clear when quoted in isolation.

### ORIGINAL (GOLEMAN'S EXACT WORDS)

In many or most moments, these minds are exquisitely coordinated; feelings are essential to thought, thought to feeling.

### QUOTATION WITH EXPLANATORY BRACKETS

"In many or most moments, these minds [emotional and rational] are exquisitely coordinated; feelings are essential to thought, thought to feeling" (Goleman 9). [This citation is arranged in MLA documentation style.]

Another way to create a smooth integration of a quotation into your sentence is to delete some words, always using an ellipsis where the deletion occurs. You also might delete any part of the quotation that interferes with conciseness and the focus you intend in your sentence. When you use an ellipsis, make sure that the remaining words accurately reflect the source's meaning and that your sentence structure still flows smoothly.

### ORIGINAL (GOLEMAN'S EXACT WORDS)

These two minds, the emotional and the rational, operate in tight harmony for the most part, intertwining their very different ways of knowing to guide us through the world (9).

### QUOTATION WITH ELLIPSIS

Goleman contends that, generally, "these two minds, the emotional and the rational, operate in tight harmony . . . to guide us through the world" (9). [This citation is arranged in MLA documentation style.]

In the preceding example, the words "for the most part, intertwining their very different ways of knowing" have been deleted from the original material so that the quotation is more concise and focused.

## 33h.2 Using quotations to enhance meaning

Perhaps the biggest complaint instructors have about student research papers is that sometimes quotations are simply stuck in, for no apparent reason. Whenever you place words between quotation marks, they take on special significance for your message as well as your language. Without context-setting information in the paper, the reader can't know exactly what logic leads the writer to use a particular quotation.

Furthermore, always make sure your readers know who said each group of quoted words. Otherwise, you've used a *disembodied quotation* (some instructors call them "ghost quotations"), which reflects poorly on your writing.

**SOURCE**

Wright, Karen. "Times of Our Lives." Scientific American Sept. 2002: 58-66. [This source information is arranged in MLA documentation style.]

**ORIGINAL (WRIGHT'S EXACT WORDS)**

In human bodies, biological clocks keep track of seconds, minutes, days, months and years. (66)

**INCORRECT (DISEMBODIED QUOTATION)**

The human body has many subconscious processes. People don't have to make their hearts beat or remind themselves to breathe. "In human bodies, biological clocks keep track of seconds, minutes, days, months and years" (Wright 66).

**CORRECT**

The human body has many subconscious processes. People don't have to make their hearts beat or remind themselves to breathe. However, other processes are less obvious and perhaps more surprising. Karen Wright observes, for example, "In human bodies, biological clocks keep track of seconds, minutes, days, months and years" (66).

Rarely can a quotation begin a paragraph effectively. Start your paragraph by relying on your TOPIC SENTENCE, based on your own thinking. Then, you can fit in a relevant quotation somewhere in the paragraph, if it supports or extends what you have said.

Another strategy for working quotations smoothly into your paper is to integrate the name(s) of the author(s), the source title, or other information into your paper. You can prepare your reader for a quotation using one of these methods:

- Mention in your sentence directly before or after the quotation the name(s) of the author(s) you're quoting.
- Mention in your sentence the title of the work you're quoting from.
- Give additional authority to your material. If the author of a source is a noteworthy figure, you gain credibility when you refer to his or her credentials.
- Mention the name(s) of the author(s), with or without the name of the source and any author credentials, along with your personal introductory lead-in to the material.

Here are some examples, using the original source material from Karen Wright on page 549, of effective integration of an author's name, source title, and credentials, along with an introductory analysis.

**AUTHOR'S NAME**

**Karen Wright explains that** "in human bodies, biological clocks keep track of seconds, minutes, days, months and years" (66).

**AUTHOR'S NAME AND SOURCE TITLE**

**Karen Wright explains in "Times of Our Lives" that** "in human bodies, biological clocks keep track of seconds, minutes, days, months and years" (66).

**AUTHOR'S NAME AND CREDENTIALS**

**Karen Wright, an award-winning science journalist, explains that** "in human bodies, biological clocks keep track of seconds, minutes, days, months and years" (66).

**AUTHOR'S NAME WITH STUDENT'S INTRODUCTORY ANALYSIS**

**Karen Wright reviews evidence of surprising subconscious natural processes, explaining that** "in human bodies, biological clocks keep track of seconds, minutes, days, months and years" (66).

**ALERT:** After using an author's full name in the first reference, you can decide to use only the author's last name in subsequent references. This holds unless another source has that same last name. ◆

**EXERCISE 33-1** Working individually or with a group, read the following original material, from page 60 of "What Makes You Who You Are" by Matt Ridley in *Time* (2 June 2003). Then, read items 1 through 5 and explain why each is an incorrect use of a quotation. Next, revise each numbered sentence so that it correctly uses a quotation. End each quotation with this MLA-style parenthetical reference: (Ridley 60).

#### ORIGINAL (RIDLEY'S EXACT WORDS)

Human beings differ from chimpanzees in having complex, grammatical language. But language does not spring fully formed from the brain; it must be learned from other language-speaking human beings. This capacity to learn is written into the human brain by genes that open and close a critical window during which learning takes place. One of those genes, FoxP2, has recently been discovered on human chromosome 7 by Anthony Monaco and his colleagues at the Wellcome Trust Centre for Human Genetics in Oxford. Just having the FoxP2 gene, though, is not enough. If a child is not exposed to a lot of spoken language during the critical learning period, he or she will always struggle with speech.

#### UNACCEPTABLE USES OF QUOTATIONS

1. Scientists are learning more about how people learn languages. "Human beings differ from chimpanzees in having complex, grammatical language" (Ridley 60).

2. People might assume that individuals can acquire speaking abilities through hard individual work, "but language must be learned from other language-speaking human beings" (Ridley 60).

3. Helping the language learning process "by genes that open and close a critical window during which learning takes place" (Ridley 60).

4. In 2002, one gene important for language development "has recently been discovered on human chromosome 7 by Anthony Monaco and his colleagues" (Ridley 60).

5. Parents should continually read to and speak with young children, because "if children are not exposed to a lot of spoken language during the critical learning period of childhood, they will always struggle with speech" (Ridley 60).

**EXERCISE 33-2**   Working individually or with your peer-response group, do the following:

1. For a paper that argues how a person should choose a spouse, write a two- to three-sentence passage that includes your own words and a quotation from the following paragraph, from page 70 of "What's Love Got to Do with It?" by Anjula Razdan in *Utne* (May-June 2003). After the quoted words, use this parenthetical reference: (Razdan 70).

**ORIGINAL (RAZDAN'S EXACT WORDS)**

> Fast forward a couple hundred years to a 21st-century America, and you see a modern, progressive society where people are free to choose their mates, for the most part, based on love instead of social or economic gain. But for many people, a quiet voice from within wonders: Are we really better off? Who hasn't at some point in their life—at the end of an ill-fated relationship or midway through dinner with the third "date-from-hell" this month—longed for a matchmaker to find the right partner? No hassles. No effort. No personal ads or blind dates.

2. For a paper arguing that biologists need more funding to speed up our understanding of the earth's living creatures before many more of them become extinct, quote from the Wilson material in Exercise 33-6 (section 33j). Be sure to include at least one numerical statistic in your quotation. (For documentation purposes, keep in mind that Wilson's article appears on pages 29–30 in the original source.)

3. Write a two- to three-sentence passage that includes your own words and a quotation from a source you're currently using for a paper assigned in one of your courses. If you have no such assignment, choose any material suitable for a college-level research paper. Your instructor might request a photocopy of the material from which you're quoting, so make a copy to have on hand.

## 33i How can I write good paraphrases?

A **paraphrase** precisely restates in your own words and your own writing style the written or spoken words of someone else. Select for paraphrase only the passages that carry ideas you need to reproduce in detail. Because paraphrasing calls for a very close approximation of a source, avoid trying to paraphrase more than a paragraph or two; for longer passages, use SUMMARY instead. Expect to write a number of drafts of your paraphrases, each time getting closer to effectively rewording and revising the writing style so that you avoid PLAGIARISM. Box 33.6 provides guidelines for writing paraphrases.

Here's an example of an unacceptable paraphrase and an acceptable one.

**SOURCE**

Hulburt, Ann. "Post-Teenage Wasteland?" New York Times Magazine 9 Oct. 2005: 11–12. [This source information is arranged in MLA documentation style.]

**ORIGINAL (HULBURT'S EXACT WORDS)**

[T]he available data suggest that the road to maturity hasn't become as drastically different as people think—or as drawn out, either. It's true that the median age of marriage rose to 25 for women and

---

**SUMMARY BOX** 33.6

## Guidelines for writing paraphrases

1. Decide to paraphrase authorities on your subject to support or counter what you write in your paper.

2. Never use a paraphrase to present your THESIS STATEMENT or a TOPIC SENTENCE.

3. Say what the source says, but no more.

4. Reproduce the source's sequence of ideas and emphases.

5. Use your own words and writing style to restate the material. If some technical words in the original have no or awkward synonyms, you may quote the original's words—but do so very sparingly. For example, you can use the term *human chromosome 7* if you're paraphrasing the original source by Matt Ridley in Exercise 33-1.

6. Never distort the source's meaning as you reword and change the writing style.

7. Expect your material to be as long as, and often longer than, the original.

8. Integrate your paraphrases smoothly into your writing.

9. Avoid plagiarism (33b–33d).

10. Enter all DOCUMENTATION precisely and carefully.

---

almost 27 for men in 2000, from 20 and 23, respectively, in 1960. Yet those mid-century figures were record lows (earnestly analyzed in their time). Moreover, Americans of all ages have ceased to view starting a family as the major benchmark of grown-up status. When asked to rank the importance of traditional milestones in defining the arrival of adulthood, poll respondents place completing school, finding full-time employment, achieving financial independence and being able to support a family far above actually wedding a spouse or having kids. The new perspective isn't merely an immature swerve into selfishness; postponing those last two steps is good for the future of the whole family (11).

**UNACCEPTABLE PARAPHRASE (UNDERLINED WORDS ARE PLAGIARIZED)**

<u>Data suggest that the road to maturity</u> hasn't changed as much as people think. True, <u>the median age of marriage</u> was 25 for women and 27 for men in 2000, up from 20 and 23 in 1960. <u>Yet those</u> 1960 <u>figures were record lows.</u> Furthermore, Americans have stopped regarding beginning a family as the signpost of <u>grown-up status.</u> When they were <u>asked to rank the</u>

importance of traditional benchmarks for deciding the arrival of
adulthood, people rated graduating from school, finding a full-time job,
gaining financial status, and being a breadwinner far above marrying or
having kids. This new belief isn't merely immature selfishness; delaying
those last two steps is good for the future of the whole family (Hulburt 11).

**ACCEPTABLE PARAPHRASE**

According to Ann Hulburt, statistics show that people are wrong when
they believe our society is delaying maturity. She acknowledges that
between 1960 and 2000, the median age at which women married rose from
20 to 25 (for men it went from 23 to 27), but points out that the early figures
were extreme lows. Hulburt finds that Americans no longer equate
adulthood with starting a family. Polls show that people rank several
other "milestones" above marriage and children as signaling adulthood.
These include finishing school, securing a full-time job, and earning
enough to be independent and to support a family. Hulburt concludes that
we should regard postponing marriage and children not as being selfish
or immature but as investing in the family's future (11). [This citation is
arranged in MLA documentation style.]

The first attempt to paraphrase is not acceptable. The writer simply
changed a few words. What remains is plagiarized because the passage
keeps most of the original's language, has the same sentence structure as
the original, and uses no quotation marks. The documentation is correct,
but its accuracy doesn't make up for the unacceptable paraphrasing. The
second paraphrase is acceptable. It captures the meaning of the original
in the student's own words.

**EXERCISE 33-3**    Working individually or with your peer-response group, read
the original material, a paragraph from page 49 of *Uniforms: Why We Are
What We Wear* by Paul Fussell (Boston: Houghton, 2002). Then, read the
unacceptable paraphrase, and point out each example of plagiarism. Finally,
write your own paraphrase, starting it with a phrase naming Fussell and ending it with this parenthetical reference: (49).

**ORIGINAL (FUSSELL'S EXACT WORDS)**

Until around 1963, part of the routine for Levi's wearers was
shrinking the trousers to fit, and the best way to do that was to put
them on wet and let them dry on your body. This gave the wearer the
impression that he or she was actually creating the garment, or at
least emphasizing one's precious individuality, and that conviction did
nothing to oppose the illusion of uniqueness precious to all American
young people (49).

**UNACCEPTABLE PARAPHRASE**

Paul Fussell says that until around 1963 Levi's wearers used to shrink new trousers to fit. The best way to do that was to put them on wet and let them dry while wearing them. Doing this created the impression that wearers were actually creating the garment or emphasizing their precious individuality. It reinforced the illusion of uniqueness precious to all American teens (49).

**EXERCISE 33-4**   Working individually or with your peer-response group, do the following:

1. For a paper on the place of censorship in the coverage of military conflicts, paraphrase the following paragraph from page 65 of *Regarding the Pain of Others* by Susan Sontag (New York: Farrar, 2003). Start with words mentioning Sontag, and end with this parenthetical reference: (65).

**ORIGINAL (SONTAG'S EXACT WORDS)**

There had always been censorship, but for a long time it remained desultory, at the pleasure of generals and heads of state. The first organized ban on press photography at the front came during the First World War; both the German and French high commands allowed only a few selected military photographers near the fighting. (Censorship of the press by the British General Staff was less inflexible.) And it took another fifty years, and the relaxation of censorship with the first televised war coverage, to understand what impact shocking photographs could have on the domestic public. During the Vietnam era, war photography became, normatively, a criticism of war. This was bound to have consequences: Mainstream media are not in the business of making people feel queasy about the struggles for which they are being mobilized, much less of disseminating propaganda against waging war.

2. In one of your sources for a current research assignment, locate a paragraph that is at least 150 words in length and write a paraphrase of it. If you have no such assignment, choose any material suitable for a college-level paper. Your instructor may request that you submit a photocopy of the original material, so make a copy to have on hand.

## 33j   How can I write good summaries?

A **summary** differs from a PARAPHRASE (33i) in one important way: A paraphrase restates the original material completely, but a summary provides only the main point of the original source. A summary is much shorter than a paraphrase. Summarizing is the technique you'll probably use most frequently in writing your research paper, both for taking notes and for integrating what you have learned from sources into your own writing.

As you summarize, you trace a line of thought. This involves deleting less central ideas and sometimes transposing certain points into an order more suited to summary. In summarizing a longer original—say, ten pages or more—you may find it helpful first to divide the original into subsections and summarize each. Then, group your subsection summaries and use them as the basis for further condensing the material into a final summary. You'll probably have to revise a summary more than once. Always make sure that a summary accurately reflects the source and its emphases.

When you're summarizing a source in your CONTENT NOTES, resist the temptation to include your personal interpretation along with something the author says. Similarly, never include in your summary your own judgment about the point made in the source. Your own opinions and ideas, although they have value, don't belong in a summary. Instead, jot them down immediately when they come to mind, but separate them clearly from your summary. Write your notes so that when you go back to them you can be sure to distinguish your opinions or ideas from your summary. On a computer, highlight your personal writing with a screen of yellow or some other color, or use an entirely different font for it. Box 33.7 provides guidelines for writing good summaries.

---

## SUMMARY BOX 33.7

### Guidelines for writing summaries

1. Use summaries from authorities on your subject to support or refute what you write in your paper.

2. Identify the main points you want to summarize and condense them using your own words without losing the meaning of the original source.

3. Never use a summary to present your THESIS STATEMENT or a TOPIC SENTENCE.

4. Keep your summary short.

5. Integrate your summaries smoothly into your writing.

6. Avoid PLAGIARISM (33b–33d).

7. Enter all DOCUMENTATION precisely and carefully.

---

Here's an example of an unacceptable summary and an acceptable one.

**SOURCE**

Tanenbaum, Leora. Catfight: Women and Competition. New York: Seven Stories P, 2002. 117-18. [This source information is arranged in MLA documentation style.]

**ORIGINAL (TANENBAUM'S EXACT WORDS)**

Until recently, most Americans disapproved of cosmetic surgery, but today the stigma is disappearing. Average Americans are lining up for procedures—two-thirds of patients report family incomes of less than $50,000 a year—and many of them return for more. Younger women undergo "maintenance" surgeries in a futile attempt to halt time. The latest fad is Botox, a purified and diluted form of botulinum toxin that is injected between the eyebrows to eliminate frown lines. Although the procedure costs between $300 and $1000 and must be repeated every few months, roughly 850,000 patients have had it performed on them. That number will undoubtedly shoot up now that the FDA has approved Botox for cosmetic use. Even teenagers are making appointments with plastic surgeons. More than 14,000 adolescents had plastic surgery in 1996, and many of them are choosing controversial procedures such as breast implants, liposuction, and tummy tucks, rather than the rhinoplasties of previous generations.

**UNACCEPTABLE SUMMARY (UNDERLINED WORDS ARE PLAGIARIZED)**

Average Americans are lining up for surgical procedures. The latest fad is Botox, a toxin injected to eliminate frown lines. This is an insanely foolish waste of money. Even teenagers are making appointments with plastic surgeons, many of them for controversial procedures such as breast implants, liposuction, and tummy tucks (Tanenbaum 117-18).

**ACCEPTABLE SUMMARY**

Tanenbaum explains that plastic surgery is becoming widely acceptable, even for Americans with modest incomes and for younger women. Most popular is injecting the toxin Botox to smooth wrinkles. She notes that thousands of adolescents are even requesting controversial surgeries (117-18). [This citation is arranged in MLA documentation style.]

The unacceptable summary above has several major problems: It doesn't isolate the main point. It plagiarizes by taking much of its language directly from the source. Examples of plagiarized language include all the underlined phrases. Finally, the unacceptable summary includes the writer's interpretation ("This is an insanely foolish waste of money") rather than objectively representing the original. The acceptable summary concisely isolates the main point, puts the source into the writer's own words, calls attention to the author by including her name in the summary, and remains objective throughout.

**EXERCISE 33-5**   Working individually or with your peer-response group, read the original material from pages 23–24 of *Diversity: The Invention of a Concept* by Peter Wood (San Francisco: Encounter, 2003). Then, read the unacceptable summary. Point out each example of plagiarism. Finally, write your own summary, starting it with a phrase mentioning Wood and ending it with this parenthetical reference: (23-24).

### ORIGINAL (WOOD'S EXACT WORDS)

Among the many meanings of diversity, let's for the moment distinguish two: the actual racial and ethnic condition of America, which I will call *diversity I,* and the diversiphile ideal of how American society should recognize and respond to its racial and ethnic composition, which I will call *diversity II.* In principle, it ought to be easy to distinguish between these two meanings. One refers to the facts, the other to hopes or wishes. *Diversity I* is the sort of thing that we might expect could be counted, or at least approximated, with wide agreement. We know with reasonable certainty, for example, that about 13 percent of the U.S. population considers itself of African descent. We can and do argue with one another over the significance of this fact, but the fact itself is not seriously in dispute.

*Diversity II,* by contrast, is an ideal. It expresses a vision of society in which people divide themselves into separate groups, each with profound traditions of its own, but held together by mutual esteem, respect and tolerance. It would be futile, however, to look for general agreement about the exact details of this ideal.

### UNACCEPTABLE, PLAGIARIZED SUMMARY

Peter Wood distinguishes between *diversity I,* the actual racial and ethnic condition of America, and *diversity II,* the diversiphile ideal of how American society should recognize and respond to its racial and ethnic composition. *Diversity I* could be counted or approximated with wide agreement. *Diversity II* is an ideal vision of society, but there can be no general agreement about the exact nature of this ideal (23-24).

**EXERCISE 33-6**   Working individually or with your peer-response group, do the following:

1. Summarize the following paragraph from pages 29–30 of "Vanishing Before Our Eyes" by Edward O. Wilson in *Time* (24 Apr. 2000). Start your summary with a phrase mentioning the author, and end with this parenthetical reference: (29-30).

### ORIGINAL (WILSON'S EXACT WORDS)

By repeated sampling, biologists estimate that as few as 10% of the different kinds of insects, nematode worms, and fungi have been discovered. For bacteria and other microorganisms, the number could be well below 1%. Even the largest and most intensively studied organisms are incompletely cataloged. Four species of mammals, for example, have recently been discovered in the remote Annamite Mountains along the Vietnam-Laos border. One of them, the saola or spindlehorn, is a large cowlike animal distinct enough to be classified in a genus of its own. Earth, as far as life is concerned, is still a little-known planet.

2. Write a summary of your paraphrase of the Sontag material in Exercise 33-4. Use the parenthetical reference given there.

3. Write a summary of a passage from a source you're currently using for a paper assigned in one of your courses. If you have no such assignment, choose any material suitable for a college-level research paper. Your instructor might request a photocopy of the material you're summarizing, so make a copy to have on hand.

## 33k  Which verbs can help me weave source material into my sentences?

The verbs listed in Box 33.8 can help you work quotations, paraphrases, and summaries smoothly into your writing. Some of these verbs imply your position toward the source material (for example, *argue, complain, concede, deny, grant, insist,* and *reveal*). Other verbs imply a more neutral stance (for example, *comment, describe, explain, note, say,* and *write*). For many examples of effective use of such verbs, see the student research papers presented in sections 34e.2, 35h.2, and 38j.3.

**SUMMARY BOX 33.8**

### Verbs useful for integrating quotations, paraphrases, and summaries

| | | |
|---|---|---|
| acknowledges | concedes | discusses |
| agrees | concludes | distinguishes |
| analyzes | confirms | between/among |
| argues | connects | emphasizes |
| asks | considers | endeavors to |
| asserts | contends | establishes |
| balances | contradicts | estimates |
| begins | contrasts | explains |
| believes | declares | expresses |
| claims | demonstrates | finds |
| comments | denies | focuses on |
| compares | describes | grants |
| complains | develops | illuminates |

**Verbs useful for integrating quotations, paraphrases, and summaries**

| | | |
|---|---|---|
| illustrates | organizes | says |
| implies | points out | sees |
| indicates | prepares | shows |
| informs | promises | signals |
| insists | proves | specifies |
| introduces | questions | speculates |
| maintains | recognizes | states |
| means | recommends | suggests |
| negates | refutes | supports |
| notes | rejects | supposes |
| notices | remarks | thinks |
| observes | reports | wishes |
| offers | reveals | writes |

# Chapter 34

## MLA DOCUMENTATION WITH CASE STUDY

Here are two directories. The first lists examples of MLA in-text parenthetical citations. The second lists examples of MLA Works Cited entries.

### MLA-STYLE DIRECTORY

#### MLA Parenthetical Citations



#### MLA Works Cited List

**BOOKS**



*continued* ➢

*continued* ➤

## 34a What is MLA style?

A DOCUMENTATION STYLE* is a standard format that writers follow to tell readers what SOURCES they used in conducting their research and how to find those sources. Different disciplines follow different documentation styles. The one most frequently used in the humanities (Chapter 38) is from the Modern Language Association (MLA).

MLA style requires you to document your sources in two connected, equally important ways.

1. Within the text of the paper, use parenthetical documentation, as described in section 34b. Section 34c shows twenty models of in-text parenthetical documentation, each for a different type of source.
2. At the end of the paper, provide a WORKS CITED list of the sources you used in your paper. Title this list "Works Cited." It should include only the sources you've actually used in your research paper, not any you've consulted but haven't used. Section 34d gives instructions for composing a Works Cited list, followed by ninety-three models, each based on different kinds of sources (book, article, Web site, and so on) that you might use.

For an example of a research paper that uses MLA-style parenthetical documentation and a Works Cited list, see section 34e.2. As you read the research paper, notice how the two requirements for crediting sources work together so that readers can learn the precise origin of QUOTATIONS, PARAPHRASES, and SUMMARIES. If you need more information than we cover in this chapter, consult the *MLA Handbook for Writers of Research Papers,* Sixth Edition (New York: Modern Language Association of America, 2003), by Joseph Gibaldi.

## 34b What is MLA in-text parenthetical documentation?

MLA-style **parenthetical documentation** places SOURCE information in parentheses within the sentences of your research papers. Also called an *in-text citation,* this information is given each time that you quote, summarize, or paraphrase source materials. It signals materials used from outside sources and enables readers to find the originals.

If you include an author's name (or, if none, a shortened title of the work) in the sentence to introduce the source material, you include in parentheses only the page number where you found the material:

---

*Words printed in SMALL CAPITAL LETTERS are discussed elsewhere in the text and are defined in the Terms Glossary at the back of the book.

> According to Brent Staples, IQ tests give scientists little insight into
> intelligence (293). [Author name cited in text; page number cited in
> parentheses.]

For readability and good writing technique, try to introduce names of authors (or titles of sources) in your own sentences. If you don't include this information in your sentence, you need to insert it before the page number, in parentheses. There is no punctuation between the author's name and the page number:

> IQ tests give scientists little insight into intelligence (Staples 293). [Author
> name and page number cited in parentheses.]

When possible, position a parenthetical reference at the end of the quote, summary, or paraphrase it refers to—preferably at the end of a sentence, unless that would place it too far from the source's material. When you place the parenthetical reference at the end of a sentence, insert it before the sentence-ending period.

If you're citing a quotation enclosed in quotation marks, place the parenthetical information after the closing quotation mark but before sentence-ending punctuation.

> Coleman summarizes research that shows that "the number, rate, and
> direction of time-zone changes are the critical factors in determining the
> extent and degree of jet lag symptoms" (67). [Author name cited in text; page
> number cited in parentheses.]

The one exception to this rule concerns quotations that you set off in BLOCK STYLE, meaning one inch from the left margin. (MLA requires that quotations longer than four typed lines be handled this way.) For block quotations, put the parenthetical reference after the period.

> Bruce Sterling worries that people are pursuing less conventional medical
> treatments, and not always for good reasons:
>
> > Medical tourism is already in full swing. Thailand is the golden
> > shore for wealthy, sickly Asians and Australians. Fashionable
> > Europeans head to South Africa for embarrassing plastic
> > surgery. Crowds of scrip-waving Americans buy prescription
> > drugs in Canada and Mexico. (92)

## 34c What are MLA guidelines for parenthetical documentation?

This section shows examples of how to handle parenthetical documentation in the text of your research papers. The directory at the beginning of this chapter corresponds to the numbered examples in the following pages. Most of these examples show the author's name or the title included in the parenthetical citation, but remember that it's usually more effective to include that information in your sentences in the research paper itself.

### 1. Paraphrased or Summarized Source—MLA

According to Brent Staples, IQ tests give scientists little insight into intelligence (293). [Author name cited in text; page number cited in parentheses.]

In "The IQ Cult," the journalist Brent Staples states that IQ tests give scientists little insight into intelligence (293). [Title of source, author name, and author credentials cited in text; page number cited in parentheses.]

IQ tests give scientists little insight into intelligence (Staples 293). [Author name and page number cited in parentheses.]

### 2. Source of a Short Quotation—MLA

Given that "thoughts, emotions, imagination and predispositions occur concurrently . . . [and] interact with other brain processes" (Caine and Caine 66), it is easy to understand why "whatever [intelligence] might be, paper and pencil tests aren't the tenth of it" (Staples 293).

Coles asks, "What binds together a Mormon banker in Utah with his brother, or other coreligionists in Illinois or Massachusetts?" (2).

### 3. Source of a Long Quotation—MLA

A long quotation in MLA style consists of more than four typed lines. It's set off block style, indented one inch or ten spaces from the left margin. Never put quotation marks around a set-off quotation because the indentation and block style communicate that the material is quoted. At the end of an indented quotation, place the parenthetical reference after the end punctuation mark.

Gray and Viens explain how, by tapping into a student's highly developed spatial-mechanical intelligence, one teacher can bolster a student's poor writing skills:

> The teacher asked that during "journal time" Jacob create a tool dictionary to be used as a resource in the mechanical learning center. After several entries in which he drew and described tools and other materials, Jacob confidently moved on to writing about other things of import to him, such as his brothers and a recent birthday party. Rather than shy away from all things

linguistic--he previously had refused any task requiring a
pencil--Jacob became invested in journal writing. (23-24)

### 4. One Author—MLA

Give an author's name as it appears on the source: for a book, on the title
page; for an article, directly below the title or at the end of the article.

One test asks four-year-olds to choose between one marshmallow now or
two marshmallows later (Gibbs 60).

Many nonprint sources also name an author; for CDs or DVDs, for example, check the printed sleeve or cover. For an online source, look at
the beginning or end of the file for a link to the author, or at the site's
home page. (For more information about citing electronic sources, see
items 18 through 20.)

### 5. Two or Three Authors—MLA

Give the names in the same order as in the source. Spell out *and*. For
three authors, use commas to separate the authors' names.

As children get older, they begin to express several different kinds of
intelligence (Todd and Taylor 23).

Another measure of emotional intelligence is the success of inter- and
intrapersonal relationships (Voigt, Dees, and Prigoff 14).

### 6. More Than Three Authors—MLA

If your source has more than three authors, you can name them all or use
the first author's name only, followed by *et al.*, either in a parenthetical
reference or in your sentence. In MLA citations, do not underline or italicize *et al.*

Emotional security varies, depending on the circumstances of the social
interaction (Carter et al. 158).

**ALERTS:** (1) The abbreviation *et al.* stands for "and others". The
Latin term *et* means "and" and requires no period. The term *al* is an abbreviation of *alii*, so it requires a period. (2) When an author's name followed by *et al.* is a subject, use a plural verb.

Carter et al. have found that emotional security varies, depending on the
circumstances of the social interaction (158). ◆

### 7. More Than One Source by an Author—MLA

When you use two or more sources by an author, include the relevant
title in each citation. In parenthetical citations, use a shortened version

of the title. For example, in a paper using two of Howard Gardner's works, *Frames of Mind: The Theory of Multiple Intelligences* and "Reflections on Multiple Intelligences: Myths and Messages," use *Frames* and "Reflections." Shorten the titles as much as possible, keeping them unambiguous to readers and starting them with the word by which you alphabetize each work in your Works Cited list. Separate the author's name and the title with a comma, but do not use punctuation between the title and the page number. When you incorporate the title into your own sentences, you can omit a subtitle, but never shorten the main title.

> Although it seems straightforward to think of multiple intelligences as multiple approaches to learning (Gardner, Frames 60-61), an intelligence is not a learning style (Gardner, "Reflections" 202-03).

### 8. Two or More Authors with the Same Last Name—MLA

Use each author's first initial and full last name in each parenthetical citation. This is the only instance in MLA style where you use an initial in a parenthetical reference. If both authors have the same first initial, use the full name in all instances.

> According to Anne Cates, psychologists can predict how empathetic an adult will be from his or her behavior at age two (41), but other researchers disagree (T. Cates 171).

### 9. Work with a Group or Corporate Author—MLA

When a corporation or other group is named as the author of a source you want to cite, use the corporate name just as you would an individual's name.

> In a five-year study, the Boston Women's Health Collective reported that these tests are usually unreliable (11).

> A five-year study shows that these tests are usually unreliable (Boston Women's Health Collective 11).

### 10. Work Listed by Title—MLA

If no author is named, use the title in citations. In your own sentences, use the full main title and omit a subtitle, if any. For parenthetical citations, shorten the title as much as possible (making sure that the shortened version refers unambiguously to the correct source), and always make the first word the one by which you alphabetize it. "Are You a Day or Night Person?" is the full title of the article in the following citation.

> The "morning lark" and "night owl" connotations are typically used to categorize the human extremes ("Are You" 11).

### 11. Multivolume Work—MLA

When you cite more than one volume of a multivolume work, include the relevant volume number in each citation. Give the volume number first, followed by a colon and one space, and then the page number(s).

> By 1900, the Amazon forest dwellers had been exposed to these viruses (Rand 3: 202).

> Rand believes that forest dwellers in Borneo escaped illness from retroviruses until the 1960s (4: 518-19).

### 12. Material from a Novel, Play, Poem, or Short Story—MLA

Literary works frequently appear in different editions. When you cite material from literary works, providing the part, chapter, act, scene, canto, stanza, or line numbers usually helps readers locate what you are referring to more than page numbers alone. Unless your instructor tells you not to, use arabic numerals for these references, even if the literary work uses roman numerals.

For novels that use them, give part and/or chapter numbers after page numbers. Use a semicolon after the page number but a comma to separate a part from a chapter.

> Flannery O'Connor describes one character in The Violent Bear It Away as "divided in two--a violent and a rational self" (139; pt. 2, ch. 6).

For plays that use them, give act, scene, and line numbers. Use periods between these numbers. For short stories, use page numbers.

> Among the most quoted of Shakespeare's lines is Hamlet's soliloquy beginning "To be, or not to be: that is the question" (3.1.56).

> The old man in John Collier's short story "The Chaser" says about his potions, "I don't deal in laxatives and teething mixtures . . ." (79).

For poems and plays that use them, give canto, stanza, and line numbers. Use periods between these numbers.

> In "To Autumn," Keats's most melancholy image occurs in the lines "Then in a wailful choir the small gnats mourn / Among the river swallows" (3.27-28).

### 13. Bible or Sacred Text—MLA

Give the title of the edition you're using, the book (in the case of the Bible), and the chapter and verse. Spell out the names of books in sentences, but use abbreviations in parenthetical references.

He would certainly benefit from the advice in Ephesians to "get rid of all bitterness, rage, and anger" (New International Version Bible, 4.31).

He would certainly benefit from the advice to "get rid of all bitterness, rage, and anger" (New International Version Bible, Eph. 4.31).

## 14. Work in an Anthology or Other Collection—MLA

You may want to cite a work you have read in a book that contains many works by various authors and that was compiled or edited by someone other than the person you're citing. Your in-text citation should include the author of the selection you're citing and the page number. For example, suppose you want to cite the poem "Several Things" by Martha Collins, in a literature text edited by Pamela Annas and Robert Rosen. Use Collins's name and the title of her work in the sentence and the line numbers (see item 12) in a parenthetical citation.

> In "Several Things," Martha Collins enumerates what could take place in the lines of her poem: "Plums could appear, on a pewter plate / A dead red hare, hung by one foot. / A vase of flowers. Three shallots" (2-4).

## 15. Indirect Source—MLA

When you want to quote words that you found quoted in someone else's work, put the name of the person whose words you're quoting into your own sentence. Give the work where you found the quotation either in your sentence or in a parenthetical citation beginning with *qtd. in*.

> Martin Scorsese acknowledges the link between himself and his films: "I realize that all my life, I've been an outsider. I splatter bits of myself all over the screen" (qtd. in Giannetti and Eyman 397).

> Giannetti and Eyman quote Martin Scorsese as acknowledging the link between himself and his films: "I realize that all my life, I've been an outsider. I splatter bits of myself all over the screen" (397).

## 16. Two or More Sources in One Reference—MLA

If more than one source has contributed to an idea, opinion, or fact in your paper, cite them all. Suppose, as in the following example, that three sources all make the same point. An efficient way to credit all is to include them in a single parenthetical citation, with a semicolon separating each block of information.

> Once researchers agreed that multiple intelligences existed, their next step was to try to measure or define them (West 17; Arturi 477; Gibbs 68).

## 17. Entire Work—MLA

References to an entire work usually fit best into your own sentences.

In <u>Frames of Mind</u>, Gardner proposes a revolutionary expansion of our understanding of human intelligence.

## 18. Electronic Source with a Name or Title and Page Numbers—MLA

The principles that govern in-text parenthetical citations of electronic sources are exactly the same as the ones that apply to books, articles, or other sources. When an electronically accessed source identifies its author, use the author's name for parenthetical references. If no author is named, use the title of the source. When an electronic source has page numbers, use them exactly as you would the page numbers of a print source.

> Learning happens best when teachers truly care about their students' complete well-being (Anderson 7).

## 19. Electronic Source with Paragraph or Screen Numbers—MLA

When an electronic source has numbered paragraphs or screens (instead of page numbers), use them for parenthetical references, with two differences: (1) Use a comma followed by one space after the name (or title); and (2) use the abbreviation *par.* for a reference to one paragraph or *pars.* for a reference to more than one paragraph, followed by the number(s) of the paragraph(s) you are citing. Note that the practice of numbering paragraphs or screens is rare.

> Artists seem to be haunted by the fear that psychoanalysis might destroy creativity while it reconstructs personality (Francis, pars. 22-25).

> The renovation cost $25 million, according to Conklin (screen 5).

## 20. Electronic Source Without Page or Paragraph Numbers—MLA

Many online sources don't number pages or paragraphs. Simply refer to those works in their entirety. Here are two examples referring to "What Is Artificial Intelligence?" by John McCarthy; this Web site does not use page numbers or paragraph numbers. Include the name of the author in your sentence; it is also helpful to include the title.

> According to McCarthy, the science of artificial intelligence includes efforts beyond trying to simulate human intelligence.

> In "What Is Artificial Intelligence?" John McCarthy notes that the science of artificial intelligence includes efforts beyond trying to simulate human intelligence.

## 34d What are MLA guidelines for a Works Cited list?

In MLA-STYLE DOCUMENTATION, the Works Cited list gives complete bibliographic information for each SOURCE used in your paper. Include only the sources from which you quote, paraphrase, or summarize. Never include sources that you consulted but don't refer to in the paper. Box 34.1 gives general information about the Works Cited list. The rest of this chapter gives models of many specific kinds of Works Cited entries.

---

**SUMMARY BOX** 34.1

### Guidelines for an MLA-style Works Cited list

**TITLE**

Use "Works Cited" (without quotation marks) as the title.

**PLACEMENT OF LIST**

Start a new page numbered sequentially with the rest of the paper, following the Notes pages, if any.

**CONTENT AND FORMAT**

Include all sources quoted from, paraphrased, or summarized in your paper. Start each entry on a new line and at the regular left margin. If the entry uses more than one line, indent the second and all following lines one-half inch (or five spaces) from the left margin. Double-space all lines.

**SPACING AFTER PUNCTUATION**

When typewriters were common, it improved readability to leave two spaces after punctuation at the end of a sentence. Computers have made this practice no longer necessary. The *MLA Handbook* uses one space, as does this book. Either style is acceptable. However, you should use two spaces if that's the style your instructor prefers. Always put only one space after a comma or a colon.

**ARRANGEMENT OF ENTRIES**

Alphabetize by author's last name. If no author is named, alphabetize by the title's first significant word (ignore *A*, *An*, or *The*).

**AUTHORS' NAMES**

Use first names and middle names or middle initials, if any, as given in the source. Don't reduce to initials any name that is given in full. For one author or the first-named author in multiauthor works, give the last name first. Use

➤

## Guidelines for an MLA-style Works Cited list

the word *and* with two or more authors. List multiple authors in the order given in the source. Use a comma between the first author's last and first names and after each complete author name except the last. After the last author's name, use a period: Fein, Ethel Andrea, Bert Griggs, and Delaware Rogash.

Include *Jr., Sr., II,* or *III* but no other titles and degrees before or after a name. For example, an entry for a work by Edward Meep III, MD, and Sir Richard Bolton would start like this: Meep, Edward, III, and Richard Bolton.

### CAPITALIZATION OF TITLES

Capitalize all major words and the first and last words of all titles and subtitles. Don't capitalize ARTICLES (*a, an, the*), PREPOSITIONS, COORDINATING CONJUNCTIONS (*and, but, for, nor, or, so, yet*), or *to* in INFINITIVES in the middle of a title.

### SPECIAL TREATMENT OF TITLES

Use quotation marks around titles of shorter works (poems, short stories, essays, articles). Underline titles of longer works (books, periodicals, plays).

For underlining, use an unbroken line like this. Don't underline a period or comma at the end. MLA prefers underlined roman type to italic type, so use underlining unless your instructor specifically requires italics.

When a book title includes the title of another work that is usually underlined (as with a novel, play, or long poem), the preferred MLA style is not to underline the incorporated title: Decoding Jane Eyre. For an alternative that MLA accepts, see item 20 in 34d.1.

If the incorporated title is usually enclosed in quotation marks (such as a short story or short poem), keep the quotation marks and underline the complete title of the book: Theme and Form in "I Shall Laugh Purely": A Brief Study.

Drop *A, An,* or *The* as the first word of a periodical title.

### PLACE OF PUBLICATION

If several cities are listed for the place of publication, give only the first. MLA doesn't require US state names no matter how obscure or confusing the city names might be. For an unfamiliar city outside the United States, include an abbreviated name of the country or Canadian province.

➤

**SUMMARY BOX** **34.1** *continued*

## Guidelines for an MLA-style Works Cited list

### PUBLISHER

Use shortened names as long as they are clear: *Random* for *Random House.* For companies named for more than one person, name only the first: *Prentice* for *Prentice Hall.* For university presses, use the capital letters *U* and *P* (without periods): Oxford UP; U of Chicago P

### PUBLICATION MONTH ABBREVIATIONS

Abbreviate all publication months except *May, June,* and *July.* Use the first three letters followed by a period (*Dec., Feb.*) except for September (*Sept.*).

### PARAGRAPH AND SCREEN NUMBERS IN ELECTRONIC SOURCES

Some electronic sources number paragraphs or screens instead of pages, although many electronic sources include no such information. If paragraphs are numbered, at the end of the publication information give the total number of paragraphs followed by the abbreviation *pars.:* 77 pars. If screens are numbered, give the total number of screens as the final information in the entry. If the source does not number pages, paragraphs, screens, or anything else, omit information about the length of the source.

### PAGE RANGES

Give the page range—the starting page number and the ending page number, connected by a hyphen—of any paginated electronic source and any paginated print source that is part of a longer work (for example, a chapter in a book, an article in a journal). A range indicates that the cited work is on those pages and all pages in between. If that isn't the case, use the style shown next for discontinuous pages. In either case, use numerals only, without the word *page* or *pages* or the abbreviation *p.* or *pp.*

Use the full second number through 99. Above that, use only the last two digits for the second number unless to do so would be unclear: 113-14 is clear, but 567-602 requires full numbers.

### DISCONTINUOUS PAGES

A source has discontinuous pages when the source is interrupted by material that's not part of the source (for example, an article beginning on page 32 but continued on page 54). Use the starting page number followed by a plus sign (+): 32+.

➤

**SUMMARY BOX** 34.1 *continued*

### Guidelines for an MLA-style Works Cited list

**URLS IN ELECTRONIC SOURCES**

For online sources accessed through a URL, the URL is required in the Works Cited entry, enclosed in angle brackets <like this>. Put the URL after the access date and before the period at the end of the entry. If your computer automatically creates a hyperlink when you type a URL (the text changes color, the URL is underlined, or both) use the command "Remove Hyperlink," which you can find on the "Insert" menu in Microsoft Word. If the URL is very long and complicated, just give the URL for the site's search page. (MLA doesn't specify what constitutes long and complicated, but a reasonable guideline is that if a URL ends in a string of seemingly random characters, or numerous underscores or slashes, consider shortening it.)

## 34d.1 Following MLA guidelines for specific sources in a Works Cited list

The Works Cited directory at the beginning of this chapter corresponds to the numbered entries in this section. Not every possible documentation model is shown in this chapter. You may find that you have to combine features of models to document a particular source. You'll also find more information in the *MLA Handbook for Writers of Research Papers*.

**BOOKS**

Citations for books have three main parts: author, title, and publication information (place of publication, publisher, and date of publication). Figure 34.1 (p. 576) illustrates where to find this information and the proper citation format.

**1. Book by One Author—MLA**

Bradway, Becky. Pink Houses and Family Taverns. Bloomington: Indiana UP, 2002.

**2. Book by Two or Three Authors—MLA**

Edin, Kathryn, and Maria Kefalas. Promises I Can Keep: Why Poor Women Put Motherhood before Marriage. Berkeley: U of California P, 2005.

Lynam, John K., Cyrus G. Ndiritu, and Adiel N. Mbabu. Transformation of Agricultural Research Systems in Africa: Lessons from Andreiya. East Lansing: Michigan State UP, 2004.

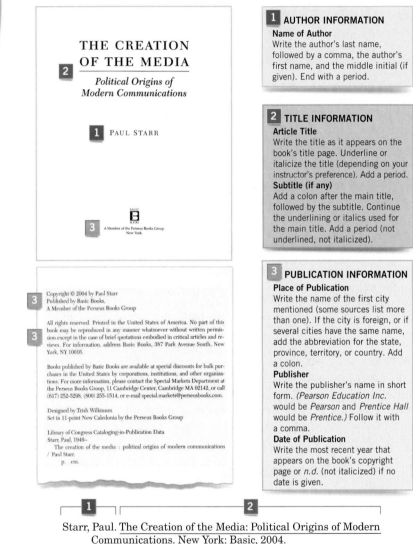

**1 AUTHOR INFORMATION**
**Name of Author**
Write the author's last name, followed by a comma, the author's first name, and the middle initial (if given). End with a period.

**2 TITLE INFORMATION**
**Article Title**
Write the title as it appears on the book's title page. Underline or italicize the title (depending on your instructor's preference). Add a period.
**Subtitle (if any)**
Add a colon after the main title, followed by the subtitle. Continue the underlining or italics used for the main title. Add a period (not underlined, not italicized).

**3 PUBLICATION INFORMATION**
**Place of Publication**
Write the name of the first city mentioned (some sources list more than one). If the city is foreign, or if several cities have the same name, add the abbreviation for the state, province, territory, or country. Add a colon.
**Publisher**
Write the publisher's name in short form. *(Pearson Education Inc.* would be *Pearson* and *Prentice Hall* would be *Prentice.)* Follow it with a comma.
**Date of Publication**
Write the most recent year that appears on the book's copyright page or *n.d.* (not italicized) if no date is given.

Starr, Paul. The Creation of the Media: Political Origins of Modern Communications. New York: Basic, 2004.

Figure 34.1 Locating and citing sources in a book

### 3. Book by More Than Three Authors—MLA

Give only the first author's name, followed by a comma and the phrase *et al.* (abbreviated from the Latin *et alii*, meaning "and others"), or list all names in full and in the order in which they appear on the title page.

Saul, Wendy, et al. Beyond the Science Fair: Creating a Kids' Inquiry
    Conference. Portsmouth: Heinemann, 2005.

### 4. Two or More Works by the Same Author(s)—MLA

Give author name(s) in the first entry only. In the second and subsequent entries, use three hyphens and a period to stand for exactly the same name(s). If the person served as editor or translator, put a comma and the appropriate abbreviation (*ed.* or *trans.*) following the three hyphens. Arrange the works in alphabetical (not chronological) order according to book title, ignoring labels such as *ed.* or *trans.*

Gardner, Howard. Intelligence Reframed: Multiple Intelligences for the 21st
    Century. New York: Basic, 1999.

---. Multiple Intelligences: The Theory in Practice. New York: Basic, 1993.

### 5. Book by Group or Corporate Author—MLA

Cite the full name of the corporate author first, omitting the first articles *A*, *An*, or *The*. When a corporate author is also the publisher, use a shortened form of the corporate name in the publication information.

American Psychological Association. Publication Manual of the American
    Psychological Association. 5th ed. Washington: APA, 2001.

Boston Women's Health Collective. Our Bodies, Ourselves for the New
    Century. New York: Simon, 1998.

### 6. Book with No Author Named—MLA

If there is no author's name on the title page, begin the citation with the title. Alphabetize the entry according to the first significant word of the title but ignoring *A*, *An* or *The*.

The Chicago Manual of Style. 15th ed. Chicago: U of Chicago P, 2003.

### 7. Book with an Author and an Editor—MLA

If your paper refers to the work of the book's author, put the author's name first; if your paper refers to the work of the editor, put the editor's name first.

Brontë, Emily. <u>Wuthering Heights</u>. Ed. Richard J. Dunn. New York: Norton, 2002.

Dunn, Richard J., ed. <u>Wuthering Heights</u>. By Emily Brontë. New York: Norton, 2002.

#### 8. Translation—MLA

Kundera, Milan. <u>The Unbearable Lightness of Being</u>. Trans. Michael Henry Heim. New York: Harper, 1999.

#### 9. Work in Several Volumes or Parts—MLA

If you're citing only one volume, put the volume number before the publication information. If you wish, you can give the total number of volumes at the end of the entry. MLA recommends using arabic numerals, even if the source uses roman numerals (*Vol. 6* rather than *Vol. VI*).

Chrisley, Ronald, ed. <u>Artificial Intelligence: Critical Concepts</u>. Vol. 1. London: Routledge, 2000. 4 vols.

#### 10. One Selection from an Anthology or an Edited Book—MLA

Give the author and title of the selection first and then the full title of the anthology. Information about the editor starts with *Ed.* (for "Edited by"), so don't use *Eds.* when there is more than one editor. Give the name(s) of the editor(s) in normal order rather than reversing first and last names. Give the page range at the end.

Trujillo, Laura. "Balancing Act." <u>Border-Line Personalities: A New Generation of Latinas Dish on Sex, Sass, and Cultural Shifting</u>. Ed. Robyn Moreno and Michelle Herrera Mulligan. New York: Harper, 2004. 61-72.

#### 11. More Than One Selection from the Same Anthology or Edited Book—MLA

If you cite more than one selection from the same anthology, you can list the anthology as a separate entry with all the publication information. Also, list each selection from the anthology by author and title of the selection, but give only the name(s) of the editor(s) of the anthology and the page number(s) for each selection. Here, *ed.* stands for "editor," so it is correct to use *eds.* when more than one editor is named. List selections separately in alphabetical order by author's last name.

Gilbert, Sandra M., and Susan Gubar, eds. <u>The Norton Anthology of Literature by Women</u>. New York: Norton, 1985.

Kingston, Maxine Hong. "No Name Woman." Gilbert and Gubar 2337-47.

Welty, Eudora. "The Petrified Man." Gilbert and Gubar 2322-32.

### 12. Signed Article in a Reference Book—MLA

A "signed article" means that the author of the article is identified. If the articles in the book are alphabetically arranged, you don't need to give volume and page numbers.

Burnbam, John C. "Freud, Sigmund." The Encyclopedia of Psychiatry, Psychology, and Psychoanalysis. Ed. Benjamin B. Wolman. New York: Holt, 1996.

### 13. Unsigned Article in a Reference Book—MLA

Begin with the title of the article. If you're citing a widely used reference work, don't give full publication information. Instead, give only the edition and year of publication.

"Ireland." The New Encyclopaedia Britannica: Macropaedia. 15th ed. 2002.

### 14. Second or Later Edition—MLA

If a book isn't a first edition, the edition number appears on the title page. Place the abbreviated information (*2nd ed., 3rd ed.,* etc.) between the title and the publication information. Give only the latest copyright date for the edition you're using.

Gibaldi, Joseph. MLA Handbook for Writers of Research Papers. 6th ed. New York: MLA, 2003.

### 15. Anthology or Edited Book—MLA

In the following example, *ed.* stands for "editor," so use *eds.* when more than one editor is named; also see items 9 and 11.

Purdy, John L., and James Ruppert, eds. Nothing But the Truth: An Anthology of Native American Literature. Upper Saddle River: Prentice, 2001.

### 16. Introduction, Preface, Foreword, or Afterword—MLA

Give first the name of the writer of the part you're citing and then the name of the cited part, capitalized but not underlined or in quotation marks. After the book title, write *By* or *Ed.* and the full name(s) of the book's author(s) or editor(s), if different from the writer of the cited material. If the writer of the cited material is the same as the book author, include only the last name after *By.* Following the publication information, give inclusive page numbers for the cited part, using roman or arabic numerals as the source does.

Hesse, Doug. Foreword. The End of Composition Studies. By David W. Smit. Carbondale: Southern Illinois UP, 2004. ix-xiii.

When the introduction, preface, foreword, or afterword has a title (as in the next example), include it in the citation before the section name.

Fox-Genovese, Elizabeth. "Mothers and Daughters: The Ties That Bind."
Foreword. <u>Southern Mothers</u>. Ed. Nagueyalti Warren and Sally Wolff.
Baton Rouge: Louisiana State UP, 1999. iv-xviii.

## 17. Unpublished Dissertation or Essay—MLA

State the author's name first, then the title in quotation marks (not underlined), then a descriptive label (such as *Diss.* or *Unpublished essay*), followed by the degree-granting institution (for dissertations), and, finally, the date. Treat published dissertations as books.

Byers, Michele. "<u>Buffy the Vampire Slayer</u>: The Insurgence of Television
as a Performance Text." Diss. U of Toronto, 2000.

## 18. Reprint of an Older Book—MLA

Republishing information can be found on the copyright page. Give the date of the original version before the publication information for the version you're citing.

O'Brien, Flann. <u>At Swim-Two-Birds</u>. 1939. Normal: Dalkey Archive, 1998.

## 19. Book in a Series—MLA

Goldman, Dorothy J. <u>Women Writers and World War I</u>. Lit. and Soc. Ser.
New York: Macmillan, 1995.

Mukherjee, Meenakshi. <u>Jane Austen</u>. Women Writers Ser. New York:
St. Martin's, 1991.

## 20. Book with a Title Within a Title—MLA

The MLA recognizes two distinct styles for handling normally independent titles when they appear within an underlined title. (Use whichever style your instructor prefers.) When using the MLA's preferred style, do not underline the embedded title or set it within quotation marks.

Lumiansky, Robert M., and Herschel Baker, eds. <u>Critical Approaches to Six
Major English Works</u>: Beowulf <u>through</u> Paradise Lost. Philadelphia:
U of Pennsylvania P, 1968.

However, because MLA also accepts a second style for handling such embedded titles, you can set the normally independent titles within quotation marks and underline them.

Lumiansky, Robert M., and Herschel Baker, eds. <u>Critical Approaches to Six
Major English Works</u>: "Beowulf" through "Paradise Lost." Philadelphia:
U of Pennsylvania P, 1968.

### 21. Bible or Sacred Text—MLA

<u>Bhagavad Gita</u>. Trans. Juan Mascaro. Rev. ed. New York: Penguin, 2003.

<u>The Holy Bible: New International Version</u>. New York: Harper, 1983.

<u>The Qur'an</u>. Trans. Abdullah Yusuf Ali. 13th ed. Elmhurst: Tahrike Tarsile Qur'an, 1999.

### 22. Government Publication—MLA

For government publications that name no author, start with the name of the government or government body. Then name the government agency. *GPO* is a standard abbreviation for *Government Printing Office,* the publisher of most US government publications.

United States. Cong. House. Committee on Resources. <u>Coastal Heritage Trail Route in New Jersey</u>. 106th Cong., 1st sess. H. Rept. 16. Washington: GPO, 1999.

United States. Cong. Senate. Select Committee on Intelligence. <u>Report on the U.S. Intelligence Community's Prewar Intelligence Assessment of Iraq</u>. 108th Cong., 1st sess. Washington: GPO, 2004.

### 23. Published Proceedings of a Conference—MLA

Harris, Diana, and Laurie Nelson-Heern, eds. <u>Proceedings of the National Education Computing Conference, June 17-19, 1981</u>. Iowa City: Weeg Computing Center, U of Iowa, 1981.

### PERIODICAL PUBLICATIONS

Citations for periodical articles contain three major parts: author information, title information, and publication information (usually year of publication and page range). Figure 34.2 (p. 582) shows a citation for an article in a journal with continuous pagination (see item 32).

### 24. Signed Article in a Daily Newspaper—MLA

Omit *A, An,* or *The* as the first word in a newspaper title. Give the day, month, and year of the issue (and the edition, if applicable). If sections are designated, give the section letter as well as the page number. If an article runs on nonconsecutive pages, give the starting page number followed by a plus sign (for example, *23+* for an article that starts on page 23 and continues on page 42).

Killborn, Peter T. "A Health Threat Baffling for Its Lack of a Pattern." <u>New York Times</u> 22 June 2003, natl. ed.: A14.

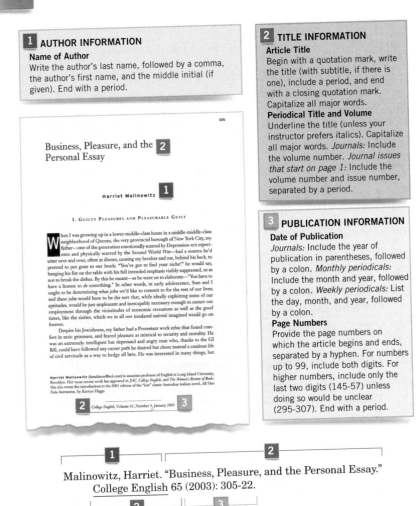

Figure 34.2 Locating and citing sources for a journal article

The following text boxes appear in the figure:

**1 AUTHOR INFORMATION**
**Name of Author**
Write the author's last name, followed by a comma, the author's first name, and the middle initial (if given). End with a period.

**2 TITLE INFORMATION**
**Article Title**
Begin with a quotation mark, write the title (with subtitle, if there is one), include a period, and end with a closing quotation mark. Capitalize all major words.
**Periodical Title and Volume**
Underline the title (unless your instructor prefers italics). Capitalize all major words. *Journals:* Include the volume number. *Journal issues that start on page 1:* Include the volume number and issue number, separated by a period.

**3 PUBLICATION INFORMATION**
**Date of Publication**
*Journals:* Include the year of publication in parentheses, followed by a colon. *Monthly periodicals:* Include the month and year, followed by a colon. *Weekly periodicals:* List the day, month, and year, followed by a colon.
**Page Numbers**
Provide the page numbers on which the article begins and ends, separated by a hyphen. For numbers up to 99, include both digits. For higher numbers, include only the last two digits (145-57) unless doing so would be unclear (295-307). End with a period.

The citation shown reads:

Malinowitz, Harriet. "Business, Pleasure, and the Personal Essay." College English 65 (2003): 305-22.

## 25. Unsigned Article in a Daily Newspaper—MLA

"A Crusade to Revitalize the City Opera." New York Times 25 Jan. 2001, late ed.: B6.

If the city of publication is not part of the title, put it in square brackets after the title, not underlined.

"Hackers Hit Northwestern Computer Net." Pantagraph [Bloomington]
26 Mar. 2005: A5.

## 26. Editorial, Letter to the Editor, or Review—MLA

After the author's name or title, provide information about the type of
publication.

"Downtown's Architectural Promise." Editorial. New York Times 4 Aug. 2003:
A12.

Hansen, Roger P. Letter. Sierra Jan.-Feb. 2003: 8.

Shenk, David. "Toolmaker, Brain Builder." Rev. of Beyond Big Blue:
Building the Computer That Defeated the World Chess Champion,
by Feng-Hsiung Hsu. American Scholar 72 (Spring 2003): 150-52.

## 27. Signed Article in a Weekly or Biweekly Periodical—MLA

Brink, Susan. "Eat This Now!" US News and World Report 28 Mar. 2005: 56-58.

## 28. Signed Article in a Monthly or Bimonthly Periodical—MLA

Langewiesch, William. "Anarchy at Sea." Atlantic Monthly Sept. 2003: 50-80.

## 29. Unsigned Article in a Weekly or Monthly Periodical—MLA

"The Price Is Wrong." Economist 2 Aug. 2003: 58-59.

## 30. Article in a Collection of Reprinted Articles—MLA

First include the original publication information, then *Rpt.* and information about the place the article was republished.

Brumberg, Abraham. "Russia after Perestroika." New York Review of Books
27 June 1991: 53-62. Rpt. in Russian and Soviet History. Ed. Alexander
Dallin. Vol. 14 of The Gorbachev Era. New York: Garland, 1992. 300-20.

Textbooks used in college writing courses often collect previously
printed articles.

Rothstein, Richard. "When Mothers on Welfare Go to Work." New York Times
5 June 2002: A20. Rpt. in Writing Arguments: A Rhetoric with Readings.
Ed. John D. Ramage, John C. Bean, and June Johnson. New York:
Longman, 2004. 263.

## 31. Article in a Looseleaf Collection of Reprinted Articles—MLA

Give the citation for the original publication first, followed by the citation for the collection.

Hayden, Thomas. "The Age of Robots." US News and World Report 23 Apr. 2001: 44+. Applied Science 2002. Ed. Eleanor Goldstein. Boca Raton: SIRS, 2002. Art. 66.

## 32. Article in a Journal with Continuous Pagination—MLA

"Continuous pagination" means that page numbers within a volume continue from one issue to the next. For example, if the first issue of a journal with continuous pagination ends on page 228, the second issue starts with page 229. Give only the volume number before the year. Use arabic numerals for all numbers.

Tyson, Phyllis. "The Psychology of Women." Journal of the American Psychoanalytic Association 46 (1998): 361-64.

## 33. Article in a Journal That Pages Each Issue Separately—MLA

When each issue begins with page 1, give both the volume number (26) and the issue number (3), separated by a period.

Adler-Kassner, Linda, and Heidi Estrem. "Rethinking Research Writing: Public Literacy in the Composition Classroom." WPA: Writing Program Administration 26.3 (2003): 119-31.

## 34. Abstract in a Collection of Abstracts—MLA

To cite an abstract, first give information for the full work: the author's name, the title of the article, and publication information about the full article. If a reader could not know that the cited material is an abstract, write the word *Abstract*, not underlined, followed by a period. Give publication information about the collection of abstracts. For abstracts identified by item numbers rather than page numbers, use the word *item* before the item number.

Marcus, Hazel R., and Shinobu Kitayamo. "Culture and the Self: Implications for Cognition, Emotion, and Motivation." Psychological Review 88 (1991): 224-53. Psychological Abstracts 78 (1991): item 23878.

## MISCELLANEOUS PRINT AND NONPRINT SOURCES

## 35. Published or Unpublished Letter—MLA

Begin the entry with the author of the letter. Note the recipient, too.

Brown, Theodore. Letter to the author. 7 Dec. 2005.

Williams, William Carlos. Letter to his son. 13 Mar. 1935. Letters of the Century: America 1900-1999. Ed. Lisa Grunwald and Stephen J. Adler. New York: Dial, 1999. 225-26.

## 36. Microfiche Collection of Articles—MLA

A microfiche is a transparent sheet of film (a *fiche*) with microscopic printing that needs to be read through a special magnifier. Each fiche holds several pages, with each page designated by a grid position. A long document may appear on more than one fiche.

Wenzell, Ron. "Businesses Prepare for a More Diverse Work Force." St. Louis
Post Dispatch 3 Feb. 1990: 17. NewsBank: Employment 27 (1990): fiche 2,
grid D12.

## 37. Map or Chart—MLA

The Caribbean and South America. Map. Falls Church: AAA, 1992.

## 38. Report or Pamphlet—MLA

Use the format for books, to the extent possible.

National Commission on Writing in America's Schools and Colleges.
The Neglected "R": The Need for a Writing Revolution. New York:
College Board, 2003.

## 39. Legal Source—MLA

Include the name of the case, the number of the case (preceded by *No.*), the name of the court deciding the case, and the date of the decision.

Brown v. Board of Ed. No. 8. Supreme Ct. of the US. 8 Oct. 1952.

## 40. Interview—MLA

Note the type of interview—for example, "Telephone," "Personal" (face-to-face), or "E-mail."

Friedman, Randi. Telephone interview. 30 June 2005.

For a published interview, give the name of the interviewed person first, identify the source as an interview, and then give details as for any published source: title; author, preceded by the word *By;* and publication details.

Winfrey, Oprah. "Ten Questions for Oprah Winfrey." By Richard Zoglin.
Time 15 Dec. 2003: 8.

## 41. Lecture, Speech, or Address—MLA

Kennedy, John Fitzgerald. Address. Greater Houston Ministerial Assn.
Rice Hotel, Houston. 12 Sept. 1960.

## 42. Film, Videotape, or DVD—MLA

Give the title first, and include the director, the distributor, and the year. For older films that were subsequently released on videocassettes or

DVDs, provide the original release date of the movie *before* the type of medium. Other information (writer, producer, major actors) is optional but helpful. Put first names first.

Shakespeare in Love. Screenplay by Marc Norman and Tom Stoppard. Dir.
  John Maddon. Prod. David Parfitt, Donna Gigliotti, Harvey Weinstein,
  Edward Zwick, and Mark Norman. Perf. Gwyneth Paltrow, Joseph
  Fiennes, and Judi Dench. 1998. DVD. Miramax, 2003.

It Happened One Night. Screenplay by Robert Riskin. Dir. and Prod. Frank
  Capra. Perf. Clark Gable and Claudette Colbert. 1934. Videocassette.
  Columbia, 1999.

### 43. Musical Recording—MLA

Put first the name most relevant to what you discuss in your paper (performer, conductor, the work performed). Include the recording's title, the medium for any recording other than a CD (*LP, audiocassette*), the name of the issuer (*Vanguard*), and the year the work was issued.

Smetana, Bedrich. My Country. Czech Philharmonic Orch. Cond. Karel Anserl.
  LP. Vanguard, 1975.

Springsteen, Bruce. "Lonesome Day." The Rising. Sony, 2002.

### 44. Live Performance—MLA

All My Sons. By Arthur Miller. Dir. Calvin McLean. Center for the Performing
  Arts, Normal, IL. 27 Sept. 2005.

### 45. Work of Art, Photograph, or Musical Composition—MLA

Cassatt, Mary. La Toilette. Art Institute of Chicago.

Mydans, Carl. General Douglas MacArthur Landing at Luzon, 1945. Soho Triad
  Fine Art Gallery, New York. 21 Oct.-28 Nov. 1999.

Don't underline or put in quotation marks music identified only by form, number, and key.

Schubert, Franz. Symphony no. 8 in B minor.

Underline any work that has a title, such as an opera or ballet or a named symphony.

Schubert, Franz. Unfinished Symphony.

To cite a published score, use the following format.

Schubert, Franz. <u>Symphony in B Minor (Unfinished)</u>. Ed. Martin Cusid.
New York: Norton, 1971.

## 46. Television or Radio Program—MLA

Include at least the title of the program (underlined), the network, the
local station and its city, and the date of the broadcast.

<u>Not for Ourselves Alone: The Story of Elizabeth Cady Stanton and Susan B.
Anthony</u>. Writ. Andrei Burns. Perf. Julie Harris, Ronnie Gilbert, and Sally
Kellerman. Prod. Paul Barnes and Andrei Burns. PBS. WNET, New York.
8 Nov. 1999.

For a series, also supply the title of the specific episode (in quotation
marks) before the title of the program (underlined) and the title of the
series (neither underlined nor in quotation marks).

"Episode One." <u>The Forsyte Saga</u>. By John Galsworthy. Adapt. Stephen
Mallatratt and Jan McVerry. Prod. Sita Williams. Masterpiece Theatre.
PBS. WGBH, Boston. 6 Oct. 2002.

## 47. Image or Photograph in a Print Publication—MLA

To cite an image or a photograph that appears as part of a print publication (perhaps as illustration for an article), give the photographer (if
known), the title or caption of the image, and complete publication
information, as for an article. If the image has no title, provide a brief
description.

Greene, Herb. "Grace Slick." <u>Rolling Stone</u> 30 Sept. 2004: 102.

## 48. Advertisement—MLA

American Airlines. Advertisement. ABC. 24 Aug. 2003.

Canon Digital Cameras. Advertisement. <u>Time</u> 2 June 2003: 77.

## ELECTRONIC SOURCES FROM DATABASES OR SUBSCRIPTION SERVICES

Online sources fall into two categories: (1) those you access through a
DATABASE or online service to which your library subscribes, such as EBSCO
or FirstSearch, or an online service to which you personally subscribe, such
as America Online; and (2) those you access by entering a specific URL
(Internet address). For source material reached through a database or subscription service, give the information listed on the following page:

- Details about the source (author, title, print source if any, publication date).
- The name of the database, underlined.
- The name of the service.
- The name of the library (if you accessed it through a library's service).
- The date you accessed the work.
- The URL of the service, in angle brackets (if you must break a URL at the end of a line, break only after a slash).
- A keyword, if you used one.

### 49. Subscription Service: Article with a Print Version—MLA

Jackson, Gabriel. "Multiple Historic Meanings of the Spanish Civil War."
Science and Society 68.3 (2004): 272-76. Academic Search Elite. EBSCO.
Milner Lib., Illinois State U. 7 Mar. 2005 <http://www.epnet.com>.

VandeHei, Jim. "Two Years after White House Exit, Clinton Shaping
Democratic Party." Washington Post 21 June 2003, final ed.: A1. Academic
Universe. LexisNexis. Bobst Lib., New York U. 5 May 2005 <http://
web.lexisnexis.com/>.

Figure 34.3 illustrates citing an article that has a print version but has been accessed through a subscription service.

### 50. Subscription Service: Abstract with a Print Version—MLA

The example below is for the same abstract shown in item 34, but here it is accessed from an online database (*PsycINFO*) by means of a library subscription service. The name of the library shows where the source was accessed, and *10 Apr. 2004* is the date it was accessed. The entry ends with the specific URL used.

Marcus, Hazel R., and Shinobu Kitayamo. "Culture and the Self: Implications
for Cognition, Emotion, and Motivation." Psychological Abstracts 78
(1991). PsycINFO. Ovid. Milner Lib., Illinois State U. 10 Apr. 2004
<http://gateway.ovid.com/ovidweb.cgi>.

### 51. Subscription Service: Material with No Print Version—MLA

Siemens, Raymond G. "A New Computer-Assisted Literary Criticism?"
Computers and the Humanities 36 (2002). America Online. 12 Nov. 2002.

### 52. Subscription Service Access with a Keyword: Article in a Periodical with a Print Version—MLA

Citations for electronic sources that don't have URLs contain at least seven major parts: author, title, publication information, title of database,

MLA

**1** **AUTHOR INFORMATION**

**Name of Author**

Write the author's last name, followed by a comma, the author's first name, and the middle initial (if given). End with a period.

**2** **TITLE INFORMATION**

**Article Title**

Begin with a quotation mark, write the title (with subtitle, if there is one), include a period, and end with a closing quotation mark. Capitalize all major words.

**Periodical Title, Volume, and Issue**

Capitalize all major words in the title and underline it. Write the volume number, period, and issue number. Do not punctuate after the title or issue number.

**3** **PUBLICATION INFORMATION**

**Print Publication Date**

*Journals:* Include the year of publication in parentheses, followed by a colon. *Monthly periodicals:* Include the month and year, followed by a colon. *Weekly periodicals:* List the day, month, and year, followed by a colon.

**Page Numbers**

Provide the page numbers on which the article begins and ends. End with a period. If the subscription service database provides only a first page number, follow it with a hyphen, a space, and a period.

**Database Name**

Underline the database. End with a period.

**Subscription Service Name**

Include the name of the library subscription service. Do not underline.

**Name of Library**

Include the library's name and a period.

**Access Date**

Provide the day, month, and year you accessed the article. Do not add a period.

**URL**

Place the URL for the database in angle brackets, followed by a period.

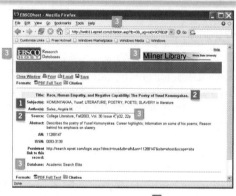

Salas, Angela M. "Race, Human Empathy, and Negative Capability: The Poetry of Yusef Komunyakaa." College Literature 30.4 (2003): 32- . Academic Search Elite. EBSCO. Milner Lib., Illinois State U. 15 May 2005 <http://web11.epnet.com>.

**Figure 34.3 Locating and citing sources for an online listing of a journal article**

name of vendor or computer service, access date, and keyword. Electronic versions of sources that also appear in print start with information about the print version. Here's an entry for a journal article accessed through a computer service; it also has a print version.

Wynne, Clive D. L. " 'Willy' Didn't Yearn to Be Free." <u>New York Times</u> 27 Dec.
2003: Op-ed page. <u>New York Times Online</u>. America Online. 29 Dec. 2003.
Keyword: nytimes.

Information applying to the print version of this article in the *New York Times* ends with *Op-ed page,* and information about the online version starts with the title of the database, *New York Times Online. America Online* is the service through which the database was accessed, and *29 Dec. 2003* is the access date. The keyword *nytimes* was used to access *New York Times Online,* as noted after the access date.

### 53. Subscription Service Access Showing a Path—MLA

When you access a source by choosing a series of keywords, menus, or topics, end the entry with the "path" of words you used. Use semicolons between items in the path, and put a period at the end.

Futrelle, David. "A Smashing Success." <u>Money.com</u> 23 Dec. 1999. America
Online. 26 Dec. 1999. Path: Personal Finance; Business News; Business
Publications; Money.com.

### OTHER INTERNET SOURCES

This section shows models for online sources accessed through Internet browsers, such as Web sites, FTP and Gopher sites, electronic mailing lists, and discussion groups. For such sources, provide as much of the following information as you can.

- The author's name, if given.
- In quotation marks, the title of a short work (Web page, brief document, essay, article, message, and so on); or underlined, the title of a book.
- Publication information for any print version, if it exists.
- The name of an editor, translator, or compiler, if any, with an abbreviation such as *Ed., Trans.,* or *Comp.* before the name.
- The underlined title of the Internet site (scholarly project, database, online periodical, professional or personal Web site). If the site has no title, describe it: for example, *Home page.*
- The date of electronic publication (including a version number, if any) or posting or the most recent update.
- The name of a sponsoring organization, if any.
- The date you accessed the material.

- The URL in angle brackets (< >), with a period after the closing bracket. If the URL is too long or complicated, simply use the URL of the site's search page or of a subscription service, followed by *Keyword* or *Path* and the links you followed. If you must break a URL at the end of a line, break only after a slash.

### 54. Online Book—MLA

Chopin, Kate. The Awakening. 1899. PBS Electronic Library. 10 Dec. 1998. PBS.
    13 Nov. 2004 <http://www.pbs.org/katechopin/library/awakening>.

### 55. Online Book in a Scholarly Project—MLA

Herodotus. The History of Herodotus. Trans. George Rawlinson. Internet
    Classics Archive. Ed. Daniel C. Stevenson. 11 Jan. 1998. MIT. 15 May 2003
    <http://classics.mit.edu/Herodotus/history.html>.

### 56. Online Government-Published Book—MLA

Start with the name of the government or government body, and then name the government agency, the title, the work's author (if known), the publication date, the access date, and the URL.

United States. Cong. Research Service. Space Stations. By Marcia S. Smith.
    12 Dec. 1996. 4 Dec. 2003 <http://fas.org/spp/civil/crs/93-017.htm>.

MLA also permits an alternative format, with the author's name first, then title, then government body.

Huff, C. Ronald. Comparing the Criminal Behavior of Youth Gangs and
    At-Risk Youths. United States. Dept. of Justice. Natl. Inst. of Justice.
    Oct. 1998. 4 Dec. 2003 <http://www.ncjrs.org/txtfiles/172852.txt>.

### 57. Article in an Online Periodical—MLA

Figure 34.4 illustrates how to cite an article in an online periodical.

Didion, Joan. "The Day Was Hot and Still. . . ." Rev. of Dutch: A Memoir
    of Ronald Reagan, by Edmund Morris. New York Review of Books
    4 Nov. 1999. 5 Dec. 1999 <http://www.nybooks.com/articles/
    article=preview?article_id=320>.

Eisenberg, Anne. "The Kind of Noise That Keeps a Body on Balance." New York
    Times on the Web 14 Nov. 2002. 23 May 2005 <http://tech2.nytimes.com>.

Gold, David. "Ulysses: A Case Study in the Problems of Hypertextualization of
    Complex Documents." Computers, Writing, Rhetoric and Literature 3.1
    (1997): 37 pars. 4 Dec. 1999 <http://www.cwrl.utexas.edu/currents/
    cwrl/v3nl/dgold/title.htm>.

## 1 AUTHOR INFORMATION
**Name of Author**
Write the author's last name, followed by a comma, the author's first name, and the middle initial (if given). End with a period.

## 2 TITLE INFORMATION
**Article Title**
Begin with a quotation mark, write the title (with subtitle, if there is one), include a period, and end with a closing quotation mark. Capitalize all major words.
**Periodical Title, Volume, and Issue**
The periodical's title should be underlined (unless your instructor prefers italics). Capitalize all major words. Do not add punctuation. Include volume information and issue number (if given).

## 3 PUBLICATION INFORMATION
**Print Version Information**
Include print publication date and page numbers.
**Online Version Information**
Include online publication date if different from original print publication date.
**Access Date**
Provide the date you accessed the article.
**URL**
Place the URL for the article in angle brackets. End with a period.

Lewis, Ricki. "Chronobiology Researchers Say Their Field's Time Has Come."
The Scientist 9.24 (1995): 14. 25 Mar. 2005 <http://www.the-scientist.com/
1995/12/11/14/1>.

Figure 34.4 Locating and citing sources for an article in an online journal

Keegan, Paul. "Culture Quake." Mother Jones Nov.-Dec. 1999. 13 Nov. 2002
    <http://www.mojones.com/mother_jones/ND99/quake.html>.

## 58. Professional Home Page—MLA

Provide as much of the following information as you can find.

- If available, include the name of the person who created or put up the home page. If first and last names are given, reverse the order of the first author's name.
- For a professional home page, include the name of the sponsoring organization.
- Include the date you accessed the material.
- Include the URL in angle brackets (< >), with a period after the closing bracket.

American Association for Artificial Intelligence. 17 Mar. 2005 <http://
    www.aaai.org>.

## 59. Personal Home Page—MLA

Follow guidelines for professional home pages, with the following changes. Give the name of the person who created the page, last name first. Include the page's title, if there is one, underlined; if there is no title, add the description *Home page,* not underlined, followed by a period.

Hesse, Doug. Home page. 1 Nov. 2005 <http://www.ilstu.edu/~ddhesse/>.

## 60. Page from a Web Site or Online Article with No Print Version—MLA

Provide as much information as you can.

"Protecting Whales from Dangerous Sonar." National Resources Defense
    Council. 9 Nov. 2005. 12 Dec. 2005 <http://www.nrdc.org/wildlife/
    marine/sonar.asp>.

## 61. Entire Internet Site—MLA

WebdelSol.Com. Ed. Michael Neff. 2005. 11 Nov. 2005 <http://
    www.webdelsol.com/>.

## 62. Academic Department Home Page—MLA

Write the name of the academic department, followed by the words *Dept. home page.* (Do not put any words in quotations or in italics.) Also include the name of the institution, the date you accessed the page, and the URL.

English. Dept. home page. Rutgers U. 26 Feb. 2005 <http://english.rutgers.edu/>.

### 63. Course Home Page—MLA

St. Germain, Sheryl. Myths and Fairytales: From Inanna to Edward
Scissorhands. Course home page. Summer 2003. Dept. of English,
Iowa State U. 20 Feb. 2005 <http://www.public.iastate.edu/
~sgermain/531.homepage.html>.

### 64. Government or Institutional Web Site—MLA

PA Department of Education. 12 Dec. 2005. Pennsylvania Department of
Education. 15 Dec. 2005 <http://www.pde.state.pa.us>.

### 65. Online Poem—MLA

Browning, Elizabeth Barrett. "Past and Future." Women's Studies Database
Reading Room. U of Maryland. 9 June 2003 <http://www.mith2.umd.edu/
WomensStudies/ReadingRoom/Poetry/>.

### 66. Online Work of Art—MLA

Provide artist, title of work, creation date (optional), the museum or individual who owns it, the place, the access date, and the URL.

van Gogh, Vincent. The Starry Night. 1889. Museum of Modern Art, New York.
5 Dec. 2003 <http://www.moma.org>. Keyword: Starry Night.

In this example, the URL is for the Museum of Modern Art. The keyword "Starry Night" is what a researcher types into a search box on the
museum's Web site. (The specific URL for the painting is long and
complicated.)

### 67. Online Image or Photograph—MLA

As with images from print publications (see item 47), include information about the photographer and title, if known. Otherwise, describe the
photograph briefly and give information about the Web site, the access
date, and the URL.

"Sears Tower." The Sears Tower in Chicago. 17 Aug. 2005 <http://
www.thesearstower.com/index.html>.

### 68. Online Interview—MLA

Pope, Carl. Interview. Salon 29 Apr. 2002. 27 Jan. 2005 <http://archive.salon.com/
people/interview/2002/04/29/carlpope/index_np.html>.

MLA

### 69. Online Film or Film Clip—MLA

Columbus, Chris, dir. <u>Harry Potter and the Sorcerer's Stone</u>. Trailer. Warner
  Brothers, 2001. 5 May 2004 <http://hollywood.com>.

### 70. Online Cartoon—MLA

Harris, Sidney. "We have lots of information technology." Cartoon.
  <u>New Yorker</u> 27 May 2002. 9 Feb. 2005 <www.cartoonbank.com>.

### 71. Online Television or Radio Program—MLA

Chayes, Sarah. "Concorde." <u>All Things Considered</u>. 26 July 2000. Natl. Public
  Radio. 7 Dec. 2001 <http://www.npr.com/programs/atc/archives>.

### 72. Online Discussion Posting—MLA

To cite an online message, give the author's name (if any), the title of the
message in quotation marks, and then *Online posting*. Give the date of
the posting and the name of the bulletin board, if any. Then give the access date and, in angle brackets, the URL.

Firrantello, Larry. "Van Gogh on Prozac." Online posting. 23 May 2005.
  Salon Table Talk. 7 June 2005 <http://tabletalk.salon.com/
  webx?50@931.xC34anLmwOq.1@.773b2ad1>.

Be cautious about using online postings as sources. Some postings contain cutting-edge information from experts, but some contain trash. Unfortunately, it is nearly impossible to find out whether people online are
who they claim to be.

### 73. Real-Time Communication—MLA

Give the name of the speaker, a title for the event ("Virtual First Year
Composition: Distance Education, the Internet, and the World Wide
Web"), the forum (DaMOO), date, access date, and URL.

Bleck, Bradley. Online discussion of "Virtual First Year Composition: Distance
  Education, the Internet, and the World Wide Web." 8 June 1997. DaMOO.
  27 Feb. 1999 <http://lrc.csun.edu/DaMOO/cw/brad.html>.

### 74. E-Mail Message—MLA

Start with the name of the person who wrote the e-mail message. Give
the title or subject line in quotation marks. Then describe the source
(*e-mail*) and identify the recipient. End with the date.

Thompson, Jim. "Bob Martin's Opinions." E-mail to June Cain. 11 Nov. 2004.

### 75. Part of an Online Book—MLA

Teasdale, Sara. "Driftwood." Flame and Shadow. 1920. Project Gutenberg. Ed.
      A. Light. 1 July 1996. E-text 591. 9 June 2005 <http://www.gutenberg.org/
      etext/591>.

### 76. Signed Article in an Online Newspaper or News Site—MLA

If the article is signed, begin with the author's name, last name first.

Wilson, Janet. "EPA Fights Waste Site Near River." Los Angeles Times 5 Mar.
      2005. 7 Mar. 2005 <http://www.latimes.com/news/science/environment/
      la-me-moab05.html>.

If the article is unsigned, begin with the article title.

"Remnant of Revolutionary War Washes Ashore." CNN.com 28 Mar. 2005.
      29 Mar. 2005 <http://www.cnn.com/2005/TECH/science/03/28/
      great.bridge.ap/index.html>.

### 77. Anonymous Online Article—MLA

"Too Smart to Marry." Atlantic Online 14 Apr. 2005. 7 Mar. 2005 <http://
      www.theatlantic.com/doc/200504/primarysources.html>.

### 78. Online Review—MLA

Holden, Stephen. Rev. of Hotel Rwanda, dir. Terry George. New York Times
      on the Web 22 Dec. 2004. 7 Mar. 2005 <http://movies2.nytimes.com/mem/
      movies/review.html>.

### 79. Online Abstract—MLA

Avery, Christopher, et al. "A Revealed Preference Ranking of U.S. Colleges
      and Universities." NBER Working Paper No. W10803. Abstract. 11 Oct.
      2004 <http://ssrn.com/abstract=601105>.

### 80. Online Editorial—MLA

"Redistricting Rampage." Editorial. washingtonpost.com 7 Mar. 2005.
      7 Apr. 2005 <http://www.washingtonpost.com/wp-dyn/articles/
      A12612-2005Mar6.html>.

### 81. Online Letter to the Editor—MLA

Freeman, Mark H. "Oscar Afterthoughts." Letter. washingtonpost.com
      5 Mar. 2005. 7 Mar. 2005 <http://www.washingtonpost.com/wp-dyn/
      articles/A8726-2005Mar4.html>.

### 82. Posting on a Blog—MLA

Silliman, Ron. "Monday, March 7, 2005." Silliman's Blog: A Weblog Focused
on Contemporary Poetry and Poetics 7 Mar. 2005. 14 May 2005 <http://
www.ronsilliman.blogspot.com>.

### 83. Electronic Sound Recording or Sound Clip—MLA

Komunyakaa, Yusef. "My Father's Love Letters." Listening Booth. Academy
of American Poets. 27 Apr. 2005 <http://www.poets.org/viewmedia.php/
prmMID/15928>.

### 84. Online Advertisement—MLA

Samsung. Advertisement. RollingStone.com 8 Nov. 2005 <http://
rollingstone.com>.

### 85. Online Manuscript or Working Paper—MLA

deGrandpre, Andrew. "Baseball Destined to Die in Hockey Town." Unpublished
article, 2002. 7 Mar. 2005 <http://www.andrewdegrandpre.com/
unpublished_exposl.html>.

### 86. Podcast—MLA

A podcast is an audio recording that is posted online. Include as much of
the following information as you can identify: author, title, sponsoring organization or Web site, date posted, date accessed, URL.

"Business Marketing with Podcast: What Marketing Professionals Should
Know." Podcast. Podblaze.com 13 Oct. 2005. 19 Oct. 2005
<http://business.podblaze.com/>.

#### OTHER ELECTRONIC SOURCES

### 87. Nonperiodical Publication on CD, DVD, or Magnetic Tape—MLA

Citations for publications on DVD, CD-ROM, or other recording formats follow guidelines for print publications, with two additions: list the
publication medium (for example, *CD*), and give the vendor's name.

Perl, Sondra. Felt Sense: Guidelines for Composing. CD-ROM. Portsmouth:
Boynton/Cook, 2004.

### 88. Video Game or Software—MLA

Chessmaster Vers. 10. San Francisco: Ubisoft, 2004.

### 89. CD-ROM Database: Abstract with a Print Version—MLA

Marcus, Hazel R., and Shinobu Kitayamo. "Culture and the Self: Implications for Cognition, Emotion, and Motivation." Psychological Abstracts 78 (1991): item 23878. Abstract. PsycLIT. CD-ROM. SilverPlatter. Sept. 1991.

All of the information through *item 23878* is for the print version of this source. The volume number is 78, and the abstract's number is 23878. All of the information from *PsycLIT* to the end of the entry is for the electronic version of the source. *PsycLIT* is the name of the CD-ROM database, and *SilverPlatter* is the name of the producer of the CD-ROM. The CD-ROM was issued in September 1991.

### 90. CD-ROM: Article in a Periodical with a Print Version—MLA

"The Price Is Right." Time 20 Jan. 1992: 38. Time Man of the Year. CD-ROM. New York: Compact, 1993.

Information for the print version ends with the article's page number, 38. The title of the CD-ROM is *Time Man of the Year*, its producer is the publisher Compact, and its copyright year is 1993. Both the title of the print publication and the title of the CD-ROM are underlined.

### 91. CD-ROM: Selection in a Book with a Print Version—MLA

"Prehistoric Humans: Earliest Homo sapiens." Guinness Book of Records 1994. London: Guinness, 1994. Guinness Multimedia Disk of Records. CD-ROM. Vers. 2.0. Danbury: Grolier Electronic, 1994.

*Vers. 2.0* signals that this CD-ROM was updated; the producer changes version numbers rather than giving update dates.

### 92. CD-ROM: Material with No Print Version—MLA

"Artificial Intelligence." Encarta 2003. CD-ROM. Redmond: Microsoft, 2003.

*Encarta 2003* is a CD-ROM encyclopedia with no print version. "Artificial Intelligence" is the title of an article in *Encarta 2003*.

### 93. Work in More Than One Publication Medium—MLA

Shamoon, Linda, et al., eds. Coming of Age: The Advanced Writing Curriculum. Book. Coming of Age Course Descriptions. CD-ROM. Portsmouth: Boynton, 2000.

This book and CD-ROM come together. Each has its own title, but the publication information—*Portsmouth: Boynton, 2000*—applies to both.

## 34d.2  Using content or bibliographic notes in MLA style

In MLA style, footnotes or endnotes serve two specific purposes: (1) You can use them for content (ideas and information) that does not fit into your paper but is still worth relating; and (2) you can use them for bibliographic information that would intrude if you were to include it in your text. Place a note number at the end of a sentence, if possible. Put it after any punctuation mark except the dash. Do not put any space before a note number, and put one space after it. Raise the note number a little above the line of words, as shown in the following examples.

**TEXT OF PAPER**

Eudora Welty's literary biography, One Writer's Beginnings, shows us how both the inner world of self and the outer world of family and place form a writer's imagination.[1]

**CONTENT NOTE—MLA**

[1] Welty, who valued her privacy, always resisted investigation of her life. However, at the age of seventy-four, she chose to present her own autobiographical reflections in a series of lectures at Harvard University.

**TEXT OF PAPER**

Barbara Randolph believes that enthusiasm is contagious (65).[1] Many psychologists have found that panic, fear, and rage spread more quickly in crowds than positive emotions do, however.

**BIBLIOGRAPHIC NOTE—MLA**

[1] Others who agree with Randolph include Thurman 21, 84, 155; Kelley 421-25; and Brookes 65-76.

## 34e  A student's MLA-style research paper

### 34e.1  Researching and writing the paper

On the following page, you'll see student writer Andrei Gurov's assignment for an MLA-style research paper.

MLA

Write an MLA-style research paper on the general subject of "memory." You are required to write 1,800 to 2,000 words, using a variety of sources. Your final paper is due in six weeks. Interim deadlines for parts of the work will be announced. To complete this assignment, you need to engage in three interrelated processes: conducting research, understanding the results of that research, and writing a paper based on the first two processes. Consult the *Simon & Schuster Handbook for Writers,* especially Chapters 31–33 for guidance on how to complete this assignment, and Chapter 34 for guidance on MLA-style parenthetical citations and Works Cited entries. You may also consult the MLA Web site at <http://www.mla.org>.

Andrei's instructor also assigned a bonus exercise asking students to chronicle their research processes in a brief informal narrative. This exercise could help students see what worked well for them and what didn't, and then they could apply that knowledge when researching future papers. The following is from Andrei's narrative about how he researched his topic and sources for his MLA-style paper about déjà vu.

I started by immediately filling in the research schedule suggested in section 31b of our handbook. I also looked for ideas in Box 31.2: Finding General Ideas for Research. In the past, brainstorming has worked well for me, so I just started listing anything that came to mind about the assigned topic of "memory" (e.g., how much memory is on my iPod, past vacations, my sister's wedding, relatives, when I broke my collarbone, forgetfulness, flashbacks). I had a lot of personal memories to write about, but those wouldn't have worked because I couldn't have done formal research on them.

So, I turned to the Web and searched Google using the keyword "memory." The computer screen practically exploded with 326 million hits, and they generally pointed to four large

*continued* ➤

categories: brain memory, computer memory, entertainment venues, and music. I didn't expect so many directions. In an attempt to narrow this down, I tried some Boolean NOT instructions, but even eliminating "computer + music + entertainment + girls" made little difference. Then I realized I hadn't used Google Scholar, which has been recommended for academic research. So, I tried again, and although I reduced the number of hits, I still would've spent a lifetime trying to sort through all of these resources.

I knew I needed something else to spark ideas. As advised by Box 31.2 in my handbook, I decided to flip through other textbooks. My anthropology book came with a study skills guide that offered some tips about memory retention. That could've been a topic, but it really didn't interest me enough to want to learn more about it. My intro sociology textbook had some information about eyewitness testimony and false memory--both pretty interesting, so I kept those topics in reserve. Then, a chapter in my intro psychology textbook (Saul Kassin's <u>Psychology</u>, 4th ed.) turned up a topic that I'd always been curious about: déjà vu. I'd experienced that weird feeling of being somewhere before--even though I'd never been there in my life--and was really curious to know what caused it. So, I decided to narrow my formal research question to "What is known today about the experience of déjà vu?"

Back in front of the computer, I did online searches using "déjà vu." Google Scholar brought up 14 million hits. AltaVista brought up only music DVDs. I went to good old Yahoo and got mostly music DVDs along with a few popular press articles. Searching with Mozilla Firefox, I typed in

*continued* ➤

"memory + deja vu" and got 726,000 hits, which, under the circumstances, seemed relatively small. But very few of the resources seemed as relevant as the ones on the first few pages of Google Scholar. To help me determine how scholarly many of the online resources were, I went to the library and skimmed Alan S. Brown's 2004 scholarly book The Déjà Vu Experience and Weiten's Psychology: Themes and Variations. I found I'd been fooled three times out of eleven. When I read the printouts, I knew almost immediately that two of the three unreliable sources were bad, but figuring out the third one took me a while longer.

In my research, I took notes and carefully recorded my sources. (I created a lot of new documents on my computer and gave each a descriptive name that I'd understand.) Then, I organized the notes into folders. At that point, I felt ready to do some planning. I knew my audience was mainly my instructor, but because my first draft was going to be peer-edited, I wanted to make sure my paper also appealed to other students in my class. I wasn't too sure about which purpose I wanted to tackle. Originally, I had wanted to write with a persuasive purpose and argue against the concept of déjà vu having anything to do with witchcraft, reincarnation, and that stuff. But the more I read, the more I became convinced that I wanted to educate people about the scientific aspects of déjà vu experiences. Therefore, I switched to an informative purpose.

I used the note documents that I had created, making sure that I kept track of when I was quoting, summarizing, and paraphrasing (I hardly paraphrased at all). As much as

*continued* ➤

possible, I kept revising so that I could work into my sentences the author and document title because I preferred to include only page numbers in my parenthetical citations. Having had a bad experience in high school with losing track of my sources, I kept a separate document as my working bibliography, which would make it easier to list each of my sources in my Works Cited list at the end of my paper.

At this stage, I felt ready to write my first draft. I sat on the floor and surrounded myself with all my printed notes sorted into categories. I then wrote a very rough draft with numbers where I thought notes would fit. Next, I went to the computer and strung my paper together. Unfortunately, but not too surprisingly, my first draft ran on for too many pages. It was time to cut. My major cuts had to do with (a) at least two pages about other terms related to déjà vu but not the same as déjà vu, and (b) a table reporting an unscientific survey I had taken of the déjà vu memories of each member in a family of fifteen.

I then worked through the paper and worked on conciseness of language (I found lots of repetition) and tried to draft my concluding paragraph. It was a struggle. I had to synthesize complicated material in a fairly limited space. I kept wanting to introduce new information, but I knew that would only set me off track and confuse readers. If you look at the next page of this narrative, you'll see my first try at a concluding paragraph, which I show in block format. (You can compare it with the one in my final draft at the end of my paper on page 622.) I rejected it because it's closer to a conclusion that might work, if it were better organized, at the

*continued* ➤  603

end of a paper about the paranormal and déjà vu. It definitely didn't work for the paper I wrote.

> We know more today than we did hundreds of years ago about the phenomenon of déjà vu. But there is more to be learned. In the last two decades, the real investigations have begun. Alan S. Brown seems to be the researcher who has led the field into an age of enlightenment, and many more mentioned in this paper are his fellow researchers. No longer can people settle for explanations that involve reincarnation and visits from the dead. No longer can we accept that spirits from the "other side" are coming back to visit us in the form of visions.

Overall, my research and writing process went well. In giving an account of it, I've simplified the details to keep the assignment brief. However, I will say that learning how to brainstorm ideas and how to do keyword searches effectively definitely saved me some anxiety, time, and effort in getting the topic and the information I needed.

## 34e.2 Formatting the MLA-style research paper

### TITLE PAGE

MLA style doesn't call for a title page for research papers or any other types of writing. Many instructors, however, do require one. If you're asked to use a title page, follow the format of the example on page 605. Never assign a page number to a title page.

Whether or not you use a title page, use the headings shown on the first page of the sample research paper on page 608. If you're required to hand in a formal outline with your paper, place the outline after the title page, unless told to do otherwise by your instructor.

**Title page of Andrei Gurov's MLA-style research paper**

One-third
down from
top of page

Déjà Vu: At Last a Subject for Serious Study

Double-space
title if more
than one line

by

Andrei Gurov

Lowercase
"by" and
double-space

Professor Ryan

Instructor

University of Middle Byrd

Institution

English 101, Section A4

Course and section

12 December 2005

Date order:
day month year

## PAGE 1 OF PAPER WITH OR WITHOUT A TITLE PAGE

On the first page of your paper, in the upper right corner, type your last name, followed by a space, and then followed by the numeral 1 placed one-half inch below the top edge of the page and one inch in from the right margin. Next, at the left margin, one inch in from the left side, type the four lines with the information shown on the first page of the sample paper on page 608. Finally, type your paper's title centered one double space below the last of the four lines that you just finished typing flush left.

Double-space after the title, and start your paper, indenting the first line of the first—and all—paragraphs five character spaces. The indent in Microsoft Word is a hanging indent of 0.5″ for "first line."

## OUTLINES

Even though MLA doesn't officially endorse using outlines, some instructors, including Andrei Gurov's, require that students submit formal outlines with their research papers. In this handbook, you'll find examples of two formal outlines in section 2r. The traditional formal outline follows long-established conventions for using numbers and letters to show relationships among ideas. A less traditional formal outline includes these elements but also includes the planned content for a research paper's introductory and concluding paragraphs. Both the traditional and the less traditional outlines can be sentence outlines (composed entirely of complete sentences) or topic outlines (composed only of words and phrases). In your outlines, however, never mix the two styles.

The outline on page 607 is for Andrei Gurov's research paper about déjà vu. To format the outline, he used the less traditional outline, which was what his instructor preferred and asked her class to use. In the name–page number line in the upper right corner of his outline, Andrei typed his last name, left one space, and then typed the lower-case roman numeral *i* for the page number, the conventional way of indicating any page that comes before the first page of the essay itself. He placed that information one-half inch from the top of the page and made sure it ended one inch in from the right edge of the paper. He then left a half-inch space below the name-number heading and centered the word *Outline.* The thesis statement in the outline matches the last sentence of the first paragraph of his paper (see p. 608).

Even if your instructor doesn't require an outline, you'll probably find that developing one to go with a later draft of your paper will help you clarify the overall organization and logic of your research paper (or, indeed, any essay you write). Examining the paper's "skeleton" enables you to focus on the overall shape of the paper and may reveal gaps in your paper's development that you can fill in.

1"

Outline

Double-space

I.   Introduction

   A.  The meaning of the term <u>déjà vu</u>

   B.  <u>Thesis statement</u>: Although a few people today still prefer to believe that feelings of déjà vu have mysterious and supernatural origins, recent research in cognitive psychology and the neurosciences has shed much rational light on the phenomenon.

II.  Percentage of people who report experiencing déjà vu

III. Misunderstandings of the phenomenon of déjà vu

   A.  Precognition

   B.  False memory

IV.  New psychological and medical theories of déjà vu

   A.  Human sight's two pathways

   B.  Implanted memories

      1.  Natural: from old memories long forgotten

      2.  Manipulated: from subliminal stimulation

      3.  Inattentional blindness

V.   Conclusion

   A.  Many years of paranormal explanations of déjà vu

   B.  Scientific research after 1980

   C.  Much promise for further research

## PAGE NUMBERING AFTER THE FIRST PAGE OF THE PAPER

In the upper right corner, type your last name, followed by a space, and then followed by the arabic numeral of the page in sequence (2, 3, and so on). Place this name-number heading one-half inch below the top edge of the page and one inch in from the right margin. Number the pages consecutively, including the last page of your Works Cited. Many writers use the "header and footer" word processing function that inserts last names and sequential page numbers, updating automatically. This feature is especially convenient during revision, when your writing causes your pages to fall differently than they originally did.

MLA

Put identifying information in upper left corner.

Andrei Gurov

Professor Ryan

English 101, Section A4

12 December 2005

Center title.

Déjà Vu: At Last a Subject for Serious Study

"Brain hiccup" might be another name for déjà vu, French for "already seen." During a moment of déjà vu, a person relives an event that in reality is happening for the first time. The hiccup metaphor seems apt because each modern scientific explanation of the déjà vu phenomenon involves a doubled event, as this paper will demonstrate. However, such modern scientific work was long in coming.

Quotation marks around phrases show they appeared separately in the source.

In his article "The Déjà Vu Illusion," today's leading researcher in the field, Alan S. Brown at Southern Methodist University, states that "for over 170 years, this most puzzling of memory illusions has intrigued scholars" but was hampered when

The ellipsis indicates words omitted from a quotation.

"during the behaviorist era . . . the plethora of parapsychological and psychodynamic interpretations" multiplied rapidly (256). Thus, notions of the supernatural and magic halted the scientific study of déjà vu for almost two centuries. By the first quarter of the twentieth century, it began again slowly. Although a few people today still prefer to believe that feelings of déjà vu have mysterious or supernatural origins, recent research in cognitive psychology and the neurosciences has shed much rational light on the phenomenon.

Some people report never having experienced déjà vu, and the percentages vary for the number of people who report having lived through at least one episode of it. In 2004, Brown

*continued* ➤

(Proportions shown in this paper are adjusted to fit space limitations of this book. Follow actual dimensions discussed in this book and your instructor's directions.)

## Commentary

1. **Computer tip.** Following MLA style, Andrei uses his last name and the page number as a header (meaning "at the top" of his pages) throughout the paper. He doesn't use a footer (meaning "at the bottom" of his pages). To do this, he accesses the "header and footer" option in the "View" choice on the toolbar in his Microsoft Word word processing program and inserts the proper information so that it will appear automatically on each page.

2. **Introductory strategy.** Andrei hopes to attract his readers' interest by making up the unusual phrase "brain hiccups," which ties into the dual visual processing that he describes later in his paper. He also refers briefly to the paranormal and immediately discredits it by quoting the leading modern researcher into déjà vu, Alan S. Brown.

3. **PROCESS NOTE:** I use a quotation from Brown's journal article "The Déjà Vu Illusion," so I include the page number in parentheses.

4. **Thesis statement.** The last sentence of Andrei's introductory paragraph is his THESIS STATEMENT. He drafted two preliminary thesis statements, shown in section 31l. The thesis statement is a bridge from his introduction to the rest of his paper and helps his readers anticipate the main message of his paper. All of his topic sentences have to tie into his thesis statement.

reports that of the subjects he has interviewed, an average
of 66 percent say that they have had one or more déjà vu
experiences during their lives (<u>Experience</u> 33). However,                    5

in early 2005 in "Strangely Familiar," Uwe Wolfradt reports
that "various studies indicate that from 50 to 90 percent of
the people [studied] can recall having had at least one such                       6
déjà vu incident in their lives."                                                  7

  Perhaps part of the reason for this variation in the
range of percentages stems from a general misunderstanding
of the phrase <u>déjà vu</u>, even by some of the earlier scientific               8
researchers twenty or more years ago. Indeed, in today's
society, people throw around the term <u>déjà vu</u> without
much thought. For example, it is fairly common for someone
to see or hear about an event and then say, "Wow. This                             9
is déjà vu. I had a dream that this exact same thing
happened." However, dreaming about an event
ahead of time is a different phenomenon known as
<u>precognition</u>, which relates to the paranormal experience
of extrasensory perception. To date, precognition has never
been scientifically demonstrated. As Johnson explains about
dreams, however,

  . . . there is usually very little "data," evidence, or         10
  documentation to confirm that a Precognition has
  taken place. If a person learns about some disaster
  and THEN [author's emphasis] tells people that                  11
  he/she has foreseen it the day before, that may
  or may not be true, because there is usually not

*continued* ➤

## Commentary

5. **Summarizing and citing a source by an author of two different sources used in this paper.** Andrei summarizes the percentage information that Brown gives in his book *The Déjà Vu Experience*. Then Andrei cites his source with a shortened title and page number. He includes a title because he has been drawing on two of Brown's writings for this paper—one book and one journal article that he accesses online—and he knows that he needs to make a clear distinction between them whenever he cites them.

6. **The writer inserting words to fit a quotation into the writer's sentence.** Nothing is wrong with Uwe Wolfradt's sentence, but Andrei needs to add the word *studied* to make the meaning clear within his research paper. To do this in proper MLA form, Andrei put his added word in brackets to indicate that he is adding the word—that is, the word is not in the original text by Uwe Wolfradt.

7. **Figuring out a page number from an online source.** Andrei found the article "Strangely Familiar" by Uwe Wolfradt online through his search using <http://www.googlescholar.com>. Even though the citation for the article on the opening screen page says that the page spread is pages 32–37, and Andrei might feel quite safe in assuming that his information is on the first page—namely, page 32—he can't be sure, so he can't include a page number.

8. **PROCESS NOTE:** I kept being distracted about using the word déjà vu as a term or as the name of an experience. As I was drafting, I purposely overlooked the problem, but I circled each use so that I could tackle the issue on my final draft.

9. **PROCESS NOTE:** I'm fairly certain that my instructor will know that this quotation is not from a source, but it's rather one I made up from everyday speech.

10. **No capital letter to start block-indented quotation.** Andrei took this quotation from the middle of a sentence in the source, so he can't start it with a capital letter. The ellipsis indicates he omitted words to make the quotation fit stylistically.

11. **How "[author's emphasis]" is used.** Whenever a source uses a typographical technique of emphasis—such as italics or all capital letters—the writer who quotes that source is required to indicate that the emphasis belongs to the source, not to the writer. In MLA style, "[author's emphasis]" is required so that the reader won't think the emphasis has been made by the writer of the paper.

corroborative confirmation of what the person claims. 12

Thus, precognition, a phenomenon talked about frequently but one that has never held up under scientific scrutiny, is definitely not the same as déjà vu.

False memory is another phenomenon mislabeled déjà vu. It happens when people are convinced that certain events took place in their lives, even though the events never happened. This occurs when people have strong memories of many unrelated occurrences that suddenly come together into a whole that's very close to the current experience. It seems like a déjà vu experience. This occurs from the "converging elements of many different but related experiences. When this abstract representation, which has emerged strictly from the melding together of strongly associated elements, happens to correspond to the present experience, a déjà vu may be the outcome" (Brown, Experience 160). To illustrate lab-induced false memory, Brown in Experience cites investigations in which subjects are shown lists of words related to sleep; however, the word sleep itself is not on the list. In recalling the list of words, most subjects insist that the word sleep was indeed on the list, which means that the memory of a word that was never there is false memory. This is exactly what happens when well-intentioned eyewitnesses believe they recall certain criminal acts even though, in fact, they never saw or experienced the events at all (159).

In the last twenty years especially, new theories have come to the fore as a result of rigorous work from

13

14

*Introductory phrase smoothly leads into direct quotation.*

*Put only page number in parentheses when author is named in text.*

*continued* ➤

## Commentary

12. **MLA style for a block-indent quotation.** MLA style requires that when a quotation takes up four or more lines in a research paper that it be set off in a block. A block indent calls for all lines to be indented ten spaces from the left margin. It has to end with a period. Then the source information has to come after the period in parentheses. Because Andrei's online source did not provide page, paragraphs, or screen numbers, he could not include a parenthetical citation after the quotation.

13. **PROCESS NOTE:** I want to use Brown in two different ways in this paragraph because I've drawn on Brown as a major reference throughout my paper. I don't want to only use quotations or only summaries. Here I use a quotation but don't call attention to the source. I place all source information in parentheses after the end of the quotation. I include a shortened version of the title of the source because I've used two different sources by the same author to write this paper.

14. **PROCESS NOTE:** To follow up on Process Note 13, this time I summarize Brown's words and fit in his name and the shortened title of the source.

psychological and medical points of view. In <u>Experience</u>,    15
Brown surveys the literature and concludes that this relatively
young field of investigation is dividing itself into four
categories: (1) dual processing, (2) memory, (3) neurological,
and (4) attentional. This paper briefly discusses the first and    16
second as each relates to the third. Next, this paper discusses
the fourth as it relates to the second.

       Brain-based studies of the human sense of sight are one
heavily researched theory of déjà vu that has been partially
explained in the last two decades. Such studies focus on
the dual pathways by which the sight of an event reaches the

> **Put author and page number in parentheses when author is not named in the sentence.**

brain (Glenn; Carey F1). For example, the left hemisphere    17
processes information from the right eye and the right
hemisphere processes information from the left eye. The
brain is incapable of storing data with respect to time and
is only able to "see" events in relation to others. Each
eye interprets data separately, at the same precise time.
According to research, the human brain can perceive two

> **Paragraph summarizes several pages of source material, as parenthetical citation shows.**

visual stimuli at one instant as long as they are "seen" less    18
than 25 milliseconds apart. Since the human brain is capable
of interpreting both signals within this time, when events are
perceived normally, they are seen and recognized by the brain
as one single event (Weiten 69, 97-99, 211).

       Occasionally, however, the neurological impulses that    19
carry data from each eye to the brain are delayed. As Johnson
explains, the person might be fatigued or have had his or her
attention seriously distracted (as when crossing the street at a
dangerous intersection). As a result, one signal may reach the

*continued* ➤

## Commentary

15. **PROCESS NOTE:** I now need to write a paragraph of transition from what was *not* déjà vu to what was. My plan is to write about two types of phenomena that aren't déjà vu, and then write about three types of phenomena that are. I checked my outline to make sure I was adhering to my plan.

16. **PROCESS NOTE:** Every time I type the word *attentional* (using Microsoft Word) into my paper, a red wavy line pops up under it, which means a misspelling. However, because the word is spelled that way consistently in all my sources, I've just ignored the red wavy line and added the word, with confidence, to my personal dictionary provided by the Microsoft Word program.

17. **Two sources for one piece of information.** When two sources contain the same information, MLA style permits the citing of both sources. Each source is given with its page number; don't provide a page number if you're using a one-page source or an online source with no page numbers. A semicolon divides the sources.

18. **Words used in a non-literal way.** The words *see* and *seen* here do not carry their literal meaning related to conscious sight. Rather, they refer to subconscious sight. Therefore, they belong in quotation marks.

19. **PROCESS NOTE:** Earlier in the paper, I devoted two paragraphs to each of two non-déjà vu topics. Now, I'm giving more attention to each of the three types of legitimate déjà vu phenomena that I've chosen to discuss (dual pathways of sight, implanted memories, and inattentional blindness). This paragraph is the second I'm writing about dual pathways of sight.

brain in under 25 milliseconds, while the other signal is slowed and reaches the brain slightly more than 25 milliseconds later. Even a few milliseconds' delay makes the second incoming signal arrive late--and, without fail, the brain interprets the stimuli as two separate events rather than one event. The person thus has the sensation of having seen the event before because the brain has recognized the milliseconds-later event as a memory.

Implanted memories is another well-researched explanation for the déjà vu phenomenon. Examples of this originate in both the natural and the lab-induced experiences of people. For instance, perhaps a person walks into the kitchen of a new friend for the first time and, although the person has never been there before, the person feels certain that he or she has. With hypnosis and other techniques, researchers could uncover that the cupboards are almost exactly like those that the person had forgotten were in the kitchen of the person's grandparents' house and that the scent of baking apple pie is identical to the smell the person loved when walking into the grandparents' home during holidays (Carey F1).

Wolfradt describes a lab-induced experiment in which psychologist Larry L. Jacoby in 1989 manipulated a group of subjects so that he could implant a memory that would lead to a déjà vu experience for each of them. He arranged for his subjects to assemble in a room equipped with a screen in front. He flashed on the screen one word so quickly that no one was consciously aware they had seen the word. Jacoby

20

21

*continued* ➤

## Commentary

20. **PROCESS NOTE:** I'm now starting to write about the second of the three types of déjà vu that I'm covering in this paper. I'm intentionally using the word *another* in my topic sentence to bridge from dual pathways of sight to implanted memories. Because there are so many concepts and examples of them in this paper, I'm trying to be very clear in my transitions.

21. **PROCESS NOTE:** Specific examples are very important to me as I write this paper. It's far too easy for me to write on and on about theory and concepts. As I'm writing this paper, I find myself often cutting generalizations to make room for details. When I've read my sophomore and junior friends' papers from when they were freshmen, I'm surprised to see how few specifics and concrete details they put in their freshman composition papers—and their grades and the comments they got reflect this fact.

was certain, however, that the visual centers of the brain of each subject had indeed "seen" the word. Later, when he flashed the word leaving it on the screen long enough for the subjects to consciously see it, everyone indicated they had seen the word somewhere before. All the subjects were firmly convinced that the first time they had seen the word, it absolutely was not on the screen at the front of the room they were in. Some became annoyed at being asked over and over. Since Jacoby's work, lab-induced memory research has become very popular in psychology. In fact, it has been given its own name: <u>priming</u>.

Inattention, or what some researchers call "inattentional 22
blindness," is also an extensively researched explanation for the déjà vu experience. Sometimes people can see objects without any impediment right before them but still not process the objects because they're paying attention to something else (Brown, <u>Experience</u> 181). The distraction might be daydreaming, a sudden lowering of energy, or simply being drawn to another object in the environment. As David Glenn explains in "The Tease of Memory":

> Imagine that you drive through an unfamiliar town
> but pay little attention because you're talking on a
> cellphone [sic]. If you then drive back down the same   23
> streets a few moments later, this time focusing on
> the landscape, you might be prone to experience
> déjà vu. During your second pass, the visual
> information is consciously processed in the
> hippocampus [of the brain] but feels falsely "old"

continued ➤

## Commentary

22. **PROCESS NOTE:** When I wrote my first draft, I felt that my discussion of implanted memories was pretty weak. I did some further research and was happy to find enough information to write this additional paragraph in my second draft. It is, to me, a dramatic demonstration of laboratory-manipulated implanted memory.

23. **Using [sic].** This quotation spells "cell phone" as one word. Therefore, Andrei uses [sic] to tell his readers that he knows this is a misspelling.

because the images from your earlier drive still
linger in your short term memory.                                    24

The busy lifestyle today would seem to lead to many
distractions of perception and thus to frequent experiences
of déjà vu; however, these are no more frequently reported
than any other causes reported concerning déjà vu.

One compelling laboratory experiment studying              25
inattention is described by Carey in "Déjà Vu: If It All Seems
Familiar, There May Be a Reason." He recounts a test with
many college students from Duke University in Durham,
North Carolina. The students were asked to look at a group of
photographs of the campus of Southern Methodist University
in Dallas, Texas, that were flashed before them at a very quick
speed. A small black or white cross was superimposed on
each photograph, and the students were instructed to find the
cross and focus on it (F6). Brown in Experience explains that
the researchers assumed that the quick speed at which the
photographs had been shown would result in no one's having
noticed the background scenes. A week's time passed, and the
same students were shown the pictures again, this time
without the crosses. Almost all insisted that they had been
to the college campus shown in the photos, which was
physically impossible for that many students since they lived
in Durham, North Carolina, and the college in the photographs
was in Dallas, Texas (182-83). This means that the scenes in
the photographs did indeed register in the visual memories
of the students in spite of the quick speed and the distraction
of looking only for the crosses.

*continued* ➤

## Commentary

24. **PROCESS NOTE:** Here's how I wasted a day of researching for this paper. I know it's not unusual for freshmen to go off the topic and waste their time, so I am trying to stay very conscious of what I am doing so that I can learn what NOT to do in the future. What happened was that I was becoming aware that psychologists have named many phenomena that are closely related to déjà vu, each somewhat different from it and from each other. For example, Brown in <u>Experience</u> names over twenty relatives of déjà vu, while other sources name as few as eight. This captured my interest, but once I got into writing up the information, I began to realize that I was going off my topic. I'll list here some that had potential but that, in the end, I never used in my paper:

- *Déjà eprouvé:* A sense that this act has already been attempted and didn't work out.

- *Déjà senti:* A mental feeling that one is *feeling* something again. It is limited to feeling, and does not include a sense of being in a place.

- *Déjà visité:* The knowledge of a large place, such as an entire village, but knowing still that one has never been there.

- *Jamais vu:* This is the opposite of déjà vu. Even though one knows something has happened before, the experience feels completely unfamiliar.

- *Presque vu:* This is the sense of almost, but not quite, remembering something—as in "it's on the tip of my tongue."

25. **PROCESS NOTE:** To stay on the topic, I needed a third type of déjà vu— for which I used inattentional blindness—to drive home my thesis statement.

26

**Concluding paragraph summarizes paper.**

The worlds of psychology and neurology have learned much since the age of paranormal interpretations of déjà vu experiences, starting around 1935. That is when rational science energetically began its disciplined investigations of brain-based origins of the déjà vu phenomenon. Concepts such as dual processing of sight, implanted memories, and inattentional blindness, among other theories, have gone far in opening the door to the possibilities of many more inventive theories to explain incidents of déjà vu. The leading researcher in the field today, Alan S. Brown, is among the strongest voices urging a vast expansion of investigations into this still relatively unexplored phenomenon. He is optimistic this will happen, given his whimsical remark to Carlin Flora of Psychology Today: "We are always fascinated when the brain goes haywire."

*continued* ⟩

# Commentary

26. **PROCESS NOTE:** In my second draft, I decided to check whether all my topic sentences tied together with each other. I remembered that neither the introductory nor the concluding paragraphs have topic sentences.

   **THESIS STATEMENT:** Although a few people today still prefer to believe that feelings of déjà vu have mysterious or supernatural origins, recent research in cognitive psychology and the neurosciences has shed much rational light on the phenomenon.

   (1) Some people report never having experienced déjà vu, and the percentages vary for the number of people who report having lived through at least one episode of it.

   (2) Perhaps part of the reason for this variation in the range of percentages stems from a general misunderstanding of the phrase déjà vu, even by some of the earlier scientific researchers twenty or more years ago.

   (3) False memory is another phenomenon mislabeled déjà vu.

   (4) In the last twenty years especially, new theories have come to the fore as a result of rigorous work from psychological and medical points of view.

   (5) Brain-based studies of the human sense of sight are one heavily researched theory of déjà vu that has been partially explained in the last two decades.

   (6) Occasionally, however, the neurological impulses that carry data from each eye to the brain are delayed.

   (7) Implanted memories is another well-researched explanation for the déjà vu phenomenon.

   (8) Wolfradt describes a lab-induced experiment in which psychologist Larry L. Jacoby in 1989 manipulated a group of subjects so that he could implant a memory that would lead to a déjà vu experience for each of them.

   (9) Inattention, or what some researchers call "inattentional blindness," is also an extensively researched explanation for the déjà vu experience.

   (10) One compelling laboratory experiment studying inattention is described by Carey in "Déjà Vu: If It All Seems Familiar, There May Be a Reason."

## Works Cited

Works Cited begins on a new page. Double-space throughout.

Brown, Alan S. The Déjà Vu Experience: Essays in Cognitive
    Psychology. New York: Psychology P, 2004.

---. "The Déjà Vu Illusion." Current Directions in Psychological
    Science 13 (2004): 256-59.

List sources in alphabetical order.

Carey, Benedict. "Déjà Vu: If It All Seems Familiar, There
    May Be a Reason." New York Times 14 Sept. 2004:
    F1+. LexisNexis. Milner Lib., Illinois State U. 11 Nov. 2005
    <http://web.lexis-nexis.com>.

Flora, Carlin. "Giving Déjà Vu Its Due." Psychology Today
    Mar.-Apr. 2005: 27. Academic Search Premier. EBSCO.
    Milner Lib., Illinois State U. 7 Nov. 2005 <http://
    weblinks3.epnet.com>.

Glenn, David. "The Tease of Memory." Chronicle of Higher
    Education 23 July 2004: A12.

Johnson, C. "A Theory on the Déjà Vu Phenomenon." 8 Dec.

Divide a URL only after a slash.

    2001. 20 Nov. 2005 <http://mb-soft.com/public/
    dejavu.html>.

Thompson, Rebecca G., et al. "Persistent Déjà Vu: A Disorder
    of Memory." International Journal of Geriatric Psychiatry
    19 (2004): 906-07.

Weiten, Wayne. Psychology Themes and Variations. Belmont:
    Wadsworth, 2005.

Wolfradt, Uwe. "Strangely Familiar." Scientific American
    Mind 16.1 (2005): 32-37. Academic Search Elite. EBSCO.
    Milner Lib., Illinois State U. 7 Nov. 2005 <http://
    www.epnet.com>.

27
28
29
30

## Commentary

27. **Working versus final bibliography.** In keeping with MLA style, Andrei developed a working bibliography using those sources referred to in his research paper. His bibliography contained over twice the number of sources in his Works Cited. He dropped sources he considered less authoritative and ones that were not specifically targeted to the subjects that he chose to discuss related to déjà vu.

28. **Balance of source types.** Andrei's final list of Works Cited contains nine works, four from online databases and five from print sources—a proportion that is typical of today's college-level research papers.

29. **What is LexisNexis?** LexisNexis is an online database, available to students through their college library, that contains a large number of research and other scholarly collections, including the LexisNexis Academic and Library Solutions. Originally a document service for law students and lawyers, it now includes areas of study such as government, business, and environmental issues.

30. **What is EBSCO?** EBSCO is a widely used online database in English studies and the humanities. It's available to students through their college library and gives access to over one hundred reference databases, thousands of online journals, lists of book titles at some libraries, linking services, and much more.

# Chapter 35

## APA DOCUMENTATION WITH CASE STUDY

*continued* ➤

APA

## 35a    What is APA documentation style?

The American Psychological Association (APA) sponsors a DOCUMENTA-TION system widely used in the social sciences. APA style involves two equally important features that need to appear in research papers.

1. Within the body of your paper, use **in-text citations**, in parentheses, to acknowledge your SOURCES. This chapter explains the proper way to provide APA in-text citations. Section 35b explains how they work, and section 35c shows sixteen models, each of which gives one or more examples of different types of sources.

2. At the end of the paper, provide a list of the sources you used—and only those sources. Title this list, which contains complete bibliographic information about each source, **References**. It needs to appear on a separate page at the end of your research paper. It includes only the sources you've actually used in your paper, not any you've consulted but haven't used. Section 35f gives instructions for composing your References pages, followed by sixty-three models, each based on a different kind of source (book, article, Web site, and so on) that you might use.

For an example of a research paper that uses APA-style in-text citations in parentheses and a References list, see section 35h. As you read the paper, notice how the two requirements for crediting sources work together so that readers can learn the precise origin of the material that is quoted, paraphrased, and summarized.

## 35b    What are APA parenthetical in-text citations?

The APA-STYLE DOCUMENTATION guidelines here follow the recommendations of the *Publication Manual of the American Psychological Association,* Fifth Edition (Washington, DC: American Psychological Association, 2001), which is the most current edition. For possible updates to information, you may wish to check the APA's Web site at <http://www.apastyle.org> or the APA's *Concise Rules of APA Style* (Washington, DC: American Psychological Association, 2005).

APA style requires parenthetical IN-TEXT CITATIONS that identify a SOURCE by the author's name (or a shortened version of the title if there is no author) and the copyright year. For readability and a good writing style, you can often incorporate the name, and sometimes the year, into your sentence. Otherwise, place this information in parentheses, located as close as possible to the material you quote, paraphrase, or summarize. Your goal is to tell readers precisely where they can find the original material.

APA style requires page numbers for DIRECT QUOTATIONS and recommends them for PARAPHRASES and SUMMARIES. Some instructors expect you to give page references for paraphrases and summaries, and others don't; so find out your instructor's preference to avoid any problems in properly crediting your sources.

Put page numbers in parentheses, using the abbreviation *p.* before a single page number and *pp.* when the material you're citing falls on more than one page. For a direct quotation from an electronic source that numbers paragraphs, give the paragraph number (or numbers). Handle paragraph numbers as you do page numbers, but use *para.* or ¶ (the symbol for paragraph) rather than *p.* or *pp.* If no paragraph numbers appear in the source, look for other ways to identify the location, such as sections introduced by main headings.

The APA *Publication Manual* recommends that if you refer to a work more than once in a paragraph, you give the author's name and the date at the first mention and then give only the name after that. An exception occurs if you're citing two or more works by the same author, or if two or more authors have the same last name. In such cases, each separate citation must include the date to identify which work you're citing.

## 35c What are APA guidelines for in-text citations?

The following numbered examples show how to cite various kinds of sources in the body of your research paper. Remember, though, that you often can introduce source names, including titles when necessary, and sometimes even years, in your own sentences rather than in the parenthetical IN-TEXT CITATIONS.

### 1. Paraphrased or Summarized Source—APA

People from the Mediterranean prefer an elbow-to-shoulder distance from each other (Morris, 1977). [Author name and date cited in parentheses; note comma.]

Desmond Morris (1977) notes that people from the Mediterranean prefer an elbow-to-shoulder distance from each other. [Author name cited in text; date cited in parentheses.]

### 2. Source of a Short Quotation—APA

A recent report of reductions in SAD-related "depression in 87 percent of patients" (Binkley, 1990, p. 203) reverses the findings of earlier studies. [Author name, date, and page reference in parentheses immediately following the quotation.]

Binkley (1990) reports reductions in SAD-related "depression in 87 percent of patients" (p. 203). [Author name followed by the date in parentheses incorporated into the words introducing the quotation; page number in parentheses immediately following the quotation.]

### 3. Source of a Long Quotation (and Format of Quotation)—APA

Incorporate a direct quotation of fewer than forty words into your own sentence and enclose it in quotation marks. Place the parenthetical in-text citation after the closing quotation mark and, if the quotation falls at the end of the sentence, before the sentence-ending punctuation. When you use a quotation longer than forty words, set it off in block style indented one-half inch or five spaces from the left margin. Never enclose a set-off quotation in quotation marks because the placement in block style carries the message that the material is quoted. Place the parenthetical reference citation one space after the end punctuation of the last sentence.

**DISPLAYED QUOTATION (FORTY OR MORE WORDS)**

Jet lag, with its characteristic fatigue and irregular sleep patterns, is a common problem among those who travel great distances by jet airplane to different time zones:

> Jet lag syndrome is the inability of the internal body rhythm to rapidly resynchronize after sudden shifts in the timing. For a variety of reasons, the system attempts to maintain stability and resist temporal change. Consequently, complete adjustment can often be delayed for several days—sometimes for a week—after arrival at one's destination. (Bonner, 1991, p. 72)

### 4. One Author—APA

In a parenthetical reference in APA style, a comma and a space separate a name from a year, and a year from a page reference. (Note: Examples 1 through 3 are also citations of works by one author.)

> One of his questions is "What binds together a Mormon banker in Utah with his brother, or other coreligionists in Illinois or Massachusetts?" (Coles, 1993, p. 2).

### 5. Two Authors—APA

If a work has two authors, give both names in each citation.

> One report describes 2,123 occurrences (Krait & Cooper, 1994).

> The results that Krait and Cooper (1994) report would not support the conclusions Davis and Sherman (1992) draw in their review of the literature.

When you write a parenthetical in-text citation naming two (or more) authors, use an ampersand (&) between the final two names, but write out the word *and* for any reference in your own sentence.

## 6. Three, Four, or Five Authors—APA

For three, four, or five authors, use the last names of all the authors in the first reference. In all subsequent references, use only the first author's last name followed by *et al.* (a Latin term meaning "and others"). Note that *et al.* is followed by a period and is not italicized.

**FIRST REFERENCE**

In one anthology, 35% of the selections had not been anthologized before (Elliott, Kerber, Litz, & Martin, 1992).

**SUBSEQUENT REFERENCE**

Elliott et al. (1992) include 17 authors whose work has never been anthologized.

## 7. Six or More Authors—APA

For six or more authors, name the first author followed by *et al.* in all in-text references, including the first.

These injuries can lead to an inability to perform athletically, in addition to initiating degenerative changes at the joint level (Mandelbaum et al., 2005).

## 8. Author(s) with Two or More Works in the Same Year—APA

If you use more than one source written in the same year by the same author(s), alphabetize the works by their titles for the References list and assign letters in alphabetical order to the years—(1996a), (1996b), (1996c). Use the year-letter combination in parenthetical references. Note that a citation of two or more such works lists the years in alphabetical order.

Most recently, Jones (1996c) draws new conclusions from the results of 17 sets of experiments (Jones, 1996a, 1996b).

## 9. Two or More Authors with the Same Last Name—APA

Include first initials for every in-text citation of authors who share a last name. Use the initials appearing in the References list. (In the second example, a parenthetical citation, the name order is alphabetical, as explained in item 12.)

R. A. Smith (1997) and C. Smith (1989) both confirm these results.

These results have been confirmed independently (C. Smith, 1989; R. A. Smith, 1997).

## 10. Work with a Group or Corporate Author—APA

If you use a source in which the "author" is a corporation, agency, or group, an in-text reference gives that name as author. Use the full name

631

in each citation, unless an abbreviated version of the name is likely to be familiar to your audience. In that case, use the full name and give its abbreviation at the first citation; then, use the abbreviation for subsequent citations.

> This exploration will continue into the 21st century (National Aeronautics and Space Administration [NASA], 2004). [In subsequent citations, use the abbreviated form, NASA, alone.]

## 11. Work Listed by Title—APA

If no author is named, use a shortened form of the title for in-text citations. Ignoring *A, An,* or *The,* make the first word the one by which you alphabetize the title in your References. The following example refers to an article fully titled "Are You a Day or Night Person?"

> Scientists group people as "larks" or "owls" on the basis of whether individuals are more efficient in the morning or at night ("Are You," 1989).

## 12. Reference to More Than One Source—APA

If more than one source has contributed to an idea or opinion in your paper, cite the sources alphabetically by author in one set of parentheses; separate each block of information with a semicolon, as in the following example.

> Conceptions of personal space vary among cultures (Morris, 1977; Worchel & Cooper, 1983).

## 13. Personal Communication, Including E-Mail and Other Nonretrievable Sources—APA

Telephone calls, personal letters, interviews, and e-mail messages are "personal communications" that your readers can't access or retrieve. Acknowledge personal communications in parenthetical references, but never include them in your References list at the end of your research paper.

> Recalling his first summer at camp, one person said, "The proximity of 12 other kids made me—an only child with older, quiet parents—frantic for eight weeks" (A. Weiss, personal communication, January 12, 2005).

## 14. Reference to an Online Source—APA

If an online source doesn't provide page numbers, use the paragraph number, if available, preceded by the abbreviation *para.* If you can't decipher a page or paragraph number, cite a heading and a paragraph number after it, if possible.

> (Anderson, 2003, para. 14)

> (Migueis, 2002, Introduction, para. 1)

### 15. Other References to Retrievable Online Sources—APA

When you quote, paraphrase, or summarize an online source that is available to others, cite the author (if any) or title and the date as you would for a print source, and include the work in your References list.

> It's possible that similarity in personality is important in having a happy marriage (Luo & Clonen, 2005, p. 324).

### 16. Source Lines for Graphics and Table Data—APA

If you use a graphic from another source or create a table using data from another source, provide a note at the bottom of the table or graphic, crediting the original author and the copyright holder. Here are examples of two source lines—one for a graphic from an article, the other for a graphic from a book.

#### GRAPHIC FROM AN ARTICLE—APA

*Note.* The data in columns 1 and 2 are from "Bridge Over Troubled Waters? Connecting Research and Pedagogy in Composition and Business/Technical Communication," by J. Allen, 1992, *Technical Communication Quarterly, 1*(4), p. 9. Copyright 1992 by the Association of Teachers of Technical Writing. Adapted with permission of the author.

#### GRAPHIC FROM A BOOK—APA

*Note.* From *The Road to Reality: A Complete Guide to the Laws of the Universe* (p. 270), by R. Penrose, 2005, New York: Alfred Knopf. Copyright 2004 by R. Penrose. Reprinted with permission of the publisher.

## 35d  What are APA guidelines for writing an abstract?

As the APA *Publication Manual* explains, "an abstract is a brief, comprehensive summary" (p. 12) of a longer piece of writing. The APA estimates that an abstract should be no longer than about 120 words. Your instructor may require that you include an abstract at the start of a paper; if you're not sure, ask. Make the abstract accurate, objective, and exact. Actually, as you study the social sciences, you may become familiar with effective abstracts because many disciplines have online abstracts of longer sources. See 35g for guidelines on formatting an Abstract page. The student paper in 35h.2 has an abstract you can study as an example.

## 35e  What are APA guidelines for content notes?

Content notes in APA-style papers add relevant information that can't be worked effectively into a text discussion. Use consecutive arabic numerals for note numbers, both within your paper and on any separate page following the last text page of your paper. Try to arrange your sentence so that the note number falls at the end. Use a numeral raised slightly above the line of words and immediately after the final punctuation mark. See 35g for instructions on formatting the Footnotes page.

## 35f What are APA guidelines for a References list?

The REFERENCES list at the end of your research paper provides complete bibliographic information for readers who may want to access the sources you draw on for your paper.

Include in a References list all the sources you QUOTE, PARAPHRASE, or SUMMARIZE in your paper so that readers can find the same sources with reasonable effort. Never include in your References list any source that's not generally available to others (see item 13 in 35c). Box 35.1 presents general format guidelines.

---

**SUMMARY BOX 35.1**

### Guidelines for an APA-style References list

**TITLE**

The title is "References" (centered without quotation marks, italics, or underlining).

**PLACEMENT OF LIST**

Start a new page. Number it sequentially with the rest of the paper and place it immediately after the body of the paper.

**CONTENTS AND FORMAT**

Include all quoted, paraphrased, or summarized sources in your paper that are not personal communications, unless your instructor tells you to include all the references you have consulted, not just those you have to credit. Start each entry on a new line, and double-space all lines. APA recommends that student papers follow journal formatting by using a *hanging indent* style: The first line of each entry begins flush left at the margin, and all other lines are indented. The hanging indent makes source names and dates more prominent. Type the first line of each entry full width, and indent subsequent lines one-half inch. The easiest way to do this is using the word processor's ruler bar.

Shuter, R. (1977). A field study of nonverbal communication in Germany, Italy, and the United States. *Communication Monographs, 44,* 298–305.

---

## Guidelines for an APA-style References list

### SPACING AFTER PUNCTUATION

APA calls for one space after end-punctuation marks.

### ARRANGEMENT OF ENTRIES

Alphabetize by the author's last name. If no author is named, alphabetize by the first significant word (ignore *A, An,* or *The*) in the title of the work.

### AUTHORS' NAMES

Use last names, first initials, and middle initials, if any. Reverse the order for all authors' names, and use an ampersand (&) before the last author's name: Mills, J. F., & Holahan, R. H.

Give names in the order in which they appear on the work (on the title page of a book or under the title of an article or other printed work). Use a comma between each author's last name and first initial and after each complete name except the last. Use a period after the last author's name.

### DATES

Date information follows the name information and is enclosed in parentheses. Place a period followed by one space after the closing parenthesis.

For books, articles in journals that have volume numbers, and many other print and nonprint sources, the year of publication or production is the date to use. For articles from most general-circulation magazines and newspapers, use the year followed by a comma and then the exact date that appears on the issue (month and day for daily and weekly publications, month alone for monthly and bimonthly publications, and season for quarterly publications). Capitalize any words and use no abbreviations. Individual entries that follow show how much information to give for various sources.

### CAPITALIZATION OF TITLES

For book, article, and chapter titles, capitalize the first word, the first word after a colon between a title and subtitle, and any proper nouns. For names of journals and proceedings of meetings, capitalize the first word, all nouns, verbs, adverbs, and adjectives, and any other words four or more letters long.

### SPECIAL TREATMENT OF TITLES

Use no special treatment for titles of shorter works (poems, short stories, essays, articles). Italicize titles of longer works (books, names of newspapers or journals). If an italic typeface is unavailable, draw an unbroken line beneath the title *and* beneath the punctuation.

Don't drop any words, such as *A, An,* or *The,* from the titles of periodicals (such as newspapers, magazines, and journals).

## Guidelines for an APA-style References list

### PUBLISHERS

Use a shortened version of the publisher's name except for an association, corporation, or university press. Drop *Co., Inc., Publishers,* and the like, but retain *Books* or *Press.*

### PLACE OF PUBLICATION

For US publishers, give the city and add the state (use the two-letter postal abbreviations listed in most dictionaries and in Box 30.4 in 30k) for all US cities except Baltimore, Boston, Chicago, Los Angeles, New York, Philadelphia, and San Francisco. For publishers in other countries, give city and country spelled out; no country name is needed with Amsterdam, Jerusalem, London, Milan, Moscow, Paris, Rome, Stockholm, Tokyo, and Vienna. However, if the state or country is part of the publisher's name, omit it after the name of the city.

### ABBREVIATIONS OF MONTHS

Don't abbreviate the names of months in any context.

### PAGE NUMBERS

Use all digits, omitting none. For references to books or newspapers only, use *p.* and *pp.* before page numbers. List all discontinuous pages, with numbers separated by commas: pp. 32, 44–45, 47–49, 53.

### REFERENCES ENTRIES: BOOKS

Citations for books have four main parts: author, date, title, and publication information (place of publication and publisher). Each part ends with a period.

AUTHOR    DATE    TITLE
Wood, P. (2003). *Diversity: The invention of a concept.*

PUBLICATION INFORMATION
San Francisco: Encounter Books.

### REFERENCES ENTRIES: ARTICLES

Citations for periodical articles contain four major parts: author, date, title of article, and publication information (usually, the periodical title, volume number, and page numbers). Each part ends with a period.

AUTHOR    DATE    ARTICLE TITLE
Wood, W., Witt, M. G., & Tam, L. (2005). Changing circumstances, disrupting

VOLUME   PAGE
PERIODICAL TITLE    NUMBER   RANGE
habits. *Journal of Personality and Social Psychology, 88,* 918–933.

## Guidelines for an APA-style References list

### REFERENCES ENTRIES: ELECTRONIC AND ONLINE SOURCES

Styles for documenting electronic and online sources continue to evolve. The 2001 APA *Publication Manual* (pp. 268–281) and the APA Web page <http://www.apastyle.org/elecref.html> are the best sources for up-to-date advice on these formats. Here are two examples of entries. The first is for an abstract on CD-ROM, a searchable "aggregated database" (that is, a compilation of resources grouped for directed or simplified access). You aren't required to document how you accessed the database—via portable CD-ROM, on a library server, or via a supplier Web site—but you are required to include a "retrieval statement" that accurately names the source (in this case, the database) and lists the date of retrieval. (If there is an item or accession number, place it in parentheses.)

AUTHOR · DATE · ARTICLE TITLE
Marcus, H. F., & Kitayamo, S. (1991). Culture and the self:

Implications for cognition, emotion, and motivation.

JOURNAL TITLE AND PUBLICATION INFORMATION · RETRIEVAL INFORMATION
*Psychological Abstracts, 78.* Retrieved October 2, 2005, from the

PsycINFO database (Item 1991-23978-001).

The second example is for an article in a newspaper consulted on the World Wide Web. The retrieval statement gives the access date and the URL, which "names" the source.

AUTHOR · DATE · ARTICLE TITLE
Overbye, D. (2005, June 28). Remembrance of things future: The mystery

ONLINE NEWSPAPER TITLE · RETRIEVAL INFORMATION
of time. *The New York Times.* Retrieved December 11, 2005, from

http://www.nytimes.com

Notice that the only punctuation in the URL is part of the address. Don't add a period after a URL.

The following samples of entries may appear in an APA References list. You can find others in the *Publication Manual of the American Psychological Association* or at <http://www.apastyle.org>.

## PRINT SOURCES

### 1. Book by One Author—APA

Note that all entries use the hanging indent style: The first line of an entry is flush to the left margin, and all other lines in the entry are indented one-half inch.

Bradway, B. (2002). *Pink houses and family taverns*. Bloomington: Indiana
    University Press.

### 2. Book by Two Authors—APA

Edin, K., & Kefalas, M. (2005). *Promises I can keep: Why poor women put
    motherhood before marriage*. Berkeley: University of California Press.

### 3. Book by Three or More Authors—APA

For a book by three to six authors, include all the authors' names. For a book by more than six authors, use only the first six names followed by *et al.*

Lynam, J. K., Ndiritu, C. G., & Mbabu, A. N. (2004). *Transformation of
    agricultural research systems in Africa: Lessons from Kenya*. East
    Lansing: Michigan State University Press.

### 4. Two or More Books by the Same Author(s)—APA

Arrange references by the same author chronologically, with the earlier date of publication listed first.

Gardner, H. (1993). *Multiple intelligences: The theory in practice*. New York:
    Basic Books.

Gardner, H. (1999). *Intelligence reframed: Multiple intelligences for the 21st
    century*. New York: Basic Books.

### 5. Book by a Group or Corporate Author—APA

Cite the full name of the corporate author first. If the author is also the publisher, use the word *Author* as the name of the publisher.

American Psychological Association. (2001). *Publication manual of the
    American Psychological Association* (5th ed.). Washington, DC: Author.

Boston Women's Health Collective. (1998). *Our bodies, ourselves for the new
    century*. New York: Simon & Schuster.

### 6. Book with No Author Named—APA

*The Chicago manual of style* (15th ed.). (2003). Chicago: University of Chicago Press.

### 7. Book with an Author and an Editor—APA

Brontë, E. (2002). *Wuthering heights* (R. J. Dunn, Ed.). New York: Norton.

### 8. Translation—APA

Kundera, M. (1999). *The unbearable lightness of being* (M. H. Heim, Trans.). New York: HarperPerennial. (Original work published 1984)

### 9. Work in Several Volumes or Parts—APA

Chrisley, R. (Ed.). (2000). *Artificial intelligence: Critical concepts* (Vols. 1–4). London: Routledge.

### 10. One Selection from an Anthology or an Edited Book—APA

Give the author of the selection first. The word *In* introduces the larger work from which the selection is taken. Note that names are inverted only in the author position; in all other circumstances, they are written in standard form.

Trujillo, L. (2004). Balancing act. In R. Moreno & M. H. Mulligan (Eds.), *Borderline personalities: A new generation of Latinas dish on sex, sass, and cultural shifting* (pp. 61–72). New York: HarperCollins.

### 11. Selection from a Work Already Listed in References—APA

Provide full information for the already-cited anthology (first example below), along with information about the individual selection. Put entries in alphabetical order.

Gilbert, S., & Gubar, S. (Eds.). (1985). *The Norton anthology of literature by women.* New York: Norton.

Kingston, M. H. (1985). No name woman. In S. Gilbert & S. Gubar (Eds.), *The Norton anthology of literature by women* (pp. 2337–2347). New York: Norton.

### 12. Signed Article in a Reference Book—APA

Use *In* to introduce the larger work from which the selection is taken.

Burnbam, J. C. (1996). Freud, Sigmund. In B. B. Wolman (Ed.), *The encyclopedia of psychiatry, psychology, and psychoanalysis* (p. 220). New York: Holt.

### 13. Unsigned Article in a Reference Book—APA

Ireland. (2002). In *The new encyclopaedia Britannica: Macropaedia* (15th ed.,
Vol. 21, pp. 997–1018). Chicago: Encyclopaedia Britannica.

### 14. Second or Subsequent Edition—APA

A book usually doesn't announce that it's a first edition. However, after
the first edition, the edition number appears on the title page. In your
entry, place the abbreviated information (*2nd ed., 3rd ed.,* and so on)
after the title and in parentheses.

Gibaldi, J. (2003). *MLA handbook for writers of research papers* (6th ed.). New
York: Modern Language Association.

### 15. Anthology or Edited Book—APA

Purdy, J. L., & Ruppert, J. (Eds.). (2001). *Nothing but the truth: An anthology of
Native American literature.* Upper Saddle River, NJ: Prentice Hall.

### 16. Introduction, Preface, Foreword, or Afterword—APA

If you're citing an introduction, preface, foreword, or afterword, give its
author's name first. After the year, give the name of the part cited. If the
writer of the material you're citing is not the author of the book, use the
word *In* and the author's name before the title of the book.

Fox-Genovese, E. (1999). Foreword. In N. Warren & S. Wolff (Eds.), *Southern
mothers.* Baton Rouge: Louisiana State University Press.

### 17. Unpublished Dissertation or Essay—APA

Byers, M. (2000). Buffy the Vampire Slayer: *The insurgence of television as a
performance text.* Unpublished doctoral dissertation, University of
Toronto, Ontario, Canada.

### 18. Reprint of an Older Book—APA

O'Brien, F. (1998). *At Swim-Two-Birds.* Normal, IL: Dalkey Archive Press.
(Original work published 1939)

You can find republishing information on the copyright page.

### 19. Book in a Series—APA

Give the title of the book but not of the whole series.

Goldman, D. J. (1995). *Women writers and World War I.* New York: Macmillan.

### 20. Book with a Title Within a Title—APA

Never italicize a title within a title, even though it would appear in italic
typeface if it were by itself. (See also item 17.)

Lumiansky, R. M., & Baker, H. (Eds.). (1968). *Critical approaches to six major English works:* Beowulf *through* Paradise Lost. Philadelphia: University of Pennsylvania Press.

### 21. Government Publication—APA

Use the complete name of a government agency as author when no specific person is named.

U.S. Congress. House Subcommittee on Health and Environment of the Committee on Commerce. (1999). *The nursing home resident protection amendments of 1999* (99-0266-P). Washington, DC: U.S. Government Printing Office.

U.S. Senate Special Committee on Aging. (1998). *The risk of malnutrition in nursing homes* (98-0150-P). Washington, DC: U.S. Government Printing Office.

### 22. Published Proceedings of a Conference—APA

Harris, D., & Nelson-Heern, L. (Eds.). (1981, June). *Proceedings of the National Education Computing Conference.* Iowa City: University of Iowa, Weeg Computing Center.

When citing a specific department or other university facility, put the name of the university first.

### 23. Signed Article in a Daily Newspaper—APA

Use the abbreviation *p.* (or *pp.* for more than one page) for items from newspapers.

Killborn, P. T. (2003, June 22). A health threat baffling for its lack of a pattern. *The New York Times,* p. A14.

### 24. Unsigned Article in a Daily Newspaper—APA

Changes sought in medical services for veterans. (2003, August 5). *The New York Times,* p. A10.

### 25. Editorial, Letter to the Editor, or Review—APA

Downtown's architectural promise. (2003, August 4). [Editorial]. *The New York Times,* p. A12.

Hansen, R. P. (2003, January/February). [Letter to the editor]. *Sierra,* 8.

Shenk, D. (2003, Spring). Toolmaker, brain builder. [Review of the book *Beyond Big Blue: Building the computer that defeated the world chess champion*]. *The American Scholar,* 72, 150–152.

### 26. Signed Article in a Weekly or Biweekly Periodical—APA

Give year, month, and day for a periodical published every week or every two weeks. Don't use the abbreviation *p.* (or *pp.*) for magazines or journals.

Brink, S. (2005, March 28). Eat this now! *U.S. News & World Report,* 56–58.

### 27. Signed Article in a Monthly or Bimonthly Periodical—APA

Give the year and month(s) for a periodical published every month or every other month. Insert the volume number, italicized with the periodical title. Put the issue number in parentheses; don't italicize it, and don't put a space before it.

Langewiesche, W. (2003, September). Anarchy at sea. *The Atlantic, 292*(2), 50–80.

### 28. Unsigned Article in a Weekly or Monthly Periodical—APA

The price is wrong. (2003, August 2). *The Economist, 368,* 58–59.

### 29. Article in a Looseleaf Collection of Reprinted Articles—APA

Hayden, T. (2002). The age of robots. In E. Goldstein (Ed.), *Applied Science 2002. SIRS 2002,* Article 66. (Reprinted from *U.S. News & World Report,* pp. 44–50, 2001, April 23).

### 30. Article in a Journal with Continuous Pagination—APA

Give only the volume number after the journal title, and italicize the volume number.

Tyson, P. (1998). The psychology of women. *Journal of the American Psychoanalytic Association, 46,* 361–364.

### 31. Article in a Journal That Pages Each Issue Separately—APA

Give the volume number, italicized with the journal title. Give the issue number in parentheses; don't italicize it and leave no space before it.

Adler-Kassner, L., & Estrem, H. (2003). Rethinking research writing: Public literacy in the composition classroom. *WPA: Writing Program Administration, 26*(3), 119–131.

### 32. Published and Unpublished Letters—APA

In the APA system, unpublished letters are considered personal communication inaccessible to general readers, so they don't appear in the References list. Personal communications are cited only in the body of the paper (see also item 36).

Williams, W.C. (1935). Letter to his son. In L. Grunwald & S. J. Adler (Eds.), *Letters of the century: America 1900–1999* (pp. 225–226). New York: Dial.

### 33. Map or Chart—APA

*The Caribbean and South America* [Map]. (1992). Falls Church, VA: American
Automobile Association.

### 34. Report or Pamphlet—APA

Student Environmental Coalition. (2005). *Reduce, reuse, recycle* [Brochure].
Normal, IL: Author.

### 35. Legal Source—APA

Include the name of the case, the citation (usually a volume number,
publication title, and page) or a record number, the name of the court
deciding the case (if other than the US Supreme Court), and the year of
the decision. The following example shows the citation for a published
case. See Appendix D of the APA *Publication Manual* for other types of
legal citations.

Brown v. Board of Educ., 347 U.S. 483 (1954).

**NONPRINT SOURCES**

### 36. Interview—APA

In APA style, a personal interview is considered personal communication
and is not included in the References list. Cite the interview in the text
with a parenthetical notation saying that it's a personal communication.

Randi Friedman (personal communication, June 30, 2005) endorses this view.

Because a published interview is recoverable by readers, treat it as
you would a journal or magazine article, depending on its place of
publication.

Zoglin, R. (2003, December 15). Ten questions for Oprah Winfrey. *Time*, 8.

### 37. Lecture, Speech, or Address—APA

Kennedy, J. F. (1960, September 12). Speech to the Greater Houston Ministerial
Association, Rice Hotel, Houston, TX.

### 38. Motion Picture—APA

Capra, F. (Director/Producer). (1934). *It happened one night* [Motion picture].
United States: Columbia Pictures.

Capra, F. (Director/Producer). (1999). *It happened one night* [Videocassette].
(Original motion picture released 1934)

Madden, J. (Director), Parfitt, D., Gigliotti, D., Weinstein, H., Zwick, E., &
Norman, M. (Producers). (2003). *Shakespeare in love* [DVD]. (Original
motion picture released 1998)

### 39. Music Recording—APA

Smetana, B. (1975). *My country* [Recorded by the Czech Philharmonic Orchestra with K. Anserl conducting]. [Record]. London: Vanguard Records. (1975)

Springsteen, B. (2002). Lonesome day. On *The rising* [CD]. New York: Columbia Records.

### 40. Live Performance—APA

Miller, A. (Author), & McLean, C. (Director). (2005, September 27). *All my sons* [Theatrical performance]. Center for the Performing Arts, Normal, IL.

### 41. Work of Art, Photograph, or Musical Composition—APA

Cassatt, M. (1891). *La toilette* [Artwork]. Chicago: Art Institute of Chicago.

Mydans, C. (1999, October 21–November 28). *General Douglas MacArthur landing at Luzon, 1945* [Photograph]. New York: Soho Triad Fine Art Gallery.

Schubert, F. (1822). *Unfinished symphony* [Musical composition].

### 42. Radio or Television Broadcast—APA

Burns, K. (Writer/Producer), & Barnes, P. (Producer). (1999, November 8). *Not for ourselves alone: The story of Elizabeth Cady Stanton and Susan B. Anthony* [Television broadcast]. New York and Washington, DC: Public Broadcasting Service.

If you're citing a television series produced by and seen on one station, cite its call letters.

### 43. Information Services—APA

Chiang, L. H. (1993). *Beyond the language: Native Americans' nonverbal communication.* (ERIC Document Reproduction Service No. ED368540)

### 44. Advertisement—APA

Swim at home. (2005). [Advertisement]. *The American Scholar 74*(2), 2.

### 45. Images—APA

If you're reproducing an image in your paper, follow the guidelines for graphics in item 16 in 35c. Include the citation in the body of your paper. If you're only referring to an image, cite the photographer or illustrator (if known), the title (or a brief description of the image), and source information.

Arthur Miller in 1961. (2005). [Photograph]. *The American Scholar 74*(2), 123.

## ELECTRONIC AND ONLINE SOURCES

Treat information from online sources that your readers can't readily retrieve for themselves—e-mail messages and discussion list communications, for example—as personal communications (see items 32 and 36). Never include them in your References list. If you have a scholarly reason to cite a message from a newsgroup, forum, or electronic mailing list that is available in an electronic archive, then document the following: an author name; the exact date of the posting; the subject line or "thread" (don't italicize it) followed by an identifier in square brackets—for example, [Msg 23]; and a "Message posted to" statement that lists the URL of the message or of the archive. Following is an example:

Hesse, D. (2003, August 1). Research on large class size [Msg 192]. Message
    posted to http://lists.asu.edu/archives/wpa-l.html

In general, APA recommends giving author, title, and publication information as for a print source. This information is followed by a "retrieval statement" that leads the reader as directly as possible to your source.

In contrast to MLA style, APA style doesn't require angle brackets around URLs in retrieval statements. Also, APA allows you to break a URL either after a slash or before a period.

### 46. Article from an Encyclopedia on CD-ROM—APA

Artificial intelligence. (2003). In *Encarta 2003*. Retrieved December 10, 2005,
    from the Encarta database.

The retrieval statement gives the retrieval date in full and the name of the database. The entry ends with a period.

### 47. Computer Software or Video Game—APA

Provide an author name, if available. Standard software (Microsoft Word) and program languages (C++) don't need to be given in the References list. Provide the name and, in parentheses, the version number in the text.

Chessmaster 10. (2004). [Video game]. San Francisco: Ubisoft.

### 48. Books Retrieved from Databases on the Web—APA

Provide information about the print version, if available, as in the first example, which cites the printed version of *The Education of Henry Adams*. The retrieval statement gives the access date, the name of the database, and the URL of the specific work.

Adams, H. (1918). *The education of Henry Adams*. New York: Houghton Mifflin.
    Retrieved December 4, 2004, from the Project Bartleby database:
    http://www.columbia.edu/acis/bartleby/159/index/html

Chopin, K. (1899). *The awakening*. Retrieved December 12, 2005, from the PBS database: http://www.pbs.org/katechopin/library/awakening

### 49. Article in a Periodical on the Web—APA

Parrott, A. C. (1999). Does cigarette smoking cause stress? *American Psychologist, 54*, 817–820. Retrieved December 7, 2005, from http://www.apa.org/journals/amp/amp5410817.html

### 50. Exact Electronic Copy of a Journal Article, Retrieved from a Database—APA

If you find online an exact duplicate of a print source (an exact image of the page as published, perhaps as a PDF file), use the same reference form as for the print version. However, if you view the work only in its electronic form, add [Electronic version] after the title.

Vazire, S., & Gosling, S. (2004). E-perceptions: Personality impressions based on personal Web sites [Electronic version]. *Journal of Personality and Social Psychology, 87*, 123–132.

### 51. Online Version of an Article from a Print Source, Retrieved from a Database—APA

If you're using an electronic version of a print source but you suspect that this version is in a format different from the original (for example, it lacks conventional print formatting, page numbers, and so on), then list the date and the source from which you retrieved it.

Vazire, S., & Gosling, S. (2004). E-perceptions: Personality impressions based on personal Web sites. *Journal of Personality and Social Psychology, 87*, 123–132. Retrieved April 10, 2005, from the PsycINFO database.

### 52. Personal or Professional Site on the Web—APA

Hesse, D. (2005, November). Home page. Retrieved December 22, 2005, from http://www.ilstu.edu/~ddhesse/

American Association for Artificial Intelligence. (2005, March). Retrieved March 17, 2005, from http://www.aaai.org

### 53. File Transfer Protocol (FTP), Telnet, or Gopher Site—APA

Taine, H. A. (2001, April). *The French Revolution Volume II*. Retrieved October 21, 2002, from ftp://ibiblio.org/pub/docs/books/gutenberg

After the retrieval data, supply the FTP, telnet, or gopher search path.

## 54. Synchronous Communications (MOO, MUD, IRC)—APA

Give the name of the speaker, a title for the event, the date of the event or posting, the access date, and the URL.

Bleck, B. (1997, June 8). Online discussion of *Virtual first-year composition: Distance education, the Internet, and the World Wide Web*. Retrieved February 27, 1999, from http://lrc.csun.edu/DaMOO/cw/brad.html

## 55. Web Discussion Forum—APA

Higa, S. (2002, June 26). A potential bookmark [Msg. 483]. Message posted to http://groups.yahoo.com/group/Modern_Era/messages/483

## 56. Electronic Mailing List (Listserv)—APA

Haswell, R. (2005, October). A new graphic/text interface. Message posted to Writing Program Administrators electronic mailing list, archived at http://lists.asu.edu/archives/wpa-l.html

APA advises using *electronic mailing list*, as Listserv is the name of a specific software.

## 57. Newsgroup—APA

Boyle, F. (2002, October 11). Psyche: Cemi field theory: The hard problem made easy [Msg 1]. Message posted to news://sci.psychology.consciousness

## 58. Course Home Page—APA

St. Germain, S. (2003, Summer). Myths and fairytales: From *Inanna* to *Edward Scissorhands*. Retrieved February 20, 2005, from http://www.public.iastate.edu/~sgermain/531.homepage.html

## 59. Academic Department Home Page—APA

Rutgers University English Department (2005). Home page. Retrieved February 26, 2005, from http://English.rutgers.edu

## 60. Online Advertisement—APA

Samsung. (2005, November). [Advertisement]. Retrieved November 7, 2005, from http://rollingstone.com

## 61. Posting on a Blog—APA

Silliman, R. (2005). Monday, March 7, 2005. *Silliman's blog: A Weblog focused on contemporary poetry and poetics*. Retrieved April 2, 2005, from http://www.ronsilliman.blogspot.com

### 62. Online Digital Recording—APA

Komunyakaa, Y. (2005). My father's love letters. Retrieved March 7, 2005, from

the Academy of American Poets Web site: http://www.poets.org/poems/

poems.cfm?prmID=2065

### 63. Podcast—APA

A podcast is an audio recording that is posted online. Include as much of the following information as you can identify: author, title, sponsoring organization or Web site, date posted, date accessed, and URL.

Business marketing with podcast: What marketing professionals should know

(2005, October 13). Retrieved October 19, 2005, from the Podblaze Web

site: http://business.podblaze.com/

## 35g What are APA format guidelines for research papers?

Ask whether your instructor has instructions for preparing a final draft. If not, you can use the APA guidelines here. For an illustration of these guidelines, see the student paper in 35h.2.

### GENERAL INSTRUCTIONS—APA

Use 8 1/2-by-11-inch white paper. The APA *Publication Manual* recommends double-spacing for a final manuscript of a student research paper. Set at least a one-inch margin on the left (slightly more if you submit your paper in a binder) and leave no less than one inch on the right and at the bottom.

Leave one-half inch from the top edge of the paper to the title-and-page-number line (*header*). Leave another one-half inch (or one inch from the top edge of the paper) before the next line on the page, whether that's a heading (such as "Abstract" or "Notes") or a line of your paper.

**ALERT:** Most word processing programs set the top and bottom margins at one inch as their default. Also, they generally set the "header" function at a default of one-half inch. Therefore, formatting the margins for your paper is probably less troublesome than it might seem. You simply need to check the default settings. ◆

Use indents of one-half inch for the first line of all paragraphs, except in an abstract, the first line of which isn't indented. Don't justify the right margin. Indent footnotes one-half inch.

## ORDER OF PARTS—APA

Number all pages consecutively. Use this order for the parts of your paper:

1. Title page
2. Abstract (if required)
3. Body of the paper
4. References
5. Appendixes, if any
6. Footnotes, if any
7. Attachments, if any (questionnaires, data sheets, or other material your instructor asks you to include)

## TITLE-AND-PAGE-NUMBER LINE FOR ALL PAGES—APA

Use a title-and-page-number line on all pages of your paper. Leaving a margin of one-half inch from the top edge of the paper, type the title (use a shortened version if necessary), leave a five-character space, and then type the page number. End the title-and-page-number line one inch from the right edge of the paper. Ask whether your instructor wants you to include your last name in this title-and-page-number line. The "header" feature on a word processing program will help you create the title-and-page-number line easily.

## TITLE PAGE—APA

Use a separate title page. On it, begin with the title-and-page-number line described above, using the numeral 1 for this first page. Then, center the complete title vertically and horizontally on the page. Use two or more double-spaced lines if the title is long. Don't italicize or underline the title or enclose it in quotation marks. On the next line, center your name, and below that center the course title and section, your professor's name, and the date.

**ALERTS:** (1) Use the following guidelines for capitalizing the title of your own paper and for capitalizing titles you mention in the body of your paper. (For capitalization of titles in the References list, see Box 35.1.)

(2) Use a capital letter for the first word of your title and for the first word of a subtitle, if any. Start every noun, pronoun, verb, adverb, and adjective with a capital letter. Capitalize each main word in a hyphenated compound word (two or more words used together to express one idea): *Father-in-Law, Self-Consciousness.*

(3) Don't capitalize articles (*a, an, the*) unless one of the other capitalization rules applies. Don't capitalize prepositions and conjunctions unless they are four or more letters long. Don't capitalize the word *to* used in an infinitive. ◆

APA

### ABSTRACT—APA

See 35d for advice about what to include in an abstract of your paper. Type the abstract on a separate page, using the numeral 2 in the title-and-page-number line. Center the word *Abstract* one inch from the top of the paper. Don't italicize or underline it or enclose it in quotation marks. Double-space below this title, and then start your abstract, double-spacing it. Don't indent the first line.

### SET-OFF QUOTATIONS—APA

Set off (display in BLOCK-STYLE form) quotations of forty words or more. Double-space to start a new line for the quoted words, indenting each line of the (double-spaced) quotation one-half inch or five spaces from the left margin. Don't enclose the quoted words in quotation marks.

If you're quoting part of a paragraph or one complete paragraph, don't indent the first line more than one-half inch. But if you quote two or more paragraphs, indent the first line of the second and subsequent paragraphs one inch from the text margin.

When the quotation is finished, leave one space after the sentence-ending punctuation, and then give the parenthetical citation. Begin a new line to resume your own words.

### REFERENCES LIST—APA

Start a new page for your References list immediately after the end of the body of your paper. Use a title-and-page-number line. Drop down one inch from the top of the paper and center the word *References*. Don't italicize, underline, or put it in quotation marks. Double-space below it. Start the first line of each entry at the left margin, and indent any subsequent lines one-half inch from the left margin. Use this "hanging indent" style unless your instructor prefers a different one. Double-space within each entry and between entries.

### NOTES—APA

Whenever you use a content note in your paper (35e), try to arrange your sentence so that the note number falls at the end. The ideal place for a note number is after the sentence-ending punctuation. Use a numeral raised slightly above the line of words and immediately after the final punctuation mark.

Put any notes on a separate page after the last page of your References list. Use a title-and-page-number line. Then, center the word *Footnotes* one inch from the top of the paper. Don't italicize or underline it or put it in quotation marks.

On the next line, indent one-half inch and begin the note. Raise the note number slightly (you can use the superscript feature in your word processing program), and then start the words of your note leaving no space. If the note is more than one typed line, don't indent any line after the first. Double-space throughout.

## 35h A student's APA-style research paper

The final section of this chapter presents a student research paper prepared to conform to APA style. We discuss the researching, planning, drafting, and revising processes of the student, Shawn Hickson, and show the final draft of the paper, including its abstract.

---

### Case Study

Shawn Hickson was given this assignment for a research paper in a second-term writing class: Write a research paper of 1,250 to 1,700 words about an aspect of contemporary life that interests you. For guidance, refer to the *Simon & Schuster Handbook for Writers,* Chapters 31 through 33. Use the documentation style of the American Psychological Association (APA) explained in Chapter 35. Your topic and working bibliography are due in two weeks. An early draft of your paper is due two weeks later. (Try to get that early draft close to what you hope will be your last draft, so that comments from me and from your peers can concretely help you write an excellent final draft.) Your final draft is due one week after I've returned your early draft (with comments) to you.

---

## 35h.1 Researching and writing the paper

When Shawn Hickson read his assignment, he was both pleased and intimidated by the amount of choice he had. He started PLANNING by listing several broad topics, finding that he was most interested in current technologies: cell phones, pagers, video games, computers, and MP3 players. He added to his list by thinking how each of these influenced several areas of life: school, work, entertainment, social life, communication. He recalled a lecture from a sociology course about how people today communicated more extensively than at any other point in history, yet they were spending less time together in person. This led to an early research question, "How do face-to-face interactions compare with cell phone or online interactions?" While he personally thought online dating services were strange, he was intrigued that they seemed to be popular among many people. He wondered, then, what role physical appearances played.

Shawn checked to see whether he could find enough sources useful for research on this topic. From his home computer, he went to his college's library home page. He searched the catalog with several keywords, including "physical appearance," "relationships," "dating," "physical attraction," and "Internet dating." He also used combinations of these terms in a Boolean search and generated a list of books, including several that hadn't been checked out. Next, he turned to online databases, which generated citations for dozens of journal, magazine, and newspaper articles. Some of them had full-text versions online, and he printed those that looked promising. Then, he went to his college library to check out several books and to review some other materials that were available only in the library.

Shawn also used the Google search engine to browse his keywords. However, he tended to turn up dating sites and bulletin boards. He thought some were entertaining and might be interesting as examples, but he ultimately decided they didn't have enough substance to use for this particular paper.

From all the sources he identified, Shawn compiled a WORKING BIBLIOGRAPHY, typing sources into a file on his computer. The working bibliography that he submitted consisted of twenty-nine SOURCES, though he had reviewed and rejected about ten others, including several he eliminated because they were of poor quality or seemed too technical for him to grasp easily. Shawn didn't intend to use all twenty-nine sources, but he wasn't yet sure where his drafting would go. Not surprisingly, his instructor urged him to reduce the list once DRAFTING began; otherwise, Shawn would risk writing too little about too much. His instructor also recommended a colleague in the psychology department who had a scholarly interest in what attracted people to each other. Shawn arranged a brief interview with the psychology instructor, who directed him to some classic studies on the topic.

After spending several hours reading his sources and taking some content notes, Shawn began to weed out material. He narrowed his list to sixteen sources, took detailed notes on each, and began to group his material into emerging subtopics. Eventually, he dropped five of the sources.

Shawn realized that he'd still need to narrow the TOPIC sufficiently to shape a THESIS STATEMENT. The narrowing process worried him because he had been told in other college courses that his topics for research papers were too broad. He was determined this time to avoid that same problem.

To start drafting his paper, Shawn spread his note cards around him for easy reference, but he felt somewhat overwhelmed by the amount of information at hand, and he wrote only a few sentences. To break through, he decided to type a DISCOVERY DRAFT (Box 2.6) to see what he had absorbed from his reading and notetaking. That very rough draft became his vehicle for many things, including creating an effective thesis statement, inserting source information according to APA documentation style, and checking the logical arrangement of his material.

Revising for Shawn started with his thesis statement, a process that helped him further narrow his focus. He started with "Physical appearances affect people's responses to each other," which his research supported but which was extremely broad and bland. His next version served him well: "When people meet face to face, they form opinions based on physical characteristics including age, attractiveness, ethnicity, and appearance of wealth, but when they meet online they have to form opinions using other criteria." This thesis proved very useful in revising the discovery draft into a true first draft, but the process made it clear to Shawn that he was covering too much for a 1,250- to 1,750-word research paper, and he dropped some material. He decided first to inform readers about the affect of appearances (or their absence) on first meetings and then to explore why people responded as they did. For his final draft, Shawn used this more focused thesis statement: "The presence or absence of physical characteristics during first meetings can influence how people respond to each other."

Shawn had to attend very closely to the details of correct parenthetical IN-TEXT CITATIONS (35b and 35c) within his paper and a correct REFERENCES list (35f and 35g) at the end. Because he'd used MLA DOCUMENTATION STYLE in other courses, he made sure not to confuse the two styles. For example, he saw that APA-style parenthetical citations include the year of publication (whereas MLA-style citations don't). For format and style details of the References list at the end of his paper, he found Box 35.1 especially helpful.

As Shawn checked the logical arrangement of his material, he dropped some aspects of physical appearance when he finally narrowed his topic sufficiently. A couple of hours at the computer led him to develop examples beyond attractions in dating, including how teachers and parents treat children whom they judge to be cute, and how gender and ethnicity influence people's expectations. Shawn learned from his research experiences the difference between researching a topic too broadly (and therefore gathering too many sources for the assignment) and researching a few aspects of a topic in depth by focusing on selected sources. His final draft, which appears on the following pages, draws on eleven sources, a number that is down considerably from the twenty-nine with which he started.

## 35h.2 Analyzing the research paper

Shawn's paper, including his title page and abstract page, is shown here. For guidelines on writing an abstract, see 35d and 35g.

Use five spaces between shortened title and page number in the header.

↑ 1/2"

Effect of Physical Cues 1 ←→ 1"

Use the first page for the title page.

The Effect of Physical Cues on New Relationships

Shawn Hickson

General Psychology 131

Professor M. Staley

May 10, 2005

Center the title, student name, course, instructor, and date on the page. Use double spacing.

*APA*

---

1" ↓ ↑ 1/2"

Effect of Physical Cues 2 ←→ 1"

## Abstract

Place abstract, if required, on the second page.

Communication via the Internet has allowed people to form friendships and relationships in new ways. Research shows that individuals respond to new acquaintances at least partly according to how attractive they perceive the new friends to be. The absence of physical cues in Internet chat rooms or e-mail discussions means that people form impressions that are less affected by superficial factors. As the Internet changes, however, these differences may diminish.

Double-space

1"

*continued >*

Effect of Physical Cues    3

The Effect of Physical Cues on New Relationships

Over the past 20 years, the Internet has enabled people to meet others from around the world with a few simple keystrokes. Occasionally, these interactions extend beyond the confines of chat rooms and e-mail discussions, so that individuals arrange to meet in person. Of course, people have learned to be cautious because others online can easily misrepresent themselves and their intentions. Nonetheless, lasting friendships, romances, and even marriages have resulted from first interactions that have happened online. Surprisingly, research shows that compared with people who meet face to face, those who meet on the Internet develop a greater liking for each other (McKenna, Green, & Gleason, 2003). This result is an example of a larger phenomenon: The presence or absence of physical characteristics during first meetings can influence how people respond to each other.

Judging People by Appearances

It can be troubling to know that something as shallow as someone's physical attractiveness can affect how people treat that person. However, the truth is that even if people do not mean to judge others based on their appearance, they tend to do so. Dion, Berscheid, and Walster (1972) showed research participants pictures of stereotypically attractive and unattractive individuals and then asked them to judge the people in the photographs according to several personality traits. The researchers found that the more attractive a person was judged to be, the more desirable traits that person was judged to have. For example, people might believe that

**APA STYLE:** 1-inch margins; double-space throughout

**INTRODUCTION**

**APA-STYLE IN-TEXT CITATION:** Doesn't require page numbers for a paraphrase or summary; check whether your instructor prefers that you include them

**THESIS STATEMENT:** Gives paper's focus

**FIRST HEADING**

**PARAGRAPH 2:** Provides background information

**APA-STYLE INTEGRATED CITATION:** Author name cited in text; date cited in parentheses

**APA**

continued ➤

(Proportions shown in this paper are adjusted to fit space limitations of this book. Follow actual dimensions discussed in this book and your instructor's directions.)

APA

beautiful women are smarter or that handsome men are more clever. Several studies found that individuals assume that attractive people will agree with them more often than those who are unattractive; they assume that the attractive person will be more like them (Miyake & Zuckerman, 1993).

**PARAGRAPH 3:**
Provides further examples of thesis

Even when people are young, appearance colors how others perceive them. Studies of preschoolers show that both peers and teachers treat children differently on the basis of their physical appearances. Both expect attractive children to be more active socially, and teachers believe that attractive children have more academic potential (Kachel, 1996). Perhaps more astounding, some controversial research shows that children's physical appearances may affect how their very own parents treat them (Bakalar, 2005).

**PARAGRAPH 4:**
Provides information and bridges to next paragraph

Attractiveness has a different importance for men and women. While both sexes value physical attractiveness in brief relationships, men tend to view it as vital in long-term relationships. In contrast, women tend to regard other qualities more highly, especially financial stability and high social status (Singh, 2004).

**PARAGRAPH 5:**
Summarizes research findings

However, for men and women alike, physical cues at the first meeting can shape not only impressions but also behaviors. Snyder, Tanke, and Berscheid (1977) showed male participants a picture of either an attractive or an unattractive female and then asked the men to rate her personality traits. Results of this initial rating were very similar with those obtained by Dion et al. (1972). Snyder's group next took the study one step further. Each male participant then had a

*continued* ➤

Effect of Physical Cues    5

phone conversation with a female participant who he thought was the female from the picture. In these conversations, men treated their phone partners as if the women possessed the characteristics they believed went along with the photograph. However, the men really knew nothing about the women; they had assigned the women traits simply on the basis of a photograph. Even more interesting, women responded in a manner that was consistent with the images that were being projected onto them. Attractive women who were treated as if they were unattractive actually behaved as if they were, and vice versa. What happened was a clear example of a self-fulfilling prophecy (Snyder et al., 1977). Judgments based on appearance clouded other realities.

Meeting on the Internet

Meeting people online, especially through e-mail or in a chat room, obviously differs from meeting them face to face because there are no physical cues, only other people's words. Do people meeting in that environment engage one another differently? A study conducted by McKenna et al. (2003) suggests that they do. McKenna and colleagues divided participants into two groups: an experimental group and a control group. All participants had two separate conversations, one in person and the other online. Both conversations took place with the same person. Those in the control group knew this, but those in the experimental group believed they were talking with two different people. Participants in both groups then rated the quality of the interactions on three factors: (a) the quality of the conversations, (b) the degree to which they

*Replaces names with* et al. *because this is second reference to same work with multiple authors*

**SECOND HEADING**

**PARAGRAPH 6:** *Explains research found on the Internet*

*Creates clarity by using letters in parentheses to identify factors*

*continued* ➤

657

felt they had gotten to know the other person, and (c) how well
they liked the other person in general. For the control groups,
the ratings were similar in all categories, for both in-person
and online conversations. However, differences emerged with
the participants who thought they had been interacting with
two different people, not the same person: They consistently
rated the Internet partner higher in all three categories.

**PARA-GRAPH 7: Interprets findings summarized in previous paragraph**

One probable explanation for this occurrence is that
Internet interactions do away with traditional physical
judgments. Attractiveness, extreme shyness, speech
impediments, and many other superficial factors can hinder
people from expressing their true selves and accepting others
who are deficient in one area or another (McKenna et al., 2003).
Because early judgments determine how two people will
interact, a physical meeting makes it harder for some
individuals to become comfortable and disclose themselves at
the same level as they would in a situation where physical
cues don't matter.

**PARAGRAPH 8: Explains interests of people meeting online**

By the time people engage in online romantic
relationships, according to researcher Malin Sveningsson
(2002), they have already established a written relationship
based on common interests. They know each other on a basis
other than that of physical characteristics. Most people who

**APA-STYLE IN-TEXT CITATION: Requires page number for direct quotation; uses p. not page**

enter chat rooms do so with the hope of making "contact with
people, getting into a rewarding discussion, or just small-
talking and having a good time in general" (p. 49). Those who
meet on Internet chat sites or electronic mailing lists nearly
always come together over a shared interest. A chat room

*continued* ➤

frequenter named Richard explained his reasons for taking part in online conversations: "When you enter a place like that, you just want somebody to talk to . . . so you actively [look] for people who [have] something to say. And all the time you [make] comments just to find someone who [has] something to tell" (p. 50). Women and men are nearly equal in their use of the Internet for purposes of community. The Cyber Dialogue group found that about 27% of women and 31% of men first went to the Internet to "join an online community" and that 85% of women and 82% of men came to believe that "the Internet community is an important part" of their lives (Hawfield & Lyons, 1998). It appears, then, that the primary motivation for both men and women is not physical but rather communicative.

Attractiveness is hardly the only physical quality by which men and women judge others. Broad features of identity such as race, gender, and ethnicity can also trigger uninformed responses. Researcher Lisa Nakamura (2002) found that when a person's race is revealed on the Internet, he or she can be just as subject to prejudicial assumptions as if the reality had been revealed face to face. Because of this, some people online deliberately try to mask their race or sex. They want others to judge them by what they say and think rather than by how they look, especially in a first encounter.

Whether Internet communication will continue to support first meetings that occur purely in writing is uncertain. With the increased use of digital images and audio, the Internet has begun to provide more and more physical cues. Participants in chat rooms tend to request images earlier as a sign of

*Shawn uses brackets in quotation to show that he (not the speaker) has altered wording to improve clarity*

*Uses statistics to illustrate example*

**APA**

**PARAGRAPH 9:** Gives other factors that influence relationships

**PARAGRAPH 10:** Explains how increased use of images and sounds changes nature of online meetings

*continued* ➤

interest. People can post false photographs or videos, of course, but deception complicates any desired face-to-face meeting later on. Further, the sound of a person's voice shapes others' perceptions. When voice communication over the Internet becomes more prevalent, it is likely that our stereotypical notions will return. Dr. Clifford Nass of Stanford University has predicted that when voice becomes a part of online interaction, people will "apply gender stereotypes" (Eisenberg, 2000, para. 6). Nass says that people tend to interpret the female voice as being "less accurate," with deeper male voices projecting authority. Some voices are perceived as more attractive than others, too.

APA-STYLE IN-TEXT CITATION: Includes paragraph or screen number for direct quotation from online source without numbered pages

## Conclusions

CONCLUSIONS: Final segment summarizes main points and looks to the future

Research on Internet relationships suggests that communication without visual cues can increase people's acceptance of one another. In face-to-face meetings, people form impressions based solely on physical appearance, impressions that influence both the way they treat others and the way those people respond. People who are treated well, for example, tend to take on positive characteristics. Because Internet conversations rely more heavily on the quality of communication than on superficial factors, meeting online allows people to suspend judgments based on appearance. This advantage may disappear as images and sounds increasingly accompany online meetings. Perhaps society would be healthier if people judged others not by their looks but by their character as expressed in words and ideas; however, the current tendency to treat stereotypically attractive and unattractive people differently shows the remoteness of that ideal.

*continued ➤*

Effect of Physical Cues     9

References

Bakalar, N. (2005, May 3). Ugly children may get parental short shrift. *The New York Times,* p. F7.

Dion, K., Berscheid, E., & Walster, E. (1972). What is beautiful is good. *Journal of Personality and Social Psychology, 24,* 285–290.

Eisenberg, A. (2000, October 12). Mars and Venus on the Net: Gender stereotypes prevail. *New York Times on the Web.* Retrieved April 7, 2005, from http://www.nytimes.com/2000/10/12/technology/12VOIC.html

Hawfield, K., & Lyons, E. (1998). Conventional wisdom about women and Internet use: Refuting traditional perceptions. Retrieved March 25, 2005, from http://elab.vanderbilt.edu/research/papers/html/studentprojects/women/conventional_wisdom.html

Kachel, J. (1996, March). Good looks count during childhood. *Brown University Child and Adolescent Newsletter, 12*(3). Retrieved April 7, 2005, from Academic Search Elite database.

McKenna, K. Y., Green, A. S., & Gleason, M. E. (2003). Relationship formation on the Internet: What's the big attraction? *Journal of Social Issues, 58,* 9–31.

Miyake, K., & Zuckerman, M. (1993). Beyond personality impressions. *Journal of Personality, 61,* 411–436.

Nakamura, L. (2002). *Cybertypes: Race, ethnicity, and identity on the Internet.* New York: Routledge.

Singh, D. (2004). Mating strategies of young women: Role of physical attractiveness. *Journal of Sex Research, 41,* 43–54.

Begins References on new page

Double-spaces throughout

Lists References in alphabetical order by author

Provides a source that appears only on the Web

continued ➤

Effect of Physical Cues     10

Snyder, M., Tanke, E. D., & Berscheid, E. (1977). Social

perception and interpersonal behavior: On the

self-fulfilling nature of social stereotypes. *Journal*

*of Personality and Social Psychology, 35,* 656–666.

Sveningsson, M. (2002). Cyberlove: Creating romantic

relationships on the Net. In J. Fornäs, K. Klein,

M. Ladendorf, J. Sundén, & M. Sveningsson, (Eds.),

*Digital borderlands: Cultural studies of identity and*

*interactivity on the Internet* (pp. 48–78). New York: Lang.

**Provides source information for chapter in a book**

*APA*

# Chapter 36

## CHICAGO MANUAL (CM) AND COUNCIL OF SCIENCE EDITORS (CSE) DOCUMENTATION

This chapter presents two more systems of documentation (in addition to MLA STYLE in Chapter 34 and APA STYLE in Chapter 35). They are the styles of the University of Chicago Press (CM) and the Council of Science Editors (CSE). The following directory provides a list of the CM-style entries you'll find in this chapter. For the CSE directory, turn to page 678.

*continued* ➢

# CM-STYLE DOCUMENTATION

## 36a   What is CM-style documentation?

*The Chicago Manual of Style* (CM) endorses two styles of documentation. One CM style is an author-date style, similar to the APA style of IN-TEXT CITATIONS (Chapter 35), that includes a list of sources usually titled "Works Cited" or "References." The other CM style uses a **bibliographic note system**. This system gives information about each source in two places: (1) in a footnote (at the bottom of a page) or an endnote (on a separate page following your paper) and, (2) if required, in a BIBLIOGRAPHY that begins on a separate page. We present the bibliographic note system here because it's often used in courses in such humanities subjects as art, music, history, philosophy, and sometimes English. Within the bibliographic note system, there are two sub-styles: "full" and "abbreviated."

### THE FULL BIBLIOGRAPHIC NOTE SYSTEM IN CM STYLE

The CM full bibliographic note system requires you to give complete information, in a footnote or an endnote, the first time you cite a source. Because you're giving full information, you don't need to include a bibliography page. If you cite a source a second time, you provide shortened information that includes the last name(s) of the author(s) and the key words in the work's title. The following example uses the full bibliographic note system.

**TEXT**

Ulrich points out that both Europeans and Native Americans told war stories, but with different details and different emphases.[3]

**FULL FOOTNOTE (SAME PAGE) OR ENDNOTE**
**(SEPARATE PAGE FOLLOWING TEXT)**

3. Laurel Thatcher Ulrich, *Age of Homespun: Objects and Stories in the Creation of an American Myth* (New York: Knopf, 2001), 269.

**SECOND CITATION OF THIS SOURCE**

6. Ulrich, *Age of Homespun*, 285.

## THE ABBREVIATED BIBLIOGRAPHIC NOTE SYSTEM, PLUS BIBLIOGRAPHY, IN CM STYLE

In the abbreviated bibliographic note system, even your first endnote or footnote provides only brief information about the source. You provide complete information in a bibliography, which appears as a separate page at the end of the paper. Following is an example using the abbreviated bibliographic note system.

**TEXT**

Ulrich points out that both Europeans and Native Americans told war stories, but with different details and different emphases.[3]

**ABBREVIATED FOOTNOTE (SAME PAGE) OR ENDNOTE**
**(SEPARATE PAGE FOLLOWING TEXT)**

3. Ulrich, *Age of Homespun*, 269.

**BIBLIOGRAPHY (SEPARATE PAGE AT END OF THE PAPER)**

Ulrich, Laurel Thatcher. *Age of Homespun: Objects and Stories in the Creation of an American Myth*. New York: Knopf, 2001.

**ALERT:** Use either the full or the abbreviated bibliographic note style, but don't mix them. Ask your instructor which style he or she prefers. Remember that CM style requires a separate bibliography only if you use the abbreviated notes style. ◆

Box 36.1 (p. 666) provides guidelines for compiling CM-style bibliographic notes.

## Guidelines for compiling CM-style bibliographic notes

### TITLE AND PLACEMENT OF NOTES

If you're using endnotes, place them all on a separate page, before your bibliography. Center the heading "Notes," without using italics, underlining, or quotation marks, an inch from the top of the page. If you're using footnotes, place them at the bottom of the page on which the source needs to be credited. Never use a title above any note(s) at the foot of the page. CM generally uses blank space (not a line) to divide the footnote(s) from the body text.

### TITLE AND PLACEMENT OF BIBLIOGRAPHY

The abbreviated notes style requires a bibliography, which begins on a separate page at the end of the paper, following the endnotes page. An inch from the top of the page, center the heading "Bibliography" or "Works Cited" (either is acceptable in CM style). Don't underline the heading or put it in quotation marks.

### FORMAT FOR ENDNOTES AND FOOTNOTES

Include an endnote or a footnote every time you use a source. Number notes sequentially throughout your paper whether you're using endnotes or footnotes. Use superscript (raised) arabic numerals for the footnote or endnote numbers in your paper. Position note numbers after any punctuation mark except the dash. The number comes best at the end of a sentence, unless that position would be so far from the source material that the citation would be confusing. Don't use raised numbers in the endnote or footnote itself. Place the number followed by a period, on the same line as the content of the note. Single-space both within each note and between notes. Indent each note's first line about three-tenths of an inch (0.3″ tab), which equals about three characters, but place subsequent lines flush left at the margin.

### SPACING AFTER PUNCTUATION

A single space follows all punctuation, including the period.

### AUTHORS' NAMES

In endnotes and footnotes, give the name in standard (first-name-first) order, with names and initials as given in the original source. Use the word *and* before the last author's name if your source has two or three authors. For more than three authors, list only the first followed by *and others*. In the bibliography, invert the name: last name, first name. If a work has two or more authors, invert only the first author's name. If your source has up to ten authors, give all the authors' names. If your source has eleven or more authors, list only the first seven and use *et al.* for the rest.

## Guidelines for compiling CM-style bibliographic notes

**CAPITALIZATION OF SOURCE TITLES**

Capitalize the first and last words and all major words.

**SPECIAL TREATMENT OF TITLES**

Use italics for titles of long works, and use quotation marks around the titles of shorter works. Omit *A, An,* and *The* from the titles of newspapers and periodicals. For an unfamiliar newspaper title, list the city (and state, in parentheses, if the city isn't well known): *Newark (NJ) Star-Ledger,* for example. Use postal abbreviations for states.

**PUBLICATION INFORMATION**

Enclose publication information in parentheses. Use a colon and one space after the city of publication. Give complete publishers' names or abbreviate them according to standard abbreviations in *Books in Print*. Omit *The* before and *Co., Inc.,* and so on after a name. Spell out *University* or abbreviate to *Univ.* Never use *U* alone. Also spell out *Press*. Never use *P* alone. Don't abbreviate publication months.

**PAGE NUMBERS**

For inclusive page numbers, give the full second number for 2 through 99. For 100 and beyond, give the full second number only if a shortened version would be ambiguous: 243–47, 202–6, 300–404. List all discontinuous page numbers. (See "First Endnote or Footnote: Book" toward the end of this box.) Use a comma to separate parenthetical publication information from the page numbers that follow it. Use the abbreviations *p.* and *pp.* with page numbers only for material from newspapers, for material from journals that do not use volume numbers, and to avoid ambiguity.

**CONTENT NOTES**

Try to avoid using CONTENT NOTES. If you must use them, use footnotes, not endnotes, with symbols rather than numbers: an asterisk (*) for the first note on that page and a dagger (†) for a second note on that page.

**FIRST ENDNOTE OR FOOTNOTE: BOOK**

For books, include the author, title, publication information, and page numbers when applicable.

   1. Eudora Welty, *One Writer's Beginnings* (Cambridge, MA: Harvard University Press, 1984), 25–26, 30, 43–51, 208.

**SUMMARY BOX** **36.1** *continued*

## Guidelines for compiling CM-style bibliographic notes

### FIRST ENDNOTE OR FOOTNOTE: ARTICLE

For articles, include the author, article title, journal title, volume number, year, and page numbers.

1. D. D. Cochran, W. Daniel Hale, and Christine P. Hissam, "Personal Space Requirements in Indoor versus Outdoor Locations," *Journal of Psychology* 117 (1984): 132–33.

### SECOND MENTION IN ENDNOTES OR FOOTNOTES

Second (or later) citations of the same source can be brief. See 36b for an explanation.

## 36b What are CM guidelines for bibliographic notes?

The CM directory that appears at the beginning of this chapter corresponds to the sample bibliographic note forms that follow. In a few cases, we give sample bibliography forms as well. If you need a model that isn't here, consult *The Chicago Manual of Style*, Fifteenth Edition (Chicago: University of Chicago Press, 2003), which gives footnote, endnote, and bibliography forms for a multitude of sources.

### PRINTED AND RECORDED SOURCES

### 1. Book by One Author—CM

*Footnote or Endnote*

1. Eudora Welty, *One Writer's Beginnings* (Cambridge, MA: Harvard University Press, 1984).

*Bibliography*

Welty, Eudora. *One Writer's Beginnings*. Cambridge, MA: Harvard University Press, 1984.

The format for the bibliography is the reverse of the format for the note, in which first lines indent. In bibliographic form, the first line is placed flush left to the margin and the second and other lines are indented three-tenths to one half inch (0.3″–0.5″ tab). Notice also where periods replace commas and where parentheses are omitted.

## 2. Book by Two or Three Authors—CM

*Footnote or Endnote*

1. Edward E. Gordon and Elaine H. Gordon, *Literacy in America: Historic Journey and Contemporary Solutions* (Westport, CT: Praeger, 2003).

2. John K. Lynam, Cyrus G. Ndiritu, and Adiel N. Mbabu, *Transformation of Agricultural Research Systems in Africa: Lessons from Kenya* (East Lansing: Michigan State University Press, 2004), 41.

*Bibliography*

Lynam, John K., Cyrus G. Ndiritu, and Adiel N. Mbabu. *Transformation of Agricultural Research Systems in Africa: Lessons from Kenya.* East Lansing: Michigan State University Press, 2004.

In a bibliography entry, invert only the name of the first author listed.

## 3. Book by More Than Three Authors—CM

1. Wendy Saul and others, *Beyond the Science Fair: Creating a Kids' Inquiry Conference* (Portsmouth, NH: Heinemann, 2005), 72.

## 4. Multiple Citations of a Single Source—CM

For subsequent references to a work you've already named, use a shortened citation. Give the last name of the author, the title of the work, and the page number, all separated by commas. Shorten the title if it's longer than four words. This example shows the form for a subsequent reference to the work fully described in item 1.

1. Welty, *One Writer's Beginnings*, 25.

If there are more than three authors for a source, use only the name of the first author, followed by *and others* or *et al.* The following example shows the shortened citation for the work in item 3.

2. Saul et al., *Beyond the Science Fair*, 72.

If you cite two or more authors with the same last name, include first names or initials in each note.

3. Eudora Welty, *One Writer's Beginnings*, 25.

4. Paul Welty, *Human Expression*, 129.

If you cite the same source as the source immediately preceding, you may use *ibid.* (capitalized at the beginning of a note), followed by a comma and the page number, instead of repeating the author's name and the title.

5. Ibid., 152.

### 5. Book by a Group or Corporate Author—CM

1. American Psychological Association, *Publication Manual of the American Psychological Association*, 5th ed. (Washington, DC: American Psychological Association, 2001).

2. Boston Women's Health Collective, *Our Bodies, Ourselves for the New Century* (New York: Simon & Schuster, 1998).

If a work issued by an organization has no author listed on the title page, give the name of the organization as the author of the work. The organization may also be the publisher of the work.

### 6. Book with No Author Named—CM

1. *The Chicago Manual of Style*, 15th ed. (Chicago: University of Chicago Press, 2003).

Begin the citation with the name of the book.

### 7. Book with an Author and an Editor—CM

1. Emily Brontë, *Wuthering Heights*, ed. Richard J. Dunn (New York: Norton, 2002).

In this position, the abbreviation *ed.* stands for "edited by," not "editor." Therefore, *ed.* is correct whether a work has one or more than one editor. (Also see items 10 and 16.)

### 8. Translation—CM

1. Milan Kundera, *The Unbearable Lightness of Being*, trans. Michael Henry Heim (New York: HarperPerennial Library, 1999).

The abbreviation *trans.* stands for "translated by," not "translator."

### 9. Work in Several Volumes or Parts—CM

The following notes show ways to give bibliographic information for a specific place in one volume of a multivolume work. Use whichever you prefer, staying consistent throughout a paper.

1. Ernest Jones, *The Last Phase*, vol. 3 of *The Life and Work of Sigmund Freud* (New York: Basic Books, 1957), 97.

1. Ernest Jones, *The Life and Work of Sigmund Freud*, vol. 3, *The Last Phase* (New York: Basic Books, 1957), 97.

If you're citing an entire work in two or more volumes, use the form shown below.

> 2. Ronald Chrisley, ed., *Artificial Intelligence: Critical Concepts*, 4 vols. (London: Routledge, 2000).

## 10. One Selection from an Anthology or an Edited Book—CM

> 1. Ernest Galarza, "The Roots of Migration," in *Aztlan: An Anthology of Mexican American Literature*, ed. Luis Valdez and Stan Steiner (New York: Knopf, 1972), 127–32.

Give page numbers for the cited selection.

## 11. More Than One Selection from an Anthology or an Edited Book—CM

If you cite more than one selection from the same anthology or edited book, give complete bibliographical information in each citation.

## 12. Signed Article in a Reference Book—CM

> 1. John C. Burnbam, "Freud, Sigmund," in *The Encyclopedia of Psychiatry, Psychology, and Psychoanalysis*, ed. Benjamin B. Wolman (New York: Henry Holt, 1996), 220.

## 13. Unsigned Article in a Reference Book—CM

> 1. *Encyclopaedia Britannica*, 15th ed., s.v. "Ireland."

The abbreviation *s.v.* stands for *sub verbo*, meaning "under the word." Capitalize the heading of the entry only if it's a proper noun. Omit publication information except for the edition number.

## 14. Second or Later Edition—CM

> 1. Anthony F. Janson, *History of Art*, 6th ed. (New York: Abrams, 2001).

Here the abbreviation *ed.* stands for "edition." Give the copyright date for the edition you're citing.

## 15. Anthology or Edited Book—CM

> 1. Eduardo del Rio, ed., *The Prentice Hall Anthology of Latino Literature* (Upper Saddle River, NJ: Prentice Hall, 2002).

Here the abbreviation *ed.* stands for "editor." For a source with two or more editors, use the plural *eds.*

### 16. Introduction, Preface, Foreword, or Afterword—CM

1. Elizabeth Fox-Genovese, foreword to *Southern Mothers*, ed. Nagueyalti Warren and Sally Wolff (Baton Rouge: Louisiana State University Press, 1999).

If the author of the book is different from the author of the cited part, give the name of the book's author or editor after the title of the book, preceded by the word *by* or *ed.* (for "edited by").

### 17. Unpublished Dissertation or Essay—CM

1. Michele Byers, "*Buffy the Vampire Slayer:* The Insurgence of Television as a Performance Text" (PhD diss., University of Toronto, 2000), 23–24.

List the author's name first, then the title in quotation marks (not italicized), a descriptive label (such as *PhD diss.* or *master's thesis*), the degree-granting institution, the date, and finally the page numbers you're citing.

1. Peter Leslie Mortensen, "Meet the Press: Reading News Coverage of Research on Writing" (paper presented at the annual meeting of the Modern Language Association, Washington, DC, December 29, 2005).

To cite a paper read at a meeting, give the name of the meeting in parentheses, along with the location and the date.

### 18. Reprint of an Older Book—CM

1. Marian Anderson, *My Lord, What a Morning* (1956; repr., Urbana: University of Illinois Press, 2002).

Republishing information is located on the copyright page. List the original date of publication first, followed by the publication information for the reprint.

### 19. Book in a Series—CM

1. Dorothy J. Goldman, *Women Writers and World War I*, Literature and Society Series (New York: Macmillan, 1995).

If the series numbers its volumes and the volume number isn't part of the title, you would include the volume number after the series title. Separate the volume number from the series title with a comma.

### 20. Book with a Title Within a Title—CM

1. Aljean Harmetz, *The Making of "The Wizard of Oz"* (New York: Hyperion, 1998).

If the name of a work that's usually italicized appears in an italicized title, put quotation marks around it. If the name of a work that's usually in quotation marks appears in an italicized title, keep it in quotation marks.

### 21. Government Publication—CM

1. House Committee on Resources, *Coastal Heritage Trail Route in New Jersey*, 106th Cong., 1st sess., 1999, H. Rep. 16.

If a government department, bureau, agency, or committee produces a document, cite that group as the author. In a bibliography entry, the author is often identified as *U.S. Congress*, followed by either *House* or *Senate* and the committee or subcommittee, if any, before the title of the document.

### 22. Published Proceedings of a Conference—CM

1. Anne Dobyns, "Civil Disobedience and the Ethical Appeal of Self-Representation," in *Rhetorical Democracy: Discursive Practices of Civic Engagement,* ed. Gerald A. Hauser and Amy Grim (Mahwah, NJ: Erlbaum, 2003), 131–36.

Treat published conference proceedings as you would a chapter in a book.

### 23. Signed Article in a Daily Newspaper—CM

1. Peter T. Kilborn, "A Health Threat Baffling for Its Lack of a Pattern," *New York Times,* sec. A, June 22, 2003, national edition.

Many newspapers print more than one edition a day and reposition the same articles on different pages. CM style recommends that, when applicable, you identify the specific edition (such as *Southeastern edition* or *final edition*); make this the last information in the entry, preceded by a comma. For a paper that specifies sections, use *sec.* before the section's letter or number or use *section* for a section's name (such as *Weekend section*). If a paper gives column titles, you may use the title (not italicized or in quotation marks) in addition to or in place of the article title. Separate all items with commas.

### 24. Editorial, Letter to the Editor, or Review—CM

1. "Downtown's Architectural Promise," editorial, *New York Times,* sec. A, August 4, 2003.

2. Roger P. Hanson, letter to the editor, *Sierra,* January/February 2003, 8.

3. Joan Didion, "The Day Was Hot and Still . . . ," review of *Dutch: A Memoir of Ronald Reagan,* by Edmund Morris, *New York Review of Books,* November 4, 1999, 4–6.

Before page numbers, use a comma for popular magazines and a colon for journals.

### 25. Unsigned Article in a Daily Newspaper—CM

1. "Changes Sought in Medical Services for Veterans," *New York Times*, sec. A, August 5, 2003.

### 26. Signed Article in a Weekly or Biweekly Magazine or Newspaper—CM

1. Christine Gorman, "How to Age Gracefully," *Time*, June 6, 2005, 73–74.

For general-readership weekly and biweekly magazines and newspapers, give the month, day, and year of publication. Separate page numbers from the year with a comma.

### 27. Signed Article in a Monthly or Bimonthly Periodical—CM

1. Tom Bissell, "A Comet's Tale: On the Science of Apocalypse," *Harper's*, February 2003, 33.

For general-readership monthly and bimonthly magazines, give the month and year of publication. Separate page numbers from the year with a comma.

### 28. Unsigned Article in a Weekly or Monthly Periodical—CM

1. "The Price Is Wrong," *Economist*, August 2, 2003, 58–59.

### 29. Article in a Collection of Reprinted Articles—CM

1. Thomas Hayden, "The Age of Robots," in *Applied Science*, Social Issues Resources Series (Boca Raton, FL: Social Issues Resources, 2002).

Cite only the publication actually consulted, not the original source. If you use a bibliography, cite its location in both the reprinted publication you consulted and the publication where the article first appeared.

### 30. Article in a Journal with Continuous Pagination—CM

1. Phyllis Tyson, "The Psychology of Women Continued," *Journal of the American Psychoanalytic Association* 46, no. 2 (1998): 361–64.

### 31. Article in a Journal That Pages Each Issue Separately—CM

1. Linda Adler-Kassner and Heidi Estrem, "Rethinking Research Writing: Public Literacy in the Composition Classroom," *WPA: Writing Program Administration* 26, no. 3 (2003): 119–31.

The issue number of a journal is required if each issue of the journal starts with page 1. In this example, the volume number is 26 and the issue number, abbreviated *no.*, is 3.

## 32. Personal Interview—CM

1. Randi Friedman, interview by author, September 30, 2005, Austin, Texas.

For an unpublished interview, give the name of the interviewee and the interviewer, the date of the interview, and the location of the interview. CM style recommends that you incorporate this information into the text, rather than place it in a note.

## 33. Published and Unpublished Letters—CM

1. William Carlos Williams to his son, 13 March 1935, in *Letters of the Century: America 1900–1999*, ed. Lisa Grunwald and Stephen J. Adler (New York: Dial, 1999), 225–26.

2. Theodore Brown, letter to author, December 7, 2005.

For an unpublished letter, give the name of the writer, the name of the recipient, and the date the letter was written.

## 34. Film, Videotape, or DVD—CM

1. Marc Norman and Tom Stoppard, *Shakespeare in Love*, DVD (1998; New York: Miramax Films/Universal Pictures, 2003).

2. Robert Riskin, *It Happened One Night*, VHS (1934; Hollywood: Columbia Pictures, 1999).

In note 1, the first information gives the authors of the screenplay. If the point of the note was about the director or the producers, then the title would appear first and *"directed by"* or *"produced by"* would follow a comma after the title along with the relevant names.

## 35. Sound Recording—CM

1. Bedrich Smetana, *My Country*, Czech Philharmonic, Karel Anserl, Vanguard SV-9/10.

Bedrich Smetana is the composer, and Karel Anserl is the conductor.

2. Bruce Springsteen, "Lonesome Day," on *The Rising*, Sony CD B000069 HKH.

## 36. Computer Software—CM

1. *Dreamweaver*, Ver. MX, Macromedia, San Francisco, CA.

Place the version or release number, abbreviated *Ver.* or *Rel.*, directly after the name of the software. Then, list the company that owns the rights to the software, followed by that company's location.

### 37. ERIC Information Service—CM

1. Hunter M. Breland, *Assessing Writing Skills* (New York: College Entrance Examination Board, 1987), ERIC, ED 286920.

*ERIC* stands for *Educational Resources Information Center.*

### 38. Secondary Source—CM

1. Mary Wollstonecraft, *A Vindication of the Rights of Woman* (1792), 90, quoted in Caroline Shrodes, Harry Finestone, and Michael Shugrue, *The Conscious Reader*, 4th ed. (New York: Macmillan, 1988), 282.

When you quote one person's words, having found them in another person's work, give information as fully as you can about both sources. CM style recommends, however, that original sources be consulted and cited whenever practical.

2. Caroline Shrodes, Harry Finestone, and Michael Shugrue, *The Conscious Reader*, 4th ed. (New York: Macmillan, 1988), 282, quoting Mary Wollstonecraft, *A Vindication of the Rights of Woman* (1792), 90.

#### ELECTRONIC SOURCES

If there is a print version of the source (as in item 42), provide information about that source. Also include information about how to find the electronic version. Unlike some other documentation styles (such as MLA), CM style doesn't generally recommend including access dates, nor does it use angle brackets around URLs. Following are examples in CM style of a few common types of electronic sources. For additional types, consult *The Chicago Manual of Style.*

### 39. Source from a CD-ROM or DVD—CM

If you're citing a portion of a CD-ROM or DVD, include the author (if named) and title of that portion, then the title of the disk, the publisher, and the date. The following example omits the author's name.

1. "Artificial Intelligence," *Encarta Reference Library Premium 2005*, DVD. Microsoft, 2005.

### 40. Online Book—CM

Include the author's name, the title, and access information—in this case, the name of the organization that sponsors the site, and the URL.

1. Kate Chopin, *The Awakening* (Washington, DC: PBS, 1998), http://www.pbs.org/katechopin/library/awakening.

### 41. Article from a Periodical Available Only Online—CM

Include the author, title of the article, title of the publication, volume and issue number (if given), publication date, and URL.

1. Veronica Austen, "Writing Spaces: Performances of the Word," *Kairos* 8, no. 1 (2003), http://english.ttu.edu/kairos/8.1/binder2.html?coverweb/austen/austen.html.

## 42. Article Accessed Through a Database—CM

Include the author, title of the article, title of the publication, volume and issue numbers (if given) of the original publication, the original publication date, and the URL of the database through which you accessed the article. CM style recommends that you include an access date when citing information retrieved through a database. Insert the access date in parentheses after the URL, followed by a period.

1. Gail Dutton, "Greener Pigs," *Popular Science* 255, no. 5 (November 1999): 38–39, http://proquest.umi.com (accessed September 2, 2005).

## 43. Source from an Internet Site—CM

Provide the author's name, the title of the Web page, the title or owner of the site, and the URL. When no specific author is listed, you may use the owner of the site as the author, as in the following example. Include an access date if your source is likely to be updated frequently, as is often the case with Internet sites.

1. American Association for Artificial Intelligence, "AI Overview," American Association for Artificial Intelligence, http://www.aaai.org/AITopics/html/overview.html (accessed December 22, 2005).

## 44. Electronic Mailing List—CM

1. T. Caruso, e-mail to Calls for Papers mailing list, June 30, 2002, http://www.cfp.english.upenn.edu/archive/2002-09/0041.html.

## 45. E-Mail Message—CM

1. Jim Thompson, e-mail message to author, November 11, 2005.

### GRAPHICS

Place the credit line for a table or illustration from another source next to or directly below the reproduced material. (If you intend to publish your paper, you must obtain permission to reprint copyrighted material from its source.) Spell out the terms *map, plate,* and *table,* but abbreviate *figure* as *fig.*

Reprinted by permission from Dennis Remington, A. Garth Fisher, and Edward Parent, *How to Lower Your Fat Thermostat: The No-Diet Reprogramming Plan for Lifelong Weight Control* (Provo, UT: Vitality House International, 1983), 74, fig. A2–1.

CM

## CSE-STYLE DOCUMENTATION

### 36c    What is CSE-style documentation?

The Council of Biology Editors is also known as the Council of Science Editors, or CSE. The information in this chapter adheres to the style guidelines in the sixth edition of *Scientific Style and Format* (1994); however, at the time of writing this handbook, the CSE is preparing a seventh edition. For up-to-date information, go to the organization's Web site at <http://www.councilscienceeditors.org>.

The CSE endorses two documentation systems widely used in mathematics and the physical and life sciences. The first system uses name-year parenthetical references in the text of a paper, together with an alphabetically arranged Cited References (or References) list. This kind of IN-TEXT CITATION system tied to a required BIBLIOGRAPHY is similar to both MLA STYLE (Chapter 34) and APA STYLE (Chapter 35).

The second CSE system marks citations in the text of a paper with numbers that correlate with a numerically arranged Cited References list. Read on to learn how the numbered reference system, sometimes referred to as a *citation-sequence system,* works:

1. The first time you cite each source in your paper, assign it an arabic number in sequence, starting with 1.

2. Mark each subsequent reference to that source with the assigned number.

3. Use superscript (raised) numbers for source citations in your sentences, although numbers in parentheses are also acceptable.

4. Don't use footnotes or endnotes to credit your sources. Use only a Cited References list, and number the entries in the order of their appearance in your paper. Start with the number 1, followed by a period, and then the content of the citation. Never list sources alphabetically. Never underline or use italics for titles of works.

Here's an example of a sentence that includes in-text citations and the corresponding cited references.

**IN-TEXT CITATIONS**

Sybesma[1] insists that this behavior occurs periodically, but Crowder[2] claims never to have observed it.

**CITED REFERENCES**

1. Sybesma C. An introduction to biophysics. New York: Academic; 1977. 648 p.

2. Crowder W. Seashore life between the tides. New York: Dodd, Mead; 1931. New York: Dover Reprint; 1975. 372 p.

Thereafter, throughout your paper, follow each citation of Sybesma's *Introduction to Biophysics* by a superscript [1] and each citation of Crowder's *Seashore Life* by a superscript [2].

When you're citing more than one reference—for example, a new source and three previous sources as well as a source from your first page—list each source number, followed by a comma with no space. Use a hyphen to show the range of numbers in a continuous sequence, and put all in superscript: [2,5–7,9]

Box 36.2 gives guidelines for compiling a Cited References list.

**SUMMARY BOX 36.2**

**CSE**

# Guidelines for compiling a CSE-style Cited References list

**TITLE**

Use "Cited References" or "References" as the title (no underlining, no italics, no quotations marks).

**PLACEMENT OF LIST**

Begin the list on a separate page at the end of the research paper. Number the page sequentially with the rest of the paper.

## Guidelines for compiling a CSE-style Cited References list

**CONTENT AND FORMAT OF CITED REFERENCES**

Include all sources that you quote, paraphrase, or summarize in your paper. Center the title one inch from the top of the page. Start each entry on a new line. Put the number, followed by a period and a space, at the regular left margin. If an entry takes more than one line, indent the second and all other lines under the first word, not the number. Single-space each entry and double-space between entries.

**SPACING AFTER PUNCTUATION**

CSE style specifies no space after date, issue number, or volume number of a periodical, as shown in the models in 36d.

**ARRANGEMENT OF ENTRIES**

Sequence and number the entries in the precise order in which you first used them in the body of your paper.

**AUTHORS' NAMES**

Reverse the order of each author's name, giving the last name first. For book citations, you can give first names or use only the initials of first and (when available) middle names; for journal citations, use only initials. (CSE style recommends you use only initials when your list includes both book and journal citations.) Don't use a period or a space between first and middle initials. Use a comma to separate the names of multiple authors identified by initials; however, if you use full first names, use a semicolon. Don't use *and* or *&* with authors' names. Place a period after the last author's name.

**TREATMENT OF TITLES**

Never underline titles or enclose them in quotation marks. Capitalize a title's first word and any proper nouns. Don't capitalize the first word of a subtitle unless it's a proper noun. Capitalize the titles of academic journals. If the title of a periodical is one word, give it in full; otherwise, abbreviate the title according to recommendations established by the *American National Standard for Abbreviations of Titles of Periodicals.* Capitalize a newspaper title's major words, giving the full title but omitting *A, An,* or *The* at the beginning.

**PLACE OF PUBLICATION**

Use a colon after the city of publication. If the city name could be unfamiliar to readers, add in parentheses the postal abbreviation for the US state or Canadian province. If the location of a foreign city will be unfamiliar to readers, add in parentheses the country name, abbreviating it according to International Organization for Standardization (ISO) standards. Find ISO abbreviations at <http://un.org/Depts/cartographic/english/geoinfo/geoname.pdf>.

**SUMMARY BOX** 36.2 *continued*

## Guidelines for compiling a CSE-style Cited References list

### PUBLISHER

Give the name of the publisher, without periods after initials, and use a semi-colon after the publisher's name. Omit *The* at the beginning or *Co., Inc., Ltd.,* or *Press* at the end. However, for a university press, abbreviate *University* and *Press* as *Univ* and *Pr,* respectively, without periods.

### PUBLICATION MONTH

Abbreviate all month names longer than three letters to their first three letters, but do not add a period.

### INCLUSIVE PAGE NUMBERS

Shorten the second number as much as possible, making sure that the number isn't ambiguous. For example, use 233–4 for 233 to 234; 233–44 for 233 to 244; but 233–304 (not 233-04) for 233 to 304.

### DISCONTINUOUS PAGE NUMBERS

Give the numbers of all discontinuous pages, separating successive numbers or ranges with a comma: 54–7, 60–6.

### TOTAL PAGE NUMBERS

In the citation for an entire book, the last information unit gives the total number of book pages, followed by the abbreviation *p* and a period.

### FORMAT FOR CITED REFERENCES ENTRIES: BOOKS

Citations for books usually list author(s), title, publication information, and pages (either total pages when citing an entire work or inclusive pages when citing part of a book). Each unit of information ends with a period.

1. Primrose SB, Twyman RM, Old RW. Principles of gene manipulation. London: Blackwell; 2002. 390 p.

### FORMAT FOR CITED REFERENCES ENTRIES: ARTICLES

List author(s), article title, and journal name and publication information, and follow each section with a period. Abbreviate a journal's name only if it's standard in your scientific discipline. For example, *Exp Neurol* is the abbreviated form for *Experimental Neurology.* In the following example, the volume number is 184, and the issue number, in parentheses, is 1. Notice there is no space after the semicolon, before the parentheses, or after the colon.

1. Ginis I, Rao MS. Toward cell replacement therapy: promises and caveats. Exp Neurol 2003;184(1):61–77.

**CSE**

## 36d What are CSE guidelines for sources on a list of references?

The CSE directory on page 678 corresponds to the sample references that follow. If you need a model not included in this book, consult *Scientific Style and Format*. If you're looking for examples for citing electronic and online sources, consult a recent issue of a journal in the discipline in which you're writing.

### 1. Book by One Author—CSE

1. Hawking SW. Black holes and baby universes and other essays. New York: Bantam Books; 1993. 320 p.

Use one space but no punctuation between an author's last name and the initial of the first name. Don't put punctuation or a space between first and middle initials (*Hawking SW*). Do, however, use the hyphen in a hyphenated first and middle name (for example, *Gille J-C* represents *Jean-Claude Gille* in the next item).

### 2. Book by More Than One Author—CSE

1. Wegzyn S, Gille J-C, Vidal P. Developmental systems: at the crossroads of system theory, computer science, and genetic engineering. New York: Springer-Verlag; 1990. 595 p.

### 3. Book by a Group or Corporate Author—CSE

1. Chemical Rubber Company. Handbook of laboratory safety. 3rd ed. Boca Raton (FL): CRC; 1990. 1352 p.

### 4. Anthology or Edited Book—CSE

1. Heerman B, Hummel S, editors. Ancient DNA: recovery and analysis of genetic material from paleontological, archeological, museum, medical, and forensic specimens. New York: Springer-Verlag; 1994. 1020 p.

### 5. One Selection or Chapter from an Anthology or Edited Book—CSE

1. Basov NG, Feoktistov LP, Senatsky YV. Laser driver for inertial confinement fusion. In: Bureckner KA, editor. Research trends in physics: inertial confinement fusion. New York: American Institute of Physics; 1992. p 24–37.

### 6. Translation—CSE

1. Magris C. A different sea. Spurr MS, translator. London: Harvill; 1993. 194 p. Translation of: Un mare differente.

### 7. Reprint of an Older Book—CSE

1. Carson R. The sea around us. New York: Oxford Univ Pr; 1951. New York: Oxford Univ Pr; 1991. 288 p.

### 8. All Volumes of a Multivolume Work—CSE

1. Crane FL, Moore DJ, Low HE, editors. Oxidoreduction at the plasma membrane: relation to growth and transport. Boca Raton (FL): CRC; 1991. 2 vol.

### 9. Unpublished Dissertation or Thesis—CSE

1. Baykul MC. Using ballistic electron emission microscopy to investigate the metal-vacuum interface [dissertation]. Orem (UT): Polytechnic Univ Pr; 1993. 111 p. Available from: UMI Dissertation Express, http://tls.il.proquest.com/hp/Products/DisExpress.html, Document 9332714.

### 10. Published Article from Conference Proceedings—CSE

1. Tsang CP, Bellgard MI. Sequence generation using a network of Boltzmann machines. In: Tsang CP, editor. Proceedings of the 4th Australian Joint Conference on Artificial Intelligence; 1990 Nov 8–11; Perth, AUS. Singapore: World Scientific; 1990. p 224–33.

### 11. Signed Newspaper Article—CSE

1. Kilborn PT. A health threat baffling for its lack of a pattern. New York Times 2003 Jun 22;Sect A:14.

*Sect* stands for *section.* Note that there is no space between the date and the section.

### 12. Unsigned Newspaper Article—CSE

1. [Anonymous]. Supercomputing center to lead security effort. Pantagraph (Bloomington, IL) 2003 Jul 4;Sect A:7.

### 13. Article in a Journal with Continuous Pagination—CSE

1. Aldhous P. More heat than light. Nature 2003;420:730.

Give only the volume number (*420*), not an issue number, before the page numbers. Note that there is no space between the year and the volume or the volume and the page.

### 14. Article in a Journal That Pages Each Issue Separately—CSE

1. Ginis I, Rao MS. Toward cell replacement therapy: promises and caveats. Exp Neurol 2003;184(1):61–77.

Give both the volume number and the issue number (here, *184* is the volume number and *1* is the issue number).

**CSE**

### 15. Journal Article on Discontinuous Pages—CSE

1. Richards FM. The protein folding problem. Sci Am 1991;246(1):54–7, 60–6.

### 16. Article with Author Affiliation—CSE

1. DeMoll E, Auffenberg T (Department of Microbiology, University of Kentucky). Purine metabolism in *Methanococcus vannielii*. J Bacteriol 1993;175:5754–61.

### 17. Entire Issue of a Journal—CSE

1. Whales in a modern world: a symposium held in London, November 1988. Mamm Rev 1990 Jan;20(9).

The date of the symposium, November 1988, is part of the title of this issue.

### 18. Article with No Identifiable Author—CSE

1. [Anonymous]. Cruelty to animals linked to murders of humans. AWIQ 1993 Aug;42(3):16.

### 19. Map—CSE

1. Russia and post-Soviet republics [political map]. Moscow: Mapping Production Association; 1992. Conical equidistant projection; 40 × 48 in.; color, scale 1:8,000,000.

### 20. Unpublished Letter—CSE

1. Darwin C. [Letter to Mr. Clerke, 1861]. Located at: University of Iowa Library, Iowa City (IA).

### 21. Video Recording—CSE

1. Nova—The elegant universe [DVD]. Boston: WGBH; 2004. 2 DVDs: 180 min, sound, color.

### 22. Slide Set—CSE

1. Human parasitology [slides]. Chicago: American Society of Clinical Pathologists; 1990. Color. Accompanied by: 1 guide.

### 23. Electronic Sources—CSE

The CSE guidelines for citing electronic sources follow the *National Library of Medicine Recommended Formats for Bibliographic Citation*, available at <http://www.nlm.nih.gov/pubs/formats/internet.pdf>.

In general, the CSE style book advises that you cite electronic sources by including the author's name, if available; the work's title; the type of medium, in brackets, such as [Internet] or [electronic mail on the Internet]; the title of the publication if there's a print version or, if not, the place of publication and the publishing organization; the date the original was published or placed on the Internet; the date you accessed the publication, preceded by the word *cited* enclosed in brackets; and the address of the source, if from the Internet or a database. Omit end punctuation after an Internet address.

1. Overbye D. Remembrance of things future: the mystery of time. The New York Times on the Web [Internet]. 2005 Jun 28 [cited 2005 Dec 11]. Available from: http://www.nytimes.com/2005/06/28/science/28time.html

**CSE**

# Writing Across the Curriculum —and Beyond

# Chapter 37

---

## COMPARING THE DISCIPLINES

### 37a  What is Writing Across the Curriculum?

Writing Across the Curriculum refers to the writing you do in college courses beyond first-year composition. Good writing in various subject areas, such as history, biology, or psychology, has many common features. However, there are also important differences. A lab report for a chemistry course, for example, differs from a paper for a literature course. This section will help you adapt general principles of writing so you'll be successful in writing across the curriculum.

People commonly group academic disciplines into three broad categories: the humanities, the social sciences, and the natural sciences. Each has its own knowledge, vocabulary, and perspectives on the world; its own specialized assignments and purposes; its own common types of SOURCES; and its own expected documentation styles. Think of learning to write in a discipline as starting to become a member of a specialized audience, beginning to know what existing members know and to write as they write.

No matter what differences exist among the academic disciplines, writing processes and strategies interconnect and overlap across the curriculum. Types of writing such as SUMMARIES, ANALYSES, and SYNTHESES are common in various disciplines. Box 37.1 compares elements of the academic disciplines.

To understand some of the differences among the disciplines, consider these three quite different paragraphs about a mountain.

#### HUMANITIES

The mountain stands above all that surrounds it. Giant timber—part of a collage of evergreen and deciduous trees—conceals the expansive mountain's slope, where cattle once grazed. At the base of the mountain, a cool stream flows over rocks of all sizes, colors, and shapes. Next to the outer bank of the stream stands a shingled farmhouse, desolate, yet suggesting its active past. Unfortunately, the peaceful scene is interrupted by billboards and chairlifts, landmarks of a modern, fast-paced life.

**SUMMARY BOX** 37.1

## Comparing the disciplines

| DISCIPLINE | TYPES OF ASSIGNMENTS | PRIMARY SOURCES | SECONDARY SOURCES | USUAL DOCUMENTATION STYLES |
|---|---|---|---|---|
| **HUMANITIES** e.g., history, languages, literature, philosophy, art, music, theater | essays, response statements, reviews, analyses, original works such as stories, poems, memoirs | literary works, manuscripts, paintings and sculptures, historical documents, films, plays, photographs, artifacts from popular culture | reviews, journal articles, research papers, books | MLA, CMS |
| **SOCIAL SCIENCES** e.g., psychology, sociology, anthropology, education | research reports, case studies, reviews of the literature, analyses | surveys, interviews, observations, tests and measures | journal articles, scholarly books, literature reviews | APA |
| **NATURAL SCIENCES** e.g., biology, chemistry, physics, mathematics | research reports, research proposals, science reviews | experiments, field notes and direct observations, measurements | journal articles, research papers, books | often CSE but varies by discipline |

**SOCIAL SCIENCES**

Among the favorite pastimes of North American city dwellers is the "return to nature." Many outdoor enthusiasts hope to enjoy a scenic trip to the mountains, only to be disappointed. They know they have arrived at the mountain that they have traveled hundreds of miles to see because huge billboards are directing them to its base. As they look up the mountain, dozens of people are riding over the treetops in a chairlift, littering the slope with paper cups and food wrappers. At the base of the mountain stands the inevitable refreshment stand, found at virtually all American tourist attractions. Land developers consider such commercialization a way to preserve and utilize natural resources, but environmentalists are appalled.

**NATURAL SCIENCES**

The mountain rises approximately 5,600 feet above sea level. The underlying rock is igneous, of volcanic origin, composed primarily of granites and feldspars. Three distinct biological communities are present on the mountain. The community at the top of the mountain is alpine, dominated by very short grasses and forbs. At middle altitudes, the community is a typical northern boreal coniferous forest community, and at the base and lower altitudes, deciduous forest is the dominant community. This community has, however, been highly affected by agricultural development along the river at its base and by recreational development.

These examples illustrate that each discipline has its own perspective and emphasis. The paragraph written for the humanities describes the mountain from the writer's perspective—personal, yet representative of a wider human response. The paragraph written for the social sciences focuses on the behavior of people as a group. The paragraph written for the natural sciences reports observations of natural phenomena.

When you write papers for courses in different disciplines, keep in mind both the strategies important for all academic writing situations and the characteristics needed in specific disciplines, as summarized in Box 37.2.

Consider the following examples of how various different disciplines can interconnect.

- In a humanities class, you might read *Lives of a Cell,* a collection of essays about science and nature written by the noted physician and author Lewis Thomas. As you consider the literary style of the writer, you also think deeply about biology and other sciences.

- In a philosophy class exploring the concept of infinity, you might read selections from *A Brief History of Time* by the astronomer Stephen Hawking.

- In an art history class discussing the Italian Renaissance, you might read social and political histories to understand how artists at the time earned a living and how that influenced their choice of subject matter.

- In an education course, you might read court decisions and laws to understand how and why schools must meet the needs of people with disabilities.

## SUMMARY BOX 37.2

### Strategies important in all academic writing situations

1. Consider your PURPOSE, AUDIENCE, and TONE (Chapter 1).
2. Use the WRITING PROCESS to PLAN, SHAPE, DRAFT, REVISE, EDIT, and PROOFREAD (Chapter 2).
3. Develop a THESIS STATEMENT (Chapter 2).
4. Arrange and organize your ideas (Chapter 2).
5. Determine what kind of evidence you need for the paper (Chapters 2–3).
6. Determine whether you need primary or secondary sources (37b).
7. Analyze features of the writing required in the assignment (37c).
8. Develop paragraphs thoroughly (Chapter 3).
9. Critically read, think, synthesize, and write (Chapter 4).
10. Reason well; use good logic (Chapter 4).
11. Write effective sentences (Chapters 16–19).
12. Choose words well (Chapters 19–21).
13. Use correct grammar (Chapters 7–15).
14. Spell correctly (Chapter 22).
15. Use correct punctuation and mechanics (Chapters 23–30).
16. Use the appropriate documentation style, if you use sources (Chapters 34–36).

## 37b What are primary research and secondary research in the disciplines?

PRIMARY SOURCES offer you firsthand exposure to texts or information, providing the exciting experience of discovering material on your own. Primary sources differ considerably between the disciplines. In the humanities, primary sources are original creative works, including novels, stories, poems, autobiographies, plays, films, musical compositions, and works of art (Chapter 38). In the social and natural sciences, primary sources may include books and articles in which researchers report findings from their research studies for the first time. You might also complete your own primary research, conducting experiments, surveys, or careful observations (Chapter 39).

SECONDARY SOURCES are scholarly writings that SUMMARIZE, ANALYZE, or SYNTHESIZE primary sources. In the humanities, secondary sources offer analysis and interpretation of primary works. In the social and natural sciences, secondary sources summarize, then synthesize findings, and draw parallels that offer new insights.

## 37c   What can help me write assignments in various disciplines?

A useful strategy for writing assignments in different disciplines is to analyze successful writings that match the requirements of your assignment. After all, the expectations for a proposal you might write for a marketing course will probably differ from those for an essay in a history class. Instructors sometimes provide models for such papers or point you to similar published works. Following are some types of questions that will help you analyze model writings.

1. Are papers divided by subheadings or not?
2. Are specific parts required? Is there a specified format?
3. Does the paper require sources? If so, do writers tend to place most of their sources in one place (for example, near the beginning), or do they place sources throughout?
4. Is the tone informal or very formal? Do writers use first person or third person?
5. Is the writing characterized by explanations and discussions that are full and expansive or concise and terse?
6. To what extent are writers expected to include their opinions or personal experiences, and to what extent are they expected to rely on objective analyses or source materials?
7. What are typical introduction and conclusion strategies in model sources?

## 37d   How do I use documentation in the disciplines?

Writers use DOCUMENTATION to credit the sources they've used and to help their readers learn more. A writer who neglects to credit a source is guilty of PLAGIARISM (Chapter 33).

DOCUMENTATION STYLES differ among the disciplines. In the humanities, most fields use the documentation style of the Modern Language Association (MLA), as explained and illustrated in Chapter 34. The student research paper in that chapter and the student literary analysis in 38j.3 use MLA documentation style. Occasionally, the humanities use CM (Chicago Manual) style, as explained and illustrated in Chapter 36. In the social sciences, most fields use the documentation style of the American Psychological Association (APA), as explained and illustrated in Chapter 35. The student research paper in Chapter 35 uses APA documentation style. In the natural sciences, documentation styles vary widely, although the Council of Science Editors (CSE) style is frequently used (see Chapter 36). Ask each of your science and technology instructors about the particular documentation style required for his or her assignments.

# Chapter 38

## WRITING ABOUT THE HUMANITIES AND LITERATURE

### 38a   What are the humanities?

The humanities consist of a set of disciplines that seek to represent and understand human experience, creativity, thought, and values. These disciplines include literature, languages, philosophy, and history, although some colleges group history with the social sciences. Also, many colleges consider the fine arts (music, art, dance, theater, and creative writing) part of the humanities, while other colleges group them separately.

### 38b   What types of sources do I use in the humanities?

In the humanities, existing documents or artifacts are PRIMARY SOURCES, and the writer's task generally is to analyze and interpret them. Typical primary source material for humanities research could be a poem by Billy Collins, the floor plans of Egyptian pyramids, or the early drafts of musical scores. A humanities class assignment might invite you to create primary sources yourself. For example, in a studio art class, you paint, draw, or sculpt. In a music composition class, you create pieces of music.

Some humanities papers will require SECONDARY SOURCES. These are articles and books that someone has written to explain or interpret a primary source. For example, suppose you're writing about a movie you saw. The movie is a primary source. If you consult a review of that movie, the review would be a secondary source.

### 38c   What types of papers do I write in the humanities?

Because the humanities cover an impressively broad range of knowledge, writing in the humanities covers many types and purposes. These include responses, narratives, interpretations, critiques, and analyses of works or objects or ideas. In practice, many writing assignments in the humanities require you to combine these activities, but we present each of them individually here for ease of reference.

## SUMMARIES

Occasionally your instructor will request an objective summary of a text; you might need to tell the plot of a novel or present the main points of an article. Generally, however, summary is a means to a larger end. For example, writing an interpretation often requires you to summarize parts of the source so that your points about it are clear.

## SYNTHESES

SYNTHESIS relates several texts, ideas, or pieces of information to one another (4c). For example, you might read several accounts of the events leading up to the Civil War and then write a synthesis that explains what caused that war. Or you might read several philosophers' definitions of morality and then write a synthesis of the components of a moral life.

## RESPONSES

In a response, you give your personal reaction to a work, supported by explanations of your reasoning. For example, do you think Hamlet's behavior makes sense? What is your reaction to America's dealings with Hitler in the 1930s? Do you agree with Peter Singer's philosophical arguments against using animals in scientific experiments? Even though a response is a personal reaction, think of it as writing to inform or, even, to argue; provide reasons for your response so your readers understand clearly why you believe as you do and so that they're convinced your response is reasonable. Some instructors want you to justify your response with references to a text, while other instructors do not. Clarify what your instructor wants before you begin.

## NARRATIVES

When you write a NARRATIVE, you construct a coherent story out of separate facts or events. In a history class, for example, you might examine news events, laws, diaries and journals, and related materials to create a chronological version of what happened. You might do the kind of work that a biographer does, gathering isolated events in people's lives, interviews with those people, or others who knew them, letters or other writings, and related SOURCES, all to form a coherent story of their lives.

## INTERPRETATIONS

An interpretation explains the meaning or significance of a particular text, event, or work of art. For example, what does Plato's *Republic* suggest about the nature of a good society? What message does Picasso's painting *Guernica* convey about the nature of war? What was the significance of the 9/11 tragedy for Americans' sense of security? What is the view of family life in Jonathan Franzen's novel *The Corrections?* You present your point of view and explain your reasoning, and the quality of your reasoning determines how successfully you've conveyed your point.

## CRITIQUES

In a critique (also called a CRITICAL RESPONSE or a review), you present judgments about a particular work, supported by your underlying reasoning. For example, movie, book, music, and art reviews present a writer's carefully reasoned, well-supported opinion of a work. Critical responses and reviews may focus on the literary form, or genre, of a work (for example, "How well does this poem satisfy the conventions of a sonnet?" or "Is this painting an example of Expressionism or Impressionism?"). Responses or reviews may focus on a work's accuracy, logic, or conclusions ("Is this history of the development of hip hop music complete and accurate?"). Finally, responses or reviews may analyze a work's relations to other works ("Is the remake of *Pride and Prejudice* better or worse than earlier film versions?") or a work's similarities to and differences from the "real" world ("To what extent do television comedies accurately portray young adult life?").

## ANALYSES

When you engage in analysis, you examine material by breaking it into its component parts and discovering how the parts interrelate. You examine and explain texts, events, objects, or documents by identifying and discussing important elements in them. These elements can include matters of form (how the work is put together) or of ideas (what the work means). The humanities use a number of **analytic frameworks**, or systematic ways of investigating a work. Box 38.1 summarizes some common analytic frameworks used most notably in literary analysis. Nearly all writing in the humanities depends on analysis to some extent.

---

### SUMMARY BOX 38.1

### Selected analytic frameworks used in the humanities

#### RHETORICAL

Examines how and why people use LOGIC, EMOTION, and ETHOS to create desired effects on specific audiences, in specific situations (see Chapter 4).

#### FEMINIST

Focuses on how women are presented and treated, concentrating especially on power relations between men and women.

## Selected analytic frameworks used in the humanities

### CULTURAL/NEW HISTORICAL

Explores how social, economic, and other cultural forces influence the development of ideas, texts, art, laws, customs, and so on. Also explores how individual texts or events provide broader understandings of the past or present.

### DECONSTRUCTIONIST

Assumes that the meaning of any given text is not stable or "in" the work. Rather, meaning always depends on contexts and the interests of those in power. The goal of deconstruction is to produce multiple possible meanings of a work, usually to undermine traditional interpretations.

### FORMALIST

Centers on matters of structure, form, and traditional literary devices (plot, rhythm, images, symbolism, DICTION; see Box 38.3, pp. 701–702).

### MARXIST

Assumes that the most important forces in human experience are economic and material ones. Focuses on power differences between economic classes of people and the effects of those differences.

### READER-RESPONSE

Emphasizes how the individual reader determines meaning. The reader's personal history, values, experiences, relationships, and previous reading all contribute to how he or she interprets a particular work or event.

---

**38d** Which documentation style do I use to write about the humanities?

Most fields in the humanities use the documentation style of the Modern Language Association (MLA), as explained and illustrated in Chapter 34. Some disciplines in the humanities use Chicago Manual (CM) style, as explained in Chapter 36. Writers use documentation to give credit to the sources they've used. A writer who neglects to credit a source is guilty of PLAGIARISM.

**EXERCISE 38-1** Consider how you could use some of the frameworks in Box 38.1 to analyze the photograph in Figure 38.1 (p. 698).

Figure 38.1   Use analytic frameworks to view this photograph.

## 38e   What is literature?

Literature includes fiction (novels and short stories); drama (plays, scripts, and some films); poetry (poems and lyrics); as well as nonfiction with artistic qualities (memoirs, personal essays, and the like). Since ancient times, literature has represented human experiences, entertained readers, and enlarged people's perspectives about themselves, others, and different ways of life.

## 38f   Why write about literature?

Writing about literature generates insights about your reading. It helps you understand other people, ideas, times, and places. It shows you how authors use language to stir the imaginations, emotions, and intellects of their readers. Finally, writing is a way to share your own reading experiences and insights with other readers.

## 38g   What general strategies can help me write about literature?

When you write about literature, you want to read the work closely as well as actively (Chapter 4). Of course, you may initially read a literary work for sheer enjoyment. However, readers often find that close, active reading actually enhances their enjoyment. Such reading involves asking what the work means, why the author made a particular choice, and why readers react to the work as they do. Boxes 38.2, 38.3, and 38.4 (pp. 701 to 703) list several questions or elements that encourage active reading.

Sometimes instructors ask students to answer questions that deal with material on a literal level, that is, to tell exactly what is said on the page. If a question asks what happens in the plot or what a passage is saying, you need to answer with a SUMMARY or PARAPHRASE of the work. If a question asks about the historical context of a work, or asks for biographical or situational information about the author, you probably need to do some research and then report exactly what you find.

More often, assignments call for making INFERENCES. Making inferences means reading "between the lines" to figure out what is implied but not stated. This reading skill is especially crucial for reading literature because it tends to "show" rather than to "tell." Inferential thinking is necessary when your instructor asks you to discuss why a character does something for which the author provides no explicit reason. It's necessary when your instructor asks you to explain the effect of images in a poem, to discuss how a work implies the author's stance on a social issue, or to analyze how the author depicts the role of women, men, or specific ethnic groups. Student Michael Choi's paper, at the end of this chapter, has many examples of inferential thinking, including the significance of several words, phrases, and images ("consecrated," "garland of thorns," "limboed" and so on).

Writing effective papers about literature involves more than summarizing the plot. It involves CRITICAL THINKING and SYNTHESIS. In such papers, you state a CLAIM (an observation or a position about the work of literature) and convince your readers that the thesis is reasonable. To be effective, your papers must be thorough and well-supported. For support, you make direct references to the work, by SUMMARIZING, PARAPHRASING, and QUOTING specific passages (33h–33j) and by explaining precisely *why* and *how* the selected passages support your interpretation.

## 38h How do I write different types of papers about literature?

When you read a literary work closely, look for details or passages that relate to your thesis. Mark up the text as you read by selectively underlining passages or by writing notes, comments, or questions in the margin. Alternatively, take notes separately, on paper or on a computer. Figure 38.2 shows Michael Choi's notes on part of the poem "Blackberries." The complete poem is on pages 704–705.

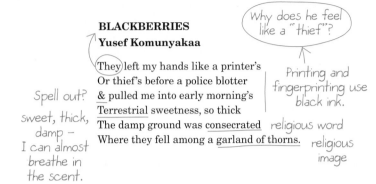

Figure 38.2 A student's margin notes

## WRITING A PERSONAL RESPONSE

In a personal response paper, you explain your reaction to a literary work or some aspect of it. You might write about why you did or did not enjoy reading a particular work; discuss whether situations in the work are similar to your personal experiences; explain whether you agree or disagree with the author's point of view and why; or answer a question or explore a problem that the work raised for you. For example, how do you react if a likable character breaks the law? As with all effective papers about literature, you need to explain your response by discussing specific passages or elements from the text.

## WRITING AN INTERPRETATION

An interpretation explains the message or viewpoint that you think the work conveys. Most works of literature are open to more than one interpretation. Your task, then, is not to discover the single right answer. Instead, your task is to determine a possible interpretation and provide an argument that supports it. The questions in Box 38.2 can help you write an effective interpretation paper.

## WRITING A FORMAL ANALYSIS

A formal analysis explains how elements of a literary work function to create meaning or effect. Your instructor may ask you to concentrate on one of these elements (for example, "How does the point of view in the story contribute to its meaning?") or to discuss how a writer develops a theme through several elements (for example, "How do setting, imagery, and symbolism reveal the author's viewpoint?"). The paper by student Michael Choi (see 38j.1) is an example of an interpretation based on a formal analysis. Box 38.3 describes some of the major literary elements that you might expect to use in formal analyses.

**SUMMARY BOX** 38.2

## Questions for an interpretation paper

1. What is a central theme of the work? For example, in the poem "Blackberries," a central theme might be shame.

2. How do particular parts of the work relate to the theme? For example, in "Blackberries," the smirking children in the car make the boy shamefully aware of his stained hands.

3. If patterns exist in the work, what might they mean? Patterns include repeated images, situations, words, and so on. In "Blackberries," the words "consecrated," "garland of thorns," and "forgiveness" form a pattern.

4. What meaning does the author create through the elements listed in Box 38.3?

5. Why might the work end as it does?

**SUMMARY BOX** 38.3

## Major elements of formal analysis in literary works

| | |
|---|---|
| **PLOT** | Events and their sequence |
| **THEME** | Central idea or message |
| **STRUCTURE** | Organization and relationship of parts to each other and to the whole |
| **CHARACTERIZATION** | Traits, thoughts, and actions of the people in the plot |
| **SETTING** | Time and place of the action |
| **POINT OF VIEW** | Perspective or position from which the material is presented—by a narrator, a main character, or another person either in the plot or observing the plot |
| **STYLE** | How words and sentence structures present the material |
| **IMAGERY** | Descriptive language that creates mental pictures for the reader |
| **TONE** | Author's attitude toward the subject of the work—and sometimes toward the reader—expressed through choice of words, imagery, and point of view (Chapter 1) |
| **FIGURE OF SPEECH** | Unusual use or combination of words, as in metaphor and simile, for enhanced vividness or effect |

SUMMARY BOX **38.3** *continued*

## Major elements of formal analysis in literary works

| | |
|---|---|
| **SYMBOLISM** | Meaning beneath the surface of the words and images |
| **RHYTHM** | Beat, meter |
| **RHYME** | Repetition of similar sounds for their auditory effect |

To prepare to write a formal analysis, read the work thoroughly, looking for patterns and repetitions. Write notes as you read to help you form insights about these patterns and repetitions. For example, if you need to analyze a character, you want to pay attention to everything that character says or does, everything that other characters say about him or her, and any descriptions of the character.

### WRITING A CULTURAL ANALYSIS

A cultural analysis relates the literary work to broader historical, social, cultural, and political situations. Instructors might ask you to explain how events or prevailing attitudes influence the writing of a work or the way readers understand it. For example, they might ask, "How did Maxine Hong Kingston's experience as a Chinese American affect the way she tells her story in *The Woman Warrior?*" or "How do differences between the institution of marriage in the early nineteenth century and today affect readers' interpretations of *Pride and Prejudice?*" Box 38.4 lists some common focuses for cultural analysis.

### 38i What special rules apply to writing about literature?

When you write about literature, certain special elements come into play.

### 38i.1 Using present and past tense correctly

Always use the PRESENT TENSE when you describe or discuss a literary work or any of its elements: *George Henderson* [a character] **takes** *control of the action and* **tells** *the other characters when they may speak.* The present tense is also correct for discussing what the author has done in a specific work: *Because Susan Glaspell* [the author] **excludes** *Minnie and John Wright from the stage as speaking characters, she* **forces** *her audience to learn about them through the words of others.*

Use a PAST-TENSE VERB to discuss historical events or biographical information: *Susan Glaspell* **was** *a social activist who* **was** *strongly* **influenced** *by the chaotic events of the early twentieth century.*

**SUMMARY BOX** 38.4

## Major topics for cultural analysis

**GENDER**   How does a work portray women or men and define—or challenge—their respective roles in society?

**CLASS**   How does a work portray relationships among the upper, middle, and lower economic classes? How do characters' actions or perspectives result from their wealth and power—or the lack thereof?

**RACE AND ETHNICITY**   How does a work portray the influences of race and ethnicity on the characters' actions, status, and values?

**HISTORY**   How does a work reflect—or challenge—past events and values in a society?

**AUTOBIOGRAPHY**   How might the writer's experiences have influenced this particular work? Similarly, how might the times in which the writer lives or lived have affected his or her work?

**GENRE**   How is the work similar to or different from other works of its type (plays, sonnets, mysteries, comic novels, memoirs, and so on)?

## 38i.2  Using your own ideas and secondary sources

Some assignments call for only your own ideas about the literary work that is the subject of your essay. In such cases, you're dealing only with a PRIMARY SOURCE, the original creative work (a poem, play, story, novel, memoir, or diary). Other assignments require you additionally to use SECONDARY SOURCES, books and articles in which experts discuss some aspect of the literary text or other material related to your topic.

You might use secondary sources to support your own ideas, perhaps by drawing on the ideas of a scholar who agrees with you or debating the ideas of a scholar who disagrees with you. Or, if you think that you have a new or different interpretation, you might summarize, analyze, or critique what others have written, to provide a framework for your own analysis. You can locate secondary sources by using the research process discussed in Chapters 31 and 32. A particularly important resource for research about literature is the *MLA International Bibliography*, which is the most comprehensive index to literary scholarship.

As with all source-based writing, you need to DOCUMENT primary sources and secondary sources because you want to ensure that readers never mistake someone else's ideas as yours. Otherwise, you're PLAGIARIZING (see Chapter 33). Most literature instructors require students to use the DOCUMENTATION STYLE of the Modern Language Association (MLA) that we described in Chapter 34. However, check with your instructor before you begin to conduct your research.

## 38j Sample student essays

This section includes three student essays of literary analysis. Two do not use SECONDARY SOURCES (38j.1 and 38j.2) and one does use them (38j.3). All three essays use MLA STYLE DOCUMENTATION.

### 38j.1 Student essay interpreting images in a poem

Michael Choi, a student in a literature course, fulfilled an assignment to write an interpretation of the images and metaphors in Yusef Komunyakaa's poem "Blackberries." When Michael first read "Blackberries," several of the images puzzled him. He wondered how they connect to an apparently simple scene of a boy picking, eating, and selling blackberries. In the process of writing his essay, Michael came to understand how those previously puzzling images and metaphors help to shape the poem's deeper meaning. His final draft is reproduced here.

#### LEARNING ABOUT THE POET, YUSEF KOMUNYAKAA

Yusef Komunyakaa is an African-American poet who was born in 1947 and raised in Louisiana. His father was a carpenter. Komunyakaa was educated at the University of Colorado, at Colorado State University, and at the University of California–Irvine. He served a tour of duty in Vietnam and was awarded the Bronze Star. In 1994, he won the Pulitzer Prize for poetry—one of the most prestigious honors a poet can receive in the United States—for his book *Neon Vernacular*. Here is his poem "Blackberries."

#### BLACKBERRIES

#### Yusef Komunyakaa

They left my hands like a printer's
Or thief's before a police blotter
& pulled me into early morning's
Terrestrial sweetness, so thick
The damp ground was consecrated                    5
Where they fell among a garland of thorns.
Although I could smell old lime-covered
History, at ten I'd still hold out my hands

& berries fell into them. Eating from one
& filling a half gallon with the other,                                    10
I ate the mythology & dreamt
Of pies & cobbler, almost
Needful as forgiveness. My bird dog Spot
Eyed blue jays & thrashers. The mud frogs
In rich blackness, hid from daylight.                                      15
An hour later, beside City Limits Road
I balanced a gleaming can in each hand,
Limboed between worlds, repeating *one dollar*.
The big blue car made me sweat.
Wintertime crawled out of the windows.                                     20
When I leaned closer I saw the boy
& girl my age, in the wide back seat
Smirking, & it was then I remembered my fingers
Burning with thorns among berries too ripe to touch.

## A student's essay about literature

Michael Choi

Professor May

English 100

8 November 2005

Images, Metaphors, and Meaning in "Blackberries"

In Yusef Komunyakaa's poem "Blackberries," the poet describes himself as "limboed between worlds" (line 18). At that moment, he is a boy standing beside City Limits Road--a symbolic line between the city and the country--selling berries that he has just picked. Yet the boy is also caught between his familiar natural world and a world of wealth and privilege. One of the poem's key issues is whether the boy is responsible for his situation. Komunyakaa uses a rich set of images and metaphors to suggest the boy's complicated position.

Some plain and direct images connect the boy to the world of nature. As he picks blackberries, the poet describes the "bird dog Spot" watching blue jays and thrashers (13-14), and he mentions "mud frogs" hiding in the dark (14-15). Readers form an impression of a rustic boy trying to earn some money from a countryside that is familiar and comfortable to him. He eats as he fills "gleaming" half-gallon cans (17) and dreams of "pies & cobbler" (12). The day is "thick" with "terrestrial sweetness" (4), and the atmosphere is peaceful, almost sleepy.

When the boy moves beyond the country to the City Limits Road to sell his harvest, however, his pleasant morning

*continued* ➤

(Proportions shown in this paper are adjusted to fit space limitations of this book. Follow actual dimensions given in this book and in your instructor's directions.)

is shattered. After a customer drives up, the boy says, "The big blue car made me sweat" (19). Partly, he sweats because the car's air-conditioning makes him aware of heat that had not bothered him until that very moment. Komunyakaa uses the strong image that "Wintertime crawled out of the windows" to heighten the contrast between the artificial environment of the car and the natural environment of the boy (20). More importantly, the boy sweats because he is suddenly self-conscious. He feels uncomfortable at the gap between himself and "the boy / & girl my age, in the wide back seat" (21-22). The emphasis on the air-conditioning and the width of the seat make clear that these children come not only from the city but also from wealthier circumstances. When they smirk at him, he remembers his berry-stained fingers. Those stained hands are a metaphor for how different he is from the children in the car, both socially and economically. He feels ashamed.

Yet, should he feel this way? Several complicated images and metaphors in the poem make this question difficult to answer. For example, at the beginning, the poet says that the berries "left my hands like a printer's" (line 1). This image not only calls attention to the inky stains on his hands but also likens berry picking to printing. Both are forms of honest manual labor. Furthermore, picking ripe berries is similar to the messy job of shedding ink-saturated type from a printing press--the typesetting method used before computers. This printing metaphor suggests a subtle connection between the boy's work and the poet's work. Komunyakaa immediately

continued ➤

complicates the first image with a second that compares the boy's hands to a "thief's before a police blotter" (2). The common element between the two metaphors is the ink, which in the second is used for fingerprinting.

Note that the person whose fingerprints are being taken by the police is not simply a "suspect" but rather a thief (2). The person is already guilty of a crime. Has the boy been stealing berries that do not belong to him, and does he feel guilty when he is caught? This possible interpretation does not completely fit the encounter with the big blue car. The "smirking" response of the children in the car seems snobbish (23). Rather than accusing him of being a thief, the children make fun of him for getting dirty while picking berries, which they can buy in cool comfort. For his efforts, which even involve his "fingers / Burning with thorns" (23-24), the boy receives ridicule. The reader's sympathies lie with the boy selling the berries. Even if he did steal the berries, his crime does not seem that great.

Another set of metaphors, more mythic in nature, suggests an answer to the question of whether the boy should feel guilty. The boy reports that he "could smell old lime-covered / History" as he picks and eats (7-8). While lime might refer to a bright shade of green or to the citrus fruit, another meaning seems to apply here. The chemical substance lime has two uses. Farmers use it to reduce acidity in soil, where it serves as a kind of fertilizer. Alternatively, quicklime spread over the bodies of dead animals speeds their decomposition. To cover history in lime, therefore, means either to cultivate it or to bury it. Later, the boy states that he "ate the mythology &

*continued* ➢

Choi 4

dreamt / of pies & cobbler" (11-12). Obviously, no one can literally eat mythology. This metaphor suggests that the boy is consuming the berries with little thought of any deeper significance his actions might have. There is a mythic dimension to picking blackberries, but the boy focuses on pleasant physical sensations and, eventually, the chance to make some money. Similarly, history is something to consume or ignore. If the boy is a criminal (which seems unlikely), maybe he is unaware that he is doing anything wrong. Furthermore, perhaps no one owns the berries, and he is merely "stealing" from nature.

The poem's most profound images and metaphors have religious overtones. The poet describes the ground beneath the berry bushes as "consecrated" (5). This powerful word choice characterizes the ground as holy. The berries do not fall simply among thorns but among "a garland of thorns" (6). The image of a garland suggests the crown of thorns placed upon the head of Jesus after his trial, and these images draw out the deepest meaning of the poet's being "limboed between worlds" (18). In some religious traditions, limbo is a place where souls temporarily go before entering heaven or where innocent but unbaptized babies permanently dwell. In addition to standing between the world of wealth and status that is represented by the car and the simpler world of bird dogs and mud frogs, the boy stands outside paradise. He has left and knows that he cannot go back.

Although mythic and religious elements are present in "Blackberries," Komunyakaa's poem ultimately supports

*continued* ➢

interpretations on several levels. The poet uses religious images to give depth to the boy's situation. When the boy picks the berries, he is in a peaceful, natural environment that is almost sacred, even if he does not realize it. When he sells the berries, he encounters a foreign world of wealth and privilege. Because of his background, he cannot easily join that world. Yet he cannot easily go back to his familiar ways because he now sees his actions differently. He perceives there may be something wrong with picking blackberries. Whether or not he should feel guilty, he does feel guilty. The poet is truly limboed between worlds.

Work Cited

Komunyakaa, Yusef. "Blackberries." Pleasure Dome: New and Collected Poems. Middletown: Wesleyan UP, 2001. 280-81.

## 38j.2 Student essay analyzing the characters in a drama

The following student essay analyzes the actions and interactions of the male and female characters in *Trifles,* a one-act play by Susan Glaspell (1882–1948). Glaspell was a feminist and a social activist who wrote many plays for the Provincetown Players, a theater company she co-founded on Cape Cod, Massachusetts. She wrote *Trifles* in 1916, four years before women were allowed to vote in the United States. In 1917, Glaspell rewrote *Trifles* as the short story "A Jury of Her Peers." In both versions of the work, two married couples and the county attorney gather at a farmhouse where a taciturn farmer has been murdered, apparently by his wife. The five characters try to discover a motive for the murder. In doing so, they reveal much about gender roles in marriage and in the larger society.

After reading *Trifles,* Peter Lesniak said to his instructor, "No male today could get away with saying some of the things the men in that play say." The instructor encouraged Lesniak to analyze that reaction.

---

Lesniak 1

Peter Lesniak

Professor Minoc

Drama 250

12 April 2005

Gender Loyalties: A Theme in Trifles

Susan Glaspell's play Trifles is a study of character even though the two characters most central to the drama never appear on stage. By excluding Minnie and John Wright from the stage as speaking characters, Glaspell forces us to learn about them through the observations and recollections of the group visiting the farmhouse where the murders of Minnie Wright's canary and of John Wright took place. By indirectly rounding out her main characters, Glaspell invites us to view them not merely as individuals but also as representatives in a conflict between the sexes. This conflict grows throughout the play as characters' emotions and sympathies become increasingly polarized and oriented in favor of their own gender. From this perspective, each of the male characters can be seen to stand for the larger political, legal, and domestic power structures that drive Minnie Wright to kill her husband.

That George Henderson speaks the first line of the play is no accident. Although his power stems from his position as

*continued* ➤

county attorney, Henderson represents the political, more than the legal, sphere. With a job similar to a district attorney's today, he is quite powerful even though he is the youngest person present. He takes control of the action, telling the other characters when to speak and when not to and directing the men in their search for evidence that will establish a motive for the murder. As the person in charge of the investigation, George Henderson orders the other characters about. Mrs. Peters acknowledges his skill at oratory when she predicts that Minnie Wright will be convicted in the wake of his "sarcastic" cross-examination (speech 63).

Glaspell reveals much of the conflict in the play through the heated (but civil) exchanges between George Henderson and Mrs. Hale. His behavior (according to the stage directions, that of a gallant young politician) does not mask his belittling of Minnie Wright and of women in general:

> COUNTY ATTORNEY. I guess before we're through
> she may have something more serious than
> preserves to worry about.
>
> HALE. Well, women are used to worrying over
> trifles. [The two women move a little closer
> together.]
>
> COUNTY ATTORNEY. [With the gallantry of a young
> politician.] And yet, for all their worries, what
> would we do without the ladies? [The women
> do not unbend. He goes to the sink, takes a
> dipperful of water from the pail, and pouring
> it into a basin, washes his hands. Starts to
> wipe them on the roller-towel, turns it for
> a cleaner place.] Dirty towels! [Kicks his foot

continued ➤

<u>against the pans under the sink.</u>] Not much
of a housekeeper, would you say, ladies?
(speeches 29-31)

As this excerpt shows, George Henderson seems to hold
that a woman's place is in the kitchen, even when she is
locked up miles away in the county jail. He shows so much
emotion at the discovery of dirty towels in the kitchen that it is
almost as if he has found a real piece of evidence that he can
use to convict Minnie Wright, instead of an irrelevant strip of
cloth. It is apparent that his own sense of self-importance and
prejudicial views of women are distracting him from his real
business at the farmhouse.

Sheriff Henry Peters, as his title suggests, represents the
legal power structure. Like the county attorney, Henry Peters is
also quick to dismiss the "trifles" that his wife and Mrs. Hale
spend their time discussing while the men conduct a physical
search of the premises. His response to the attorney's asking
whether he is absolutely certain that the downstairs contains
no relevant clues to the motive for the murder is a curt
"Nothing here but kitchen things" (speech 25). Ironically, the
women are able to reconstruct the entire murder, including the
motive, by beginning their inquiries with these same "kitchen
things." Sheriff Peters and the other men all completely miss
the unfinished quilt, the bird cage, and the dead bird's body.
When the sheriff overhears the women talking about the quilt,
his instinctive reaction is to ridicule them, saying, "They
wonder if she was going to quilt it or just knot it!" (speech 73).
Of course, the fact that Minnie Wright was going to knot the

*continued* ➤

quilt is probably the single most important piece of evidence that the group could uncover, since John Wright was strangled with what we deduce is a quilting knot. Although he understands the law, the sheriff seems to know very little about people, and this prevents him from ever cracking this case. His blindness is made clear when he chuckles his assent to the county attorney's observation that Mrs. Peters is literally "married to the law" (speech 145) and therefore beyond suspicion of trying to hinder the case against Minnie Wright. This assumption is completely wrong, for Mrs. Peters joins Mrs. Hale in suppressing the evidence and lying to the men.

Rounding out the male characters is Lewis Hale, a husband and farmer who represents the domestic sphere. Although Lewis Hale may not be an ideal individual, he provides a strong foil for John Wright's character. We might expect Lewis Hale, as Mrs. Hale's spouse, to be a good (or at least a tolerable) person, and, on the whole, he is. Although he, too, misses the significance of the "trifles" in the kitchen and mocks the activities of his wife and Mrs. Peters, he seems less eager than the other men to punish Minnie Wright-- possibly because he knew John Wright better than they did. Lewis Hale is clearly reluctant to provide evidence against Minnie Wright when he speaks of her behavior after he discovers the body:

> HALE. She moved from that chair to this one over
> here [Pointing to a small chair in the corner.]
> and just sat there with her hands held
> together and looking down. I got a feeling

continued ➤

Lesniak 5

that I ought to make some conversation, so I
said I had come in to see if John wanted to
put in a telephone, and at that she started to
laugh, and then she stopped and looked at
me--scared. [The county attorney, who has
had his notebook out, makes a note.] I dunno,
maybe it wasn't scared. I wouldn't like to say
it was. . . . (speech 23)

Lewis Hale is the only man who tries to bring up the
incompatibility in the Wrights' marriage, citing John
Wright's dislike for conversation and adding, "I didn't know
if what his wife wanted made much difference to John--"
(speech 9), but George Henderson cuts him off before he can
pursue this any further. Lewis Hale is a personable and
talkative man--not at all like John Wright, whom Mrs. Hale
likens to "a raw wind that gets to the bone" (speech 103).
Lewis Hale is a social being who wants to communicate with
the people around him, as his desire for a telephone party
line indicates. The Hales' functional marriage shows that
gender differences need not be insurmountable, but it also
serves to highlight the truly devastating effect that a
completely incompatible union can have on two people's
lives. Mrs. Hale reminds us that even a marriage that
"works" can be dehumanizing:

MRS. HALE. I might have known she needed help!
I know how things can be--for women. I tell
you it's queer, Mrs. Peters. We live close
together and we live far apart. We all go
through the same things--it's all just a
different kind of the same thing. (speech 136)

continued ➣

Lesniak 6

The great irony of the drama is that the women are able to accomplish what the men cannot: They establish the motive for the murder. They find evidence suggesting that John Wright viciously killed his wife's canary--her sole companion through long days of work around the house. More important, they recognize the damaging nature of a marriage based on the unequal status of the participants. Mrs. Hale and Mrs. Peters decide not to help the case against Minnie Wright, not because her husband killed a bird, but because he isolated her, made her life miserable for years, and cruelly destroyed her one source of comfort. Without hope of help from the various misogynistic, paternalistic, and uncomprehending political, legal, and domestic power structures surrounding her, Minnie Wright took the law into her own hands. As the characters of George Henderson, Henry Peters, and Lewis Hale demonstrate, she clearly could not expect understanding from the men of her community.

Lesniak 7

Work Cited

Glaspell, Susan. Trifles. The Prentice Hall Anthology of
    Women's Literature. Ed. Deborah H. Holdstein. Upper
    Saddle River, NJ: Prentice, 2000. 301-11. 1038-48.

## 38j.3  Student MLA-style research paper analyzing two poems

The student essay that follows is a literary analysis of two poems by Claude McKay that draws on SECONDARY SOURCES.

Born in 1889 on the Caribbean island of Jamaica, Claude McKay moved to the United States in 1910 and became a highly respected poet. Paule Cheek, a student in a class devoted to writing about literature, chose to write about Claude McKay's nontraditional use of a very traditional poetic form, the sonnet. A sonnet has fourteen lines in a patterned rhyme and develops one idea. In secondary sources, Cheek found information about McKay's life that she felt gave her further insights into both the structure and the meaning of McKay's sonnets "In Bondage" and "The White City." For your reference, both poems appear below.

### IN BONDAGE

I would be wandering in distant fields  
Where man, and bird, and beast, lives leisurely,  
And the old earth is kind, and ever yields  
Her goodly gifts to all her children free;  
Where life is fairer, lighter, less demanding,        5  
And boys and girls have time and space for play  
Before they come to years of understanding—  
Somewhere I would be singing, far away.  
For life is greater than the thousand wars  
Men wage for it in their insatiate lust,        10  
And will remain like the eternal stars,  
When all that shines to-day is drift and dust.  
But I am bound with you in your mean graves,  
O black men, simple slaves of ruthless slaves.  

### THE WHITE CITY

I will not toy with it nor bend an inch.  
Deep in the secret chambers of my heart  
I muse my life-long hate, and without flinch  
I bear it nobly as I live my part.  
My being would be skeleton, a shell,        5  
If this dark Passion that fills my every mood,  
And makes my heaven in the white world's hell,  
Did not forever feed me vital blood.  
I see the mighty city through a mist—  
The strident trains that speed the goaded mass,        10  
The poles and spires and towers vapor-kissed,  
The fortressed port through which the great ships pass,  
The tides, the wharves, the dens I contemplate,  
Are sweet like wanton loves because I hate.

Paule Cheek

Professor Bartlestone

English 112, Section 03

14 March 2005

Words in Bondage: Claude McKay's

Use of the Sonnet Form in Two Poems

The sonnet has remained one of the central poetic forms

of the Western tradition for centuries. This fourteen-line form is

easy for poets to learn but difficult to master. With its fixed rhyme

schemes, number of lines, and meter, the sonnet form forces

writers to be doubly creative while working within it. Many poets

over the years have modified or varied the sonnet form, playing

upon its conventions to keep it vibrant and original. One such

writer was Jamaican-born Claude McKay (1889-1948).

The Jamaica of McKay's childhood was very different

from turn-of-the-century America. Slavery had ended there in

the 1830s, and McKay was able to grow up "in a society whose

population was overwhelmingly black and largely free of the

overt white oppression which constricted the lives of black

Americans in the United States during this same period"

(Cooper, Passion 5-6). This background could not have

prepared McKay for what he encountered when he moved to

America in his twenties. Lynchings, still common at that time,

were on the rise, and during the Red Scare of 1919 there were

dozens of racially motivated riots in major cities throughout

the country. Thousands of homes were destroyed in these

riots, and several black men were tortured and burned at the

continued ➤

stake (Cooper, <u>Claude McKay</u> 97). McKay responded to these atrocities by raising an outraged cry of protest in his poems. In two of his sonnets from this period, "The White City" and "In Bondage," we can see McKay's mastery of the form and his skillful use of irony in the call for social change.

McKay's choice of the sonnet form as the vehicle for his protest poetry at first seems strange. Since his message was a radical one, we might expect that the form of his poetry would be revolutionary. Instead, McKay gives us sonnets--a poetic form that dates back to the early sixteenth century and was originally intended to be used exclusively for love poems. The critic James R. Giles notes that this choice

> is not really surprising, since McKay's Jamaican education and reading had been based firmly upon the major British poets. From the point quite early in his life when he began to think of himself as a poet, his models were such major English writers as William Shakespeare, John Milton, William Wordsworth. He thus was committed from the beginning to the poetry which he had initially been taught to admire. (44)

McKay published both "The White City" and "In Bondage" in 1922, and they are similar in many ways. Like most sonnets, each has fourteen lines and is in iambic pentameter. The diction is extremely elevated. For example, this quatrain from "In Bondage" is almost Elizabethan in its word choice and order:

*continued* ➤

> For life is greater than the thousand wars
>
> Men wage for it in their insatiate lust,
>
> And will remain like the eternal stars,
>
> When all that shines to-day is drift and dust.
>
> (lines 8-12)

If this level of diction is reminiscent of Shakespeare, it is no accident. Both poems employ the English sonnet rhyme scheme (a b a b c d c d e f e f g g) and division into three quatrains and a closing couplet. McKay introduces a touch of his own, however. Although the English sonnet form calls for the "thematic turn" to fall at the closing couplet, McKay defies convention. He incorporates two turns into each sonnet instead of one. This allows him to use the first "mini-turn" to further develop the initial theme set forth in the first eight lines while dramatically bringing the poem to a conclusion with a forcefully ironic turn in the closing couplet. Specifically, in "The White City," McKay uses the additional turn to interrupt his description of his "Passion" with a vision of "the mighty city through a mist" (9). In "In Bondage," he uses the additional turn to justify his desire to escape the violent existence that society has imposed on his people.

McKay also demonstrates his poetic ability through his choice of words within his customized sonnets. Consider the opening of "In Bondage":

> I would be wandering in distant fields
>
> Where man, and bird, and beast, lives leisurely,
>
> And the old earth is kind, and ever yields
>
> Her goodly gifts to all her children free;

continued ➤

Cheek 4

> Where life is fairer, lighter, less demanding,
>
> And boys and girls have time and space for play
>
> Before they come to years of understanding--
>
> Somewhere I would be singing, far away. (1-8)

The conditional power of <u>would</u> in the first line, coupled with the alliterative <u>wandering</u>, subtly charms us into a relaxed, almost dreamlike state in which the poet can lead us gently through the rest of the poem. The commas in the second line force us to check our progress to a "leisurely" crawl, mirroring the people and animals that the line describes. By the time we reach the eighth line, we are probably ready to join the poet in this land of "somewhere . . . far away."

Then this optimistic bubble is violently burst by the closing couplet:

> But I am bound with you in your mean graves,
>
> O black men, simple slaves of ruthless slaves.
>
> (13-14)

In "The White City" McKay again surprises us. This time, he does so by turning the traditional love sonnet upside down; instead of depicting a life made endurable through an overpowering love, McKay shows us a life made bearable through a sustaining hate:

> I will not toy with it nor bend an inch.
>
> Deep in the secret chambers of my heart
>
> I muse my life-long hate, and without flinch
>
> I bear it nobly as I live my part.
>
> My being would be a skeleton, a shell,
>
> If this dark Passion that fills my every mood,

*continued* ➤

And makes my heaven in the white world's hell,

Did not forever feed me vital blood. (1-8)

If it were not for the presence of "life-long hate" in the third line, this opening would easily pass as part of a conventional love sonnet. However, as the critic William Maxwell notes in "On White City," the first quatrain is "designed to ambush those anticipating another rehearsal of love's powers." The emotion comes from "deep in the secret chambers" of the speaker's heart (2), it allows him to transcend "the white world's hell" (7), and it is a defining "Passion." Once again, however, McKay uses the couplet to defy our expectations by making it plain that he has used the form of the love sonnet only for ironic effect: "The tides, the wharves, the dens I contemplate, / Are sweet like wanton loves because I hate" (13-14).

McKay's impressive poetic ability made him a master of the sonnet form. His language could at times rival even Shakespeare's, and his creativity allowed him to adapt the sonnet to his own ends. His ironic genius is revealed in his use of one of Western society's most elevated poetic forms to critique that same society. He held that critique so strongly that shortly after publishing these poems, McKay spent six months in the Soviet Union, where he met with Communist leaders (Hathaway 282). McKay once described himself as "a man who was bitter because he loved, who was both right and wrong because he hated the things that destroyed love, who tried to give back to others a little of what he had got from them . . ." (qtd. in Barksdale and Kinnamon 491). As these two sonnets show, McKay gave back very much indeed.

continued ➤

Works Cited

Barksdale, Richard, and Kenneth Kinnamon, eds. <u>Black</u>
<u>Writers of America: A Comprehensive Anthology</u>.
New York: Macmillan, 1972.

Cooper, Wayne F. <u>Claude McKay: Rebel Sojourner in the</u>
<u>Harlem Renaissance</u>. Baton Rouge: Louisiana State UP,
1987.

---, ed. <u>The Passion of Claude McKay</u>. New York: Schocken,
1973.

Giles, James R. <u>Claude McKay</u>. Boston: Twayne, 1976.

Hathaway, Heather. "Claude McKay." <u>The Concise Oxford</u>
<u>Companion to African American Literature</u>. Ed. William
L. Andrews, Frances Smith Foster, and Trudier Harris.
New York: Oxford UP, 2001. 282-83.

Maxwell, William. "On 'The White City.'" <u>New Negro, Old Left:</u>
<u>African American Writing and Communism between the</u>
<u>Wars</u>. New York: Columbia UP, 1999. <u>Modern American</u>
<u>Poetry</u>. 5 Mar. 2005 <http://www.english.uiuc.edu/
maps/poets/m_r/mckay/whitecity.htm>.

McKay, Claude. "In Bondage." <u>Literature: An Introduction to</u>
<u>Reading and Writing</u>. 7th ed. Ed. Edgar V. Roberts and
Henry E. Jacobs. Englewood Cliffs: Prentice, 2004. 870.

---. "The White City." <u>Literature: An Introduction to Reading</u>
<u>and Writing</u>. 7th ed. Ed. Edgar V. Roberts and Henry E.
Jacobs. Englewood Cliffs: Prentice, 2004. 1118-19.

# Chapter 39

---

## WRITING IN THE SOCIAL SCIENCES AND NATURAL SCIENCES

### SOCIAL SCIENCES

#### 39a    What are the social sciences?

The social sciences focus on the behavior of people as individuals and in groups. The field includes disciplines such as economics, education, political science, psychology, sociology, and certain courses in geography. At some colleges, history is included in the social sciences; at others, it's part of the humanities.

#### 39b    What kinds of sources do I use in the social sciences?

Some methods used in the social sciences lead to **quantitative research**, which seeks to count things or translate information into numerical data to analyze statistically. Other methods lead to **qualitative research**, which relies on careful descriptions and thorough written interpretations.

In the social sciences, PRIMARY SOURCES include surveys and questionnaires, observations, interviews, and experiments. When writing about information you gather, you analyze and explain what the sources mean or why they're significant.

#### SURVEYS AND QUESTIONNAIRES

Surveys and questionnaires systematically gather information from a representative number of individuals. For example, you might survey people to see how and why they will vote in an upcoming election, or you might interview students to explain the effects of peer pressure on behavior in high schools. To prepare a questionnaire, use the guidelines in Box 39.1.

#### OBSERVATIONS

Some writing in the social sciences requires direct observations of people's behaviors. Use whatever tools you need to take complete notes: a laptop or notebook, sketching materials, tape recorders, or cameras. In

## Guidelines for developing a questionnaire

1. Define what you want to learn.
2. Write questions to elicit the information you seek.
3. Use appropriate language when phrasing questions so that they are easy to understand (21b).
4. Make sure that your wording does not imply what you want to hear.
5. Decide whether to include open-ended questions that allow people to write their own answers.
6. Test a draft of the questionnaire on a small group of people. If any question is misinterpreted or difficult to understand, revise and retest it.

reporting your observations, tell what tools you used, because they might have influenced what you saw. For example, it would be important to state whether a photo was posed or candid because human subjects behave differently when they know they are being photographed.

### INTERVIEWS

You might interview people to gather opinions and impressions. Remember that interviews aren't always reliable because people's memories are imprecise, and their first impulse is to present themselves in the best light. Try to interview as many people as possible so that you can cross-check information.

**ALERTS:** (1) If you use abbreviations to increase your notetaking speed, be sure to write down what they stand for so that you'll be able to understand them later when you write out your observations (32c). (2) Before you interview anyone, master any equipment you might need to use so that mechanical problems don't intrude on the interview process. ◆

### EXPERIMENTS

The social sciences sometimes use data from experiments as a source. For example, if you want to learn how people react in a particular situation, you can set up that situation artificially and bring individuals (known as "subjects") into it to observe their behavior.

With all methods of inquiry in the social sciences, you need to be ethical. You're required to treat subjects fairly and honestly, not in ways that could cause them harm in body, mind, or reputation. Professional social scientists must seek explicit written permission from their subjects, and colleges have official panels to review research proposals to make sure the studies are ethical. Check with your instructor to see whether you need to have your study approved.

## 39c What are writing purposes and practices in the social sciences?

The purpose of much writing in the social sciences is explanatory. Writers try to explain both what a behavior is and why it happens. SUMMARY and SYNTHESIS (4e) are important fundamental strategies for explanatory writing in the social sciences.

ANALYSIS (Chapter 4) helps social scientists write about problems and their solutions. For example, an economist writing about financial troubles in a major automobile company might start by breaking the situation into parts: analyzing employee salaries and benefits, the selling prices of cars, and the costs of doing business. Next, the economist might show how these parts relate to the financial health of the whole company. Finally, the economist might suggest how specific changes would help solve the company's financial problems.

Social scientists often also use ANALOGY (3i) to make unfamiliar ideas clear. When an unfamiliar idea is compared to one that is more familiar, the unfamiliar idea becomes easier to understand. For example, sociologists may talk of the "culture shock" that some people feel when they enter a new society. The sociologists might compare this shock to the reaction of someone suddenly being moved hundreds of years into the future or the past.

Social scientists are particularly careful to define their KEY TERMS when they write, especially when they discuss complex social issues. For example, if you're writing a paper on substance abuse in the medical profession, you must first define what you mean by the terms *substance abuse* and *medical profession.* Does *substance* mean alcohol and drugs or only drugs? What defines *abuse,* and how do you measure it? By *medical profession,* do you mean only nurses and doctors, or hospital administrators, too? Without defining such terms, you confuse readers or lead them to wrong conclusions.

In college courses in the social sciences, your goal is usually to be a neutral observer, so most of the time you need to use the THIRD PERSON (*he, she, it, one, they*). Using the FIRST PERSON (*I, we, our*) is acceptable only when you write about your own reactions and experiences. Some writing in the social sciences overuses the PASSIVE VOICE (8o and 8p). Style manuals for the social sciences, however, recommend using the ACTIVE VOICE whenever possible.

**39d** **What are different types of papers in the social sciences?**

Instructors will sometimes assign the same kinds of writing in the social sciences we explained for the humanities in section 38c. Three additional types of papers are case studies, research reports, and research papers (or reviews of the literature).

## CASE STUDIES

A case study is an intensive study of one group or individual. If you write a case study, describe situations as a neutral observer. Refrain from interpreting them unless your assignment says that you can add your interpretation to your report. Also, always differentiate between fact and opinion (4c.2). For example, you may observe nursing home patients lying on their sides in bed, facing the door. Describe exactly what you see: If you interpret or read into this observation that patients are lonely and watching the door for visitors, you could be wrong. Perhaps because medicines are injected in the right hip, patients are more comfortable lying on their left side, which just happens to put them in a position facing the door. Such work requires FIELD RESEARCH (32c).

A case study is usually presented in a relatively fixed format, but the specific parts and their order vary. Most case studies contain the following components: (1) basic identifying information about the individual or group; (2) a history of the individual or group; (3) observations of the individual's or group's behavior; and (4) conclusions as well as possible recommendations that resulted from the observations.

## RESEARCH REPORTS

**Research reports** explain your own original research based on PRIMARY SOURCES. These may result from interviews, questionnaires, observations, or experiments. Research reports in the social sciences often follow a prescribed format: (1) statement of the problem; (2) background, sometimes including a review of the literature; (3) methodology; (4) results; and (5) discussion of findings.

## RESEARCH PAPERS (OR REVIEWS OF THE LITERATURE)

More often for students, social science research requires you to summarize, analyze, and synthesize SECONDARY SOURCES (37b). These sources are usually articles and books that report or discuss the findings of other people's primary research. To prepare a **review of literature**, comprehensively gather and analyze the sources that have been published on a specific topic. "Literature" in this sense simply means "the body of work on a subject" and not creative work. Sometimes a review of the literature is a part of a longer paper, usually the "background" section of a research report. Other times the entire paper might be an extensive review of the literature.

## 39e What documentation style should I use in the social sciences?

If you use sources when writing about the social sciences, you must credit them using documentation. The American Psychological Association (APA) is the most commonly used documentation style in the social sciences. APA style uses PARENTHETICAL REFERENCES in the body of a paper and a list of REFERENCES at the end. We describe APA documentation style in detail in Chapter 35, providing a sample student research paper using APA style in section 35h.

Chicago Manual (CM) documentation style is sometimes used in the social sciences. The CM BIBLIOGRAPHIC NOTE style is described in detail in Chapter 36.

# NATURAL SCIENCES

## 39f What are the natural sciences?

The natural sciences include disciplines such as astronomy, biology, chemistry, geology, and physics. The sciences focus on natural phenomena. Scientists form and test hypotheses, which are assumptions made to prove their logical soundness and consequences in the real world. They do this to explain CAUSE AND EFFECT (4h) as systematically and objectively as possible.

The scientific method, commonly used in the sciences to make discoveries, is a procedure for gathering information related to a specific hypothesis. The scientific method is the cornerstone of all inquiry in the sciences. Box 39.2 gives guidelines for using the scientific method.

## 39g What are writing purposes and practices in the natural sciences?

Because scientists usually write to inform their AUDIENCE about factual information, SUMMARY and SYNTHESIS are important fundamental writing techniques (4e).

Exactness is extremely important in scientific writing. Readers expect precise descriptions of procedures and findings, free of personal bias. Scientists expect to be able to *replicate*—repeat step by step—the experiment or process the researcher carried out and obtain the same outcome.

Completeness is as important as exactness in scientific writing. Without complete information, a reader can misunderstand the writer's message and reach a wrong conclusion. For example, a researcher investigating how plants grow in different types of soil needs to report these facts: an analysis of each soil type, the amount of daylight exposure for each plant, the soil's moisture content, the type and amount of fertilizer used, and all other related facts. By including all of this information,

**SUMMARY BOX** 39.2

## Guidelines for using the scientific method

1. Formulate a tentative explanation—known as a *hypothesis*—for a scientific phenomenon. Be as specific as possible.

2. Read and summarize previously published information related to your hypothesis.

3. Plan and outline a method of investigation to uncover the information needed to test your hypothesis.

4. Experiment, following exactly the investigative procedures you've outlined.

5. Observe closely the results of the experiment, and write notes carefully.

6. Analyze the results. If they prove the hypothesis to be false, rework the investigation and begin again. If the results confirm the hypothesis, say so.

7. Write a report of your research. At the end, you can suggest additional hypotheses that might be investigated.

the researcher tells the reader how the conclusion in the written report was founded in the experiment or analysis.

Because science writing depends largely on objective observation rather than subjective comments, scientists generally avoid using the FIRST PERSON (*I, we, our*) in their writing. Another reason to avoid the first person is that the sciences generally focus on the experiment rather than on the person doing the experimenting.

When writing for the sciences, you're often expected to follow fixed formats, which are designed to summarize a project and present its results efficiently. In your report, organize the information to achieve clarity and precision. Writers in the sciences sometimes use charts, graphs, tables, diagrams, and other illustrations to present material. In fact, illustrations, in many cases, can explain complex material more clearly than words can, as in Figure 39.1 on page 730.

## 39h What documentation style should I use in the natural sciences?

If you use secondary sources when you write about the sciences, you are required to credit your sources by using documentation. Documentation styles in the various sciences differ somewhat from discipline to discipline and, even, from publication to publication. Ask your instructor which style to use.

**COMMON DISEASES AND INFECTIONS WITH THEIR MICROBIAL CAUSES**

| | Bacteria | Fungus | Protozoa | Virus |
|---|---|---|---|---|
| Athlete's foot | | ▲ | | |
| Chickenpox | | | | ▲ |
| Common cold | | | | ▲ |
| Diarrheal disease | ▲ | | ▲ | ▲ |
| Flu | | | | ▲ |
| Genital herpes | | | | ▲ |
| Malaria | | | ▲ | |
| Meningitis | ▲ | | | ▲ |
| Pneumonia | ▲ | ▲ | | ▲ |
| Sinusitis | ▲ | ▲ | | |
| Skin diseases | ▲ | ▲ | ▲ | ▲ |
| Strep throat | ▲ | | | |
| Tuberculosis | ▲ | | | |
| Urinary tract infection | ▲ | | | |
| Vaginal infections | ▲ | ▲ | | |
| Viral hepatitis | | | | ▲ |

Figure 39.1  A table conveying data

The Council of Science Editors (CSE) has compiled style and documentation guidelines for the life sciences, the physical sciences, and mathematics. CSE documentation guidelines are described in sections 36c and 36d.

## 39i  How do I write different types of papers in the natural sciences?

Two major types of papers in the sciences are *reports* and *reviews*.

### 39i.1  Science reports

Science reports tell about observations and experiments. When they describe laboratory experiments, as is often the case in academic settings, they're usually called laboratory reports. Formal reports feature the eight elements identified in Box 39.3. Less formal reports, which are sometimes assigned in introductory college courses, might not include an abstract or a review of the literature. Ask your instructor which sections to include in your report.

## Parts of a science report

1. **Title.** Precisely describes your report's topic. Your instructor may require a title page that lists the title, your name, the course name and section, your instructor's name, and the date. If so, there is no recommended format in CSE style; generally, students use APA format (35g) or their instructor's.

2. **Abstract.** Provides a short overview of the report to help readers decide whether your research interests them.

3. **Introduction.** States the purpose behind your research and presents the hypothesis. Any needed background information and a review of the literature appear here.

4. **Methods and Materials.** Describes the equipment, material, and procedures used.

5. **Results.** Provides the information obtained from your efforts. Charts, graphs, and photographs help present the data in a way that is easy for readers to grasp.

6. **Discussion.** Presents your interpretation and evaluation of the results. Did your efforts support your hypothesis? If not, can you suggest why not? Use concrete evidence in discussing your results.

7. **Conclusion.** Lists conclusions about the hypothesis and the outcomes of your efforts, paying particular attention to any implications that can be drawn from your work. Be specific in suggesting further research.

8. **References.** Presents references cited in the review of the literature, if any. Its format conforms to the requirements of the documentation style preferred by your instructor.

### SAMPLE STUDENT SCIENCE REPORT

The sample science report presented on the following pages was written by a student in an intermediate course in biology. Like the sample report, yours would likely follow APA format for margins, page numbering, and title page. The text and references would follow CSE-style recommendations.

Adam Furman

Biology 201, Lab

Professor Joshua Mann

November 13, 2005

*Title of report* → The Effectiveness of Common Antibiotics

*Title of subsection* → Introduction ← *Abstract omitted on this sample*

The purpose of this experiment was to test the effectiveness of antibiotics against two common bacteria.

Antibiotics are substances that inhibit life processes of bacteria. There are two types of antibiotics. One interferes with cell wall synthesis, causing death. The other disrupts protein synthesis, thus preventing replication.

Escherichia coli is a gram-negative bacterium. It is found in the colon of many mammals, including humans. Commonly, it contaminates beef and chicken products. Staphylococcus epidermidis is a gram-positive bacterium found naturally on the skin. This bacterium is often the cause of infected burns and cuts. Both bacteria were used in this experiment.

It is hypothesized that five chemical antibiotics will be effective against both bacteria. Also hypothesized is that two natural antimicrobials, echinacea and garlic, would not work very well.

Methods and Materials

Using aseptic techniques, two petri dishes were inoculated. Staphylococcus epidermidis was used on one dish and Escherichia coli on a second dish. A sterile paper disc was saturated with Streptomycin. The disc was placed on one of

*continued* ➤

Effectiveness 2

the dishes. The process was repeated for the other dish. Both dishes were marked with identification and location of the paper discs. Each of the following was also saturated on paper discs and placed into its own zone on both dishes: sterile water (control), ampicillin, erythromycin, chloramphenicol, tetracycline, gentamycin, echinacea, and garlic.

The dishes were incubated overnight at room temperature. The zone of inhibition of growth in centimeters was measured and recorded.

Results

Streptomycin, a protein synthesis disrupter, worked effectively to prevent growth of the S. epidermidis and the E. coli. Tetracycline inhibited the reproduction of the S. epidermidis and the E. coli. Ampicillin, a common bactericide, worked better on the S. epidermidis than the E. coli, because the S. epidermidis is gram positive and the E. coli is gram negative. Gentamycin effectively prevented the growth of E. coli. Erythromycin and chloramphenicol behaved similarly to the ampicillin.

The antibiotics behaved as expected in regard to effectiveness against gram-positive and gram-negative bacteria. As hypothesized, the echinacea inhibited growth only slightly, indicating that it probably would not function as an antibiotic. The garlic had a zone of inhibition greater than expected for a non-antibiotic. Zero centimeters of inhibition from the sterile water control demonstrates that there was no contamination of the experiment.

continued ➤

Effectiveness 3 | Discussion section omitted in this sample
---|---

Conclusion

The results imply that the ampicillin would be an effective treatment against S. epidermidis infection and gentamycin would prove effective in treating an infection of E. coli.

As with any experiment, it would be wise to repeat the tests again to check for accuracy. Other antibiotics could be tested against a larger range of bacteria for broader results.

No Cited References needed in this type of science report

## 39i.2 Science reviews

A science review is a paper discussing published information on a scientific topic or issue. The purpose of the review is SUMMARY: to assemble for readers all the current knowledge about the topic or issue. Sometimes, the purpose of a science review is SYNTHESIS: to suggest a new interpretation of the old material. In such reviews, the writer must present evidence to persuade readers that the new interpretation is valid.

If you're required to write a science review, you want to (1) choose a very limited scientific issue currently being researched; (2) use information that is current—the more recently published the articles, books, and journals you consult, the better; (3) accurately PARAPHRASE (33i) and SUMMARIZE (33j) material; and (4) DOCUMENT your sources (Chapters 34–36). If your review runs longer than two or three pages, you might want to use headings to help your reader understand the organization and idea progression of your paper. See Chapters 32–33 for advice on finding and using sources.

# Chapter 40

## BUSINESS AND PUBLIC WRITING

### 40a   Who writes in the workplace?

If you plan to have a job or already have one, chances are that writing is or will be a large part of your life. Writing infuses most job situations, from corporate offices, not-for-profit agencies, schools, and health care facilities to farms and factories. People write to co-workers inside organizations; they write to customers or service providers outside them. Even people who work independently (consultants, therapists, artists, craftspeople, and so on) keep records, apply for grants, correspond with customers, and advertise their services.

Work-related correspondence needs to be professional in TONE, concise, and well informed. It can't contain slang, abbreviations, or informal words or expressions. Recipients expect it to use standard EDITED AMERICAN ENGLISH grammar, spelling, and punctuation. To be effective, always address the recipient by name, preferably last name until a relationship is established, and say straight out in the first paragraph what the communication is about.

All workplace writing benefits from moving its way through the WRITING PROCESS as it seeks to INFORM or to PERSUADE. Indeed, never before in your writing have the acts of revising, editing, and proofreading carried as much weight as they do in business writing. The slightest error reflects negatively on the writer personally and on the larger world of the company that employs the writer.

**ESL TIP:** In some cultures, work-related correspondence is often sprinkled with elaborate language, many descriptive details, and even metaphors. Most US businesses, however, expect correspondence that gets to the point quickly, is highly concise, and is written in clear language.

## 40b What are typical policies concerning business writing?

Most workplaces have policies that strictly govern their employees' use of the organization's e-mail system and stationery. As soon as you start with a new employer, speak to your supervisor about policies. Also ask for the employee manual and take time to read it carefully. If no one seems to know the official policy, always assume that the policies are strict until you're told differently. See Box 40.1 for a list of typical business writing policies for employees.

**SUMMARY BOX** 40.1

### Typical business writing policies for employees

- Companies reserve e-mail systems and any uses of company letterhead stationery for their operations only.
- Companies own all correspondence written, sent, or received via e-mail or other means, including courier or regular mail. Furthermore, their administrators and supervisors at all levels have complete access to view and save all of this correspondence.
- Companies prohibit employees from writing, sending, or receiving correspondence (by any means) with content that is potentially harmful to the company. This includes, but is not limited to, content that makes libelous comments, enters into preliminaries to contractual agreements or into contracts themselves, contains chain letters, mentions material that degrades someone in the company, disseminates confidential or embarrassing information, or reveals other offensive material.

## 40c What are legal considerations concerning business writing?

Legal considerations involving business writing involve two entities at least: you as an employee and the company for which you work.

### 40c.1 Legal considerations involving you as an employee

Because employers have complete access to your business e-mail, business letters, and business memos, they can use such documents as evidence of your job performance. You might not be aware during the normal course of your workday that your supervisors have access to your written conduct of business, but they do legally. Judge your writing, therefore, as if it were being read in a formal assessment of your work.

## 40c.2 Legal considerations involving your company

For legal purposes, your business e-mail as well as your business letters and business memos written on company letterhead stationery may be used as evidence in legal disputes, in court, and by the government, regarding you or the company you work for. In some situations, e-mails sent to customers or other parties within and outside the company may be construed as legally binding on the company; therefore, they're your responsibility.

## 40d  What are special considerations concerning business e-mail?

E-mail is the primary form of written business communication today. Therefore, use it with special care, even though you might use it quite informally in your personal life. Here are some overriding guidelines for business use.

- Find out whether personal e-mail is tolerated. (You can usually find e-mail policies in an employee manual.) Even if personal e-mail is permitted, realize that monitoring systems in most workplaces can quickly identify such e-mails. Therefore, you might want to avoid sending or receiving personal e-mails on your workplace computer.
- Scan for viruses to avoid the risk of infecting your organization's entire computer system. If you aren't sure how to do this skillfully, ask before trying to scan your first attachment.
- Ask your supervisor whether there are restrictions regarding the size of attachments that you can send or receive. (Large attachments can overload the computer system at work.) If there are restrictions, use NETI-QUETTE and alert your recipients about the size of any large attachments before you send them. In turn, ask senders to alert you before sending large ones to you.
- Protect the ID numbers and passwords you're assigned or have created to access your organization's electronic systems. As an employee, you're accountable for all activity conducted on password-protected accounts.

Some businesses automatically insert or require employees to insert a DISCLAIMER—a statement appended to the top or bottom of e-mails designed to protect the company from legal liability. The value of disclaimers is limited. Only a court of law can determine the effectiveness of such statements, but they might prove effective in limiting a company's liability in some cases. Here are two typical examples:

> This e-mail may contain confidential material. If you were not an intended recipient, please notify the sender and delete all copies. We may monitor e-mail to and from our network.

> This e-mail and any files transmitted with it are confidential and contain privileged or copyrighted information intended solely for the use of the named recipients. It may not be copied or disclosed to anyone other than the named recipients. If you have received this message in error, please notify the sender immediately, and delete this e-mail from your system.

### 40d.1 Maximizing the advantages of business e-mail systems

Most business e-mail systems are extremely convenient information storage systems. In them, you can store not only e-mail addresses but also job titles, business addresses, Web addresses, telephone and fax numbers, and notations. Steps for efficient use of e-mail systems are explained in Box 40.2.

---

**CHECKLIST BOX 40.2**

**Organizing e-mail contacts**

1. **Categories.** Place contacts into categories, allowing you to manipulate data, link it to various tasks (*committee work*) or projects (*team initiative*), and create category distribution lists. Keep such lists up to date to avoid leaving out new members or sending messages to former ones.

2. **Viewing criteria.** Use different viewing modes so you can find contacts by category, distribution list, company, or address criteria.

3. **Search features.** Input a first or last name to locate a contact or distribution group.

4. **Links.** Link your contacts with other features, such as an appointment feature, if available.

5. **Vcards.** Forward an electronic business card with an e-mail message, making it easy to share your contact information with others.

## 40d.2 Following guidelines for content of work-related e-mail

The subject line in an e-mail tells your recipients how to sort, file, and prioritize a message. Be very specific in stating your subject so that you don't show disrespect for your recipient's time. You might have to write the same people more than one e-mail about different subjects in the same day, but at least your recipients will be able to keep their records straight.

| NO (VAGUE) | YES (SPECIFIC) |
|---|---|
| Travel Approval | Approval Request for Chicago Trip |
| E-mail Policy | New E-mail Retention Policy |
| Meeting | Meeting on Annual Report Schedule |
| Schedule Change | Cancellation of Chicago Trip |

In the "Cc" or "Copies" space, insert the e-mail addresses of people who need to see your message, even when they aren't expected to respond. Never send copies to people who don't really need the information; it can backfire and simply annoy someone who already has too many messages in his or her Inbox. If you use the "Bcc" (Blind Copy) space, you're sending a copy to people without your primary recipients knowing about it. Generally, people consider blind copying rude because it's akin to talking behind someone's back. However, certain rare, delicate situations might call for it. For example, in a mass mail-out, it would be good netiquette to blind copy dozens of customers because you would be protecting their privacy by not disclosing their e-mail addresses to everyone else.

For the message of your e-mail, single-space the text, and double-space between paragraphs and before your complimentary closing. Start paragraphs flush left at the margin. When you need to include a separate document of more than a paragraph or two with your e-mail, such as a report, compose it as a separate document in your word-processing program, and attach it to your e-mail using the "Attachments" function of your e-mail service. Attached documents, rather than copied and pasted documents, look better because they maintain the original formatting (margins, spacing, italics). As you compose your message, follow the principles in Box 40.3 on page 740.

Figure 40.1 is an example of a professional e-mail.

## 40d.3 Using e-mail netiquette

**Netiquette**, a word coined from *net* and *etiquette*, refers to good e-mail manners. For example, unless your business recipients give you permission to loosen your level of formality, always address them by their full names and titles, especially when your recipients are people you've never met or corresponded with before. As important, always use GENDER-

NEUTRAL LANGUAGE. Finally, try to reply to e-mail messages within one or two days after receiving them. When you can't respond quickly, always acknowledge that you've received a message. Say when you'll reply, and don't forget to follow up.

For an example of a business e-mail, see Figure 40.1 on the following page.

## SUMMARY BOX 40.3

### Content of a business e-mail

- Keep the message of your business e-mail brief and your paragraphs short. Reading a screen is harder on the eyes than reading a print document.

- Restrict each business e-mail to one topic, even if you have to write the recipients about more than one topic in the same day.

- Start your business e-mail with a sentence that tells what your message is about.

- Put the details of your business e-mail message in the second paragraph. Supply any background information that your recipients aren't already aware of or might have forgotten.

- Conclude your e-mail in a short, final paragraph by asking for explicit information or specific action, if needed; or by restating your reason for writing (for example, keeping someone apprised of a situation or reporting on a meeting).

- If your e-mail runs longer than three to four paragraphs, add topic headings (42d) to help your readers speed through the material.

- Never write in all capital letters (WE NEED TO TAKE ACTION NOW) or all lowercase letters (i think we should check with the denver office). Not only are they annoying to read, but all capital letters are considered the written equivalent of rudely shouting. All-lowercase letters suggest laziness and a lack of respect.

- At the end of your message, before your full name and position, use a commonly accepted complimentary closing, such as *Sincerely, Cordially,* or *Regards.*

- Be cautious about what you say in a business e-mail. After all, the recipient can forward any e-mail, including ones received as blind copies, to others without your permission, even though this practice is considered unethical and rude.

- Forward an e-mail message only if you've asked the original sender for permission.

---

To: sherrel.ampadu@jpltech.com
From: Chris Malinowitz <cmalinowitz@chateauby.com>
Subject: Confirming Meeting Arrangements
Cc: dmclusky@chateauby.com
Bcc:
Attached: C:\Documents and Settings\Desktop\Chateau Menus.doc

---

Dear Ms. Ampadu:

I am writing to confirm the final arrangements for your business meeting on June 17, 2006, at our conference center.

As you directed, we will set the room in ten round tables, each seating six. We will provide a podium and microphone, an LCD projector and screen, and a white board with markers. I understand that you will be bringing your own laptop. Our technician can help you set up.

You indicated that you would like to provide lunch and refreshments at two breaks. Attached please find our menus. You will need to make your lunch selections at least 48 hours in advance.

If you have any questions or wish to make any changes, I would be pleased to accommodate your needs. Thank you for choosing The Chateau at Brickyard.

Sincerely,

Chris Malinowitz
Catering Director, The Chateau at Brickyard

Figure 40.1 A professional e-mail

## 40e How do I format and write memos?

**Memos** are usually exchanged internally (within an organization or business). Today e-mail takes the place of most memos, unless the correspondence requires a paper record or signature. The guidelines for writing e-mail (40c) also pertain to memos. The appropriate form of communication—paper memos or e-mail—depends on what's customary in your work environment.

The standard format of a memo includes two major parts: the headings and the body.

To:       [Name your audience—a specific person or group.]
From:     [Give your name and your title, if any.]
Date:     [Give the date on which you write the memo.]
Re:       [State your subject as specifically as possible in the "Subject" or "Re" line.]

The content calls for a beginning, middle, and end, with all parts holding closely to your topic. Don't ramble. If you need more than one or, at most, two pages, change your format into that of a brief report. Here are some guidelines for preparing a memo.

- **Introduction:** Briefly state your purpose for writing and why your memo is worth your readers' attention. Mention whether the recipient needs to take action, making it clear either here or at the conclusion.
- **Body:** Present the essential information on your topic, including facts the recipient needs to know. If you write more than three or four paragraphs, use headings to divide the information into subtopics so that the memo can be scanned quickly.
- **Conclusion:** End with a one- to two-sentence summary, a specific recommendation, or what action is needed and by when. Finish with a "thank you" sentence.

## 40f  How do I write business letters?

Business letters are more formal and official than business e-mails or business memos. Choose to write a business letter, rather than a business e-mail, to add appropriate weight and respect to your message, for ceremonial occasions, and to ensure that your message is placed on the record and thereby becomes part of a "paper trail." Business letters generally fall into two official categories based on their purposes.

- **Regular business letters** are business-to-business communications. These letters make up the majority of business correspondence. Always use company letterhead stationery, and follow any special guidelines for style or format that your company uses.
- **Social business letters** are letters to business colleagues on matters that serve a business-related social function, such as congratulations on an achievement, condolences in a time of loss, thank you letters, invitations to social events, and the like. Given that these letters are written in a business context, social business letters may be written on company letterhead stationery.

There are some general guidelines for addressing recipients in business letters. The old-fashioned "To Whom It May Concern" rarely reaches the right person in an organization. Use the full name of your recipient whenever possible. If you can't locate a name, either through a phone call to a central switchboard or on the Internet, use a specific category—for example, "Dear Billing Department," placing the key word "Billing" first (not "Department of Billing"). Always use gender-neutral language. Figure 40.2 is an example of a business letter from a not-for-profit group.

*ArtsFlamenco*

3B-243 West 21st Street
New York, NY 10011
artsflamenco@msn.com
www.artsflamenco.org

January 11, 2006

Mr. Antonio Alducin
Advisor, Latino Heritage Club
George Washington High School
324 Mapleview Road
Englewood, New Jersey 07631

Dear Mr. Alducin,

We enjoyed speaking with you earlier this week regarding *ArtsFlamenco*'s arts-in-education programs. We can certainly work with you to develop an after-school workshop that ties in elements of Spanish language, culture, music, and dance.

We are enclosing three program plans and their estimated costs. For your further interest, we are also including a DVD showing clips from two of our recent arts-in-education programs. After you have reviewed these materials, please contact us to discuss any questions you might have.

We very much look forward to speaking with you again.

All the best,

Jorge Navarro
President and Artistic Director

Encl: 3

*A Section 501(c)(3) New York Not-for-Profit Corporation*

**Figure 40.2  A sample business letter written in block style**

Here are guidelines for the format and content of your business letters.

- **Paper:** Use 8½ × 11 inch paper. The most suitable colors are white, off-white, and light beige. Fold your business letters horizontally into thirds to fit into a standard number 10 business envelope (9½ × 4 inches). Never fold a business letterhead stationery page in half and then into thirds.

- **Letterhead stationery:** Use the official letterhead stationery (name, address, and logo, if any) of the business where you're employed. If no letterhead stationery exists, imitate the format that others have used. If no such tradition exists, center the company's full name, address, and phone number at the top of the page, and use a larger and different font than for the content of your letter.

- **Format:** Without indents, use single spacing within paragraphs and double spacing between paragraphs. All lines start flush left, which means at the left margin. This is called **block style**. An equally acceptable alternative form is called **modified block style** in which the lines for the inside address and the body begin flush left but the heading, closing, and signature begin about halfway across the page. Box 40.4 lists the features of block style and modified block style letter formats.

Use block or modified block formats for business correspondence of a personal nature, such as job application letters, letters of complaint concerning personal matters, or letters asking for information for you personally. Use plain white paper, and if you have personal stationery, use it.

## 40g How do I write a resume?

A **resume** details your accomplishments and employment history. Its PURPOSE is to help a potential employer (the AUDIENCE) determine whether you'll be a suitable candidate for employment. To make a favorable impression, follow the guidelines for writing a resume in Box 40.5.

You'll also find an example of a resume in Figure 40.3.

# Features of block and modified block styles

### BLOCK-STYLE FORMAT

- Begin the dateline two inches below the top of the page or three lines below the last line of the letterhead, depending on the depth of the letterhead copy.
- Begin all elements at the left margin.
- Allow one inch for left, right, and bottom margins.
- Leave three blank lines between the dateline and the inside address.
- Leave one blank line between the inside address and the salutation.
- Leave one blank line between the salutation and the body.
- Type the body single-spaced and leave one blank line between paragraphs.
- Leave one blank line between the body and complimentary closing.
- Leave three blank lines between the complimentary closing and the signature block.

### MODIFIED BLOCK STYLE FORMAT

- Begin the dateline two inches below the top of the page or three lines below the last line of the letterhead, depending on the depth of the letterhead copy.
- Center:
  - Dateline
  - Complimentary closing
  - Signature block
- Allow one inch for left, right, and bottom margins.
- Leave three blank lines between the dateline and the inside address.
- Leave one blank line between the inside address and the salutation.
- Leave one blank line between the salutation and the body.
- Type the body single-spaced and leave one blank line between paragraphs.
- Leave one blank line between the body and complimentary closing.
- Leave three blank lines between the complimentary closing and the signature block.

## Guidelines for writing a resume

- Place your name, address, e-mail address, and telephone number at the top.

- Make it easy to read. Label the sections clearly, and target the resume to the position you want. Help employers see your most significant attributes as quickly and as easily as possible.

- Adjust your resume to fit your PURPOSE. For example, if you're applying for a job as a computer programmer, you'll want to emphasize different facts than you would if you're applying for a job selling computers in an electronics store.

- Use headings to separate blocks of information. Include the following headings, as appropriate: Position Desired or Career Objective; Education; Experience; Licenses and Certifications; Related Experience; Honors or Awards; Publications or Presentations; Activities and Interests; and Special Abilities, Skills, and Knowledge.

- When you list your work experience, place your most recent job first; when listing education, place your most recent degrees, certificates, or enrollments first.

- Write telegraphically. Start with verb phrases, not with the word *I*, and omit *a, an,* and *the.* For example, write "Created new computer program to organize company's spreadsheets" instead of "*I* created *a* new computer program to organize *the* company's spreadsheets."

- Include only relevant information.

- Tell the truth. Even if you get the job, an employer who discovers you lied will probably fire you.

- Include references, or state that you can provide them on request. (Be sure to have them at hand so that you can respond speedily to such a request.)

- Try to fit all of the information on one page. If you need a second page, make sure the most important information is on the first page.

- Use high-quality paper that is white, off-white, or light beige.

- Consider using minimal formatting (that is, use no bold or italic type and no columns). Employers often scan resumes into computers and then search them electronically for key words. Some also request text-only applications through online job sites.

- Proofread carefully; even one spelling error or one formatting error can eliminate you from consideration.

## MONICA A. SCHICKEL

CURRENT ADDRESS *(until 15 December 2005)*
1822 Manchester Hall
Illinois State University
Normal, IL 61761
(309) 555-7619
mnsschl@gmail.com

PERMANENT ADDRESS
704 Franklin Street
Eureka, IL 61530
(309) 555-8337
Cell: (217) 555-3236
mnsschl@gmail.com

OBJECTIVE:   Entry-level position as a graphic designer or publications assistant

### EDUCATION:

| | |
|---|---|
| 8/02–present | **Illinois State University,** Normal, IL<br>BA Graphic Design, expected December 2005<br>Minor in Technical Writing |
| 8/00–5/02 | **Illinois Central College,** East Peoria, IL<br>AA General Education, May 2002 |

### EMPLOYMENT:

| | |
|---|---|
| 6/05–present | **Publications Intern** (half-time; paid)<br>*The Pantagraph,* Bloomington, IL<br>• Design advertisements<br>• Prepare photographs for publication<br>• Lay out "Tempo" section<br>• Edit and proofread articles |
| 10/02–5/05 | **Customer Service Representative**<br>National City Bank, Normal, IL<br>• Sold accounts to customers; made all sales goals<br>• Created promotional posters for specials |
| 4/00–7/02 | **Evening Manager**<br>Video Supermarket, Peoria, IL<br>• Organized 90,000-movie inventory<br>• Supervised three clerks |

### SKILLS AND SELECTED EXPERIENCES:

- Expert in Quark, InDesign, Photoshop, Dreamweaver
- Full understanding of MS Word, Excel, PowerPoint, Publisher; Internet research; Web design
- Illustrator and photographer. Have completed several commissions; portfolio available on request
- Vice President, Student Residence Halls Association
- Cartoonist, *Daily Vidette* (student newspaper)
- Excellent customer service understanding and experience
- Fast output ability with high-quality work

REFERENCES:   Available on request

**Figure 40.3  A sample resume**

## 40h How do I write a job application letter?

A **job application letter** always needs to accompany your resume. Avoid repeating what's already on the resume. Instead, connect the company's expectations to your experience by emphasizing how your background has prepared you for the position. Your job application letter, more than your resume, reflects your energy and personality. Here are guidelines for writing a job application letter.

- Use one page only.
- Overall, think of your letter as a polite sales pitch about yourself and what benefits you can bring to the company. Don't be shy, but don't exaggerate.
- Use the same name, content, and format guidelines as for a business letter (40f).
- Address the letter to a specific person. If you can't discover a name, use a gender-neutral title such as *Dear Personnel Director.* Box 40.6 provides help for writing gender-neutral salutations.
- Open your letter by identifying the position for which you're applying.
- Mention your qualifications, and explain how your background will meet the job requirements.
- Make clear that you're familiar with the company or organization; your research will impress the employer.
- End by being specific about what you can do for the company. If the job will be your first, give your key attributes—but make sure they're relevant. For instance, you might state that you're punctual, self-disciplined, eager to learn, and hard-working.
- State when you're available for an interview and how the potential employer can reach you.
- Edit and proofread the letter carefully. If you have to hand-correct even one error, print out the letter again.

For an example of a job application letter, see Figure 40.4.

**ESL TIP:** In some cultures, job applications may include personal information, such as an applicant's age, marital status, number of children, religion, or political beliefs. In North America, however, this is not standard practice. Such personal information does not help an employer determine how well you can perform a particular job, so avoid including it in your application. ☺

Thinking, speaking, and writing using gender-neutral language is very important in the workplace, particularly when addressing recipients in memos, job application letters, and so on. Prepare yourself by following the guidelines in Box 40.6 (p. 750).

Monica A. Schickel
1822 Manchester Hall
Illinois State University
Normal, IL 61761
(309) 555-7619
mnsschl@gmail.com

November 20, 2005

Jaime Cisneros
Publications Director
R.L. Smith Consulting
2000 Wabash Avenue
Chicago, IL 60601

Dear Mr. Cisneros:

Please consider my application for the graphic designer position that your company
advertised in the *Chicago Tribune* on November 18. I believe that my professional
experiences, education, and skills prepare me well for this opportunity.

I am currently completing a paid internship at *The Pantagraph* newspaper in
Bloomington, Illinois, where I have worked as an effective member of a creative team.
My responsibilities have included designing advertisements, laying out sections of
the newspaper, and preparing photographs. Other related experience includes
commission work as an illustrator and photographer. As the enclosed resume
demonstrates, I have additional work experience in business environments.

Next month I will earn a BA in graphic design from Illinois State University,
where my course of study has included extensive work in graphic design,
photography, drawing and illustration, and digital media. Simultaneously, I will
complete a minor in technical writing that includes courses in document design
and editing, as well as writing.

I would be pleased to provide further information, including a portfolio that
demonstrates the quality of my work. I am available for an interview at your
convenience. The opportunities at R.L. Smith closely fit my background and goals,
and I look forward to discussing how I can contribute to your publications
department.

Sincerely,

*Monica A. Schickel*

Monica A. Schickel

**Figure 40.4  A sample job application letter**

**SUMMARY BOX 40.6**

## Guidelines for writing a gender-neutral salutation

1. Telephone or send an e-mail to the company to which you're sending the letter. State your reason for contacting them, and ask for the name of the person you want to receive your letter.

2. Address men as Mr., and address women as Ms., unless you're specifically told to use Miss or Mrs. If your recipient goes by another title such as Dr. or Professor, use it.

3. If you can't identify a proper name and must use a title alone, keep the title generic and gender-neutral.

   **NO**   Dear Sir: [sexist]

   Dear Sir or Madam: [sexist for both genders]

   **YES**   Dear Human Resources Officer:

   Dear Apple Sales Manager:

   For more information about gender-neutral language, see 21g.

## 40i   How do I write a business proposal?

Proposals persuade readers to follow a plan, choose a product or service, or implement an idea. A marketing specialist might propose a new product line. A teacher might propose a change in the curriculum. A leader in a not-for-profit organization might propose a way to raise funding. Proposals generally describe a project, the steps for starting and completing the project, and how much it will cost.

Readers evaluate proposals based on how well the writers have anticipated and answered their questions. If some readers have a high level of knowledge about the subject of the proposal, and others have little, then you need to explain the basic information and offer a glossary of terms. Here are some guidelines for preparing a proposal.

| | |
|---|---|
| **INTRODUCTION** | Explain the purpose and scope of the project. |
| | Describe the problem that the project seeks to solve. |
| | Lay out the solution your project will provide. |
| | Include dates for beginning and completing the work. |
| | Project the outcomes and the costs. |
| | Be accurate and precise. |
| **BODY** | What is the product or service? |
| | What resources are needed? |
| | What are the phases of the project? |

What is the detailed budget?

Precisely how is each phase to be completed?

By what date is each phase to be completed?

How will the project be evaluated?

CONCLUSION   Summarize briefly the benefits of this proposal.

Thank readers for their time.

Offer to provide further information.

## 40j   How do I prepare an informal meeting agenda?

New employees are usually expected to know from their high school or college experiences the basics of how to prepare the agenda for a simple informal meeting—that is, a meeting not conducted according to the rules of formal parliamentary procedure. The best way to begin is to study the agendas and minutes of prior meetings of the same group. The person who assigns you the task of preparing the agenda is the logical person to go to for such materials. If that person doesn't have access to the history of the group, find out who does, even if this means talking with someone who has only an oral history to tell you.

If no strategy you think of uncovers enough information, turn the meeting into one that starts with brainstorming what was done and what needs to be done. The problem is one of the collective, not of you the individual. Figure 40.5 shows you the agenda for an informal meeting prepared by an employee who had attended six previous meetings of this group.

## 40k   How do I write informal meeting minutes if I'm a new employee?

New employees are usually expected to know how to take minutes at an informal meeting—that is, a meeting not conducted according to the formal rules of parliamentary procedure. Therefore, sometimes a new employee is told without warning to take minutes at such a meeting. Few newcomers to a company enjoy having to participate in a discussion and also take notes, so in some cases, such a sudden assignment is seen as a bit of an initiation rite. Therefore, always go to meetings prepared with a laptop or a notebook, pens or pencils—and a smile.

Generally, the minutes of an informal meeting cover all important topics that were discussed, both those on the agenda and not. Exactly what is defined as "important" is hard to know if you're new to a company, so your best route is to write down just about everything that comes up. Then you can ask at least two colleagues who were at the meeting and know more about the topic than you do to advise you about what to leave out when you write up the minutes.

FORMAT OF HEADING
Name and title centered, single spaced
Double space to date and time on one line and location on one line
"Agenda" two lines below

**Human Resources Department**
**Planning Meeting for Open Enrollment Communication**

Friday, July 16, 2004, 3–4 p.m.
Michigan Avenue Conference Room

**Agenda**

**Attendees**
Margaret Alexander, HR
Joanna Bergstrom, HR Director-Organizer
Rebecca Greenfield, Freelance HR Writer/Editor
Larry Jordan, HR Services
Bob LeGorce, Finance
Bernard Moore, HR Services
Chris Papparello, Finance

| Topics | Discussion leader (time) |
|---|---|
| • Introductions/roles and responsibilities | Joanna (5 minutes) |
| • Tentative enrollment dates | Joanna and Bob (5 minutes) |
| • Possible benefits plan changes | Bob (10 minutes) |
| • Goals/strategies for communication | Bob and Chris (10 minutes) |
| • Communication elements | Joanna and Beth (25 minutes) |
| • Next steps/assignments | Joanna (5 minutes) |

REQUIRED IN INFORMAL AGENDA
Organization or department name
List of attendees
Topics to be discussed

OPTIONAL IN INFORMAL AGENDA
Statement of purpose after title of meeting
Bullets for names
Name of chair or organizer
Time allotments

Figure 40.5 An informal meeting agenda

The sample set of minutes shown in Figure 40.6 is being communicated by e-mail because the minutes-taker found out this is the traditional way the minutes of this particular group are circulated.

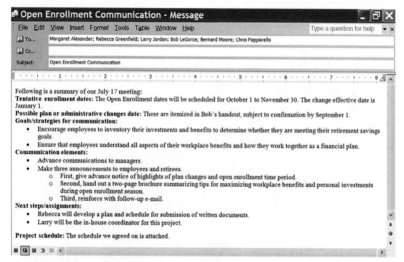

Figure 40.6 The minutes of an informal meeting

## 40l What is public writing?

**Public writing** is intended for people who are reading for reasons other than work, school, or professional obligations. Instead, they read it out of interest or a desire to keep informed. Some public writing is also known as CIVIC WRITING because you're writing to affect actions or beliefs among other citizens in a democratic society.

Examples of writing for the public include a letter or e-mail to refute a newspaper editorial, a program for a play or concert, a brochure to draw new members into a service organization, a proposal to build a town park, a fund-raising letter for a worthy cause, a script for a radio announcement, a Web site for a hobby or social cause that interests you, or an e-mail urging your representative to vote for a certain bill. Depending on your purpose, follow the guidelines for INFORMATIVE or PERSUASIVE writing. The Nature Conservancy Web site in Figure 40.7 illustrates one type of public writing situation.

In all of these examples—and you can add many more of your own— you're likely writing for an AUDIENCE that you don't know personally. You're also discussing subjects that you think affect others, not just you alone. For these reasons, public writing requires that you take special care in analyzing your audience and establishing your credibility.

Figure 40.7 A Web site as an example of public writing.

"Establishing credibility" means convincing your readers that they need or want to listen to you. Create a strong ETHOS by being accurate and honest and by explaining your connection with the readers. What do you have in common with them? How does your experience make you a reputable source—or, have you done research to become a knowledgeable source? Can you name other authorities who agree with your perspective? Readers can discern fake information quite quickly.

For example, if you're writing a letter to the editor of your local newspaper, you'll gain credibility if you begin, "As a resident of Green County for twelve years," and then state your position. By establishing yourself first as a member of your audience's community, you convey that you have a sincere and long-standing interest in the welfare of that community. Or suppose you're writing to ask one of your state senators to support a bill for a new wildlife refuge. You might present your argument on the basis of your research into the benefits and drawbacks of setting aside the land. In this way, you make yourself credible by demonstrating that you understand the complexities of the issue.

LOGOS (logical appeals) and PATHOS (emotional appeals) also play important roles in public writing. For more information about using the three persuasive appeals, see 5g.

## 40m How do I write reports for the public?

Reports for the public vary in length, format, and content. An action brief from a political organization might consist of a few pages detailing recent developments on an issue of concern, such as a proposed law. Often these are published on Web sites or distributed through e-mail messages. A product update might contain news of technological advances, along with critical reviews and, perhaps, information on where to purchase an item. An impact study might explain the effect that a proposed construction project or new policy will have on the local environment, economy, or groups of people.

Write your material in an evenhanded TONE so that your credibility is supported by your fairness. If you want to criticize something, be sure your argument is well reasoned and supported—and that it lacks BIAS or malice toward any person(s) or specific idea(s). This doesn't mean that your writing needs to be limp. Indeed, you can choose writing that's spirited, enthusiastic, and even stirring.

Figure 40.8 shows the cover and Figure 40.9 the executive summary of a report on climate changes in the Great Lakes region of North America. An executive summary is a brief overview sometimes included before a lengthy report. The report was produced by The Union of Concerned Scientists and The Ecological Society of America. The entire work was published online and as a 105-page booklet.

To write a public report, follow the guidelines in Box 40.7 (p. 757).

## 40n How do I write letters to my community or its officials?

Letters to your community or its officials allow you to influence opinions or actions. Perhaps you want to endorse a new public project or react to a proposal. When you respond to a previous piece of writing in a

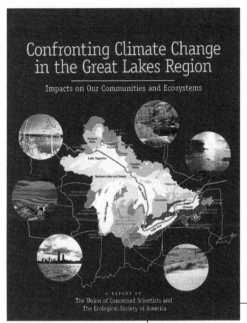

**Figure 40.8 Cover of a public report**

## Executive Summary

The Great Lakes region of the United States and Canada is a land of striking glacial legacies: spectacular lakes, vast wetlands, fertile southern soils, and rugged northern terrain forested in spruce and fir. It is also home to 60 million people whose actions can profoundly affect the region's ecological bounty and the life-sustaining benefits it provides. Now that the world is entering a period of unusually rapid climate change, driven largely by human activities that release heat-trapping greenhouse gases into the atmosphere, the responsibility for safeguarding our natural heritage is becoming urgent.

Growing evidence suggests that the climate of the Great Lakes is already changing:
- Winters are getting shorter.
- Annual average temperatures are growing warmer.
- The duration of lake ice cover is decreasing as air and water temperatures rise.
- Heavy rainstorms are becoming more common.

This report examines these trends in detail and discusses the likelihood that they will continue into the future. The consequences of these climatic changes will magnify the impacts of ongoing human disturbances that fragment or transform landscapes, pollute air and water, and disrupt natural ecosystems and the vital goods and services they provide. *Confronting Climate Change in the Great Lakes Region* explores the potential consequences of climate change, good and bad, for the character, economy, and environment of the Great Lakes region during the coming century. It also examines actions that can be taken now to help forestall many of the most severe consequences of climate change for North America's heartland.

CONFRONTING CLIMATE CHANGE IN THE GREAT LAKES REGION
*Union of Concerned Scientists • The Ecological Society of America*

**Figure 40.9 Executive summary**

## SUMMARY BOX 40.7

### Writing a public report

- Decide your purpose. Will you only inform, or will you also analyze the information you present? Or—going one step further—will you make a recommendation based on the information and your analysis?

- State your findings objectively. Though you may later bring in your opinion by recommending a course of action, your credibility depends on your first reporting accurately.

- Organize a formal report using the following sections. Depending on the purpose of your report, however, you might combine or expand any of the sections.

  - **Executive summary:** Provides a very brief summary of the entire report, including conclusions or recommendations.
  - **Introduction:** Explains the purpose of the report, describes the problem studied, and often describes or outlines the organization of the entire report.
  - **Methods:** Describes how the data were gathered.
  - **Results:** Presents the findings of the report.
  - **Discussion:** States the implications of your findings.
  - **Conclusion:** Makes recommendations or simply summarizes the findings.

publication, always begin by referring precisely to the source, using title, section, and date, if possible.

Many letters to the editor (and increasingly these are sent as e-mails) propose solutions to a community problem. These letters aim to persuade other readers that a problem exists and that a particular solution isn't only feasible but also the most advantageous of all the possible alternatives. Follow the general guidelines for writing ARGUMENTS (see Ch. 5). Use the format for a business letter or e-mail, and keep the following guidelines in mind when writing to propose a solution:

- Explain briefly the specific problem you're attempting to solve.
- Tell how your solution will solve all elements of the problem.
- Address briefly the possible objections or alternatives to your proposed solution.
- State why your solution offers the most advantages of all the alternatives.

To the Editor:

Re "Parking Plan Threatens Green Space" (news article, May 14):

For well over a century, Lincoln Park has provided a welcome oasis in downtown Springfield. In this park, office workers eat lunches, schoolchildren play on the way home, and evening concerts and other events unite the community.

It is very shortsighted, then, that the City Council now considers converting a third of the park into additional parking.

I acknowledge that parking downtown has gotten difficult. As the manager of a small shop, I know that our customers sometimes have trouble finding a parking place. However, the park itself is one of the reasons our downtown has become more popular in the past decade.

Ironically, destroying the park's attractive green space will reduce the need for more parking, which will hurt business.

A better solution is for the city to purchase the vacant property at the corner of Main and Jefferson and build a multistory garage. No doubt this option is more expensive than using the park. However, the land would be available cheaply, a multistory garage would actually provide more parking than the park land, and a preserved park would bolster business, thereby increasing tax revenues. I'm sure most citizens would prefer to leave future generations a legacy of trees, grass, and inviting beaches rather than a debt of sterile concrete.

Joel C. Bradway
Springfield, May 17, 2005

**Figure 40.10** A letter printed from a community newspaper

In the letter in Figure 40.10, a citizen argues for preserving a city park in its present form.

## 40o   What other types of public writing exist?

Many people write simply to express themselves or to entertain others. The most obvious examples are fiction, poetry, plays, film scripts, journals, and scrapbooks. In addition, many people produce newsletters, brochures, or similar documents, using not only words, but also graphic designs and images (Chapter 42).

Writing for the Internet is perhaps the broadest form of public writing, in the sense that anything you post there is available to any reader with online access. On the Internet, you might post book reviews on a bookseller's Web site or a message about an upcoming concert to a newsgroup. You might create a Web site about your talents, interests, or accomplishments, or a Web site for an organization, a social cause, or a special interest group. Chapter 43 discusses writing for the Web in detail.

## **40p**  What is a blog?

One form of public writing is the Web log (BLOG), an online journal that a writer updates on a fairly regular basis. Some writers focus their blogs on a single topic or a narrow range of topics. Others record the events of their lives, as in a diary open for the world to read.

Special software allows bloggers (blog writers) to share their thoughts online. As with a Web site, writers need access to a server to publish their work. Many Internet providers (such as Yahoo! and AOL) support blogs. Additionally, there are Web sites that not only host blogs but also allow viewers to read thousands of others. One example is <http://www.blogger.com>.

Figure 40.11 is a section of a blog written by John Lovas, a professor of writing at a California community college. John's blog combines references to his professional and personal life and includes pictures as well as words.

Figure 40.11  A sample blog

# Chapter 41

## MAKING ORAL PRESENTATIONS AND USING MULTIMEDIA

### 41a What are oral presentations?

Oral presentations, which are speeches often supported with multimedia tools, are common not only in academic disciplines across the curriculum, but also in work and public settings. Preparing a presentation and drafting a paper involve similar processes. We recommend you consult Chapters 2 through 4 for information about the writing process. The rest of this chapter will provide additional information for preparing presentations and using multimedia tools.

### 41b How does my purpose focus my presentation?

Just as writing purposes change from one situation to the next, so do speaking purposes. You might address a group of students to inform them about a film club you're starting. You might try to persuade a management group at work to adopt a new set of procedures for making purchasing decisions. Or you might give a toast at a friend's wedding to express your feelings and to entertain the wedding guests.

The three main purposes for presentations are to entertain, to INFORM and to PERSUADE (1b). In academic and work situations, the last two are most important. For an oral presentation, determine your purpose, and keep it in mind as you draft and revise your speech. Common INFINITIVE PHRASES for an informative presentation include: *to explain why, to clarify, to show how, to report, to define, to describe,* and *to classify.* Common phrases for a persuasive presentation include: *to convince, to argue, to agree with, to disagree with, to win over, to defend,* and *to influence.*

### 41c How do I adapt my message to my listening audience?

Adapting your presentation to your listening audience means grabbing and holding their interest and being responsive to their viewpoints. Consult the strategies for analyzing audiences in Box 41.1. Especially consider your listeners' prior knowledge of your topic, their desire to learn more, and whether they agree with your point of view. You'll find that your audience falls into one of three categories: *uninformed, informed,* or *mixed.* Box 41.1 suggests how to adapt your message to each type of audience.

## SUMMARY BOX 41.1

### Adapting an oral presentation to your audience

| | |
|---|---|
| **UNINFORMED AUDIENCE** | Start with the basics, and then move to a few new ideas. Define new terms and concepts, and avoid unnecessary technical terms. Use visual aids and give examples. Repeat key ideas—but not too often. |
| **INFORMED AUDIENCE** | Don't waste your audience members' time with the basics. From the beginning, reassure them that you'll be covering new ground. Devote most of your time to new ideas and concepts. |
| **MIXED AUDIENCE** | In your introduction, acknowledge the more informed audience members who are present. Explain that you're going to review the basic concepts briefly so that everyone can build from the same knowledge base. Move as soon as possible toward more complex concepts. |

Adapting your presentation to the general needs and expectations of your audience doesn't mean saying only what they might want to hear. It means rather that you need to consider their knowledge of your topic and their interest in it. You can then make your message understandable and relevant by using appropriate language and examples.

## 41d How do I organize my presentation?

As with essays, an oral presentation has three parts: INTRODUCTION, BODY, and CONCLUSION. Within the body, you present your major points, with two to three supports for each point. Drafting a SENTENCE OUTLINE gets you close to your final form and forces you to sharpen your thinking. Box 41.2 shows you a sample outline for an oral presentation.

### INTRODUCING YOURSELF AND YOUR TOPIC

All audience members want to know three things about a speaker: Who are you? What are you going to talk about? Why should I listen? To respond effectively to these unasked questions, try these suggestions.

- Grab your audience's attention with an interesting question, quotation, or statistic; a bit of background information; a compliment; or an anecdote. If necessary to establish your credibility—even if someone has introduced you—briefly and humbly mention your qualifications as a speaker about your topic.
- Give your audience a road map of your talk: Tell where you're starting, where you're going, and how you intend to get there. Your listeners need to know that you won't waste their time.

---

**SUMMARY BOX** 41.2

## Organizational outline for an oral presentation

Title: _____

Topic: _____

Specific purpose: _____

Thesis statement: _____


   I. Introduction (followed by a clear transition to point 1 in the body)
  II. Body
     A. Major point 1 and specific supporting examples (followed by a clear transition from point 1 to point 2, perhaps with a brief reference to the introduction)
     B. Major point 2 and specific supporting examples (followed by a clear transition from point 2 to point 3, perhaps with a brief reference to point 1 and the introduction)
     C. Major point 3 and specific supporting examples (perhaps with a brief reference to points 1 and 2)
  III. Conclusion (Refer to your introduction but do not repeat it verbatim or your audience will lose interest.)

---

### FOLLOWING YOUR ROAD MAP

Although much advice for writing applies to oral presentations, listening to a presentation is very different from reading an essay. When you're reading an article and lose sight of the main point, you can reread a few paragraphs. But when you're listing to a speech, you can't go back. As a result, audiences generally need help following the speaker's line of reasoning. Here are some strategies to keep your listeners' minds from wandering and to help them follow your points.

- Signal clearly where you are on your road map by using cue word transitions such as *first, second,* and *third;* or *subsequently, therefore,* and *furthermore;* or *before, then,* and *next.*
- Define unfamiliar terms and concepts, and follow up with strong, memorable examples.
- Occasionally tell the audience what you consider significant, memorable, or especially relevant, and why. Do so sparingly, at key points.
- Provide occasional summaries at points of transition. At each interval, recap what you've covered and say how it relates to what's coming next.

### WRAPPING UP YOUR PRESENTATION

Demonstrate that you haven't let key points simply float away. Try ending with these suggestions.

- Never let your voice volume fall or your clarity of pronunciation falter because the end is in sight.
- Don't introduce new ideas at the last minute.
- Signal that you're wrapping up your presentation using verbal cues, such as "In conclusion" and "Finally." When you say "finally," mean it!
- Make a dramatic, decisive statement; cite a memorable quotation; or issue a challenge. Allow a few seconds of silence, and then say "thank you." Use body language, such as stepping slightly back from the podium, and then sit down.

## 41e How do I research and write a presentation?

Doing research for an oral presentation requires the same kind of planning as doing research for written documents. To keep yourself calm and focused, divide the preparation into manageable tasks according to a realistic time line (31b). Set small goals and stick to them to give yourself enough time to research, organize, and practice your presentation. Review Chapters 31–33 for help on finding and evaluating sources, taking notes, planning a research strategy, and documenting sources. An oral presentation won't have a WORKS CITED or REFERENCES list to be read out, but your instructor might ask you to turn it in before or after you give your presentation.

Most of the preparation involved in an oral presentation is written work. Writing helps you take four important steps in your preparation: (1) to organize your thoughts; (2) to distance yourself from the ideas and remain objective; (3) to pay attention to words and language; and (4) to polish for clarity and impact.

When drafting your speech, it may help you to review Chapters 20–22 on usage and the impact and correct form of words. In particular, see section 21b for a discussion of a medium LEVEL OF FORMALITY in language, which is an appropriate level for most public speaking. Careful DICTION (21e) will make your speech both easy to listen to and memorable.

An oral presentation calls for the same careful language selection that you employ in your writing (1d). Here are some tips on using language in oral presentations.

- Recognize the power of words. For example, read this statement by Winston Churchill, made after World War II: "Never in the field of human conflict was so much owed by so many to so few." Now try substituting the word *history* for "the field of human conflict." Note that while the single word *history* is more direct, using it destroys the powerful impact of the original words.

- Never alienate your audience by using words, phrases, or examples that could offend your listeners or people connected with them.

- Use GENDER-NEUTRAL LANGUAGE by avoiding sexist terms and inappropriate words and expressions (21g).

- Present yourself with dignity in body language, tone of voice, and dress.

### 41f How do I incorporate multimedia into my oral presentation?

Multimedia elements such as visual aids, sound, and video can reinforce key ideas in your speech by providing illustrations or concrete images for the audience. If done well, they can make long explanations unnecessary and add to your credibility. Still, they can never take the place of a well-prepared presentation.

### 41f.1 Using traditional visual aids

Here are various types of visual aids and their uses. For each of them, always make text and graphics large enough for others to read and grasp at a distance.

- **Posters** can dramatize a point, often with color or images. Because you need to make sure posters are large enough for everyone in your audience to see them, they tend to work best with smaller audiences of thirty or fewer—unless you've made a truly huge poster.

- **Dry-erase boards** are preferable to chalkboards because you can use various colors that are visually appealing on them. Use them to roughly sketch an illustration or to emphasize a technical word. Doing this adds a dynamic element to your presentation, but take care not to turn your back on the audience for more than a few seconds.

- **Handouts** are useful when the topic calls for a longer text or when you want to give your audience something to refer to later. Short, simple handouts work best during a presentation, but longer, more detailed ones are more effective at the end; remember that listeners can pay more attention to what's on the page than to you, and you don't want to compete with yourself! Always include DOCUMENTATION information for any SOURCES on the handout. A strategic handout can be a useful backup just in case other technologies are missing or broken; remember to wait until everyone has one before you begin speaking about it.

- **Transparencies** require an overhead projector. You can prepare them in advance, either by hand or by using a computer and printer, which helps clarity and also allows you to incorporate visual materials. For emphasis during a presentation, you can write on transparencies with a marker.

## 41f.2 Using electronic media

Computers offer a range of possibilities for enhancing oral presentations. However, make sure that they add to your remarks rather than distract your audience. Above all, don't spend so much time developing multimedia materials that you neglect actually writing your presentation.

### POWERPOINT PRESENTATIONS

Microsoft PowerPoint® is the most widely used presentation software that creates digital slides. These slides can contain words, images, or combinations of both; they can even include sound or movie clips. To project your slides during a presentation, you need an LCD projector connected to your computer and a screen.

To design PowerPoint slides, follow the principles of unity, variety, balance, and emphasis discussed in Chapter 42. Never present so much information on each slide that your audience pays more attention to reading it than to listening to you. Also, never simply read large amounts of text from your slides; your audience will quickly—and rightfully—become bored. People have coined the phrase "death by PowerPoint" in despair at presenters who simply repeat what's written on slides, especially if the slides are an endless succession of bulleted lists. Remember the power of photographs, illustrations, or other visual materials for conveying information or making points (Chapter 6).

Figure 41.1 (p. 766) is an example of an effective PowerPoint slide prepared for a presentation about a community service project. The slide is clearly titled, well-balanced, and has an image to capture attention. It presents the points concisely and clearly.

### SOUND AND VIDEO CLIPS

A brief sound file (for example, a sentence or two from a speech) or a video clip (perhaps 20 to 30 seconds of footage from an event) can occasionally help you illustrate a point. These clips can be as simple as a CD

Figure 41.1 A sample PowerPoint slide

or a DVD or as complicated as WAV or QuickTime files on a computer. Always keep them brief and be absolutely sure that your audience will recognize immediately that they enhance your message and aren't just for show.

## 41g How do I plan for multimedia in my presentation?

Few things can frustrate you more than technology troubles. Always have a backup plan. Computers and projectors have a tendency to act up just at the times you're most nervous or the situation is most important, and few things annoy audience members more than watching people fiddle with technology. If you or a technician can't solve the problem in a minute or two, shift to your plan B, which might consist of selected transparencies, a strategic short handout, or even no multimedia at all. Plan and practice for all situations.

If you're making a PowerPoint presentation, you need to operate in advance the computer system you'll be using. If you intend to hook up your laptop computer to an LCD projector, make sure you bring with you—and practice installing—all of the connecting cables and cords. Arrive early to double-check that any technology you're planning to use is available and working, even if you've practiced with it beforehand. Learn how to turn on computers, video players, and projectors. Learn how to raise or lower the screen, if you're using one, and how to dim the lights.

## 41h What presentation styles can I use?

**Presentation style** is the way you deliver what you have to say. You may memorize it, read it, map it, or speak without notes. In general, avoid the last style until you have considerable experience giving speeches, unless otherwise instructed by your professor or someone in your workplace.

### MEMORIZING YOUR PRESENTATION

Memorized talks often sound unnatural. Unless you've mastered material well enough to recite it in a relaxed way, choose another presentation style. After all, no safety net exists if you forget a word or sentence. Fortunately, instructors rarely require you to memorize long presentations.

### READING YOUR PRESENTATION

You can bore your audience when you read your entire presentation aloud. Burying your nose in sheets of paper creates an uncomfortable barrier between you and your audience because you appear painfully shy, unprepared, or insincere. If you have no choice but to read, avoid a monotone voice. Vary your pitch and style so that people can listen more easily. In addition, try these tips.

- Become familiar with your words as much as possible so that you can look up from the pages to make frequent eye contact with your audience.
- Place the sheets of paper on a podium instead of holding them.
- Keep your hands out of your pockets. Use them to gesture instead.
- Turn your body—not just your head—to your right, left, and straight ahead so that you can look at everyone in your audience.

### MAPPING YOUR PRESENTATION

Mapping means creating a brief outline of the presentation's main points and examples and then using that outline to cue yourself as you talk. Box 41.3 (p. 768) contains additional suggestions for mapping your presentation. (For information about mapping, see 2j.)

## 41i How do I use my voice effectively?

Your voice is the focus of any oral presentation. If you're unsure whether you can be heard in a particular setting, speak briefly and then ask your listeners whether they can hear you. When you use a microphone, speak into it without raising your voice. If the sound system "screeches" with

## Preparing materials for delivering a mapped presentation

- Type your key words in a large font for easier reading.
- Highlight the most important point(s) you want to make.
- Use only one side of a page or card to avoid losing your place.
- Number your pages or cards in large type in case you drop them.
- Clearly distinguish your introduction, body, and conclusion so that your audience can follow along easily.
- Mark cues to yourself on your pages for pauses, emphasis, and use of visuals.
- Include information on your sources so that you can briefly mention them (and offer to give more details after your speech).

feedback, step away from any speaker units on the stage or around the room.

Speak naturally but clearly. Articulate your words by pronouncing the end of each word. Swallowing word endings leads to poor speech delivery. Speak slowly and deliberately—but make sure that your words have rhythm and pace so that your listeners will stay engaged. Vary your tone of voice for emphasis and clarity. Pause every now and then to let your points sink in.

## 41j How do I use nonverbal communication?

Your body language can either add to or detract from your message. Eye contact is your most important nonverbal communication tool because it communicates confidence and shows respect for your listeners. If you have to walk up to the front of a room or a podium, don't begin speaking before you get there and are looking directly at the audience. Smile or nod at your listeners as you begin. To do this smoothly, you need to memorize your first few sentences.

Use appropriate facial expressions to mirror the emotions in your message. Gestures, if not overdone, contribute to your message by adding emphasis; they are best when they appear to be natural rather than forced or timed. If you use a podium, stand squarely behind it. When gestures aren't needed, rest your hands on the podium—don't scratch your head, dust your clothing, or fidget. You may step slightly forward or backward from a microphone to indicate transitions in your message, but never sway from side to side. And, of course, dress appropriately for your audience and the type of event.

## 41k What can I do to practice for my oral presentation?

Good delivery requires practice. In preparing to speak, figure in enough time for at least four complete run-throughs of your entire presentation, using visuals if you have them. When you practice, keep the following in mind:

- Practice conveying ideas rather than particular words so that your TONE doesn't become stilted.
- Time yourself and cut or expand material accordingly.
- Practice in front of a mirror or videotape yourself. As you watch yourself, notice your gestures. Do you look natural? Do you make nervous movements that you weren't aware of as you spoke?
- Practice in front of a friend. Ask for constructive feedback by posing these questions: What was my main point? Did the points flow? Did any information seem to come from out of nowhere or not fit in with the information around it? Did I sound natural? Did I look natural? How did the visuals add to my message?

## 41l How can I overcome stage fright?

If you suffer from stage fright, remember that the more prepared and rehearsed you are, the less frightened you'll be. Your aim is to communicate, not to perform. If you worry that your audience will see that you're nervous, Box 41.4 (p. 770) suggests ways to overcome physical signs of anxiety. The truth is that once you're under way, the momentum of your presentation will take over and you'll forget to be nervous. Try it.

## 41m How do I make a collaborative presentation?

A common practice in many academic settings—and in business and public situations—is to present an oral report as part of a group. All members of the group are required to contribute in some way to the collaborative enterprise. Here are some guidelines to follow:

- Make sure, when choosing a topic or a position about an issue, that most members of the group are familiar with the subject.
- Lay out clearly each member's responsibilities for preparing the presentation. Try to define roles that complement one another; otherwise, you may end up with overlap in one area and no coverage in another.

- Agree on firm time limits for each person, if all members of the group are expected to speak for an equal amount of time. If there is no such requirement, people who enjoy public speaking can take more responsibility for delivery, while others can do more of the preparatory work or contribute in other ways.

- Allow enough time for practice. Good delivery requires practice. Plan at least four complete run-throughs of your presentation, using visuals if you use them. Although each member can practice on his or her own part alone, schedule practice sessions for the entire presentation as a group. This will help you (a) work on transitions, (b) make sure the order of presenters is effective, (c) clock the length of the presentation, and (d) cut or expand material accordingly.

- As you practice your presentation, have different group members watch in order to make suggestions, or videotape the practices. Notice your gestures. Do you look natural? Do you speak clearly and at an effective pace?

---

**SUMMARY BOX 41.4**

## Overcoming anxiety during an oral presentation

- **Pounding heart.** Don't worry: No one else can hear it!

- **Trembling hands.** Rest them on the podium, or put your hands behind your back or hold your outline or notes until the shaking stops. It will.

- **Shaky knees.** Stand behind the desk or podium. If neither is available, step forward to emphasize a point. Walking slowly from one place to another can also help you get rid of nervous energy.

- **Dry throat and mouth.** Place water at the podium. Never hesitate to take an occasional sip, especially at a transition point.

- **Quavering voice.** Speaking louder can help until this problem disappears on its own, which it always does. The sooner you ignore the quaver, the faster it will stop.

- **Flushed face.** Although you might feel as if you're burning up, audiences don't notice. The heat always fades as you continue speaking.

# Chapter 42

## DOCUMENT AND VISUAL DESIGN

### 42a What is visual design?

**Visual design** refers to the appearance of a document (how it looks), as opposed to its content (what it says). We're using the term document to refer broadly to all kinds of texts, including papers, reports, letters, brochures, flyers, posters, PowerPoint slides, and Web pages. Designing documents includes everything from choosing typefaces and heading styles, to determining the use of color, to selecting and placing photographs, illustrations, or other graphics. Chapter 6 explained how to analyze visual images, and the advice there can help you choose images for your own documents. However, visual design involves words as well as images and, more important, the relationship between the two. Note how all of the elements in the poster in Figure 42.1 work together.

Document design matters for several reasons, not least because first impressions count. As soon as readers see your document, they form an opinion about you and your project. A well-designed document shows that you respect your readers and have spent time formatting your work so that it's attractive and helps achieve your PURPOSE.

Some documents follow formats that are fairly standardized. Certain kinds of writing for work, such as letters, memos, and e-mail messages, follow customary patterns (see 40d–f). Papers you write in academic settings usually follow guidelines established by the Modern Language Association (Chapter 34); the American Psychological Association (Chapter 35); the Chicago Manual of Style; or the Council of Science Editors (both in Chapter 36). Check with your instructor about which style to use. Some instructors encourage—or even require—design elements such as photos, illustrations, and diagrams. However, before spending time and effort incorporating extensive design elements into academic work, ask your instructor whether he or she appreciates design elements.

Other document types invite more design creativity. Consider, once again, the public service announcement in Figure 42.1. Flyers, brochures, annual reports, reports on special projects, programs for concerts or plays, and so on give you considerable room for originality. Overall, the best design is always the one appropriate to the PURPOSE and writing situation at hand.

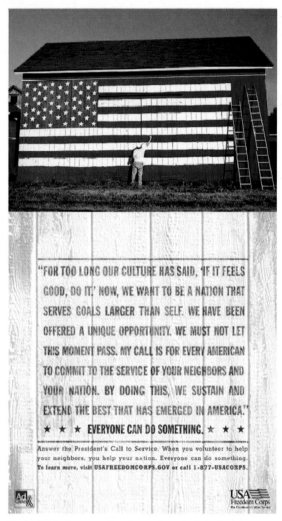

Full-color image is appealing to the eye

Images and text are balanced on page

Large typeface helps readers focus on text

Enough white space around ad text enhances readability

Different typeface sizes help highlight most important text

Figure 42.1 A poster showing various design elements

You don't have to be a graphic artist to produce well-designed documents. Although professional designers can produce work well beyond the abilities of most people, with a few tools and a little knowledge, you can produce modest yet effective documents. Just keep things simple and resist pressing beyond your abilities. Box 42.1 lists types of software that you can use to design documents.

**SUMMARY BOX** 42.1

## Computer programs used in designing documents

- **Word Processing Software:** Allows you to vary typefaces and fonts (see 42c–d), draw and insert images, and create charts, graphs, and tables. Word processing programs are sufficient for formatting most basic documents. In fact, such programs can do things once possible only with more complicated software.

- **Graphic Design Software:** Allows you to create and edit graphics and images using software such as Macromedia FreeHand and Adobe Photoshop. You can then save images in formats that are compatible with word processing and page layout software, and insert them into your document.

- **Page Layout Software:** Enables you to design sophisticated documents more easily. Programs such as Adobe InDesign and Microsoft Publisher require some effort to learn and can be fairly costly, though, so check whether computers in libraries or campus labs have this software.

## 42b What are basic principles of design?

The basic principles of design—whether for a chair, a car, a painting, a written document, or a Web page—are unity, variety, balance, and emphasis. **Unity** results from repetition and consistency. **Variety** comes from a logical, appropriate break from unity that adds interest. **Balance** refers to a sense of harmony or equilibrium. **Emphasis** directs the eye to what is most important. Box 42.2 describes how to check for these principles.

**SUMMARY BOX** 42.2

## Checklist for document design

- **Unity:** Do all elements in my document work together visually?
- **Variety:** Have I introduced design elements, where appropriate, that break up monotony, such as headings that add to clarity or illustrations that add to content?
- **Balance:** Are the parts of my document in proportion to each other?
- **Emphasis:** Does my document design draw attention to key information?

The flyer that a student produced for The Nature Club in Figure 42.2 reflects the four basic design principles. UNITY results from similar parts of the flyer sharing the same features. All of the headings in this example (except the title) use the same font and color, and all of the body text uses the same font. In addition, dates for the speakers and events are displayed in a matching indented format. Unity also emerges from the colors of the headings and the images. VARIETY in the flyer comes from the use of photographs to complement the text. Headings, colors, and font sizes are different from the main text. Variety is also one way to create EMPHASIS. For example, the title of the organization is the largest text on the page. Headings signal different types of information, and the ample use of white space allows information to stand out clearly. The contact information appears in white print over the dark image of the mountain in the lower right corner.

Finally, the page demonstrates BALANCE in many ways. Each side of the flyer contains three groups of material, with space between them: two pictures and a block of text on one side, one picture and two blocks of text on the other. The information about "Speakers" and "Events" is similar in format.

# The Nature Club

**Please join us!**
The Nature Club is open to all members of the campus community. Our purpose is to share our common enjoyment of nature and to address environmental concerns. We meet the first Wednesday of each month, 7:00 p.m., at 114 Mercer Hall.

**Spring Speakers**

**James Franklin**
Biology
"Prairie Wildlife"
January 15

**Sarah Minkowski**
Political Science
"Alaskan Refuges and Energy Policy"
February 12

**Cesar Sanchez**
The Nature Conservancy
"The Last Best Places"
March 12

**Upcoming Special Events**

- Fundraising Dance for The Nature Conservancy February 19

- Salt River Canoeing April 18

- Camping and Hiking in Grand Teton National Park June 3–10

**Sherita Jones**
State Representative
"Pending Environmental Legislation"
April 9

For more information, contact
Jesse Langland, President
The Nature Club
jklang@tnc.gkztq.edu

**Figure 42.2 A flyer for The Nature Club**

**EXERCISE 42-1** Following are two alternative versions of the flyer for The Nature Club. Each of the two has problems with unity, variety, balance, or emphasis—or a combination of all four. Work alone or in groups to identify the problems in each design.

**The Nature Club**

Please join us!

The Nature Club is open to all members of the campus community. Our purpose is to share our common enjoyment of nature and to address environmental concerns. We meet the first Wednesday of each month, 7:00 p.m., in 114 Mercer Hall.

Spring Speakers

James Franklin, Biology, "Prairie Wildlife"
January 15

Sarah Minkowski, Political Science, "Alaskan Refuges and Energy Policy"
February 12

Cesar Sanchez, The Nature Conservancy, "The Last Best Places"
March 12

Sherita Jones, State Representative, "Pending Environmental Legislation"
April 9

**Upcoming Special Events**

Fundraising Dance for The Nature Conservancy
February 19

Salt River Canoeing
April 18

Camping and Hiking in Grand Teton National Park
June 3–10

For more information, contact

Jesse Langland, President
The Nature Club
jklang@tnc.gkztq.edu

**Figure 42.3**

## The Nature Club

### Please join us!

The Nature Club is open to all members of the campus community. Our purpose is to share our common enjoyment of nature and to address environmental concerns. We meet the first Wednesday of each month, 7:00 p.m., at 114 Mercer Hall.

**Spring Speakers**

James Franklin, Biology, "Prairie Wildlife" January 15
Sarah Minkowski, Political Science, "Alaskan Refuges and Energy Policy" February 12
Cesar Sanchez, The Nature Conservancy, "The Last Best Places" March 12
Sherita Jones, State Representative, "Pending Environmental Legislation" April 9

**Upcoming Special Events**

Fundraising Dance for The Nature Conservancy February 19
Salt River Canoeing April 18
Camping and Hiking in Grand Teton National Park June 3–10

For more information, contact Jesse Langland, President: jklang@tnc.gkztq.edu

**Figure 42.4 Examples of poorly designed flyers.**

## 42c How do I design with text?

Text consists of letters and words. To format text, you need to decide which typeface—a particular style of type, such as Verdana or New Century Schoolbook—that you'll use. Also called fonts, they come in two major categories. **Serif** fonts have little "feet" or finishing lines at the top and bottom of each letter; **sans serif** (*sans* is a French term meaning *without*) don't. Times New Roman is serif; Arial is sans serif. The serifs at the bottom of each letter help guide readers' eyes through lines of text; therefore, when you're writing longer segments of text, use serif fonts. Reserve sans serif for short, isolated lines such as headings and captions.

Remember that a font can set a tone, so avoid using a playful font (**Comic Sans MS**) or a simulated handwriting font (*Kaufmann*) in academic and business writing. Fonts come in different sizes (heights) that are measured in "points" (units smaller than .02 inch). For body text in longer documents, use 10- to 12-point serif typefaces.

8 point     12 point     16 point     24 point

### 42c.1 Highlighting text

Highlighting draws attention to key words or elements of a document. You can highlight in various ways, but in all cases, use moderation.

#### BOLDFACE, ITALICS, AND UNDERLINING

*Italics* and underlining—they serve the same purpose—have special functions in writing (for example, to indicate titles of certain works, as we discuss in Chapters 34 and 35), but they're also useful for emphasis and for headings. **Boldface** is reserved for heavy emphasis.

#### BULLETED AND NUMBERED LISTS

You can use bulleted and numbered lists when you discuss a series of items or steps in a complex process or when you want to summarize key points or guidelines. A bulleted list identifies items with small dots, squares, or other shapes and symbols. Lists provide your reader with a way to think of the whole idea you're communicating. For this reason, they work particularly well as summaries.

#### COLOR

Adding color to a document can change it dramatically. In addition to including colorful visuals or BORDERS (42e), you can also change the font color or use a colored background for certain words or sections. Take time, however, to think about your reasons for adding color to your text. How does color suit the type of document? How will it help you accomplish your purpose? Use color sparingly for variety and emphasis.

## JUSTIFYING

When you make your text lines even in relation to the left or right margin, you're **justifying** them. There are four kinds of justification, or ways to line up text lines on margins: left, right, centered, and full.

> **Left justified** text (text aligns on the left)

> **Right justified** text (text aligns on the right)

> **Center justified** text (text aligns in the center)

> **Full justified** text (both left and right justified to full length, or measure, of the line of type)

Most academic and business documents are left justified, which means that the right ends of the lines are unjustified, or *ragged*. Center, right, and full justification are useful for designing shorter documents (flyers, posters, and so on) because they can attract attention.

## INDENTATION

When you move text toward the right margin, you are **indenting**. Using the ruler line in your word processing program to control indentations makes it easier to make global changes in your indentation. The top arrow of the bar sets the paragraph indentation, while the bottom arrow sets the indentation for everything else in the paragraph. MLA style Works Cited pages and APA References pages use hanging indentations in which the first line of an entry aligns at the left margin and every following line is indented. Indent bulleted and numbered lists to make them stand out, as in the list in 42d.

## SETTING MARGINS

**Margins** are the boundaries of a page, which means the white space or blank areas at the top, bottom, and sides of a paper or screen. College essays, research papers, and most BUSINESS WRITING call for one inch of space on all sides.

Narrow margins allow you to fit more information on a page but also decrease the amount of white space available. This can make a page appear cluttered, dense, and difficult to read. Wide margins let you fit less information on a page. For ACADEMIC WRITING, margins greater than one inch make your document look thin because there's less content on a page.

## 42d How do I use headings?

Headings clarify how you've organized your material and tell your readers what to expect in each section. Longer documents, including handbooks (like ours), reports, brochures, and Web pages, use headings to break content into chunks that are easier to digest and understand. In academic writing, APA style favors headings, whereas MLA tends to discourage them. Following are some guidelines for writing and formatting headings.

- **Create headings in a slightly larger type than the type size in the body of your text.** You can use the same or a contrasting typeface, as long as it coordinates visually and is easy to read.
- **Keep headings brief and informative.** Your readers can use them as cues.
- **Change the format for headings of different levels.** Think of levels in headings the way you think of items in an outline (see 2r). Level one headings show the main divisions of a document. Level two headings divide material that appears under level one headings, and so on. Changing the format for different levels of headings creates a clear outline for the reader. You can do this in various ways: You can center heads or left justify them; you can use a different font or type size; you can highlight using boldface, italics, or underlining; or you can use various combinations of capitals and lowercase letters. Always be consistent in the style you use within each document.

  Level one heading (most important)     **First-Level Head**
  Level two heading                      <u>Second-Level Head</u>
  Level three heading                    *Third-level head*

- **Use parallel structure.** All headings at the same level should be similar in kind. For example, you might make all first-level heads questions and all second-level heads noun phrases. Box 42.3 presents common types of headings, with examples showing parallel structure.

## 42e How do I use borders?

**Borders** are lines used to set apart sections of text. They can take a number of forms, from single lines of varying thickness to patterns. A single rule (a simple straight line, horizontal or vertical) can emphasize

**SUMMARY BOX 42.3**

## Common types of headings

- **NOUN PHRASES can cover a variety of topics.**

  Executive Branch of Government

  Judicial Branch of Government

- **Questions can evoke reader interest.**

  When and How Does the President Use the Veto Power?

  How Does the Supreme Court Decide Whether to Consider a Case?

- **GERUNDS and *-ing* phrases can explain instructions or solve problems.**

  Submitting the Congressional Budget

  Approving the Congressional Budget

- **Imperative sentences can give advice or directions.**

  Identify a Problem

  Draft the Bill

breaks between major sections of a long report. Borders around text serve to set off information, as in a table or chart. A sales brochure, for example, might "box in"—enclose in four borders, or *rules*—testimonials from satisfied customers, or a newsletter might set off upcoming events in a special box. Simplicity is the key. Getting too fancy can be distracting. In academic or business writing, generally use black borders. Other documents might benefit from colored borders, but use color sparingly.

## 42f   How should I incorporate graphics?

*Graphics,* also called *images* or *visuals,* can enhance document design when used appropriately. A visual can condense, compare, and display information more effectively than words, but only if its content is suitable. A graph showing how sales increased over a period of time, for example, makes the point more quickly and clearly than an explanation. A photo or drawing can illustrate or reinforce a point you want to make. Most word processing programs offer help for formatting and placing visuals, as does PowerPoint or more sophisticated layout software, such as Publisher.

## CHARTS, GRAPHS, AND TABLES

Business and scientific reports rely heavily on charts and graphs, as do some research papers. They're compact ways to present large amounts of information. The next four figures illustrate these elements.

- **Bar graphs** compare values, such as the number of different majors at a college, as shown in this graph.

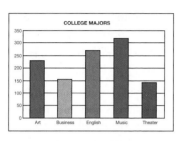

- **Line graphs** indicate changes over time. For example, advertising revenue is shown over an eight-month period in this graph.

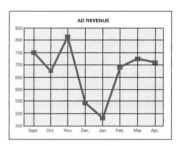

- **Pie charts** show the relationship of each part to a whole, such as a typical budget for a college student, as shown in this chart.

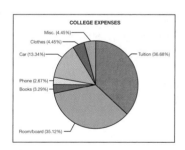

- **Tables** present data in list form, as shown here, allowing readers to grasp a lot of information at a glance.

TABLE 42.1   Total Number of Computer Lab Users by Semester

| Semester | Number of Users | Percentage (%) of Student Population |
|---|---|---|
| Spring 2005 | 2,321 | 25.8 |
| Summer 2005 | 592 | 6.6 |
| Fall 2005 | 3,425 | 38.1 |

In academic or business documents, especially lengthy ones, number figures and tables, if more than one, and number them sequentially. If possible, choose only one term in a relatively short piece of writing: *Table 1, Table 2;* or *Figure 1, Figure 2,* and so forth.

## CLIP ART

**Clip art** refers to pictures, sketches, and other graphics available on some word processing programs. It can also be downloaded from the Internet, sometimes from free sites, and sometimes for a small fee. Although clip art is rarely,  if ever, appropriate in academic writing and business writing, it can add interest to flyers, posters, newsletters, and brochures designed for certain audiences.

## PHOTOGRAPHS

In an age of digital cameras, not to mention an age when cell phones have the capacity to take pictures and send them around the world, **photographs** are everywhere. Because you can fairly easily download photographs from a digital camera, you can place them fairly easily into documents. You can also scan photographs from printed photos or from books and articles. The Internet is another source of images; several Web sites (including many at libraries) offer thousands of photographs for free. You can use the "search images" feature of a search engine like Google. Or, you can explore sites that allow you to download and use pictures for a small fee (an example is <http://www.iphoto.com>).

◢ **ALERT:** Whenever you use a photograph that you haven't taken yourself, you need to do so legally and ethically. Although the copyright law is fairly generous in allowing students to use found images for projects done strictly for courses, you should document the source of the image. If you're using a found image in a project for a wider audience beyond college, you need to get permission from the photographer or whomever owns the rights. Often, it's difficult and time-consuming to track down the photographer. That's why an online photo clearinghouse has several advantages; not only can you search what they have available, but for a small fee (often fifty cents to a dollar) you buy permission to use the photo for a limited time in your work. Finally, if there are identifiable people in a picture that you've taken yourself, you need to seek their permission to use the photograph in a public document. ◆

Once a photograph is in your computer, you can place it in your document, usually with an "Insert" or "Import" command. A modest software program, such as the pictures toolbar within Microsoft Word, can

Figure 42.9  An image that has been cropped

help you adjust a photograph by cropping it (trimming the top, bottom, or sides), rotating it, or making it larger or smaller. With a powerful program like Adobe Photoshop, you can modify colors or create special effects. Figure 42.9 shows how cropping affects an image.

For additional help in using visuals in your documents, follow the guidelines in Box 42.4.

---

**SUMMARY BOX** 42.4

### Guidelines for using visuals

- **Design all visuals to be simple and uncluttered.**

- **Include a heading or title for each visual.** Doing so helps readers quickly understand what they're seeing.

- **Never use unnecessary visuals.** Putting cute clip art on the pages of your writing won't make your reader think your work is well done. However, including a chart that summarizes your findings might.

- **Consider your audience and their sensibilities.** You don't want to offend your readers, nor do you want them to be confused.

- **Credit your source if a visual isn't your own.** Always avoid plagiarism by crediting your source using DOCUMENTATION. If you're using a visual (including a photograph) for a public purpose other than for a class project, you need written permission to use it in your work.

## **42g** What is page layout?

**Layout** is the arrangement of text, visuals, color, and space on a page. You'll want to arrange these elements so that you follow the basic principles of design (42b). Experiment with ideas for layout by creating mock-up pages on a computer or by sketching possibilities by hand. Try a variety of layouts.

You might also see if any suitable **templates** are available. A template is a professionally designed form that shows you where to place visuals in relation to text; a template has predefined typefaces, heading styles, margins, and so on. Page layout software (such as Microsoft Publisher) has a variety of templates for brochures, flyers, newsletters, and many other types of documents, and several Web sites offer them, too.

Box 42.5 explains how to position texts and visuals.

---

**SUMMARY BOX** 42.5

### Guidelines for positioning text and visuals

- Consider the size of visuals in placing them so that they don't cluster at the top or the bottom of a page. That is, avoid creating a page that's top-heavy or bottom-heavy.

- To create balance in a document, imagine it as divided into halves, quarters, or eights. As you position texts or images in the spaces, see which look full, which look empty, and whether the effect seems visually balanced.

- Use the "Table" feature of your word processing program to position text and visuals exactly where you want them. Turn off the grid lines when you're done so that the printed copy shows only the text and visuals.

- Avoid splitting a chart or table between one page and the next. If possible, the entire chart or table needs to fit on a single page. If it runs slightly more than a page, look for ways to adjust spacing or reduce words. If you have no choice but to continue a chart or table, then on the second page, repeat the title and add the word "continued" at the top.

- Use the "Print Preview" feature to see what each printed version will look like, which will help you revise before completing your final document.

- Print copies of your various layouts and look at them from different distances. Ask others to look at your layouts and tell you what they like best and least about each.

You have many options for placing images in relation to text. Figure 42.10 shows one standard kind of placement, the image centered above the words. In contrast, Figure 42.11 shows the text wrapped around the picture, which creates a better sense of connection between the two. Finally, Figure 42.12 illustrates that words can also wrap elements other than photographs, in this case a list enclosed in borders forming a box.

However, our research shows that students who are involved in a volunteer project actually achieve better grades than those who are not. One possible reason is that having too much free time actually encourages people to waste it; being busier forces them to be more organized.

Figure 42.10  An image centered above text

However, our research shows that students who are involved in a volunteer project actually achieve better grades than those who are not. One possible reason is that having too much free time actually encourages people to waste it; being busier forces them to be more organized. A more interesting reason is that volunteering for a meaningful project gives people a sense of purpose that carries over into other phases of their lives. Students who are concerned about the state of the environment, for example, draw energy from working with others who share their passion.

Figure 42.11  Text wrapped around the image

However, our research shows that students who are involved in a volunteer project actually achieve better grades than those who are not. One possible reason is that having too much free time actually encourages people to waste it; being busier forces them to be more organized. A more interesting reason is that volunteering for a meaningful project gives people a sense of purpose that carries over into other phases of their lives.

**Successful volunteers:**
-Follow their passions
-Budget their time
-Have positive outlooks
-Seek likeminded others

Figure 42.12  Text wrapped around a box

## USING WHITE SPACE

**White space**, the part of your document that has neither text nor visuals, allows readers to read your document more easily and to absorb information in chunks rather than in one big block. White space indicates breaks between ideas and thereby focuses attention on the key features of your document.

Traditionally, academic writing includes relatively little white space, except sometimes between sections of a document. For academic writing, you need to use double spacing unless your instructor requests otherwise; double spacing leaves space for comments in response to your writing. Business writing usually calls for single-spaced lines, with an added line of white space between paragraphs.

Flyers, brochures, posters, reports, Web pages, and similar documents tend to make extensive and varied use of white space because they rely heavily on graphics. Styles change over time, but most current professional designers prefer an uncluttered look with lots of white space.

# Chapter 43

## WRITING FOR THE WEB

### 43a  What is writing for the Web?

Writing for the Web means producing documents that are designed specifically to be read online. The World Wide Web consists of millions of sites (one or many connected pages) and billions of pages (a document within a site). Of course, many of the documents that appear on the Web were actually written for print publication. This includes articles in library databases (32d), online versions of newspapers and magazines, and even papers placed on the Web as Word documents and PDF (Portable Document Format) files. This chapter emphasizes producing documents designed specifically to be read online.

As your experience no doubt makes clear, Web pages are common in academic, business, and public settings. They inform, entertain, and persuade through text, images, color, and often sound and video. Because Web sites allow readers to jump from page to page to find information within a site and beyond, they provide readers with exceptional flexibility. This flexibility affects how you design a Web site because you need to consider not only how a page looks but also how it relates to others, both ones you've created and ones already online. Writing for the Web provides great flexibility because you can freely and easily change the content of your pages.

Figure 43.1 shows the home page of The Nature Club's Web site (the club whose flyer we discussed in 42b). Most of the information is similar to the information on the flyer shown there. However, notice how the headings from that flyer have now become links to other pages within the site. Links appear prominently, right under the name of the club. Visitors to this home page can tell in a glance what kinds of information the Web site contains and go directly to the pages that interest them. The

Figure 43.1  The Nature Club's home page

page also prominently lists the next event so frequent visitors to it don't have to click further for quick information.

## 43b  What is the Web writing process?

The **Web writing process** has five parts: (1) writing the content, (2) creating the structure of the content, (3) designing the layout of the material on the computer screen, (4) checking whether the Web material is usable, and (5) loading the Web site on a **server**, a computer that is always online and available to Internet users.

## 43c  How do I plan content for my Web site?

The Web differs from other media in distinct ways that affect your writing.

- Web writing calls for smaller blocks of text than print writing. Web readers prefer not to scroll down long sections of information.
- Web writing highlights the connections or links between related Web sites.
- Web writing emphasizes visual elements such as color and pictures.

As you plan your writing PURPOSE, choose your AUDIENCE, and analyze your WRITING SITUATION, ask yourself these questions:

- Will I aim to create a site that seeks to INFORM, or to PERSUADE, or to combine these purposes?
- What is the size of my Web writing project? How many pages will I want and how much content will I include in each?
- Should I include links to other Web sites? Which sites will support my purpose, perhaps with an illustration, an explanation, a reference, or so on?
- Who will my readers be? How can I help them navigate—that is, move—from one document to another?

## 43d How do I create a structure for my Web site?

**Web structure** is the organization of the content and documents that site creators include in a Web project. Almost all Web sites have a **home page**, a page that introduces the site and provides links to the other

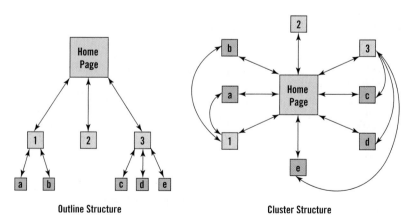

Outline Structure        Cluster Structure

Figure 43.2 Two possible Web site structures

pages that the site contains. The home page functions like a table of contents in print or, perhaps, the entryway to a building. It should be appealing and give visitors to the home page clear directions for how they can navigate your site, or move from page to page. Here are some guidelines for creating a site's structure.

- Determine all of the pages your site might contain and whether these pages should be grouped into **categories** (groups of pages all on the same topic). For example, if you want to include a page for each event that a club has sponsored, you could use the category "Special Events." People using the club's home page might click on a "Special Events" link that then directs them to pages for individual events.
- Generate a list of categories. You might use the planning techniques of BRAINSTORMING, FREEWRITING, and CLUSTERING discussed in Chapter 2.
- Plan a Web structure by drawing a map of all of your separate documents and the best way they connect to one other. Figure 43.2 shows two possible structures.
- Plan **hyperlinks**, which are direct electronic connections between two pages. Combinations of hyperlinks are the glue that holds Web writings together.

## 43e How do I design Web pages?

Once you've drafted a map of your Web site, you begin designing and creating your individual Web pages. Generally, all the pages within a site need to have the same basic design and similar navigation features to ensure that the site is unified and that users have an easy, pleasant experience. Most guidelines and principles that contribute to good design in printed documents apply equally to Web design. Use the basic design principles of unity, variety, balance, and emphasis discussed in Chapter 42.

Begin by planning a Web page's general appearance. Make decisions about the placement of texts and graphics, the use of color and white space, and what you want to emphasize. Early in your planning process, you might look at some Web sites that seem similar to what you have in mind. For example, if you're creating a site for a club or an organization, look at Web sites for clubs or organizations you know of or have heard about. Figure 43.3 (p. 790) is the home page of the National Museum of the American Indian. Notice how links appear prominently right under the attractive photograph that welcomes visitors to this home page. Readers can tell in a glance what kinds of information the Web site contains, and then go directly to the pages that interest them.

Links          Featured events          Keyword search box

Figure 43.3 The home page of the National Museum of the American Indian

Box 43.1 contains some general advice about designing Web pages.

**SUMMARY BOX** 43.1

## General advice for designing Web pages

- **Choose an appropriate title.** Make sure your page has a title that tells readers exactly what they'll find there.

- **Keep backgrounds and texts simple.** Like professional Web designers, strive for a clean, uncluttered look. Dark text on a plain light background is easiest to read, with white being the preferred background. In contrast to print documents, SANS SERIF fonts tend to be easier to read on computer screens than SERIF fonts. Avoid multiple typefaces, sizes, and colors, multiple images and graphics, and busy backgrounds.

---

**SUMMARY BOX** 43.1 *continued*

### General advice for designing Web pages

- **Use images to attract attention to important elements and to please the reader.** Readers will tend to look first at pictures and graphics on a page, so choose and then position them to reinforce your page's content.

- **Unify the pages in your site.** Keep the overall appearance of pages within one site consistent in terms of typefaces, graphics, and color. Make sure pages share some features, perhaps the same basic layout, font, color scheme, and header or **navigation bar** (the set of links on every Web page that allows users to get back to the site's home page and to major parts of the site).

- **Provide identifying information.** Generally, the bottom of a page includes the date the page is updated, or added to, along with contact information for the site's creator or administrator.

---

## 43f  How do I use Web writing software?

Web pages are written in a computer program language called **HTML**, for **H**yper**T**ext **M**arkup **L**anguage. Although it's possible to create Web pages directly using HTML, it's easier to use an HTML editor—a program that generates tags, or codes, in much the same way that word processing programs generate boldface type or other formatting. Some HTML editors are Microsoft FrontPage, Macromedia Dreamweaver, and Adobe GoLive. Your college's computer lab may have these programs or others. Also, you can download some free HTML editors; a good one is available from Mozilla at <http://www.mozilla.org>.

The most important codes are those for links. Highlight the words you want to serve as the link and then provide the URL of the page you want users to see when they click on the link.

### USING TEMPLATES, TABLES, AND FRAMES

**Templates** are predesigned Web page formats; they have places for you to insert text and images, using an established format. The advantage is simplicity and directness. You simply insert your material into the appropriate slots. The disadvantage is that the range of available formats might be limited and may not fit.

**Tables** allow you to use HTML editors to place text and images accurately. The word table here differs from the display visual shown in 42f. Unlike designing with pen and paper or with computer drawing software, HTML editors don't allow you to position materials immediately at different points on the screen. First, you have to define specific areas, and the easiest way to do this is with tables. A table divides the screen into a grid of spaces. You can then change the size of different rows, columns, or cells in the table to place blocks of text, images, links, and so on exactly where you want them. Figure 43.4 shows the basic table design underlying The Nature Club home page.

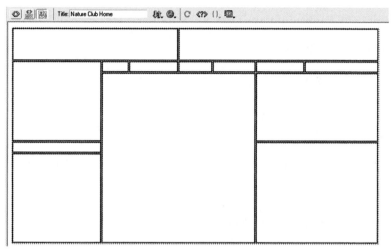

Figure 43.4 Tables used to create The Nature Club home page

Optionally, you may choose to create **frames** on your Web page. A frame is a part of a Web page that functions independently of the other parts of the page. A common use of frames is for menus of links. When a user clicks on a link, its contents appear in a new frame or box on the page, while the original frame remains unchanged. For example, in the National Science Foundation's home page (Figure 43.6, on p. 794), the column of links at the far right may be designed because a frame; while new content appears in a larger frame on the left of the page, the right frame remains unchanged. Using frames appears to be diminishing in popularity, because many sites instead use navigation bars—a line of links, often with a graphic, that occurs at the top or bottom of every page. Your HTML editor will provide advice for using tables and frames, as do various Web sites.

## 43g  How do I incorporate images into Web pages?

Web pages can include many different kinds of graphics. For example, bullets can mark off a list of items, as they do in print documents. Borders or rule lines can divide the page. You can also use photographs imported from a digital camera, scanned from print, or downloaded from the Internet, along with clip art and other graphics.

Keep in mind that photographs can require lots of digital storage space, which means they can take a long time to download, especially for people using a dial-up modem. Therefore, use only the images that enhance your page. You also want to optimize images for the Web, which means using a feature in programs such as Adobe Photoshop or Macromedia Fireworks to reduce the size of an image file to allow it to load faster.

Images in a Web page exist as separate files, so even when you cut and paste an image into a Web page, the HTML editor is including a link to the separate file that contains the image. The designer of The Nature Club Web site, for example, used Dreamweaver software. In Dreamweaver, one way to insert an image is to "Copy" the image from its source, open the Web page you're building, place your cursor in the spot you want the image to go, and use "Paste" to insert the image. When you save the page you've made, Dreamweaver will ask if you want to save the image file along with the Web page, usually in the same folder. If you don't save the image file with the Web page and put both on the server, your readers won't be able to see it.

The Web pages in Figures 43.5 and 43.6 make excellent use of images. The Guthrie Theater page (Figure 43.5) prominently features a costumed actor, her arms opened as if to welcome users to the Web site. The page designer has made the background actors in the image less visible so that the image isn't too cluttered or distracting. The image balances the main categories on the page, cleverly labeled "Act I," "Act II," and "Act III." The word "Magic" is in the largest type on the page, so it stands out beneath the image.

The National Science Foundation Web site in Figure 43.6 makes use of several images. Each relates directly to a story, attracting the reader's attention. Note, for example, the image to the far right of the Web page. The brain with the headline "The Look of Holiday Stress" hints at what users will find when they click on that image—information about how frenzied holiday activities (shopping, preparing for guests, and so on) affect the brain's chemistry.

Figure 43.5 The home page of the Guthrie Theater at <http://guthrietheater.org>

Figure 43.6 The home page of the National Science Foundation at <http://nsf.gov>

**EXERCISE 43-1**   Working alone or in a group, analyze the use of images in the Web page in Figure 43.7. For help, consult the discussions of images in Chapter 6 and visual design in Chapter 42. Optional: Choose one or more current Web sites on the Internet for your analysis.

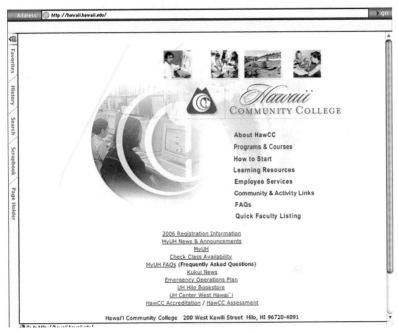

Address: http://hawaii.hawaii.edu/

**COMMUNITY COLLEGE**

About HawCC
Programs & Courses
How to Start
Learning Resources
Employee Services
Community & Activity Links
FAQs
Quick Faculty Listing

2006 Registration Information
MyUH News & Announcements
MyUH
Check Class Availability
MyUH FAQs (Frequently Asked Questions)
Kukui News
Emergency Operations Plan
UH Hilo Bookstore
UH Center West Hawai'i
HawCC Accreditation / HawCC Assessment

Hawai'i Community College   200 West Kawili Street  Hilo, HI 96720-4091

Figure 43.7  The home page of Hawaii Community College at <http://hawaii.hawaii.edu>

## 43h   What precautions do I need to take while using images I find?

Be careful and respectful using any images that you haven't created yourself, especially when copying images from the Internet. E-mail the site's creator to ask permission. Web sites usually include an e-mail address to which you can send a brief note explaining why you want to use the graphic. Generally, you'll be given free permission if you're writing for a class project or another educational purpose, but if you're writing a Web project for profit, you'll be expected to pay a fee. For the correct DOCUMENTATION format for your graphic sources, see Chapter 34 for MLA style and Chapter 35 for APA style.

## **43i** How do I edit my page and test usability?

Before you publish your Web page (that is, before you upload it to a server), edit and proofread it as carefully as you would a print document. The key difference between editing a Web page and a print document is that you also need to check that all of the interactive parts of your Web page are working properly. Before you finalize your Web page, use the checklist in Box 43.2.

---

**CHECKLIST BOX** 43.2

### Editing checklist for a Web site

- **Are any images broken?** Broken images show up as small icons instead of the pictures you want. The usual cause of broken images is mistyping the file name or failing to upload the image.

- **Do all the links work?** For each link to a page on your own site, be sure a file with that exact name exists on the server. Mistyped or mislabeled files can cause broken links.

- **Is the Web site user-friendly?** Ask your friends, classmates, or colleagues to report any sections in which information is unclear or difficult to find. They can also provide feedback about your content.

---

## **43j** How do I display my Web page?

After you've created and tested a Web page, you're ready to display it on the Web. To do this, you need two things: First, you need space on a WEB SERVER, a centralized computer always online and primarily dedicated to storing and making Web pages available. Second, you need the ability to load all of your files to that server, including the page(s) you've made and any associated graphics that you've included.

### FINDING SPACE ON THE WEB

If you have a commercial Internet Service Provider (ISP), such as America Online or Earthlink, you may be able to use it to post your Web site. Your college may offer Web space to its students, so check with your computing service office. Some services on the Internet offer free Web space as well as help in building Web pages. Try searching for "free Web hosting." Note that if you use "free" Web space, the provider may insert advertising on your page.

You'll also need some kind of File Transfer Protocol (FTP) program to upload the HTML files to your Web server. The host of your space should be able to advise you on the best way to upload files and which FTP program to use.

### UPLOADING IMAGE OR SOUND FILES

If you've used graphics, pictures, icons, or sound on your Web page, you'll also need to upload those files to the Web server where your page is now located. Otherwise, they can't be accessed by Web browsers, the programs viewers use to access your site.

Be careful to save the files with the correct extensions. Picture files normally have *.jpg* or *.gif* extensions, and sound files normally have *.wav*, *.mp3*, or *.midi* extensions. If your files don't have the correct extensions, the Web browser won't be able to process them.

After you've uploaded your Web site to a server, check it once again to make sure that all of the links are working.

### PUBLISHING YOUR PAGE

Posting a Web page is a form of publishing. Like all original writings, your Web site is automatically copyrighted. If you want to make this clear to users (to discourage PLAGIARISM, for example) include a copyright notice by typing the word *copyright*, the copyright symbol ©, the year of publication, and your name. If you want feedback, include your e-mail address. If you use material from SOURCES, credit them completely by using DOCUMENTATION; you might include a link titled "Works Cited," "References," or "Sources" that takes your readers to a separate page. Always ask for permission to use someone else's work on your Web site. Plagiarism is plagiarism (Chapter 33), whether the medium is print or electronic.

## **43k** How do I maintain my Web site?

Check and update your site regularly. The Internet is always changing, and if your page contains links to other sites, you need to make sure your links still work. You may also want to add new information, links, or features. Include a date at the bottom of your home page to let visitors know when you last updated the site. Finally, consider implementing feedback from visitors; they might tell you that information needs updating, and they might have suggestions for improving your site overall.

## How else can I publish on the Web?

Web pages are a common way to publish online, but they aren't the only way. For example, easily available and free blogging sites (such as www.blogger.com) simply have you choose a template and type your content.

**Podcasts** are short audio files (often 1 to 10 minutes) that are like radio shows distributed via the Internet. People can listen to them directly online or download them to a digital player (such as an Apple iPod) for listening later. Podcasts are oral presentations (though obviously without visual aids), and serious ones need to be carefully planned and written so that listeners can easily follow them, just as they would a speech. Note that a Podcast might also serve as a source for a paper you're writing; take care to evaluate it as you would any source. Several Podcast directories exist online, including <http://podcasts.yahoo.com>. Figure 43.8 shows the Podcast directory for National Public Radio.

**Figure 43.8 The podcast directory for National Public Radio (NPR)**

# A Message to Multilingual Writers

If you ever worry about your English writing, you have much in common with us and many US college students. Still, we recognize that because you're a multilingual writer, you face special challenges. In becoming a skilled writer in English, you need to concentrate on almost every word, phrase, sentence, and paragraph in ways native speakers of English do not.

The good news is that errors you make demonstrate that you're moving normally through the stages of second-language development. As with your progress in speaking, listening, and reading in a new language, developing writing skills takes time. The process of learning to write English is like learning to play a musical instrument. Few people can play fluently without first making many errors.

What can help you advance as quickly as possible from one writing stage to another? We recommend that you start by thinking about school writing in your first language. Recall how you were taught to present ideas in your written native language, especially when explaining information, giving specific details, and arguing logically about a topic. Then compare it to how writing American English works. Making yourself aware of the differences will help you learn English strategies more easily.

Most college essays and research papers in the United States are direct in tone and straightforward in structure. Typically, the THESIS STATEMENT (the central message of the piece of writing) is at the end of the first paragraph or, in a longer piece of writing, in the second paragraph. Each paragraph that follows relates in content directly to the essay's thesis statement. Also, each paragraph after the thesis statement needs to begin with a TOPIC SENTENCE that contains the main point of the paragraph, and the rest of the paragraph supports the point made in the topic sentence. This support consists of RENNS (3f) that provide specific details. The final paragraph brings the content to a logical conclusion that grows out of what has come before.

Always honor your culture's writing traditions and structures, for they reflect the richness of your heritage. At the same time, try to adapt to and practice the academic writing style characteristic of the United States. The *American Heritage English as a Second Language Dictionary,* which is available in paperback and hardcover, can ease your way with English words and expressions. If your college library doesn't own a copy, ask your professor to request that the reference librarian purchase a few copies for students to consult.

The *Simon & Schuster Handbook* offers three special features that we've designed specifically for you as a multilingual learner. Chapters 7 through 30 focus on the most challenging grammar issues that you face as you learn to write English. In other chapters throughout the book, ESL Tips offer you more helpful hints about possible cultural references and grammar issues. Finally, in Chapter 45, we've provided an "English Errors Transferred from Other Languages" chart. In this chart, you'll find information about trouble spots that commonly occur when speakers of certain first languages (Spanish, Russian, and so on) speak, read, or write in English.

Distinctive variations in school writing styles among people of different cultures and language groups have interested researchers for the past thirty years. Interesting differences have been observed; for example, many Spanish-speaking students feel that US school writing lacks grace because writers don't include any wide-ranging background material. In fact, US writing teachers usually consider such broad introductory material wordy and not relevant to the essay's central message. Japanese school writing customarily begins with references to nature, which US teachers think unnecessary. In some African nations, a ceremonial, formal opening always starts school writing as an expression of respect for the reader, but US teachers don't expect or want such openings.

As individuals, we greatly enjoy discovering the rich variations in the writing traditions of our students from many cultures of the world. As US writing teachers, however, our responsibilities call for us to explain what you need to do as writers in the United States. If you were in one of our classes, we would say "Welcome!" and ask you to teach us about writing in your native language. Using that knowledge, we then would respectfully teach you the US approach to writing so that we could do our best to help you succeed as a writer and learner in a US college.

Lynn Quitman Troyka
Doug Hesse

# Chapter 44

## MULTILINGUAL STUDENTS WRITING ESSAYS IN US COLLEGES

### 44a How is writing taught in US colleges?

Multilingual students who went to high school outside the United States may find that teachers and students in this country behave differently from teachers and students in their home countries. If you're one of these students, you might be surprised by the seemingly informal interaction between teachers and students in the United States. No matter how you interpret what you might see, rest assured that the casual teacher–student relationship is based on respect. Instructors still expect students to pay attention, obey class rules, and meet all assignment deadlines.

In the United States, teachers usually expect students to participate in class discussions. This can be very challenging for multilingual students if they aren't used to this style of classroom interaction, especially if they don't feel confident about speaking English. If this is the case for you, do your best to make as many contributions to class discussion as you possibly can. The more you try, the easier it will become.

When your instructors assign work, they may show you model papers. It can be very helpful to examine the parts of these sample papers to see how the authors have organized information, presented main points, and supported those main points. This is especially true if the assignment is a new type of writing for you. When you look at examples, be sure you know which aspects of the papers your teacher thinks are strong, and which aspects he or she thinks need improvement. Of course, when you analyze sample papers, you're doing so only to learn which writing techniques work well. Remember: Don't copy phrases, ideas, content, or images from them. In the United States, copying someone else's work is called PLAGIARISM, and it's ethically and legally wrong. For a detailed discussion about plagiarism, see Chapter 33.

Just as classroom expectations and writing assignments differ from culture to culture, the way that writing is taught also varies. In writing classes in US colleges, many instructors teach a process approach to writing. This approach emphasizes the steps that writers go through as they compose assignments for themselves and for college and work. The basic steps are planning, drafting, revising, editing, and proofreading. For an overview of the process approach, see Box 2.1 and Figure 2.1. For more specific details about the writing process, read Chapter 2 of this handbook.

Sometimes multilingual students become so concerned about making grammar mistakes that they neglect taking enough time to think about the ideas in their paper. Always remember that writing is about communicating ideas. To ensure you're conveying your own ideas and fulfilling the requirements of your assignments, spend as much time thinking about the content of your paper as you do working on your grammar. For help in working on thinking of ideas and expressing them, review sections 2d–2m of this handbook, which describe activities to help you come up with interesting material for your writing.

## 44b How does my past writing experience affect my writing in English?

Thinking about your own writing experiences and learning about others' can help you set goals for improving your writing. Exercises 44-1 and 44-2 can help you do both.

**EXERCISE 44-1** Think about the following sentences. For each sentence, write "True," "False," or "I'm not sure." If invited, share your answers with your instructor so he or she can learn more about your previous writing experiences. Next, write your thoughts about all or some of the statements, which can give you insight into yourself as a writer in English. Outside of class, you might also discuss your answers with one or more of your multilingual classmates or friends.

1. I am better at writing in another language than I am at writing in English.
2. I have more experience writing in another language than I do in English.
3. I feel confident about writing in English.
4. I received all of my secondary (high school) education outside the United States.
5. When I write in English, I have trouble finding the appropriate vocabulary.
6. When I write in English, I use a dictionary that translates words between English and my first language.
7. When I write in English, I use an English-English dictionary.
8. When I write in English, I use a computer spell-check program.
9. When I write in English, I use a computer grammar-check program.
10. In the past, I have written many different kinds of papers in English.

11. When I write in English, I can write fairly quickly.

12. I think I will need to write a lot for my major.

13. I think I will need to write a lot in English for my future career.

14. When I write in English, I sometimes have trouble finding vocabulary.

15. A serious problem I have with writing in English is writing correct sentences.

16. It is difficult for me to organize my ideas when I write in English.

17. I often have trouble making my papers long enough when I write in English.

18. I have trouble making my reader understand what I mean when I write in English.

19. Writing in my native language calls for a different structure than writing in English does.

20. In the past, the kinds of writing my teachers assigned were different from the kinds my college instructors assign.

21. In the past, my instructors had different expectations about my writing than my instructors have now.

**EXERCISE 44-2**    The following final draft of an essay was written by a multilingual student. Take some time to read the essay and then write a brief paper in which you discuss your own experiences writing in English and any other language(s) in which you've written. Consider using some of the ideas you came up with in your responses to Exercise 44-1. You could also describe your goals for improving your writing in English, and describe what kinds of English-language writing you think you will do in the future for your studies, your career, or outside of school and work. As you write, assume that your readers will be your instructor and perhaps your classmates. Your instructor can help you improve your writing if he or she knows more about you. Your classmates can also help you improve your writing while they learn about your writing experiences and compare them to their own.

### The Differences Between Writing in English and Japanese

I started studying English when I was a junior high school student. I learned only about grammar in school, and it is pretty tough for me to write in English compared to my native language, Japanese. I've really found a lot of difficulties since I started learning how to write in English in the United States. All of the problems that I have when I write in English relate to grammar differences, the way of expression, and the way to compose essays.

First of all, English grammar and Japanese grammar work in reverse ways. For example, we can say, "I read the book" in English. The order of the sentence is subject, predicate, and then object. On the other hand, in Japanese we say, "I the book read." As you can see, the subject is in the beginning, but the rest of the sentence has changed order (compared to English). This is the reason I get confused when I write essays in English, especially when the sentences get longer and longer and making them gets more complicated.

Second of all, the way of expression is pretty different between English and Japanese. We Japanese rarely express our feeling directly in good writing. The most excellent way of writing involves using metaphors. However, the English way of writing is entirely opposite. In English, you have to use immediate expressions and insist strongly. When I try to write an essay in English, I may think the essay is excellent because there are lots of metaphors. However, the American teacher will say, "I'm having trouble understanding what you are trying to say."

Finally, the way of composing an essay is the most different thing which makes Japanese students worry when they write English essays. It's somewhat similar to the differences I expressed in the previous paragraph, but it relates to the different kind of writing rules in different countries. In English, teachers always teach us that writing should have an introduction, body, and conclusion. However, according to the Japanese writing style, we don't have to write a thesis in the introduction, but instead we write the main idea in the conclusion. Therefore, I always forget to write my main idea in the introduction of the essay when I write in English, so it turns out to be an essay that the teacher thinks has no meaning and no opinion.

Writing in a second language is not such an easy thing. We make mistakes and solve these. And then, we make other mistakes. I think the most important thing is to figure out the rules of writing and to know what kind of writing people prefer in each country. If we can know this, and just keep writing and writing, we will overcome our difficulties at last.

## 44c How can I know what my instructor expects in my writing?

Your past writing experiences influence the way you approach writing assignments. In the next passage, a bilingual student illustrates how her past experiences influenced her interpretation of writing assignments in the United States. (Note: The original draft has been edited to improve readability.)

When I studied here, I felt puzzled with different types of writing assignments. When I wrote my first term paper, I really did not know what my professor did expect from me and how to construct my paper. My previous training in my first and second language writing taught me little about how to handle writing assignments by using composing strategies. Since language teaching in my country is exam-oriented, I learned to write in Chinese and in English basically in the same way. Under the guidance of my professor, I read a sample paper, analyzed its content and structure, and tried to apply its strengths to my own writing. Writing was not a creative process to express myself but something that was to be copied for the purpose of taking exams. As a result, when I don't have a sample for my assignments, I really don't know how to start.

Like this student, you may have difficulty understanding what your instructor expects you to do when completing a specific writing assignment. Your instructor may expect you to take a clear position on your topic. He or she may want you to use examples from your personal experience to support your ideas, use quotations and specific ideas from an assigned reading, use outside sources, or use all three. Do not hesitate to ask your instructor questions about the assignment to make sure you understand exactly what he or she expects.

**EXERCISE 44-3**   Reread the passage from Exercise 44-2. Have you ever had trouble figuring out what an instructor expected from you when he or she assigned a writing exercise? Have you ever written a paper and later found out that what you wrote was not at all what your instructor expected? Write a paragraph or two describing your experiences.

When your instructor gives you a writing assignment, you may not know how to start because you don't know much about the topic. This might be especially true if the topic that your instructor asks students to write about relates to aspects of American culture that you're not very familiar with. If you feel this is the case, you might need to talk to your instructor about the situation and try to find more information about the topic in newspapers or magazines or by discussing the topic with other students. Similarly, if you're writing about your own culture or about your home country, keep in mind that your instructor and classmates may not know very much about your culture. This means you may need to explain information for them in more detail than you would if you were writing a paper for people who share your cultural background.

**EXERCISE 44-4**   Have you ever written or read something that didn't make sense because it didn't include the necessary cultural background information? Write a paragraph or two describing your experiences and explaining the source of miscommunication. Before you begin, read the following passage by a student who describes the importance of providing background information in writing. (Note: This excerpt has been edited for readability.)

If I were writing in Chinese to Chinese readers and wanted to quote a story in Chinese history as evidence, I would simply have to mention the name of the people involved in the historic event or briefly introduce the story. However, when I am writing in English to tell the readers the same story, I have to tell the whole story in detail, even though I might only want to use a small part of it in my essay. Otherwise, the readers will surely get lost.

## 44d  How should I organize my writing?

As part of the writing process, many instructors ask students to write an OUTLINE and a THESIS STATEMENT for their papers (2q). Some writers from other countries have observed that American readers expect papers to have a standardized organization and communicate their purpose in a clear, obvious way. In some cases, this rigid structure poses challenges. For example, one bilingual student wrote that when he writes in his first language, he can use a "flexible organization" and can place his thesis "at the beginning, middle, or end of the essay" or "simply leave the thesis out and the let the reader draw the conclusion to show respect for the reader's intelligence." He explains that he finds it challenging writing in English because he must follow a "restricted organization" that presents a thesis in the first paragraph and then supporting subtopics and detailed examples.

**EXERCISE 44-5**   Are there differences between how you were taught to organize your writing in the past and how your instructors expect you to organize it now? Describe the differences in a paragraph or two, and, if you can, draw a picture that illustrates the differences. Before you begin, think back to the paragraph in Exercise 44-4 and what the student wrote about the differences organizing his papers in Chinese and English. Also, consider the following descriptions of organization in writing. (Note: Both of these examples have been edited for readability.)

**EXAMPLE 1**    Russian composition is not about composing supportive arguments around your own personal opinion, but instead is about composing a hierarchy of others' opinions on a certain topic. The process is very much like making a chain: You pick a citation and link it to another citation and so on.

**EXAMPLE 2**    From my TOEFL [Test of English as a Foreign Language] preparation class, I learned the basic framework for English writing: introduction plus body paragraphs plus conclusion, with topic sentences in the body paragraphs. I was impressed by the great difference between writing in my first language and English writing. For example, in a persuasive essay, writers from my country usually prefer to explain the problem first and then come up with their opinion. But for English writing, writers may be more likely to express the opinion at the very beginning and then give reasons to support the idea.

## 44e How can I use other writers' work to improve my writing?

If you are writing a paper based on other texts that you have read, such as a reading your teacher has given you or sources you have found for a research project, it is important to understand how directly your teacher wants you to draw on the text(s). For example, he or she may want you to read the text and simply use it as a springboard for your own ideas; however, your instructor may also expect you to read and analyze the text closely and refer to specific ideas and sentences in the source text when you write your paper. It can be especially difficult for ESL students to analyze a text closely and write about it without relying too heavily on the author's wording and sentence structure. However, in US colleges and universities, using another author's words, sentence structure, or even ideas without giving the author credit is considered to be a serious offense called PLAGIARISM, or stealing something that belongs to someone else. In contrast, in some cultures, reliance on the author's wording is not a problem, and may even be seen as a way of complimenting the author. As one bilingual student said, "When you are writing in my first language, you can always feel free to copy good sentences from other articles or writing pieces. But in the United States, it is a violation of copyright. When you are writing in English, you cannot use someone else's work without citing it."

Chapter 33 of this handbook provides detailed information about how to document sources and avoid plagiarism.

## 44f What kind of dictionary should I use?

Although it can be helpful to use a dictionary that translates words from your native language into English, sometimes such dictionaries are not adequate. One ESL student, who has problems with word choice, says that dictionaries "don't always work" because some terms are "translated literally." She goes on to explain that when she uses dictionaries, she doesn't accept just any definition. The student learns how to use it in a "real English way" and whether it is "appropriate to use in a certain context."

If you realize that you need a dictionary that does more than translating words between your native language and English, you might try an English-English dictionary, especially one that was written for non-native learners of English.

## 44g What should I do with my classmates' and instructor's comments?

As part of the writing process, you and your classmates may participate in peer response, sometimes called peer review or peer editing. You might exchange papers or sit together and read your paper to the students in your group. The purpose of peer response is to offer and receive advice about how to improve your writing from your classmates. This type of group work may be uncomfortable for you if teachers in your home country did not assign group work or expect students to critique each other's work, or if you prefer working individually. Here are some strategies to help make peer response successful for you and your classmates:

- Let your group members know you really do want them to give you advice on your paper so that you can improve its quality before you turn it in for a grade.
- Ask your group members specific questions about your writing.
- Provide other group members with specific, tactful advice about their writing.
- Talk to your instructor if you don't know whether you should follow a specific piece of advice from a classmate.
- See Box 1.5 for more information about peer response.

In addition to receiving feedback from your classmates, try to get feedback from your instructor before he or she gives your paper a grade. Instructors expect to see significant changes based on their comments. If you have questions about how to revise your writing in response to what your teacher has told you, you should talk to your instructor or a tutor.

## 44h Where can I find strategies for editing my work?

When you are satisfied with the content, organization, and development of the ideas in your paper, you should focus on language-related concerns in your writing. Chapter 45 outlines strategies for proofreading your papers.

## 44i How can I set long-term goals for my writing?

Improving your writing can take a long time, whether you are writing in your first language or in a second language. Some students find it helpful to set long-term goals for writing to help them focus on what to improve. You may want to talk to a professor in your major (or in a subject you are thinking about majoring in) so that you can ask him or her what kinds of writing you might be expected to do later, both in your college courses and in the workplace (if you plan to work in an English-speaking environment or in a context where English is used to communicate with other nonnative English speakers).

**EXERCISE 44-6** Interview a professor in your major (or in a subject you are thinking about majoring in). Ask him or her the following questions, and write a report about the answers you receive. Compare your report with that of a classmate.

1. What kinds of writing do you assign to students in your classes?
2. How do students learn how to write these assignments?
3. (Choose one or two types of writing assignments that the professor mentions.) What are the important parts of this assignment? What steps should students go through to complete this kind of assignment?
4. When you grade student writing, what aspects are most important to you?
5. What kinds of writing do graduates in this major usually do in the workplace?
6. Can you show me some examples of student writing from your courses?

# Chapter 45

## HANDLING SENTENCE-LEVEL ISSUES IN ENGLISH

### 45a How can I improve the grammar and vocabulary in my writing?

The best way to improve your English-language writing, including your grammar and vocabulary, is by writing. Many students also find it helpful to read as much as they can in English to see how other authors organize their writing, use vocabulary, and structure their sentences. Improving your writing in a second language—or a first language, for that matter—takes time. You will probably find that your ability to communicate with readers improves dramatically if you work on the ideas outlined in the previous chapter, including understanding the writing assignment and improving the organization and ideas in your writing. Sometimes, though, readers may find it hard to understand your ideas because of grammar or word choice problems in your sentences. In other cases, readers may become distracted from your ideas because you have a great many technical errors. We have designed this chapter to help you improve in these areas.

### 45b How can I improve my sentence structure?

Sometimes students write sentences that are hard to understand because of problems with overall sentence structure or length. For example, one student wrote the following sentence, which has errors.

> When the school started, my first English class was English 1020 as a grammar class, I started learning the basics of grammar, and at the same time the basic of writing, I worked hard in that class, taking by the teacher advice, try to memorize a lot of grammar rules and at the same time memorize some words I could use them to make an essay point.

To correct the structural and length errors, the student needs to do several things to improve the sentence. She needs to break it into several shorter sentences (Chapter 13). Also, she needs to revise her sentences so that they clearly connect to each other (Box 2.10). Additionally, she needs to work on her verb tenses in some phrases like "to make an essay point," which means she needs to ask for extra help at the writing center or from her instructor. After patient study and work, her revision might look like this:

> When school started, my first English class, English 1020, was a grammar class, where I started learning the basics of grammar. At the same time, I learned the basics of writing. I worked hard in that class, taking the teacher's advice and memorizing a lot of grammar rules. In addition, I memorized some words I could use in my essays to make my points.

**EXERCISE 45-1** Many different revisions of the previous example of a student's uncorrected paragraph are possible. Write a different revision of that student's paragraph.

**EXERCISE 45-2** A student wrote the following passage in a paper he wrote about his experiences learning English. Rewrite the passage, improving the student's sentence structure and punctuation. In your revision of this passage, correct any errors that you see in grammar or spelling. Afterward, compare your revision with a classmate's. Then examine a piece of your own writing to see if you need to revise any of your sentences because of problems with sentence structure. (While you are doing this, if you have any questions about correct word order in English, see Chapter 48.)

> I went to school in my country since I was three years old, I was in Arabic and French school, and that's was my dad choice because his second language is French. So my second language at that time was French. In my elementary school I started to learn how to make an essay in French and Arabic. I learned the rules and it is too deferent from English. But later on when I was in my high school I had two choices between English class and science class so I choose the science because that's was my major. After I graduate I went to American university and I start studying English and my first class was remedial English for people doesn't know anything about this language. I went to this class about two months and then I have moved to a new place and I start from the beginning as an ESL student.

## 45c How can I improve my word choice (vocabulary)?

An important aspect of writing in a second language is having enough vocabulary to express your ideas. Many students enjoy learning more and more words to be able to communicate precise meanings. For example, one English-as-a-Second-Language student explains that she has improved her writing and made it more "desirable" by using "words as tools." She also says that by using "different words every time" she "refreshes" her writing and "eliminates the routine" from it. You, too, can experiment in your writing with new words that you hear and read in other contexts. To help make sure you're using a new word in the right way, we recommend the *American Heritage English as a Second Language Dictionary,* which is available in paperback and hardback. It can ease your way with English words and expressions because it's intended specifically for multilingual learners of English.

## 45d How can I find and correct errors in my own writing?

Some multilingual writers find it easiest to find and correct their grammar errors by reading their writing aloud and listening for mistakes. This method is often preferred by students who feel their spoken English is better than their written English. Other writers like to ask a friend who is a native speaker of English to check their writing for grammatical mistakes. Still other multilingual writers prefer to circle each place where they think they've made an error and then use their handbook to check themselves.

Many multilingual writers like to keep a list of the types of grammar errors they make so that they can become especially sensitive to errors when proofreading their papers. The best system is to make a master list of the errors in categories so that the checking can be as efficient as possible.

## 45e How can I correct verb form (tense) errors in my writing?

Many multilingual writers consider verb-form errors the most difficult to correct. They want to be sure that their verb forms express the appropriate time frame for the event or situation they're describing. For a detailed discussion of verb forms, see 8b–8f.

**EXERCISE 45-3**  Read the following passage in which a student describes her experience learning to write in English. The student's instructor has underlined errors related to time frames expressed by the verbs. Correct the underlined verbs, changing them to the correct time frames.

I must have started writing when I was nine years old. I remember my father used to give us papers and watercolors and let us draw as much as we want. At the end, he made sure that we write comments about why we have sketched the way we did. The only written thing that I find dating to that period was a kind of comment about a picture which I have sketched of a village enveloped in water.

I don't remember much about the kind of writing assignments we <u>have</u> at school, whether in my native language Arabic, or in my second languages, at that time, English and French. That period is a little bit hazy in my mind. However, I remember that whenever we had the chance to go to school, we made sure that we <u>fill</u> the playgrounds with creative farewell sentences indicating that we <u>have</u> been there. It <u>is</u> our little game against the witchcraft of war and against the will of the principal, who <u>forgive</u> us easily once we <u>have</u> recited the multiplication table or <u>sing</u> the national anthem.

## 45f    How can I correct my errors in subject-verb agreement?

Subject-verb agreement means that a subject (a noun or a pronoun) and its verb must agree in number and in person. In the following two sentences, notice the difference in the way the subjects and the verbs that describe their actions agree: *Carolina runs charity marathons. They give her a sense of accomplishment.*

For more information about subject-verb agreement, review Chapter 10. To help you put subject-verb agreement rules into practice, try the next exercise.

**EXERCISE 45-4**    Examine the following student's description of his experiences learning English. The student's instructor has underlined verbs that do not agree with their subjects. Correct the underlined verb forms, changing them to agree with their subjects.

I describe the way I learned English as a natural way, where one first <u>learn</u> how to speak and communicate with others, before learning the grammar rules that <u>supports</u> a language. When I arrived in the United States, I <u>works</u> hard to improve my communications skills in English, trying to speak even when the people <u>does</u> not understand me. Also, making friends with native speakers <u>help</u> a person learn the language. One can learn from them every single minute that one <u>spend</u> with them.

Do you have similar problems with subject-verb agreement in your own writing? Examine something you've written recently to check whether your subjects and verbs agree.

## 45g    How can I correct my singular/plural errors?

In English, if you're referring to more than one noun that is a count noun, you must make that noun plural, often by adding an -s ending. If you would like more information on this topic, see Chapter 46. To help you recognize when necessary plural forms are missing, try the next exercise.

**EXERCISE 45-5**   In the following passage, a student comments on the differences between writing in English and in Chinese. The student's instructor has underlined only the first two nouns that need to be plural. Read the passage, correct the two underlined nouns, and then find and correct the other nouns in the passage that need to be plural.

> English and Chinese have many similarity. They both have paragraph, sentence, and punctuation mark, like comma, full stops, and question marks. The biggest difference is that English has an alphabet with letter, while Chinese uses symbol for writing. My mother told me that about two thousand year ago, people in China used picture to draw what they wanted to say on turtle shells. Day after day, the pictures changed and turned into the Chinese character.

Examine a piece of your own writing and make sure that you have used plural words correctly.

## 45h  How can I correct my preposition errors?

Prepositions are words such as *in, on, for, over,* and *about,* which usually show where, how, or when. For example, in the sentence *She received flowers from her friend for her birthday,* the prepositions are *from* and *for.* Unlike some other languages, English has many prepositions, and knowing which one to use can be very difficult. You can find information about using prepositions in section 7h and in Chapter 49. To practice finding and correcting preposition errors in your own writing, complete the next exercise.

**EXERCISE 45-6**   In the following passage about one student's learning experiences as a second-language learner, the student's instructor has underlined problems with preposition use. Try to correct the preposition errors. In some cases, more than one answer may be correct. If you can't find the information you need from Chapter 49 or in a dictionary, you might ask a native English speaker for help.

> I've always wanted to learn languages other than my native language. I started taking English and French lessons of school and I liked the idea of becoming fluent for at least one language. I thought English would help me a lot to the future because it could help me communicate to people from all over the world.

**What other kinds of errors might I make?**

Depending on your language background and your prior experience with writing in English, you may make errors related to the use of articles (*a, an, the*), word order (where to place adjectives and adverbs in sentences), and various verb forms and noun forms (for example, problems with noncount nouns and helping verbs). For example, the next sentence has a problem with one article and the order of an adjective: *The New York City is a place exciting.* The corrected sentence is *New York City is an exciting place.*

    Chapters 46 through 51 address grammar errors that are often made by multilingual writers. Try to keep track of your most common errors and refer to the relevant sections of this handbook for help.

**How can I keep track of my most common errors?**

One way of becoming more aware of the types of errors you make is to keep track of the errors you often make in the papers you write. You can ask your instructor or a tutor to help you identify such errors, and you can make a list of them that you update regularly. Remember the passage from Exercise 45-3 about a student's experiences learning to write? After the student examined the teacher's comments on her paper, she made a list of her errors and included a correction and a note about the error type for each. After making this list of her errors, the student writer realized that many of her errors related to verb form.

| Specific Error | Correction | Type of Error |
|---|---|---|
| as much as we <u>want</u> | wanted | verb form |
| that we <u>write</u> comments | wrote | verb form |
| about why we <u>have</u> sketched | had | verb form |
| which I <u>have</u> sketched | had | verb form |
| we <u>fill</u> the playground | filled | verb form |
| that we <u>have</u> been there | had | verb form |
| once we <u>have</u> recited | had | verb form |

**EXERCISE 45-7**   Using one or more pieces of your writing, make an error list similar to the previous one. (You could make this list on a sheet of paper or in an electronic file.) Examine the list. What are the most common types

of errors that you make? Once you have identified your common error types, refer to the relevant proofreading exercises in the previous sections of this chapter and to the relevant ones in Chapters 46 through 51. Also, remember to keep your common errors in mind when you proofread your future writing assignments.

## 45k   How can I improve my proofreading skills?

The most effective way to improve your proofreading skills is to practice frequently. Proofread your own writing and, after you have done so, ask your instructor, a tutor, or a friend who is a native English speaker to point out the location of errors that you did not see on your own. If you know you often make a particular kind of error, such as errors with subject-verb agreement (Chapter 10), ask the person helping you to check for these problems specifically. When you know which errors you've made, try to correct the errors without help. Finally, have your instructor or tutor check your corrections.

Another effective way to improve your proofreading skills is to exchange your writing with a partner. You can check for errors in his or her writing and he or she can check for errors in yours. Try Exercises 45-8 and 45-9 for more proofreading practice.

**EXERCISE 45-8**   The following passage was written by a bilingual student about her experiences learning to write in English. After you read it, rewrite it, correcting the linguistic errors you find.

> I've always faced some problem in writing in English as it took me some time to get used to it. Facing these complexities encourage me to developed my skills in English writing. My first class in English was about grammar, spelling, and writing. I realize later that grammar is hard to learn, so I knew I have to put in a lot of effort to understand it perfectly and use it properly. I also had some difficulties for vocabulary, as it was hard to understand the meaning of some word.
>
> Another thing that helped me with my English was when my mother enroll me in an English learning center that specialize in teach writing skills. After a month of taking classes, my teacher saw some improvement in my grammar and vocabulary. To test me, she asked me to write an essay on how to be successful. I was really excite of it and started write it immediately. After I finish my essay and my teacher check it, my teacher suggested that I take a few more classes for her. She taught me how to organized my ideas. After finishing these classes I realize that my writing was getting much better with time.

**EXERCISE 45-9**  In the following paragraph, a student describes the study of English at private schools in Japan. After you read the paragraph, rewrite it, correcting the errors that you find.

Recently, the number of private language schools are increased in Japan. These schools put special emphasize on oral communication skills. In them, student takes not only grammars and reading classes, which help them pass school examinations, but also speaking, listening classes. They can also study English for six year, which is same period as in public schools. Some of the teacher in these school are native speaker of English. Since these teachers do not use Japanese in the class, the students have to use the English to participate it. They have the opportunity to use the English in their class more than public school students. It is said that the students who took English in private schools can speak English better than those student who go to public schools.

The following chart contains information about errors that may be caused by a difference between your native language and English. The chart does not include all languages or all possible errors. Instead, it focuses on languages commonly spoken by ESL students in the United States, and it includes errors that often cause significant difficulties for students.

## ENGLISH ERRORS TRANSFERRED FROM OTHER LANGUAGES

| Languages | Error Topic | Sample Errors | Corrected Errors |
|-----------|-------------|---------------|------------------|
| **Singulars and Plurals (Ch. 46)** | | | |
| Chinese, Japanese, Korean, Thai | no (or optional) plural forms of nouns, including numbers | NO: She wrote many good **essay**. NO: She typed two **paper**. | YES: She wrote many good **essays**. YES: She typed two **papers**. |
| Hebrew, Italian, Japanese, Spanish | use of plural with embedded plurals | NO: We cared for five **childrens**. | YES: We cared for five **children**. |
| Italian, Spanish | adjectives carry plural | NO: They are **Americans** students. | YES: They are **American** students. |
| **Articles (Ch. 47)** | | | |
| Chinese, Japanese, Hindi, Korean, Russian, Swahili, Thai, Turkish, Urdu | no article (*a, an, the*) but can depend on whether article is definite/indefinite | NO: He ate sandwich. | YES: He ate **a** sandwich. |

*continued ➤*

| Languages | Error Topic | Sample Errors | Corrected Errors |
|---|---|---|---|
| **Word Order (Ch. 48)** | | | |
| Arabic, Hebrew, Russian, Spanish, Tagalog | verb before subject | NO: **Questioned Avi** the teenagers. | YES: **Avi questioned** the teenagers. |
| Chinese, Japanese, Hindi, Thai | inverted word order confused in questions | NO: **The book was it** heavy? | YES: **Was the book** heavy? |
| Chinese, Japanese, Russian, Thai | sentence adverb misplaced | NO: We will go home **possibly** now. | YES: **Possibly**, we will go home now. |
| **Gerunds, Infinitives, and Participles (Ch. 50)** | | | |
| French, German, Greek, Hindi, Russian, Urdu | no progressive forms or overuse of progressive forms with infinitive | NO: They **talk** while she **talk**. <br><br> NO: They **are wanting** to talk now. | YES: They **are talking** while she **is talking**. <br> YES: They **want** to talk now. |
| Arabic, Chinese, Farsi, Russian | omit forms of *be* | NO: She happy. | YES: She **is** happy. |
| Chinese, Japanese, Korean, Russian, Thai | no verb ending changes for person & number | NO: She **talk** loudly. | YES: She **talks** loudly. |
| Arabic, Chinese, Farsi, French, Thai, Vietnamese | no or nonstandard verb-tense markers | NO: He **laugh** yesterday. <br> NO: They **has arrived** yesterday. | YES: He **laughed** yesterday. <br> YES: They **arrived** yesterday. |
| Japanese, Korean, Russian, Thai, Vietnamese | nonstandard passives | NO: A car accident **was happened**. | YES: A car accident **was caused by the icy roads**. |

# Chapter 46

## SINGULARS AND PLURALS

### 46a   What are count and noncount nouns?

**Count nouns** name items that can be counted: *a radio* or *radios, a street* or *streets, an idea* or *ideas, a fingernail* or *fingernails.* Count nouns can be SINGULAR or PLURAL.

**Noncount nouns** name things that are thought of as a whole and not split into separate, countable parts: *rice, knowledge, traffic.* There are two important rules to remember about noncount nouns: (1) They're never preceded by *a* or *an*, and (2) they are never plural. Box 46.1 lists eleven categories of uncountable items, giving examples in each category.

Some nouns can be countable or uncountable, depending on their meaning in a sentence. Most of these nouns name things that can be meant either individually or as "wholes" made up of individual parts.

COUNT   You have **a hair** on your sleeve. [In this sentence, *hair* is meant as an individual, countable item.]

NONCOUNT   Kioko has black **hair**. [In this sentence, all the strands of *hair* are referred to as a whole.]

COUNT   **The rains** were late last year. [In this sentence, *rains* is meant as individual, countable occurrences of rain.]

NONCOUNT   **The rain** is soaking the garden. [In this sentence, all the particles of *rain* are referred to as a whole.]

When you are editing your writing (see Chapter 2), be sure that you have not added a plural *-s* to any noncount nouns, for they are always singular in form.

**ALERT:** Be sure to use a singular verb with any noncount noun that functions as a SUBJECT in a CLAUSE. ◆

To check whether a noun is count or noncount, look it up in a dictionary such as the *Dictionary of American English* (Heinle & Heinle). In this dictionary, count nouns are indicated by [C], and noncount nouns are indicated by [U] (for "uncountable"). Nouns that have both count and noncount meanings are marked [C;U].

**SUMMARY BOX 46.1**

## Uncountable items

| | |
|---|---|
| **GROUPS OF SIMILAR ITEMS** | clothing, equipment, furniture, jewelry, junk, luggage, mail, money, stuff, traffic, vocabulary |
| **ABSTRACTIONS** | advice, equality, fun, health, ignorance, information, knowledge, news, peace, pollution, respect |
| **LIQUIDS** | blood, coffee, gasoline, water |
| **GASES** | air, helium, oxygen, smog, smoke, steam |
| **MATERIALS** | aluminum, cloth, cotton, ice, wood |
| **FOOD** | beef, bread, butter, macaroni, meat, pork |
| **PARTICLES OR GRAINS** | dirt, dust, hair, rice, salt, wheat |
| **SPORTS, GAMES, ACTIVITIES** | chess, homework, housework, reading, sailing, soccer |
| **LANGUAGES** | Arabic, Chinese, Japanese, Spanish |
| **FIELDS OF STUDY** | biology, computer science, history, literature, math |
| **EVENTS IN NATURE** | electricity, heat, humidity, moonlight, rain, snow, sunshine, thunder, weather |

---

## 46b How do I use determiners with singular and plural nouns?

**Determiners,** also called *expressions of quantity,* are used to tell how much or how many with reference to NOUNS. Other names for determiners include *limiting adjectives, noun markers,* and ARTICLES. (For information about articles—the words *a, an,* and *the*—see Chapter 47.)

Choosing the right determiner with a noun can depend on whether the noun is NONCOUNT or COUNT (see 46a). For count nouns, you must also decide whether the noun is singular or plural. Box 46.2 (p. 822) lists many determiners and the kinds of nouns that they can accompany.

**ALERT:** The phrases *a few* and *a little* convey the meaning "some": *I have **a few** rare books* means "I have *some* rare books." *They are worth **a little** money* means "They are worth *some* money."

Without the word *a,* the words *few* and *little* convey the meaning "almost none": *I have **few** [or very few] books* means "I have *almost no* books." *They are worth **little** money* means "They are worth *almost no* money." ◆

821

## Determiners to use with count and noncount nouns

**GROUP 1: DETERMINERS FOR SINGULAR COUNT NOUNS**

With every **singular count noun**, always use one of the determiners listed in Group 1.

| *a, an, the* | **a house** | **an egg** | **the car** |
|---|---|---|---|
| *one, any, some, every, each, either, neither, another, the other* | **any house** | **each egg** | **another car** |
| *my, our, your, his, her, its, their, nouns with 's or s'* | **your house** | **its egg** | **Connie's car** |
| *this, that* | **this house** | **that egg** | **this car** |
| *one, no, the first, the second,* etc. | **one house** | **no egg** | **the fifth car** |

**GROUP 2: DETERMINERS FOR PLURAL COUNT NOUNS**

All the determiners listed in Group 2 can be used with **plural count nouns**. Plural count nouns can also be used without determiners, as discussed in section 46b.

| *the* | **the bicycles** | **the rooms** | **the idea** |
|---|---|---|---|
| *some, any, both, many, more, most, few, fewer, the fewest, a lot of, a number of, other, several, all, all the* | **some bicycles** | **many rooms** | **all ideas** |
| *my, our, your, his, her, its, their, nouns with 's or s'* | **our bicycles** | **her rooms** | **student's ideas** |
| *these, those* | **these bicycles** | **those rooms** | **these ideas** |
| *no, two, three,* etc.; *the first, the second, the third,* etc. | **no bicycles** | **four rooms** | **the first ideas** |

➤

**SUMMARY BOX** 46.2 *continued*

## Determiners to use with count and noncount nouns

**GROUP 3: DETERMINERS FOR NONCOUNT NOUNS**

All the determiners listed in Group 3 can be used with **noncount nouns** (always singular). Noncount nouns can also be used without determiners, as discussed in section 47b.

| | | | |
|---|---|---|---|
| *the* | **the rice** | **the rain** | **the pride** |
| *some, any, much, more, most, other, the other, little, less, the least, enough, all, all the, a lot of* | **enough rice** | **a lot of rain** | **more pride** |
| *my, our, your, his, her, its, their, nouns with 's or s'* | **their rice** | **India's rain** | **your pride** |
| *this, that* | **this rice** | **that rain** | **this pride** |
| *no, the first, the second, the third, etc.* | **no rice** | **the first rain** | **no pride** |

---

How do I use *one of,* nouns as adjectives, and *states* in names or titles?

### *ONE OF* CONSTRUCTIONS

*One of* constructions include *one of the* and a NOUN or *one of* followed by a DETERMINER-noun combination (*one of my hats, one of those ideas*). Always use a plural noun as the OBJECT when you use *one of the* with a noun or *one of* with an adjective-noun combination.

> **NO**    *One of the **reason** to live here is the beach.*

> **YES**    *One of the **reasons** to live here is the beach.*

> **NO**    *One of her best **friend** has moved away.*

> **YES**    *One of her best **friends** has moved away.*

The VERB in these constructions is always singular because it agrees with the singular *one*, not with the plural noun: ***One** of the most important inventions of the twentieth century **is** [not are] television.*

For advice about verb forms that go with *one of the . . . who* constructions, see 10l.

## NOUNS USED AS ADJECTIVES

Adjectives in English do not have plural forms. When you use an adjective with a PLURAL NOUN, make the noun plural but not the adjective: *the* **green** [not *greens*] *leaves*. Be especially careful when you use a word as a MODIFIER that can also function as a noun.

> The bird's wingspan is ten inches. [*Inches* is functioning as a noun.]

> The bird has a ten-inch wingspan. [*Inch* is functioning as a modifier.]

Do not add *-s* (or *-es*) to the adjective even when it is modifying a plural noun or pronoun.

> **NO**    Many **Americans** students are basketball fans.

> **YES**    Many **American** students are basketball fans.

## NAMES OR TITLES THAT INCLUDE THE WORD *STATES*

*States* is a plural word. However, names such as *United States* or *Organization of American States* refer to singular things—one country and one organization, even though made up of many states. When *states* is part of a name or title referring to one thing, the name is a SINGULAR NOUN and therefore requires a SINGULAR VERB.

> **NO**    The **United States have** a large entertainment industry.

> **NO**    The **United State has** a large entertainment industry.

> **YES**    The **United States has** a large entertainment industry.

## 46d   How do I use nouns with irregular plurals?

Some English nouns have irregularly spelled plurals. In addition to those discussed in section 22c, here are others that often cause difficulties.

## PLURALS OF FOREIGN NOUNS AND OTHER IRREGULAR NOUNS

Whenever you are unsure whether a noun is plural, look it up in a dictionary. If no plural is given for a singular noun, add *-s* to form the plural.

Many nouns from other languages that are used unchanged in English have only one plural. If two plurals are listed in the dictionary, look carefully for differences in meaning. Some words, for example, keep the plural form from the original language for scientific usage and have another, English-form plural for nonscientific contexts: *formula, formulae, formulas; appendix, appendices, appendixes; index, indices, indexes; medium, media, mediums; cactus, cacti, cactuses; fungus, fungi, funguses.*

Words from Latin that end in *-is* in their singular form become plural by substituting *-es: parenthesis, parentheses; thesis, theses; oasis, oases.*

**OTHER WORDS**

Medical terms for diseases involving an inflammation end in -*itis*: *tonsillitis*, *appendicitis*. They are always singular.

The word *news*, although it ends in *s*, is always singular: *The **news is** encouraging.* The words *people*, *police*, and *clergy* are always plural even though they do not end in *s*: *The **police are** prepared.*

**EXERCISE 46-1**   Consulting all sections of this chapter, select the correct choice from the words in parentheses and write it in the blank.

> EXAMPLE   At the beginning of every school year, all (student, students) <u>students</u> can expect (homework, homeworks) <u>homework</u> that teaches them about the toll-free No Bully hot line.

1. One of the main (reason, reasons) _____ for such a hot line is the change in tempers and violent capacities of (American, Americans) _____ students.

2. Because students are often bullied by a fellow classmate when outside the classroom, it is important that they receive (information, informations) _____ about how to react when confronted by such a threat.

3. Many a child in the (United State, United States) _____ is in danger not only of being teased and taunted by others but also of being the victim of a crime in which (blood, bloods) _____ is spilled, such as from assault or robbery.

4. Because (many, much) _____ classrooms are unsupervised after school, this (time, times) _____ becomes especially dangerous.

5. In a moment of danger, (ignorance, ignorances) _____ can be deadly, so the No Bully hot line was set up to give students (advice, advices) _____ on how to handle bullying and other threatening situations.

# Chapter 47

## ARTICLES

### 47a How do I use *a, an,* or *the* with singular count nouns?

The words *a* and *an* are called **indefinite articles**. The word *the* is called the **definite article**. Articles are one type of DETERMINER. (For more on determiners, see 7f; for other determiners, see Box 46.2 in 46b.) Articles signal that a NOUN will follow and that any MODIFIERS between the article and the noun refer to that noun.

| | |
|---|---|
| **a** chair | **the** computer |
| **a** brown chair | **the** teacher's computer |
| **a** cold, metal chair | **the** lightning-fast computer |

Every time you use a singular count noun, a COMMON NOUN that names one countable item, the noun requires some kind of determiner; see Group 1 in Box 46.2 (in 46b) for a list. To choose between *a* or *an* and *the,* you need to determine whether the noun is **specific** or **nonspecific**. A noun is considered specific when anyone who reads your writing can understand exactly and specifically to what item the noun is referring. If the noun refers to any of a number of identical items, it is nonspecific.

For nonspecific singular count nouns, use *a* (or *an*). When the singular noun is specific, use *the* or some other determiner. Box 47.1 can help you decide when a singular count noun is specific and therefore requires *the.*

**ALERT:** Use *an* before words that begin with a vowel sound. Use *a* before words that begin with a consonant sound. Go by the sound, not the spelling. For example, words that begin with *h* or *u* can have either a vowel or a consonant sound. Make the choice based on the sound of the first word after the article, even if that word is not the noun.

| | |
|---|---|
| **an i**dea | **a g**ood idea |
| **an u**mbrella | **a u**seless umbrella |
| **an h**onor | **a h**istory book ◆ |

**SUMMARY BOX 47.1**

## When a singular count noun is specific and requires *the*

- **Rule 1: A noun is specific and requires *the* when it names something unique or generally and unambiguously known.**

  **The sun** has risen above **the horizon.** [Because there is only one *sun* and only one *horizon,* these nouns are specific in the context of this sentence.]

- **Rule 2: A noun is specific and requires *the* when it names something used in a representative or abstract sense.**

  Benjamin Franklin favored **the turkey** as **the national bird** of the United States. [Because *turkey* and *national bird* are representative references rather than references to a particular turkey or bird, they are specific nouns in the context of this sentence.]

- **Rule 3: A noun is specific and requires *the* when it names something defined elsewhere in the same sentence or in an earlier sentence.**

  **The ship *Savannah*** was the first steam vessel to cross the Atlantic Ocean. [*Savannah* names a specific ship.]

  **The carpet in my bedroom** is new. [*In my bedroom* defines exactly which carpet is meant, so *carpet* is a specific noun in this context.]

  I have **a computer** in my office. **The computer** is often broken. [*Computer* is not specific in the first sentence, so it uses *a.* In the second sentence, *computer* has been made specific by the first sentence, so it uses *the.*]

- **Rule 4: A noun is specific and requires *the* when it names something that can be inferred from the context.**

  Monday, I had to call **the technician** to fix my computer again. [*A technician* would be any of a number of individuals; *the technician* implies the same person has been called before, and so it is specific in this context.]

One common exception affects Rule 3 in Box 47.1. A noun may still require *a* (or *an*) after the first use if more information is added between the article and the noun: *I bought **a sweater** today. It was **a** (not *the*) **red sweater**.* (Your audience has been introduced to *a sweater* but not *a red sweater,* so *red sweater* is not yet specific in this context and cannot take *the.*) Other information may make the noun specific so that *the* is correct. For example, *It was **the red sweater that I saw in the store yesterday*** uses *the* because the *that* CLAUSE makes specific which red sweater the writer means.

## **47b** How do I use articles with plural nouns and with noncount nouns?

With plural nouns and NONCOUNT NOUNS, you must decide whether to use *the* or to use no article at all. (For guidelines about using DETERMINERS other than articles with nouns, see Box 46.2 in 46b.) What you learned in 47a about NONSPECIFIC and SPECIFIC NOUNS can help you choose between using *the* or using no article. Box 47.1 in 47a explains when a singular count noun's meaning is specific and calls for *the*. Plural nouns and noncount nouns with specific meanings usually use *the* in the same circumstances. However, a plural noun or a noncount noun with a general or nonspecific meaning usually does not use *the*.

> Geraldo grows **flowers** but not **vegetables** in his garden. He is thinking about planting **corn** sometime. [three nonspecific nouns]

### PLURAL NOUNS

A plural noun's meaning may be specific because it is widely known.

> **The oceans** are being damaged by pollution. [Because there is only one possible meaning for *oceans*—the oceans on the earth—it is correct to use *the*. This example is related to Rule 1 in Box 47.1.]

A plural noun's meaning may also be made specific by a word, PHRASE, or CLAUSE in the same sentence.

> Geraldo sold **the daisies from last year's garden** to the florist. [Because the phrase *from last year's garden* makes *daisies* specific, *the* is correct. This example is related to Rule 3 in Box 47.1.]

A plural noun's meaning usually becomes specific by its use in an earlier sentence.

> Geraldo planted **tulips** this year. **The tulips** will bloom in April. [*Tulips* is used in a general sense in the first sentence, without *the*. Because the first sentence makes *tulips* specific, *the tulips* is correct in the second sentence. This example is related to Rule 3 in Box 47.1.]

A plural noun's meaning may be made specific by the context.

> Geraldo fertilized **the bulbs** when he planted them last October. [In the context of the sentences about tulips, *bulbs* is understood as a synonym for *tulips*, which makes it specific and calls for *the*. This example is related to Rule 4 in Box 47.1.]

## NONCOUNT NOUNS

Noncount nouns are always singular in form (see 46a). Like plural nouns, noncount nouns use either *the* or no article. When a noncount noun's meaning is specific, use *the* before it. If its meaning is general or non-specific, do not use *the*.

> Kalinda served us **rice**. She flavored **the rice** with curry. [*Rice* is a noncount noun. By the second sentence, *rice* has become specific, so *the* is used. This example is related to Rule 3 in Box 47.1.]

> Kalinda served us **the rice that she had flavored with curry**. [*Rice* is a noncount noun. *Rice* is made specific by the clause *that she had flavored with curry*, so *the* is used. This example is related to Rule 3 in Box 47.1.]

## GENERALIZATIONS WITH PLURAL OR NONCOUNT NOUNS

Rule 2 in Box 47.1 tells you to use *the* with singular count nouns that carry general meaning. With GENERALIZATIONS using plural or noncount nouns, omit *the*.

> **NO**   **The tulips** are **the flowers** that grow from **the bulbs**.

> **YES**   **Tulips** are **flowers** that grow from **bulbs**.

> **NO**   **The dogs** require more care than **the cats** do.

> **YES**   **Dogs** require more care than **cats** do.

---

### 47c   How do I use *the* with proper nouns and with gerunds?

## PROPER NOUNS

PROPER NOUNS name specific people, places, or things (see 7b). Most proper nouns do not require ARTICLES: *We visited **Lake Mead** with **Asha** and **Larry***. As shown in Box 47.2, however, certain types of proper nouns do require *the*.

## GERUNDS

GERUNDS are PRESENT PARTICIPLES (the *-ing* form of VERBS) used as nouns: ***Skating** is challenging*. Gerunds are usually not preceded by *the*.

> **NO**   **The constructing** new bridges is necessary to improve traffic flow.

> **YES**   **Constructing** new bridges is necessary to improve traffic flow.

Use *the* before a gerund when two conditions are met: (1) The gerund is used in a specific sense (see 47a), and (2) the gerund does not have a DIRECT OBJECT.

## Proper nouns that use *the*

- **Nouns with the pattern *the . . . of . . .***

  **the** United States **of** America  **the** Fourth **of** July

  **the** Republic **of** Mexico  **the** University **of** Paris

- **Plural proper nouns**

  **the** United Arab Emirates

  **the** Johnsons

  **the** Rocky Mountains [*but* Mount Fuji]

  **the** Chicago Bulls

  **the** Falkland Islands [*but* Long Island]

  **the** Great Lakes [*but* Lake Superior]

- **Collective proper nouns (nouns that name a group)**

  **the** Modern Language Association

  **the** Society of Friends

- **Some (but not all) geographical features**

  **the** Amazon  **the** Gobi Desert  **the** Indian Ocean

- **Three countries**

  **the** Congo  **the** Sudan  **the** Netherlands

---

**NO**  **The designing fabric** is a fine art. [*Fabric* is a direct object of *designing,* so *the* should not be used.]

**YES**  **Designing** fabric is a fine art. [*Designing* is a gerund, so *the* is not used.]

**YES**  **The designing of** fabric is a fine art. [*The* is used because *fabric* is the object of the preposition *of* and *designing* is meant in a specific sense.]

**EXERCISE 47-1**  Consulting all sections of this chapter, select the correct article from the words in parentheses and write it in the blank.

**EXAMPLE**  Be forewarned: (A, An, The) <u>The</u> camera as we know it may soon be obsolete.

1. At (a, an, the) _____ dawn of (a, an, the) _____ twenty-first century comes (a, an, the) _____ invention so advanced that it may rid (a, an,

the) _____ United States of America of every camera that has come before it.

2. (A, An, The) _____ digital camera, which allows photos to appear on (a, an, the) _____ computer monitor, takes up virtual space, not physical space.

3. As (a, an, the) _____ result, if you see (a, an, the) _____ bad photo on (a, an, the) _____ screen, you can simply erase (a, an, the) _____ poor photo to make room for (a, an, the) _____ new one.

4. With this new technology, (a, an, the) _____ aunt can e-mail photos to her niece or nephew, or she can post photos to (a, an, the) _____ Web page.

5. Digital cameras allow photographers to alter (a, an, the) _____ appearance of people or things, which, according to many critics, is (a, an, the) _____ chief disadvantage of (a, an, the) _____ digital camera.

**EXERCISE 47-2**   Consulting all sections of this chapter, decide which of the words in parentheses is correct and write it in the blank. If no article is needed, leave the blank empty.

EXAMPLE   For (a, an, the) _____ years, people have worked under (a, an, the) the assumption that (a, an, the) the best remedy for (a, an, the) a burn is butter.

1. This kind of treatment seems to be (a, an, the) _____ good idea because butter looks and feels like ointment, but butter doesn't contain (a, an, the) _____ antibacterial property like ointment does.

2. In using butter to treat (a, an, the) _____ burns, you are coating (a, an, the) _____ skin with debris that must be removed later to keep it from interfering with (a, an, the) _____ healing process.

3. In actuality, cold water without ice will not only ease (a, an, the) _____ pain but also prevent scarring and further damage.

4. In fact, (a, an, the) _____ person who keeps the finger submerged for at least several minutes and as long as half an hour will have (a, an, the) _____ least painful or scarred burn, according to doctors.

5. However, if (a, an, the) _____ burn is serious, (a, an, the) _____ first person to be consulted should be a doctor.

# Chapter 48

## WORD ORDER

### 48a How do I understand standard and inverted word order in sentences?

In **standard word order**, the most common pattern for DECLAR-ATIVE SENTENCES in English, the SUBJECT comes before the VERB. (To understand these concepts more fully, review 7l through 7p.)

    That book      was heavy.

With **inverted word order**, the MAIN VERB or an AUXILIARY VERB comes before the subject. The most common use of inverted word order in English is in forming DIRECT QUESTIONS. Questions that can be answered with a yes or no begin with a form of *be* used as a main verb, with an auxiliary verb (*be, do, have*), or with a MODAL AUXILIARY (*can, should, will,* and others; see Chapter 51).

#### QUESTIONS THAT CAN BE ANSWERED WITH A YES OR NO

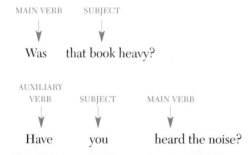

    Was    that book heavy?

    Have     you        heard the noise?

MODAL
AUXILIARY VERB — Can

SUBJECT — you

MAIN VERB — lift the book?

To form a yes-or-no question with a verb other than *be* as the main verb and when there is no auxiliary or modal as part of a VERB PHRASE, use the appropriate form of the auxiliary verb *do*.

AUXILIARY
VERB — Do

SUBJECT — you

MAIN VERB — want me to put the book away?

A question that begins with a question-forming word such as *why, when, where,* or *how* cannot be answered with a yes or no: **Why** *did the book fall?* Some kind of information must be provided to answer such a question; the answer cannot be simply yes or no because the question is not "*Did* the book fall?" Information on *why* it fell is needed: for example, *It was too heavy for me.*

### INFORMATION QUESTIONS: INVERTED ORDER
Most information questions follow the same rules of inverted word order as yes-or-no questions.

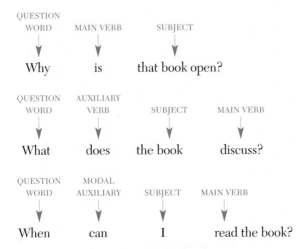

QUESTION
WORD — Why

MAIN VERB — is

SUBJECT — that book open?

QUESTION
WORD — What

AUXILIARY
VERB — does

SUBJECT — the book

MAIN VERB — discuss?

QUESTION
WORD — When

MODAL
AUXILIARY — can

SUBJECT — I

MAIN VERB — read the book?

### INFORMATION QUESTIONS: STANDARD ORDER
When *who* or *what* functions as the subject in a question, use standard word order.

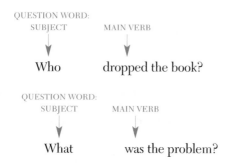

**ALERT:** When a question has more than one auxiliary verb, put the subject after the first auxiliary verb. ◆

The same rules apply to emphatic exclamations: ***Was*** *that book heavy!* ***Did*** *she enjoy that book!*

## NEGATIVES

When you use negatives such as *never, hardly ever, seldom, rarely, not only,* or *nor* to start a CLAUSE, use inverted order. These sentence pairs show the differences, first in standard order and then in inverted order.

> **I have never seen** a more exciting movie. [standard order]
>
> **Never have I seen** a more exciting movie. [inverted order]
>
> **She is not only** a talented artist **but also** an excellent musician.
>
> **Not only is she** a talented artist, **but she is also** an excellent musician.
>
> I didn't like the book, and **my husband didn't either**.
>
> I didn't like the book, and **neither did my husband**.

**ALERTS:** (1) With INDIRECT QUESTIONS, use standard word order.

> **NO** She asked **how did I drop** the book.
>
> **YES** She asked **how I dropped** the book.

(2) Word order deliberately inverted can be effective, when used sparingly, to create emphasis in a sentence that is neither a question nor an exclamation (also see 19e). ◆

## 48b How can I understand the placement of adjectives?

ADJECTIVES modify—describe or limit—NOUNS, PRONOUNS, and word groups that function as nouns (see 7f). In English, an adjective comes directly before the noun it describes. However, when more than one adjective describes the same noun, several sequences may be possible. Box 48.1 shows the most common order for positioning several adjectives.

**SUMMARY BOX 48.1**

### Word order for more than one adjective

1. **Determiners, if any:** *a, an, the, my, your, this, that, these, those,* and so on
2. **Expressions of order, including ordinal numbers, if any:** *first, second, third, next, last, final,* and so on
3. **Expressions of quantity, including cardinal (counting) numbers, if any:** *one, two, few, each, every, some,* and so on
4. **Adjectives of judgment or opinion, if any:** *pretty, happy, ugly, sad, interesting, boring,* and so on
5. **Adjectives of size or shape, if any:** *big, small, short, round, square,* and so on
6. **Adjectives of age or condition, if any:** *new, young, broken, dirty, shiny,* and so on
7. **Adjectives of color, if any:** *red, green, blue,* and so on
8. **Adjectives that can also be used as nouns, if any:** *French, Protestant, metal, cotton,* and so on
9. **The noun**

| 1 | 2 | 3 | 4 | 5 | 6 | 7 | 8 | 9 |
|-----|------|-----|------|------|-----|-----|------|----------|
| a   |      | few |      | tiny |     | red |      | ants     |
| the | last | six |      |      |     |     | Thai | carvings |
| my  |      |     | fine |      | old |     | oak  | table    |

## 48c How can I understand the placement of adverbs?

ADVERBS modify—describe or limit—VERBS, ADJECTIVES, other adverbs, or entire sentences (see 7g). Adverbs may be positioned first, in the middle, or last in CLAUSES. Box 48.2 (p. 836) summarizes adverb types, what they tell about the words they modify, and where each type can be placed.

## Types of adverbs and where to position them

| | | |
|---|---|---|
| **ADVERBS OF MANNER** | • describe *how* something is done | Nick **carefully** groomed the dog. |
| | • are usually in middle or last position | Nick groomed the dog **carefully**. |
| **ADVERBS OF TIME** | • describe *when* or *how long* about an event | **First**, he shampooed the dog. |
| | • are usually in first or last position | He shampooed the dog **first**. |
| | • include *just, still, already,* and similar adverbs, which are usually in middle position | He had **already** brushed the dog's coat. |
| **ADVERBS OF FREQUENCY** | • describe *how often* an event takes place | Nick has **never** been bitten by a dog. |
| | • are usually in middle position | |
| | • are in first position when they modify an entire sentence (see "Sentence adverbs" below) | **Occasionally**, he is scratched while shampooing a cat. |
| **ADVERBS OF DEGREE OR EMPHASIS** | • describe *how much* or *to what extent* about other modifiers | Nick is **extremely** calm around animals. [*Extremely* modifies *calm*.] |
| | • are directly before the word they modify | |
| | • include *only*, which is easy to misplace (see 14a) | |
| **SENTENCE ADVERBS** | • modify the entire sentence rather than just one word or a few words | **Incredibly**, he was once asked to groom a rat. |
| | • include transitional words and expressions (see 3g.1), as well as such expressions as *maybe, probably, possibly, fortunately, unfortunately,* and *incredibly* | |
| | • are in first position | |

**ALERT:** Do not let an adverb separate a verb from its DIRECT OBJECT or INDIRECT OBJECT. ◆

**EXERCISE 48-1**  Consulting all sections of this chapter, find and correct any errors in word order.

1. For two hundred years almost, the North Pacific humpback whales have returned to the tropic waters of Hawaii.
2. Why they are returning to these particular waters year after year?
3. The humpbacks do not accidentally arrive in Hawaiian waters; they are precise extremely in searching for this specific location, where they gather to complete their breeding rituals.
4. The whales first to arrive are sighted sometime in late November, after completing a 3,000-mile journey.
5. The humpbacks last to migrate to Hawaii arrive by December late or January early.

**EXERCISE 48-2**  Consulting all sections of this chapter, find and correct any errors in word order.

1. A beautiful few flowers began to bloom in my garden this week.
2. A neighbor asked me, "You did grow all these yourself?"
3. "Yes," I replied, "the roses are my favorite husband's, but the tulips are my favorite."
4. My neighbor, who extremely was impressed with my gardening efforts, decided to grow some flowers of her own.
5. Weeks later, as I strolled by her house, I saw her planting happily seeds from her favorite type of plant—petunias.

# Chapter 49

## PREPOSITIONS

**Prepositions** function with other words in PREPOSITIONAL PHRASES (7o). Prepositional phrases usually indicate *where* (direction or location), *how* (by what means or in what way), or *when* (at what time or how long) about the words they modify.

This chapter can help you with several uses of prepositions, which function in combination with other words in ways that are often idiomatic—that is, peculiar to the language. The meaning of an IDIOM differs from the literal meaning of each individual word. For example, the word *break* usually refers to shattering, but the sentence *Yao-Ming **broke into** a smile* means that a smile appeared on Yao-Ming's face. Knowing which preposition to use in a specific context takes much experience in reading, listening to, and speaking the language. A dictionary like the *Dictionary of American English* (Heinle and Heinle) can be especially helpful when you need to find the correct preposition to use in cases not covered by this chapter. Section 49a lists many common prepositions. Section 49b discusses prepositions with some expressions of time and place. Section 49c discusses combinations of verbs and prepositions called PHRASAL VERBS. Section 49d discusses prepostions with PAST PARTICIPLES. Section 49e discusses common expressions using prepositions.

### 49a How can I recognize prepositions?

Box 49.1 lists many common prepositions.

**SUMMARY BOX 49.1**

#### Common prepositions

| | | | | |
|---|---|---|---|---|
| about | against | around | before | between |
| above | along | as | behind | beyond |
| according to | along with | as for | below | but |
| across | among | at | beneath | by |
| after | apart from | because of | beside | by means of |

---

**SUMMARY BOX** 49.1 *continued*

## Common prepositions

| | | | | |
|---|---|---|---|---|
| concerning | in addition to | near | over | under |
| despite | in back of | next | past | underneath |
| down | in case of | of | regarding | unlike |
| during | instead of | off | round | until |
| except | in front of | on | since | up |
| except for | in place of | onto | through | upon |
| excepting | inside | on top of | throughout | up to |
| for | in spite of | out | till | with |
| from | into | out of | to | within |
| in | like | outside | toward | without |

---

**49b** **How do I use prepositions with expressions of time and place?**

Box 49.2 shows how to use the prepositions *in, at,* and *on* to deliver some common kinds of information about time and place. The box, however, does not cover every preposition that indicates time or place, nor does it cover all uses of *in, at,* and *on.* Also, the box does not include expressions that operate outside the general rules. (Both these sentences are correct: *You ride **in** the car* and *You ride **on** the bus.*)

---

**SUMMARY BOX** 49.2

## Using *in, at,* and *on* to show time and place

**TIME**

- ***in** a year or a month* (*during* is also correct but less common)

    **in** 1995          **in** May

- ***in** a period of time*

    **in** a few months (seconds, days, years)

- ***in** a period of the day*

    **in** the morning (afternoon, evening)

    **in** the daytime (morning, evening) *but* **at** night

➤

839

**Using *in*, *at*, and *on* to show time and place**

- *at* **a specific time or period of time**

  **at** noon      **at** 2:00      **at** dawn      **at** nightfall

  **at** takeoff (the time a plane leaves)

  **at** breakfast (the time a specific meal takes place)

- *on* **a specific day**

  **on** Friday      **on** my birthday

**PLACE**

- *in* **a location surrounded by something else**

  **in** the province of Alberta      **in** the kitchen

  **in** Utah      **in** the apartment

  **in** downtown Bombay      **in** the bathtub

- *at* **a specific location**

  **at** your house      **at** the bank

  **at** the corner of Third Avenue and Main Street

- *on* **a surface**

  **on** page 20

  **on** the second floor *but* **in** the attic *or* **in** the basement

  **on** Washington Street

  **on** the mezzanine

  **on** the highway

---

## 49c   How do I use prepositions in phrasal verbs?

**Phrasal verbs**, also called *two-word verbs* and *three-word verbs*, are VERBS that combine with PREPOSITIONS to deliver their meaning. In some phrasal verbs, the verb and the preposition should not be separated by other words: ***Look at*** *the moon* [not ***Look*** *the moon* ***at***]. In **separable phrasal verbs**, other words in the sentence can separate the verb and the preposition without interfering with meaning: *I **threw away** my homework* is as correct as *I **threw** my homework **away***.

    Here is a list of some common phrasal verbs. The ones that cannot be separated are marked with an asterisk (*).

**SELECTED PHRASAL VERBS**

| | | |
|---|---|---|
| ask out | get along with* | look into |
| break down | get back | look out for* |
| bring about | get off | look over |
| call back | go over* | make up |
| drop off | hand in | run across* |
| figure out | keep up with* | speak to* |
| fill out | leave out | speak with* |
| fill up | look after* | throw away |
| find out | look around | throw out |

Position a PRONOUN OBJECT between the words of a separable phrasal verb: *I threw it away.* Also, you can position an object PHRASE of several words between the parts of a separable phrasal verb: *I threw **my research paper** away.* However, when the object is a CLAUSE, do not let it separate the parts of the phrasal verb: *I threw away **all the papers that I wrote last year**.*

Many phrasal verbs are informal and are used more in speaking than in writing. For ACADEMIC WRITING, a more formal verb is usually more appropriate than a phrasal verb. In a research paper, for example, *propose* or *suggest* might be a better choice than *come up with*. For academic writing, acceptable phrasal verbs include *believe in, benefit from, concentrate on, consist of, depend on, dream of* (or *dream about*), *insist on, participate in, prepare for*, and *stare at*. None of these phrasal verbs can be separated.

**EXERCISE 49-1** Consulting the preceding sections of this chapter and using the list of phrasal verbs in 49c, write a one- or two-paragraph description of a typical day at work or school in which you use at least five phrasal verbs. After checking a dictionary, revise your writing, substituting for the phrasal verbs any more formal verbs that might be more appropriate for academic writing.

**49d    How do I use prepositions with past participles?**

PAST PARTICIPLES are verb forms that function as ADJECTIVES (50f). Past participles end in either *-ed* or *-d*, or in an equivalent irregular form (8d). When past participles follow the LINKING VERB *be*, it is easy to confuse them with PASSIVE verbs (8n), which have the same endings. Passive verbs describe actions. Past participles, because they act as adjectives, modify NOUNS and PRONOUNS and often describe situations and conditions. Passive verbs follow the pattern *be* + past participle + *by: The child **was frightened by** a snake.* An expression containing a past participle, however, can use either *be* or another linking verb, and it can be followed by either *by* or a different preposition.

- The child **seemed frightened by** snakes.
- The child **is frightened of** all snakes.

Here is a list of expressions containing past participles and the prepositions that often follow them. Look in a dictionary for others. (See 50b on using GERUNDS after some of these expressions.)

**SELECTED PAST PARTICIPLE PHRASES + PREPOSITIONS**

| | |
|---|---|
| be accustomed to | be interested in |
| be acquainted with | be known for |
| be composed of | be located in |
| be concerned/worried about | be made of (*or* from) |
| be disappointed with (*or* in someone) | be married to |
| be discriminated against | be pleased/satisfied with |
| be divorced from | be prepared for |
| be excited about | be tired of (*or* from) |
| be finished/done with | |

## **49e** How do I use prepositions in expressions?

In many common expressions, different PREPOSITIONS convey great differences in meaning. For example, four prepositions can be used with the verb *agree* to create five different meanings.

**agree to** means "to give consent": *I cannot **agree to** my buying you a new car.*

**agree about** means "to arrive at a satisfactory understanding": *We certainly **agree about** your needing a car.*

**agree on** means "to concur": *You and the seller must **agree on** a price for the car.*

**agree with** means "to have the same opinion": *I **agree with** you that you need a car.*

**agree with** also means "to be suitable or healthful": *The idea of having such a major expense does not **agree with** me.*

You can find entire books filled with English expressions that include prepositions. The following list shows a few that you're likely to use often.

**SELECTED EXPRESSIONS WITH PREPOSITIONS**

| | | |
|---|---|---|
| ability in | different from | involved with [*someone*] |
| access to | faith in | knowledge of |
| accustomed to | familiar with | made of |
| afraid of | famous for | married to |
| angry with *or* at | frightened by | opposed to |
| authority on | happy with | patient with |
| aware of | in charge of | proud of |
| based on | independent of | reason for |
| capable of | in favor of | related to |
| certain of | influence on *or* over | suspicious of |
| confidence in | interested in | time for |
| dependent on | involved in [*something*] | tired of |

# Chapter 50

## GERUNDS, INFINITIVES, AND PARTICIPLES

PARTICIPLES are verb forms (see 8b). A verb's -*ing* form is its PRESENT PARTICIPLE. The -*ed* form of a regular verb is its PAST PARTICIPLE; IRREGULAR VERBS form their past participles in various ways (for example, *bend, bent; eat, eaten; think, thought*—for a complete list, see Box 8.4 in 8d). Participles can function as ADJECTIVES (*a **smiling** face, a **closed** book*).

A verb's -*ing* form can also function as a NOUN (***Sneezing** spreads colds*), which is called a GERUND. Another verb form, the INFINITIVE, can also function as a noun. An infinitive is a verb's SIMPLE or base FORM, usually preceded by the word *to* (*We want everyone **to smile***). Verb forms—participles, gerunds, and infinitives—functioning as nouns or MODIFIERS are called VERBALS, as explained in 7e.

This chapter can help you make the right choices among verbals. Section 50a discusses gerunds and infinitives used as subjects. Section 50b discusses verbs that are followed by gerunds, not infinitives. Section 50c discusses verbs that are followed by infinitives, not gerunds. Section 50d discusses meaning changes that depend on whether certain verbs are followed by a gerund or by an infinitive. Section 50e explains that meaning does not change for certain sense verbs no matter whether they are followed by a gerund or an infinitive. Section 50f discusses differences in meaning between the present participle form and the past participle form of some modifiers.

## 50a How can I use gerunds and infinitives as subjects?

Gerunds are used more commonly than infinitives as subjects. Sometimes, however, either is acceptable.

**Choosing** the right health club is important.

**To choose** the right health club is important.

🔺 **ALERT:** When a gerund or an infinitive is used alone as a subject, it is SINGULAR and requires a singular verb. When two or more gerunds or infinitives create a COMPOUND SUBJECT, they require a plural verb. (See 7l and 10e.) ◆

## 50b When do I use a gerund, not an infinitive, as an object?

Some VERBS must be followed by GERUNDS used as DIRECT OBJECTS. Other verbs must be followed by INFINITIVES. Still other verbs can be followed by either a gerund or an infinitive. (A few verbs can change meaning depending on whether they are followed by a gerund or an infinitive; see 50d.) Box 50.1 lists common verbs that must be followed by gerunds, not infinitives.

Yuri **considered** *calling* [not *to call*] the mayor.

He **was having trouble** *getting* [not *to get*] a work permit.

Yuri's boss **recommended** *taking* [not *to take*] an interpreter to the permit agency.

---

**SUMMARY BOX** 50.1

### Verbs and expressions that must be followed by gerunds

| | | |
|---|---|---|
| acknowledge | detest | mind |
| admit | discuss | object to |
| advise | dislike | postpone |
| anticipate | dream about | practice |
| appreciate | enjoy | put off |
| avoid | escape | quit |
| cannot bear | evade | recall |
| cannot help | favor | recommend |
| cannot resist | finish | regret |
| complain about | give up | resent |
| consider | have trouble | resist |
| consist of | imagine | risk |
| contemplate | include | suggest |
| defer from | insist on | talk about |
| delay | keep (on) | tolerate |
| deny | mention | understand |

## GERUND AFTER *GO*

The word *go* is usually followed by an infinitive: *We can **go to see*** [not *go seeing*] *a movie tonight.* Sometimes, however, *go* is followed by a gerund in phrases such as *go swimming, go fishing, go shopping,* and *go driving: I will **go shopping*** [not *go to shop*] *after work.*

## GERUND AFTER *BE* + COMPLEMENT + PREPOSITION

Many common expressions use a form of the verb *be* plus a COMPLEMENT plus a PREPOSITION. In such expressions, use a gerund, not an infinitive, after the preposition. Here is a list of some of the most frequently used expressions in this pattern.

**SELECTED EXPRESSIONS USING *BE* + COMPLEMENT + PREPOSITION**

| | |
|---|---|
| be (get) accustomed to | be interested in |
| be angry about | be prepared for |
| be bored with | be responsible for |
| be capable of | be tired of |
| be committed to | be (get) used to |
| be excited about | be worried about |

We **are excited about *voting*** [not *to vote*] in the next presidential election.

Who **will be responsible for *locating*** [not *to locate*] our polling place?

⚡ **ALERT:** Always use a gerund, not an infinitive, as the object of a preposition. Be especially careful when the word *to* is functioning as a preposition in a PHRASAL VERB (see 49c): *We are committed **to changing*** [not *to change*] *the rules.* ◆

## 50c When do I use an infinitive, not a gerund, as an object?

Box 50.2 lists selected common verbs and expressions that must be followed by INFINITIVES, not GERUNDS, as OBJECTS.

She **wanted *to go*** [not *wanted going*] to the lecture.

Only three people **decided *to question*** [not *decided questioning*] the speaker.

---

**SUMMARY BOX** 50.2

### Verbs and expressions that must be followed by infinitives

| | | | |
|---|---|---|---|
| afford | consent | intend | promise |
| agree | decide | know how | refuse |
| aim | decline | learn | require |
| appear | demand | like | seem |
| arrange | deserve | manage | struggle |
| ask | do not care | mean | tend |
| attempt | expect | need | threaten |
| be left | fail | offer | volunteer |
| beg | force | plan | vote |
| cannot afford | give permission | prefer | wait |
| care | hesitate | prepare | want |
| claim | hope | pretend | would like |

---

### INFINITIVE AFTER *BE* + COMPLEMENT

Gerunds are common in constructions that use a form of the verb *be* plus a COMPLEMENT and a PREPOSITION (see 50b). However, use an infinitive, not a gerund, when *be* plus a complement is not followed by a preposition.

> We **are eager *to go*** [not *going*] camping.

> I **am ready *to sleep*** [not *sleeping*] in a tent.

### INFINITIVE TO INDICATE PURPOSE

Use an infinitive in expressions that indicate purpose: *I read a book **to learn** more about Mayan culture.* This sentence means "I read a book for the purpose of learning more about Mayan culture." *To learn* delivers the idea of purpose more concisely (see Chapter 16) than expressions such as *so that I can* or *in order to.*

### INFINITIVE WITH *THE FIRST, THE LAST, THE ONE*

Use an infinitive after the expressions *the first, the last,* and *the one*: *Nina is the first **to arrive** [not arriving] and the last **to leave** [not leaving] every day. She's always the one **to do** the most.*

**UNMARKED INFINITIVES**

Infinitives used without the word *to* are called **unmarked infinitives**, or sometimes *bare infinitives.* An unmarked infinitive may be hard to recognize because it is not preceded by *to.* Some common verbs followed by unmarked infinitives are *feel, have, hear, let, listen to, look at, make* (meaning "compel"), *notice, see,* and *watch.*

> Please let me **take** [not *to take*] you to lunch. [unmarked infinitive]
>
> I want **to take** you to lunch. [marked infinitive]
>
> I can have Kara **drive** [not *to drive*] us. [unmarked infinitive]
>
> I will ask Kara **to drive** us. [marked infinitive]

The verb *help* can be followed by a marked or an unmarked infinitive. Either is correct: *Help me **put** [or **to put**] this box in the car.*

◢ **ALERT:** Be careful to use parallel structure (see Chapter 18) correctly when you use two or more gerunds or infinitives after verbs. If two or more verbal objects follow one verb, put the verbals into the same form.

> **NO**   We went **sailing** and **to scuba dive**.
>
> **YES**   We went **sailing** and **scuba diving**.
>
> **NO**   We heard the wind **blow** and the waves **crashing**.
>
> **YES**   We heard the wind **blow** and the waves **crash**.
>
> **YES**   We heard the wind **blowing** and the waves **crashing**.

Conversely, if you are using verbal objects with COMPOUND PREDICATES, be sure to use the kind of verbal that each verb requires.

> **NO**   We enjoyed **scuba diving** but do not plan **sailing** again.
> [*Enjoyed* requires a gerund object, and *plan* requires an infinitive object; see Boxes 50.1 and 50.2 in this chapter.]
>
> **YES**   We enjoyed **scuba diving** but do not plan **to sail** again.  ◆

## 50d   How does meaning change when certain verbs are followed by a gerund or an infinitive?

**WITH *STOP***

The VERB *stop* followed by a GERUND means "finish, quit." *Stop* followed by an INFINITIVE means "interrupt one activity to begin another."

> We **stopped *eating***. [We finished our meal.]
>
> We **stopped *to eat***. [We stopped another activity, such as driving, to eat.]

## WITH *REMEMBER* AND *FORGET*

The verb *remember* followed by an infinitive means "not to forget to do something": *I must **remember to talk** with Isa. Remember* followed by a gerund means "recall a memory": *I **remember talking** in my sleep last night.*

The verb *forget* followed by an infinitive means "fail to do something": *If you **forget to put** a stamp on that letter, it will be returned. Forget* followed by a gerund means "do something and not recall it": *I **forget having put** the stamps in the refrigerator.*

## WITH *TRY*

The verb *try* followed by an infinitive means "make an effort": *I **tried to find** your jacket.* Followed by a gerund, *try* means "experiment with": *I **tried jogging** but found it too difficult.*

## 50e   Why is the meaning unchanged whether a gerund or an infinitive follows sense verbs?

Sense VERBS include words such as *see, notice, hear, observe, watch, feel, listen to,* and *look at.* The meaning of these verbs is usually not affected by whether a GERUND or an INFINITIVE follows as the OBJECT. *I **saw** the water **rise*** and *I **saw** the water **rising*** both have the same meaning in American English.

**EXERCISE 50-1**   Write the correct form of the verbal object (either a gerund or an infinitive) for each verb in parentheses. For help, consult 50b through 50e.

EXAMPLE   People like (think) <u>to think</u> that they have a good memory, but everybody shows signs of forgetfulness from time to time.

1. Think about (ride) _____ the railroad to work on a rainy Monday morning.

2. The comfortable reclining seats let passengers (take) _____ a relaxing nap on the way to work.

3. Because of the rain, commuters are forced (bring) _____ an umbrella and a raincoat, along with their usual traveling items.

4. Once they reach their destination, passengers forget that they need their umbrellas and raincoats (walk) _____ the few blocks to work.

5. (Step) _____ out into the rain makes the passengers suddenly realize that they've left their umbrellas and raincoats on the train, which has already left the station.

6. However, they need not be angry about (lose) _____ the forgotten item.

7. Many railroads have lost-and-found offices that help (reunite) _____ the rightful owners with their lost possessions.

8. After losing a possession, passengers tend (call) _____ the lost-and-found office in search of the missing article.

9. Some commuters even acknowledge (leave) _____ gifts, false teeth, wooden legs, and bicycles aboard the train.

10. Most times, people can claim their possessions either by (answer) _____ a few questions to ensure proper ownership or by (identify) _____ the lost item.

## 50f How do I choose between *-ing* and *-ed* forms for adjectives?

Deciding whether to use the *-ing* form (PRESENT PARTICIPLE) or the *-ed* form (PAST PARTICIPLE of a regular VERB) as an ADJECTIVE in a specific sentence can be difficult. For example, *I am* **amused** and *I am* **amusing** are both correct in English, but their meanings are very different. To make the right choice, decide whether the modified NOUN or PRONOUN is causing or experiencing what the participle describes.

Use a present participle (*-ing*) to modify a noun or pronoun that is the agent or the cause of the action.

Micah described your **interesting** plan. [The noun *plan* causes what its modifier describes—interest; so *interesting* is correct.]

I find your plan **exciting.** [The noun *plan* causes what its modifier describes—excitement; so *exciting* is correct.]

Use a past participle (*-ed* in regular verbs) to modify a noun or pronoun that experiences or receives whatever the modifier describes.

An **interested** committee wants to hear your plan. [The noun *committee* experiences what its modifier describes—interest; so *interested* is correct.]

**Excited** by your plan, they called a board meeting. [The pronoun *they* experiences what its modifier describes—excitement; so *excited* is correct.]

Here are frequently used participles that convey very different meanings, depending on whether the *-ed* or the *-ing* form is used.

| | |
|---|---|
| amused, amusing | depressed, depressing |
| annoyed, annoying | disgusted, disgusting |
| appalled, appalling | fascinated, fascinating |
| bored, boring | frightened, frightening |
| confused, confusing | insulted, insulting |

| | |
|---|---|
| offended, offending | reassured, reassuring |
| overwhelmed, overwhelming | satisfied, satisfying |
| pleased, pleasing | shocked, shocking |

**EXERCISE 50-2** Choose the correct participle from each pair in parentheses. For help, consult 50f.

EXAMPLE    It can be a (satisfied, satisfying) <u>satisfying</u> experience to learn about the lives of artists.

1. The artist Frida Kahlo led an (interested, interesting) _____ life.
2. When Kahlo was eighteen, (horrified, horrifying) _____ observers saw her (injured, injuring) _____ in a streetcar accident.
3. A (disappointed, disappointing) _____ Kahlo had to abandon her plan to study medicine.
4. Instead, she began to create paintings filled with (disturbed, disturbing) _____ images.
5. Some art critics consider Kahlo's paintings to be (fascinated, fascinating) _____ works of art, though many people find them (overwhelmed, overwhelming) _____.

**EXERCISE 50-3** Choose the correct participle from each pair in parentheses. For help, consult 50f.

EXAMPLE    Learning about the career of a favorite actor or actress is always an (interested, interesting) <u>interesting</u> exercise.

1. Canadian Jim Carrey is an actor-comedian with a very (fascinated, fascinating) _____ history.
2. (Raised, Raising) _____ by his parents in southern Ontario, Carrey grew up in one of the most media-rich areas in North America.
3. Biographies reveal the (surprised, surprising) _____ news that this bright and talented student dropped out of school during the tenth grade.
4. After relocating to Los Angeles in the 1980s, the (disappointed, disappointing) _____ Carrey discovered the difficulties of acting after his first (canceled, canceling) _____ TV series left him briefly out of work.
5. Carrey's career skyrocketed with his (amused, amusing) _____ appearances on *In Living Color,* a TV show that led to a string of box-office hits: *The Mask; The Truman Show; Liar, Liar;* and *Bruce Almighty.*

**EXERCISE 50-4** Choose the correct participle from each pair in parentheses. For help, consult 50f.

> EXAMPLE    Studying popular myths that turn out to be false can be a (fascinated, fascinating) <u>fascinating</u> experience.

1. While doing research for a paper about birds, I discovered some (interested, interesting) _____ information about ostriches.

2. I encountered an (unsettled, unsettling) _____ passage in a book, which said that ostriches do not, in fact, stick their heads into the sand for protection when they feel fear.

3. This myth about (frightened, frightening) _____ ostriches began among the ancient Arabs and has since been passed on by many reputable writers.

4. In reality, an ostrich does not have to do something as useless as bury its head in the sand when a predator approaches, because a (hunted, hunting) _____ ostrich can reach speeds of nearly 35 mph and can thus outrun most other animals.

5. A (threatened, threatening) _____ ostrich can also kick its way out of many dangerous situations with its powerful legs, and with its 8-foot-tall frame, it presents itself as a (frightened, frightening) _____ opponent.

# Chapter 51

## MODAL AUXILIARY VERBS

AUXILIARY VERBS are known as *helping verbs* because adding an auxiliary verb to a MAIN VERB helps the main verb convey additional information (see 8e). For example, the auxiliary verb *do* is important in turning sentences into questions. *You have to sleep* becomes a question when *do* is added: *Do you have to sleep?* The most common auxiliary verbs are forms of *be, have,* and *do.* Boxes 8.6 and 8.7 in section 8e list the forms of these three verbs.

MODAL AUXILIARY VERBS are one type of auxiliary verb. They include *can, could, may, might, should, had better, must, will, would,* and others discussed in this chapter. Modals differ from *be, have,* and *do* used as auxiliary verbs in the specific ways discussed in Box 51.1.

This chapter can help you use modals to convey shades of meaning. Section 51a discusses using modals to convey ability, necessity, advisability, possibility, and probability. Section 51b discusses using modals to convey preferences, plans or obligations, and past habits. Section 51c introduces modals in the PASSIVE VOICE.

---

**SUMMARY BOX** 51.1

## Modals and their differences from other auxiliary verbs

- Modals in the present future are always followed by the SIMPLE FORM of a main verb: *I **might go** tomorrow.*

- One-word modals have no *-s* ending in the THIRD-PERSON SINGULAR: *She **could** go with me; he **could** go with me; they **could** go with me.* (The two-word modal *have to* changes form to agree with its subject: *I **have to** leave; she **has to** leave.*) Auxiliary verbs other than modals usually change form for third-person singular: *I **do** want to go; he **does** want to go.*

**Modals and their differences from other auxiliary verbs**

- Some modals change form in the past. Others (*should, would, must,* which convey probability, and *ought to*) use *have* + a PAST PARTICIPLE. *I* **can do** it becomes *I* **could do** it in PAST-TENSE CLAUSES about ability. *I* **could do** it becomes *I* **could have done** it in clauses about possibility.

- Modals convey meaning about ability, necessity, advisability, possibility, and other conditions: For example, *I can go* means "I am able to go." Modals do not describe actual occurrences.

## **51a** How do I convey ability, necessity, advisability, possibility, and probability with modals?

### CONVEYING ABILITY

The modal *can* conveys ability now (in the present), and *could* conveys ability before (in the past). These words deliver the meaning "able to." For the future, use *will be able to.*

> We **can** work late tonight. [*Can* conveys present ability.]
>
> I **could** work late last night, too. [*Could* conveys past ability.]
>
> I **will be able to** work late next Monday. [*Will be able* is the future tense; *will* here is not a modal.]

Adding *not* between a modal and the MAIN VERB makes the CLAUSE negative: *We* **cannot** *work late tonight; I* **could not** *work late last night; I* **will not be able to** *work late next Monday.*

⬧ **ALERT:** You will often see negative forms of modals turned into CONTRACTIONS: *can't, couldn't, won't, wouldn't,* and others. Because contractions are considered informal usage by some instructors, you will never be wrong if you avoid them in ACADEMIC WRITING, except when you are reproducing spoken words. ◆

### CONVEYING NECESSITY

The modals *must* and *have to* convey a need to do something. Both *must* and *have to* are followed by the simple form of the main verb. In the present tense, *have to* changes form to agree with its subject.

> You **must** leave before midnight.
>
> She **has to** leave when I leave.

In the past tense, *must* is never used to express necessity. Instead, use *had to*.

PRESENT TENSE    We **must** study today. We **have to** study today.

PAST TENSE    We **had to** [not *must*] take a test yesterday.

The negative forms of *must* and *have to* also have different meanings. *Must not* conveys that something is forbidden; *do not have to* conveys that something is not necessary.

You **must not** sit there.  [Sitting there is forbidden.]

You **do not have to** sit there.  [Sitting there is not necessary.]

## CONVEYING ADVISABILITY OR THE NOTION OF A GOOD IDEA

The modals *should* and *ought to* express the idea that doing the action of the main verb is advisable or is a good idea.

You **should** go to class tomorrow morning.

In the past tense, *should* and *ought to* convey regret or knowing something through hindsight. They mean that good advice was not taken.

You **should have** gone to class yesterday.

I **ought to have** called my sister yesterday.

The modal *had better* delivers the meaning of good advice or warning or threat. It does not change form for tense.

You **had better** see the doctor before your cough gets worse.

*Need to* is often used to express strong advice, too. Its past-tense form is *needed to*.

You **need to** take better care of yourself. You **needed to** listen.

## CONVEYING POSSIBILITY

The modals *may, might,* and *could* can be used to convey an idea of possibility or likelihood.

We **may** become hungry before long.

We **could** eat lunch at the diner next door.

For the past-tense form, use *may, might,* and *could,* followed by *have* and the past participle of the main verb.

I **could have studied** French in high school, but I studied Spanish instead.

## CONVEYING PROBABILITY

In addition to conveying the idea of necessity, the modal *must* can also convey probability or likelihood. It means that a well-informed guess is being made.

> Marisa **must** be a talented actress. She has been chosen to play the lead role in the school play.

When *must* conveys probability, the past tense is *must have* plus the past participle of the main verb.

> I did not see Boris at the party; he **must have left** early.

**EXERCISE 51-1**  Fill in each blank with the past-tense modal auxiliary that expresses the meaning given in parentheses. For help, consult 51a.

EXAMPLE  I (advisability) <u>should have</u> gone straight to the doctor the instant I felt a cold coming on.

1. Since I (necessity, no choice) _____ work late this past Monday, I could not get to the doctor's office before it closed.
2. I (advisability) _____ fallen asleep after dinner, but I stayed awake for a while instead.
3. Even after I finally got into bed, I (ability) _____ not relax.
4. I (making a guess) _____ not _____ heard the alarm the next morning, because I overslept nearly two hours.
5. When I finally arrived at work, my boss came into my office and said, "Julie, you (necessity) _____ stayed home and rested if you are sick."

**EXERCISE 51-2**  Fill in each blank with the past-tense modal auxiliary that expresses the meaning given in parentheses. For help, consult 51a.

EXAMPLE  I (advisability) <u>should have</u> waited for a rainy afternoon to visit the Empire State Building.

1. Since I (necessity, no choice) _____ work all week, Sunday was my only free day to visit the Empire State Building.
2. I (advisability) _____ known that because it was such a clear, beautiful day, everyone else would want to visit this New York City landmark, too.
3. The lines for the elevator were terribly long, and even though I am physically fit, I (ability) _____ not possibly climb the eighty-six flights of stairs to the observation deck near the top of the building.
4. The other visitors to the Empire State Building (probability) _____ noticed how impatient I was becoming by the look on my face.

5. Then I heard the security guard say to the woman in line ahead of me, "You (advice, good idea) _____ come yesterday. Because of the light drizzle, hardly anyone was here."

## 51b How do I convey preferences, plans, and past habits with modals?

**CONVEYING PREFERENCES**

The modal *would rather* expresses a preference. *Would rather*, the PRESENT TENSE, is used with the SIMPLE FORM of the MAIN VERB, and *would rather have*, the PAST TENSE, is used with the PAST PARTICIPLE of the main verb.

We **would rather see** a comedy than a mystery.

Carlos **would rather have stayed** home last night.

**CONVEYING PLAN OR OBLIGATION**

A form of *be* followed by *supposed to* and the simple form of a main verb delivers a meaning of something planned or of an obligation.

I **was supposed to meet** them at the bus stop.

**CONVEYING PAST HABIT**

The modals *used to* and *would* express the idea that something happened repeatedly in the past.

I **used to** hate going to the dentist.

I **would** dread every single visit.

**ALERT:** Both *used to* and *would* can be used to express repeated actions in the past, but *would* cannot be used for a situation that lasted for a period of time in the past.

**NO**  I **would** live in Arizona.

**YES**  I **used to** live in Arizona. ◆

## 51c How can I recognize modals in the passive voice?

Modals use the ACTIVE VOICE, as shown in sections 51a and 51b. In the active voice, the subject does the action expressed in the MAIN VERB (see 8n and 8o).

Modals can also use the PASSIVE VOICE (8p). In the passive voice, the doer of the main verb's action is either unexpressed or is expressed as an OBJECT in a PREPOSITIONAL PHRASE starting with the word *by*.

| PASSIVE | The waterfront **can be seen** from my window. |
|---|---|
| ACTIVE | **I can see** the waterfront from my window. |
| PASSIVE | The tax form **must be signed** by the person who fills it out. |
| ACTIVE | The person who fills out the tax form **must sign** it. |

**EXERCISE 51-3**  Select the correct choice from the words in parentheses and write it in the blank. For help, consult 51a through 51c.

EXAMPLE   When I was younger, I (would, used to) <u>used to</u> love to go bicycle riding.

1. You (ought to have, ought have) _____ called yesterday as you had promised you would.
2. Judging by the size of the puddles in the street outside, it (must be rained, must have rained) _____ all night long.
3. Ingrid (must not have, might not have been) _____ as early for the interview as she claims she was.
4. After all the studying he did, Pedro (should have, should have been) _____ less frightened by the exam.
5. I have to go home early today, although I really (cannot, should not) _____ leave before the end of the day because of all the work I have to do.

**EXERCISE 51-4**  Select the correct choice from the words in parentheses and write it in the blank. For help, consult 51a through 51c.

EXAMPLE   We (must have, must) <u>must</u> study this afternoon.

1. Unfortunately, I (should not, cannot) _____ go to the movies with you because I have to take care of my brother tonight.
2. Juan (would have, would have been) _____ nominated class valedictorian if he had not moved to another city.
3. You (ought not have, ought not to have) _____ arrived while the meeting was still in progress.
4. Louise (must be, must have been) _____ sick to miss the party last week.
5. Had you not called in advance, you (may not have, may not have been) _____ aware of the traffic on the expressway.

# Terms Glossary

This glossary defines important terms used in this handbook, including the ones that are printed in small capital letters. Many of these glossary entries end with parenthetical references to the handbook section(s) or chapter(s) where the specific term is fully discussed.

**absolute phrase** A phrase containing a subject and a participle that modifies an entire sentence. (7o) *The semester [subject] being [present participle of be] over, the campus looks deserted.*

**abstract noun** A noun that names something not knowable through the five senses: *idea, respect.* (7b)

**academic writing** Writing you do for college classes, usually intended to inform or to persuade. (1c)

**action verbs** Strong verbs that increase the impact of your language and reduce wordiness. *Weak verbs,* such as *be* or *have,* increase wordiness. (16e)

**active voice** An attribute of verbs showing that the action or condition expressed in the verb is done by the subject, in contrast with the *passive voice,* which conveys that the action or condition of the verb is done to the subject. (8n, 8o)

**adjective** A word that describes or limits (modifies) a noun, a pronoun, or a word group functioning as a noun: *silly, three.* (7f, Chapter 11)

**adjective clause** A dependent clause, also known as a *relative clause.* An adjective clause modifies a preceding noun or pronoun and begins with a relative word (such as *who, which, that,* or *where*) that relates the clause to the noun or pronoun it modifies. Also see *clause.* (7p)

**adverb** A word that describes or limits (modifies) verbs, adjectives, other adverbs, phrases, or clauses: *loudly, very, nevertheless, there.* (7g, Chapter 11)

**adverb clause** A dependent clause beginning with a subordinating conjunction that establishes the relationship in meaning between the adverb clause and its independent clause. An adverb clause modifies the independent clause's verb or the entire independent clause. Also see *clause, conjunction.* (7p)

**agreement** The required match of number and person between a subject and verb or a pronoun and antecedent. A pronoun that expresses gender must match its antecedent in gender also. (Chapter 10)

**analogy** An explanation of the unfamiliar in terms of the familiar. Like a simile, an analogy compares things not normally associated with each other; but unlike a simile, an analogy does not use *like* or *as* in making the comparison. Analogy is also a rhetorical strategy for developing paragraphs. (3i, 21d, 41b)

**analysis** A process of critical thinking that divides a whole into its component parts in order to understand how the parts interrelate. Some times called *division,* analysis is also a rhetorical strategy for developing paragraphs. (3i, 4b, 38h, 39f)

**analytic frameworks** Systematic ways of investigating a work. (38c)

**antecedent** The noun or pronoun to which a pronoun refers. (9l–9s, 10o–10t)

**APA style** See *documentation style*.

**appeals to reason** Tools a writer uses to convince the reader that the reasoning in an argument is sound and effective; there are three types—logical, emotional, and ethical appeals. (5j)

**appositive** A word or group of words that renames a preceding noun or noun phrase: *my favorite month,* **October***.* (7n)

**argument** A rhetorical attempt to convince others to agree with a position about a topic open to debate. (1b, Chapter 5)

**articles** Also called *determiners* or *noun markers*, articles are the words *a, an,* and *the. A* and *an* are indefinite articles, and *the* is a definite article; also see *determiner*. (7f, Chapter 47)

**assertion** A statement. In a thesis statement, an assertion expresses a point of view about a topic; in an argument, an assertion states the position you want to argue. (2q, 5c)

**audience** The readers to whom a piece of writing is directed; the three types include *general audience, peer audience,* and *specialist audience*. (1c)

**auxiliary verb** Also known as a *helping verb*, an auxiliary verb is a form of *be, do, have, can, may, will,* or certain other verbs, that combines with a main verb to help it express tense, mood, and voice. Also see *modal auxiliary verb*. (8e)

**balanced sentence** A sentence composed of two parallel structures, usually two independent clauses, that present contrasting content. (18b)

**base form** See *simple form*.

**bias** In writing, a distortion or inaccuracy caused by a dislike or hatred of individuals, groups of people, or ideas. (4c.2)

**bibliographic notes** In a note system of documentation, a *footnote* or *endnote* gives the bibliographic information the first time a source is cited. (33f, 34d.2, Chapter 36)

**bibliography** A list of sources used or consulted for research writing. (Chapters 34, 35, and 36)

**block style** Style used in writing business letters. Block style uses no indents, single spacing within paragraphs and double spacing between paragraphs. All lines start flush left, which means at the left margin. (40f)

**blog** Shortened form of "**Web log**," a kind of online journal. (1a, 1h)

**body paragraphs** Paragraphs that provide the substance of your message in a sequence that makes sense. (3c)

**Boolean expressions** In a search engine, symbols or words such as And, Or, Not, and Near that let you create keyword combinations that narrow and refine your search. (2l, 32d.1)

**borders** Lines used to set apart sections of text. (42e)

**brainstorming** Listing all ideas that come to mind on a topic and then grouping the ideas by patterns that emerge. (2h)

**bureaucratic language** Sometimes called *bureaucratese;* language that is overblown or overly complex. (21m)

**business writing** Writing designed for business, including letters, memos, resumes, job application letters, and e-mail messages. (1d, 3a, Chapter 40)

**case** The form of a noun or pronoun in a specific context that shows whether it is functioning as a subject, an object, or a possessive. In modern English, nouns change form in the possessive case only (city = form for subjective and objective cases; city's = possessive-case form). Also see *pronoun case*. (9a–9k)

**cause and effect** The relationship between outcomes (effects) and the reasons for them (causes). Cause-and-effect analysis is a rhetorical strategy for developing paragraphs. (3i, 4h, 4j)

**chronological order** Also called *time order,* an arrangement of information according to time sequence; an organizing strategy for sentences, paragraphs, and longer pieces of writing. (3h)

**citation** Information that identifies a source quoted, paraphrased, summarized, or referred to in a piece of writing; *in-text citations* appear within sentences or as *parenthetical references.* Also see *documentation.* (Chapters 33 and 34)

**civic writing** Writing done to influence public opinion or to advance causes for the public good. (40l)

**claim** States an issue and then takes a position on a debatable topic related to the issue. A claim is supported with evidence and reasons, moving from broad reasons to specific data and details. (5a)

**classical argument** An argument with a six-part structure consisting of introduction, thesis statement, background, evidence and reasoning, response to opposing views, and conclusion. (5e)

**classification** A rhetorical strategy for paragraph development that organizes information by grouping items according to underlying shared characteristics. (3i)

**clause** A group of words containing a subject and a predicate. A clause that delivers full meaning is called an *independent* (or *main*) *clause.* A clause that lacks full meaning by itself is called a *dependent* (or *subordinate*) *clause.* Also see *adjective clause, adverb clause, nonrestrictive element, noun clause, restrictive element.* (7p)

**cliché** An overused, worn-out phrase that has lost its capacity to communicate effectively: *flat as Kansas, ripe old age.* (21j)

**climactic order** Sometimes called *emphatic order,* an arrangement of ideas or other kinds of information from least important to most important. (3h, 5e )

**clip art** Refers to pictures, sketches, and other graphics available on some word processing programs. (42f)

**clustering** See *mapping.*

**coherence** The clear progression from one idea to another using transitional expressions, pronouns, selective repetition, or parallelism to make connections between ideas. (3c.4, 3g)

**collaborative writing** Students working together to write a paper. (2x)

**collective noun** A noun that names a group of people or things: *family, committee.* Also see *noncount noun.* (7b, 10j, 10t)

**colloquial language** Casual or conversational language. Also see *slang.* (21i)

**comma fault** See *comma splice.*

**comma splice** The error that occurs when only a comma connects two independent clauses; also called a *comma fault.* (Chapter 13)

**common noun** A noun that names a general group, place, person, or thing: *dog, house.* (7b)

**comparative form** The form of a descriptive adjective or adverb that shows a different degree of intensity between two things: *bluer, less blue; more easily, less easily.* Also see *positive form, superlative form.* (11e)

**comparison and contrast** A rhetorical strategy for organizing and developing paragraphs by discussing similarities (*comparison*) and differences (*contrast*). It has two patterns: *point-by-point* and *block organization.* (3i)

**complement** An element after a verb that completes the predicate, such as a direct object after an action verb or a noun or adjective after a linking verb. Also see *object complement, predicate adjective, predicate nominative, subject complement.* (7n)

**complete predicate** See *predicate.*

**complete subject** See *subject*.

**complex sentence** See *sentence types*.

**compound-complex sentence** See *sentence types*.

**compound construction** A group of nouns or pronouns connected with a coordinating conjunction. (9d)

**compound noun** See *subject*.

**compound predicate** See *predicate*.

**compound sentence** See *coordinate sentence, sentence types*.

**compound subject** See *subject*. (7l, 10e)

**compound word** Two or more words placed together to express one concept. (22g)

**conciseness** An attribute of writing that is direct and to the point. (Chapter 16)

**concrete noun** A noun naming something that can be seen, touched, heard, smelled, or tasted: *smoke, sidewalk*. (7b)

**conjunction** A word that connects or otherwise establishes a relationship between two or more words, phrases, or clauses. Also see *coordinating conjunction, correlative conjunction, subordinating conjunction*. (7i)

**conjunctive adverb** An adverb, such as *therefore* or *meanwhile*, that communicates a logical connection in meaning. (7g)

**connotation** An idea implied by a word, involving associations and emotional overtones that go beyond the word's dictionary definition. (21e.2)

**contraction** A word where an apostrophe takes the place of one or more omitted letters. (27d)

**coordinate adjectives** Two or more adjectives of equal weight that modify a noun. (24e)

**coordinate sentence** Two or more independent clauses joined by either a semicolon or a comma with coordinat-

ing conjunction showing their relationship; also called a *compound sentence*. Also see *coordination*. (17b)

**coordinating conjunction** A conjunction that joins two or more grammatically equivalent structures: *and, or, for, nor, but, so, yet*. (7i, 13c.3, 17b, 17c)

**coordination** The use of grammatically equivalent forms to show a balance or sequence of ideas. (17a–17d, 17i)

**correlative conjunction** A pair of words that joins equivalent grammatical structures, including *both . . . and, either . . . or, neither . . . nor, not only . . . but* (or *but also*). (7i)

**count noun** A noun that names an item or items that can be counted: *radio, streets, idea, fingernails*. (7b, 46a, 46b)

**critical reading** A parallel process to critical thinking where you think about what you're reading while you're reading it. (4d)

**critical response** Formally, an essay summarizing a source's central point or main idea. It includes a *transitional statement* that bridges this summary and the writer's synthesized reactions in response. (4f)

**critical thinking** A form of thinking where you take control of your conscious thought processes. (4a, 4b, 38g)

**cumulative adjectives** Adjectives that build meaning from word to word: *distinctive musical style*. (24e)

**cumulative sentence** The most common structure for a sentence, with the subject and verb first, followed by modifiers adding details; also called a *loose sentence*. (19e)

**dangling modifier** A modifier that attaches its meaning illogically, either because it is closer to another noun or pronoun than to its true subject or because its true subject is not expressed in the sentence. (14d)

**declarative sentence** A sentence that makes a statement: *Sky diving is exciting.* Also see *exclamatory sentence, imperative sentence, interrogative sentence.* (7k)

**deduction, deductive reasoning** The process of reasoning from general claims to a specific instance. (4i)

**definite article** See *articles.*

**definition** A rhetorical strategy in which you define or give the meaning of words or ideas. Includes *extended definition.* (3i)

**demonstrative pronoun** A pronoun that points out the antecedent: *this, these; that, those.* (7c, 7f)

**denotation** The dictionary definition of a word. (21e.1)

**dependent clause** A clause that cannot stand alone as an independent grammatical unit. Also see *adjective clause, adverb clause, noun clause.* (7p, 12b)

**description** A rhetorical strategy that appeals to a reader's senses—sight, sound, smell, taste, and touch. (3i)

**descriptive adjective** An adjective that names the condition or properties of the noun it modifies and (except for a very few, such as *dead* and *unique*) has comparative and superlative forms: *flat, flatter, flattest.*

**descriptive adverb** An adverb that names the condition or properties of whatever it modifies and that has comparative and superlative forms: *happily, more happily, most happily.* (7g)

**determiner** A word or word group, traditionally identified as an adjective, that limits a noun by telling how much or how many about it. Also called *expression of quantity, limiting adjective,* or *noun marker.* (7f, 46b, Chapter 47)

**diction** Word choice. (21e)

**digital portfolio** A collection of several texts in electronic format that you've chosen to represent the range of your skills and abilities. (1h)

**direct address** Words naming a person or group being spoken to. Written words of direct address are set off by commas. (24g) *The answer,* **my friends,** *lies with you. Go with them,* **Gene.**

**direct discourse** In writing, words that repeat speech or conversation exactly and so are enclosed in quotation marks. (15e, 24g, 28b)

**direct object** A noun or pronoun or group of words functioning as a noun that receives the action (completes the meaning) of a transitive verb. (7m)

**direct question** A sentence that asks a question and ends with a question mark: *Are you going?* (23a, 23c)

**direct quotation** See *quotation.*

**direct title** A title that tells exactly what the essay will be about. (2u)

**discovery draft** A first draft developed from focused freewriting. (2s)

**disclaimer** A statement appended to the top or bottom of e-mails designed to protect the company from legal liability. (40d)

**documentation** The acknowledgment of someone else's words and ideas used in any piece of writing by giving full and accurate information about the person whose words were used and where those words were found. For example, for a print source, docmentation usually includes names of all authors, title of the source, place and date of publication, and related information. (33a–33k, Chapters 34–36)

**documentation style** A system for providing information about the source of words, information, and ideas quoted, paraphrased, or summarized from some source other than the writer. Documentation styles discussed in this handbook are MLA, APA, CM, CSE, and COS. (31h, Chapters 34–36)

**document design** A term for the placement of tables, graphs, and other illustrations on printed and online material. (Chapter 37)

**double negative** A nonstandard negation using two negative modifiers rather than one. (11c)

**drafting** A part of the writing process in which writers compose ideas in sentences and paragraphs. *Drafts* are versions—*first* or *rough, revised,* and *final*—of one piece of writing. (2s)

**edited American English** English language usage that conforms to established rules of grammar, sentence structure, punctuation, and spelling; also called *standard American English.* (21c)

**editing** A part of the writing process in which writers check the technical correctness of grammar, spelling, punctuation, and mechanics. (2v)

**elliptical construction** The deliberate omission of one or more words in order to achieve conciseness in a sentence. (7p, 15h, 16d.3)

**emotional appeal** Rhetorical strategy which employs the use of descriptive language and concrete details or examples to create a mental picture for readers, leading them to feel or understand the importance of a claim. Greek name is *pathos.* (5g)

**essential element** See *restrictive element.*

**ethical appeal** Rhetorical strategy intended to reassure readers that the writer is authoritative, honest, fair, likable, and so on. Greek name is ethos. (5g)

**euphemism** Language that attempts to blunt certain realities by speaking of them in "nice" or "tactful" words. (21l)

**evaluate** A step in the critical thinking process where you judge the quality of the material you are assessing. (4b, 4c.3, 4g)

**evidence** Facts, data, examples, and opinions of others used to support assertions and conclusions. Also see *sources.* (4g)

**exclamatory sentence** A sentence beginning with *What* or *How* that expresses strong feeling: *What a ridiculous statement!* (7k)

**expletive** The phrase *there is (are), there was (were), it is,* or *it was* at the beginning of a clause, changing structure and postponing the subject: *It is Mars that we hope to reach.* [Compare: *We hope to reach Mars*]. (16c)

**expository writing** See *informative writing.*

**expressive writing** Writing that reflects your personal thoughts and feelings. (1b.1)

**faulty parallelism** Grammatically incorrect writing that results from nonmatching grammatical forms linked with coordinating conjunctions. (18e)

**faulty predication** A grammatically illogical combination of subject and predicate. (15g)

**field research** Primary research that involves going into real-life situations to observe, survey, interview, or be part of some activity. (32c, 32i)

**figurative language** Words that make connections and comparisons and draw on one image to explain another and enhance meaning. (21d)

**finite verb** A verb form that shows tense, mood, voice, person, and number while expressing an action, occurrence, or state of being.

**first person** See *person.*

**focused freewriting** A technique that may start with a set topic or may build on one sentence taken from earlier freewriting. (2g)

**formal outline** An outline that lays out the topic levels of generalities or hierarchies that marks them with Roman numerals, letters, numbers indented in a carefully prescribed fashion. (2r)

**frames** A part of a Web page that functions independently of the other parts of the page. (43f)

**freewriting** Writing nonstop for a period of time to generate ideas by free association of thoughts. Also see *discovery draft.* (2g)

**fused sentence** See *run-on sentence.*

**future perfect progressive tense** The form of the future perfect tense that describes an action or condition ongoing until some specific future time: *I will have been talking.* (8j)

**future perfect tense** The tense indicating that an action will have been completed or a condition will have ended by a specified point in the future: *I will have talked.* (8i)

**future progressive tense** The form of the future tense showing that a future action will continue for some time: *I will be talking.* (8j)

**future tense** The form of a verb, made with the simple form and either *shall* or *will*, expressing an action yet to be taken or a condition not yet experienced: *I will talk.* (8g)

**gender** The classification of words as masculine, feminine, or neutral. (10s, 21g)

**gender-free language** See *gender-neutral language.*

**gender-neutral language** Also called *gender-free language* or *nonsexist language,* it uses terms that do not unnecessarily say whether a person is male or female, as with *police officer* instead of *policeman.* (10s, 21g)

**generalization** A broad statement without details. (1b.3, 1d)

**gerund** A present participle functioning as a noun: ***Walking*** *is good exercise.* Also see *verbal.* (7e, 47c, Chapter 50)

**helping verb** See *auxiliary verb.*

**homonyms** Words spelled differently that sound alike: *to, too, two.* (22f)

**home page** The opening main page of a Web site that provides access to other pages on the site categories. (43d)

**HTML** (**H**yper **T**ext **M**arkup **L**anguage) A computer program language used for Web pages. (43f)

**hyperbole** See *overstatement.*

**hyperlink** Connection from one digital document to another online. (43d)

**idiom** A word, phrase, or other construction that has a different meaning from its literal meaning: *He lost his head. She hit the ceiling.* (Chapter 49)

**illogical predication** See *faulty predication.*

**imperative mood** The mood that expresses commands and direct requests, using the simple form of the verb and often implying but not expressing the subject, you: *Go.* (8l)

**imperative sentence** A sentence that gives a command: *Go to the corner to buy me a newspaper.* (7k, 12b.3)

**incubation** The prewriting technique of giving ideas time to develop and clarify. (2m)

**indefinite article** See *articles, determiner.*

**indefinite pronoun** A pronoun, such as *all, anyone, each,* and *others,* that refers to a nonspecific person or thing. (7c, 7f, 10i)

**independent clause** A clause that can stand alone as an independent grammatical unit. (7p)

**indicative mood** The mood of verbs used for statements about real things or highly likely ones: *I think Grace is arriving today.* (8l, 15d)

**indirect discourse** Reported speech or conversation that does not use the exact structure of the original and so is not enclosed in quotation marks. (15e, 24h)

**indirect title** Hints at an essay's topic; tries to catch the reader's interest by presenting a puzzle that can be solved by reading the essay. (2u.3)

**indirect object** A noun or pronoun or group of words functioning as a noun that tells to whom or for whom the action expressed by a transitive verb was done. (7m)

**indirect question** A sentence that reports a question and ends with a period: *I asked if you are leaving.* (23a, 23c, 48a)

**indirect quotation** See *quotation.*

**induction** The reasoning process of arriving at general principles from particular facts or instances. (4i)

**inductive reasoning** A form of reasoning that moves from particular facts or instances to general principles. (4i)

**inference** What a reader or listener understands to be implied but not stated. (4c.2)

**infinitive** A verbal made of the simple form of a verb and usually, but not always, *to* that functions as a noun, adjective, or adverb. Infinitives without the word *to* are called *unmarked* (or *bare*) *infinitives.* (7e, 8k, Chapter 50)

**infinitive phrase** An infinitive, with its modifiers and object, that functions as a noun, adjective, or adverb. Also see *verbal phrase.* (7e)

**informal language** Word choice that creates a tone appropriate for casual writing or speaking. (1d, 21h)

**informal outline** Non-traditional outline that doesn't follow the rules of a *formal outline.* (2r)

**informative writing** Writing that gives information and, when necessary, explains it; also known as *expository writing.* (1b.2)

**intensive pronoun** A pronoun that ends in *-self* and that emphasizes its antecedent. Also called *reflexive pronoun: Vida **himself** argued against it.* (7c)

**interjection** An emotion-conveying word that is treated as a sentence, starting with a capital letter and ending with an exclamation point or a period: *Oh! Ouch!* (7j, 24j)

**interrogative pronoun** A pronoun, such as *whose* or *what,* that implies a question: **Who** *called?* (7c, 12b.1)

**interrogative sentence** A sentence that asks a direct question: *Did you see that?* (7k)

**in-text citation** Source information placed in parentheses within the body of a research paper. Also see *citation, parenthetical reference.* (34b, 35b)

**intransitive verb** A verb that does not take a direct object. (8f)

**invention techniques** Ways of gathering ideas for writing. Also see *planning.* (2g–2m)

**inverted word order** In contrast to standard order, the main verb or an auxiliary verb comes before the subject in inverted word order. Most questions and some exclamations use inverted word order. (10h, 19f, Chapter 47)

**irony** Words used to imply the opposite of their usual meaning. (21d)

**irregular verb** A verb that forms the past tense and past participle in some way other than by adding *-ed* or *-d.* (8d)

**jargon** A particular field's or group's specialized vocabulary that a general reader is unlikely to understand. (21k)

**justify** When used as a design term, it refers to aligning text evenly along both the left and right margins. (42c.1)

**key terms** In an essay, the words central to its topic and its message. (5d)

**keywords** The main words in a source's title or the words that the author or editor has identified as central to that source. Use keywords in searching for sources online or in library databases. (32d.1)

**layout** The arrangement of text, visuals, color, and space on a page. (42g)

**levels of formality** Word choices and sentence structures reflecting various degrees of formality of language. A formal level is used for ceremonial and other occasions when stylistic flourishes are appropriate. A medium level, neither too formal nor too casual, is acceptable for most academic writing. (21b)

**levels of generality** Degrees of generality used to group or organize information or ideas as you write, as when moving from the most general to the most specific. Conversely, *levels of specificity* move from the most specific to the most general. (2o)

**levels of specificity** Degrees of specificity used to group or organize information or ideas as you write, as when moving from the most specific to the most general. Conversely, *levels of generality* move from the most general to the most specific. (2o)

**limiting adjective** See *determiner.*

**linking verb** A main verb that links a subject with a subject complement that renames or describes the subject. Linking verbs, sometimes called *copulative verbs,* convey a state of being, relate to the senses, or indicate a condition. (8a, 8c)

**logical appeal** Rhetorical strategy that intended to show readers that the reasoning depends on formal reasoning, including providing evidence and drawing conclusions from premises. Greek name is *logos.* (5g)

**logical fallacies** Flaws in reasoning that lead to illogical statements. (4j)

**main clause** See *independent clause.*

**main verb** A verb that expresses action, occurrence, or state of being and that shows mood, tense, voice, number, and person. (7d, 8b)

**mapping** An invention technique based on thinking about a topic and its increasingly specific subdivisions; also known as *clustering* or *webbing.* (2j)

**margins** The boundaries of a page, which means the white space or blank areas at the top, bottom, and sides of a paper or screen. (42c.1)

**mechanics** Conventions governing matters such as the use of capital letters, italics, abbreviations, and numbers. (Chapter 30)

**memo or memorandum** A brief form of business correspondence with a format that is headed with lines for "To," "From," and "Subject" and uses the rest of its space for its message. (40e)

**metaphor** A comparison implying similarity between two things. A metaphor does not use words such as *like* or *as,* which are used in a simile and which make a comparison explicit: *a mop of hair* (compare the simile *hair like a mop*). (21d)

**misplaced modifier** Describing or limiting words that are wrongly positioned in a sentence so that their message is either illogical or relates to the wrong word or words. Also see *squinting modifier.* (14a)

**mixed construction** A sentence that unintentionally changes from one grammatical structure to another, incompatible one, so that the meaning is garbled. (15f)

**mixed metaphors** Incongruously combined images. (21d)

**MLA style** See *documentation style, parenthetical reference.*

**modal auxiliary verb** One of a group of nine auxiliary verbs that add information such as a sense of needing, wanting, or having to do something or a sense of possibility, likelihood, obligation, permission, or ability. (8e, Chapter 51)

**modified block style** An alternative to block style, in modified block style the lines for the inside address and the body begin flush left but the heading, closing, and signature begin about halfway across the page. (40f)

**modifier, modify** A word or group of words functioning as an adjective or adverb to describe or limit another word or word group. Also see *misplaced modifier*. (7n, Chapter 11, 19d)

**mood** The attribute of verbs showing a speaker's or writer's attitude toward the action by the way verbs are used. English has three moods: imperative, indicative, and subjunctive. Also see *imperative mood, indicative mood, subjunctive mood*. (8l, 8m)

**multimodal** The use of a combination of words and images. (6c)

**narrative** A rhetorical strategy that tells a story; a narrative deals with what is or what has happened. (3i)

**navigation bar** The set of links on every Web page that allows users to get back to the site's home page and to major parts of the site. (43e)

**netiquette** Coined from the word etiquette, netiquette is good manners when using e-mail, the Internet, and online sites such as bulletin boards, chatrooms, etc. (40d.3)

**noncount noun** A noun that names a thing that cannot be counted: *water, time.* Also see *collective noun*. (7b, Chapters 46 and 47)

**nonessential element** See *nonrestrictive element*.

**nonrestrictive clause** See *nonrestrictive element*.

**nonrestrictive element** A descriptive word, phrase, or dependent clause that provides information not essential to understanding the basic message of the element it modifies and so is set off by commas. Also see *restrictive element*. (24f)

**nonsexist language** See *gender-neutral language*.

**nonspecific noun** A noun that refers to any of a number of identical items; it takes the indefinite articles *a, an*. (47a)

**nonstandard English** Language usage other than what is called *edited American English*. (21c)

**noun** A word that names a person, place, thing, or idea. Nouns function as subjects, objects, or complements. (7b)

**noun clause** A dependent clause that functions as a subject, object, or complement. (7p)

**noun complement** See *complement*.

**noun determiner** See *determiner*.

**noun phrase** A noun and its modifiers functioning as a subject, object, or complement. (7o)

**number** The attribute of some words indicating whether they refer to one (*singular*) or more than one (*plural*). (8a, 10b, 15b, Chapter 45)

**object** A noun, pronoun, or group of words functioning as a noun or pronoun that receives the action of a verb (*direct object*); tells to whom or for whom something is done (*indirect object*); or completes the meaning of a preposition (*object of a preposition*). (7m)

**object complement** A noun or adjective renaming or describing a direct object after verbs such as *call, consider, name, elect*, and *think: I call the most obsessive joggers* **fanatics**. (7n)

**objective case** The case of a noun or pronoun functioning as a direct or indirect object or the object of a preposition or of a verbal. A few pronouns change form to show case (*him, her, whom*). Also see *case*. (Chapter 9)

**outline** Technique for laying out ideas for writing. An outline can be formal or informal. (2r, 3ll)

**overstatement** Deliberate exaggeration for emphasis; also called *hyperbole*. (21d)

**paragraph** A group of sentences that work together to develop a unit of thought. They are the structured elements of an essay, which is composed of an *introductory paragraph, body paragraphs,* and a *concluding paragraph.* Also see *shaping.* (2n, Chapter 3)

**paragraph arrangement** Ordering sentences by specific techniques to communicate a paragraph's message. (3h)

**paragraph development** Using specific, concrete details (RENNS) to support a generalization in a paragraph; rhetorical strategies or patterns for organizing ideas in paragraphs. (3f, 3i)

**parallelism** The use of equivalent grammatical forms or matching sentence structures to express equivalent ideas and develop coherence. (3g.4, Chapter 18)

**paraphrase** A restatement of someone else's ideas in language and sentence structure different from those of the original. (33i)

**parenthetical reference** Information enclosed in parentheses following quoted, paraphrased, or summarized material from a source to alert readers to the use of material from a specific source. Parenthetical references, also called *in-text citations,* function together with a list of bibliographic information about each source used in a paper to document the writer's use of sources. Also see *citation.* (34b)

**participial phrase** A phrase that contains a present participle or a past participle and any modifiers and that functions as an adjective. Also see *verbal phrase.* (7o)

**passive construction** See *passive voice.*

**passive voice** The form of a verb in which the subject is acted on; if the subject is mentioned in the sentence, it usually appears as the object of the preposition *by:* **I was frightened by** the thunder. [Compare the active voice: *The thunder **frightened me**.*] The passive voice emphasizes the action, in

contrast to the *active voice,* which emphasizes the doer of the action. (8n–8p)

**past participle** The third principal part of a verb, formed in regular verbs, like the past tense, by adding *-d* or *-ed* to the simple form. In irregular verbs, it often differs from the simple form and the past tense: *break, broke, broken.* (7e, 8b, 50f)

**past perfect progressive tense** The past perfect tense form that describes an ongoing condition in the past that has been ended by something stated in the sentence: *I had been talking.* (8j)

**past perfect tense** The tense that describes a condition or action that started in the past, continued for a while, and then ended in the past: *I had talked.* (8g, 8i)

**past progressive tense** The tense that shows the continuing nature of a past action: *I was talking.* (8j)

**past subjunctive** The simple past tense in the subjunctive mood. (8m)

**past tense** The tense that tells of an action completed or a condition ended. (8g)

**past-tense form** The second principal part of a verb, in regular verbs formed by adding *-d* or *-ed* to the simple form. In irregular verbs, the past tense may change in several ways from the simple form. (8b, 8d)

**peer-response group** A group of students formed to give each other feedback on writing. (1c.1)

**perfect infinitive** Also called *present perfect participle,* a tense used to describe an action that occurs before the action in the main verb. (8k)

**perfect tenses** The three tenses—the present perfect (*I have talked*), the past perfect (*I had talked*), and the future perfect (*I will have talked*)—that help show complex time relationships between two clauses. (8g, 8i)

**periodic sentence** A sentence that begins with modifiers and ends with the independent clause, thus postponing the main idea—and the emphasis—for the end; also called a *climactic sentence*. (19e)

**person** The attribute of nouns and pronouns showing who or what acts or experiences an action. *First person* is the one speaking (*I, we*); *second person* is the one being spoken to (*you, you*); and *third person* is the person or thing being spoken about (*he, she, it, they*). All nouns are third person. (8a, 10b)

**personal pronoun** A pronoun that refers to people or things, such as *I, you, them, it.* (7c, 9n)

**persuasive appeal** Rhetorical strategies which appeal to the emotions, logic, or ethics of readers. (5g)

**persuasive writing** Writing that seeks to convince the reader about a matter of opinion. It is also known as *argumentative writing.* (1b.3, Chapter 5)

**phrasal verb** A verb that combines with one or more prepositions to deliver its meaning: *ask out, look into.* (49c)

**phrase** A group of related words that does not contain both a subject and a predicate and thus cannot stand alone as an independent grammatical unit. A phrase functions as a noun, verb, or modifier. (7o)

**plagiarism** A writer's presenting another person's words or ideas without giving credit to that person. Documentation systems allow writers to give proper credit to sources in ways recognized by scholarly communities. Plagiarism is a serious offense, a form of intellectual dishonesty that can lead to course failure or expulsion. (1e, 33b, 33c)

**planning** An early part of the writing process in which writers gather ideas. Along with shaping, planning is sometimes called *prewriting.* (Chapter 2)

**plural** See *number.*

**podcasts** Brief sound files that are shared over the Internet, somewhat like online radio broadcasts. (1h, 43l).

**positive form** The form of an adjective or adverb when no comparison is being expressed: *blue, easily.* Also see *comparative form, superlative form.* (11e)

**possessive case** The case of a noun or pronoun that shows ownership or possession: *my, your, their,* and so on. Also see *case, pronoun case.* (Chapter 9, 27a–27c)

**predicate** The part of a sentence that contains the verb and tells what the subject is doing or experiencing or what is being done to the subject. A *simple predicate* contains only the main verb and any auxiliary verbs. A *complete predicate* contains the verb, its modifiers, objects, and other related words. A *compound predicate* contains two or more verbs and their objects and modifiers, if any. (7l)

**predicate adjective** An adjective used as a subject complement: *That tree is **leafy**.* (7n)

**predicate nominative** A noun or pronoun used as a subject complement: *That tree is a **maple**.* (7n)

**prediction** A major activity of the *reading process,* in which the reader guesses what comes next. (4c)

**premises** In a deductive argument expressed as a syllogism, statements presenting the conditions of the argument from which the conclusion must follow. (4i)

**preposition** A word that conveys a relationship, often of space or time, between the noun or pronoun following it and other words in the sentence. The noun or pronoun following a preposition is called its *object.* (7h, Chapter 49)

**prepositional phrase** A preposition and the word it modifies. Also see *phrase, preposition.* (7h, 7o)

**presentation style** The way you deliver what you have to say. Memorization, reading, mapping and speaking with notes are different types of presentation styles. (41h)

**present infinitive** Names or describes an activity or occurrence coming together either at the same time or after the time expressed in the main verb. (8k)

**present participle** A verb's *-ing* form. Used with auxiliary verbs, present participles function as main verbs. Used without auxiliary verbs, present participles function as nouns or adjectives. (7e, 8b, 50f)

**present perfect participle** See *perfect infinitive.*

**present perfect progressive tense** The present perfect tense form that describes something ongoing in the past that is likely to continue into the future: *I have been talking.* (8j)

**present perfect tense** The tense indicating that an action or its effects, begun or perhaps completed in the past, continue into the present: *I had talked.* (8g, 8i)

**present progressive tense** The present-tense form of the verb that indicates something taking place at the time it is written or spoken about: *I am talking.* (8j)

**present subjunctive** The simple form of the verb for all persons and numbers in the subjunctive mood. (8m)

**present tense** The tense that describes what is happening, what is true at the moment, and what is consistently true. It uses the simple form (*I talk*) and the *-s* form in the third-person singular (*he, she, it talks*). (8g, 8h)

**prewriting** All activities in the writing process before drafting. Also see *planning, shaping.* (2e–2m)

**primary sources** Firsthand work: write-ups of experiments and observa-

tions by the researchers who conducted them; taped accounts, interviews, and newspaper accounts by direct observers; autobiographies, diaries, and journals; expressive works (poems, plays, fiction, essays). Also known as *primary evidence.* Also see *secondary source.* (4g.2, 32a, 32i)

**process** A rhetorical strategy in writing that reports a sequence of actions by which something is done or made. (3i)

**progressive forms** Verb forms made in all tenses with the present participle and forms of the verb *be* as an auxiliary. Progressive forms show that an action, occurrence, or state of being is ongoing. (8g, 8j)

**pronoun** A word that takes the place of a noun and functions in the same ways that nouns do. Types of pronouns are *demonstrative, indefinite, intensive, interrogative, personal, reciprocal, reflexive,* and *relative.* The word (or words) a pronoun replaces is called its *antecedent.* (7c, Chapter 9)

**pronoun-antecedent agreement** The match in expressing number and person—and for personal pronouns, gender as well—required between a pronoun and its antecedent. (10o–10t)

**pronoun case** The way a pronoun changes form to reflect its use as the agent of action (*subjective case*), the thing being acted upon (*objective case*), or the thing showing ownership (*possessive case*). (9a–9k)

**pronoun reference** The relationship between a pronoun and its antecedent. (9l–9s)

**proofread** The act of reading a final draft to find and correct any spelling or mechanics mistakes, typing errors, or handwriting illegibility; the final step of the writing process. (2w)

**proper adjective** An adjective formed from a proper noun: *Victorian, American.* (30e)

**proper noun** A noun that names specific people, places, or things and is always capitalized: *Dave Matthews, Buick*. (7b, 30e, 47c)

**public writing** Writing intended for readers outside of academic and work settings. (Chapter 40)

**purpose** The goal or aim of a piece of writing: to express oneself, to provide information, to persuade, or to create a literary work. (1b)

**quotation** Repeating or reporting another person's words. *Direct quotation* repeats another's words exactly and encloses them in quotation marks. *Indirect quotation* reports another's words without quotation marks except around any words repeated exactly from the source. Both *direct* and *indirect quotation* require *documentation* of the *source* to avoid *plagiarism*. Also see *direct discourse, indirect discourse.* (Chapter 28, 33h)

**readers** Readers are the audiences for writing; readers process material they read on the literal, inferential, and evaluative levels. (4c)

**reading process** Critical reading that requires the reader to read for *literal meaning*, to draw *inferences*, and to *evaluate*. (4c)

**reciprocal pronoun** The pronouns *each other* and *one another* referring to individual parts of a plural antecedent: *We respect **each other***. (7c)

**References** In many documentation styles, including APA, the title of a list of sources cited in a research paper or other written work. (31h, 31i, 32c, 35f)

**reflexive pronoun** A pronoun that ends in *-self* and that refers back to its antecedent: *They claim to support **themselves***. (7c)

**regular verb** A verb that forms its past tense and past participle by adding *-ed* or *-d* to the simple form. Most English verbs are regular. (8b, 8d)

**relative adverb** An adverb that introduces an adjective clause: *The lot **where** I usually park my car was full.* (7g)

**relative clause** See *adjective clause.*

**relative pronoun** A pronoun, such as *who, which, that, whom,* or *whoever,* that introduces an adjective clause or sometimes a noun clause. (7c)

**RENNS Test** See *paragraph development.* (3f)

**research question** The controlling question that drives research. (31c)

**research writing** Also called *source-based writing,* a process in three steps: conducting research, understanding and evaluating the results of the research, and writing the research paper with accurate documentation. (Chapter 31)

**restrictive clause** See *restrictive element.*

**restrictive element** A word, phrase, or dependent clause that contains information that is essential for a sentence to deliver its message. Do not set off with commas. (24f)

**revising, revision** A part of the writing process in which writers evaluate their rough drafts and, based on their assessments, rewrite by adding, cutting, replacing, moving, and often totally recasting material. (2u)

**rhetoric** The area of discourse that focuses on the arrangement of ideas and choice of words as a reflection of both the writer's purpose and the writer's sense of audience. (Chapter 1)

**rhetorical strategies** In writing, various techniques for presenting ideas to deliver a writer's intended message with clarity and impact. Reflecting typical patterns of human thought, rhetorical strategies include arrangements such as chronological and climactic order; stylistic techniques such as parallelism and planned repetition; and patterns for organizing and developing writing such as description and definition. (3i)

**Rogerian argument** An argument technique adapted from the principles of communication developed by the psychologist Carl Rogers. (5h)

**run-on sentence** The error of running independent clauses into each other without the required punctuation that marks them as complete units; also called a *fused sentence* or *run-together sentence.* (Chapter 13)

**sans serif** Font types that do not have little "feet" or finishing lines at the top and bottom of each letter. (42c)

**search engine** An Internet-specific software program that can look through all files at Internet sites. (32j)

**secondary source** A source that reports, analyzes, discusses, reviews, or otherwise deals with the work of someone else, as opposed to a primary source, which is someone's original work or firsthand report. A reliable secondary source should be the work of a person with appropriate credentials, should appear in a respected publication or other medium, should be current, and should be well reasoned. (4g.2, 32a, 32i, 38c, 39b)

**second person** See *person.*

**sentence** See *sentence types.*

**sentence fragment** A portion of a sentence that is punctuated as though it were a complete sentence. (Chapter 12)

**sentence outline** Type of outline in which each element is a sentence. (2r)

**sentence types** A grammatical classification of sentences by the kinds of clauses they contain. A *simple sentence* consists of one independent clause. A *complex sentence* contains one independent clause and one or more dependent clauses. A *compound-complex sentence* contains at least two independent clauses and one or more dependent

clauses. A *compound* or *coordinate sentence* contains two or more independent clauses joined by a coordinating conjunction. Sentences are also classified by their grammatical function; see *declarative sentence, exclamatory sentence, imperative sentence, interrogative sentence.* (7k, 7q, 17b)

**sentence variety** Writing sentences of various lengths and structures; see *coordinate sentence, cumulative sentence, periodic sentence, sentence types.* (19a)

**serif** Font types that are characterized by little "feet" or finishing lines at the top and bottom of each letter. (42c)

**server** A computer that is always online and available to Internet users. (43b)

**sexist language** Language that unnecessarily communicates that a person is male or female. For example, *fireman* is a sexist term that says only males fight fires, while *fire fighter* includes males and females. (10s, 21g)

**shaping** An early part of the writing process in which writers consider ways to organize their material. Along with planning, shaping is sometimes called *prewriting.* (2n–2r)

**shift** Within a sentence, an unnecessary abrupt change in *person, number, subject, voice, tense, mood,* or *direct* or *indirect discourse.* (15a–15c)

**simile** A comparison, using *like* or *as,* of otherwise dissimilar things. (21d)

**simple form** The form of the verb that shows action, occurrence, or state of being taking place in the present. It is used in the singular for first and second person and in the plural for first, second, and third person. It is also the first principal part of a verb. The simple form is also known as the *dictionary form* or *base form.* (8b)

**simple predicate** See *predicate.*

**simple sentence** See *sentence types.*

simple subject  See *subject.*

simple tenses  The present, past, and future tenses, which divide time into present, past, and future. (8g, 8h)

singular  See *number.*

slang  A kind of colloquial language, it is coined words and new meanings for existing words, which quickly pass in and out of use; not appropriate for most academic writing. (21a)

slanted language  Language that tries to manipulate the reader with distorted facts. (21i)

source-based writing  See *research writing.*

sources  Books, articles, print or Internet documents, other works, and persons providing credible information. In *research writing,* often called *outside sources.* (1f, Chapters 32 and 33)

spatial order  An arrangement of information according to location in space; an organizing strategy for sentences, paragraphs, and longer pieces of writing. (3h)

specific noun  A noun understood to be exactly and specifically referred to; uses the definite article *the.* (47a)

split infinitive  One or more words coming between the two words of an infinitive. (14b)

squinting modifier  A modifier that is considered misplaced because it is not clear whether it describes the word that comes before it or the word that follows it. (14a)

standard American English  See *edited American English.*

standard word order  The most common order for words in English sentences: The subject comes before the predicate. Also see *inverted word order.* (19f, Chapter 48)

stereotype  A kind of hasty generalization (a *logical fallacy*) in which a sweeping claim is made about all members of

a particular ethnic, racial, religious, gender, age, or political group. (4j)

subject  The word or group of words in a sentence that acts, is acted upon, or is described by the verb. A *simple subject* includes only the noun or pronoun. A *complete subject* includes the noun or pronoun and all its modifiers. A *compound subject* includes two or more nouns or pronouns and their modifiers. (7l)

subject complement  A noun or adjective that follows a linking verb, renaming or describing the subject of the sentence; also called a *predicate nominative.* (7n)

subjective case  The case of the noun or pronoun functioning as a subject. Also see *case, pronoun case.* (Chapter 9)

subject tree  Shows you visually whether you have sufficient content, at varying levels of generality or specificity, to start a first draft of your writing. A subject tree also visually demonstrates whether you have a good balance of general ideas and specific details. (2p)

subject-verb agreement  The required match between a subject and a verb in expressing number and person. (10b–10n)

subjunctive mood  A verb mood that expresses wishes, recommendations, indirect requests, speculations, and conditional statements. *I wish you **were** here.* (8l, 8m)

subordinate clause  See *dependent clause.*

subordinating conjunction  A conjunction that introduces an adverb clause and expresses a relationship between the idea in it and the idea in the independent clause. (7i, 13c.4, 17f, 17g)

subordination  The use of grammatical structures to reflect the relative importance of ideas. A sentence with logically subordinated information expresses the most important information in the independent clause and less important information in dependent clauses or phrases. (17e–17i)

**summary** A brief version of the main message or central point of a passage or other discourse; a critical thinking activity preceding synthesis. (4e, 33j)

**superlative form** The form of an adjective or adverb that expresses comparison among three or more things: *bluest, least blue; most easily, least easily.* (11e)

**syllogism** The structure of a deductive argument expressed in two *premises* and a *conclusion.* The first premise is a generalized assumption or statement of fact. The second premise is a different assumption or statement of fact based on evidence. The conclusion is also a specific instance that follows logically from the premises. (4i)

**synonym** A word that is very close in meaning to another word: *cold* and *icy.* (21e.2)

**synthesis** A component of critical thinking in which material that has been summarized, analyzed, and interpreted is connected to what is already known (one's prior knowledge) or to what has been learned from other authorities. (4b, 4e)

**tag question** An inverted verb-pronoun combination added to the end of a sentence, creating a question that asks the audience to agree with the assertion in the first part of the sentence. A tag question is set off from the rest of the sentence with a comma: *You know what a tag question is, **don't you?*** (24g)

**tense** The time at which the action of the verb occurs: the present, the past, or the future. Also see *perfect tenses, simple tenses.* (8g–8k)

**tense sequence** In sentences that have more than one clause, the accurate matching of verbs to reflect logical time relationships. (8k)

**thesis statement** A statement of an essay's central theme that makes clear the main idea, the writer's purpose, the

focus of the topic, and perhaps the organizational pattern. (2q)

**third person** See *person.*

**title** The part of an essay that clarifies the overall point of the piece of writing. It can be *direct* or *indirect.* (2u.3)

**tone** The writer's attitude toward his or her material and reader, especially as reflected by word choice. (1d, 4c.2, 5f)

**topic** The subject of discourse. (2c)

**topic sentence** The sentence that expresses the main idea of a paragraph. A topic sentence may be implied, not stated. (3e)

**Toulmin model** A model that defines the essential parts of an argument as the *claim* (or *main point*), the *support* (or *evidence*), and the *warrants* (or *assumptions behind the main point*). (5h)

**transition** The connection of one idea to another in discourse. Useful strategies within a paragraph for creating transitions include transitional expressions, parallelism, and the planned repetition of key terms and phrases. In a long piece of writing, a *transitional paragraph* is the bridge between discussion of two separate topics. Also see *critical response.* (3g.1, 3j)

**transitional expressions** Words and phrases that signal connections among ideas and create coherence. (3g.1)

**transitive verb** A verb that must be followed by a direct object. (8f)

**understatement** Figurative language in which the writer uses deliberate restraint for emphasis. (21d)

**unity** The clear and logical relationship between the main idea of a paragraph and the evidence supporting the main idea. (3c.4, 3d, 3e)

**unstated assumptions** Premises that are implied but not stated. (4i)

**usage** A customary way of using language. (Chapter 20)

**valid** Correctly and rationally derived; applied to a deductive argument whose conclusion follows logically from the premises. Validity applies to the structure of an argument, not its truth. (4i)

**verb** Any word that shows action or occurrence or describes a state of being. Verbs change form to convey time (*tense*), attitude (*mood*), and role of the subject (*voice*, either *active* or *passive*). Verbs occur in the predicate of a clause and can be in verb phrases, which may consist of a main verb, auxiliary verbs, and modifiers. Verbs can be described as *transitive* or *intransitive*, depending on whether they take a direct object. Also see *voice*. (Chapter 8)

**verbal** A verb part functioning as a noun, adjective, or adverb. Verbals include *infinitives, present participles* (functioning as adjectives), *gerunds* (present participles functioning as nouns), and *past participles*. (7e, Chapter 50)

**verbal phrase** A group of words that contains a verbal (an infinitive, participle, or gerund) and its modifiers. (7o)

**verb phrase** A main verb, any auxiliary verbs, and any modifiers. (7o)

**verb tense** Verbs show tense (time) by changing form. English has six verb tenses. (8g)

**visual design** Refers to the appearance of a document (how it looks), as opposed to its content (what it says). (42a)

**voice** An attribute of verbs showing whether the subject acts (*active voice*) or is acted on (*passive voice*). Verbs are sometimes referred to as *strong* or *action verbs* or *weak verbs*. (8n–8p)

**warrants** One of three key terms in the *Toulmin model* for argument; refers to implied or inferred assumptions. They are based on *authority, substance,* and *motivation*. (5h)

**Web** See *World Wide Web*.

**webbing** See *mapping*.

**Web page** On the Internet, a file of information. Such a file is not related in length to a printed page, as it may be a paragraph or many screens long. (43c)

**Web site** One page or a home page that provides links to a collection of documents or files related to the home page. (43c)

**Web structure** The organization of the content and documents that site creators include in a Web project. (43d)

**white space** The part of a document that has neither text nor visuals. (42g)

**wiki** A Web site that allows multiple readers to change its content. (1h)

**wordiness** An attribute of writing that is full of empty words and phrases that do not contribute to meaning. The opposite of *conciseness*. (16a)

**World Wide Web** The *Web*, a user-friendly computer network allowing access to information in the form of text, graphics, and sound on the Internet. (Chapter 43)

**working bibliography** A preliminary list of useful sources in research writing. (31i)

**Works Cited** In MLA documentation style, the title of a list of all sources cited in a research paper or other written work. (34a)

**writer's block** The desire to start writing, but not doing so. (2t)

**writing process** Stages of writing in which a writer gathers and shapes ideas, organizes material, expresses those ideas in a rough draft, evaluates the draft and revises it, edits the writing for technical errors, and proofreads it for typographical accuracy and legibility. The stages often overlap; see *planning, shaping, drafting, revising, editing, proofreading*. (Chapters 1 and 2)

**writing situation** The beginning of the writing process for each writing assignment as defined by four elements: topic, purpose, audience, special requirements. (2c)

# List of Boxes by Content

# Credits

## TEXT/ART

Susan Howard, "Depth of Field," *Newsday,* January 1, 1991. Copyright © 1991. Reprinted by permission of Tribune Media Services. (page 105)

Gretel Ehrlich, "Other Lives" from *The Solace of Open Spaces.* New York: Penguin Books, 1986. Copyright © 1985. (page 105)

Ruth Mehrtens Galvin, "Sybarite to Some, Sinful to Others." Used by permission of Smith College. (page 106)

Lori de Mori, "Making Olive Oil" in *Florence: Authentic Recipes for Celebrating the Foods of the World* by Lori de Mori. Copyright © 2004 by Weldon Owe Inc. and Williams-Sonoma Inc. Reprinted by permission of the publisher. (page 106)

Melissa Greene, "No Rms, Jungle Vu." (pages 106–107)

Banesh Hoffman, "My Friend, Albert Einstein," pp. 139–144. (page 107)

John Arrend Timm, *General Chemistry,* Editions McGraw-Hill Book Company Inc., third edition, 1956. (page 107)

D. Kern Holoman, "Jazz" from *Masterworks: A Musical Discovery* 1st edition by D. Kern Holoman. Copyright © 1998. Reprinted by permission of Pearson Education, Upper Saddle River, NJ. (page 108)

William Ryan, *Blaming the Victim.* New York: Random House, 1976. (page 108)

Rosanne Labonte, student. (page 109)

Warren Bennis, "Time to Hang Up the Old Sports Clichés." (page 110)

Alison Lurie, excerpt from *The Language of Clothes.* Copyright © 1981 by Alison Lurie. Reprinted by permission of Melanie Jackson Agency, L.L.C. (page 110)

Marie Winn, *The Plug-In Drug.* New York: Penguin Books, 2002. (pages 110–111)

Deborah Tannen, excerpt from *You Just Don't Understand.* Copyright © 1990 by Deborah Tannen. Reprinted by permission of HarperCollins Publishers. (page 111)

Simone de Beauvoir, *Memoirs of a Dutiful Daughter.* New York: Penguin Classics, 2001. (page 111)

James Gorman, "Gadgets." (page 111)

June Jordan, "Waiting for a Taxi" from *Technical Difficulties: African-American Notes on the State of the Union.* New York: Pantheon, 1992, pp. 161–168. (page 113)

Jane Brody, "A Hoarder's Life: Filling the Cache—and Finding It" from *The New York Times* (November 19, 1991), pp. 101–102. (page 112)

Jean Rosenbaum, M.D., *Is Your Volkswagen a Sex Symbol?* New York: Bantam Books, Random House Inc., 1973. (page 112)

"DNA Profiling Advancement: The Use of DNA Profiles in Solving Crimes," *The FBI Law Enforcement Bulletin.* (page 114)

John C. Sawhill, "The Collapse of Public Schools." Reprinted with permission. (page 114)

Ora Gygi, "Things Are Seldom What They Seem." (page 120)

Annie Dillard, "Terror at Tinker Creek." (page 124)

Paul De Palma, "http://www.when_is_enough_enough?.com" from *The American Scholar* 68, no. 1 (Winter 1999). Copyright © 1999 by Paul De Palma. (page 124)

permission of The Union of Concerned Scientists in conjunction with The Ecological Society of America. (page 757)

DeAnza College Web screen courtesy of DeAnza College, http://www.faculty.deanza.fhda.edu. (page 759)

USA Freedom Corps print advertisement courtesy of USA Freedom Corps/Ad Council. (page 772)

The Nature Club Web screen courtesy of The Nature Club. (page 787)

National Museum of the American Indian Web screen courtesy of the National Museum of the American Indian, Washington, DC. (page 790)

The Guthrie Theatre Web screen courtesy of The Guthrie Theatre. (page 794)

Hawaii Community College Web screen courtesy of the University of Hawai'i. (page 795)

## PHOTOGRAPHS

Getty Images-Photodisc (page 1)
Photos.com (page 87)
Photos.com (page 106)
Photos.com (page 108)
Rob Crandall/Stock Boston (page 116)
Photos.com (page 165)
© Gallo Images/CORBIS (page 167)
Peter Vadnai (page 171)
Scott Cunningham/Merrill Education (page 173)
Stockbyte (page 174)
Paul Conklin/Getty Images, Inc.-Taxi (page 175)
Photo 24/Brand X Pictures/Getty Images, Inc. (page 179)
Photos.com (page 183)
Anthony Marsland/Stone/Getty Images (page 192)
Corbis/Bettmann (page 203)
Alvar De Leiva/Stock Image/Getty Images, Inc. (page 223)
Photos.com (page 281)
Photos.com (page 317)
Photos.com (page 346)
Jeremy Woodhouse/Digital Vision/Getty Images, Inc. (page 350)
Ed Freeman/Image Bank/Getty Images (page 399)
Photos.com (page 409)
Andrew Olney/Photographer's Choice/Getty Images (page 411)
Photos.com (page 425)
Todd Gipstein/National Geographic/Getty Images, Inc. (page 479)
Kim Westerskov/Photographer's Choice/Getty Images (page 491)
Laurance B. Aiuppy/Taxi/Getty Images (page 687)
AP Wide World Photos (page 698)
AP Wide World Photos (page 782)
Photos.com (page 799)

# ESL Index

# Index

893

## P

**T**

*Quick Notes*

*Quick Notes*

*Quick Notes*

*Quick Notes*

*Quick Notes*

*Quick Notes*

# Everything You Need to Earn a Better Grade, *All in One Place!*

# *www.prenhall.com/troyka*

**With the purchase of this new handbook, you also receive access to a comprehensive, easy-to-use Web site.** This Web site will help you with your writing in college and beyond. Follow the instructions below for instant access.

**REGISTER for access to the Web site**

1. Go to www.prenhall.com/troyka
2. Click on the **title/edition** or **cover** of your handbook.
3. Click on **Register**.
4. Depending on whether or not you have registered for another Pearson Education Web site, select **No, I Am a New User** or **Yes, Look Me Up**.
5. Enter the code below and follow the on-screen instructions to complete the one-time registration.

> ### PSTHS-AUXIL-CLUNG-FUMED-HAUNT-WORSE

NOTE: This student access code is redeemable one time only! If you purchased a used book, go to the URL in Step 1, select your handbook, and follow the on-screen instructions for purchasing access to the Web site.

6. **LOG IN**—After you register, you can access the site at any time by logging in at www.prenhall.com/troyka and clicking on the appropriate title/edition. Enter your login name and password, click on **Log In**, and enjoy the wealth of resources available to you.

Name:

E-mail:

User name:

Password:

**Fill in the boxes above to have your user name and password always at your fingertips.**

Turn the page to see a list of resources and tools available to you with this Web site.

# Everything You Need to Earn a Better Grade, *All in One Place!*

**My Writing Plan**
- Take a **diagnostic test** to assess your writing skills.
- Build your own virtual *Writing Plan* and custom version of the eBook.
- Visit the *English Tutor Center*, which offers personal tutoring by actual English instructors.

**My eBook™**
- Search topics by table of contents or index.
- Highlight, annotate, and take notes within the eBook.

**Practice**
- Develop your writing skills using **self-grading exercises**.
- Practice editing with *Blue Pencil™* exercises.
- Learn visual rhetoric using our interactive **Visual Rhetoric Activities**.

**Research Navigator™**
- Follow a series of clear **research guidelines** as you write your paper.
- Access **25,000+ journal articles** and the *New York Times Archive*.
- Use the *AutoCite™* Works Cited generation tool.

**And More**
- Use *Exchange* to build a writing portfolio and receive feedback from your peers.
- View **videos from professionals** related to the writing they do for their jobs.
- See **sample documents** that model effective writing.

**Product and Technical Support are available 24/7 at**
**http://247.support.pearsoned.com**

• www.prenhall.com/troyka